מסורה

ArtScroll® Series

Rabbi Nosson Scherman / Rabbi Meir Zlotowitz
General Editors

Published by
Mesorah Publications, ltd

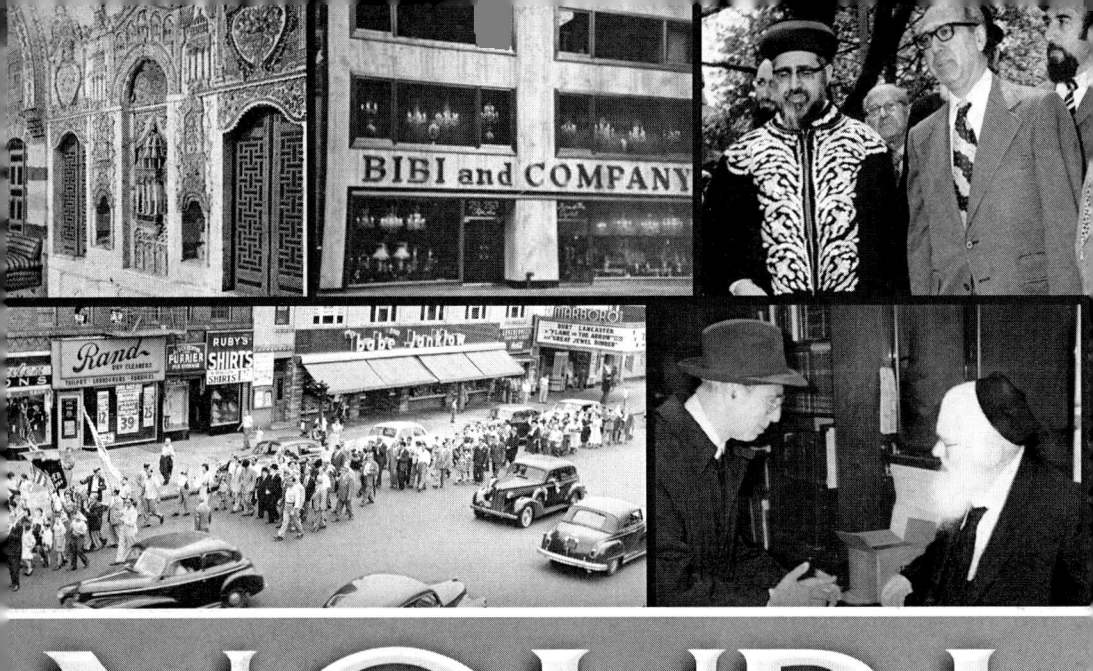

NOURI

The story of Isidore Dayan, and the growth
of a vibrant community in America

Devora Gliksman

FIRST EDITION
First Impression … March 2016

Published and Distributed by
MESORAH PUBLICATIONS, LTD.
4401 Second Avenue / Brooklyn, N.Y 11232

Distributed in Europe by
LEHMANNS
Unit E, Viking Business Park
Rolling Mill Road
Jarow, Tyne & Wear, NE32 3DP
England

Distributed in Australia and New Zealand
by **GOLDS WORLDS OF JUDAICA**
3-13 William Street
Balaclava, Melbourne 3183
Victoria, Australia

Distributed in Israel by
SIFRIATI / A. GITLER — BOOKS
Moshav Magshimim
Israel

Distributed in South Africa by
KOLLEL BOOKSHOP
Northfield Centre, 17 Northfield Avenue
Glenhazel 2192, Johannesburg, South Africa

ARTSCROLL® SERIES
NOURI
© Copyright 2016, by MESORAH PUBLICATIONS, Ltd.
4401 Second Avenue / Brooklyn, N.Y. 11232 / (718) 921-9000 / www.artscroll.com

---

ALL RIGHTS RESERVED
The text, prefatory and associated textual contents and introductions
— including the typographic layout, cover artwork and ornamental graphics —
have been designed, edited and revised as to content, form and style.

No part of this book may be reproduced
IN ANY FORM, PHOTOCOPYING, DIGITAL, OR COMPUTER RETRIEVAL SYSTEMS
— even for personal use without written permission from
the copyright holder, Mesorah Publications Ltd.
except by a reviewer who wishes to quote brief passages
in connection with a review written for inclusion in magazines or newspapers.

THE RIGHTS OF THE COPYRIGHT HOLDER WILL BE STRICTLY ENFORCED.

ISBN 10: 1-4226-1697-5 / ISBN 13: 978-1-4226-1697-0

Typography by CompuScribe at ArtScroll Studios, Ltd.
Printed in the United States of America by Noble Book Press Corp.
Bound by Sefercraft, Quality Bookbinders, Ltd., Brooklyn N.Y. 11232

In memory of

Salim Ben Luna Halevy

Yaccob Ben Gilson Halevy

Gilson Bat Letifah

Faraj Ben Rima Hacohen

Yehuda Ben Allen Halevy

Yehuda Ben Margalit

Dedicated by

Albert Ayal

נר זכרון

לזכר נשמת רעיתי ואמנו היקרה
עטרת משפחתנו האשה הצנועה

מרת רחל בת מרגלית שעיה מוגרבי ע"ה

גידלה בניה לתורה, קיבלה יסוריה באהבה
השיבה נשמתה בשם טוב ביום ו' ניסן תשע"ג

וגם לזכר נשמת אבינו וסבנו עטרת משפחתנו

מר יצחק בן ויקטוריה שעיה מוגרבי ז"ל

נפטר ביום ל' כסלו תשס"ז

ת.נ.צ.ב.ה.

משה שעיה מוגרבי ומשפחתו

In memory of

Irving Maleh

by

Jack Maleh

In honor of my silent partners,

my wife

Rachel

and children
Etty, Daniella and Eliahou.

by

Dr. Mayer Ballas

TABLE OF CONTENTS

Acknowledgments — 13

PART I

Prologue — 21

Chapter 1:
Baghdad, Ottoman Empire, c. 1895 — 23

Chapter 2:
Damascus, Syria, 1909 — 32

Chapter 3:
Lyon, France, 1914 — 41

Chapter 4:
Damascus, Syria, 1917 — 48

Chapter 5:
San Francisco, 1918 — 56

Chapter 6:
Damascus, Syria, 1918 — 62

Chapter 7:
Damascus, Syria, 1920 — 67

Chapter 8:
Lower East Side, New York, 1920 — 73

PART II

Chapter 9:
Lower East Side, New York, 1925 — 81

Chapter 10:
Bensonhurst, 1927 — 87

Chapter 11:
Bensonhurst, 1930 — 96

Chapter 12:
    Bensonhurst, 1931 — 102

Chapter 13:
    Bensonhurst, 1931 — 108

Chapter 14:
    Bensonhurst, Early 1930's — 116

Chapter 15:
    Bensonhurst, 1937 — 129

Chapter 16:
    Ahi Ezer, 1939 — 136

PART III

Chapter 17:
    Bensonhurst, November 1940 — 147

Chapter 18:
    From New York to a New World, 1941 — 156

Chapter 19:
    Syrian Boys in the Army, 1944-1945 — 168

Chapter 20:
    Bensonhurst, 1945 — 178

Chapter 21:
    In the Aftermath, 1946 — 183

Chapter 22:
    Bensonhurst, 1947 — 188

Chapter 23:
    Shanghai, China, 1946 — 193

Chapter 24:
    Ahi Ezer, 1946 — 198

Chapter 25:
    Finding Family, 1948 — 208

Chapter 26:
    Bensonhurst, 1949 — 215

PART IV

Chapter 27:
    Bensonhurst, 1951 — 227

Chapter 28:
    Ahi Ezer, 1952 — 240

Chapter 29:
    Mexico, Israel, and Beyond, 1953 — 250

Chapter 30:
   Morocco, 1955   258

Chapter 31:
   A New Face in Ahi Ezer, 1956   264

Chapter 32:
   Painful Growth, Bensonhurst, 1957   272

Chapter 33:
   Egypt, 1957   278

Chapter 34:
   Alone in Athens, 1957   282

Chapter 35:
   Beyond Paris, 1957   290

Chapter 36:
   Bensonhurst, 1958   298

Chapter 37:
   Florida, 1959   304

Chapter 38:
   Ahi Ezer, 1959   309

PART V

Chapter 39:
   Moving Forward, 1960   315

Chapter 40:
   "Oseh Hadashot, Ba'al Milhamot"   326

Chapter 41:
   "The One Thing That You Should Never Mind
   Is if Your Children Are Better Than You."   335

Chapter 42:
   "I Have to Do My Part; the Rest Is Up to Hashem."   345

Chapter 43:
   Rabbot Machashabot B'lev Ish   351

Chapter 44:
   Bensonhurst and Jerusalem, 1967   360

Chapter 45:
   "How Can We Help Our Brothers?"   366

Chapter 46:
   "We Are *L'shem Shamayim*; There Are Bound to Be Setbacks."   376

PART VI

Chapter 47:
   Simple Faith   391

Chapter 48:
 "One Who Is Accompanied Will Not Suffer Harm." 396

Chapter 49:
 "You Go With Your Children. I'm Staying With Mine." 404

Chapter 50:
 "I Just Want My Children Back." 413

Chapter 51:
 B'toch Ami Anochi Yoshabet — I Dwell Among My People 422

Chapter 52:
 In Every Generation Our Enemies Rise Up to Destroy Us 429

Chapter 53:
 Mama Rachel Cries for Her Children 438

Chapter 54:
 Blessing Is Found Only on That Which Is Hidden From the Eye 444

Chapter 55:
 "Do You See That Man? He's a *Tzaddik*." 461

Chapter 56:
 "It Seems That the Whole [Dayan] House
 Revolves Around… Me!" 473

Chapter 57:
 "Our Home Is Your Home." 483

Chapter 58:
 "If These Buildings Ever Get Built,
 It Will Be Only Through Divine Providence." 491

PART VII

Chapter 59:
 "How Can I Emulate an Angel?" 503

Chapter 60:
 And They Were Honored by His Attention… 511

Chapter 61:
 "A Shul With Money in the Bank Is a Bankrupt Shul." 524

Chapter 62:
 "In What *Zechut* Did He Merit to See Generations of Children
 and Grandchildren Who Are *Bnei Torah*?" 534

Chapter 63:
 "Your Grandfather, He Knew in What to Invest." 541

Chapter 64:
 "His Radiance Shines;
 His Ways Make You Cling to the *Shechinah*." 551

Chapter 65:
  "How Can I Express My Gratefulness to the Borei Olam?"   558
Chapter 66:
  "I Think That This Is Going to Be My Last Time…"   566
Chapter 67:
  "He Had Merits, and Brought Merits to Many…"   573
Glossary   575
Family Trees   580

ACKNOWLEDGMENTS

Several years ago, Mr. Danny Srour met one of Mr. Nouri Dayan's grandchildren. Almost as an afterthought, he told him, "You should really write a book about your grandfather. And I will be the first to help sponsor it." Six months later, the Dayan family took Mr. Srour up on his offer. Now is the time to thank Mr. Srour and all the other people who helped this book become a reality.

- Many thanks to Mr. Danny Srour, who eloquently expounded on his connection to the Dayan family: "The names — Dayan, Maslaton, and Bibi — were household names in my family. In the early 1900's, my grandmother traveled with my aunt and my father on the same boat as Hacham Murad. Thus began a relationship that continues until today. Hacham Murad Maslaton became my father's mentor, inspiring him to live a life of Torah. Nouri Dayan became one of my father's closest friends; indeed, he was like a brother. And the Bibis completed this warm circle. From Ahi Ezer on 64th Street to Ahi Ezer on 71st Street to Ahi Ezer on Ocean Parkway — we stayed a close-knit community, bound by friendship and love. As a youngster, I remember Nouri standing in front of the synagogue with his *lulav* and *etrog*, making sure that everyone had a chance to fulfill this precious mitzva. I recall how he created a late *minyan* on Sunday morning in order to attract more people to the synagogue. I relive praying Shaharit together, reciting *Tehillim* together, and then sharing breakfast together. These seemingly small acts changed our community. Nouri's impact, and that of the Dayan, Maslaton, and Bibi families, is eternal. May Hashem constantly shower these families with blessings, Amen!"

- Thank you to Mrs. Adele Bibi and the family of Mr. Joe R. Bibi, who have contributed significantly toward this project in the memory of their husband and father. Joe's sudden passing shocked the Syrian community of Flatbush to which he had always been devoted. Joe was the son of Reuben and Esther Bibi, and certainly inherited their beautiful character traits but, in many ways, he was also the communal heir of his Uncle Dave and Cousin Nouri. As Dave handed over the mantle of leadership to Nouri, Nouri did the same to his great-nephew Marvin Azrak who, as president of Ahi Ezer, partnered with Joe as chairman of the board. Together, they led Ahi Ezer as the congregation expanded its services toward the community in an unprecedented manner. In addition, for many years, Joe served as the vice president of Shaare Zion and was often regarded as the peacemaker. He was one of the founders of Mikdash Melech and of the Deal Synagogue. With all of his accomplishments, Joe remained inordinately humble; he didn't know the word "I." He refused honor while honor chased him, yet he never allowed it to catch up. Joe was also the historian of the family. His interviews enhanced the documentary films produced by The Sephardic Heritage Museum. Equally significant was his enthusiasm for this project. As he reviewed various sections, he was inordinately pleased with the way his family history had come alive in a readable and riveting way. His recollections formed the basis for the opening chapters of this book and for many other parts. His approval was heartwarming. Sadly, Joe passed away before the project was completed. May his children, grandchildren, and great-grandchildren be blessed and continue in his ways.
- As those who witnessed the incredibly beautiful relationship that their father had with "Uncle Izzy" — who was actually their cousin — the children of Mr. Dave Bibi appreciated the value of this project and gave a contribution in his memory. Dave was Nouri's uncle but also his father-figure, particularly in regard to community leadership. In the early 1930's, David became involved with fundraising for the Ahi Ezer Congregation. By 1939, at not yet 30 years of age, he became its president. He was also instrumental in establishing the Ahi Ezer Girls Yeshiva. David Bibi was a man of incredible foresight, most clearly seen when he spearheaded the purchase of various properties which ultimately were used as senior citizen housing and for the Sephardic Community Center. In his quiet and humble manner, Dave aided families and businesses in need, not only financially, but also by giving of his valuable time and advice. He was a true philanthropist and a unique individual. At home, he was a loving and caring husband, devoted father and grandfather, who earned the

admiration and respect of his family and of everyone who knew him. His legend will live on and hopefully inspire others to emulate his actions.

- Many thanks to Mr. Albert Levy and the Levy family. As Mr. Albert Levy describes: "The Levy family has been involved with Ahi Ezer since it was located on 64th Street. As the youngest of three brothers, I had more time to devote to the synagogue (my older brothers, Aaron and Benny, had to work to help support the family). I feel that it is an inborn trait of the tribe of Levi, to which we belong, to work in the *k'nees* and for the *k'nees*. My involvement came naturally, but it was nurtured by Nouri. I can still see him in my mind's eye, as he read *Tehillim*, as he organized *minyanim*, as he sat at committee meetings. Nouri and Mr. Dave Bibi were our role models in how to serve the community. Mr. Bibi would often say: 'For the *k'nees*, one must give from his heart.' And Nouri would say: 'We are *l'shem Shamayim*; don't worry, Hashem will help.' They happily passed on the reins of leadership to the next generation, to Mr. Marvin Azrak and Mr. Joe Bibi. Marvin was calm, levelheaded, and powerful. His untimely passing was a tremendous loss. After he passed away, my older brother Aaron became more involved in the synagogue and benefited greatly from Joe Bibi's constant guidance, virtually up until his last day on this world. Ahi Ezer has had a tremendous impact on our lives and our community, and much of the credit belongs to these great leaders."

- Thank you to Mr. Abe Farah and his family who generously contributed to this project in dedication not only to Nouri, but also in memory of Hacham Sion Maslaton. At the young age of 18, Abe came from Syria to America, alone and lost. He eagerly awaited Friday nights when he and his friends ate at Hacham Sion's table and partook of the elaborate meal that his wife Vicky so lovingly prepared. Abe's wife, Stella, arrived under similar circumstances. She gratefully accepted the Maslaton hospitality and spent many wonderful weeks in their home. Hacham Sion introduced Abe to Stella. He and Vicky married off the young couple and remained a constant source of support. May this book be a tribute to their memories.

We are also grateful to the following contributors:
- Mr. Jacques Doueck who made a donation in honor of his father, Mr. Moshe J. Doueck. Jacques elaborates: "Father, you worked together with your good friend and role model, Nouri Dayan, for the good of Ahi Ezer. For forty years you sold the *aliyot* in Ahi Ezer on the

holidays. You always sat next to Nouri on Shabbat afternoons and was inspired by his pleasant ways and how he encouraged young boys to read *Tehillim*. Father, may you go from strength to strength. At the age of 87 you made your first *siyum Mishnayot*. Regarding this, Rabbi Shlomo Churba wrote: 'It is written in the Gemara that poor people cannot excuse themselves from learning Torah because Hillel sets an example of learning even amid poverty. Similarly, wealthy businessmen cannot use the excuse that they are too busy with their work, because Rabbi Elazar ben Charsom was even wealthier and he was still able to learn. Mr. Moshe Doueck proves that nobody can excuse themselves from studying Torah by saying that they cannot learn since they did not begin when they were young.' May Hashem continue to bless you with long life, good health, and happiness, and may you merit to see many generations of *bnei Torah*."

- Jack and Marilyn Bibi, who contributed in honor of their father, Reuben Bibi.
- Jeffrey and Heather Deutsch and their families, who donated to this project in honor of their mother Florence (Bibi) Deutsch and their grandfather Reuben Bibi.
- The Azrak family, in memory of Ramon and Marvin Azrak.
- Charles and Brenda Saka and their family, in memory of Mr. David Bibi and Mr. Nouri Dayan: "They were visionaries and leaders of our great community, giants among men, who taught us all to be givers and doers. We are blessed to have had them as role models. May our community continue to carry on their legacy."
- Allen and Esther Saka and their family, who made a donation in memory of Hacham Sion Maslaton and Mr. Ezra (Nouri) Dayan: "These men inspired our family and brought us closer to Hashem and our holy Torah."
- Dr. Robert Matalon, Dr. Albert Matalon, Mr. Morris Gindi, the Mizrahi Family, Mr. Bunny Escava, Mr. Seymour Escava, Rabbi Saul Wolf, Mr. Joe Bijo, Dr. Isaac Mohadeb, Mr. Morris Cohen, Mr. Jack Azar, Mr. Victor Sutton, Mr. Jack Fallak, and Mr. Ruby J. Bibi who all gave generous donations.

This book could not have been completed without the dedication and help of Rabbi Shlomo Dayan, whose research, particularly in regard to photographs, has been invaluable. In addition, Rabbi Moshe Laniado's guidance and advice contributed tremendously to the completion of this book. We appreciate and value his contribution. Special thanks to our supporting staff: Mrs. Sara Leah Haber for her exceptional research and

Mrs. Sara Handel for transcribing many interviews. Many thanks to the Sephardic Heritage Museum for providing a private showing of their video depicting the arrival of the Syrians at the turn of the century. In addition, we thank everyone who contributed photographs, particularly Henry Hamra for his rare pictures of Syria, the Mirrer Yeshiva, and Kevarim.com.

It has been a privilege to work with the ArtScroll staff. Rabbi Meir Zlotowitz and Rabbi Nosson Scherman have been very encouraging, particularly in recognizing the value in the message that this book has to offer. We are grateful for their support. Thank you to Mrs. Mindy Stern, who edited the book and was instantly enthusiastic. Her reaction was heartwarming. It is always a pleasure to work with Mr. Mendy Herzberg, whose efficiency is unparalleled. Thank you to Mrs. Rivky Kapenstein for the aesthetically pleasing page design and to Mrs. Esther Feierstein for her meticulous proofreading. May they and the entire ArtScroll family have continued success.

May HaKadosh Baruch Hu bless this project, and everyone who made it happen, with success.

PART I

PROLOGUE

The house had just been completed. After all that construction, all they needed to purchase was gates for the porches.

"I'm going to get a few estimates," Rabbi David Ozeirey told his wife, Barbara. He then proceeded to call the numbers on his list. After a few phone calls to various metalworkers, he reached Mr. Faks.

"Hello, is this Mr. Faks?"

"Yes, who is speaking?"

"My name is David Ozeirey and I'm calling to get an estimate for a gate on my porch and…"

"Who is this? Did you say David Ozeirey? Isn't your father-in-law Mr. Nouri Dayan?"

"Yes, he is…"

"Well, I will be right over. What is your address? I will be doing the job…"

"Wait, I'm not sure… I mean I want to see… you know, your workmanship, quality, style, price…"

"Never mind, I'll be right over," answered Mr. Faks. "Wait for me!"

Within 20 minutes, Mr. Faks arrived with his tape measure and other paraphernalia and set to work immediately.

"Mr. Faks, hold it! I'm not sure about anything yet," Rabbi Ozeirey protested.

"Listen here, Rabbi, and listen carefully. I use the best materials and deliver the best quality workmanship, and the price? Well, why do you think I came here so fast? Many years ago, I arrived here from Syria, broke, penniless, like a dog. Nobody would even look at me. I didn't know what to do with myself. And then, your father-in-law found me. You know what he did? He put money in my pocket, and gave me a job, but that wasn't all that he gave me. He also gave me a way of life. I wasn't religious. He showed me how to live, what to do and what not to do — with love. Because of him, my family is religious today. He took my kids, and put them in yeshiva for free. Today, my daughter is religious and covers her hair. I will never forget this man all my life!"

Rabbi Ozeirey wondered where all this was leading.

"I worked for his company until it closed down. I had to look for a new job and I went into this business and became successful right away. My first order was for 300 high-end steel medallions. They were very costly, beautiful, and ornate. However, the company only took 296 medallions and left me with four of them. I have them stored away for years, and didn't want to part with them. I set them aside for someone special, someone I love. And I love Mr. Dayan! I will give you these medallions for free. As for the rest of the bars, I will only charge you cost price — and my work is high quality. But for Mr. Dayan, anything."

Mr. Faks showed a skeptical Rabbi Ozeirey the medallions.

"But they look old and dirty…"

"Don't worry," Mr. Faks reassured him, "I know my business — I will make them look like new and then I will glaze them with a special treatment that will keep them rust-free and shiny for years to come. This is my small way of paying back Mr. Dayan for all the good he did for me — I love that man — I can never really pay him back…"

Indeed, Mr. Faks did a beautiful job, for cost price, plus the unique medallions.

But to Rabbi David and Barbara Ozeirey, the beautiful gates represent something far more precious: the incomparable legacy of Mr. Nouri Dayan.

Who was this unique man who, many years after he left this world, still evokes awe and gratitude in hundreds of people?

"A *tzaddik*," declared Rav Ben Sion Abba Shaul, Rosh Yeshiva of Porat Yosef Yeshiva in Yerushalayim, upon seeing him.

How did this man, orphaned as a baby, deprived of a normal childhood, become a devoted servant of G-d, community leader, and tireless soldier for his people?

Let us find out.

Chapter 1:
BAGHDAD, OTTOMAN EMPIRE, C. 1895[1]

He was a young man. When he bent over his craft, he could have passed for one of the many craftsmen working steadily at his trade, be he Jew or Arab. It was when he stood up to his full height, straight and tall, with clear dark eyes, that one saw his innate nobility. Yosef Bibi was a cut above his peers.

He paused over the smooth sheet of metal, a smooth silver plate, very shiny and very valuable. He ran his long slender fingers over the glossy surface. It was time to take that plain piece of metal and transform it into something beautiful. It was time to embark on an artistic journey that was painstaking and tedious but ultimately exhilarating.

Yosef loved this part of the job. It was akin to taking a blank piece of paper and writing, sentence after sentence, until, suddenly there was a riveting story where before there had been nothing. He had already mapped out his plan. He knew exactly how he wanted the finished product to look. It was time to begin.

He took his burin, a thin rod, similar to a screwdriver, and placed it over the pattern he had outlined. Then he took a hammer and gave a little tap. That was the first indentation. He moved the instrument slightly forward — *tap, tap* — now the line was a centimeter long. *Tap, tap, tap* — the circle was deeper than the line but not deep enough to penetrate the silver. *Tap, tap* — an arch appeared. *Tap, tap, tap* — another circle. A cluster of

---

1. Most of Part I has been based on family lore that has been passed down from generation to generation. Two interviews that were particularly helpful were that of Mr. Joe Bibi of Brooklyn and Mrs. Ruchoma Levy of Israel, grandchildren of Yosef Obadia Bibi. Details were supplemented by general research of the era. Ages of the protagonists are based on Ellis Island and family records. The dates of the given chapters are approximate.

grapes was taking shape. Yosef was totally focused on his work. A customer had ordered a very specific design. The silver was expensive. He couldn't afford to mess up.

Not that he usually did. At 23 years old, Yosef Bibi was already a master craftsman. He had traveled as far as Bombay, India where he was hired by the wealthy Sassoon family — "the Rothschilds of the Middle East" — to do restoration work on the community's religious artifacts (*Sifrei Torah* cases, *brit* trays, candlesticks, etc.), all of which were silver, copper, or brass.

Silver was the metal of choice during prosperous times. Ornaments and vessels made of silver were easy to repair and, after a quick polish, looked like new. Copper was a much cheaper alternative but it was often too weak to be used on its own and had to be mixed with other minerals that turned it into brass. Brass and copper required heavy polishing and much patience to make them sparkle as they should. Yosef labored for many weeks until all the community vessels and ornaments were restored.

The work in Bombay enhanced Yosef's reputation as a master craftsman. He spent many months away from his family, living among strangers — warm and friendly strangers, but strangers all the same. Nonetheless, the work suited him. Yosef was quiet but industrious. He enjoyed his own company and was grateful to G-d Who had given him a talent with which to make an honest living.

When he returned to Baghdad, he continued working with his father and brothers on the ground floor of their home, where most Baghdadians had their businesses. One of the Bibi family's specialties was their *Sefer Torah* cases. According to Sephardic tradition, these cases were made of metal and were works of art, usually custom-made to serve as a tribute to beloved, departed family members. Much thought went into which *pesukim* to engrave on the surface of the case, so that they reflected the love of Torah and the devotion to G-d of those in whose honor the case was being dedicated.

In good times, the cases were made of solid silver. In difficult times, silver-plated brass or copper was used. Working with silver-plated brass was different from working with solid silver. The engraver pounded and chiseled at the thick metal until a beautiful design made of flowers, scrolls, stars, and rosettes, intertwined with Hebrew letters, emerged. He then melted a thin coating of silver and poured it over the copper to create a silver look. When even that was too expensive, the artisan used colored paints rather than the silver coating, resulting in a different but also beautiful look.

But the copper cases were very heavy; two people were needed to lift one case. So the Bibis stopped making copper cases and looked for other inexpensive alternatives to solid silver. Yosef experimented with a combination of materials — thick, richly colored velvet — and silver. He

An old Sephardic
Sefer Torah case made of copper,
inlaid with silver

A *fanoose*

staggered the silver pieces so that there was significantly less silver being used, but the effect was very regal.[2]

The Bibis also designed the elaborate *ner tamid* found in all Sephardic synagogues of that time. The typical *ner tamid* design was that of a *fanoose*, an upside-down dome elaborately elongated to create a dramatic effect. The inverted dome was topped with a saucer designed to be filled with water and oil. The water kept the oil afloat so that when its floating wicks were lit, their flame would be highly visible. Three chains suspended the *fanoose* from the ceiling, creating an elegant look. The Bibis took pride in beautifying the synagogues of their community.

I'm very fortunate, Yosef ruminated as he worked. *I earn a living while engaging in a craft that I enjoy…*

He had come to a tricky part in the design. It was time to heat the metal just enough to make it pliable — too much heat and the metal would liquefy, too cool and the metal would not budge. He worked carefully, patiently, stretching the silver so that the center of the design would be raised while

---

[2]. "I think that the Sephardic tradition of having metal cases for their *Sifrei Torah* evolved because of the hot, Middle Eastern climate. The metal cases protected the parchment from the elements. The Ashkenazic environment was cooler, less conducive to rotting. Our cases were expensive, so people invested much time, thought, and creativity into designing them," commented Mr. Joe Bibi in 2012.

Baghdad, Ottoman Empire, c. 1895

the background would be lowered. There, he had done it. He examined his work with a critical eye: Had he achieved the three-dimensional effect that the customer ordered? The cluster of grapes lay flat in the background, allowing the letters to protrude in a way that emphasized their importance. He nodded to himself. Yes, it was good. He went on to the next phase of the project.

Tap, tap, tap.

He examined the results from a different angle.

Tap, tap.

He compared it to the original plan.

Tap, tap, tap.

"So, how are you doing, old man?"

Yosef looked up and smiled at his friend, Yaakob.[3] At 23 years old, Yosef was used to being teased. In their community, people married young, and his single status was an open invitation to comment. He gave a brief nod and went back to his work.

"Listen, Bibi *habibi,* I have a great idea. The Bakal family, next door, they have a wonderful girl. I'm telling you, it's a match made in Heaven."

Yosef broke into a wide grin and put down his burin. *"Ya, habibi* — you must be joking. What, you want me to marry a baby? How old is she? 10?"

"Of course not, Yosef. You think I would suggest a child? She's much older than that. She's…" Yaakob started counting his fingers, "at least 13."

"Thirteen? I think I'll pass. Thanks anyway." Yosef once again bent over his work.

"Yosef, is he bothering you?" piped up 7-year-old Selim,[4] Yosef's little brother, from the other end of the room.

"It's fine," Yosef drawled, already tap tapping.

In addition to the religious ornaments and objects, Sephardic Jewry decorated their synagogues with intricately engraved metalwork such as these doors to the heichal (aron kodesh).

---

3. Syrian Jewry traditionally pronounce the "bet" and "vet" as a "bet." Therefore, Yaakov is pronounced Yaakob, Reuven was Reuben, and Rivka was Ribka, which ended up sounding almost like Rebecca. Sephardic Jewry refers to Ma'ariv as Arbit.

4. It was common among Middle Eastern Jews to use the Arabic versions of their Jewish names. Hence Solomon became Selim.

"I don't give up so quickly, you know…"
Yosef grunted.
"I'm going to talk to your parents…"
This time Yosef didn't even acknowledge his comment.

The Bakal family was just as well known in the community as the Bibis. They, too, were hardworking people who made an honest living, while upholding their Jewish traditions. They lived in the building next door to the Bibis and similarly had their business in the same building where they lived. On the ground floor, they had a large warehouse where they stored their products. The middle floor was their living quarters and on their roof was their "factory."

The Bakals had a dried fruit and vegetable business. They bought produce in season and laid them on the roof, where the sun dried them out. They knew just how much sugar and flavorings to add so that their products would last for many months. The sugar served as a preservative and the flavorings ensured that the fruits and vegetables remained tasty. They stored them in their warehouse on the ground floor, where it was cool, and then they would sell them at a large profit many months later, when those very fruits and vegetables were out of season and unobtainable.

Once an idea germinates, it can take on a life of its own and that is what happened to the little "suggestion" that Yosef's friend presented. As it turned out, Farha (Farch'ha) Bakal was already 14, almost an old maid by Middle Eastern standards. While she was 9 years younger than Yosef, this age gap wasn't uncommon, and since there were so many other reasons that the match seemed promising, one thing led to another and soon they were married. The new Bibi couple began their life together in Baghdad, the city of their birth.

Baghdad's first Jews arrived after the destruction of the First Bet HaMikdash in 3338 (586 BCE). In the next 2,500 years, the situation of the Jews of that region fluctuated between periods of great prosperity and great persecution.[5] By the 16th century, the Jewish community reestablished itself and, under the Ottoman Empire, slowly emerged as a center for Middle Eastern Jewry, even creating satellite communities in China, India, Syria, and Egypt. This gave Baghdad's Jews useful business connections that stretched from the Far East, all the way across the Ottoman Empire, and turned Baghdad into a wealthy and prosperous Jewish center, the second largest and most influential of all the Jewish communities in the Ottoman Empire.

---

5. In 1353, Tarlemane decimated the Jewish population and for the next century and a half, there was no real Jewish community in Baghdad *(The Jews of the Middle East and North Africa in Modern Times,* Columbia University Press, p. 352). Much of the historical information in this chapter has been culled from the aforementioned book. Some of the information on the Ben Ish Hai has been taken from the book *Ari MiBavel.*

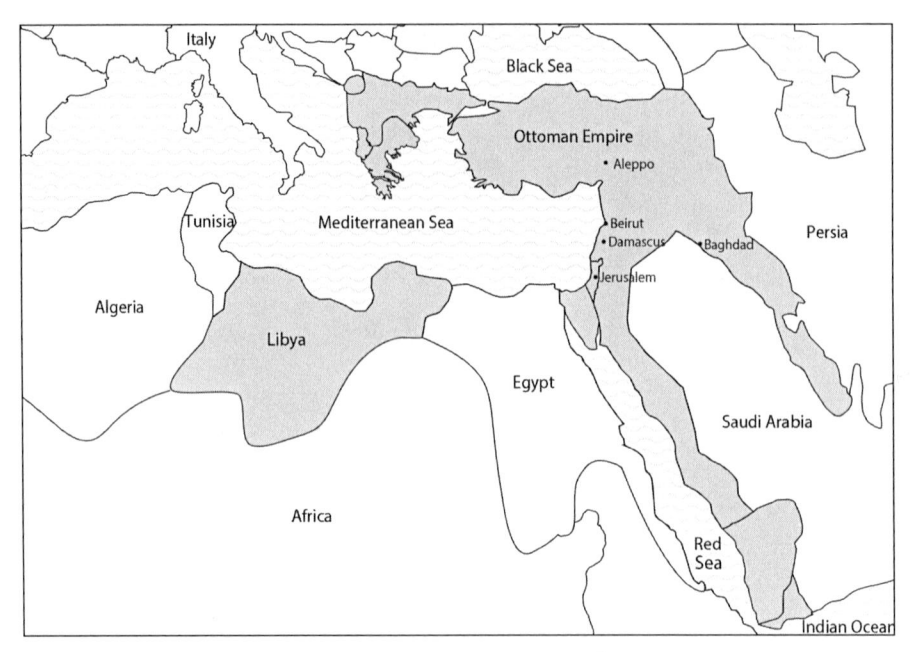

The Ottoman Empire as of 1890[6]

During the 1800's, Jewish life in Baghdad reached a height it had not enjoyed since the period of the Geonim. By 1889, there were about 25,000 Jews among a population of 100,000 Muslims and 5,000 Christians. A large part of this growth was due to the presence of one of the greatest Sephardic leaders of the generation, Rav Yosef Chaim, author of the popular *sefer Ben Ish Hai*.

The Ben Ish Hai refused to accept a community position, but he remained the de facto leader by virtue of his greatness. His word begged obedience and the community flocked to hear his lectures every day. He would speak to the public for an hour, teaching Torah in a way that both laymen and scholars learned something. He was known for his uncompromising adherence to the Law, but since he gave over his teachings with so much love, his people accepted his instructions willingly.

The Shabbat *derashot* of the Ben Ish Hai attracted over 4,000 men and women every week. After Minha in the Bet Knesset HaGadol, everyone

---

6. For almost 400 years, the Ottoman Empire covered much of the Middle East, North Africa, and Central Asia. At its peak, it bordered Iran (Persia) on the Middle Eastern side, the Austro-Hungarian Empire on the European side, and included Greece and most of the land along the Mediterranean Sea. At the time of our story, it had lost a large portion of its land but still included Iraq, Syria, Lebanon, Eretz Yisrael (Palestine), and Jordan — none of which existed as independent countries until after the collapse of the Ottoman Empire. These countries were formed roughly according to the regions into which they were subdivided during Ottoman rule. Nonetheless, as long as it was one empire, Jews moved often and freely from one region to the other.

would assemble in the adjoining Beit Knesset HaKatan, packing the large room and the balcony. He usually quoted the *Zohar*, giving a basic understanding of the text and then branching out as he wove in practical halachic instruction with ethical lessons in his 3-hour lecture. The crowd hung onto every word.

Farha Bakal regularly attended these *derashot*, and spoke reverently of the awesome experience for the rest of her life. She was a fitting partner for Yosef Bibi, who was known for his piety and his love of learning. Perhaps he too had been influenced by the Ben Ish Hai and his *derashot*, for Yosef Bibi had an unusual affinity for the *Zohar* and learned from it often. Late at night, when most people were long sleeping, Yosef was chanting from his worn *sefer*, swaying back and forth to the rhythm of his melody.

Under the leadership of the Ben Ish Hai, almost all of Baghdad's Jews observed Shabbat, even as secular influences subtly crept into their society.[7] They served their neighboring communities as well, providing them with rabbanim, *dayanim*, *shohatim*, *soferim*, and *melamedim*. Even the Baghdadian laymen bolstered those communities as they moved from one area to the other in search of better business opportunities.

Hacham Yosef Haim (1832-1909) was fondly known as the Ben Ish Hai, after one of the many *sefarim* that he authored. The Ben Ish Hai was often referred to as the Rambam of the East because of the universal acceptance that he garnered from all corners of the region. "Had he lived during the time of the Temple, it would never have been destroyed," declared Rabbi David Hai HaCohen, "for, unlike then, when the Jews disregarded the admonitions of the prophets, the entire Baghdad community obeyed the Ben Ish Hai." His expertise in all parts of Torah was legendary.

Such was the case with Yosef Bibi. Shortly after his marriage, Yosef decided that it was time to leave Baghdad. He set his sights on Damascus, a much poorer and much smaller city than Baghdad, but a place where he felt they would do better financially. The Jews of Damascus were known for their exquisite engraving and, simply by reputation, they had formed a monopoly on metalwork in that area of the Middle East. They owned and operated large engraving factories with master craftsmen who trained apprentices and were paid not only for their work, but for training new workers. These facto-

---

7. At the funeral of the Ben Ish Hai, Rabbi Shimon Aaron Abba Agasi protested the new incursions in traditional Judaism: publicly desecrating Shabbat, eating forbidden foods in non-Jewish restaurants, attending theater, and women dressing immodestly [Western style].

The Bet Knesset HaGadol, where Farha Bibi listened to the lectures of the Ben Ish Hai

ries were staffed exclusively by Jews. Customers from all over that region of the Middle East came to Damascus for their engraving needs.

Baghdad was in Iraq and Damascus was in Syria, but both were part of the Ottoman Empire and travel between the two areas was common. There were definite differences between the Jews of the two regions, but their traditions were almost identical. Language was probably the greatest barrier; the Arabic dialects of the two regions were different enough to be confusing.

A Damascus engraving factory

Yosef had always been ambitious and unafraid of change. He wasn't daunted by the thought of learning a new language, meeting new people, forging new business contacts, and creating life anew. His new wife, Farha, loyally supported his vision, even though it couldn't have been easy for her to leave her own family behind.

A rare view of the entrance to *Haret al Yahud* (the Jewish Quarter) of Damascus, referred to as the *Hara* or *Al-Amin*, at the turn of the 20th century, around the time that the Bibis moved there

The young Bibi couple packed up their modest belongings and set out to establish a new life in Damascus.

An aerial view of the *Hara*

Baghdad, Ottoman Empire, c. 1895 / 31

Chapter 2:
DAMASCUS, SYRIA, 1909

Moonlight peeked through the windows that faced the courtyard of the sleepy Jewish Quarter, casting a bit of light into the large room. The room was dimly lit. A small *wan-naseh* stood on the table, its few wicks floating in oil glowing softly in the darkness. A man and woman sat near each other, alone in thought.

They had come to Damascus barely fifteen years earlier, young and idealistic, eager to build their home. They encountered an ancient city with a vibrant Jewish Quarter, a labyrinth of narrow alleyways marked by simple doorways that opened into comfortable homes. From the outside, those homes seemed exceedingly modest, and yet, behind those yellow painted stucco walls were high-ceilinged rooms, some with delicately engraved woodwork and marble finishes, relics of a wealthy era when money flowed freely through the courtyards of *Al-Amin*.

Those prosperous years were long gone as most of Damascus Jewry struggled to make a living. Spacious homes were divided among several families and, though the high ceilings still lent an aura of wealth, chipped marble and rubbed-out wood couldn't feed empty stomachs. All that was left from the once wealthy commercial center was a struggling working class that was grateful for small comforts: life among family and friends, a vibrant religious atmosphere, and a warm and familiar society that revolved around the *hohsh*, the communal courtyard.

The homes of Damascus Jewry faced the narrow street on one side, and the *hohsh* on the other. The *hohsh* was where the children played while the women drew water from the communal cistern and chatted about life, rejoiced in good news, and commiserated with each other's pain.

The Jews of Syria generally built their homes and their synagogues with simple exteriors to avoid *ayin hara*, though the interiors were often opulent. This is the entrance to the famous Eliyahu HaNavi synagogue.

The *hohsh* was where men met one another at the end of a long workday and caught up on the news and maybe even exchanged an insight they saw in the *Zohar*. Jewish homes never had windows facing the street. All windows faced the *hohsh*, perhaps indicating a silent understanding that Syrian Jewry opened windows to each other, but were closed to non-Jewish society.

Damascus Jewry didn't consciously isolate themselves from the world around them. They merely kept to themselves, creating a self-contained society. They had their own butchers, grocers, and bakers. They inhabited their own world of shared values, where everyone believed in G-d, everyone ate kosher food, everyone kept the Shabbat holy, and everyone prayed in the Bet Knesset. Some Jews were more learned and some were less. Some Jews were more pious and some were less. But everyone revered the Hachamim and aspired to be good Jews. [8]

---

8. Already twenty-five years earlier, Rabbi Yehuda Cohen sharply rebuked the people of Damascus regarding relaxed standards of modesty among the women (*Yehuda Yaaleh, Perashat Shoftim,* and *Mishlei* 31) and breeches in keeping Shabbat (ibid. *Kedoshim*). Nonetheless, he praises the city as a whole, stating that most of its people are truly G-d fearing and want only to follow His Will.

Damascus, Syria, 1909

According to Syrian tradition, this synagogue was built on the site where Eliyahu HaNavi parted from his student Elisha. The community built a monument over that spot, gated it off, and built a magnificent synagogue over it. For centuries, Jews flocked to the 2,000-year-old synagogue to pray for salvation, and many miracles were attributed to prayers said there. Some of the many chandeliers that adorned the synagogue can be seen in this picture.

Certainly, Arab culture influenced the food, music, and lifestyle of Damascus Jewry. But it was a subtle influence that crept into Jewish society over generations, without their active participation in Muslim society.[9] There were just enough cultural ties between the two groups so that the Jews of Damascus felt at home in their host country without actually being friends with their Muslim neighbors. Yet that sweet sense of security was slowly dissipating.

---

9. "There was no mixing between Jews and non-Jews in Damascus. Our lives were completely separate" (Mr. Basil Cohen). On the other hand, most Syrian Jewish food is actually Syrian, as are the names of the dishes. Even today, Arabic words and expressions are part of Syrian Jewish vocabulary.

From their shops, the Jews of Damascus noticed that fewer customers placed large orders and more people looked to fix their old possessions rather than order new things. They understood that their economic difficulties were a reflection of the upheavals occurring throughout the Empire.[10] They discussed these changes in the *hohsh*, cautiously wondering what would happen to their comfortable relationships as their Arab neighbors grew increasingly frustrated with their difficult lives.

For Yosef and Farha Bibi, their move to Damascus had been blessed. Their family had expanded to include four children: one girl and three boys. They were regular Damascenes, at home in their new community that was both warm and welcoming. But the daily economic struggle tempered their joy.

This is the street entrance to a house in Bet Farhi, the most elaborate Jewish home in the Jewish Quarter during the 1800's. Note how simple the exteriors of the Damascus houses were.

Joy. Farha allowed herself to dwell on that feeling, a small smile playing at her lips. Just a few months earlier she thought her heart would burst with joy as, barely fifteen years after her own wedding, she handed over her lovely Shafika to be the child bride of a fine young man, Yisrael Dayan. She could hardly believe that, sometime soon, she would, G-d willing, become a grandmother.

A gusty wail broke the silence and Farha hurried to the cradle in the corner of the room. She picked up her own baby, David, and rocked him softly in her arms until he fell back asleep. *Hashem has been good to us*, Farha admitted to herself, as she watched his tiny chest rise up and down with his soft breathing. Her baby boy was scheduled to become a baby uncle and the prospect of the two generations growing up together was exhilarating.

Yes, Hashem has been good to us. But Farha couldn't bring herself to say those words aloud. Not now. Not when she and Yosef had just arrived

---

10. The slow collapse of the Ottoman Empire, the opening of the Suez Canal, the deluge of foreign imports due to the ease of transportation, and national unrest, all contributed to the economic depressions of the 1890's.

The *hohsh* pictured here is one of the many courtyards of Bet Farhi. Note all the windows facing into the courtyard (while none face the street).

at a very painful decision. She returned to the table and sat back down, once again silent. Neither she nor Yosef was particularly talkative, but this wasn't their usual companionable quiet. This was silence borne of contemplation. They had made a decision and now they pondered its implications.

"I think that I will have to take Reuben," Yosef stated.

"Reuben? But he is doing so well in the Beirut school…" Farha was dismayed.

"I know… I know…"

There was a longer silence.

"But you realize that I will need his help?"

Farha sighed. *He has made up his mind. They will both go. I will be giving up my husband and my son.* But, as usual she was silent.

Yosef drummed on the table, lost in thought. *The Ribbono shel Olam has been good to me. I'm 43 years old and healthy. I have a wonderful wife, a daughter, and three healthy sons. Shafika has married a fine young man from an excellent family. And now this wonderful opportunity has fallen into my lap… and yet it's so difficult to be happy…*

He glanced around the familiar room where they sat together. Recognition of his blessings couldn't erase the poverty that screamed from every corner of the dimly-lit room. The walls needed a painting. There was barely any furniture and what they did have was shabby. The jars of pickled vegetables were almost empty. The wooden cupboards didn't contain much more than was visible outside of them.

Compared to the rest of the Damascus community, the Bibis were comfortable. Their son attended school and they always had bread on their table. But that "prosperity" was merely an illusion; this new business opportunity had knocked on the Bibi door at precisely the right time.

There was another matter weighing on Yosef's mind, but this he dared not share with Farha. There was much unrest within the Ottoman Empire. The Young Turks had overthrown the Sultan a year and a half earlier. Nine months later, a counter coup, though brutally squashed, reinforced the message that the new Turkish government would use its military might to consolidate power. And it was definitely gaining power. While ostensibly championing for justice, peace, and Western ideals, the Young Turks were a militant group and there was a subtly sinister undertone to their activities.

Yosef wasn't a gossiper and neither was Farha. When he chose not to tell her about the many young and not-so-young Jewish men who had been abruptly summoned to serve in the revamped Turkish army, he wasn't hiding anything from her. He was simply choosing not to share the latest tidbit of news. After hearing rumors of the brutality of the Young Turks, Yosef had no illusions about what life for a Jew in the Turkish military was sure to be like. No wonder many men were stealthily slipping out of the country...[11]

"How will you meet up with Reuben?" Farha interrupted her husband's thoughts.

Yosef blinked. *Right, we were in the middle of a conversation. Where were we?* He wrinkled his brow in concentration. *Reuben... she's right, how will I get him out of the country?*

"How are you traveling?" Farha interrupted again.

Now Yosef became more focused. "As of now, our first destination is Tunisia. The best way to get there is to go by train to the port of Tripoli in Lebanon and, from there, by boat."

"Reuben is in Beirut. That is pretty close to Tripoli, right?"

"It's..." As Yosef spoke, a plan was taking shape in his mind.

Yes... this might just work...

Reuben clutched the crumpled letter in his hand. He had read it so many times, he practically knew it by heart. And now the day had arrived...

"Ready, *habibi*?" his friend slapped him on the shoulder.

"Ready as I'll ever be," Reuben answered ruefully. He slung his arm over his friends' shoulders and they made their way down the streets, laughing and singing, a bunch of teenagers having a good time. They walked part of the way, hitched a ride for the other part, until finally they

---

11. "The rate of emigration from all parts of the Turkish Empire increased considerably in 1907–1908 with the rise and accession to power of the "Young Turks" movement... The new regime sought to modernize and strengthen the Turkish Empire by creating a larger and more effective army. As a result, the customary exemption of Christians and Jews from military service through the payment of a small tax was abolished ..." (*Magic Carpet: Aleppo-In-Flatbush*, by Joseph Sutton, pp. 6-7).

Trablois (also known as Tripoli)
is the second largest city in Lebanon and its most popular port.

saw the shimmering Mediterranean, strikingly blue against the brilliantly lit sky. Reuben stared, drinking in the picture perfect scene.

"Beautiful," he whispered.

"What, the water?" interrupted one of his more boisterous friends, breaking the spell. "Or the hunks of metal over there?" he pointed.

Reuben followed his finger. They were still a few miles from the port but they could already see several large ships in the distance. There were also smaller boats around and lots of activity. As he and his friends drew closer, they saw many travelers waiting to board the ferry boats that would take them to the ships waiting offshore.

"We need that one," Reuven pointed to the right. The name on the side of the ship matched the one on the crumpled letter he still held in his pocket. He drew in a long breath, "Let's go!"

He and his friends quickly undressed and left their clothing on the beach. Then they entered the water, laughing and playing, throwing coins into the water and challenging each other to find them. To the rest of the world, they were a bunch of college kids having fun in the sun and no one paid them much attention. Gradually, they advanced until they reached the opposite side of the boat from where the passengers were boarding. They grabbed hold of a rope dangling on the side and used it to help hoist Reuben up. Quickly, he scaled the side of the boat until he reached the top, and then he sprinted over the side, onto the deck.

Eight boys swam out to the boat. Seven boys swam back to shore. Nobody noticed the discrepancy.

I hope they made it back, thought Reuben as he scrambled to hide until the boat disembarked. He wasn't really afraid for his friends; they were good swimmers. As for himself, his father had his ticket waiting for him. But until the boat left, there was still the possibility that the Turkish customs officials would find him. If that happened, even his coveted college deferment would not save him from army duty. *I'll lay low for a while. Then I will look for Papa…*

Yosef found his cabin and put away his suitcases. *I wonder if Reuben made it…* he mused. *He must be soaking… and not dressed properly…* Yosef took one of his small bags, emptied it, and repacked it with a shirt and pants, socks and shoes. *This will do for now…* Then he began to walk slowly around the deck.

The ship had raised its anchor and was gliding smoothly toward the horizon. Reuben felt the gentle motion and he realized that they were on their way. The question remained, how would he find his father?

At this rate, I'll become seasick from walking, Yosef thought grimly, as he circled the deck once more.

"Papa, psst…"

Yosef stopped short.

"Over here… Papa…"

Yosef turned slowly. There was Reuben, wet and half dressed, but grinning with success. "Here," Yosef opened the handbag and pulled out the shirt and pants, socks and shoes. "Put this on, quickly!"

Reuben dressed quickly and then father and son embraced. They made their way to their cabin where they would discuss everything that Yosef had not been able to write in the letter.

"So you see, it's a long-term contract," Yosef explained over sweet *ka'ak* that his wife had sent along for the journey.

"How 'long term'?"

Yosef ticked off his fingers, "We begin in Tunisia. They are introducing an event they are calling the Camel Festival.[12] They are hoping that it will be similar to the World's Fair in that it will attract international interest.[13] While the fair itself will not last long, there is a lot of preparation

---

12. Later known as the Festival of the Sahara, the very first Camel Festival was held in 1910, when Tunisia was under French rule. It has become the country's oldest and most famous annual festival.
13. The Nationalist Movement of the 1800's gave birth to grand international exhibitions, where nations displayed their accomplishments, while ostensibly promoting world peace and friendship. The first World's Fair was held in London in 1869. It was followed by similar events held across the world. The World's Fair became the venue to celebrate international events (such as the opening of the Suez Canal), to inaugurate groundbreaking

Damascus, Syria, 1909

before and after the fair and therefore our contract requires us to be there for almost two years…"

"And then?" prompted Reuben.

"And then we move on to France for another exhibition, and from there we will be heading to America to join in the World's Fair of 1915…"

Reuben began doing the math in his head. *It's 1910… the end of the last exhibition will be just before 1916… this trip could easily stretch to… What about my schooling?*

"Papa, this is at least six years."

Yosef looked steadily at his son, as if waiting for him to continue.

"I mean, do we really have to do this? Six years is a long time."

"Do you think that I don't realize that six years is a long time?" Yosef kept his tone measured. He realized that Reuben wasn't asking questions in order to challenge his judgment. He just wanted to understand why his life was being turned upside down so suddenly.

"Reuben, business in Damascus has been very slow. People cannot afford to buy silver or copper utensils. They are not even fixing their old and broken items. No one has money for luxuries. And then this fell into my lap — a long-term contract, do you realize what this is? For the next few years, I don't have to wait in my shop, praying that someone will knock on the door with something to fix. I don't have to come home and notice the bare cupboards, feeling that I have failed to provide for Mama and the children. True, we will have to work long hours, but we will be paid simply for setting up our booth, regardless of how many customers come that day. And the pay is good. I will be able to send home money…" his voice trailed off.

Reuben averted his eyes. He understood his father's decision; the family needed to eat. And yet he and his father were embarking on a long and lonely journey.

The anticipated six years would stretch much longer than they imagined.

They would not see the rest of the family for ten years.

---

discoveries (like the first intercontinental telephone call), and to display unique works of art that often became national landmarks (such as the Eiffel Tower).

Chapter 3:
LYON, FRANCE, 1914

Dear Papa and Reuben,

Damascus is… well, it's still Damascus. Nothing as interesting and exotic as the new places that you have seen, though I guess there is something to be said for familiarity. Yisrael sends regards. The children are coming along nicely. Shimon is beginning kitab (school)[14] soon and we are all very excited. Sara is a lovely young lady with long dark curls and baby Rachel makes sure her needs are heard. Baruch Hashem for her lovely smile. It makes all the work worthwhile…

I stop by the house almost every day since Mama watches the children when I go out to work. It's good to see her and the boys. Moshe is becoming quite a scholar — his head is always buried in a sefer. I must tell you about your very special David. The other day, Mama sent him out to the bakery to buy bread. He is a very mature 5-year-old and Mama felt he was ready for this bit of independence. She waited for him to return, but there was no David in sight. You remember how far the bakery is from our house — he should have been back in a half hour. Mama was getting very nervous. Suddenly, David burst into the house — without any bread! "Where were you?" asked Mama. "Well, I took the money and I bought bread. But, on the way home, I saw people who looked hungry so I gave them the bread. Then I went back to the bakery to buy more bread. As I walked home, I saw more people who looked hungry, so I gave them the bread. Then I went back to the bakery and bought more bread but…" David looked so puzzled as he lifted his empty hands, "…now I have no more money and no bread!" Mama

---

14. *Kitab* is Arabic for school, probably from the same Hebrew root for writing (*kaf, taf, bet*).

didn't know whether to hug him or smack him. He is such a good boy, with such a big heart...[15]

In a dank, dimly-lit room, a lonely father drank in the words of his only daughter as she tried to draw him into their lives back in Damascus. Shafika was the writer in the family and thank goodness for that. Through her, Yosef lived the lives of the children whose childhood was quickly passing him by and the grandchildren whom he had never seen. They were all waiting for him to return to the Old Country, a place that seemed to exist in a different lifetime.

It's good to hear that the boys are doing well, Yosef thought. He never let on how difficult it had been to leave them when they were so young. He prayed that they grow up to be upright Jews, despite the absence of a father in their lives.

"One day," he muttered to himself, "one day, we will be together."

"What did you say, Papa?" asked Reuben, as he polished a brass ash tray that a customer had brought in. On the table was a motley collection of serving trays, candlesticks, perfume dispensers, and oil lamps. Some items needed engraving, other needed repairs or polishing. It was after hours and any extra work they did on their own time was pure profit. Night work was difficult in their dimly-lit room, but they did their best and touched up their efforts in the morning.

"Nothing," Yosef answered, as he slid the papers back into the envelope.

Reuben knew that this wasn't so, but he didn't push the conversation. Whatever had been said had not been meant for his ears. Besides, he had been trained not to question his elders, certainly not his father.

I bet it was something about home, thought Reuben as he rubbed the tray even more vigorously. *He's always like that, after reading a letter. He misses everyone, just like I do...*

But they would not discuss it. Yosef stoically put on a cheerful front and Reuben followed along. Neither dared complain. They had work. They sent money home. They were more fortunate than many other people whom they knew.

The work in France was similar to what they had done in Tunisia, though each fair had its unique flavor. The Bibis set up an engraving booth where people came and watched them as they worked. Yosef was tall and slim, with a gentlemanly air about him. He had a short, trimmed beard, and wore the traditional Arab *tarboush* that completed the exotic look. He

---

15. Though no actual letters remain from this period, the Bibi family tradition is that the only communication from the family in Syria to their father and brother overseas was through letters. We have recreated letters based on the spirit and stories of that time.

smiled at the spectators and then proceeded to show them how an ordinary piece of silver could become a striking piece of art in minutes. People brought items they purchased at other booths and asked Yosef to engrave their names and, no matter what the language, Yosef created a beautiful design with the letters. A customer brought in a simple vase, Yosef would sketch a design and — voila! — there emerged a beautiful and unique product.

The locals brought their metal pots and pans that were bent out of shape and, as they watched, Yosef hammered them back to life and then polished them so that they looked like new. If a customer brought in an urn that was dented, first he would try to fix the dent. But if that didn't work, he would dent it in other places and then create a design so that suddenly the dent wasn't a damage but part of the design. With each new challenge, Yosef continued to expand his artistic repertoire.

Yosef Bibi

Meanwhile, Reuben took orders.

Reuben had come a long way since attending the one room *kitab* in Damascus. His parents had sent him to the Alliance school,[16] where he learned how to read, write, and speak English, Arabic, and French. His

---

16. The *Alliance Israelite Universelle*, also known as KYACH (*Kol Yisrael Chaveirim*), founded in France in 1860, was formed to combat anti-Semitism and help world Jewry. The officers and directors of the organization were secular Jews and their efforts were either rebuffed or appreciated, depending on the community (*Rabbi Samson Raphael Hirsch*, Mesorah Publ., p. 181). The Alliance built schools, mainly in Sephardic countries, through which they introduced Western culture. Many Sephardic communities welcomed these schools, unaware that their European teaching philosophy deemphasized religion, and therefore subtly undermined tradition. Only after several decades did Rabbanim recognize the dangerous effects that these schools were having on their communities and they denounced the schools (*Aleppo – City of Scholars*, Mesorah Publ., p. 52). Nonetheless, in Damascus, the school was accepted by the religious community. Hacham Murad Maslaton, the spiritual leader of Ahi Ezer Cong. in Damascus, taught in the Alliance school and received an award for excellence in education.

Lyon, France, 1914

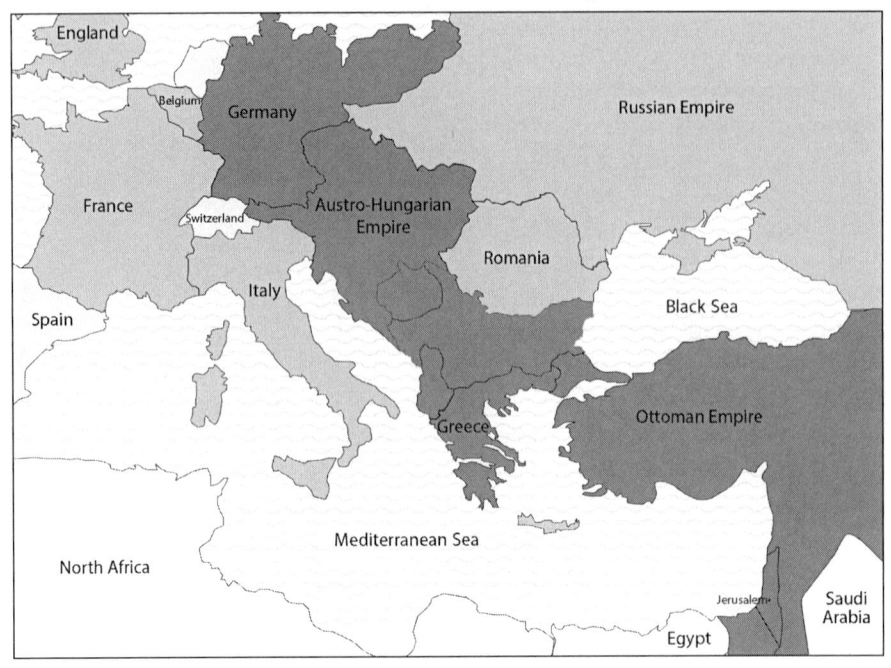

World War I began when Serbia challenged Austria-Hungary, providing an opportunity for Germany/Austria-Hungary to teach a lesson to France and Russia, their historical enemies. The conflict snowballed until almost all of Europe, parts of Asia and Africa, and eventually America were involved. When the war finally ended, leaving unprecedented destruction in its wake, it became known as the Great War. Its "greatness" was recognized in the sheer scope of area it encompassed, in the enormous amounts of casualties suffered all over the world, and in the way it turned powerful empires into weak nations in a span of four years. World War I destabilized Europe and paved the way for World War II.

teachers had been so impressed with his academic success, they convinced his parents to send him to the American University in Beirut.[17]

"Such a mind must be cultivated," insisted his teachers in a letter to the Turkish government requesting that he be exempted from the draft.

At the ripe old age of 13, Reuben received a draft exemption[18] and a university scholarship. But then the contract came up and that was the end of his higher education. While Yosef was grateful for his son's companionship, it was Reuben's proficiency in languages that had been the motivating factor in taking him along on the trip. Yosef knew only Arabic and Hebrew and it was very difficult for him to communicate with customers or business associates. Reuben's assistance was invaluable.

---

17. The American University of Beirut was the first American college to be established outside the United States. It was founded in 1866 and the language of instruction was English.

18. Legally, only men over 18 years old were drafted. Nonetheless, many boys and men, regardless of age, simply disappeared, kidnaped by the Young Turks to serve in the army. The coveted exemption was insurance against a random abduction (ed.).

And that was before the outbreak of war.

"Explain it to me, Reuben, what is happening?"

"It's complicated, Papa. The Serbians assassinated Archduke Ferdinand of Austria-Hungary…"

"Why did they do that?" Yosef interrupted.

"Politics," Reuben shrugged, "you know how it is. Anyway, Austria-Hungary declared war on Serbia. Russia and France came to Serbia's defense. Germany ran to help Austria-Hungary and now…"

"And now Turkey has entered the picture."

"Against France," Reuben added.

"Turkey against France," Yosef repeated, and then fell silent.

Turkey against France… and we are Turkish citizens… in France…

"I don't like this, Reuben," Yosef spoke with uncharacteristic force. "We are Turkish citizens in a country at war with Turkey. We must leave now…," and, as an afterthought, he added, "besides, we have to be in California soon."

"I know Papa, but it's not so simple. I thought that we could just buy ship tickets and be on our way. No luck. American policy states that a shipping company may not sell ship tickets to foreigners without entry visas, which we don't yet have. Meanwhile, I showed the shipping company our passports and they made all sorts of suspicious noises. I couldn't wait to have those passports back in my hands. I just don't want them to call the police."

"But this is ridiculous. We are here legally and we should be able to leave legally."

"Papa, there is a war going on — 'legal' no longer matters. Everybody is suspicious of foreigners, especially foreigners with Turkish passports."

Yosef Bibi took in a long breath, and expelled the air slowly. *This is crazy… we must get out of here… but how?*

"I think we should travel to Marseilles where there is an American consulate. We can apply for entry visas and hope for the best. And Marseilles is right on the water. Maybe we can bribe a sailor to get us onto a ship…"

Reuben threw up his hands in exasperation. "Anything is better than sitting here waiting to be arrested."

"Arrested? For what?"

"Papa, what I said before — we can get arrested for spying."

"Spying? We are not spies."

"No, we are not. But with my knowledge of languages and our foreign passports, what do you expect people to think? We have been here too long. People who used to smile at me, now scrutinize me. Maybe I'm being overly suspicious but I really think that we must leave Lyons. Besides, we can peddle in Marseilles just as we have been doing here. I don't think we will earn much more money, but it will be difficult to earn much less," Reuben answered ruefully, alluding to the not-very-profitable pushcart peddling they had been engaging in ever since the exposition had closed.

Yosef and Reuben headed to Marseilles and continued to search for ways to leave France while earning some petty cash on the side. One contact lead to another. Finally they spotted a glimmer of hope on the horizon.

The office of the American consul buzzed with activity. The Bibis were not the only foreigners in France looking to get to America. Reuben waited impatiently as different scenarios, some implausible and some impossible, flitted in his mind. *Maybe he'll just, on the spot, approve our visa applications… Nah, why should he do that?*

The door opened and a secretary motioned to Reuben, "You may go in now."

Reuben nodded his thanks and slid into the room. The consul was focused on the paper in front of him. Even sitting, he appeared tall and commanding. Reuben hoped that he had a soft side to him as well.

"Okay," declared the consul, pushing away the paper he had been looking at and giving Reuben his full attention, "What brings you here today, my fine young man?"

In careful, halting English, Reuben described the predicament that he and his father faced. Then he thrust the paper his father had signed four years earlier across the desk. "This is the contract. See, we are supposed to be in Tunisia in 1910, in France in 1913, and in San Francisco in 1915. Now, here are our passports. They are both stamped Tunisia — 1910, and France — 1913. And now we want to leave France and travel to San Francisco to be there for the World's Fair of 1915."

The consul scrutinized the contract. Then he compared it to the passports. Then he looked up at Reuben.

"How do you speak French and English so well?"

"I attended the American University in Beirut." Reuben pulled out some more papers. "Here are my transcripts."

The consul studied the new papers. He kept on looking from one document to another, examining each one in turn.

Reuben began to panic. *I have to convince him that I'm saying the truth.*

"I know that my story seems strange. How often do you have Turkish citizens in France who speak English, French, and Arabic fluently? But I'm speaking the truth. We are not spies. We are regular people, trying to earn a living, and we just happened to get stuck in the wrong place at the wrong time. You must believe me…"

The consul continued studying the papers.

"We must be in San Francisco by next month. We have an obligation… if we don't get to San Francisco on time, our employer will be furious…"

Reuben just let the words flow, not caring if his monologue came across as simple babbling. "

Finally, the consul looked up. "I believe you," he said. He scribbled a visa and stamped it. "Here," he said, "go buy your ship tickets. And leave as soon as possible. I'm not sure how much longer the French government will be allowing civilian ships to sail."

He stood up and extended his hand for a handshake.

"Thank you," Reuben clasped the outstretched hand.

"Take care," the consul smiled.

Reuben nodded. But in his heart he knew that it wasn't in his own hands to take care of himself. He and his father were embarking on a dangerous and lonely journey with only G-d as their hope.

Chapter 4:
DAMASCUS, SYRIA, 1917

My beloved ones! How are all of you? Yishtabach Shemo, Reuben and I are well. What can I say? The world is very big and no two places are the same. San Francisco is unlike any other city I have ever visited. Its weather is very similar to Damascus — mild in the winter, and hot in the summer — but that is where their similarities begin and end.

San Francisco is a very young city.[19] Its youthfulness creates a sense of life, optimism, and hope. One feels creative and energetic just being here. Perhaps it's the Fair that fosters this energy. The World's Fair is like nothing I have ever experienced. Just the Fair's ground is a mini city, covering many dunams of land, with enormous buildings that are alive with activity until way into the night. And how, you might ask, can that be? Does not darkness curtail the festivities? As soon as dusk dims the sky, electric lights turn the night to day. While I'm no newcomer to electricity — I wrote to you about its popularity when we were in France — I would never have dreamed that electricity could produce so much power. As I work in my booth, job after job, I barely notice the passage of time for the lighting tricks me into thinking it's still day. Amazing as it might sound, the light seems to exist from nowhere.[20]

Once in a while, we wander around to see the exhibits, such as a model of the Panama Canal, built on the banks of the Pacific Ocean. I have been told

---

19. San Francisco was an obscure outpost of a few hundred pioneers until it became part of the United States in 1846. Within the next decade, the sleepy little town became a major city.
20. The World's Fair of 1915 was most famous for its lighting. A startup company, known as General Electric, used it as a forum to promote this "miraculous" technology. The massive exhibition area was illuminated at night by soft, indirect lighting that seemed to have no source.

that Pacific means peaceful, and that is truly an apt name. I watch the deep blue waters, still and silent against the sun that seems to be always shining, and I feel languid, tranquil. The tumultuous Atlantic conveyed energy and movement. The Pacific exudes peace.

Reuben is pulled toward the air shows where people fly — yes, fly! — in airplanes. Seeing these fascinating metal birds in operation is an experience. The airplanes at the Fair are large machines, built to seat one or two people, with boards extending in either direction, almost like wings, and another board in front that turns so fast, you cannot even see it moving. Somehow — Reuben could probably explain this better than me — everything combines to lift the machine off the ground, and into the air. It sounds unbelievable, but it really is true. A person could spend a week at the Fair and not tire of the wonders that are here.

But life is far from fun and games. We work very long hours. It's fortunate that I specified in the original contract that I would work only until an hour before sundown on Fridays and only after sundown on Saturday night. In America, such a schedule is unheard of. I have met fellow Jews in the Bet Knesset who come to pray on Shabbat, and then go to work! Jewish life here is very different from what I'm used to back home. We miss everyone and yearn to see you.

Give the children kisses and tell them that we love them.

Yours, Yosef

Shafika finished reading her father's letter and folded the paper back into the envelope, very thoughtful. *I won't tell Mama that the letter is dated a year and a half ago. She's so excited about receiving news — any news — I can't disappoint her...*

The Panama Pacific International Exposition, also referred to as the World's Fair of 1915, was held in celebration of the opening of the Panama Canal in August of 1914 and in commemoration of almost ten years since the infamous San Francisco earthquake. Pictured here is an admission ticket.

"Thank you for stopping by to read the letter," Farha smiled gratefully. The rare letters from Yosef and Reuben were her lifeline. They gave her hope that, some day, her family would be whole again.

"It's fine," Shafika returned, smiling in an attempt to mask her fatigue. In the seven years her father had been away, the child bride had blossomed into a capable young woman, mother to four lovely children: Shimon, Sara, Rachel, and the youngest, a newborn — little Ezra. Shafika was tall and striking, witty and talented and enterprising. But the difficulties of war had taken its toll on the young mother, though she tried not to let her mother see her pain.

Her husband, Yisrael Dayan, had just been drafted into the Turkish army. His absence left her with a gnawing ache in her heart, and that wasn't her only problem.

The Young Turks had imposed mandatory forced labor on the young female population to make up for the lack of male workers. The factory hours were long and didn't leave Shafika much time to peddle her eggs, which was the only real income that she earned. Compounding her pain was that she was forced to report to work on Shabbat. She and her friend Sara (Cohen) Maslaton tried to devise tricks to make it appear as if they were working while not actually desecrating the Shabbat. They were beaten more than once when their charade was discovered.[21]

Shafika left the house early in the morning and returned late at night, bone weary and with barely a few liras to show for her efforts. She missed her father and brother in far-off America, where life sounded exciting and optimistic.

"Papa sounds so upbeat," Shafika commented as she prepared to leave. "America seems to agree with him."

Her mother gave a noncommittal shrug. "I'm sure that he wants to come home."

"Oh, certainly. I just mean that there is so much hope and promise in his words. While here..." Shafika stopped abruptly. "I must go now. I left the children sleeping because I knew that you were anxious to hear what Papa wrote. I hope that no one woke up." She took baby Ezra from her mother's arms, gave her mother a peck on the cheek and slipped outside.

The smooth stone courtyard of the Jewish Quarter was dark, but Shafika could still feel the gritty sand through the thin soles of her slippers. Damascus was warm and pleasant most of the year but, summertime, the desert dust pushed its way insidiously into their houses. In better times, Shafika was forever cleaning. She beat the carpets, and dust swirled around. She

---

21. "I spent many hours speaking with my grandmother, Sara Maslaton, when she lived in our house. While helping prepare food, or just relaxing, she would tell me stories of the past. This was one of the stories that she told me" (Mrs. Carol [Dayan] Harari Raful).

swept the floor, and a little later there was another pile of dust at her feet. If she didn't wipe down the furniture once a day, the dust turned to grime and then she really had a hard time getting it off.

Now she wished that she had time for all the chores that had once seemed so tedious. She would happily beat rugs and sweep floors rather than spend hours at a factory sewing machine, earning almost nothing. Better yet, imagine if she could join her father and experience the wonders of the World's Fair, the glory of the Pacific Ocean. If she could only sprout wings and fly off to America, even for one day!

Too bad Yisrael does not share my dreams, Shafika sighed.

Yisrael Dayan was a good man, an excellent husband. She was happy with him and she understood him. He had his whole world in Damascus. Here he was surrounded by his parents and nine siblings — a real clan. Besides, when times were good, Damascus was truly a lovely place in which to live.

The local Bedouins referred to Damascus as paradise, a sentiment echoed in the ancient texts. When leaving the desert and entering the city, one was greeted by green gardens, blossoming citrus trees, and gurgling water fountains, an oasis of life in the middle of the desert. No wonder Damascus had been a preferred stop for traders traveling by caravan from Europe to the Far East for so many centuries.

One of the beautiful scenic gardens in Damascus

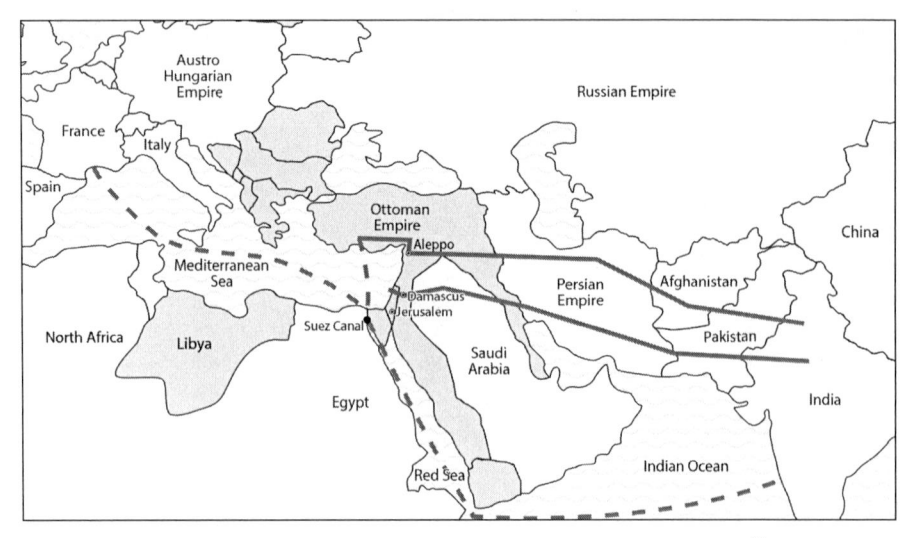

Trade route from Europe and the far East to the Ottoman Empire[22]

Even when Damascus had been a commercial hub, life was slow-paced and relaxed. There was always time to visit a friend or relative and share a cup of tea and *ka'ak*, the popular Syrian sugar cookies. As the economy suffered, the easygoing attitude remained, despite the financial difficulties. This suited Yisrael, who had simple aspirations: As long as they had food for the day and they were allowed to live as Jews, he was satisfied.

But even having food for the day was no longer as simple as it had been a few years earlier. There was just no money — nothing. Every lira was a struggle. Gone were the days when Raphael Stambouli hosted Baron Alphonse de Rothschild in his magnificent estate and the Farhis doled out the salaries of all the pashas of Syria from their opulent palace. Their fabulous wealth had been their own but they were always ready to help out their less fortunate brothers. The old people would rehash all the old legends, reminisce nostalgically, and then sigh and shake their heads. There was no one around to relieve the poverty that was crushing the spirit of the new generation.

---

22. *Al-Sham* is Arabic meaning northern. Damascus, one of the most famous cities in the Middle East, is located north of most of its Middle Eastern neighbors, who would refer to it as *as-Sham* — up north. Both Aleppo and Damascus were "caravan towns." Aleppo was on the trade route from Europe and the Near East (Ottoman Turkey) to the Middle East (Baghdad / Persia or Palestine / Egypt). Damascus was also on the trade route, but usually as part of the sea route. European traders sailed the Mediterranean Sea until they reached a port, like that of Tripoli, Lebanon. The land route from there to other parts of the Middle and Far East often went through Damascus. The opening of the Suez Canal coupled with the advancements in steamship travel made it profitable for European countries to ship merchandise from Europe, across the Mediterranean Sea, through the Suez Canal, around the Persian Gulf, bypassing both Aleppo and Damascus, with devastating economic effects.

In the 1800's, the wealthy Jews of Damascus lived a grandiose life with palatial homes, expensive furnishings, and gold vessels. Above is a glimpse of the renovated Bet Farhi, an estate that spanned 25,000 square meters.

Shafika shook her head, as if to rid it of negative thoughts. She let herself into her small apartment. With one hand, she held her baby, and with the other, she opened the door. She stepped inside, relieved by the quiet stillness that greeted her. Her three other children were sound asleep on mattresses on the floor. Shafika gave her baby a quick hug and settled him into his crib over in the corner of the room. Then she paused and took in the peaceful scene.

Below is Bet Stambouli, which was equally ornate, though not as spacious. The twenty-five wealthy Jewish merchants and bankers were the richest people in Damascus. They were also known for their exceptional hospitality, kindness, and charity.

Shimon, her big "man" — all of 5 years old — was breathing deeply, his thick lashes resting black against his cheeks. *Even sleeping, he is long and lanky, like his father*, Shafika noted fondly as she silently adjusted his blanket, a small smile playing at her lips. She moved on to 4-year-old Sara, whose long black curls lay in disarray against her pillow. How lovely she had looked in the portrait they had taken just a

Damascus, Syria, 1917

few weeks earlier, before Yisrael left. And then there was Rachel, her mushroom haircut framing her still babyish features.

Shafika felt a pang that her husband wasn't at her side, watching the children grow. He assured her that he would be allowed home every once in a while and she hoped that what he said was true. For now, the children were her greatest comfort. She spent another minute just gazing at each child as they slept and then she walked over to the small wooden desk she reserved for her projects.

Shafika was exceptionally bright and talented. Despite her grueling schedule, she wasn't content to sit back and allow her soul to sleep. She enjoyed sharpening her G-d-given skills, expanding her knowledge of life and of the world. No matter how tired she was, every night, by the dim light of the *wan-naseh*, she pored over Reuben's old textbooks, laboring long and hard. She taught herself to read, write, and speak Arabic, English, and Hebrew, a feat almost unheard of in their community where most girls couldn't read or write in any language. She knew that her language skills could ultimately be a business asset, but that wasn't her sole motivation. Shafika enjoyed learning. When she used her knowledge to benefit others, she derived additional pleasure.

As many Damascus men slipped out of the country of their birth, they sent letters from all over the world, but mainly from England and America. Sometimes those letters were in Arabic. Other times the letters were in English or French because many of those young men had never learned enough Arabic to read and write properly and, in their new country of residence, they had to rely on others to help them write letters that were inevitably written in the language of the writer. Shafika was happy to help her friends and neighbors by reading and translating the letters and helping them compose letters in return. In this way, her language skills benefited others, not just herself.

Yisrael and Shafika Dayan with three of their children: Sara, Rachel, and Ezra

But wouldn't it be nice if I had those electric lights that Papa writes about? thought Shafika, as she peered ruefully at the printed page in front of her. It was no use. After an hour of straining to see, she grew weary, and her head became muddled. She headed for bed and fell into a dreamless sleep. Like her mother, Farha, she swallowed her pain and waited stoically for the day when her family would be whole again.

Chapter 5:
SAN FRANCISCO, 1918

"Hey Ruby, what's up?"
Reuben Bibi pulled his motorcycle up to the curb, braking into a neat park. His father was already in the shop, though normally they came to work together. People had gotten used to the strange sight of his dapper father, sitting ramrod straight in his business suit, clinging to his son on the back of his motorcycle, as they sped from the modest room they slept in to their storefront on Sutter Street. Yosef Bibi remained as practical in America as he had been back in Damascus. If this was a convenient way to travel, then why not?

Reuben swung his leg over the seat and kicked down the kickstand so that the motorcycle stood more securely. He gave the "Pirate," his motorized buddy, a fond pat and turned his attention to the friendly voice.

"And how have you been, old friend?" Reuben returned, slapping him on the back.

"Come, I'll tell you about it in the shop. Your Pop is probably waiting for you."

Reuben nodded in agreement and the two friends walked inside. Yosef Bibi was already at work. He looked up at his son and, seeing that he had company, nodded in greeting but didn't enter the conversation. He went over to the table that held some unfinished projects, picked one out, and settled down to work.

"I've been traveling around, Ruby, selling a little here and there, trying to make contacts. It's not easy."

Reuben nodded. Almost a quarter of his life had already been spent on the road trying to eke out a living, and he was all of 23 years old!

"I really want to settle down. Find a wife. Build a family..."

Reuben noticed a strange stillness emanating from his father's corner. *Is he listening?* Reuben didn't want to look up and see. His father had a hard time with English. Had he stopped working in order to concentrate on the conversation? Then he heard the *tap tapping* resume. His father was back at work.

"Really Reuben, it's getting to me. This life is not a life. Alone, on my own, for years on end... I mean, at least you have your father. People like me..."

Again Reuben noticed the silence from his father's end of the room. He ignored its implications and went right on working as he spoke.

"Why don't you get married?" Reuben suggested.

"Haven't met anyone. You know how it is. Back in the Old Country, your mother picked out a nice girl... from inside the corner *hohsh*... someone she watched grow up..." He shook his head, "Anyway, I gotta go. Sorry for unloading on you, pal. See ya around."

Yosef and Reuben Bibi in America

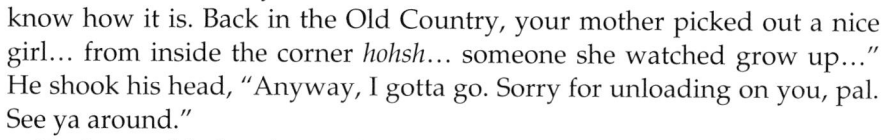

Reuben nodded and waved good-bye.

As soon as their visitor was out of earshot, Yosef spoke up, "He's right."

Reuben shrugged.

Yosef persisted, "He is right. It's time for him to get married. It's time for you to get married. And it's not going to happen here in San Francisco."

"Papa, the war just ended. We still have not heard from the family back home. We have no idea how they are managing or anything else that has been going on in their lives. Is it really the right time to be thinking about me getting married?"

"Yes, it is."

Reuben looked up at his father and when he saw the steely determination in his eyes, he knew that the argument was lost. His father had decided that it was time for him to marry. Period.

The next few weeks were very busy. The Bibis had opened their shop on 406 Sutter Street when the World's Fair closed in December of 1915. The

San Francisco, 1918 / 57

standard practice of taking a train to New York and then a ship to Europe and from there to an Ottoman port was out of the question while Europe was in the thick of war. Yosef and Reuben waited out the war years in San Francisco, building up their business, saving their nickels and dimes for when they would reestablish contact with the family.

The Bibi business was very profitable. San Francisco had come a long way since its years as a remote outpost for idealistic pioneers. When the discovery of gold in 1848 prompted a deluge of fortune hunters in 1849, Jews were among the starry-eyed dreamers. Yet many of the Jewish '49ers quickly changed their dream of finding gold to the practical business of providing for the miners. Over the years, these Jewish peddlers became business magnates, and they helped turn the gold rush town into a burgeoning metropolis and a business center.

As the gold rush tapered off and San Francisco developed into a more normal society, art and culture became its main hallmarks. This was a boon for the Bibis, who found that they could make a respectable living in San Francisco long after their exposition contract had expired. Yosef Bibi's delicate custom-engraving and unique silver art were in great demand and the father and son team never had a shortage of customers. Now Yosef wanted to give it all up and start from scratch at the other end of the country.

"You will never find a good Sephardic girl here," Yosef stubbornly maintained.

That was true. There were very few Sephardim in San Francisco. Yosef Bibi wasn't about to let his son become swallowed into the Ashkenazic community when there was a growing community of Sephardim on the

These pictures are taken from Yosef Bibi's promotional pamphlet. The advertisement described his work as: "... *Bibi Syrian chasing can be done on vases, flowerpots, trays, silverware, candlesticks, candelabras, lamps, and numerous other objects whether they be of gold, silver, brass, copper, nickel, or any other metal of any shape or thickness. Although it requires great skill and years of experience to do this work, the price is but a trifle compared with that charged for the American chasing...*"

other side of the fruited plain. He was grateful to the San Francisco community for their warmth and they respected him for his adherence to his religious principles, but the time had come to part.

Reuben shrugged. Yosef continued talking, "No one is pushing you into anything. But among our own kind, the wheels will turn, and something good will come along. You will see."

Reuben knew that it was pointless to air his concerns when his father was so determined, but he still wondered if his father was being practical in wanting to give up their profitable business and build up a reputation from scratch.

Yosef was idealistic and enterprising when it came to business and he was just as idealistic and enterprising when it came to religion. He kept his beard and always had his head covered (though he had switched his *tarboush* for a western fedora), two Jewish trademarks that many of his co-religionists had abandoned. He prayed with a *minyan* whenever possible, was uncompromising in his determination never to work on Shabbat, and ate very simply so as not to encounter problems of *kashrut*. He always carried his *Zohar* with him, a custom he began as a young man back in Baghdad, and whenever he had a spare moment, he would read from it. By now he knew the book practically by heart. Without ever preaching, Yosef Bibi exuded piety and integrity and won the respect of other religious Jews.

Though Reuben had become a more westernized adult in dress and mentality, he also refused to work on Shabbat, prayed regularly, and was loyal to Jewish law. He understood that his father's determination to seek out a match for him in New York stemmed from his desire to see that he marry a girl with the appropriate religious ideals who also came from a similar background. The only solution, difficult as it seemed, was to leave their burgeoning business and head east, even if it meant starting all over again.

And that is just what they did.

A few weeks later, Yosef and Reuben Bibi found themselves on the Lower East Side of Manhattan. They had traveled miles away from San Francisco, in more ways than one.

Reuben lay in his narrow, uncomfortable bed, and gazed at his surroundings. A thin stream of moonlight allowed him to see the peeling paint that he knew was a dingy shade of grey, though he assumed that at one point it might have been white. The room was cold. But if he closed the window all the way, it would smell from too many people occupying too little space.

Ah, the wonders of New York!

He turned over on his side and tried to dream of sunny California, where fresh clean air smelled of the sea and sunshine bathed everything in its warm glow. True, there were days there that had been unbearably hot, but overall, sunny California lifted his spirits and made life seem lovely.

On the other hand, his father had been right: It was good to be among their own kind again.

Twenty years had passed since the first Syrian Jewish immigrants came to America. They were followed by others, also intrepid idealists, who came either for business or to escape the Turkish army. By 1918, there was an established community that was beyond the tag-along stage, when they joined any congregation that allowed them begrudging entry. They were beyond holding Shabbat services in a bar whose owner allowed their small group free use of his premises because he didn't open anyway until 12 in the afternoon. They had already held services on the street, in tenement hallways, and finally, in their own rented apartment on Orchard Street. Their community was a far cry from the ancient home they had left behind, but it was a growing community of its own.

Reuben enjoyed hearing Syrian spoken in the synagogue and meeting people he remembered from Damascus. Everyone was excited to reconnect with one another and even the foreign faces welcomed the newcomers as their own. Their back-slapping bear hugs warmed Reuben's heart almost as much as the San Francisco sun.

Most of the men they met were kindred souls, living alone as their families struggled back in Syria. All the newcomers were poor, very poor. Typically, the Syrians rented the top floor apartments of the six-story tenement buildings. The higher the floor, the cheaper the price. And of course, there were no elevators.

Despite the poverty and the loneliness, there was a cautious optimism that passed grudgingly from person to person. People who had come twenty years earlier were idolized. They recounted the same pushcart-peddling tales that all the newcomers were going through and pointed out how from there they rose up the financial ladder and were now successful businessmen. Jacob Mizrahi already owned three linen stores on the boardwalk of Atlantic City. The Oriental Jobbers, founded by a group of early Syrian immigrants, ran a thriving storefront on 54 Alex Street.

Yosef and Reuben Bibi were more fortunate than most. They began American life on a contract with guaranteed income, and their subsequent years in San Francisco had been profitable as well. They had a trade that was less volatile and less strenuous than peddling. And they came to the same conclusion as most of their friends: Life in America wasn't easy, but it held a lot more promise than what they left back in Syria.

While the Bibis had come to New York in search of a bride for Reuben, they tacitly agreed that they were there to stay. 71 Allen Street had become their new home and now that the Great War was over, it was time for the family to join them. They sent a letter to Syria, outlining their plans. They waited for a reply. None was forthcoming.

What was going on? The war had ended months ago. Why hadn't Shafika written?

Chapter 6:
DAMASCUS, SYRIA, 1918

She was tall and slim and very pretty, dressed in white clothes that were light and airy, suitable for the desert climate that was warm even in the winter. She turned her head slightly to glance behind her. There was no one there. But that eerie feeling that someone was following her persisted. She walked faster.

Business had been good that day.

They like me, Shafika silently acknowledged, without pride. She had perfected her English over the years and, even though she had a heavy accent, the Europeans who lived in Damascus gravitated to her stall. Granted, her eggs were no better than anyone else's. But they were not any worse either, so why not do business with someone with whom you could easily communicate?

Yet Shafika was uneasy. She had noticed the hooded looks of some of her Arab competitors. *They are jealous,* she reflected, her brow involuntarily creasing. What should she do? She couldn't afford to give up her livelihood. And why should she? True, she had an advantage over her Arab neighbors. But it wasn't simply luck that had created that advantage. She had worked hard to learn English, and she had taken that hard work and used it to help others. She was proud of her knowledge, not in an arrogant way, but in happy appreciation of the gifts G-d had given her. Only today, after noticing the hostile looks of her Arab competitors, did she suddenly wish she was a little less talented.

This too will pass, Shafika consoled herself. She heard a rustling behind her, and stiffened. *What was that?* She didn't know whether she should turn around or ignore it. *I just want to go home to my children,* she thought with rising panic. She quickened her pace.

Yisrael Dayan plodded forward, as if battling the desert sand that swirled violently around him and colored the sky a dull shade of tan. There was no sun in sight; no rain either. Hot winds replaced the usually murderous rays, heralding cooler weather, but Yisrael wasn't certain that the substitution was an improvement. Gritty sand invaded his eyes, nose, and mouth despite the white cloth shielding his face. The air was thick, foggy with dust that stuck in his throat. And yet, all the discomfort in the world was better than active combat. He shuddered at the memory. Would he have to go out to battle once again? Perhaps the war would end before his company was assigned active duty.

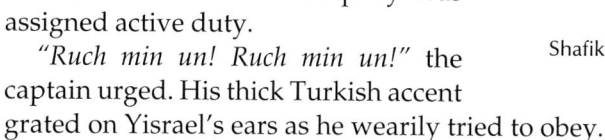

Shafika (Ruchoma) Bibi Dayan

"*Ruch min un! Ruch min un!*" the captain urged. His thick Turkish accent grated on Yisrael's ears as he wearily tried to obey.

Move, move, move… he hated it. How he wished he was back home, settled. His family had lived in Syria for generations, first in Aleppo, now in Damascus. There he was surrounded by his parents, brothers, and sisters and, of course, his wife and her family. No matter what difficulties existed, everything seemed manageable when one felt settled.

I'm so different from Papa, came the unbidden thought. His father-in-law seemed to enjoy the change of pace, the thrill of visiting new countries, the chance to expand his experiences. *Perhaps it's just what he is used to,* Yisrael reflected. It seemed that his father-in-law was always moving — Baghdad, India, Damascus, Tunisia, France, and America. His father-in-law had been on the road for close to eight years and while they had only heard sporadically from him ever since the war broke out, his early letters were all positive and upbeat.

Now he was in America.

America — now that was something that Yisrael really couldn't understand. It was so distant, so foreign. How could anyone coming from his world feel comfortable in a faraway land? All he knew about America was that pale people ruled in a foreign tongue and money beckoned all who sought it.

Yisrael shook his head as he trudged along. *So strange.* Forced to fight in a war whose goals were not necessarily good for him and his people,

Damascus, Syria, 1918 / 63

Yisrael still felt comfortable in familiar territory. The many Arabic dialects that existed throughout the Ottoman Empire demarcated the differences between nations, but united them as well. As Yisrael and his comrades traipsed the deserts from Syria to Iraq, they encountered plenty of prejudice from one group to another, and the primitive, filthy living conditions in the army were breeding grounds for disease.[23] There was death all over — from enemy fire, from illness, and from some of the soldiers' sheer inability to weather the brutal regimen of army life. Yet there was comfort in being in familiar territory among those who were culturally similar. This was despite the difficulty of being a Jew in a non-Jewish army.

Yisrael Dayan

The Young Turks had introduced many governmental reforms to the Ottoman Empire, but their operational methods were brutal and cruel and very shocking to the Jewish recruits who were used to genteel ways. It was a providential anomaly that, for now, the wrath of the Turks was aimed at the Armenians rather than the Jews.[24] Certainly, there were times that his Jewishness made him fearful but, overall, Yisrael's difficulties were similar to that of anyone else at war. He was tired, hungry, dirty, and spiritually depleted.

I just want to go home, he sighed as he plodded on.

Farha puttered quietly around the kitchen. Two flickering flames did little to illuminate the darkness, but she didn't mind. Nighttime was for sleeping. Her bed beckoned.

She checked on the children. Moshe and David — her 12- and 10-year-old boys — were fast asleep. Shimon, Sara, and Rachel — her grandchildren — were also fast asleep. She stroked each one lovingly on the cheek, finally stopping by the crib where the baby slept. His name was Ezra, but he had

---

23. Rabbi Solomon Maimon cited these concerns in a family newsletter. It seems that there were multiple reasons why being drafted into the Turkish army was considered dangerous.
24. During WWI, up to 2 million Christians in the Ottoman Empire were killed or disappeared. This is known as the 1915 Genocide or the Armenian Genocide (Armenians were the main victims). This was considered a "successful" genocide, as it emptied Ottoman Turkey of its Christian population, leaving it almost completely Muslim. The Jews were not singled out for cruelty at this time but the overall barbaric behavior of the Turks was frightening.

not been well and the Hacham recommended adding the name Nouri, "my light." Indeed, Farha felt a special attachment to her youngest grandchild.

Nouri, she whispered softly, *my light...*

She held herself back from picking up the sleeping child and cradling him in her arms, but she couldn't pull herself away from his crib.

Nouri, light of my life, you are so young, so sweet, so innocent... She bent down and held his hand, caressing the tiny fingers. *So young... too young to remember your wonderful mother... too young to have her image imprinted on your mind and heart forever... too young...* She stifled a cry and went to snuff out the flames.

Thank goodness they are obedient children, she sighed as she readied herself for bed. They knew not to ask too many questions. They accepted her words calmly. Mama had a high fever, she had told them. She went to the doctor. The doctor sent her to the hospital. No, she would not be coming back.

But soon Yisrael would come home, G-d willing, and then she would have to review all the unpleasant details all over again. Suddenly Farha could hear the wailing of the Rabbi as he conducted the funeral, and the cries of her friends and family as they accompanied the coffin to its final resting place. She relived it all: identifying her only daughter's remains, arranging the funeral, sitting *shiba'a* while taking care of the children...

All alone, she shivered under the covers, hugging herself for comfort. *I have been so alone.* Everything had been on her shoulders, including protecting the little ones from the traumatic news. She was indescribably weary, sapped of all emotional strength. *If only Yosef were here!* Farha firmly squashed the thought. Yosef was far away. She would have to be strong and deal with life's pain alone.

Yisrael stared at his comrades in disbelief. It was all over, just like that?

"Just go home," his friend said. "We have lost. The Turkish army is in total disarray. We are free."

Indeed, something had changed. His commanding officer was nowhere in sight. His fellow soldiers were openly making plans to go home, though no real orders had been issued. There was disorganization and confusion but one thing was clear: No one was staying around waiting to be told what to do.

He trekked by foot, thoughts of his young family waiting for him at home spurring him on. With each step, he put his miserable past behind, plodding forward toward the future.

Shafika, Shimon, Sara, Rachel, Ezra. He marched to the rhythm of their names, a faint smile playing at his lips. The older ones would certainly remember him; he had been allowed home a number of times over the years. But the baby, he had been so little when he saw him last. *I wonder*

The British entering Damascus in 1918

who he looks like, now that he is older... Yisrael smiled at the thought and tried to move quicker. He had already walked for four hours. Only two more to go.

What will I tell him? Farha was distracted and her hands worked on their own, slicing and cutting the vegetables and then serving the children. She smiled perfunctorily as Moshe gave a *d'bar Torah*, as David pumped his niece Sara up and down on his knee, as Shimon sang the Shabbat *pizmonim*. Watching her children and grandchildren enjoying Shabbat together was comforting, but it wasn't enough.

What will I tell him? The pesky thought would not go away. She had just returned from joining in rejoicing with her neighbor whose son had returned from the now defunct Turkish army. Surely her son-in-law would be returning soon as well.

What will I tell him? She looked around at her precious children and grandchildren, physically undernourished, but nurtured by love.

What will I tell him?

There was a knock at the door. Slowly the knob turned. Yisrael stepped through the door — dirty and disheveled — but smiling. The children pounced on him and he hugged them all in return. But his eyes searched the room, and then settled on his mother-in-law, a question in his gaze. Where was Shafika?

Chapter 7:
DAMASCUS, SYRIA, 1920

"Yisrael, I have an idea for you…"

Yisrael looked up from his black Turkish coffee, his eyes guarded. How he had craved the bitter brew during the endless nights spent in makeshift tents, without water to wash up or a mattress to sleep on. Then he dreamt of the simple comforts of life: a cup of coffee, a piece of fresh pita, his wife's encouraging smile. He finally had his coffee and his pita but, under the circumstances, both were tasteless.

"Yisrael, I have a sister… a wonderful girl…"

Yisrael didn't answer. Could anyone replace Shafika? She had been so fine, talented, and clever…

"Please Yisrael, listen to me. My sister is a very special girl. She would have been married long ago but, as a Rabbi's daughter, people were wary. They thought she'd be too pious, too demanding, too religious. But I know you, Yisrael… and I know your father. There are not many people as pious as your father. And your mother, she is also very special. You will like my sister and she will like you…"

"My mother-in-law wants us all to go with her to America," Yisrael interrupted. "She'll find me a wife there. At least that's what she thinks."

"And you?"

Yisrael made a face. America didn't attract him any more now than it did months ago. He hated change. And he couldn't imagine a greater change than moving to America. He would have to leave his parents and siblings and, while he was fond of his in-laws, they couldn't replace his warm and close-knit family. He would be exchanging the land of his birth for a land that was different from Syria in every way: climate, language, and culture. His family had lived in Syria forever. He wasn't used to wandering. He

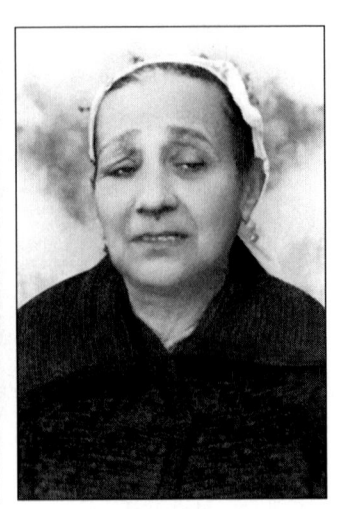

Shimon Dayan, Yisrael Dayan's father, was a learned man who made a living as a carpenter in Damascus and later in Eretz Yisrael. He and his wife Sara were known for their piety.

didn't have the emotional strength for the drastic change his mother-in-law wanted.

"I'm telling you, Yisrael, this is perfect. I mean, she's my sister. I would not recommend it if I didn't think it was good. I want it to be good for both of you…"

Yisrael shrugged, noncommittal, and rose from his spot. He was grateful to his friend for his almost daily visits. No doubt, his gentle pressure was helping pull him out of the rut that he had fallen into since learning about his wife's death. But he had heard enough for one day.

"Don't you at least want to know her name?"

Yisrael gave a half smile which his friend interpreted as an invitation.

"Miriam," he injected quickly, "last name Peretz — like me… and she can't wait to meet you."

Yisrael shook his head and walked away.

Persistence paid off and eventually Yisrael agreed to a meeting. His mother-in-law was unhappy. Miriam was 26 years old. In their circles that was considered an old maid, proof that there was something "wrong." But Yisrael dismissed her concerns. His goal was to marry a woman who would be a good mother to his children and he would only be able to determine that after he met her.

After one meeting, Yisrael was impressed. Miriam was the daughter of Hacham Moshe Peretz, one of the Hachamim who served on the Damascus Bet Din. Hacham Moshe was known for his exceptional fear of sin. It was said about him that he once lent a friend a pot before Pesah and the man forgot to return it until after Pesah. Hacham Moshe refused to take the pot back as he had sold all his *hametz* before Pesah and didn't have in mind to sell this pot and had actually waived his claim to ownership.

Miriam was modest and religious, as befitting the Hacham's daughter. She was warm and pleasant and Yisrael felt that she would raise his children with love. She dreamed of moving to Palestine, an idea that suited Yisrael far more than America. He discussed the idea with his parents and they were very enthusiastic. They, too, were seeking to move to Eretz Yisrael. For Yisrael, the prospect of relocating with his parents and siblings was much more attractive than moving on his own.

It was time for Yisrael to have a talk with his mother-in-law, though he didn't relish the task. The children had been living with their grandmother for over a year and even before then, Farha had been very active in their lives during the years he had been in the army. She would not find it easy to part with the children.

While he understood her feelings, he wasn't prepared for her reaction.

He chose a quiet evening, after the children had gone to sleep. He wasn't accustomed to talking much with his mother-in-law, especially about something so delicate. Farha was a reticent woman; she listened more than she spoke. She was a natural introvert, but there was also a language barrier. Though she moved to Damascus from Baghdad as a young adult, she never mastered the Damascus Arabic, which was different from Baghdadian Arabic. Her nature plus the discomfort with the language kept her quiet. This had worked well in the past, as she and her son-in-law went about their responsibilities without wasting time on needless conversation. Now Yisrael wished that one of them had the gift of small talk. A little easygoing banter might lighten the tension that stretched between them as he spoke to the stony face across from him.

Farha listened. She didn't nod in agreement, or bristle in disagreement. Her face remained surprisingly expressionless.

"No."

Yisrael was shocked at the strength of that one word.

"Mama, I understand…"

"No, you don't," Farha cut in. "You don't understand what it means to have lost a daughter."

"That is true," Yisrael conceded, "and Shafika was special."

"These children are all that I have left from her," Farha stated. "You cannot take them away from me."

Yisrael sighed. "What do you suggest that I do?"

"Exactly what I proposed earlier. Papa will send the papers and money for all of us to go to America."

"I don't want to go to America."

"Want?" she interjected sharply. "Did I want to lose my daughter? We don't always get what we want in this world."

"I'm not going to America," Yisrael stated quietly.

Damascus, Syria, 1920 / 69

"You are not taking the children away from me," Farha declared.

"They are my children."

"They are my grandchildren."

"I'm their father."

Farha raised herself to her full height, which wasn't very tall. She pushed back her chair. "We will speak in the morning."

"I will not change my mind."

"Maybe someone will help you see reason."

Yisrael shook his head as his mother-in-law left the room.

The next few weeks were fraught with tension. Yisrael was learning that the quiet, middle-aged woman he had always thought of as being soft and gentle had an obstinate streak that couldn't be bridged. Every day she came up with another argument. He was getting tired of fielding her attacks but he had too much respect for her to ignore her completely.

"What about Nouri?"

"Who?" Yisrael was still not used to the name change.

"Ezra," she said impatiently. "Nouri."

"What about him?" He answered her question with a question, exasperated. *What kind of convoluted argument did she have now?*

"Nouri is 2 years old and he is still not walking properly. The doctors say that it's because he is severely bow-legged. They have no way to help him here."

Yisrael knew about the problem. So the child didn't walk yet. He was sure that there were other children who walked late. The problem would surely sort itself out, despite the doomsayers.

Suddenly, Farha became uncharacteristically talkative. "I wrote to Papa. He has done investigations in America. He says that they have treatments there. He says that in America they will be able to help him. Eretz Yisrael is wonderful but right now they don't have the same medical care that they have in America…"

Yisrael rolled his eyes. *Was there no end to her ridiculous reasoning?*

"I'm not going to America. Not to get married. Not to get treatment for Ezra. I'm marrying Miriam. We are going to Palestine. And Ezra — I mean Nouri — will be fine."

"He is so young… Nouri needs extra care…"

"He needs his father," Yisrael cut in sharply.

"You will come."

"I will not!"

Farha took a deep breath and tried to speak calmly.

"You will have the other children, Shimon, and Sara, and Rachel. I know that children need a father… and no one can replace you… but Papa will also be there and he will love him like his own children…" Farha was following Yisrael around the house as he suddenly, almost violently, flung open the door.

The nerve of her to even suggest such a thing!

"All the children are coming with me," Yisrael stated angrily, banging the door as he left.

There was silence. Farha sighed. She had one more idea.

"Good morning, Yisrael, and how are you feeling today?"

Yisrael gave a cursory nod. He wasn't very interested in another conversation with his mother-in-law.

"I see that you are not willing to listen to reason," she stated matter-of-factly. "Fine. Get married. Move to Palestine. But let me have Rachel and Nouri. They are both so little. I'm the only mother they remember. It will be too difficult for them to adjust to a new mother and a new land."

Yisrael shook his head in disbelief. She still didn't get it?

"Or maybe you want to let me have the two older ones — Shimon and Sara. They are like my own children. You will get two and I will get two. What do you think?"

Yisrael remained speechless.

"Here," Farha withdrew a letter with a dramatic flourish, "I made us an appointment with the Bet Din. If I cannot convince you, maybe they will."

Yisrael grabbed the letter from her hand and scanned its contents. He could hardly believe what he was reading. His mother-in-law was taking him to Rabbinical court over custody of his children. How could she!?

But when he looked up at the grim set of her lips and her pain-filled eyes, he sighed. Perhaps the Bet Din decision would enable his poor mother-in-law to make peace with reality. The children were his and he was taking them with him to Palestine and he didn't think that any Bet Din in the world would order him differently.

Yisrael walked out of the courthouse rubbing his eyes in disbelief. They both won. They both lost.

Farha (Bakal) Bibi

Damascus, Syria, 1920

They could barely look at each other. He reviewed the testimony in his mind…

I'm the father. I want my children…

I'm the grandmother. I have raised these children as my own for years.

I'm marrying a wonderful woman. She will be their new mother…

The children are very attached to me; they hardly know their father…

The children will relearn who I am; there is no replacement for a father…

The oldest is like my son! He is a brother to my children…

I cannot give up my oldest child…

The youngest one is a cripple. In America there is treatment…

He will be fine. It's more important for him to be with his father and his brothers and sisters…

Let little Nouri come to America with a sister for companionship… I only want what is best for the children…

And then came the decision. Rachel would remain with her father and siblings. Nouri would go with his grandmother to America so that he could receive proper medical treatment.

Yisrael was walking in a daze. How could a father agree to such a drastic separation from his child? When would he see him again? But Yisrael wasn't being given a choice. The Bet Din had decided: Nouri was going to America.[25]

Farha prepared to leave with a heavy heart. Who knew if she would ever see her precious grandchildren again?

At least I have Nouri… my light.

Though at his age he could not know it, Nouri would never see his father again.

---

25. "According to my aunt, Tziyona (married to my father's brother Shimon), the original decision of the Bet Din was to allow my Grandma Farha to take one child. Initially, my grandfather, Yisrael, agreed to send Shimon, his oldest son, but then quickly changed his mind. If he had to send away a child, he would send the one who needed medical attention. My Uncle Shimon commented that perhaps, had he been taken to America, he would have become the successful businessman!" (Mrs. Sara [Dayan] Salem).

Chapter 8:
LOWER EAST SIDE, NEW YORK, 1920

When Yosef and Reuben arrived in New York, Yosef headed straight for the *k'nees*. True, he needed a *minyan*, but he was also on the lookout for a suitable match for Reuben. He made inquiries among his new friends and, with Reuben's agreement, decided on Esther Mizrahi, the daughter of Isaac Mizrahi, one of the founders of Ahi Ezer, the synagogue of Damascus Jewry.

Isaac Mizrahi was from a Damascus family that had moved to Beirut and from there to America. He was a skilled drapery designer, who specialized in heavy damask fabrics. He had built up a respectable business but his real passion was Jewish books. Whenever he had a few extra dollars, he would buy another *sefer* and had amassed a respectable library. This pull toward the spiritual and the scholarly suited both Yosef and Reuben.

There was only one problem. Esther was only 16, which, by Syrian standards, was considered old. But by American standards, it was quite young. Americanized Isaac Mizrahi didn't want his daughter to get married just yet. So he shipped her off to Atlantic City to work for his brother, Jacob.

Jacob Mizrahi was a legend in the Syrian community. He had come to America ten years before most other Syrians and was long past hauling his *shenta* (suitcase stuffed with merchandise) from hotel to hotel on the boardwalk, trying to interest hoteliers in his wares. With much ingenuity, perseverance, and Providence, he graduated from door-to-door peddling and opened his own store… and then another store, and another.

Esther had spent several summers working for her uncle and now she joined his sales staff for the winter season as well. She was good-natured and bright and made the most of what she knew would be a short venture into the world of business. While her uncle's success came from hard work

Isaac Mizrahi

and the good grace of the Almighty, Esther soon realized that there was a lot of psychology to the art of selling. She kept her eyes and mind open, eager to learn about life.

In one of his stores, Uncle Jacob had a safe that he had bought from a bank that had gone out of business. There he stored an expensive line of hand-crocheted linen, of which he put only one napkin on display in a locked glass case. One day, a woman came into the store and she saw the napkin.

"What is that?" she asked Esther, who was manning the store.

"Oh, it's not for you," Esther answered nonchalantly. "It's too expensive."

The woman kept looking at the napkin. "It's so pretty…"

Esther tried to remember all Uncle Jacob's instructions as she furtively sized the woman up, while not appearing too eager to make a sale. "You have good taste. You should see the tablecloth… what size table do you have?"

"Ten feet."

Okay, this is a woman with a large house. But Esther still stayed cool. "Mmmmm… what does your husband do?" she asked.

"He's a doctor," she answered.

"Oh… well maybe tell him to come around and I will explain to him the quality of this particular set. You see, it's not the kind of item that you purchase every day…" By now Esther had really whet the customer's appetite.

"Come around? My husband is right over here. Let me call him over."

The doctor came in and, like most men, didn't really see anything particularly special about the napkin, except that his wife liked it.

"Honey, you like the napkin?" he asked her.

"Oh, yes!"

That was the cue that Esther was waiting for. "I'll call my uncle to come and show you the tablecloth."

Uncle Jacob came down, all businesslike. "Are you sure that you are interested in this? It's very expensive…"

By now, the woman looked desperate. "Yes, yes!"

He turned to Esther, "Go lock the door. I can't let anyone in the store while I open the safe." Then he went to the back of the room, pulled open a curtain, and revealed the safe. He entered the code, turned the knobs, and cranked open the door very slowly and deliberately, talking as he unrolled the material, explaining how valuable and rare it was. By then the customer was hooked and he knew he made a sale.

Hand-embroidered linens were very expensive, though not necessarily so expensive that they needed to be kept in a vault. There was a lot of showmanship involved to encourage a customer to spend so much money. The customer felt important if he purchased something held under lock and key and offered only to exclusive clients. Jacob Mizrahi understood the psychology of selling and used it to build up his business.

Esther learned to understand people and deal with them by combining insight with practicality. She did what she had to do, happily and naturally, rising to any occasion, while smoothing out the rough edges that were always a part of life.

Meanwhile Yosef and Reuben settled in New York. They found an apartment on Eldridge Street, just opposite the famous Eldridge Street Synagogue.

The Eldridge Street Synagogue, built in 1886 by Eastern European immigrants, was an inviting oasis in the crowded and claustrophobic Lower East Side of Manhattan. It had a 70-foot-high ceiling, stunning stained-glass windows, elaborate brass fixtures and hand-stenciled walls. It begged its visitors to escape into a wondrous world where they could be proud of their religion and forget about their miserable living conditions as they basked in abundant air, light, and space.

The Eldridge Street Synagogue was a center of

The Eldridge Street Synagogue

acclimation for newly arrived immigrants. It was where poor Jews came to find a meal or secure a loan, where all Jews came to pick up a business tip, or find out about job and housing opportunities. It was the hub of Orthodox Jewry on the Lower East Side. The High Holidays drew so many people, police were stationed on the streets to control the crowds.

Nonetheless, by the time Yosef and Reuben moved to Eldridge St., the block had turned predominately Syrian, though the Ashkenazic synagogue still had robust attendance. The main Ashkenazic migration to America had occurred twenty to thirty years earlier. As they became financially stable, the Ashkenazim moved out of the Lower East Side and the Syrians began moving in. Slowly, whole buildings were taken over by Syrian Jews.

From Eldridge Street to Essex Street, Norfolk Street to Hester Street, building after building turned from Ashkenazi to Syrian. It was hard to get into a "good" (meaning, mainly Syrian) building. Predictably, the vacant apartment was on the sixth floor. The buildings had no elevators; running water and bathrooms were on the street floor, and the apartments were small and dingy. But the new arrivals took what was available because once they were "in," when an apartment on a lower floor became vacant, those on a higher floor could move to a lower floor, and, once again there would be a sixth-floor vacancy for the newest arrivals. Yosef and Reuben became securely part of "Little Syria" as they worked to bring over the rest of the family.

Reuben and Esther Bibi

The year drew to a close and Reuben and Esther became engaged. The families scheduled the wedding for August, hoping that by then the family from Syria would have arrived. Indeed, on June 8, 1920, Farha, Moshe, and David Bibi, together with Yosef's brother Selim and his family, and little Nouri, orphaned of his mother and now far from his father, were reunited with Yosef and Reuben.

The reunion was bittersweet. Everyone was happy to see one another, but ten years had passed and much had changed during that time. Moshe and David had been babies when their father had left. They were now teenage boys meeting their father, practically for the first time. Their older brother Reuben was also a virtual stranger to them. And no one mentioned Shafika, Yosef's beloved daughter, or the grandchildren he would never meet.

They hugged and kissed and cried. Then they moved on to prepare for the upcoming wedding. It was comforting to have a joyous occasion to celebrate after so much pain. And it was comforting to unite in the New Country with friends from the Old Country. With Hacham Murad (Mordechai) Maslaton — newly arrived from Syria — performing the ceremony and the familiar Syrian language passing from tongue to tongue, Farha could shut her eyes and pretend that she was back home.

L-R: Dave, Nouri, and Moshe (Morris) shortly after coming to America. Note the braces on Nouri's legs. This was the standard treatment for bow-leggedness at the time.

Then she would open her eyes and face reality: America would never be her home. She would have to find strength in the familiar rather than dwell on the differences. Farha counted her blessings, chief among them that little Nouri was still at her side. A standard part of the Ellis Island inspection required all 2-year-olds to walk. A 2-year-old child who couldn't walk was judged to be crippled and denied entry. In an unusual stroke of Providence, "crippled" Nouri, who had been awarded to his grandmother because he needed medical attention for this very disability, passed the inspection designed to weed out children with his problem!

Clearly, the Almighty was proclaiming: Nouri belongs in America.

Lower East Side, New York, 1920 / 77

PART II

Chapter 9:
LOWER EAST SIDE, NEW YORK, 1925

It was the Seder night.

Yosef Bibi sat tall and straight and surveyed the long, narrow table in front of him. To his right sat his wife Farha, and his sons Reuben, Morris (Moshe), and Dave (David). They were fine young men — kind and considerate, industrious and responsible. Reuben's wife, Esther, wasn't feeling well, so she wasn't in the room, but their two little children, Lillian and Moe, were beginning the night sitting quietly at the end of the table. To Yosef's left was Nouri, the grandson who was like his own child. Next to Nouri sat Yosef's brother Selim and his wife and their three children.[1]

A room filled with family, how wonderful! Five years had passed since the Bibi family was reunited and yet they never forgot the ten years they spent apart.

For the Bibis, the holiday of Pesah was particularly poignant. While they had not left Syria in a desperate bid to save their lives, they had left a land where they were shackled by poverty to make their new home in a land of hope. The land of hope was also a land of challenges: The new immigrants struggled to hold onto the heritage that they loved in a land that was pushing them to forget their past.

Pesah was an island of tradition in a sea of modernity. For two glorious nights, the family was back in Syria, eating their traditional foods and singing their heartfelt *pizmonim*. For those two days, they forgot about the unexpected poverty they met on the Lower East Side (if the streets were paved in gold, prying it up from the pavement was proving to be very difficult). They forgot about the frenzied life they led, the hustle and bustle of

---

1. There were also probably other guests, particularly men who were in New York without their families. Mr. Joe Bibi recalled their Sedarim always being crowded with people. Other interviewees also mentioned having as many as forty guests as being typical of Syrian hospitality.

The 1925 directory listing the addresses of Yosef Bibi, Reuben, and their business

trying to earn a buck, and the constant pull to become more "American." For those two days they joined together and rejoiced in being Syrian Jews with a rich and vibrant heritage. Shabbat served this purpose on a weekly basis but Pesah, with its emphasis on tradition and on family, was an even more powerful opportunity.

Yosef and Farha never regretted moving to America, yet they were mindful of what they missed in the life they had left back in Syria. They missed a world that was far more slow-paced and calm than the hectic streets of the Lower East Side. They missed the Middle Eastern culture of natural courtesy and esteem; Americans seemed brash and rough by comparison. They missed the comfort of mixing among people with whom they shared generations of cultural ties.[2]

---

2. In contrasting the Syrian immigrant experience with that of the Ashkenazim, Sutton (p. 148) writes: "Hundreds upon hundreds of thousands of Jews *did* flee the country [Russia] and when the majority of them came to the *Goldene Medina*, they harbored a feeling bordering on hatred for their former homelands..." This statement is not entirely true, as there was plenty of nostalgia among the Ashkenazim as well, much of it over-drama-

The Sea Beach railroad station at 66th Street, in 1914

Nonetheless, they were forward-looking people, eager to focus on the future rather than live in the past. From year to year, as they watched their family grow and prosper, they became cognizant of the great ways of the Almighty Who led them out of Syria, a land that held nostalgic memories but also profound pain. They never spoke of the daughter who lay buried far away with no one to visit her grave. They never spoke of the missing grandchildren that Providence had pulled away from them to a different Promised Land.[3] They held tightly to their faith, rejoiced in their heritage, and walked stoically toward the future. At the start of the Pesah Seder, as all waited expectantly for Yosef to begin, they saw their happiness reflected in each other's eyes. They were grateful that they were together, a growing family, celebrating around one table, united in their love for one another.

Yosef began Kiddush and everyone followed along. Within a half hour, the little children were running around, wine had spilled, and the adults were valiantly trying to keep the older children involved. Yet the magic remained. The warmth of family was like a comfortable blanket that covered them all. The men sang and spoke *dibrei Torah*. The women tried to pay attention while taking care of the little ones scurrying underfoot. And then, amid it all, wailing was heard from the bedroom off to the side, and then a triumphant shout.

"*Mabrook*! (Congratulations!)" cried the midwife. "It's a boy!"

Reuben rushed to see how his wife was faring while the rest of the room exploded in joy. A week later, the child was named Yosef Reuben Bibi after his father and grandfather, the first of many grandchildren to bear

---

tized in their disillusionment with America. Yet there was a definite attitude difference. Ashkenazic immigrants were homesick for familiarity, but they were angry at Russia for the abuse and persecution that forced them to leave (*World of Our Fathers*, Irving Howe, pp. 27,71). While: "When they [Syrian Jews] came to America it was with a bitter-sweet recollection of a peaceful and familiar life, which was still being lived by family and friends they had left behind. They felt that they were *in exile*" (Sutton, p. 148).

3. This reticence was accepted as a matter of course. Reuben's children, who grew up with their grandparents and uncles, never heard about Nouri's parents or other siblings until they were young adults. Even then, they learned only the basic details (ed.).

Spacious 65th Street and 20th Avenue, in 1924

the name Yosef. The Bibi family was already an important presence in the Syrian community and they would continue to affect the community in many positive ways.

By 1925, most of the Syrian community had moved out of the Lower East Side to better locations. The post-war "Roaring Twenties" gave way to an economic boom in America. As the Syrian community prospered, they sought better living conditions. A large group moved to Williamsburg, but they didn't stay there long. Eventually, almost the entire Syrian Jewish community relocated to Bensonhurst, colloquially known as "See Beej" in Arabic-accented English. The recently built BMT Sea Beach Line that connected Brooklyn to Manhattan via Bensonhurst made the rural neighborhood a residential option for people who worked in Manhattan. Hence, they called the neighborhood "See Beej" after the transportation system that made living there possible.

"See Beej" was, quite literally, a breath of fresh air. Large residential homes and streets of multi-family row houses bordered large swatches of open fields with vegetable farms and trees. There were also blocks of tall apartment buildings with spacious apartments that were airy and well lit. The immigrants inhaled the scent of freshly cut grass and air that had not been polluted by too many people living in quarters that were too crowded, and they didn't want to leave. The poorer families searched among the apartment buildings or nearby row houses to find something to rent. The richer families bought large, private houses that dwarfed the homes they had grown up in back in Syria.

A modest rentable was still a world away from the Lower East Side slums. Moving from a sixth- or even fourth-floor tenement apartment to a one-story walkup on top of a storefront was much more than a step up, it was a whole different life. Even the tallest apartment building had indoor plumbing, large windows facing wide streets, and small grassy backyards. They were very different from the typical Lower East Side apartments where one room might face the street but all the others either overlooked a concrete courtyard, the neighbor's apartment, or had no windows at all. People hung their laundry out their windows in Bensonhurst just as they did on the Lower East Side, but on the Lower East Side the heavily congested lines blocked the sun and air from the apartments below, while in Bensonhurst there was plenty of space to go around.

So "Little Syria" of the Lower East Side transferred to "See Beej."

Their arrival was preceded by the Ashkenazim (and Italians) who had settled in this "upper class" neighborhood not many years earlier. Bensonhurst was a Jewish enclave with many shuls, enough to suit a range of personalities and ideologies. All the shuls were Orthodox but the level of observance within those congregations varied. Nonetheless, the Jewish spirit was vibrant and religious. It provided the perfect backdrop for the arriving Sephardim.[4]

Reuben and Esther Bibi moved to Bensonhurst almost immediately after their marriage in 1920. His parents followed several years later in 1925, a move that, in Esther's opinion, was long overdue. As soon as she met her future mother-in-law, practically straight off the boat, Esther realized that her role as Reuben's wife would entail involvement in the greater Bibi family. On a practical level, it would just be easier if they lived nearby.

In Syria, women stayed home where they did all the cooking and cleaning, and took care of the children. The men were the ones who went to the *souk* (market), either for shopping or for business. Some women did needlework at home, which was considered acceptable. But unless, G-d forbid, a woman was a widow, the Middle Eastern woman stayed home.

This had changed somewhat with the advent of the Great War and the drafting of much of the male population. Then, many women had been forced into roles that they historically avoided.

But not Farha Bibi.

When Yosef and Reuben left Syria in 1910, Farha relied on her son-in-law to help out with the shopping and errands. As her little boys grew up, they took over those roles, and Shafika had also been around to help. Farha Bibi had spent almost her whole life at home, and that was back in the Middle East where she had been born and raised. No one expected her to make a total change in lifestyle at 50 years old, in a new country among a foreign culture.

Esther realized early on that all the things American women did naturally would be her job as the woman of the Bibi home. Doctor appoint-

---

4. Though the Sephardim remained insular, praying in their own shuls and living in a very small and specific group of streets, the Ashkenazic presence provided them with religious amenities that they would not have had on their own such as a kosher butcher, bakery, and *mikva*.

Lower East Side, New York, 1925 / 85

Nouri — "Izzy" — Dayan

ments, government offices, apartment hunting — these would all fall on Esther's shoulders. At barely 20 years old, Esther weathered her responsibilities with affable good nature. And it was only natural that when her little nephew Nouri turned 6, Esther would be the one to take him to register at the local public school.

"I really can't," Esther explained to Reuben over supper the night before registration. "It's just too hard to go — with the baby and all. Mama agreed to take him."

Reuben nodded; he knew that his Esther would make some kind of arrangement. Her stepmother, Sara Mizrahi, was a special person, and it was just like her to offer to take Nouri and ease Esther's burden. Sara had lived in America for years and spoke English fluently so she had no qualms about taking care of the registration... until she actually did it.

"What is his first name?" the secretary asked the middle-aged woman in front of her.

"Nouri."[5]

The secretary tapped her pen impatiently against her desk. "I mean his English name."

Sara Mizrahi was unnerved. She had not expected this problem and had no idea what to do. The boy was Nouri. Who was she to give him another name?

"Ma'am, we cannot stay here all day."

Think, Sara, think! No one wants you to come back and do this all over again. Just give him a name.

"Isidore," she blurted out. *A popular American-Jewish name,* she reasoned.

When she came home and told Esther what had happened, Esther reassured her, "It's fine, Ma, it's not as if anyone is going to call him that. It's only a formality."

But once the little boy went to school, Isidore became Izzy, which was easier on the American tongues than Nouri.

And that was how Ezra, who was Nouri, became Isidore, often called Izzy.

---

5. The Syrian pronunciation of the "r" sound, rolled on the tongue properly, comes out as a cross between an "r" and a "d" and sounds almost unpronounceable to someone unfamiliar with the sound.

Chapter 10:
BENSONHURST, 1927

"Watch, Izzy, I'm going to win!" 18-year-old Dave Bibi shot a penny toward the cabinet, joining the others clustered nearby. His little niece and nephews — Lillian, Moe, and Joe — watched their uncle with adoration.

Ten-year-old Nouri measured the shot and good-naturedly agreed that his uncle deserved the pot. They played another few rounds to the delight of their young audience.

"That's all folks," Dave declared, dusting off his pants as he stood up. Nouri followed him toward the dining room where Reuben and Morris were reading *Zohar* with their father. He took a seat and listened to the discussion while Dave walked into the kitchen. His mother was rolling dough, fast as only a Syrian housewife knew how.

"Smells good," he told his mother in Arabic.

Farha smiled and continued to roll. She then cut rounds of dough with the inside of a glass, filled each round with salty cheese, folded them in half to form half moons, and pressed the edges down with a fork. Farha enjoyed the monotony of motion that was soothing in its familiarity. The scent of the baking *sambousak* was nourishment for her soul. One of her little grandchildren wandered into the kitchen, and Farha stopped for a moment to pinch her cheek.

"Take," she urged in Arabic, holding out a fresh pastry. "Eat, my darling."

Lillian needed no convincing.

"Mama, she should really wait until we are ready to eat. Or else, she'll be eating all day." Esther had just come into the kitchen, holding the baby.

Farha shrugged. "She looked hungry," she answered.

"Smelling your *sambousak* would make anyone hungry," Esther noted fondly.

"Um hmm," Dave agreed, his mouth full of crumbs.

Farha merely smiled. Esther looked around and realized that if she didn't lend a hand, their Fourth of July lunch would never get moving. Reuben worked practically every day of the week. The national holiday was a welcome vacation, a time for the family to be together. Within a half hour she had the table set, vegetables cut, bread and dips set out, and all the children washed up and ready to eat. Her father-in-law sat at the head of the table with little Joe on his lap.

"Nouri, please wash a tomato and bring it to me," requested Yosef Bibi. While Nouri had become Izzy to the more Americanized younger generation, he remained Nouri to his grandparents and to others as well.

Josef Bibi's *Sefer Torah* in its handmade case

Nouri went to the kitchen, washed a tomato and brought it to his grandfather. While balancing Joe on his knee, Yosef took the tomato and sliced off the top. Then he scooped out the juice and spooned it into his grandson's mouth. "It's good," he told the child, "yes?" Joe wasn't sure if it was the tomato juice that was so good or the warmth of being fed on his grandfather's lap.

Jdedda and *Stetta* (Arabic for grandfather and grandmother), as Yosef and Farha were fondly called, were from a generation that didn't easily articulate their feelings. Their emotions were apparent through their actions rather than their words. Farha's face lit up when her children and grandchildren walked through the door and she would run to give them something to eat. Yosef's warmth was apparent in the way he spoke, in the attention he gave to his children and grandchildren, and in his obvious desire to be with them.

Just as his joy wasn't expressed orally, neither was his pain. Quietly, without fanfare, Yosef had a *Sefer Torah* written in his daughter's memory and adorned it with an original case, similar to the type he had been

The breastplate on the case, which is inscribed: Dedicated in the memory of my father Abdullah and [my mother] Salcha, my brother David, my brother Reuben, and my brother Moshe

On the engraving on the inside of the crown, he dedicates the *Sefer Torah* in the memory of his daughter Shafika, and he indicates that both Reuben and David had passed away young. There he also dedicates the *Sefer Torah* in the memory of his two sisters, Bolisa and Simcha.

famous for back in Syria. He also donated a beautiful *parochet* for the *Aron* and designed a *ner tamid*, all in her memory.

While preparing this tribute to his daughter, he also decided to memorialize other members of his family. On the case, he engraved the names of his parents and siblings who had passed away. This quiet act reminded the Bibi brothers that, in their family, pain was stoically accepted but never forgotten. Though they doubtless knew that all three of them had been named for their uncles who died young, it was a topic that no one spoke about.

Yosef began this project at a time when money was still very tight. The Bibis lived in a rented row house apartment above a storefront, the cheapest type of housing available in Bensonhurst. True, both Morris and Dave worked as delivery boys and their income was a help. Nonetheless, Yosef's tribute to his daughter required active cooperation from the rest of the family, for they would all have to pinch pennies to pay for the project. Yosef was focused and determined. The *Sefer Torah* was bought but the ornaments were the work of his own hands, a labor of love that testified to

Moussa Zalta, one of the earliest Damascus immigrants, and his family when they came to America

the deep pain he felt over the death of his daughter, almost a decade after the fact.

The Bibi family was very close-knit. *Jdedda* and *Stetta* lived on 59th Street with Morris, Dave, and Nouri. Reuben and Esther Bibi lived on 62nd Street, and Uncle Selim and Aunt Frieda lived on 60th Street.

The neighborhood was full of extended family and friends who had also relocated from the Lower East Side. Isaac and Sara Mizrahi, Esther Bibi's parents, lived on 66th Street. Moussa Zalta and his family — friends from Damascus — lived on 65th Street. Hacham Murad Maslaton, the spiritual leader of Ahi Ezer, lived on 66th Street. His father-in-law, Hacham David Cohen, also lived nearby.

The transplantation of the Syrian Jewish community to Bensonhurst was a resounding success (though some Syrians remained on the Lower East Side for many more years). Within five years, almost entire blocks turned Syrian as families looked to live near other "SY"[6] families. The transplanted Syrian community took their culture with them. Their lives revolved around their businesses, their families, and their religion, though not necessarily in that order.

The economic prosperity of the '20s didn't lull the new immigrants into a false sense of security. They took nothing for granted and worked very hard to cultivate their businesses and achieve financial security. At

---

6. Fellow Syrians began referring to each other as "SY" as opposed to "J-dub," which referred to Ashkenazim who spoke "JW," an Americanized reference to Yiddish (Jewish).

K'nees Racqy	K'tab al Atik	
K'nees Menasha	K'nees Shamah	K'nees Elmyan

Some of the beautiful Damascus synagogues;
all were elaborately decorated with Italian marble, intricate carvings, and original mosaics.

the same time, they looked to establish respectable religious institutions, though it would be many years before they had anything near what they had left behind in Syria.

The new "American Syrians" were proud of their past.

While the community in New York was far more *Halab* (Allepan) than *Sham* (Damascus),[7] the Damascus community, of whom the Bibis were a

---

7. Rabbi Petachiya of Regensburg explains the origin of *Halab*: "Because upon this mountain *Abraham Abinu* herded his sheep. There were steps leading down the mountain slope, which he descended in order to distribute milk — *halab* — to the poor." The Arabic equivalent of *halab* is *haleb*, which was written "Alep" in French and "Aleppo" in Italian, hence Aleppo (*Aleppo – City of Scholars*, pp. 9-10). See map on p. 52 for an understanding of why Damascus was called "*Sham*."

Bensonhurst, 1927 / 91

part, had a rich heritage characterized by sincere devotion to G-d as seen in their reverence for their hachamim, their concern for their fellow Jews, and the centrality of the Bet Knesset — colloquially referred to as the *"k'nees"* — in their lives.

The *k'nees* had always been the hub of the community. Even in very difficult times, Damascus Jewry invested in their synagogues, creating beautiful houses of worship that inspired pride in their religion. Back in Damascus, when one stepped into a *k'nees*, one stepped into a different world — a royal world. Suddenly, one felt conscious that he was about to speak to the King.

The new immigrants did not have a fraction of the funds needed to recreate the majesty that existed thousands of miles away; their new places of worship were far more simple. They dreamed of a fortunate future when G-d would shine His goodness upon them and they would respond with devotion to Him. For now, they were happy and proud of their growing community.

By 1927 there were four established Sephardic synagogues in Bensonhurst, each with its own *kitab*: Magen David (the *Halabi* center), Ahi Ezer (the *Shammi* center), K'nees Betesh, and K'nees Sutton (home-based synagogues founded by wealthy businessmen who wanted their homes to be places of prayer and learning as was customary back in Syria). The children of the community went to public school, attended *kitab* afterward, and usually attended one of the four synagogues on Shabbat.

People felt very secure in living the Syrian Jewish version of the American dream: work hard, achieve financial security, but don't forget G-d and His people along the way. In the early years of the community, this formula seemed to work. Overall, the community retained their religiosity, took care of one another, and slowly achieved financial stability.[8] Perhaps a contributing factor toward its success was the existence of the "old school" — people in the community who continued to live in America as they had lived in Syria.

Yosef Bibi was a prime example. Over a decade and a half had passed since he had left Syria, and he still sported a beard, prayed three times a day, and always had his *Zohar* with him. At 60 years old, he was energetic and spry and saw little value in sleeping his days away. Late at night, after putting in a full day of work, Yosef took his beloved *Zohar*, sat by an open window that overlooked the street, and read aloud, in the distinctive Hebrew of Baghdad, hour after hour. People emerging from the train as they returned home from work as late as 2 a.m. would hear chanting,

---

8. There were subtle changes happening but, overall, in the 1920's and 1930's, the Syrian Jewish community kept Shabbat (some more liberally than others), ate only kosher (some more strictly than others), and attended synagogue (some more regularly than others).

the silent streets making room for the lone voice that could be heard two blocks away.

"There goes the night watchman," a night worker commented to his friend.

"Does he ever sleep?" his companion wondered.

"I hope not," answered his friend. He, like many others, found comfort in the Hebrew words he didn't understand. Someone was keeping G-d's word alive, night after night.

Nouri relaxed to the rhythm of his grandfather's voice. It lulled him to sleep and it soothed him if he woke up in the middle of the night. The words of the *Zohar*, chanted in the traditional sing-song unique to Baghdad's Jews, would always be powerfully precious to the young boy.

And then, one day, the chanting stopped.

The hearse passed by the house where the women were gathered at the window.

They let out a loud wail. It was heard long after the black car disappeared down the block.[9]

The hearse stopped at Ahi Ezer. Hacham Murad Maslaton eulogized the *niftar* outside the *k'nees*.

"The importance of eulogizing the dead is well known," he told the mourners, "to the point where we shed rivers of tears, particularly when the deceased is a righteous man, a man who loved Torah, learned Torah, and whose fear of Heaven was a deep internal fear that emanated from his heart and soul. He pursued *tzedaka* and *hesed* openly and hiddenly. Look at the beautiful *Sefer Torah*, the *parochet*, and the *ner tamid*, that he donated to beautify our Bet Knesset! They are the fruits of his own labor that are exceedingly precious, how much more so when the labor of one's hands is accompanied by *yirat Shamayim*. Even when he suffered, the words of Torah never stopped flowing from his lips. How fitting is it that we cry over his passing and use our pain to do *teshuva*…"

He then performed *hatarat nedarim* and publicly asked the *niftar* for forgiveness from everyone. The long blast of the *shofar* signaled that the ceremony was about to end. Then the children recited Kaddish and the funeral party proceeded to the Montefiore Cemetery on Farmer's Boulevard.

The week of *shiba'a* passed in a haze of visitors, all coming to hear about Yosef Bibi and commiserate with the Bibi family. For Farha, the loss of her partner of 37 years was profoundly painful. She had been a child bride who left everything familiar to forge a new path with her dashing and

---

9. Syrian women didn't attend funerals, as per the *Zohar*. This *minhag* might also be based on a Gemara [*Sanhedrin* 20b], although there it seems to be referring to a woman going to the cemetery itself.

Bensonhurst, 1927

talented husband. Neither of them had parents nearby to lean on, nor did they have the comfort of familiar surroundings. Their dependence on each other created a special bond that ten years of separation didn't weaken. It was only seven years since they had reunited on American shores.

Seven short years, and Yosef was gone.

For Reuben, his father's absence left a gaping hole in his life. For ten years he and his father had been inseparable. They ate together, prayed together, worked together, and moved together. They traveled continents with only each other for company. They learned to understand each other, to nurture each other, and together, they paved the way for the rest of the family. Even after he married, Reuben saw his father every day as a partner in their business, *J. Bibi and Son*. Their bond was extraordinarily strong.

Nouri, not long after his grandfather's passing

For Morris and Dave, losing their father seven years after they met him was a double blow. All those years growing up in Damascus, living through the uncertainty of war, the pain of poverty, and the pity of their neighbors who clucked sympathetically over the little boys who didn't know their father, the Bibi boys clung to the wonderful picture of Papa in America with whom they would soon be reunited. They had not been orphans; they were just biding their time until they would all be together. That time together proved to be painfully short.

And then there was Nouri.

For Nouri, now 10 years old, the week of mourning was a week of sadness and uncertainty: sadness over losing his grandfather, uncertainty about his own position. He had been an orphan before and was an orphan still. Nothing had really changed. On the other hand, his grandfather was the only "father" he had ever known. Was he not like a son who lost his father? But, as he looked over at his uncles with their torn clothing and stubbly chins, he knew he was different.

Suddenly, in his own home, surrounded by people who loved him, Nouri felt inexplicably alone. He wasn't a brother to Reuben, Morris, and Dave. They were brothers to each other but he was merely a nephew. He wasn't a brother to Reuben's children. They were siblings to each other but he was merely a cousin. His status was always different from everyone else.

He was Nouri, the orphan: surrounded by family, but also alone.

Chapter 11:
BENSONHURST, 1930

"My heart is aflame with feelings of joy," Nouri began his bar mitzva speech, "for I am about to express my gratitude. To whom? To the King of all kings. He brought me into this world. He created me from nothing. He formed me in a wondrous fashion. He made me whole in body and limb. He made me grow and mature, day after day, until I reached where I am today, a man among men. From this day forward, I am obligated to fulfill everything the Torah commands me to do, and to abandon everything the Torah forbids me to do. Because of this, I have to thank Him so much for all the great kindness He has shown me from the time I was born until this day. Therefore, I am announcing in public: Thank you. Thank you, Hashem, the Creator of the world!"

Nouri continued his twenty-one-page bar mitzva speech along the same vein. The content of the speech wasn't surprising: Hacham Murad Maslaton infused all his pupils with a clear recognition of and connection to their Creator. What set Nouri apart from the rest was his earnest acceptance of all that he had learned.

If there was anyone who had an excuse to be sad or moody, to demand answers from his Creator and to question His ways, it could have been Nouri. He had been thrust into a world of adults, raised by grandparents who loved him implicitly but who, in their pain, also allowed many disconcerting gaps in his identity to exist. No one spoke about his mother; mentioning her name was too painful. No one spoke about his father, who he knew was alive, but to him seemed dead. No one acknowledged his being different for they wanted him to be one of the gang, which he was… almost.

Yet the opening lines of his bar mitzva *derasha* truly personified the adult that Nouri was becoming. At 13, Nouri was already full of love and gratitude to his Creator. His opening declaration wasn't merely lip service; it was his personal pledge of allegiance to G-d.

How did Nouri the orphan come to such a deep appreciation of his Creator at such a young age? Doubtless his grandfather, Yosef Bibi, had been a profound influence. Yosef's life had taken sharp turns and included much pain, and yet he had not questioned his Creator, rather redoubled his devotion to Him. But he passed away when Nouri was a young boy who still needed direction.

Hacham Murad, as a young man

Hacham Murad Maslaton became the primary influence in Nouri's life.

Hacham Murad was quickly becoming a legend in his own community.

"First kiss the hand of the Hacham. Then you kiss mine," ordered Moussa Zalta, one of the founders of the Ahi Ezer community.

Moussa's attitude reflected the community's unusual reverence for Hachamim. If a Syrian Jew was walking down the block and he spotted Hacham Murad walking in the opposite direction, he would reverse course, kiss the Hacham's hand, and accompany him to his destination. A Syrian Jew was never frustrated that he had gone out of his way, even if he was in a hurry. Accompanying the Hacham was a privilege. Being in his presence was a joy.

While walking with Hacham Murad, there was no idle chatter, no coarse language, not because anyone said anything, but simply because such behavior was suddenly uncouth. Hacham Murad's gentle demeanor and purity of soul affected those around him. One simply had to act godly in the presence of someone who was clearly His representative.

Hacham Murad had arrived from Syria in 1920 with his wife, Sara, and their five children: Rachel, Joseph, Betty, Rebecca, and Sion. Their youngest two children — Jack and Esther — were born in America. Within a few years of their arrival, Rachel married Ezra Tawil and Joe married Sophie

Hacham Yaakob   Hacham Ezra   Hacham Yehuda

The Maslaton family had lived in Damascus for many generations. They were a Rabbinic family, with many famous scholars dotting their family tree. Among the more famous members of the Maslaton family were the following: Hacham Eliyahu Tarrab-Maslaton was a revered Rabbi. His son, Hacham Ezra, served on the Bet Din together with Hacham Yitzchak Aboulafia and the Sabba Kaddisha. His son, Hacham Yehuda, served as a Rabbi in Egypt. Hacham Yaakob was the Av Bet Din of Beirut and a brother of Hacham Murad.

Cohen, and both couples moved near their parents. The Maslaton home was a warm and lively place, where the married children (and then the grandchildren) stopped by regularly, and where the youngest Maslatons were barely older than their nieces and nephews. Yet it was Hacham Murad's spiritual purity that defined his home.

In all situations, Hacham Murad conveyed holiness. When surrounded by little children — his own or those that he taught — those children became docile, respectful, as if they too could sense that they were in the presence of someone great. Adults and children revered Hacham Murad for reasons that they could not define but truly appreciated. Nouri in particular gravitated to his teacher.

From the time that Nouri was a little boy, he loved to learn with Hacham Murad. Like his peers, he began with *aleph-bet* and then progressed to the *ta'amim*. He learned to read all of Tanach flawlessly and had a good grasp of its lessons. He learned to translate whatever he learned into Arabic in the traditional sing-song chant that had been handed down from teacher to pupil for generations.

Unlike most of his contemporaries, Nouri continued to allot time for learning every day, even after he became a bar mitzva. This was unusual, especially during those Depression years, when teenaged boys worked overtime to help bring in income and spiritual pursuits fell by the wayside. Life was regimented, full, but uncomplicated. People worked hard, counted their pennies, and had very little time left over for idleness. Their main leisure outlet was socializing on Shabbat or at occasional *semahot*.

This picture was taken at the bar mitzva of the grandson of Hacham Yehudah Maslaton. Both were killed during World War II. They ran back to the synagogue, which was the target of a German bombardment, and they died in the blast. The Rabbis in the middle row, from L-R: unknown, Hacham Yehudah, Rabbi Nahum Effendi (Chief Rabbi of Egypt), and Rabbi Toledano. Sitting in the front are two grandsons of Hacham Yehuda: Shlomo is on the right and Yehuda – proudly wearing his bar mitzva watch — is on the left. The two young girls on the sides are granddaughters of Hacham Yehuda: Frida is on the right and Lily is on the left. Behind the Rabbis are family and friends of Hacham Yehuda.

Nouri's days were similarly full and simple but more spiritual in nature. He rose early in the morning and ran off to Ahi Ezer where he prayed with a *minyan* even as a young boy. Afterward, he dashed back home for a quick breakfast that *Stetta* had waiting for him. From there, it was on to P.S. 226 on 60th Street and 23rd Avenue, where he studied until 3 in the afternoon. In those days, everyone went to public school. Probably about 60 percent of the school was Jewish, about 15 percent Sephardic. The balance was a mix of Italian and Polish.

At 3 o'clock Nouri headed back to Ahi Ezer for Minha and lessons with Hacham Murad who taught him together with his son Sion, thereby forging a *habruta*/friendship between the two youths. Sion and Nouri became an inseparable pair — "twins," joked people in the community. Sundays and summers and stolen occasions throughout the year found Nouri hanging around the Maslaton house where the doors were always open.

In the course of the evening, Nouri would eat supper, do his homework, and return to Ahi Ezer for Arbit and more learning. He was a quiet

Bensonhurst, 1930 / 99

Maslaton Family, 1925: Hacham Murad is holding his son Jack, and his wife, Sara, is holding baby Esther. Rebecca, Betty, and Sion Maslaton are standing in the background. The two married Maslatons— Rachel and Joe — are not in this picture. They both lived in Bensonhurst, though Joe was often out of town on business.

Joe Maslaton, a traveling salesman, was known to enter a town and immediately find the local Rabbi so that he would have where to eat and from whom to learn.

presence, never demanding, never questioning, always with a shy smile that warmed everyone around him. And then, one day, he was confronted with an answer to a question that he never asked.

"Hello, Izzy. How is it going?"

Nouri gave Uncle Reuben a smile, and nodded as he unwound his *tefillin* from his arm. The two of them met in Ahi Ezer almost every morning. Neither of them had time for a real conversation but that didn't matter. They touched base in their own way, without much talk but with natural care and concern for each other.

"Can you spare a minute?" Reuben asked casually.

Nouri was surprised at the change of routine. "Sure," he said as he followed his uncle over to a chair on the side.

"Izzy, you know that I wasn't in Syria when Mama and you left. I don't know what happened between her and your father. We all know that this is a

100 / NOURI

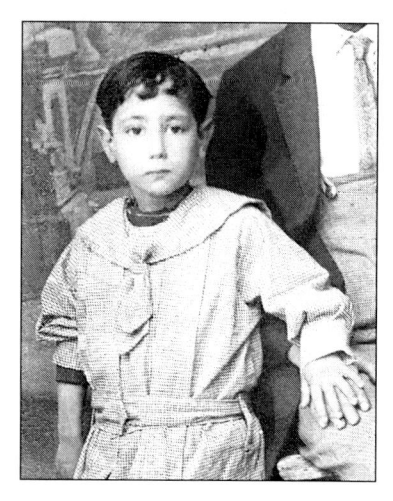

Sion Maslaton, back in Syria. The future leader of Ahi Ezer showed spiritual potential at a very young age when, on the boat to America, he refused to eat any food that his father would not eat (because of its questionable kosher status) even though his father told him that it was permissible for him.

very painful subject and no one is interested in bringing it up…" Reuben paused.

Nouri waited patiently. So far, nothing new had been said.

"But Izzy, you have a father. And your father probably wants to know his son. I tracked him down. This is his address in Eretz Yisrael. I think that you should write him a letter." Reuben handed Nouri a scrap of paper and slipped away.

Write a letter to my father, Nouri thought in wonder. *My father. Right, I have a father.*

Chapter 12:

BENSONHURST, 1930

"Where's Izzy?" Morris asked Dave late one evening. He had just returned from a trip up north — Boston, New Hampshire, Connecticut, Vermont — and he had not yet seen his "kid brother."

"Dunno. I also just came in," Dave answered, putting away his things.

The two brothers had just started their own company, Bibi Brothers. After their father passed away, they realized that they needed to earn more than the delivery boy wages they had been getting. Reuben was continuing their father's business but he needed all the income that business provided to support his growing family. It was their job — Morris's and Dave's — to provide for themselves, their mother, and Nouri, even though they were mere teenagers.[10]

Bibi Brothers began selling fireplaces and their accessories. The standard home heating system in the 1930's was a wood-burning fireplace. After many years of use, the metal sheeting that lined the opening to the chimney — the actual fireplace — had to be replaced. This was one part of the business. Fireplace accessories — bellows, nets, brushes, and andirons — were another part of the business. Of these items, the andiron was the most interesting and essential. While supporting the firewood, interesting andirons lent character to the entire room.

Technology propelled society forward and many middle-class earners began installing gas furnaces and radiators in their houses. Yet their houses had been built with fireplaces and chimneys and no one wanted to reconstruct their homes in order to fill in the holes. They opted to place an

---

10. As late as the 1940's, few Sephardic immigrants finished high school. No one attended college. Advanced education was an investment of time and money, which few people could spare.

electric log in the unused spot, creating the look and atmosphere of a burning hearth, without the soot and ash of the wood-burning fireplaces. The Bibis sold these artificial fireplaces as well.

The Bibis were industrious people who faced life with unfailing optimism. Times are hard? Work harder. And do it without complaining. While they did have clients in New York, both of the brothers spent weeks on the road. Morris traveled to New England while Dave headed to Pennsylvania, Delaware, Washington D.C., and Virginia. They would spend a week on the road and then return to New York and process their orders, establish new business contacts, and take care of the paperwork. The weeks in New York gave them family time and, in Morris's case, time to revitalize himself spiritually, which was why he was so eager to see Nouri.

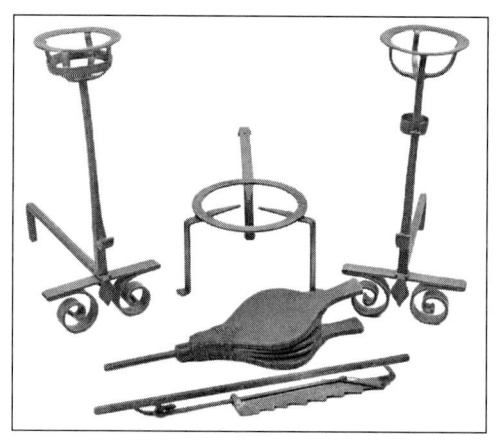

A bellows is an instrument designed to release a stream of air that fans the fire; the andirons hold the wood in place. The brush in the foreground was used to clean the accumulated soot.

Morris was the scholar in the family. From the time he was a little boy, back in Syria, he loved to learn Torah. When he came to America, he gravitated to Hacham Murad, learning with him whenever he had a free moment. Reuben and Dave also enjoyed reading the *perasha* and the *Zohar* but Morris thirsted for Torah knowledge beyond the simple meaning of

Artistic andirons became very fashionable. These Hessian soldier andirons were a Bibi specialty.

Bensonhurst, 1930 / 103

the text. He became alive as he learned and he infused others with that excitement.

That was why he sought out Nouri. After his father's death, 18-year-old Morris felt additional responsibility toward his nephew. Whenever he came home from a trip, he learned with him, remained attuned to his progress, and encouraged him to strive for higher goals.

Some people think I have no father. I think I have four! mused Nouri as he reviewed the material that Morris instructed him to review. A letter from his real father was resting in his dresser, its return address something that still surprised him. Nouri had been signing his name Isidore Sumak, as he had been registered in school. Only after receiving a letter from his father, signed Yisrael Dayan, did he learn that "Sumak" was some kind of mistake. He casually questioned his grandmother.

Nets or screens kept the soot out of the room.

David Bibi

"Oh," she answered, "it means redhead. Someone in the family must have been a redhead."

That was all the information she offered and Nouri didn't press her further, but from that day on, he signed his name Izzy Dayan. Nouri glanced again at the thin blue airmail letter and made a mental note to answer it that night. Neither he nor his father were big letter writers but their sporadic communication was precious to both of them.

Four fathers, ruminated Nouri, with a small smile. *Not bad.*

There was his real father, whom he yearned to meet one

104 / NOURI

day. And then there were his three uncles. Each of Nouri's uncles cared deeply for their nephew and took responsibility for him. Their mother, Farha, Nouri's grandmother, was a quiet presence who had created a warm and stable atmosphere where her love for her family was palpable. Her sons gave that love strength.

Dave was Nouri's "big brother," but he was actually so much more. He was closest to him in age, though at eight years apart they were certainly not equals. It wasn't simply the age difference that put Dave in a plane above Nouri. Already in his youth, David Bibi commanded attention. He had a quiet charisma that pulled people to him. They trusted him. His warmth for others was genuine and deep. His forthright honesty and integrity made him a true friend and a valuable role model for his younger nephew.

Morris Bibi

Morris was Nouri's father in spiritual matters, not because he was that much older than Dave, but because that was his natural role. He was always learning and teaching. Nouri was his prime student.

Reuben was the patriarch of the family. He took responsibility for everyone. He gave subtle advice to his brothers, visited his mother often, and kept an eye on his nephew. He was also supporting a family of six children which, during those Depression years, wasn't easy.

Reuben continued the business that he had founded with his father on Allen Street. In 1920, they had moved the business to Greenwich Village, where it continued for nine years. Initially, they dealt mainly in silver and brass manufacturing.

Then the Depression hit.

Like he had done in France when the exposition closed, Reuben was back to refurbishing old items, or buying them, fixing them, and reselling them. For the customer, buying a renovated item was much cheaper than buying the same item new. But there was never enough business and

Bensonhurst, 1930 / 105

Reuben Bibi

Reuben's inventory kept decreasing.

He could no longer afford the rent in Greenwich Village, so he moved to Greenwich Avenue. Then he moved to 33rd Street off 5th Avenue. Then he moved to Lexington Avenue. He still barely scraped together enough income to feed his family.

Despite the setbacks, Reuben remained innovative, ambitious, and always willing to experiment. He taught himself about electricity and began to manufacture electric floor lamps and table lamps with unique, handmade shades. He experimented with wrought iron, a cheaper alternative to brass that also required less polishing. He often made his products from castaway materials that he could pick up for nearly nothing. A lot of work went into every project. Reuben compensated by working overtime, often 15 hours a day.

He came into the shop seven days a week: Sunday to Thursday, Friday until an hour before sunset, and Saturday night. On winter Fridays, he headed to Ahi Ezer straight from the train. He left his money and any other *muktza* in Ahi Ezer until after Shabbat. When Shabbat ended, right after Arbit, he collected his *muktza* and went back to his shop in Manhattan, where he worked until very late at night, fixing and polishing merchandise. He did this all day Sunday as well. He worked very hard and lived very frugally but, overall, he was grateful to be able to provide for his family.

Even during those difficult years, there were joyful moments, like when Hacham Murad's daughter Rebecca became engaged to Morris Bibi. Morris was Hacham Murad's prized pupil. They learned together on a level far more advanced than almost anyone else in the community. When Morris became engaged to Rebecca, it was as if Hacham Murad was taking his own son to be his son-in-law.

Farha was equally joyous. Her son, Morris, was marrying the Hacham's daughter. How her husband Yosef must be rejoicing from on high! He had been inordinately proud of his son the scholar and it was gratifying to have Morris's scholarship valued. Furthermore, the Maslatons and the Bibis shared deep ties that went back to Damascus when Sara Maslaton (Hacham Murad's wife) had been a friend of Farha's daughter, Shafika. Their bond deepened as new immigrants in America, learning about their new country while clinging to the old. For Farha, a match with the

Maslatons was like joining family with family. She looked forward to the wedding in happy anticipation.

Providence had other plans.

Chapter 13:
BENSONHURST, 1931

Once again they sat together quietly — Reuben, Morris, and Dave — on low stools, wearing torn shirts, sporting stubbly chins. Nouri was there, too. They were together, yet he was apart. They were sons; he wasn't.

When the *shiba'a* was over, they all sat together again, this time on regular chairs. "You're moving in with me," Reuben announced. "We are one family."

No one protested. Morris was getting married in a few weeks. Dave had no plans to marry yet, but marriage was obviously not far off. That left Nouri.

"Thank you," answered the 14-year-old boy, and then he slipped away.

They don't have to do this, ruminated Nouri as he packed his things. *They have a bunch of kids… Money is tight… They have a big house, but taking all of us in will make it a lot smaller… They are not my parents… But I have nowhere to go… Morris and Dave are often on the road… I'm too young to be on my own… They could send me to an orphanage… I'm just grateful to them for their kindness…*

This would be Nouri's attitude to his uncles and their families for the rest of his life.

Reuben Bibi and his family lived in a newly built, two-story house on a lot that spanned almost the whole block — from 62nd to 63rd Street. Though the lot was large, the house was a modest size. Downstairs was the living room, dining room, and kitchen. Upstairs were three bedrooms, one of which was accessible not only through the apartment, but through a hallway that lined the length of the house, down the steps to a private entrance.

Wedding of Morris and Rebecca Bibi

Reuben and Esther and baby Ely had one bedroom. The other five children shared another bedroom. The third bedroom, the one with the private entrance, went to Morris and Dave. Nouri had a cot in the kitchen.

Morris married Rebecca Maslaton. They made a small affair since Morris and his brothers were in mourning for their mother. The young couple made their home in Bensonhurst.

Meanwhile, Nouri had finished junior high and looked to contribute to his upkeep in a responsible manner. He became a delivery boy, working mainly for his uncles, Morris and Dave, and he gave over all his wages to his aunt and uncle. If he wanted some pocket money for something personal, he would take on an extra job.

Even at that young age, Nouri was already quietly inspiring others.

"Jack," called Nouri to Hacham Murad's little son one day, "c'mere."

Jack grinned at his older brother's good friend.

"I have a job for you. Want to earn a nickel every day?"

Jack's eyes grew wide. A nickel! Imagine how much candy he could buy with a nickel a day!

Bensonhurst, 1931 / 109

Jack and Esther, with their older sisters, Betty and Rebecca, cousins (the Zonana girls are the children of Jemilla Zonana, Sara Maslaton's sister), and niece: Back row, L-R: Frieda Zonana, Betty Kubie, Sara Zonana, Rebecca Bibi, Vicky Zonana. Front row, L-R: Jack and Esther and their niece, Sara (Joe's daughter).

Jack Maslaton, standing with some of his family. His parents and brother-in-law, Morris Bibi, are behind him. His sister Esther is beside him.

"Come with me, I'll show you how." Nouri led Jack down the block toward the Bibi home where he lived. "See that window over there?"

Jack peered up and nodded.

"That's our kitchen window. I sleep on a cot, in the kitchen. I'm nervous that I might not wake up on time for 4:30 *selihot* every morning.[11] A lot of people don't go because it's so early and then they are tired and have a difficult time working the rest of the day. I want to get up for *selihot* but I don't want to impose on anyone at home. If you wake me up every morning — you know, give a whistle — I'll pay you a nickel."

"But how am I going to get up so early?"

Nouri smiled, "That's easy. Ask your father to wake you. He never misses."

Jack thrust out his hand, "A deal!"

Every morning of that month of Elul, Jack asked his father to wake him for *selihot* and then, instead of turning back over and going to sleep, Jack jumped out of bed and ran down the block to wake Nouri.

"Thank you," Nouri whispered, leaning his head out the window. In a flash, he was downstairs, ready to walk with Jack to Ahi Ezer. Jack happily collected his nickels, blissfully unaware that Nouri took on an extra job as a window washer to pay his "salary."

After a week on the job, Jack grew puzzled. As soon as he whistled, Nouri appeared, as if he were up already. If so, why was he paying him to wake him?

---
11. Sephardic custom is to say early morning *selihot* the entire month of Elul.

"You are doing me such a big favor," Nouri would reassure him.

Jack shrugged, and pocketed his nickels. Only many years later did it hit him that Nouri had found an ingenious way of getting him to attend *selihot*. By "hiring" Jack as his alarm clock, he steered him in the right direction. That was Nouri, always trying to influence others to be better, but only in ways that were pleasant and subtle, not heavy and demanding.

Jack and Esther,
with their older sister, Rebecca Bibi

Then Dave found himself a bride — Milo Salem — the daughter of Eli Abu Yom Tov "Nikchari" Salem, the neighborhood grocer and one of the most beloved and respected members of the greater Syrian community. Stepping into Abu Yom Tov's store was like stepping into the Old Country: large open sacks of rice, lentils, and other legumes strewn across the floor, barrels of green and black olives, and baskets of fresh vegetables, all weighed on an ancient scale that looked like it came from the Old Country. The average American non-Jew walked into the tiny, overcrowded store, looked around, bewildered, and walked right out. Hence, Abu Yom Tov's store remained uniquely Syrian.

Dave and Milo Bibi

Dave moved out of Reuben's home and Nouri moved into the boys' room with Joe Mizrahi, "Jerusalem Joe," as they called Esther's cousin from Eretz Yisrael. Eight months later Joe moved out and the sleeping

Bensonhurst, 1931 / 111

arrangements changed again. Reuben's oldest son, Moey, moved in with Nouri, freeing up space in the children's room for the new baby. But the kids were getting older, and bigger children take up more space. Reuben had an idea.

"Listen here, Joey," Reuben addressed his second son, gesturing around Nouri's narrow room. "We are going to build a bunk bed for this room." Reuben stole an hour here and there from his busy day until he and Joey finished building the bunk bed. Then Joey and his younger brother, Ikey, moved into the "big boys" room. He and Moey slept on the new bunk bed, Ikey slept on the couch, while Nouri slept on the pull out.

Dave Bibi's father-in-law, Abu Yom Tov Salem, was admired for his piety and righteousness, often seen from the quiet acts of kindness he did from his humble grocery.

At night, the Bibi house became quiet. Electricity was expensive and people generally went to sleep when the sun set. By then they were tired from their busy day that had started when the sun came out and ended when it went to sleep.

Except for Nouri.

While the Bibi house slept, Nouri was up in bed with a little flashlight and a large *sefer* and he would read and read and read. His roommates learned to sleep with that sliver of light poking through the darkness. They respected Nouri's diligence and would inevitably fall asleep as Nouri continued to read by flashlight, hour after hour, night after night. Usually it was a *sefer*, but sometimes it was an English book that looked thick, impressive, and scholarly.

Joey watched him from the top bunk, and yawned. *I don't think he has ever put his book down before I fell asleep,* he noted sleepily. A minute later, Joey was out cold while Nouri continued to read.

"Breakfast, everyone!" called Esther Bibi from the kitchen. "Moey, you having toast? What about the rest of you?"

"Ma, I need a note for the teacher," Moey mentioned while chomping on his toast. Lillian wrinkled her nose in disapproval at his manners. Moe grinned and slowly opened his mouth to give her a better view of its contents.

"Euwwww" shrieked Lillian. "Ma, did you see what he just did?"

Joey blithely poured himself some orange juice. Ikey tumbled into the kitchen, tripping over his untied shoelaces, and then he howled in pain. Charlotte ran into the kitchen to see what all the commotion was about. Nouri was crouching in the fridge looking for something.

"Moey, stop bothering your sister. Lillian, if you keep on carrying on like that, Daddy will hear you all the way in Manhattan. Joey, just tie Ikey's shoes for goodness sake. Izzy, why are you still by the fridge? What are you looking for?" Esther was struggling to butter toast and keep the peace while holding baby Florence.

"Oh, nothing," Nouri answered. "I just thought that maybe there was some leftovers from last night. I can help myself."

Esther shrugged her shoulders and shifted the baby. She had to get the kids moving or else everyone would be late for school. She was too busy to argue. "Help yourself."

And he did. Wherever possible, Nouri tried to be self-sufficient. He looked to alleviate the burden he felt that he caused his aunt and uncle. No one enjoyed last night's leftovers, so Nouri felt more comfortable eating that, rather than fresh toast or eggs for breakfast. Esther did all that she could to make Nouri feel like a real son and brother, but Nouri always held himself slightly apart. Only the older children, who remembered their home before Nouri arrived, picked up on his slight separateness. To the younger Bibis he was a total brother.

Nouri related to his uncle and aunt like a son to his parents. He addressed them as Dad and Mom, and he respected them implicitly. He sought to please them and to learn from them.

"Izzy, I'm going over to Grandpa. We like to read *Zohar* together Saturday night. Joey is also coming. Want to join?" invited Reuben.

Isaac Mizrahi, Esther's father, had always been warm and welcoming to Nouri. After a moment of consideration, Nouri nodded. "Sure," he said.

So began a tradition that lasted for many years. Isaac Mizrahi welcomed his children and grandchildren into his large living room, lined floor to ceiling

In Isaac Mizrahi's home

Bensonhurst, 1931 / 113

with glass enclosed bookcases. While his collection of *sefarim* was famous, Saturday night was reserved for reading the *Zohar* in the traditional Arab vernacular favored by Syrian Jewry. His wife would come in with hot cups of black coffee and homemade *ka'ak*, refreshments for the body, while the men refreshed their souls.

Nouri became a real part of his Uncle Reuben's family and he appreciated the warmth and effort that went into making that happen. The Bibi home was a happy place to be. Esther was a wonderful, no-nonsense woman, who raised her large brood with discipline and love. Reuben spent most of his days at work, but his strong and solid personality gave his home direction. He was a visionary with confidence in the future and he transmitted that confidence to his children. Sunday mornings, he often took the kids on an outing before going in to the shop.

"Big things are happening," he would say, on the way to one of his favorite places, Floyd Bennett Field. Airplanes were the darlings of the decade as intrepid pilots sought to prove that their specially designed aircrafts could travel cross-country, trans-Atlantic, and even as far as the North Pole. Officially opened in 1931, Floyd Bennett Field was the first municipal airport in New York City. The new airfield's modern, electrically illuminated, concrete runways were a tremendous improvement over the dim dirt paths of most airports. Its modern amenities attracted dare-devil pilots from all over the world and hundreds of spectators would come to watch a much publicized takeoff. Fifteen years had passed since Reuben saw his first takeoff at the San Francisco World's Fair and he was still fascinated.

"See that bird?" He pointed to the striking airplane with red tubing and bright yellow wings and the words *Red Devil* painted along the side. "I remember when those were the coolest things around… come, maybe they'll let us take a ride." And with a little negotiating, the pilot agreed.

After a quick ride overhead, Reuben took them back on the train. The kids got off in Bensonhurst and Reuben continued down to Manhattan. The Bibi boys came running home, breathless about their adventure in the sky. Their 10-minute journey became the talk of the community.

Reuben was fascinated with technology and how it was changing their lives from one day to the next. He was certain that these changes would continue to benefit people and he encouraged his children to be brave and to face new ideas with confidence.

Esther and Reuben were optimistic people with big hearts. They had a large family — much larger than the typical American home — and money was always tight, and yet they transmitted hope and confidence to the children. There was only bread and potatoes for supper? Maybe tomorrow there would be money for a more substantial meal. And if not, why complain? How would that help anyone?

Even during those lean years, the Bibis always had guests at their table. Reuben was the *mesader* in Ahi Ezer, the official who gave out the *aliyot*, and he was always on the lookout for strangers. When he spotted a new face, he would call him up for an honor, and then he would invite him to his home. Having spent 10 years on the road, far from family, he understood the loneliness of a traveler, and hoped to assuage some of that pain with a Shabbat meal in a homelike atmosphere.

Pesah, the Bibi home was overflowing with people. Most of their guests came just for the Seder and then walked home. But when the children inevitably dozed off during the night, Reuben hauled them into one of the bedrooms, and laid them out widthwise on the bed — six, seven, eight across — in order to fit more children in. There was always room for another guest and no one was turned away.

Nouri

Nouri learned from his uncle that anything is possible and that life is about doing what you are supposed to do, no questions asked. Acts of kindness are intrinsic to being a Jew, so one must find ways to do kindness, either with money or without money. Reuben was one of the few immigrants fluent in written Arabic and English. He would translate letters and documents that new immigrants brought to him, giving generously of his time.

Nouri watched and absorbed. For now, he was on the taking end. But he yearned for the day when he would be the one to give.

Bensonhurst, 1931

Chapter 14:
BENSONHURST, EARLY 1930'S

Esther Maslaton was restless. She wandered into the kitchen. Her mother was checking some rice. *Not very interesting,* Esther moped. She itched another scab.

"Don't do that," Sara said sharply, not even glancing up. "You want to be stuck with marks all over your face?"

How did she see that? Esther scuttled out of the kitchen and back to her room. For lack of anything else to do she laid down. *Bored, bored, bored, bored!* But her mother was busy and all she seemed to do was get in her way, or get scolded for scratching. Sick children were meant to dutifully lie in bed and amuse themselves and not bother their mothers who had the same amount of work as usual. Now that Esther was feeling basically well but not allowed to leave the house until the pox went away, she was climbing the walls.

Hey, that's an idea. Why not climb the walls? They needed a painting anyway...

Then she heard the shrill of the doorbell. *Should I get it? I am not supposed to be going out...*

Then there was loud banging... and ringing... and banging... and yelling...

"Who is carrying on like that?" her mother called from the kitchen.

"Sounds like Jack."

"What's wrong with him, banging and yelling like a madman? Go tell him to come up."

Yay! I can go outside. Esther ran down the steps accompanied by more ringing and banging and yelling, and then some strange popping sounds and something breaking. *Was that glass?* She yanked open the door.

Sara in Syria,
with her daughter Betty,
in better times

With her son Sion,
in difficult times

In America

Sara [Cohen] Maslaton also became a revered community figure. This feisty woman had been orphaned at 12 and then married at 13. She suffered through the poverty of World War I, when her family almost starved, and buried three babies, but she never lost faith in G-d and went on to raise an exemplary family.

"Fire," panted Jack, red-faced. "Run and tell Mama. There is a fire on the first floor."

"Mama," Esther hollered, running up the steps, "fire! Come outside."

Sara Maslaton heard Esther and joined her running down the steps and outside.

Pop! Shatter!

Everyone on the street joined the Maslatons as they watched another window burst from the heat. The flames licked the wooden frames until they were totally consumed. By the time the fire trucks arrived, the two-family home was a burnt-out shell.

Bensonhurst, Early 1930's

"Thank G-d, no one was hurt," Sara murmured. That might have easily not been the case had Jack not come home at that precise moment. She sighed. They would have to move, again.

This was the Maslatons' third (or was it fourth?) apartment in America in the twelve years since they arrived. Their move from the Lower East Side to Bensonhurst had been a step up but, since many landlords wanted to upgrade their property without paying for the renovations, arson had become a way of life. This was not the only apartment from which fire had evicted the Maslatons — though in terms of getting out in the nick of time, it was the most dramatic event. The owners reasoned that most people smelled fire and got out in time and meanwhile, the insurance companies covered the cost of fixing up the property because no one could prove that it was not an accidental fire.

As for their belongings, well, the Maslatons had not amassed many possessions in their years in America. Sparse wardrobes were hastily put together — sometimes with the help of kind community members who heard about the fire — and the same went for their modest collection of kitchenware. It was more the act of reorganizing their lives that was draining and difficult.

Stoic Sara had weathered many challenges in her life, yet she continued to face every situation with strength and practicality and faith. From 66th Street to 72nd Street to 60th Street and on, she just picked up and resettled. Hacham Murad relied on her implicitly and trusted her to find a solution to every problem. When he brought home some new faces that had showed up in *k'nees* on Shabbat, he just assumed that she would find a way to stretch their meager food supply to accommodate them. Ditto for a place to sleep. The doors of the Maslaton home were always open.

For Nouri Dayan, this was certainly the case.

Nouri practically grew up in the Maslaton home. He was not the only one to find warmth, love, and guidance in the simple Bensonhurst apartment that kept changing addresses.

The whole Ahi Ezer community felt connected to the Maslaton home. Because the congregation was small — maybe a few dozen families of which many members were related[12] — the *k'nees* atmosphere was that of one big happy family who lived together, prayed together, and (occasionally) fought together.

The neighborhood role models, who had spent most of their lives in the Old Country, were sadly disappearing. Hacham David Cohen, Hacham Murad's

---

12. As of 1925, Magen David had over 400 households as members. Ahi Ezer was much smaller, under 50 families. The Cohens, Bibis, and Maslatons were all related, as were others in the congregation.

father-in-law, had passed away the year before. Like his friend Joseph Bibi, Hacham David had kept his beard, even in America, and learned *Zohar* regularly. Until his last days on this world he was almost always seen with a *sefer* in his hand. He and Joseph Bibi were true examples of centuries-old Damascus Jewry: pious men who worked for a living, but always made time for Torah, and didn't allow modernity to affect their spirituality.

Hacham David's wife, Salha, outlived her much-older husband and was a much-beloved community matriarch. This rare woman, who raised a family of orphans with love and devotion, never merited biological children of her own. She was the only woman in the neighborhood who always covered her hair and dressed so completely modest, one could have placed her back in the Old Country.

Hacham David Cohen (sitting on the left) his wife Salha (sitting on the right). Zaki Cohen is sitting in the middle and his siblings, Basil and Jamila (Zonana), are standing behind them. Basil Cohen brought his brother-in-law, Hacham Murad Maslaton, to America to serve as the spiritual leader of Ahi Ezer. Note the *sefer* that Hacham David is holding.

The Cohen family was a crucial part of the foundation of Ahi Ezer.

Back in Syria, the Cohens were well known for their scholarship and piety. The men chose spouses from like-minded families (they had married into the Maslaton family several times) or married cousins. Though most of the family had left the Old Country, they retained their high level of religiosity wherever they settled. Moussa and Zaki Cohen, nephews of Hacham David, became role models in Ahi Ezer, as did Hacham David's son, Zaki. To differentiate between the two Zaki Cohens, one was known as Zaki *"zegir,"* the younger one, while the other was Zaki *"kebir,"* the older one.

It was no secret: The Maslaton, Cohen, and Bibi families were on a higher spiritual plane than most of their kinsmen. They were the pious scholars of Ahi Ezer. They were the people to whom the community looked up.

Salha Cohen, Sara Maslaton's stepmother, married her husband the day that he finished the *shloshim* for his late wife. This unusual woman earned the love and respect of all her stepchildren.

Though the new generation did not grow beards, they carried on the traditions of their fathers and spent their (rare) free time in the synagogue, praying or learning or helping out the community.

The bulk of the congregation had much simpler religious aspirations.

Right up in the front row were the older men, wizened fellows who were very sincere in their loyalty to G-d, despite their lack of Jewish knowledge. Moussa Zalta, David Didia, Moussa Zagha, and Nissim Sabin sat next to each other, all the time.

These old-timers never missed Shabbat services, dutifully listened to the Hacham's *derasha*, and then carried on about the latest news in Arabic. Having never had much of a background in learning, even back in Syria, they were limited in America where they were overburdened with making a living and navigating a whole new culture.[13]

Then there was Ibrahim "Belleh," whose last name became Americanized as Bailey. Ibrahim Bailey was the sexton of Ahi Ezer and probably the most colorful character in the community. He was very tall, very large, and very much a Middle Eastern immigrant. Having never mastered English, his guttural Arabic sounded almost frightening to the Americanized children of the community who both loved and feared him

---

13. While Basil Cohen declared that there was no Shabbat desecration in Damascus, he acknowledged that not everyone knew the intricacies of halacha, possibly because they left learning when they were young in order to help make a living for their families. Most of the Ahi Ezer community had a very simple grasp of Jewish Law but their belief in G-d and reverence for their *hachamim* was outstanding. Mr. Victor Didia recalls the struggles of the older generation: "They were socially isolated due to the language barrier. They had nothing to read in Arabic — not one newspaper, magazine, or flyer. They did not understand the radio. They were very dependent on their children to help them navigate America, and on their few friends for a social structure. They had no way to grow, not in general or Jewish knowledge. It was very sad."

for, in addition to keeping the synagogue clean and neat, Ibrahim Bailey was their "bus driver."

Rain or shine, Ibrahim Bailey marched the streets of Bensonhurst, lugging his pushcart behind him, with ten or even twelve children squashed inside, singing songs as he wheeled them as fast as he could. The first few children were zoomed down the block. As his load grew heavier, he slowed down. After he finally deposited the first shift at the doors of Ahi Ezer, he began his next route.

If it was raining, he covered the children with a tarp. If it was snowing, he replaced his pushcart with a sled. All day, he was running around the neighborhood, chauffeuring the children back and forth. There were intervals during the day when no one had to be picked up nor did anyone have to be taken home. Then he would rest in the upstairs room of the *k'nees*, which was allotted to him for personal use. Along the walls hung the sabers and swords that he had used as a soldier in the Turkish army. The children loved to speculate as to what Ibrahim Bailey actually did with his exotic weapon collection... but they were fond of the eccentric sexton whose appearance at their doorsteps was as predictable as the rising of the morning sun.

These solid but simple men transmitted Old Country values — hard work and an unquestioning belief in G-d — though America never really became their home.

Their children, even those born in the Old Country, were in a different league.

David Didia's sons, Morris and Jimmy, had become successful businessmen who shed their Arabic accents and could read and write English. The Zaghas and Zaltas were also fluent in both languages, as were Morris and Dave Bibi. Though they did not realize it at the time, they were the bridge between the old and the new.

When Morris Bibi bought a car, the Maslatons were intrigued. When he drove the whole family up to Niagara Falls, Sara smilingly agreed that though she

The Maslaton Family at Niagara Falls

Bensonhurst, Early 1930's / 121

did not know the language (and never would) there were some very nice advantages to America.

When Dave Bibi volunteered to raise money to spruce up the *k'nees*, Hacham Murad was indulgently optimistic. When he succeeded in making those improvements, Hacham Murad was grateful. Thus began a trend that would continue for many years: As soon as the younger generation married they were encouraged to help the community through volunteerism. This was the only way. The community was very small; only if everyone gave of themselves would they be able to create a true spiritual center.

And so they gave of themselves, even when times were very, very, tough.

Most of the Syrians started off as peddlers in the textile industry and worked their way up. They gravitated toward this mode of business because it allowed them to observe Shabbat. Unlike factory workers, peddlers and salesmen could adjust their workday hours and choose not to work on Shabbat, especially once a salesman opened his own store.

The pressure to earn a living and the temptation of American culture was enormous. Syrian Jews fell into a pattern of laxity, not as a rebellion against Judaism, but as people overwhelmed by the glitter of a New World coupled with the sheer energy needed to survive. They were impressed by the success stories they heard and wondered if being a little more "American" would also propel them to the top. They grew weary of the race, too tired to fight the rope pulling them toward a new value system, while staring back wistfully at their leaders whom they loved and revered.

They had numerous venerable leaders, some who were in America for only a few years, and others who led for decades. Rabbi Meir Vaknin, Chief Rabbi of Teveria, was a renowned scholar who lived on the Lower East Side during the years of the Great War. He had come to America to raise money for the Holy Land and was unable to return until after the war ended. The Syrian community was in awe of his greatness. For the four years that he was part of their community, there was no Shabbat desecration.

Rabbi Haim Tawil stepped in where Rabbi Vaknin left off. He served as Chief Rabbi of the Syrian Jewish community from shortly after the War until 1933. It was his influence that created the religious center of the *Halabi* community, the Magen David Synagogue and Talmud Torah. He immigrated to Eretz Yisrael and Rabbi Yaakob Kassin became the next Chief Rabbi.

Rabbi Yaakob Kassin was a young man of 33 when he came to America, but he was already famous for his Talmudic scholarship and mastery of Kabbalah. He was born in Yerushalayim in 5660 (1900) and had learned with some of the greatest scholars who lived there. His appointment as overall leader of the Syrian community was greeted with much joy.

Hacham Yaakob Kassin immediately set out to raise the level of Torah scholarship among his people, appearing at the *kitab* regularly to test the children and monitor their progress. He sought to unite Syrian Jewry in New York through its Rabbinic leadership. Perhaps the most powerful effect of that successful unification was the establishment of the ban against accepting *geirim* (converts).

Coming from Eretz Yisrael, it was easy for Rabbi Kassin to pick up on the nuances of religious laxity that was subtly creeping into the community, and he realized early on that those laxities could easily lead to problems far greater than people imagined. When people were lax about prayer and dress, it was a problem. When people were lax about Shabbat and *kashrut*, it was a bigger problem. But when people were lax about conversions, it was a problem that could easily destroy the community with no way to reverse its ramifications.

Rabbi Kassin wasn't an implacable zealot. He was an understanding person who influenced with encouraging words and a lot of warmth. But when it came to conversions he was a fierce warrior who unified his fellow Rabbis for battle and would not back down.

Rabbi Meir Vaknin (1885-1975) was born in Teveria, where he became one of the members of the community's Sephardic Bet Din. In 1901, he traveled overseas to raise money for the community, eventually ending up in New York, where he served as the Rabbinic leader of the Syrian community for five years. He authored several *sefarim* and was known as a very holy man.

In the early 20th century, the rabbis of Argentina, led by Rabbi Shaul Sutton, drafted a proclamation prohibiting the acceptance of converts under all and any circumstances. They saw that gentiles were converting to Judaism for marriage purposes only, without any religious sincerity, and were therefore not kosher Jews. They realized that having these pseudo-Jews as part of their communities paved the way for assimilation. Being that it was virtually impossible to weed out all imposters, they imposed a ban against accepting all converts.

Rabbi Kassin prevailed upon his predecessor, Rabbi Haim Tawil, to support a similar proclamation for the Syrian community in America. He saw

Bensonhurst, Early 1930's

Hacham Moshe Dweck is sitting to the left of
Rabbi Kassin. Mr. I. Shalom is the first on the right.

In addition to Hacham Yaakob Kassin and Hacham Murad Maslaton, the original signers of the proclamation were (L-R): Hacham Haim Tawil [d. 1942], Hacham Moshe Gindi, the Rabbi of K'nees Betesh [1888-1954], and Hacham Moshe Dweck [d. 1945], a revered community scholar.

what was happening to Ashkenazic Jewry and, while Syrian Jewry was by nature more clannish and more traditional minded, he was afraid that if they accepted converts, assimilation would soon follow. Rabbi Kassin appealed to the Rabbinic leaders of the community to issue a joint proclamation, banning any gentiles, whether they converted or not, from the community. Hacham Murad gave his full-hearted support.

This edict, commonly referred to as the *Takanah*, not only served to protect the community from intermarriage, it also sent a powerful message of unity to all members of the Syrian community. They saw that their leaders were ready and able to join forces to protect their people. The *Takanah* didn't do away with the growing religious laxity, but it created an iron wall around the community, keeping its members inside and the gentile world outside.[14]

Meanwhile, Nouri was growing up.

He had already been working for his uncles for a few years. He often contemplated the future — and sometimes the past — especially when he received a rare letter from his family.

Nouri scanned its contents again: *Shimon, Sara, and Rachel — his full siblings — were doing well. They had all married and were building families of their own. His half-siblings, children born to his father after his second marriage, Moshe, Yehoshua, and Mordechai, were teenagers, growing up quickly.*

He leaned back on his pillow and closed his eyes.

Letters from Eretz Yisrael always made him contemplative. What would have happened had he gone with his father to Eretz Yisrael? He would never have known his wonderful grandparents, who were no longer with him but were still a part of him. Would he have known his uncles? Air travel was slowly becoming more common and they all spoke about one day making the trip over the ocean.

But it's already too late, sighed Nouri, rolling over on his stomach, as if squashing the thought. *Papa is already gone.*

Not long after he had made contact with his father, he received the news of his passing. True to the reticent nature of the Bibi family, he received the bare-bone facts: His father became ill, passed away a little while later, and was buried in the cemetery in Tel Aviv. There was no real explanation why a 48-year-old man, still in his prime, was no longer among the living.

Nouri continued to write the family, continued to dream of meeting them, but it was a very different dream than those of that short period when he thought he would one day meet his father. At some point in his adolescence, he erased the residue of those early hopes, recognizing that his orphanhood had nothing to do with geography. Nouri was just as much an orphan in America as he would be if he were in Eretz Yisrael.

Besides, there were plenty of other orphans around. Almost none of the people he knew had the typical American-dream childhood presented in school readers: two parents, a steady income, a house, a dog, and just enough grit and perseverance, honesty and integrity, to feel that those gifts were well earned.

---

14. This proclamation has been reaffirmed numerous times, with more Sephardic congregation leaders adding their signatures. The Syrian community credits their unusually low rate of assimilation to strict adherence to this proclamation.

Bensonhurst, Early 1930's / 125

L-R: Nouri Dayan and Sion Maslaton, as young men

Among his own people there was a different attitude. Parents were a gift, given to some for long term, and taken away early from others. Financial stability was never, *ever*, a given, no matter how hard one worked, no matter how much determination one had. Everything was part of G-d's plan, plain and simple.

And one does not question G-d.

"Nouri, don't you think it's time to move on?"

To where? wondered the 17-year-old. *I have nowhere to go…*

"How much are you making as a delivery boy? It's a dead-end job. How are you ever going to get married without a decent salary?"

Oh, that is what he is talking about…

"Here is what you are going to do," explained Joe Maslaton patiently to his kid brother Sion and to Nouri. "I will help you rent a storefront in Boro Park. Both of you will have to put up some money as well. I do selling for huge linen companies. Through my connections, I can get you good prices. You'll buy low and sell high — that's how business works. Slowly, you will build up a company."

To Sion and Nouri, this sounded like a plan. Neither of them wanted to travel cross-country selling linens like Joe, or fireplaces and their accessories like Morris and Dave. Selling from a storefront seemed much more attractive. Also, they had both reached the age where formal learning in *kitab* ended. Being together in the store many hours a day would allow the two *habrutot* time to learn with each other. So they invested the little they

126 / NOURI

had, borrowed some money, set up their storefront, and waited for business to boom. As time went on, they noticed that they had plenty of time for learning. This was great for their spiritual situation but not for business.

When they finally realized that the Depression climate of the 1930's wasn't a great time for a start-up business, it was too late. The business went bankrupt. They would have to start over again.

Luckily, Morris and Dave Bibi stepped in to help them.

"Okay, Izzy, here's the plan. We all know that Reuben has golden hands. It's a shame for him to spend time on selling and keeping books when he should be devoting all his efforts to manufacturing and fixing items that can be sold at a profit. Morris and I have decided to split up. Morris is opening his own business in fireplaces and their accessories, mainly importing bellows from England. I think he'll give Sion a job. It will be good for both of them. Reuben and I want to do something different. Maybe we'll start out with similar items…"

Nouri listened quietly. He had no real affinity for the fireplace business. As a kid, he had helped Morris lug fireplaces up three or four stories in old, Lower East Side apartment buildings that didn't have elevators. *Boy, were those things heavy*, recalled Nouri.

"… Times are changing. There are new technologies being developed all the time. I want to travel around, see what I can buy cheap, see what Reuben can create from what I find, and then we'll see where our ideas take us. You, Izzy, are organized and well thought out. You'll run the office — you know, taking care of the books, keeping the records, all that stuff — I'll do the buying and Reuben will run the manufacturing department. We'll pool our resources and put a down payment on property on 65th Street

Sion Maslaton in Morris Bibi's factory, English Bellows

Bensonhurst, Early 1930's / 127

and 17th Avenue. That will be our factory, our offices, and our storefront. Being local will save us time and money. When we need to travel, we will, but our base will be right here in Bensonhurst. How does this sound to you?" asked Dave Bibi.

Nouri admired his uncle and felt that they could work well together. Besides, he was in debt from his first start-up company and he was out of a job. What choice did he have?

"Why not?" smiled Nouri.

"Deal?" asked Dave, stretching out his hand.

"Deal," agreed Nouri, clasping his uncle's hand in his.

And that was how Bibi and Company opened.

Chapter 15:

BENSONHURST, 1937

From opening day, Bibi and Co. was a family business. Even when Bibi and Co. began employing outsiders, the overwhelming majority of the staff was family. The business was founded on trust, shared values, optimism, and idealism.

Bibi and Co. began with the familiar fireplace accessories but with a different twist. Morris and Dave had been middlemen, buying fireplaces and accessories from larger companies and selling to individuals. Morris continued in that line but Dave and Reuben set up the new business differently. Reuben designed and created original products, creating a larger profit margin in the process.

In the early years, Reuben worked predominately with brass, iron, and sometimes copper. Brass was the metal of choice for fireplace accessories. Copper was usually too weak on its own; as a fireplace accessory, it would simply melt. Brass was stronger but much heavier. It also required a lot of work to make it usable. The foundry delivered a large block of brass (a combination of copper and other minerals) which had to be cast into a mold, then cooled, then ground, then polished, and then lacquered. The mold had to be designed with the right amount of thickness; if the brass was cast too thin, the item would not hold up. Reuben's goal was to create sturdy, attractive, and interesting products that would enhance the room with the fireplace at its center.

The same machinery used to produce fireplace accessories was ideal for all sorts of metal products. People liked to adorn their fireplaces with chrome and copper candelabras to set on its mantle. Reuben designed these lamps along with doorknockers, ashtrays, and candlesticks of either brass or copper. He produced table lamps and floor lamps as well. A

Selim Bibi (Joseph Bibi's brother) made these painted brass candlesticks.

His son, Eddie, made this menorah.

Back row, L-R: Reuben Bibi, a deaf worker who was with the company for many years, unknown, Saul Tawil. Middle row: Toufic Attie (in the suit and large kippah), Joe Cohen, Mickey Carey, Isaac (Zaki) Cohen, Nouri. Front row: Dave Bibi and Meyer Cohen. The three other people in the front are unknown.

When it first opened, Bibi and Co. hired primarily family, as is seen in this picture. Even later on, when employees set out on their own, many of the Bibis continued in the family tradition and chose businesses with an artistic angle.

customer could enter Bibi and Co. and pick out a total design for his living room or den, matching the fireplace accessories with lamps, ashtrays, and candlesticks.

Meanwhile, Dave scavenged around for new ways to bring more profits into the business. He imported artistic lamps and gift items from China so that customers who came into Bibi and Co. could choose decorative items of a totally different style. That business connection abruptly ended when war broke out between China and Japan in 1937. Dave Bibi remained ever optimistic, sure that another business opportunity would come his way. Then, one day, Bibi and Co. got the break that they needed.

"May I speak to Mr. Bibi?" asked Mr. O'Brien.

Mr. O'Brien was a familiar face to Bibi and Co. He was an antique dealer who had often used Reuben's services in refurbishing merchandise for resale.

"Dave Bibi here. How can I help you?"

Mr. O'Brien held an electric candelabra, a beautiful piece with crystal arms and glass prisms hanging down. "See this? We used to import these crystal parts from Czechoslovakia and put them together to make lamps and candelabras. But with all the trouble going on over there, we can't get anything from Czechoslovakia anymore.[15] Think you can manufacture something like this?"

Dave deferred to Reuben, who studied the candelabra from every angle.

"Leave it here a few days," he said. "I'll see what I can do."

For Reuben, this was an intriguing challenge. For the next few days he walked around Kresge's and Woolworth's, studying their glassware. He picked up an ashtray and turned it upside down. Now it resembled the bottom of the base. He took four salt-and-pepper shakers, removed their covers, stacked them as pillars and had the next level of the base. He found a dessert dish with a cut-glass design that was almost the exact pattern as the top of the base of the original. He bought several of each piece and took them back to the factory and worked on assembling the parts into a solid base. He had one of his workers manufacture the metal arms. Now he had to arrange for the electrical components.

Reuben had been dealing in wrought-iron lamps for years. His favorite contact was Mr. Levitan, a lamp dealer who bought close-out lamp parts, used what he needed, and discarded the rest.

"How can I help you today, Mr. Bibi?" asked Mr. Levitan.

"Anything in the warehouse that you are discarding?"

"I got a whole roomful of stuff."

"How much you want for it?"

"What do you mean? Each piece is a different price."

"I mean, how much do you want for the whole room?"

Reuben bought the whole roomful of lamp parts for $200. Mr. Levitan was thrilled because this was scrap, sitting around and taking up space because he had not gotten around to taking it out to the garbage. Normally he would have paid someone to cart away all his junk and here Reuben was paying for it and carting it away. Reuben was thrilled because he was confident that he would be branching out into electrical lighting. He

---

15. The German occupation of Czechoslovakia began with the Nazi annexation of Sudetenland in October 1938.

tinkered with the wires, the sockets, the switches, until he finally had a beautiful copy of the candelabra that Mr. O'Brien had requested.

"This is beautiful," enthused Mr. O'Brien. "Can you make some more?"

Slowly, Bibi and Co. began specializing in candelabras that could be outfitted either for candles or electricity. Mr. O'Brien continued to show Reuben new styles and models and challenge him to produce good copies. One of those models had a crystal arm shaped like an "S."

How am I going to do this? wondered Reuben, as he studied the unique piece.

He headed back to Kresge's and Woolworth's but found nothing there. Then he went to a hardware store where they were selling bathroom items. One of their products was a long glass rod. Reuben had an idea.

"I want to buy this glass rod," he told the salesman. Then he stopped himself, "Actually, I don't want to buy it. I want to know who you buy it from."

One contact led to another and soon Reuben was in Hicksville, Long Island, meeting the manufacturer. "You see this rod that you are manufacturing? I need the exact same thing, but in an "S" shape. Can you do it?"

The man studied the rod. "Never did something like this before."

"Try it," urged Reuben.

The glass manufacturer worked for a while and then came out with a perfect "S" rod.

"Great," beamed Reuben. "I'll take a whole case."

Reuben drove the case of rods back to Brooklyn, but as soon as he assembled all the parts to the candelabra, the rod broke. He headed back to Long Island to the manufacturer.

"You did a great job, but your glass is breaking."

"Well, we usually put a pipe in the middle. As a bathroom piece, it holds up."

Reuben was thoughtful. "When I was a kid back in Damascus, I used to watch the sword maker at his work. He would hammer away at the blade, thrust it into fire, hammer again, and again, and then, he would thrust the sword into a cold barrel of water. Why did he do that?"

The glass manufacturer answered, "When you beat the metal, the molecules scatter. When you thrust it into hot, then into cold, the molecules join in a certain way, and strengthen the material."

"That's what we got to do!" Reuben declared.

The man was puzzled.

"Make the rod again. Right after the glass is heated up, submerge it into cold water to strengthen it."

"I never heard of anything so crazy in my life," the glazier said.

"Just do it," Reuben insisted.

The glazier shrugged his shoulders and did as he was told. Then Reuben took the finished "S" rod and dropped it on the wooden floor. It bounced like a rubber ball. Reuben beamed. He had found the solution to his problem.

From one innovative idea to the next, the business grew.

"I'm heading out to Philadelphia," Dave Bibi announced.

"What for?" asked Nouri.

"I used to go there to sell fireplaces and andirons. There are some really gorgeous houses out there. Wealthy people redo their homes every once in a while. Maybe they'll sell me their old chandeliers. Those things were massive, full of gorgeous crystals. In today's market, they're worth a fortune."

The crystal market in America was basically dead. America had never produced their own crystals; they always imported from Germany (Bohemian crystal) and Czechoslovakia. Trade between America and those countries had ground to a standstill and businesses that used crystals in their products were stuck. Reuben insisted that in order to produce the copies that Mr. O'Brien wanted, he needed real crystals, which couldn't be ordered for any price. Dave was banking on his new idea as the solution to their problem.

He wasn't disappointed.

"C'mon fellas, unload the car and bring everything inside."

Moe Bibi and his brother Joe (Reuben's boys) carried in a huge chandelier.

The early Bibi and Co. catalogues featured mainly table-top candelabras and hurricane lamps. Hurricane lamps were basically candelabras but, instead of arms holding bulbs, they had a "hurricane globe" for the light source. All Bibi's candelabras and lamps were designed to use candles but could also be "electrified" by running a wire through the hollow main column and installing an electrical socket in the globe. A large saucer-like glass "bobache" — originally made to catch the wax from the candles but often used as an ashtray — cradled the globe, with crystal prisms dangling from the saucer.

Bensonhurst, 1937 / 133

"See," declared Dave triumphantly, "I told you it was a great idea. You would not believe how little I paid for this. This beauty was designed for twenty-four candles. With electricity becoming more popular, who wants to bother with lighting all those candles and then dealing with the melted wax? The lady of the house was happy to get rid of it. There must be hundreds of crystals on this thing. With a little polishing, the crystals will be as good as new. We can dismantle the whole thing and use the crystals to adorn other lamps and candelabras — maybe even a chandelier if we get a special order."

Reuben agreed. Bibi and Co. suddenly had a terrific source of crystals. From one chandelier, Reuben could manufacture a whole line of hurricane lamps, a popular adornment for the fireplace mantle. Luxury electrical items were a new frontier and the Bibis entered the business at just the right time.

Within two years, the business had taken off in a big way.

The Bibis still lived frugally, but instead of shopping off pushcarts on the Lower East Side, they graduated to real stores like Lerner's. Before the holidays, they would troop to S. Klein on 14th Street in Manhattan, one of the most popular stores for guaranteed, *shatnez*-free suits.

Financial stability was a very gradual process. Like Nouri and his uncles, Reuben Bibi's kids quit school after junior high because they had to work.

Reuben Bibi and family. Back row, L-R: Joe, Lillian, Reuben, Esther, Ike, Moe.
Front row, L-R: Ely, Florence, Sara, Charlotte.

They joined the business as teenagers, doing whatever they were told to do. They swept the factory floor, took out the garbage, made deliveries with the drivers, and washed the windows. They kept their eyes and ears open and slowly learned the business. Gradually, they were given more responsibility, but no one — even children of successful businessmen — was given a free ride.

It was an era where people were motivated to accomplish, in business and in life. Certainly, the Bibi home was a constant hub of activity. By 1939, Reuben and Esther had ten children plus Nouri living in the same cramped quarters. They always had guests at their Shabbat table and sometimes during the week as well. Everyone was treated as part of the family, but none as much as Nouri.

Nonetheless, Nouri looked forward to the day when he would have his own home and family.

Chapter 16:
AHI EZER, 1939

Ahi Ezer Congregation had come very far from their humble beginnings on the Lower East Side.

One of the many examples of that growth was felt on Sukkot. Back on the Lower East Side, everyone ate in the synagogue sukka of the Ashkenazim. In Bensonhurst, Ahi Ezer finally had a sukka of its own. The Singerracci family (Italian immigrants who had joined Ahi Ezer) constructed a large sukka from 18-20 doors, assembled on a platform, in the garden adjacent to the *k'nees*. On the first two days of Yom Tov, the sukka was packed as nearly all of the congregation came for Kiddush and *mazza* (the traditional Kiddush buffet).

Even more amazing was the appearance of private sukkot popping up in the neighborhood. Zaki Cohen built a sukka in his house by removing the skylight and placing *se'kach* there instead. Reuben Bibi's sukka was right outside his kitchen. Along its wooden walls, he painted scenic murals depicting the streets of Venice with waterways and gondoliers. Friends and neighbors came to admire the intricate artwork that was clearly a labor of love.

Nonetheless, the *k'nees* sukka remained a community fixture. Mainly on Yom Tov itself, Ahi Ezer congregants came to the sukka to eat and meet, and certainly to spend some extra time with Hacham Murad who was often in the sukka learning. On Hol Ha'moed, the sukka was empty most of the day. Zaki-*kebir* was one of the rare congregants who didn't work on Hol Ha'moed. After prayers, he would stop off in the *k'nees* sukka to chat with the old-timers. Moussa Zalta also lingered; he had no reason to rush to his barbershop when only a few gentiles would come in for a snip. Besides, his son Sam had come for a visit.

"Always be honest, Sam, always be good. Don't become like everyone else. Be better." Hacham Murad urged the young man softly, holding his hand as he spoke. Sam Zalta loved the old-timers, revered his parents, but was carving out a new future for himself. He returned to the old neighborhood for an injection of nostalgia that would help keep him on the straight and narrow.

He thinks that I'm good, that I'm honest, that I can be better than everyone else, Sam thought as he peered into his teacher's eyes, *a giant of a man in a short body. An angel. Should I not believe an angel?*

"Sam, are you listening?"

A blast of autumn wind rustled the simple white tablecloths.

"Sam, you must always do the right thing. Deep down, you know what is right. You are a good man, Sam, a good man. Choose to do what is right."

Sam once more raised the hand clasped in his to his mouth and kissed it. As he left the sukka with his father, he contemplated the words of the Hacham. They were the same words he had heard as a child in *kitab*, as a teenager popping in and out of *k'nees*, and as a young man facing the world. Those same words, said so simply, so softly, and with so much confidence, remained imprinted on his soul.

After all, should he not remember the words of an angel?

The unusual love and respect that Ahi Ezer congregants had for their Hacham was so great, they practically rose from their chairs when they mentioned his name. He had earned that love and devotion through his holy ways. Hacham Murad was soft-spoken and even-tempered — always. When he walked in the street, he kept his head slightly bowed and his eyes lowered, as written in the *Igeret HaRamban*. If he had to leave the room during prayer, he would walk in only at a part where everyone was standing, lest someone rise for his honor.

Hacham Murad rarely walked in the street, one regular exception being Erev Shabbat. Then, one of his children would accompany him to a store, early in the morning, before any women were out shopping, and he would purchase something special, *"lichbod Shabbat Kodesh."* This

Hacham Murad;
note his slightly averted eyes.

trip wasn't combined with other errands — his devoted Sara took care of that — but was dedicated solely to honoring the Shabbat. He was exceedingly careful with all his actions, until he had spiritually elevated even his day-to-day behavior. If he wanted to try out a pen, he would write the word "Amalek" and then cross it out repeatedly. *Ah*, the pen worked... and in the act he blotted out the name of "Amalek."

People from all over the greater Syrian community — *Halabi* and *Shammi* — came to Hacham Murad for blessings, particularly when they despaired. When a child returned home from school too frightened to talk, his parents brought him to Hacham Murad to perform the *"re'ee,"* a mystical ceremony where the Hacham whispered some words from the Hida's *sefer* and the child's speech was restored.

Hacham Haim Yosef David Azulai, the Hida (1724-1806), learned from some of the greatest scholars of the day, including Rav Shalom Sharabi and the Ohr HaHaim Hakadosh, both outstanding Kabbalists.

Occasionally, Ashkenazim also came to Hacham Murad for his blessing, but that was rare, though his reputation as a holy person continued to spread.

Across the street from Ahi Ezer lived Rabbi Menachem Binyamin Ben Zion Rottenberg-Halberstam, the Voideslaver-Sanzer Rebbe, to whom everyone in Bensonhurst referred simply as the "Gaon." Hacham Murad regularly used the *mikva* housed in the Gaon's *shteibel*, and a warm relationship developed between the two men.

The Gaon was a genuine Chassidic Rebbe, who conducted a lively *tisch* where the atmosphere was very different than the *k'nees* of Hacham Murad. Sephardic Jews revered *hachamim* — all *hachamim*: Chassidic, Litvish, Sephardic. Naturally, some Ahi Ezer regulars occasionally made their way to the *shteibel* to join in the Gaon's *tisch*, a unique and deeply spiritual experience. This never bothered Hacham Murad, who truly believed that a person should go wherever he could benefit spiritually.

Hacham Murad was the Rabbi, the *hazzan*, and the *ba'al ko'rei*. His meticulously prepared *derashot* encompassed many esoteric ideas. His *tefillot* were unusually inspiring, not because he was a musical wonder, but because they emerged from the depth of his soul. There was no showmanship, no dramatics, just his sweet and clear enunciation of the words, like a son tearfully pleading with his father. His mastery of the Sephardic cantillation as he read from the Torah was flawless. Nonetheless, while he performed all his duties with simple aplomb, it was his humility that remained his defining characteristic.

In his humility, Hacham Murad was truly happy when Hacham Yaakob Kassin took on the leadership of Magen David. The *Halabi* congregation was large and growing and needed a dynamic and strong Rabbi. Hacham Murad gladly stood side by side with the much younger Rabbi whenever community unity was called for. He also began sending all halachic questions to Hacham Yaakob. Rabbi Kassin had learned in the famous Yeshiva Porat Yosef, where he distinguished himself as a *talmid hacham* and *mekubal*. Hacham Murad was certain that he must be better equipped to answer halachic questions. Yet everyone knew of the tremendous respect that Hacham Yaakob had for Hacham Murad, as he often deferred to him publicly.

In his humility, Hacham Murad spent most of his day teaching little children, most under the age of 10. The bulk of his remaining time was spent

The Voideslaver-Sanzer Rebbe (1881-1957), Rabbi Menachem Binyamin Ben Zion Rottenberg-Halberstam, immigrated to the United States in 1922 and opened his *shteibel* in Bensonhurst. As a great-grandson of the Divrei Chaim, he personified Sanzer Chassidus during his years in Voideslav and later in America.

Hacham Yaakob Kassin (middle) and Hacham Murad (left)

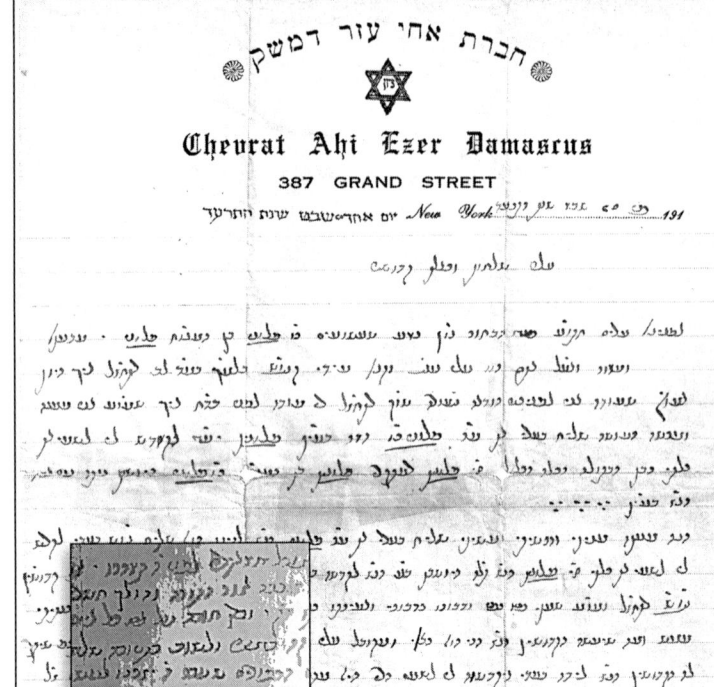

This is a letter that Hacham Murad wrote on synagogue stationery years earlier. Ahi Ezer had been founded by Damascus immigrants who had settled on the Lower East Side back in 1914. The original location was 387 Grand Street. Note the nous al'lam *script and how very different it is from Ashkenazic script.*

giving classes to laymen on Tanach or *Chok l'Yisrael* (few men had the energy to concentrate on more complicated material at the end of a long workday), despite the fact that, almost from the moment he stepped onto American soil, Hacham Murad was recognized as a *talmid hacham* with expertise regarding Sephardic tradition.

The family still reminisced over that very first query that he had received — a short, handwritten letter that Hacham Murad couldn't decipher because it wasn't written in the *nous al'lam* script common among Sephardic Jewry. From the return address, written in English, his neighbor explained that the letter was from the Chief Rabbi of New York, Rabbi Sholom Elchanan Yaffe.

Hacham Murad wrote his reply in Rashi letters, apologizing that he couldn't read what the Rav had written. Rabbi Yaffe replied — also in

Rashi letters — by rewriting the entire question, which had to do with the proper way to write a divorce according to Sephardic tradition. Hacham Murad promptly answered this question that few Sephardic Rabbis in America were equipped to answer.

While Hacham Murad slowly earned the admiration from those outside his community, his most loyal followers remained his congregants, particularly the Bibi brothers.

The Bibi brothers were a tight-knit trio, united by more than blood. They were genuine, sincere Jews, devoted to G-d, each in his own way. Reuben was raising a large family, and yet he never let his myriad duties distract him from his spirituality. Like his father before him, the *Zohar* was his steady companion and he was always interested in hearing another *d'bar Torah*.

Rabbi Sholom Elchanan Yaffe (5618-5684 / 1858-1923) learned in the Volozhiner Yeshiva and was ordained by the Netziv and Rav Yitzchak Elchanan Spector. He served as a Rav in various cities in Lithuania until 1890, when he moved to America. He authored several *sefarim*.

Morris took that devotion one step further and became a real Torah scholar.

Dave was different.

Dave liked to take action, not in a loud way, but with concrete plans and goals. He was the engine behind Bibi and Co. He had endless optimism and was always willing to hear new ideas and to change course, if necessary. The infectious enthusiasm he had for his business, he used for community service and religious life as well. In 1939, when he was barely 30 years old, Dave Bibi became the third president of Ahi Ezer.

Dave Bibi exuded strength, charisma, and success. These G-d-given gifts could have easily swayed him into becoming haughty and proud. And yet he never was. He had been trained well by his mentor, Hacham Murad, and was inordinately humble. He used his exceptional leadership qualities to lead and he became one of the most beloved and admired members of the community.

In the early 1920's, the Ahi Ezer community purchased a house on 64th Street and 21st Avenue to be used as a synagogue. The running expenses of the synagogue included the monthly mortgage payments, utilities (water, electricity, and gas) and stipends for the Rabbi and the sexton. By 1936, the main room was crowded and had to be extended. This was an additional expense. While the treasurer — for many years it was Reuben Bibi — did the actual banking and paid the bills, it was the president who made sure that there was money for expenses. That often meant fundraising, the duty of the president. David Bibi was always fundraising, yet everybody loved him. How was this possible?

"Izzy, I need you to come with me today, to raise money for the synagogue."

Nouri dutifully put on his coat. Though he was an equal partner in the business, Nouri considered Dave his boss, and he obeyed his commands like an obedient soldier. In truth, he probably would have done so even had Dave not been his boss. Nouri viewed all of his uncles as father figures and he respected them accordingly.

"This fella, he's *Halabi*. But he is very wealthy and there is no reason that he should not help us out as well. A synagogue is a synagogue." Dave parked the car and motioned Nouri to follow him.

Nouri watched as Dave engaged the owner of the house in warm conversation, chatting for just the right amount of time. The man seemed sympathetic. He reached for his wallet and opened it.

That was pretty easy, thought Nouri, glancing admiringly at his uncle who had tackled an uncomfortable job with such aplomb. The man leafed through a wad of bills and pulled one out. Nouri's eyes widened.

One dollar? That's it? Nouri was astounded. A sweeping look around the house indicated that its owner was very wealthy. Dave had made such a compelling case, and this was all that the man would give?

David rose and held out his hand. "Thank you very much. May you have much success in all that you do."

"I don't get it," blurted Nouri, closing the car door. "You were so warm and friendly — and this guy — he's loaded! And all he gave you was a dollar, and you thanked him like he gave you a million. Why?"

"Why? What do you mean 'why'?" David looked sternly at his nephew. "No one is required to give us anything. When someone gives, we must be grateful, no matter how much or how little he gives." Dave paused, "Izzy, our job is to plead our case. How much we receive is in G-d's hands, but there is never an excuse for rude or ungracious behavior."

Nouri remained silent as Dave drove back to the factory. He parked the car, turned off the engine, and then picked up the conversation as if they had been talking the whole time. "Besides, just wait till next time. This same guy — he's going to give us a big donation."

"Why do you think so? I would not bother going back to him at all. Giving a dollar... it's almost as if he were making fun of us..."

Dave shook his head and smiled. "You'll see. Next time he'll give more. It always pays to be a gentleman."

A few months later, Dave took Nouri with him again to the same house and they walked out with a very nice donation.

"How did you know?" Nouri persisted.

"These are my rules of fundraising: never assume anyone has to give you anything, always be grateful, and always be a gentleman. You will never lose out."

With all his fundraising efforts, one might have thought that Dave felt absolved of any other charitable obligations. Nothing was further from the truth. After the first month of the business's existence, Dave called Reuben and Nouri together.

"Let's go down the numbers. How much did we spend? How much did we earn? How much are our salaries? Now let's take off …" Dave went on to explain that he wanted to set up a charity fund and that all the partners would donate immediately from their salaries into the fund. If they could only do 10 percent, then it would be 10 percent, but the goal was to donate as much as possible.

Dave didn't believe in stealing the show for himself. If he was doing a worthy mitzva — like donating charity — than why not get others involved as well? His conviction was inspiring. When he took Nouri on fundraising trips, it wasn't for moral support. He wanted him to see how it's done so that Nouri would eventually be comfortable doing it on his own.

Nouri found himself learning from Dave all the time. In the synagogue — where they sat right next to each other, in the first row — he learned that you can be the president of the synagogue and the owner of a successful business, but you run to greet a stranger, find him a seat, make him welcome, and invite him to your house. In business, he learned that you can be out of town, on a business trip, without a *minyan*, in the middle of making a deal, but if it was time to pray, you go back to the hotel room and you talk to G-d, like a child talking to his father. In community service, he learned that you can be running around and raising money — during work hours, when you could be cutting one more deal — and yet you still make sure to give above and beyond your charity obligations. More than anything else, he learned that by being a good Jew, you can inspire others, simply by example.

Nouri learned all this, and more, from Dave Bibi.

Dave was a simple Jew with a heart full of love for G-d and His People.

"*Su'let?* (Did you pray?)" Reuben asked Nouri.

The two men walked together to the *k'nees* on Shabbat afternoon, to be on time first for *Mishmara*,[16] then Minha, then *seuda shelishit*, then Hacham

---

16. This is an old Syrian custom where the congregation reads the *perasha* of the following week together with selections from *Nabi*, *Ketubim*, and *Mishnayot* (specific to the coming

Murad's *derasha*, and then Arbit. It was the same schedule, the same people, day in, day out. Reuben, Dave, and Nouri sat together — same row, same order. Whenever Morris walked in from Flatbush, he joined them. On the other side of the room, front row, were still the two "Moussas" — with David Didia and Nissim Sabin.

Row after row of familiar faces.

Week after week of a familiar schedule.

And Nouri loved everything about it. Ahi Ezer was his home. Not just because he had prayed there for as long as he could remember. Not just because Uncle Reuben was the *mesader* and Uncle Dave was the president. Not just because of his special relationship with Hacham Murad who had taken a pointed interest in him from when his grandfather had passed away years earlier. Ahi Ezer was Nouri's home because he chose to make religion the most important part of his life and that was being carried out in Ahi Ezer.

While the two decades in America had brought much growth to the Syrian Jewish community, along with that growth came change that wasn't always so positive. Hacham Murad began keeping Arak around for Kiddush rather than his usual wine. As the *mesader*, Reuben Bibi was adept at creating honors, other than *aliyot*, for people whose Sabbath observance was questionable.[17]

In this turbulent era where most young men were choosing to de-emphasize practical religion in their lives, Nouri was unique. He realized that belief in G-d required loyalty to Him. Loyalty meant keeping one's own needs and desires subservient to His service. Nouri never looked for the easy way out of religious responsibilities and was quick to take on higher religious standards. While he was quiet about his religious convictions, they didn't go completely unnoticed.

Those closest to Nouri recognized the sincerity in his soul.

---

perasha). Hacham Murad would begin the reading and then the men and boys around the table each took a turn. By the end of the year, they finished all of Tanach and Mishnayot.

17. Wine that is touched by a Sabbath desecrator becomes forbidden. Arak is liquor [*Yoreh De'ah* 123]. "Hacham Murad would not allow a Shabbat desecrator to be called up to the Torah. My father found other ways to honor these people so that they would still feel happy coming to shul. Many of their children or grandchildren eventually became *shomrei Shabbat*" (Mr. Joe Bibi).

PART III

Chapter 17:
BENSONHURST, NOVEMBER 1940

Brriiing!

"Get the door," called Esther Bibi from deep inside one of the bedrooms upstairs.

At four and a half, little Evelyn hesitated. Usually, there were plenty of other hands around, ready to open up. But her mother was taking care of baby Rita — who, in her humble opinion, cried way too often — and all the others were in school or at work.

It is probably just the postman, she decided, reaching for the doorknob.

Her eyes widened when she saw the uniformed man in front of her.

"I am looking for Isidore Dayan."

"Isidore, who?"

The man peered at the little girl, who looked truly puzzled, and then checked his roster again. "Dayan," he said, "Isidore Dayan."

"I am sorry, sir, there is no Isidore Dayan here. We only have an Isidore Bibi."

The man looked back at his list, his brows scrunched in thought. "Are you sure?"

"Positive," nodded the little girl.

The man shrugged his shoulders and left.

A few minutes later, Esther came down holding baby Rita, bathed and dressed in fresh clothing. *Finally quiet*, Evelyn noted with satisfaction.

"Who was by the door?" Esther asked, setting the baby down.

"A funny man in a uniform."

"Oh?" Esther raised a brow, "What did he want?"

Evelyn shook her head. "It was a mistake. He wanted an Isidore Dayan but I explained to him that we only have an Isidore Bibi."

Esther smiled. "He meant Izzy. But don't worry, I'm sure he'll be back."

Izzy's name is not Bibi? Evelyn was confused. *Does that mean that Izzy is not my brother?*[1]

Sure enough, the draft notice found its way back to the Bibi house, even addressed to Isidore Dayan. While America had not yet entered the war, the government had just passed the Selective Training and Service Act (STSA) of 1940 requiring all men between the ages of 21 and 45 to register with the army. A national lottery would determine which of these men would actually be called up to serve a one-year term. The precinct on Bay Parkway and 85th Street was seeing a steady stream of Sephardic men and boys coming to register.

Jack and Esther Maslaton as teenagers

"It is just a formality," worried wives and mothers reassured one another.

It certainly seemed that way. Almost a year had passed since war broke out in Europe and, except for the ever-changing news from the front, America seemed unaffected. Why would they — why should they — join in a battle a half a world away? Besides, President Roosevelt, the man who most of America idolized for having pulled America out of the Depression years, seemed bent on keeping America out of the war.

"*Yishtabah Shemo*, we must pray to Him that they do not draft our boys," sighed Hacham Murad.

Young Jack, just shy of 17, wondered at this oft-repeated comment. He revered his father and trusted his wisdom but somehow… He glanced sidewise at his father and saw the pain and worry etched in the wrinkles that were multiplying by the week. Wasn't his fear a bit overdone?

"But why, Papa?" Jack blurted out. "We are not talking about the Turkish army…" Images of Ibrahim Bailey and his saber collection flashed through Jack's mind. Every Simhat Torah, the eccentric sexton donned an elaborate Arab costume and treated the congregation to a sword-wielding dance that

---

1. Reuben and Esther welcomed Nouri so completely that the younger children were unaware that he was not their brother. Several Bibis still remember the shocking moment when they discovered that fact.

was enough to convince all the children to be ready and waiting when he came to pick them up for *kitab*.

"I mean, this is America!" Jack declared with pride.

Everyone knew that America was a wonderful country — purple mountains majesty, and all that. His parents often praised the land that had freed them from the impossible poverty of the past. True, his father's eyes were sometimes wistful and Jack wondered if it was because he was comparing religious life in the New World to that of the Old Country. But, overall, they were happy that they came and he knew that his father would not deny that truth.

"Yaakob," murmured Hacham Murad, "it is not so simple."

Jack at his bar mitzva

Jack shook his head. "I just don't understand the fear. I mean, none of us think — or want — America to get involved, but if they do, and we get drafted, would it be so terrible? When our people did all that they could to avoid the Turkish army — even fleeing the country if they had to — it was because, as Jews, one never knew when a Turkish sword would end up in a Jewish back "by accident."[2] America is not like that. Americans respect different religions. That is what democracy is all about. They might not love us, but they certainly do not hate us."

Hacham Murad shook his head wordlessly, almost imperceptibly.

Jack persisted. "Papa, back in Syria, when the Arabs went to war, their battle was not our battle. We always knew that whoever won, our fate as Jews would not change. Here, it is different. If America enters the war, it will be because this war is a war against democracy. It is one madman trying to take over the world and rule it the way he wants. If America enters the war, it will be to protect us, to protect our rights."

Hacham Murad raised an eyebrow. "Since when have you become such an expert on American policy?" was his gentle rebuke.

Jack flushed. He knew that his comments were far from an expert opinion. He was simply parroting what he read in the papers, heard on the

---

2. Though, in general, Jews had good relations with their Arab host countries, the deterioration of the Ottoman Empire created unrest and contributed to sporadic anti-Semitic altercations.

radio, and picked up as he listened to the men in the *k'nees*. And, to be honest, it was the latter group that had the most influence on his way of thinking.

The war: It was all everyone was speaking about. And EVERYONE agreed that if anyone should want to join the army, it should be the Jews. The Jews were the ones who had prospered so astronomically in the past fifty years in America. Where was their gratitude to this warm and welcoming land of opportunity if not to go to battle for it? It was the Jews that Hitler was threatening to destroy. Where was their backbone, their gumption, their determination to slay the monster that was bent on destroying them? Are the Jewish people cowards?

And why was it that only his father, one lone voice from the Old Country, saw the situation differently than everyone else?

Jack and Esther at his bar mitzva

Nouri

"Candle-lighting time!" called out Morris.

Rebecca Bibi nodded and quickly finished her last-minute preparations. Morris hummed a tune as he slid into his jacket and straightened his tie. Nouri had come for Shabbat and he was waiting at the door to go with his uncle to the *k'nees*.

He's already a man, Morris noticed with a jolt as they headed toward 501 Avenue R, to the small rented room where the few Syrians in Flatbush prayed. *I was 25 when I got married. Nouri must be... goodness, he's pushing 24...*

Nouri noticed that his uncle seemed very thoughtful. Not that either of them were chatterboxes,

Morris and Rebecca Bibi with Jack Maslaton

but on Friday night, on the way to *k'nees*, Morris usually had something more uplifting to offer than absolute silence. But the *k'nees* was right around the corner and soon they were thoroughly immersed in prayer.

Afterward, there was a lot of back-slapping and hand-shaking as everyone wished each other a *Shabbat Shalom*. The faces were all familiar, though back in Bensonhurst, Nouri had met these Magen David congregants only occasionally. Morris was one of the early Sephardim in Flatbush where there was no *k'nees Sham* and *k'nees Halab*; there were barely enough people to keep one *k'nees* going. So Morris had joined the *Halabim* and was a respected member of the group.

Morris and Rebecca enjoyed having guests. After almost nine years of marriage, they had still not been blessed with children. Both were warm, generous-hearted people, who naturally found other outlets for giving. Morris had "the candy car." All the Bibi children knew that a trip in Uncle Morris's car yielded sweet results. Rebecca rejoiced with every baby boy born, even as she awaited her own. She presented the happy parents with a beautiful, hand-crocheted *kippah*, designed for the baby to wear at his *brit*.

Shabbat afternoon before Minha, the Bibi house turned into a mini Bet Midrash. The one-room *k'nees* on Avenue R did not have room for much more than a small *aron kodesh, siddurim, humashim,* and chairs, but not many *sefarim*. Morris Bibi had a nice library and therefore his home became the natural venue for learning. He was joined by Eli Laniado, Jack Hidary, and

Bensonhurst, November 1940 / 151

Hacham Murad, Morris Bibi, and Rabbi Kassin, learning together on vacation

Ezra Hedaya. The men learned until just before Minha. Then they walked together to the *k'nees* for prayers.[3]

Morris Bibi was always learning: with his father-in-law, Hacham Murad, with Hacham Matloub Abadi, and with Hacham Yaakob Kassin (from whom he learned *shehita*). In Nouri, Morris recognized the scholar's soul. Though Nouri spent more time with Reuben and Dave, the relationship he had with Morris was, in some ways, stronger. Their personalities were similar. Their pull to piety was similar. Their love of learning was similar.

By the time Shabbat ended, Morris Bibi had come up with an idea.

He was surprised to hear that Nouri had been thinking along the same lines.

"Isn't she too young?" Nouri had asked his good friend, Solomon Maimon, a week earlier.

Solomon had come to the Maslaton home in a clear stroke of Providence.

As per his custom, Joe Maslaton "found" Hacham Abraham Maimon, the leader of the Turkish congregation in Seattle, on one of his travels. He returned to the Hacham's house many times, always ending his visit inviting his hosts to his home on the East Coast. One day, Solomon, Hacham Abraham's son, showed up at Joe's doorstep, tacitly accepting his invitation. He had come to learn in Yeshiva University and the opportunity to spend Shabbat at Joe's had been an added attraction.

---

3. This mini Bet Midrash continued until the group outgrew their room on Avenue R. The Hedaya family donated a building on the corner of Ocean Parkway and Kings Highway and named their synagogue Sha'arei Zion. They sold that building in 1957 and bought property at 2030 Ocean Parkway. Sha'arei Zion became the Syrian center, with several *minyanim*, and many *shiurim* and learning programs.

Solomon began coming to Joe Maslaton every holiday and almost every Shabbat. He became an adopted member of the family, joining them when they went to Hacham Murad on the holidays. The services at Ahi Ezer were different from the Turkish custom but similar enough for Solomon to feel very at home. The same applied to the way Hacham Murad conducted himself, how he spoke, and what he taught.

Solomon's studies in the yeshiva introduced him to a higher level of Gemara learning, which exposed a weakness inherent in the Sephardic tradition. The Sephardic way was to spend many years mastering proper reading of all of Tanach, and slowly progressing to Mishnayot and then Gemara, similar to the method described in the Mishna (*Abot* 5:21). By 7 years old, most of the community children were familiar with reading all of Tanach and *Zohar*. But since most boys went out to work by the time they were 13, they did not progress beyond the simple understanding of the Gemara. Solomon realized that his new friends, Sion Maslaton and Nouri Dayan, had probably never been exposed to the type of Gemara learning he was experiencing in yeshiva. Out of gratitude for their hospitality and a desire to enrich the lives of his friends, he offered to learn with them every Sunday.

The three young men learned together every week. As the learning sessions progressed, their relationship with one another deepened. When Nouri had that niggling idea in the back of his mind, he first mentioned it to Solomon.

"I mean, I just thought it would be good — you know, nice home and all…"

Property of Museum of History & Industry, Seattle

"The Sunday learning sessions lasted throughout the five years I spent in Yeshiva University. Every once in a while, when I opened my mailbox at the yeshiva, I found an unmarked envelope with money inside. I knew it was from Nouri, even though he never said anything. He was appreciative of those classes and determined to give me a *matan b'seser*," recalled Rabbi Solomon Maimon in 2014.

Bensonhurst, November 1940 / 153

Nouri was an informal member of the Maslaton family even before his marriage. The Cohens, Maslatons, and Zonanas were all cousins. Top row, L-R: Ray Cohen, (unknown), Ray Zonana, Frieda Zonana. Middle row, L-R: Vicky Zonana, Sophie Maslaton [slightly crouched], Nouri, Sion Maslaton. Sitting in the front, chin on her hand, is Esther Maslaton.

A great home. And it's about time you had your own home... Solomon thought.

"But, well... she's so young," Nouri's voice trailed off. "What will people say?"

"What do you care what people say?" Solomon answered with a laugh. "People like to talk. It is a great idea and I think you should go ahead with it."

But Nouri was still dragging his feet, unsure what to do. So when Morris came up with the same idea, it was the opening that Nouri had been looking for... only he was still hesitant.

Morris decided that his nephew needed a little push.

"So, here is what you do. You take my car — here are the keys — and pick her up to take her for a drive."

Nouri eyed the keys resting on the table suspiciously.

"Go on. Take them. They're not going to bite... and neither will she."

Nouri was not so sure.

Morris was beginning to lose his patience. "Come on, we are not talking about a stranger, for goodness sake. She's my sister-in-law, remember? Her father is your mentor. Her brother is your best friend. She's everything you could want in a wife. You even thought of it yourself. Why all the nerves?"

Nouri stared at his uncle in disbelief. Ten years of marriage was clearly the recipe for severe amnesia. Which young man would not be shaking in his boots before his first date, especially when the girl is the daughter of the man he respected most in the world? But when Morris began humming *Makhelot Aam* (the traditional wedding tune), Nouri knew he had enough. He grabbed the keys and left the house.

Nouri and Esther (Maslaton) Dayan

The first spin around the block went reasonably well. Morris patiently explained that the next time, he would actually have to take her somewhere. Ever obedient, Nouri did as he was told, and the next date also went well. A few weeks later, it was all over. Nouri Dayan was engaged to Esther Maslaton.

Nouri the orphan would soon have his own home.

Bensonhurst, November 1940

Chapter 18:
FROM NEW YORK TO A NEW WORLD, 1941

Things fell into place quickly. Nouri had been a de facto member of the Maslaton home for years. Marriage only made that bond stronger. He popped over to his in-laws regularly, to see if they needed anything, perhaps a nail banged into the wall, or a leaky faucet repaired. *Erev Shabbat*, he would take his father-in-law shopping for the *lichbod Shabbat* treats he always bought. And, when Nouri was called up to appear before the draft board, his mother-in-law fasted, just as she fasted when her own son, Sion, was called up.

Nouri, Sion, and then Jack, were called up more than once. Each time they returned home, Hacham Murad and Sara Maslaton were visibly relieved.

"It is not just the danger," Hacham Murad explained. America had barely begun fighting and few casualties had been reported. No one had really tasted that aspect of war yet. "A gentile army is no place for Jewish boys. How will they keep *kashrut*? How will they keep Shabbat? What about prayer? And how about the constant interaction with *goyim*?"

I had not thought about it that way... Jack listened but was still bothered. Focusing on his father's last sentence, Jack interjected, "And how about when we attend public school? Don't we interact with them there? I mean, we aren't in Syria anymore..."

Hacham Murad shook his head, but he realized that defining the dangers of a Jew in a gentile army to his American-born son was going to be a challenge. Syrian Jews in America were proudly patriotic and very optimistic that they could fight alongside their countrymen and still retain their Jewish identity and religiosity. Perhaps this perception stemmed from a marked difference between their old lives in Syria and their new lives

The broader Syrian community, 1943

in America. In Syria, Jews interacted with their Arab neighbors mainly in business, rarely educationally or socially. In America, despite years of being together with gentiles in public school, the community retained its Jewish identity, mainly because of its self-imposed insularity. Even in public school, SYs stuck together; socializing with gentiles was taboo.

The glue that held the Syrian community together was their religion and their culture. They met at the *k'nees*, talked about whose *kibbe* (traditional meat-filled dumplings) they liked best, made fun of gefilte fish, and sang Arabic music. After junior high school, most of the community youth went to work to help out the family, effectively ending their foray into gentile society. On the surface, they emerged from this system unscathed, their religiosity intact.[4]

Then came the draft.

... I clearly remember the day I received my invitation from the President. I left home amid the tears and farewells of friends and family... During a selectee's first month in the army, he undergoes the most complete mental and physical renovation imaginable. He is thrown in with a collection of men from all walks of life — some illiterate, some profane, some utterly despondent, and some with far above average intelligence... He rises at 5 a.m. and has a hearty breakfast — a conglomeration of something or another and an unidentified liquid. He has nothing to do until 6:30 so he sits around, scrubs toilets, and mops floors... The army either makes or breaks a man fast. One must submit to menial duties and indulge

---

4. This was an illusion. In 1939, Mr. I. Shalom and Mr. Moe Haber spearheaded a meeting to create jobs for youth who did not want to work on Shabbat and to galvanize the community to fight Sabbath desecration. They were acknowledging that Sabbath observance was a problem (*Community Reporter*).

From New York to a New World, 1941 / 157

in physical efforts beyond his wildest imagination… Then the glorious day comes when he realizes he is a soldier. With it comes a renewed interest in life… There is a lot of sweat, pain, and heartbreak between these lines. That's what it takes to make the soldier of today… [Isaac Sasho Levy, *Victory Bulletin,* August 1943].

Slowly, the army became the teacher of its soldiers. Some of its lessons were positive: a soldier's life revolved around courage, loyalty, discipline, obedience, and teamwork. But there were other messages as well, and it was those messages that hardened many Syrian Jewish soldiers, turning their Judaism from a strong faith in G-d based on simple belief and tradition, into a religious identity that they were wearily fond of but could not be bothered to develop.

The United States entered the war shortly after Nouri's marriage. The draft age widened to include all males between 18 and 64 and the length of service changed from one year to the duration of the war. Now that the United States was formally at war, the call-up list rose exponentially.

The draft board had a priority list: Young, unmarried men were preferable to married men, especially those with children. The first time Nouri was called up, he was dismissed because he was wearing glasses. The second time he was called up, he was dismissed because he was married. The third time he was called up, he was dismissed because he had a child. But he had other friends who were drafted even though they wore glasses, or were married, or had a child. So Nouri just thanked Hashem, though it was only many years later that he truly understood the degree to which he had to be thankful.

Many neighborhood boys were drafted. Letters from the front showed how quickly Syrian boys were melting into the army pot. SY boys became part of the crowd and assuaged their loneliness with friendships they would never have made back home. Those who had been lax about formal prayer before being drafted became even more lax in the army. Ditto for other areas of religion. It took a lot of determination and conviction to remain strong.

Hacham Murad prayed that that conviction not be tested.

Jack Maslaton sweated as he waited for his interview. He had been told what *sugya* to prepare and he had done exactly as instructed. He mentally reviewed the information that he had learned with his father, as the minutes ticked by. Finally, a friendly Rabbi greeted him cordially and called him into his office. He began asking him basic questions — full name, father's name, mother's name, etc. — and writing down the answers. Then came the real questions.

"So, let us begin with the basics. Explain the concept of *yush*."

"Excuse me," Jack asked, confused. "Can you repeat that?"

"Yush."

What is he talking about? Jack wondered wildly.

The Rabbi stared at the boy waiting in front of him. *This is such an elementary question! If he cannot answer this, then how in the world can I sign him on as a student in our yeshiva?* The silence stretched.

Finally, Jack tried again. "Can you repeat it one more time? Please?"

"*Yush*," the Rabbi enunciated the word slowly.

Jack shook his head miserably.

He left Yeshiva University without the coveted paper listing him as a Rabbinical student. That paper was his main chance at an exemption. [5]

"Don't worry Jack, they'll never draft you, even without that piece of paper," his friends consoled him.

"Look at you, so short and scrawny…"

"And those glasses! My goodness, they'll take one look at those thick glasses and disqualify you immediately…"

And yet, he kept getting called up, and sent home with a warning to make sure to respond to the next call-up notice. As more boys were drafted, their enthusiasm about going overseas waned. Some boys were the sole supporters of their homes and they worried how their families would manage without their income. Others finally realized that war was a dangerous game, as reports of casualties trickled in slowly. Some boys began dodging their call-up notices.

"Listen, Rabbi, we want to make a deal," explained the head of the draft board to Hacham Murad when he came down to plead with them to leave Jack home. "Let Jack go willingly, and we will make sure that he will never see the battlefield. You see what is going on. He keeps getting called up, and we keep finding ways to exempt him. But this will not continue. Eventually, he'll be drafted. Let's send him off now and we'll get him a cushy job, right here at Fort Hamilton. What do you say?"

Yeah, and once the Rabbi's son stops looking for ways out of the army, others will also go more willingly, understood Jack, though he was unsure that his father recognized the motives of the draft board.

Hacham Murad sighed. The atmosphere in America was turning subtly anti-Semitic. There were plenty of gentiles who felt that, if not for the Jews, there would be no war. They held them responsible for all the chaos in the world. If sending Jack would make them happy — and they were offering him unbelievable terms — was there much of a choice?

So Jack reported for service in early 1942. Indeed, the first few months passed uneventfully. He was given a job right in the neighborhood, at Fort

---

5. He was told to prepare the *sugya* entitled "*yee'oosh shelo mida'at.*" The Ashkenazic / Yiddish pronunciation was so different from the Sephardic pronunciation that he simply did not understand what he was being asked.

Hamilton Parkway, where he worked the large flashlights that scanned the skies for enemy planes. He was even allowed to sleep at home and the army gave him a car to drive back and forth from the base to home.

The army cars for civilian use were very cheaply made. The rubber tires were synthetic and wore out quickly so that Jack was often delayed by flat tires. If he came home one or two hours after he was expected, it was never cause for alarm. Hacham Murad and Sara just assumed that he had another flat tire. Then, one evening, his usual hour delay stretched into two hours, three hours, and then four hours...

What happened to Jack?

Jack Maslaton in the US Army

"Come on, Private, onto the truck."

"What is going on?" Jack asked, as the truck rolled away.

"Quiet!"

"But where are we going?" Jack persisted, as they sped away.

"You are being shipped off on a secret mission."

"Officer, I have a special deal. I am not supposed to be shipped off!"

"Private, see that boat? You will either board it, or be shot right here."

Yessiree, thought Jack as he reluctantly boarded the boat.

Jack sat among his unit, quietly worrying. *I have to get out of here. My parents must be worried sick, and for good reason. I am not trained for battle! Where are they taking me and what will they do with me?*

Feeling that he had no choice, Jack continued pestering his superiors until they finally took him to the captain. The captain listened to his story, and agreed that taking Jack had been a mistake. "But I am not turning back," he stated firmly.

"But I don't know how to do anything," Jack protested.

"We'll train you as a medic, right here, aboard the ship," decided the captain.

Jack felt his stomach turn. That was the end of his "cushy" tour of duty. He was about to participate in some of the most dangerous battles of World War II, beginning with the invasion of Normandy.

Back in Bensonhurst, it was Tisha b'Ab in the spring.

After many hours of calling the army base (where no calls were being answered because the staff was too busy shipping off the soldiers), the Maslatons finally heard the news that they dreaded: Jack had been shipped overseas.

Sara Maslaton was crying. Hacham Murad was subdued.

They had not had the opportunity to bid Jack good-bye, to pack him up with goodies that would not sustain his body but might sustain his soul, or to bless him one last time before he went off to war.

"We will pray," whispered Hacham Murad.

Sara nodded, but she knew that she would do more than pray: She would fast every Monday and Thursday, as a *shemira* that Jack return safely — physically and spiritually whole.

Jack Maslaton, in uniform, at home with cousins. L-R: Ray (Cohen) Weinberg, Nettie (Cohen) Kastel, Jack, Ray (Zonana) Hesney, Frieda (Zonana) Daniels. The two children in the front are Moshe — "Mersh" — Cohen and Adele Cohen.

Front row, L-R: Saul Tawil (Ray [Maslaton] Tawil's son), Rebecca (Maslaton) Bibi, and Jack. Back right is Moe Bibi.

From New York to a New World, 1941 / 161

This is no place for a good Jewish boy, lamented Jack silently, as raucous laughter was punctuated by an expletive. He finally understood how unusually foresighted his father had been.

For Jack Maslaton, the years in the army were a grueling ordeal. He was a sensitive soul, unused to the coarseness of army life, particularly since the tension of war brought out the worst sides of people. He and his army buddies were tired, filthy, hungry, and constantly wrestling with the niggling feeling that that day might be their last. Some men pushed away their worries with crass discussions, exchanging ideas that were so morally abhorrent that Jack felt defiled. When he lay in his pup tent, he felt very alone, one Jew in his unit of gentiles.

The "Pup Tent" was so small, only a puppy could fit in comfortably. Standing in front is Mickey Kairy.

The differences between him and them were immeasurable.

Yet to remain apart was unthinkable. A main part of army discipline was how each unit was a cohesive group of buddies, friends who felt responsible for one another. He had to be one of the guys, even though he did not want to belong.

Jack (front right), the lone Jew in his unit

Army schedule usually did not allow for formal prayer. One day, Jack was granted a furlough. Before he left the army barracks, he decided that he would find a quiet spot to pray properly, with his *tallit* and *tefillin*. In the middle of his prayers, he suddenly realized that he had an audience. Two privates and a captain were watching him. He finished quickly and then faced them.

"Private Maslaton," barked the captain, "what exactly were you doing?"

"I was praying, sir."

"Nonsense," he roared, "no one prays like that."

Jack was silent. *How do I answer that?*

"Give me those straps," snapped the captain.

Jack was not about to hand over his *tefillin*, yet he did not want to be court-marshaled for insubordination. "Please, sir, these are my phylacteries. Why must I hand them over?"

"Don't try any funny business with me. I will have no suicides on my watch."

"Suicide? I have no idea what you are talking about."

"Are you telling me that you are not using those straps to choke yourself to death? I mean, I know war is hard, but we don't want any of that stuff here."

"Captain, I want very much to stay alive. That is why I am praying to G-d. These…" Jack began winding the *tefillin* off his arm, "are part of our prayer ritual."

"Who are you?" the captain asked suspiciously, "and what are your prayer rituals?"

"I am an Orthodox Jew, sir, and we pray wearing…"

"Fine, fine," the captain waved him away, "pray all you want. Only no funny business, you hear?" Jack nodded and rolled his straps off his arm, relieved. *Thrown together, but worlds apart. When I wear the uniform, I am one of them. But when they see the real me, they think I belong in the zoo!*

"Medic, medic!" was the refrain that kept Jack and his partner on their toes.

As they ran over to the latest wounded soldier, Jack could not help but notice that even under fire, fellow soldiers crawled toward their dead comrades, not to drag the body away for burial, but to slip off a watch or a ring and pocket it for themselves.

How different are we, the nation of G-d!

As Jack and his partner dragged a wounded friend to the waiting ambulance, he averted his eyes from the corpses lying around, each one representing another young life abruptly ended. He felt for the soldiers who would likely be buried in unmarked graves, with only a religious symbol as a marker. He could hear the wails across the ocean, as families were informed that a son, brother, or husband would never return home.

Jack with his "buddies." Keeping apart was not an option.

Looting the body was not even a passing thought.

He ate very little.

"I am a vegetarian," Jack would tell his buddies, and only ate vegetables and bread. Then, when his mother sent him a roll of salami, his senior officer graciously took it for himself. "I know that you're a vegetarian," he told him.

Jack had nothing to answer.

In their own way, Jack's gentile army buddies loved him. They gave him their extra potatoes and vegetables and he gave them his meat. They pulled him along on their day off, insisting that he have "fun" with them, although their idea of fun was very different from his idea of fun. Jack was in a constant balancing act as he tried to keep his soul pure while not appearing aloof or snobby.

Keeping Shabbat was rarely an option. In a war, everyone was on duty seven days a week. If Jack could ever keep Shabbat, he did, even when it involved some very creative thinking. But his main weapon to protect his spirituality was prayer. He could pray in his heart all day, every day, and he knew that his family was praying for him as well. He often pulled up the memory of his father's tears on Yom Kippur, the image of him imploring G-d for mercy, as a child begging his father.

Surely G-d would protect the child of one who served Him so faithfully!

"A letter from Jack," Sara Maslaton announced excitedly.

The news spread quickly, and soon much of the Maslaton family huddled around the table as Hacham Murad unfolded the letter. But the letter was streaked with black marker where the censor had done his job and, from the readable gaps, it was very hard to understand what was going on, other than that Jack was "alive and well." So Hacham Murad wrote back that he could not understand his letter because it was so heavily censored.

Jack's next letter was a real puzzle.

"He is repeating himself... I am fine... I am eating well... again and again, the same old thing," murmured Hacham Murad. "What is he trying to tell me?"

After reading the seemingly silly repetitive phrases, Hacham Murad smiled. "Now I understand!" he said. "It is a code. See..." And Hacham Murad proceeded to show the family how Jack had cleverly revealed more about life in the army.

To my dear son Yaakob,

... Always tell me when you receive the food that we send for I rejoice [knowing] that you have eaten and become satisfied from it. Today, Mama went to the post office to send you a package... almonds, ka'ak... and other foods for you to enjoy... Regarding [what you wrote previously] that you have been careful not to shave with a razor and now you are [pained because you are] forced to do so, know my son, that HaKadosh Baruch Hu desires the heart and He is not unduly strict on us. Nonetheless, I am pleased about what you are doing, that you are stringent on yourself wherever possible. Hashem will help you in all that you do to give Him honor. May you always be happy. With His help, very soon, there will be Salvation, and we will be able to serve Hashem thousandfold...

Your father,
Mordechai Maslaton s"t

Jack did everything he could to protect his religiosity. In his letters home, he posed his questions to his father, who answered what he was asked and then added much more. When Chanukah came, Hacham Murad wrote about lighting candles. When Pesah arrived, he asked him if the army would be providing matza. When summer came along, he warned him that if the weather was hot, he should not fast on Tisha b'Ab. He informed him about family and community news, especially when it could impact him all the way across the ocean, like when Selim Bibi's daughter bore a son while the child's father was in the army...

...And if you meet him, remind him that his child needs a pidyon ha'ben. As a Kohen, you, Yaakob, have an obligation to help him with this mitzva. Here is what you must do...

And Hacham Murad proceeded to explain to Jack how to perform the ceremony without the child being present.

Hacham Murad's letters were filled with warmth and love, all transmitted through *pesukim* and *dibrei Hazal*. Yet he did not hesitate to inject softly worded rebuke, like the time Jack wrote letters to all his siblings except one…

>…Please write to him as soon as possible. You do not want to cause jealousy among your brothers and sisters…

Or the time Hacham Murad found out from someone else that Jack was suffering from blisters on his hands…

>…My thoughts are confused [due to the distress of hearing the news secondhand]. Therefore I am requesting that you let me know immediately about your health…

Or when Jack mentioned how he did not want to inconvenience his parents by giving them lists of food that they should send him…

>…Know, my child, that when parents send their children packages, it is not a strain. It is our pleasure. So please tell us what you need…

Letters were a soldier's lifeline. Though normal life seemed so far away, it was comforting to be a part of it, even for only the few minutes it took to read the letter.

>…Your mother and I are planning to go [on vacation to the mountains] for two weeks. With Hashem's help, you will join us in the coming year, may He inscribe us for another year of life. I must tell you that it is not my desire to be mebatel Talmud Torah [by going on vacation]. It is just that many people tell me that I must go for at least two weeks for my health. Through healing the body, there will also be a healing of the soul that will enable me to continue to learn and to teach… Nouri, Esther, and the children will also be going [on vacation] to the same place they went last year… David Bibi and his family will be going there as well…

Eddie Bibi, out in the snow with his rifle, preparing to fight

The sheer normalcy of the news was comforting, because life on the front was anything but normal. When they were in the middle of active combat and darkness fell, they lay down in the open fields — forget about beds — without shelter from

the snow or rain, without protection from the wind and swirling dust. The bare ground was their pillow; the vast sky, their blanket. They waited for sleep to transport them to a different world where there was no blood, no pain, and no death around them.

But usually, Jack could not find comfort in dreams. Even as he slept, he saw corpses parading before him: gentile bodies with crosses hanging from their necks, Jewish bodies with a Magen David dangling. That was how they dragged them off the battlefields. Europe was dotted with "American" cemeteries, lines of graves, marked by crosses. Then, at the very end, there were the Jewish graves, indicated by the Magen David. It was amazing how a symbol that had always filled him with warmth now filled him with dread.

There was no peace in sleep, when all around there was war.

And when morning came, and Jack opened his eyes, the first thing he saw was the thin layer of snow that covered his face.

Ah, life in the army.

Chapter 19:
SYRIAN BOYS IN THE ARMY, 1944-1945

Hello Folks,

How are you all? I am feeling great... Well folks, now that I am thoroughly (gosh, that was a hard word to spell) satisfied that I was granted my furlough and even more so, thankful that I saw Grandma, Uncle Faraq, Aunt Zhia, and Aunt Salha, and countless other relatives and friends, whom if I put their names down, it would take two full pages... So now, all that I am waiting for, G-d willing, is the day that I will walk into the home of Mr. and Mrs. Isaac D. Cohen and family, at 2020 62nd St., give you all a hearty embrace, sit down, and look about me, while pinching myself to see whether I am dreaming or not. I will gather my senses and clear my throat because, from then on, folks, I am going to do nothing but talk, talk, talk.

Talk about the first time I have ever been up in a plane and seeing the beautiful scenery of Palestine from 20,000 feet.

Talk about the six-hour plane trip from the desolate, scorching desert, which is Iran, to the beautiful, cool, fragrant orange blossoms, which is Palestine.

Talk about the expression on Grandma's face when she first saw me, and then the expression of joy when she found out that I was her daughter Regina's son.

Talk about that Saturday night when me, Uncle Faraq, Cousins Meyer and Albert were singing the songs of Mosa'ei Shabbat.

Talk about the wonders and beauty of Jerusalem...

Last but not least, folks, I am waiting for the day when I can tell you about that wonderful trip back to the States, and seeing that enchanting,

L-R: Zaki Cohen, Joe Cohen, Meyer Cohen, Hacham Murad

exotic, lovely, lady of mine — that grand old gal, the Statue of Liberty. Here is hoping, praying, and wishing that great day isn't far off...

Your loving son,
Meyer

In one of the many ironies of war, some Syrian boys ended up back in the Middle East! The entire Cohen/Maslaton family was in an uproar: Meyer (Zaki Cohen's son) had visited Grandma Nitza (her husband, Hacham Meir Maslaton, had already passed away) and Uncle Faraq. They had moved to Eretz Yisrael years before but Regina had already left to America to marry her cousin Zaki. It was over thirty years since Regina had seen her mother. Her children had never met their grandparents, aunts, uncles, and cousins. And now, in an unbelievable stroke of Providence, Meyer was meeting the family he had never thought he would meet.

From America to Australia, from Iran to Italy, SY boys were serving in the American army. They were deployed all over the world and their experiences varied greatly. Later on, when exchanging war stories, they learned that some areas of deployment were like summer camp compared to others. Clearly, the "randomness" of ending up in the line of fire as opposed to guarding a border where there was no fighting going on, made G-d's hand glaringly apparent.

For most soldiers, upbeat letters and smiling photographs masked the horrors of serving in a real and vicious war. The soldiers wanted it that way. Everyone back home was worried enough, why exacerbate their

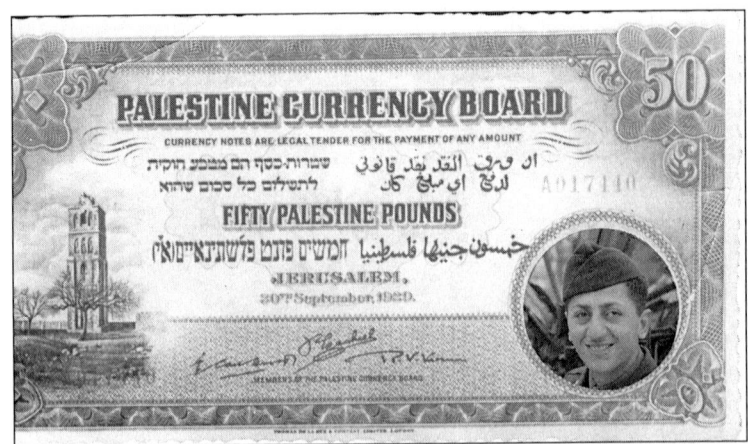

Meyer Cohen goes to Palestine to meet Grandma Nitza Maslaton and family. He sends back this souvenir.

nerves? Meanwhile, they were learning firsthand that war was ugly and cruel and that bravery, courage, and discipline were not so easy to master.

No soldier would return home the same way that he left.

The years of war crawled slowly forward. The Syrian community emptied of its young men. Moe Bibi, Reuben's eldest son, was called up. After basic training, he was sent to Omaha Beachhead, the deceptively American-sounding code name for a section on the coast of Normandy. History would rank D-Day as the turning point of World War II, but for Moe Bibi, a combat engineer, all he knew was that he was being sent on a dangerous mission. He was trained to clear away mines and lay down metal nettings to create roadways for the tanks. Following through with the mission for which he was trained (while under enemy fire) was downright frightening.

Uncle Faraq Maslaton, son of Hacham Meir

The Invasion of Normandy was the largest amphibious operation in world history, involving the deployment of over 160,000 troops. The units that were hardest hit were those that were sent to Omaha Beachhead. And of the troops sent to Omaha Beachhead, the most casualties came from the combat engineers. Moe Bibi knew that he was lucky to be alive. He was not ready to share that revelation with the folks back home.

Americans kept up with the casualty lists, stoically grim, even though they knew very few of the gory

170 / NOURI

Meyer's twin brother, Joe Cohen, is pictured here in uniform with his mother Regina, and his sisters, Ray and Nettie.

details. People were naturally subdued as everyone had a husband, son, or brother serving. There were almost no weddings; there were no males to marry. It was as if life stood still as families lived from letter to letter, hoping that their men were safe.

> *...Last week, we conducted special prayers and supplications in the k'nees. We blew the shofar and we recited Tehillim for the war to end. We practically shook up all of New York [with our cries]: Hashem, enough of our suffering!*

In almost every other letter to Jack, Hacham Murad described the prayers that were taking place regularly, the heartfelt appeals for Heavenly compassion, and the deep feelings they had for the soldiers at war. He did not just write to Jack. Hacham Murad wrote to other boys from the community, words of blessing, encouragement, and hope.

And the soldiers needed it. Though D-Day had turned the tide, there were bloody battles still waiting to be fought. In fact, the bloodiest of them all came toward the end of the war. It was dubbed the Battle of the Bulge.

"Run for your lives," one of the generals screamed.

Jack bolted awake. *Where are we? What is going on?*

All around him, soldiers were scrambling to their feet, pulling on their boots over the rumpled uniforms they had slept in. It was December 16, 1944. The French forest was cold and windy and very dark. The Americans heard the Germans coming at them but they did not know where they were coming from.

Jack ran… then stopped. *Where am I supposed to go?* He thought wildly.

Soldiers were running in all directions, yet they could not all be going to the right place. Some of them were surely running straight into enemy territory. The attack had come as a complete surprise. No one knew what to do.

"Hey you, Jew boy. Follow me."

Syrian Boys in the Army, 1944-1945

Syrian boys in the army. L-R: David Salem, Chick Esses, Joe Dweck, Al Gindi, Joe Semah, Joe Cohen.

Jack turned around. It was that big guy from Texas, the one who had caught him praying with his *tefillin* and bombarded him with questions. Now, he motioned that Jack follow him.

I hope he knows where he is going, Jack prayed.

Sure enough, the Texan led him back to American lines, and away from the German attackers. When they reached safety, Jack slid onto the ground, exhausted. Then he took out a pocket calendar that he kept with him always and checked a niggling idea in his mind. Yes, it was written right there, in clear black letters.

"*Vaihi Yaakob*" he whispered in wonder, "and Yaakob (Jack) lives."[6]

In whose merit was he alive?

His father's tears?

His mother's fasting?

The mitzva of *tefillin*?

Did it really matter?

The Battle of the Bulge, so called because the progression of this battle caused the Allied front lines to "bulge" inward, lasted from December 16, 1944 until January 25, 1945.

Every minute is a miracle, Jack ruminated as he administered sulfa medication to a groaning soldier. Bombs were falling all over the place.

---

6. The Torah portion of that week began with those words.

Every fifth bomb lit the sky, allowing the enemy to see exactly where they were. Six weeks of dodging bullets and caring for those who had not dodged successfully, made one humbly grateful to G-d for every minute of survival. Jack would never forget the time he fled from one area to another and, upon returning two hours later, saw that the ambulance he had abandoned was a bombed-out wreck. There was so much death and destruction all around, he felt as if he were holding his breath, waiting for it to end.

Am I going to survive? he wondered, as he stood on line before the German officer. *This is crazy... a few minutes ago we were in control, and now this?*

Indeed, just as the Americans were certain of victory, the Germans managed to wrest control over some of the area that had just been occupied by the Americans. Logically, Jack knew that this was temporary. The sudden fog made it impossible for the Americans to bomb, but as soon as the fog lifted, the Americans would be back in control. But what about until then? Jack trembled as he watched the Germans in action.

They were separating the American Jewish soldiers from the non-Jews.

This is insane... okay, they have control now, but for how long? They should be running away... they know they are losing... and all they can think about is how to mistreat the Jews?

Jack made a split-second decision. He slipped out of line and hurriedly buried his *tefillin* (which he had on him) and his dog-tags. When he reached the German officer, he stared stonily ahead. "I am an American," he declared.

The German officer looked at him suspiciously, but let him go.

Four hours later, the Germans were running for their lives.

And yet for those few hours, they preferred to persecute the Jews rather than save their own lives by running from the Americans, Jack noted ruefully to himself. *Madmen!*

L-R: Hymie Zonana, Dave Cohen, Sam Sabin, Alan Nesser, and Moe Bibi

Syrian Boys in the Army, 1944-1945 / 173

Indeed, the fanatical hatred of the Germans toward the Jews was madness. Their preoccupation with that hatred distracted them from the war itself and ultimately contributed to its end. When the infamous Battle of the Bulge finally ended, the rest of the war proceeded in a much calmer fashion. Nonetheless, it would take several more months until the Allied victory was complete. Ironically, it was then that the full trauma of the war hit Jack in a way he would never forget.

British, Russian, and American troops closed in on the German army from all sides, stealthily taking control of the shrinking Weimar Republic. As each army, from its angle, took over land, they liberated the area they conquered and established temporary rule. Much of the gentile population welcomed the Allied arrivals, either because they hoped to be treated well by the new rulers, or because they were weary of a war that had sucked the life out of their conquered countries.

None were as grateful as the prisoners of the infamous concentration camps.

The Soviets freed the first camp, Majdanek, on July 23, 1944, as the ovens of Auschwitz were in constant operation. The camp was virtually empty, as the SS had already sent the prisoners to camps farther into German-occupied land. But the camp was completely intact because the Nazis had not had the time to destroy the evidence of their cruelty. The Soviets meticulously filmed every part of the camp to show the world that the gas chambers and crematoriums were not prisoner hallucinations, but truly existed.

Six months later, the Soviets liberated Auschwitz, which by then was virtually empty. Three months later, the British and American troops overran Germany and liberated the rest of the camps. Buchenwald was the first camp to be liberated by the Americans. Jack's battalion was stationed nearby. He and his army buddies decided to hitch a ride to Buchenwald to see if all the wild stories were true.

Going there was easy.

Returning to real life afterward was much more difficult.

"Come…"

Jack and his friend stared at the emaciated man, uncomprehendingly.

"Come here…" The man had switched to another language, but the two Americans were still confused. He clawed at Jack's sleeve, his blue tipped nails a macabre adornment to his stick fingers.

"He wants to show us something," Jack told his friend. They followed the walking skeleton as he dragged himself weakly to a large room.

The room was dark and dirty with ash. There were six ovens, deep cavernous holes, visible because their doors were hanging open. For a minute it reminded Jack of a matza factory, but there was no white dust around, and

The ovens at Buchenwald

the smell of burning flesh that emanated from the cold room was unmistakable. He looked at his guide in confusion. *What is he trying to show us?*

The man tried to talk but the words did not come out. Neither did the tears that seemed stuck in his throat. He just shook his head back and forth, his eyes pleading to these American soldiers that they understand what he could not bring himself to say. A voice from behind him interrupted the silent conversation.

"He is showing you the ovens where they burnt his family..."

Jack whirled around to face an American soldier he did not recognize.

"They gassed them, and then turned them into ash. All the Jews. I speak Yiddish. I understand what he is saying. I am a Jew." The last sentence came out as a hoarse cry.

Jack fought back the lump in his throat, "Me too."

Jack walked out of the crematorium room shaking. *It's like being drunk*, he realized. *Everything looks fuzzy. I feel unsteady as I walk. I just don't want to think.*

Syrian Boys in the Army, 1944-1945 / 175

Mickey Carey in front of the ovens

He barely saw the stick figures sitting and lying all over the place. He distractedly put cigarettes in their open hands, until he had none left to give out. He blocked out the stench of human excrement, decaying bodies, and the faint smell of burnt skin that lingered even though the ovens were cold. He turned around to give the camp one last look before he left, and he saw the chimneys of the crematorium, thankfully still.

Jack, in Germany

"They would show the prisoners the smoke and tell them, there are your parents, wives, children..." the voice of that American soldier echoed in his ears.

Jack felt like he wanted to yell or scream: *A factory made to kill people... to butcher human beings! Animals! Killing human beings... burning their bodies... taunting their families... animals!*

But no sound came out. And no sound would come out for the next few weeks as American operations wound down in Germany. It was with utter

176 / NOURI

detachment that Jack noted Germany's well-kept roads, pretty houses, normal electricity, and indoor plumbing. The streets were squeaky clean even though there was no sanitation department; energetic German women swept the gutter and sidewalk in front of their houses once a week. Of all the countries he had been to — England, France, Belgium, Czechoslovakia — Germany was, by far, the most modern and aesthetically appealing.

Germany: the most civilized country, with the highest standard of living in all of Western Europe. Cultured Germany had produced the most depraved human beings. Animals!

He stared at the huge German flag that he took from one of their bases: *I am going to take this flag, this symbol of German culture, and drape it across Bay Parkway so that all the cars will ride over it endlessly, until it is frayed beyond recognition. This is what I think of "cultured" Germany.*

That is what he would tell his father when he finally returned home.

Chapter 20:
BENSONHURST, 1945

Davie Tawil spotted his Uncle Jack on the way to *k'nees*. They ran over to each other and Jack picked up his nephew and called out, exultantly, "I can't believe that I am alive!"

His joy was mirrored in all the familiar faces that greeted him on the street, in the *k'nees*, and at the neighborhood grocery. The GIs were back and the Syrian community of Bensonhurst rejoiced, only it was a bittersweet rejoicing.

The numbers that were bandied about were shocking: six million. With all the horrific reports floating around during the war years, few were truly prepared for the terrible reality. The survivors straggling into the United States did not have to elaborate; their tortured eyes told their story. And the Syrian community commiserated, though they realized that they would never completely understand their pain.

Yet for the families who had returning soldiers, there was palpable relief. No one forgot the soldiers who would never return home. No one forgot the millions who had perished. Nonetheless, each soldier who returned was cause for celebration. The people decorated their houses and made parties. They got together and just talked.

Then they went back to regular life.

Only it was not so simple.

"Jack, tell me about the army. Tell me about the war," begged little Davie Tawil.

Jack looked at his nephew unseeingly.

What should I tell him? About the town that I saw that once had a big Jewish community but is now empty? "Where are the synagogues?" I asked the people. And all those evil gentiles looked at me with hate in their eyes and pretended not to know. "Listen, Captain," I told my superior, "I know the Jewish people. They would have buried their religious artifacts — their Sifrei Torah, their books — they would not just abandon them. Where are these synagogues?" So the captain called in the local mayor. "Do you want to eat?" he asked him. The man nodded. Then the captain pointed to me. "Show this man what he wants to see." And he showed us where the synagogue had been. And the captain got a bulldozer and dug up the ground. And we found the Sifrei Torah and the sefarim.

And when Jack finished speaking, he was spent, but Davie was fascinated.

"You have to write a book. You have to tell over the stories," the young boy insisted.

Jack shook his head and, young as he was, Davie saw the sadness in his eyes, a sadness that had not been there a few short years earlier.

"I don't want to write. I don't want to talk," Jack answered softly. "I just want to forget."

Nouri wound his *tefillin* and gave them a kiss as he put them away. He glanced around the *k'nees*. Jack was back. He looked the same, didn't he? Well, at least he was in the *k'nees* and that was great, but where were all the others?

The SY veterans returned from war, but they had changed. They had left as confident, fine young men who were motivated and optimistic. Most had not been religiously inclined, but they revered the Hacham and they all agreed that sitting together with family and friends at *mazza* on Shabbat was the highlight of the week.

They came back from the war… different. They were hardened men. Their smiling eyes had a jaded look. Their everyday language was… different. They smiled, they laughed, but there was something broken — sad — even in their laughter. After their initial welcome, many of them chose to stay home rather than return to the *k'nees*. Formal prayer? Why? No one prayed harder than a soldier in a foxhole. They had seen G-d up close, they believed in Him. G-d certainly understands why they just felt no pull to the *k'nees*.

Hacham Murad saw what was happening and immediately called a meeting. His eyes glanced at their faces — boys who had become men, but whom he still thought of as boys. He had officiated at the marriages of their parents. He had been *sandak* at their *brit milas*. He taught all of them to read, to learn, to put on *tefillin*. And yet their familiar faces were different than he remembered.

He prayed inwardly that G-d place the correct words in his mouth. He told them, "Ahi Ezer has purchased a site to build a new Bet Knesset — for you. We have begun, and you will finish. It's for you, so that you can come, every day, and pray… for if not, why is it being built? It must be a place of Torah learning with many classes. Let us try to improve ourselves in *limud Torah* and *yirat Shamayim*, and you will merit that even your children will succeed in these areas…"

Hacham Murad's words were warm and sincere. All of the young men were moved. But were they moved enough to make real changes in their lives?

To Nouri's chagrin, this wasn't usually the case.

"Why?" he wondered aloud, over breakfast one morning.

His wife, Esther, shrugged. "They went through a lot. Who can judge them?"

"I'm not judging them — you know that. I just…"

Esther nodded. She understood what he felt without him saying anything. There was that sense of helpless futility. It was like seeing a person destroy himself.

"Give them time…"

Nouri shook his head. "That is what I'm afraid of. The more time that elapses, the harder it is to go back to a religious life. I mean, let's be realistic, a few years in the army, where there is no Shabbat, no *kashrut*… they have gotten used to living this way. And it's not as if everyone was very religious before they went. A lot of our boys kept things out of habit, not out of knowledge. So when you pick up different habits, bad habits…"

Esther had no answer. Nouri was right. How does one suddenly re-adopt practices that he abandoned? And there were so many other factors. With all the GIs returning at once, there was a huge job shortage, especially since many women had entered the workforce when the men had been at war.

"Tell a veteran without a job that he should only look for work that will allow him to keep Shabbat, and he will look at you as if you are nuts. He hasn't been keeping Shabbat for three years! Now, when he so desperately

The community boys loved and revered their holy Rabbi, but would that awe be enough to convince them to go back to the lives they had left? Here is a rare picture of Hacham Murad Maslaton, praying. Note that he is wearing both Rashi and Rabbeinu Taam tefillin, together, in accordance with the Sephardic tradition. The Shulhan Aruch [O"C 34:2] writes that only those on a high spiritual level should wear Rabbeinu Taam tefillin. Therefore, among Sephardim in those years, only the hachamim wore both, and they wore them together.

needs a job — to earn money, to regain his focus in life, to re-enter the normal world — we are telling him to limit himself so drastically?" Nouri was talking more to himself than to Esther. "We have to do something. And we have to do it now. Maybe Dave will have an idea."

Paradoxically, the war years had been very good to Bibi and Co. At one point they had made so much money, they didn't want to put it all in the bank. They couldn't shake the Depression era mentality they had all grown up with: Banks couldn't be trusted.

So they took stacks of bills and cheerfully buried them in the backyard. Having never learned advanced science,[7] they had no idea of the ramifications of their actions. A few months later, when they went to dig up those bills, they were left with nothing more than scraps of paper. All the bills had decomposed.

Luckily, the business was doing so well, this minor setback didn't hurt them. They forged ahead, churning out new ideas, and constantly expanding. Now it was time to look at that expansion and see how they could use their burgeoning business to help others, especially those in their community.

"Lamps," Dave said decisively, "we'll set them up in the lamp business."

"But that's our territory," Reuben interjected.

"There's plenty of business for all of us," Dave answered.

Reuben shrugged. Dave was the one who was out there. If he said that there was enough business for everyone, who was he to argue?

"Let's call them in for a meeting," Nouri suggested. He was excited that his nascent idea was already bearing fruit. In short order, ten of his young friends were gathered at Bibi and Co.

Dave chaired the meeting, explaining to them that Bibi and Co. was interested in helping them launch a new company called Promotional Lamp Co. What he didn't explain was that not only was he giving them the merchandise and the expertise, he was actually setting them up in competition with himself!

"Lamps are a cheap commodity. For $2, you can sell a decent pair of lamps and make a profit. The ten of you will become equal partners. We will give you offices here, teach you the ropes, and when the business begins to show a profit, you will continue on your own. What do you think?"

They thought it was great. Maybe even too great.

---

7. Another fascinating aspect of this generation was the degree to which they were self-taught. Most of Reuben Bibi's knowledge of science and engineering came from his own experience in trial and error. Neither Dave, nor Morris, nor Nouri attended school past junior high, yet they all became successful businessmen and prominent members of the Syrian community.

"What's the deal? Why are you doing this?" one of the men asked.

"No deal — well, maybe one little thing…"

The hardened vets looked at each other knowingly. After all their rounds of employment opportunities, they knew that if something sounded too good, it usually was. In the weeks since their return back home, their collective self-esteem had risen quite high with the warm welcome and then fallen quite low when they came face to face with their dismal earning potential.

"No working on the Shabbat," Dave stated blandly, "and stop every day to pray Minha and Arbit together."

"That's it?"

"That's it."

The boys eyed one another. Religious coercion? Perhaps. Did they care? Not really. They had nothing against returning to religious life if they could.

A short while later, Promotional Lamp Co. was up and running.[8]

It made no difference — *Halabi*, *Shammi*, Ashkenazi — the word was out: You are a nice person who cannot find work? Go to Bibi and Co. You want to keep Shabbat and no one will give you a job? Go to Bibi and Co. Even gentiles who were down on their luck somehow found out about Bibi and Co. — like the two deaf-mutes who became the most devoted workers the company ever had.

Giving everyone jobs wasn't as simple as it sounds. It often meant training people in fields that they had no experience in, which meant expending time that could be used to build the business, and instead using that time to build people, who sometimes went out on their own afterward and created competitive businesses — with Dave Bibi's blessings!

David was the power behind the company, but Reuben Bibi was often the one left coaching the new recruits, a job he did with patience and good will.[9] And Nouri had to make the whole system work.

The three partners were consistently united in their mission: Bibi and Co. would not exist solely for itself but as a vehicle to help others.

Perhaps that was why business continued to boom.

---

8. It's unclear exactly who thought of this idea: Dave, Nouri, or both together. They were always working to help the community. In the words of Mickey Carey, "All the SY's worked for Bibi." Mr. Joe Bibi commented on this venture: "The business was a good beginning for them. They were all bosses, not underpaid laborers. It gave them self-esteem, and helped them get on their feet. But the alliance didn't last long. Instead of getting together and finding a proper niche for each person (head of sales, head of bookkeeping, etc.), each one thought he was the overall boss and, within two years, the business collapsed. Mickey Carey, Meyer Cohen, Isaac Cabbaso, Al Azar, and Eddie Bibi were part of the original ten." When it fell apart, Mr. Dayan commented, "At least we kept them from working on Shabbat."

9. "I knew nothing about electricity: What? You need to connect the wires? Reuben Bibi hired me, taught me, took me with him to install chandeliers, and eventually sent me out on my own" (Mr. Meyer Cohen).

Chapter 21:
IN THE AFTERMATH, 1946

"I want to go to Europe," Dave Bibi announced to Reuben and Nouri.

"What for?" Reuben asked, intent on assembling a chandelier.

"The war is over. Europe is open, but a mess. There must be tons of nice things just lying around, waiting for someone to grab them up and market them."

Reuben grunted, still focused on his work.

"A bargain hunter's paradise, I'm sure of it," Dave insisted.

Reuben looked up at Nouri, "What do you say?"

Nouri shrugged, "Dave's the purchasing expert. Let him go for it."

Reuben nodded, and then went right back to work.

Dave beamed.

Dave had not left America since he arrived from Syria when he was 11 years old. At 38, he was still young and adventurous, in business and in life. While he recognized that Bibi and Co. had blossomed through Divine Providence, he didn't downplay the role that optimism, innovation, creativity, and sheer chutzpah had played.

Here goes more of the same, he thought to himself as he stepped out of the dinky, European hotel and onto an unfamiliar street where all he heard were languages that he didn't understand. For a moment, he wondered how he would communicate. Then he straightened himself and forged ahead. He would speak English and they would have to understand.

In its heyday, Czechoslovakia had been the king of crystals. A bit of that regality still surfaced occasionally, when gorgeous turrets popped out of nowhere, and suddenly, a grand palace was visible, right next to a bombed-out ruin. One could picture elaborate crystal chandeliers hanging from their ceilings. The signs of war were everywhere, but that wasn't what was on Dave Bibi's mind. He was scanning the street signs, hoping they would lead him to the government building he sought. There it was: Department of Trade and Commerce. He walked right inside.

While ostensibly not communist, the Czechoslovakian government had appropriated loads of property — for the good of the people, of course — and had warehouses full of merchandise with no idea what to do with it. The government needed cash — desperately. They decided to sell their wares to private investors.

"Do you have any crystals?" Dave Bibi inquired.

"Of course," sniffed the government clerk.

"May I see them?"

"Sir, that is not the way we do things. We have 180 cases of crystals, of various qualities. We cannot let everyone go through our boxes. Whoever gives us a reasonable offer must take the whole batch. These are excellent crystals, I give you my word."

"I'm sure that you do," Dave answered smoothly, "but I must see at least a sample. Now."

The clerk looked Dave Bibi up and down. *Not a tall man, but he cuts an impressive figure anyway... very possible that he has the funds he had claimed when we scheduled this appointment.* The clerk called over a different employee and spoke to him in rapid Czech. A few minutes later, the employee returned, straining under the weight of a heavy box. With a motion, the clerk invited Dave to have a look.

Careful to retain a poker face, Dave fingered one crystal, examining it closely. *This is good, really good!* He put it back in the box and took out another, not allowing his rising excitement to show. *This one box alone is incredible!* He realized that there was no guarantee about the rest of the merchandise. He mentally began going down the figures and finally named a price that, if even half of the boxes were these types of crystals, was exceptionally low. The clerk nodded and went to speak to his superior.

They closed the deal that afternoon.

"Do you have anything else for sale?" inquired Dave.

The clerk sent him on to the ceramics department. There they showed him delicate porcelain dishes that he had never seen in America. Once again, Dave quoted a ridiculously low price, which was accepted on the spot. Now he was all fired up with enthusiasm for a new niche for Bibi and Co.: the giftware department.

Dave traveled to Austria, France, Belgium, and Italy. In each country, he sniffed for specialties. The Limoges region in France was famous for their elegant, hand-painted, porcelain dishes. When the 1930's introduced more minimalist styling, the elaborate Limoges pieces fell out of favor and the factories in the region shut down one by one. David discovered the

Sansom family, also French experts in ceramics. He hired them to make Limoges style pieces, which he marketed under the Bibi logo. These pieces became an essential part of the giftware department.

In Venice, Italy, he found paperweights, beautiful glass pieces, that were blown with a flower burst inside. They were very pretty, very marketable, and very different from anything he had seen in America. Dave bought a whole shipment. After several weeks in Europe, he headed home, cautiously happy with his trip.

Bibi and Co. was expanding.

They bought a building on 5th Avenue and 28th Street in Manhattan to use as a retail showroom. They set up a display window where they featured their unique hurricane lamps, chandeliers, and giftware. On the second floor, they stored additional merchandise. They also hired more workers for the growing business.

Joe Bibi, Reuben's second son, drafted and discharged, was eager to re-enter the workforce, back to his old job at Bibi and Co. Dave Bibi put him in charge of the new Manhattan showroom, though he popped in all the time to supervise. Joe was young and inexperienced, but he was also forward thinking and hardworking, and became an important employee. He kept the showroom window full of a dazzling array of products that drew the attention of window shoppers, as well as serious buyers.

Inevitably, it drew the attention of job seekers as well.

"May I speak to the owner?"

Joe looked up from his work, nonplussed. The man who had spoken in very halting English was clearly not a customer. *Could he be looking for a job? Impossible.*

To 21-year-old Joe, the thin, short, balding man standing patiently in front of him was near retirement age. *Not a day less than 60*, was his mental estimate. But, being the respectful young man that he was, Joe went to call his Uncle Dave, who approached the man, hand outstretched.

"Dave Bibi," he introduced himself. "How can I help you?"

"Alexander Levy, but most people call me Sandro. I am looking for a job."

If Dave was surprised, he did not let it show.

"Where are you from?" he asked casually.

"Milan, Italy."

Dave was intrigued. The Levys of Italy were a famous family, known for their expertise in the arts, especially Venetian art goods.

"What did you do back in Italy?" Dave asked in genuine interest.

"I was a museum director, that is, up until the war..." He shrugged his shoulders. "Let me shorten my sad tale to the bare facts: I lost my whole family in the war and ended up in a DP camp, sick and broken. A sweet

In the Aftermath, 1946 / 185

young girl had pity on me and nursed me back to health. I married her and we have a lovely child. I need a job to support them."

Joe watched every movement. *His clothing is shabby, but his taste is conservative. Clearly, a gentleman who had come upon hard times. He has character; his demeanor exudes breeding.*

As Sandro discussed Venetian art, Joe listened. *He is a worldly man. His English is stilted but excellent for a fresh refugee. He takes time to get the words out, but if one has patience, he is certain to learn something. He carries himself well, and he speaks like a professor, especially when it comes to his areas of expertise.*

Joe's eyes wandered to his uncle's face. Dave was listening intently, and Joe recognized an expression he had seen many times before. *Uncle Dave feels sorry for the man... but there is no way he can pay him the type of salary he deserves...*

"How much is your rent?" Dave asked.

Sandro named the figure and Dave wrote it down.

"How much do you pay for food? Basic utilities?"

Sandro silently calculated his monthly expenses and then threw out a number.

"Okay. So here we have your monthly expenses for food and shelter. On top of that, I can add $25 so that your costs will be covered with a decent amount to spare. I know that you are really worth ten times more than this. You are overqualified, and that is why you are finding it so difficult to get a job. Businesses like mine are not hiring workers for this kind of money. We can get decent workers for much cheaper. I want to help you out. I wish I could pay you more, but this is the most that I can do."

Sandro stood up and offered Dave Bibi his hand. "Thank you very much. When can I begin working?"

Dave smiled as he clasped Sandro's hand in his. "Right now," he said. "Joe," he indicated his nephew, "is going to be your new boss."

I am what...?! Joe did not know what to do with himself.

Sandro turned to Joe and gave a little bow. "At your service."

Joe had the good grace to smile.

So began Joe's foray into "business school."

Sandro's arrival was just the beginning.

"Joe, meet Mr. Hamburger," Dave Bibi motioned to the newcomer. "Mr. Hamburger used to work in finance back in Germany. I just hired him as your financial assistant. I am sure that you and he will work well together."

Joe was speechless. Not that he ever had a choice about who worked for him, but how in the world did all these old folks find his Uncle Dave? He had no doubt that Mr. Hamburger had been offered the same deal as Sandro — enough money for expenses with a decent amount left over — despite the fact that Bibi and Co. did not really need the extra help.

What am I going to do with him? wondered Joe.

Mr. Hamburger and Dave were still talking amiably. Dave showed him where he could put his derby and the umbrella that he held in the crook of his arm. Joe peered out the window to reassure himself of what he knew to be true. Yup, there was the sun, shining with all its might, nary a cloud in sight. Would he ever have the guts to ask this Mr. Hamburger why he carried an umbrella on a bright and sunshiny day?

It's part of the uniform, Joe decided a few days later as Mr. Hamburger walked into the showroom, straight-backed and formal, the umbrella embedded in the crook of his arm. The derby was at the same exact angle every day. His clothes were old but expensive, and the fine cut was so noticeable that even though he was not wearing tails, his whole bearing made it seem like he was. When Mr. Hamburger nodded in greeting, his thick red mustache crinkled up at the ends.

Despite his unusual staff (which continued to grow with the addition of other interesting workers, some who were qualified and some who were not) Joe learned to appreciate his uncle. Slowly he realized that his kindness had created a win/win situation: These elderly gentlemen found a secure income while Joe Bibi was earning a free BA in business school.

G-d was certainly smiling His approval.

Chapter 22:
BENSONHURST, 1947

"Mr. Bibi, there's a telephone for you, in the candy store."

Dave Bibi glanced at Nouri. "I think it's about time we get our own line."

"Do you want me to look into it?" Nouri asked.

Dave nodded as he handed the child messenger a nickel. He walked quickly out the factory and down the block, where the phone was sure to be dangling from the cord as the caller on the other end waited for him to pick up.

The little boy looked shyly at Nouri, "And will I get a quarter for saying *Tehillim*?"

Nouri smiled, "Sure, come over here." He led him to his office and took out a *Tehillim* with large print. "Go on now, you can say it right outside the store. When you finish, come back for your quarter."

The little boy took the small book and went outside.

"A quarter?" Reuben asked, looking up from his work. "It used to be a nickel."

Nouri shrugged, "Inflation."

Ever since he had started earning money as a teenager, Nouri always allotted part of his earnings to his pet projects, like the nickels he gave out to little children on Hanuka and Purim, just to make them happy. When Bibi and Co. bought the Bensonhurst building on 65th Street, he began paying children to say *Tehillim*. With a few pennies, a child was kept gainfully occupied while his Hebrew reading improved, his fluency in *Tehillim* expanded, and who knew how much holiness was created through a child's prayers! Nouri never launched a grand campaign. Nor was he expecting grand results. He just wanted to bring a little more holiness into their lives and into the world.

Nouri had a special place in his heart for children, not in an outgoing or boisterous way, but in a way that was deep and genuine. Unlike other adults, for whom children are often invisible, Nouri saw the children as delightful people and independent beings. When he met children in the street, he gave them the same hearty greeting he gave their fathers. In his concern for them, he came up with ideas to help them grow and develop.

Certainly, some of this warmth came from his having been an orphan. He understood what love, attention, and validation could do for a child, even when it came from outside the immediate family unit. He was forever grateful to all the people in his life who helped him grow and develop. His generosity of spirit wasn't only a tribute to himself, but to them as well.

Bibi and Co.'s Manhattan showroom

Nouri occasionally went to the Manhattan showroom, but the main part of his day was spent in Bensonhurst. The Bensonhurst building was a happening place. The factory was loud and busy, as Dave sketched designs, and Reuben implemented those plans while supervising a roomful of factory workers. There was plenty of talk and banter but, overall, the workers were focused and productive.

The Czechoslovakian crystals proved to be a fabulous investment. True, many of the boxes were junk, and most of the good stuff wasn't 100 percent perfect, but overall, these were antique crystals, cut with many facets, unlike any others that existed on the market. Bibi and Co. fixed them, polished them, and assembled them in lighting fixtures in ways that any imperfections went unnoticed. For the first decade of the business, Bibi and Co. had marketed their unique products only through "Mom and Pop" stores. Now they had the means to create whole lines of hurricane lamps and chandeliers to market on a broader scale. They photographed their products, hired a salesman, and began selling to a large department store in Philadelphia.

As the business expanded, so did the scope of jobs, particularly in the Bensonhurst building. They needed factory workers, assemblymen, electricians, deliverymen, and truck drivers. They hired secretaries, salesmen, inventory workers, and bookkeepers. And Nouri's job was to keep the whole place running smoothly.

This suits me fine, Nouri mused one day in satisfaction.

Being consistently in Bensonhurst meant that he never missed a *minyan*; he even organized *minyanim* in the business during the winter months when Minha was very early. He often popped over to the *k'nees* or to his in-laws to see if anyone needed his help, and was readily available to the community kids who stopped by to say *Tehillim* and get their quarters. Occasionally, he would wander outside to see if there were any children loitering around, and then he'd grab them and haul them into the factory to say *Tehillim* and be rewarded.

By 1948, the Bibi catalogue featured chandeliers in addition to candelabras and hurricane lamps, but the big difference was in the lighting source. In the new models, electric bulbs were standard, though all of them could be outfitted for candles as a special order and at a $2 discount. They also added table lamps, floor lamps, wall brackets, and giftware.

Even as they expanded, Bibi and Co. remained essentially a family business. Beyond close relatives, any Jew in need was considered family. There were so many different parts of the business, Dave Bibi could find almost anyone a suitable job.

The reverse was also true: People considered a job at Bibi and Co. to be a respectable means of earning a living. There was more than one accomplished scholar on Bibi's employee roster, men who would have preferred learning and teaching Torah but, for whatever reason, sought a different means of support.

While Dave Bibi welcomed these employees warmly, positions in Bibi and Co. were limited in terms of upward mobility. Some people would benefit from becoming independent, yet they didn't have the capital to start out or maintain a business.

"Nouri, we have to do something," Dave approached Nouri one day at work.

Nouri continued counting the envelopes he was holding, a small smile playing at his lips.

"About what?" he asked, laying the stack of paychecks aside.

Dave's chiseled features radiated strength and confidence. He was one of those people whose age you could never guess. His hair was jet black, his eyes were alive with enthusiasm, and the energy he generated shouted: young, young, young! Yet, his aristocratic demeanor, his poise and self-assurance, were that of someone much older.

I'm proud to be his nephew, Nouri realized. And he knew that he was much more than that. He was Dave's protégée, kid brother, son, and business partner all rolled into one. He was also his foil. Where Dave instantly commanded attention, Nouri's boyish grin and infectious smile won hearts in a much softer, understated way. The two men complemented each other and were inordinately comfortable together. Just as significantly, they genuinely liked each other. Perhaps that was why when one of them had an idea, the other was almost certain to be enthusiastic as well.

"I was thinking about creating a free loan society," Dave began. "We can offer people in the community a one-time loan of — let's say — $1,000, and the borrower could use that money to start off a business, or just to tide himself over until his new business makes a profit."

"$1,000 is a lot of money…"

"It's really the minimal for a startup company."

Nouri agreed. They decided that the loan would be open-ended.

"Pay us back when you can," Dave and Nouri reassured their "customers." Of course they went through all the usual motions: There had to be a co-signer, the co-signer had to be someone from the community, and all parties had to sign. Other than that, the fund operated on trust. People paid back at their own pace, some quickly and others less so. There were those who paid back and re-borrowed at the same time, essentially creating a revolving loan, with many people taking years to repay the original sum. But there was always money in the fund from those who paid back quickly or from Dave and Nouri who made sure that the well never ran dry. Dave and Nouri never questioned why someone didn't repay their loan. It was clear to them that if the borrower could repay, he would, and if he couldn't, then their kindness would have to stretch a little longer.

They constantly thanked G-d that their growing business made their philanthropy possible, though there were always the usual bumps along the way.

Like when the unions kidnaped Zaki Cohen.

"You better shape up," growled the burly Italian who had just roughed him up. "Tell your boss that he better work with us, or else!"

But Bibi and Co. didn't want to unionize. While they understood that the unions came into being to protect the worker — and they well remembered the years when immigrant workers were used and abused by greedy

Bensonhurst, 1947 / 191

bosses — they balked at being forced to join. They treated their employees just fine, probably better than most union shops. Their pay scale was fair; most of their employees earned higher salaries than union workers. If they unionized, Bibi and Co.'s expenses would rise, not to the benefit of the employees. So they tried to hold out, but one incident after another had them wondering how long they would last.

"They smashed the showroom window again," Dave reported one morning. "I'm going down to see the damage."

One rock hurled through the huge window left chandeliers, lamps, and giftware smashed among the window shards. The merchandise was a clear loss. Then there was the cost of clean-up, the cost of a new window, and the store had to be boarded up until the window was repaired. Such damage was a big expense and there was almost nothing they could do to stop the terrorization. Eventually, Bibi and Co. gave in to the unions, yet their experience taught them a great deal: Even successful businesses have their ups and downs, sometimes one must give in in order to move on, and don't let the hitches in life color the world black.

Chapter 23:
SHANGHAI, CHINA, 1946

"I'm telling you, Joe, I have never seen anyone like them." Chinese-born Solomon Nathan wasn't usually so effusive, but this time he was truly impressed. "Most of these boys are older than us, but some of them are our age. And they sit and sway over those Gemaras a whole day. It's unbelievable."

Joe Jacobs nodded in agreement. The Mirrer Yeshiva had relocated to Shanghai and immediately affected the entire community simply by being there. They lived in the Hongkou section — a short walk from the old Iraqi community on Sima Road — and the yeshiva was housed in the Bet Aharon synagogue, adjacent to the Iraqi community.[10]

The years that the Mirrer Yeshiva spent in Shanghai were years of growth for themselves and for the Shanghai community. Though they spent most of their time learning in their Bet Midrash, they also reached out to their Sephardic brothers, offering classes and even one-on-one tutoring.

But they had never intended to stay there. Shanghai was on the other side of the world — literally. It was cut off from all major centers of Jewry. When World War II ended, the European refugees eagerly awaited their immigration papers for America, Eretz Yisrael, Canada, and other places. By 1946, almost no one from the Mirrer Yeshiva was left in Shanghai.

The Mirrer *bachurim* who arrived in America didn't forget their Sephardic friends back in Shanghai. They realized that if the Iraqi Jews stayed in China, within a few generations they would become assimilated. With the help of Agudath Israel, they worked on getting visas for anyone

---

10. Most of the Iraqi community had come to Shanghai at the turn of the century. They were traditional Jews who ate kosher and tried to keep Shabbat, but there were very few Torah scholars.

The majestic Bet Aharon synagogue was full and completely functional until a short time before the Mirrer Yeshiva came. "We had moved to a different area where a new shul had been built," explained Mr. Joe Jacobs. "The old shul was temporarily empty... and then the Mirrer Yeshiva came and filled its sanctuary with the sounds of Torah."

who agreed to leave. The Jacobs boys — Joe, his brother, and cousins — gratefully accepted the invitation. Solomon Nathan and Isaac Levy joined as well.

"Don't worry," Rabbi Dovid Shmuel Schachter, one of the *bachurim* who had given classes back in Shanghai, wrote to the Sephardic boys. "There is a wonderful Sephardic community in Bensonhurst, Brooklyn. You will feel at home there. Trust me."

You will feel at home... trust me. Sure.

Joe Jacobs sat next to his brother, Sol, in the back of the synagogue. He looked around the room. The faces were already familiar. *They should be, by now,* he thought ruefully to himself. The thought was vaguely unsettling. After a month of coming to the same *k'nees* every Shabbat, he still didn't know one person. No one had extended a hand in greeting. No one had even asked him his name. It was as if he and his companions were invisible. At first, they had not really minded. They had each other; they were not lonely. Only it would have been nice to be acknowledged, at least a little.

"We don't have to keep coming here," Sol commented to the others as they walked home.

"Where should we go for prayers? To the Ashkenaz?"

"Hold it, Joe, don't get so excited. Who said anything about Ashkenaz? I heard that there is another synagogue — a small one — on 64th Street. It's also Sephardic. We can check it out. If we like it, fine. If not, we can go back to the old one."

Joe turned over the suggestion in his mind. Try out another place? He was tired of being a stranger. On the other hand, maybe there he would be welcomed. Maybe there he would find a home. Maybe there he would stop being a stranger.

The next week, the Jacobs boys walked up 64th Street scanning the addresses.

This is a synagogue? They looked at each other warily. After the majestic Shanghai synagogues, the first synagogue in Bensonhurst was a weak comparison. But this little house was... well, it was a house, not a synagogue. As they observed men greeting each other in Arabic, and proceeding inside, they knew that they had not made a mistake. This *was* the synagogue they were looking for.

"After you," Sol extended his hand in a grand gesture.

Joe took a deep breath and walked up the stoop. He opened the door and stepped into the vestibule. *Neat, clean, so far so good.* He walked farther inside where men were already humming tunes for Kabbalat Shabbat. There were several rows of seats, modest chairs that did their job, the *teba* (*aron kodesh*) was in the middle, and the lectern was up front. Though far from grand, it was a synagogue, plain and simple — literally.

He motioned to Sol that he was going to the back of the room, his usual spot. Sol followed him, picking up two *siddurim* along the way. Just as they were getting comfortable, a very distinguished-looking man rose from his seat in the front, turned around and scanned the room. His eyes stared toward the back.

Joe turned around to see if there was anything behind him that warranted interest. The women's sanctuary was empty. *Nothing there.*

As he turned to face the front again, he watched this man walk quickly to the back of the room, right to where he and Sol were standing. He thrust his hand forward in greeting, and with a warm and welcoming smile, introduced himself. "*Shabbat Shalom,* Dave Bibi here. Please come sit up front. I have seats for you over there."

Joe and Sol were too shocked to protest. They meekly followed Mr. Bibi to the front row. They joined in the prayers, still overwhelmed. After the services, Dave Bibi introduced them around. They met his brother Reuben, his nephew Nouri, and some of the other men. Their names were a blur, but the meal that they ate at Dave's house wasn't. They savored every bit of the home-cooked food and the amazingly warm atmosphere. There was no question in either one's mind: they would be returning for services the next morning.

As soon as they walked in the next morning, there was Dave Bibi, rushing to greet them and usher them into seats next to him. The other men in the row beamed equally warm smiles, though the newcomers had yet to remember all their names.

"We are on for lunch, yes?" Dave asked quickly as he unfolded his *tallit.* Joe and Sol looked at each other and nodded, remembering the delightful meal of the previous night.

Shanghai, China, 1946

They enjoyed the prayers. They were a bit different from what they were used to but familiar enough to be comforting. When the services ended, the entire room seemed to flow out of the *k'nees* behind the Rabbi.[11] Sol raised an eyebrow in question, but Dave Bibi just motioned that they follow the crowd. They walked out of the *k'nees*, down the street, and kept on walking. It was a mini-parade of people, talking softly as they accompanied the Rabbi to his house on 60th Street. Here too, the young men were moved by the generosity and warmth that seemed to overflow from all corners of that tiny apartment.

Hacham Murad sat at the head of the large table. He scanned the room with his dark eyes, his penetrating gaze solemn, warm, and welcoming all at once. The table was decked out with a huge selection of Sephardic foods. There was *ka'ak*, Syrian potato salad, Israeli salad, olives, beets with tehina, *kibbe*, and other delicacies. Hacham Murad made Kiddush. Once the blessings were said, he motioned that everyone partake of the food, and a small smile played at his lips as he watched their enjoyment.

They ate and they sang, the spirited *bakashot* and *zemirot* echoing outside.[12] After a while, Sara Maslaton brought out glasses of Arak with plates of hard-boiled eggs that had baked in the *hamin* overnight and had become a deep tan color. That was the final course, the silent signal that *mazza* was ending. A few minutes later, all the guests filed past the Hacham to wish him Shabbat Shalom.

Majesty, marveled Joe, *we are in the presence of majesty*.

Mazza at the Hacham's house was followed by lunch at Dave Bibi's home. The Jacobs boys returned to their basement apartment buoyant. They even returned to the synagogue for Minha and Arbit. Again, they were greeted at the door, this time by Nouri Dayan, already a familiar face.

"What about a job?" asked Nouri after Arbit on Mosa'ei Shabbat. Nouri was quieter than Dave, but just as warm and concerned.

Joe shrugged. "Legally, it's very difficult. I'm here on a tourist visa and so I'm not allowed to work."

Nouri nodded thoughtfully. "Let me see what I can do. Make sure to come here for Shaharit in the morning and we'll talk."

Every day, Nouri had a different idea, a new plan. Slowly, each of the boys found jobs. Then, one day, Rabbi Schachter showed up. The boys were thrilled to see their old friend and mentor, who was going to be

---

11. Actually, it was mainly family. In those years, most of the congregation was related, and so it seemed like the whole shul was there.
12. "*Bakashot* are specific to Shabbat and are usually said early in the morning, before prayers. We would sing some of those at *mazza* anyway. *Zemirot* are non-specific to Shabbat, but are part of our community traditions," explained Mr. Irwin Dayan.

giving classes in Ahi Ezer. He also joined them as a guest at the homes of Nouri and his uncles.

But it was the pre-Sukkot argument that really solidified their places in Ahi Ezer.

"You will be my guests for the whole Yom Tov," Dave Bibi announced happily.

"Wait a minute," Reuben Bibi interjected, "you can't grab them for the whole holiday. I also want them to come to me."

Suddenly the brothers were arguing over who should have the privilege of hosting the Jacobs boys. A slow grin spread over Joe's face as he listened to them negotiate. He felt warm all over. *These men really care about us…*

When the Bibis finally turned to him beaming, having successfully negotiated that the boys would go to Dave for the first days and to Reuben for the second days, Joe could only nod. He was speechless from emotion.

I'm finally home. Ahi Ezer is home.

Chapter 24:
AHI EZER, 1946

As in the case of every home, the dynamics of a home change with time. The children grow up, the old guard passes away, its needs are different than before, and true growth takes place with that acknowledgment.

So it happened in Ahi Ezer. A new generation of children was attending *kitab*. Among the new attendees were the Dayan children. Nouri's oldest child, Yisrael (Irwin), was named after his father. The next child, Ruchoma (Carol), was named after his mother (Shafika is the Arabic nickname for Ruchoma). As sad as it was to have his first two children named after the parents he never knew, their births were an enormous comfort: This was his concrete tribute to his father and mother.

Like their father, the Dayan children "lived" in Ahi Ezer. From a very young age, they were around — for prayers, for *seuda shelishit*, for anything. Mosa'ei Shabbat, the men would linger for a class in *Humash*, to learn some halachot together, or read the *Zohar*. Irwin and Carol hung around with the rest of the kids, their cousins and others. They were a variety of ages, but it didn't matter. They were one community. They were a unit.

The little *k'nees* still had a distinctly Old World feel to it, mainly due to its seminal figures. When Hacham Murad came to the New Country, he brought the Old Country with him. In the few suitcases that he took on that awful journey, he packed his *Sefer Torah*, encased in its silver-plated case, and six *shofarot*. Now his *Sefer Torah* was in the *heichal [aron kodesh]* of Ahi Ezer. The *shofarot* he kept at home and brought them to the *k'nees* only for the holidays.

Hacham Murad was faithful to the *Shammi* traditions. He followed the same order of the prayers (even when the available *siddurim* were different) and sang the same tunes. Ahi Ezer didn't hire famous *hazzanim*, not for the

High Holidays and not for entertainment. The Hacham was the *hazzan* and *ba'al ko'rei* on Shabbat and the holidays; his brother-in-law, Zaki Cohen, was the *hazzan* during the week. The synagogue services were an opportunity to forge a connection to one's Creator. Who better to lead the services than people who truly lived with that connection?

Hacham Murad continued with the same *minhagim* from the Old Country, even those that had been abandoned by similar congregations around the world. For example, in the weeks between Pesah and Shabu'ot, the women would come to the *k'nees* Shabbat afternoon to hear *Pirkei Abot*. The elders of the congregation — Basil Cohen, Zaki-*kebir* and Zaki-*zegir* Cohen, and others — sat by the *teba* and sang each Mishna in a special, ancient tune. Then Nouri and Jack translated each Mishna into Arabic, explaining the lessons to be learned. The women loved this tradition. The tune was moving and nostalgic and they finally understood something that was going on in the *k'nees*.

Irwin and Carol

Lag ba'Omer in Ahi Ezer was an experience.[13] The entire community assembled in the social hall of the *k'nees*. The hall was set up with a large canopy, like a *huppah,* and from it, there were chains on which were suspended cups, filled with oil and wicks. As it was the anniversary of the death of Rabbi Shimon bar Yochai, first they read from the *Zohar*, the *sefer* Kabbalah that he authored, and then they sang the *pizmonim* about him. Meanwhile, Dave Bibi auctioned off the privilege of lighting the candles. Each candle represented the name of a great *tzaddik*, beginning with the *Abot* — Abraham, Yis'hak, and Yaakob — and going on through the ages. Whoever bid on a candle would step up to light it. People tried to buy names that corresponded to their deceased loved ones. The excitement of the bidding, the lighting, and the singing, created a warm and uplifting atmosphere. When all the lights were lit, the scene was impressive. Then the people brought out refreshments and showed a film of Eretz Yisrael, reminding everyone that

---

13. "This was an old Sephardic *minhag* that we referred to as 'the lighting of the lights.' In those years, we were the only ones who did it," recalled Mr. Irwin Dayan. This tradition is similar to the lighting of bonfires prevalent in other communities.

Ahi Ezer, 1946 / 199

Nouri with Irwin and Carol in Prospect Park

all the lights were in memory of great people, but we yearned to see them in person, in Eretz Yisrael, with the coming of the Redemption.

People who rarely came to Ahi Ezer during the year came on Tisha b'Ab. In that small, humble synagogue, there was a genuine sadness. As soon as one walked through the door, he felt the heaviness of the day. There was an intense feeling as they said the *kinnot*. There was emotion and passion as the congregation sang together. Afterward, the old timers gathered around and read *sefer Iyov*, with flawless cantillation, and an understanding of the sorrows that the Jewish people have gone through, and can still go through, unless we repent and bring the Redemption.[14]

The combination of Old World figures and Old World customs is what gave the synagogue its unique flavor, even as it became progressively more American.

But times were changing.

Hacham Murad was aging. He no longer had the strength to teach from morning until night. He began training his son, Sion, to assist him.

Sion Maslaton had always been inclined toward learning. He and Nouri had been regular *habrutot* for as long as they could remember. Though no

---

14. Similarly, at home, with or without other people, Hacham Murad perpetuated the *Shammi* traditions. He conducted his own *seuda rebi'it*, where he sang all the *piyutim* with immense feeling. Mrs. Carol [Dayan] Raful recalls: "Rabbi Dovid Twersky, the Skverer Rebbe from Boro Park, told my husband that he was in Hacham Murad's house during one *melaveh malkah* (*seuda rebi'it*) and was overwhelmed by the holy atmosphere."

A new generation: Some of Hacham Murad's grandchildren, sons and daughters of Betty (Maslaton) Kubie, Sion Maslaton, and Sara (Maslaton) Dayan, together in a park. L-R [back row]: Sarah Maslaton (later Sankary), Helen Kubie, Irwin Dayan. Standing, middle row: Joel Kubie, Carol Dayan (later Raful), Miriam Maslaton (later Ozeri). Sitting, middle row: Ruth Kubie (later Antebi), Max Maslaton, Lorette Kubie. Sitting, front: Murray Kubie, Rachel Maslaton (later Salem).

one mentioned anything outright, Hacham Murad was clearly grooming Sion as his successor.

His older brother, Joe, was also pulled toward spirituality but because he had been on the road, practically from the time he was a teenager, he never had time to develop his own Torah knowledge. Yet Joe contributed to the spiritual growth of the Ahi Ezer community in other ways. He returned from his trips with enthusiastic reports of Jewish communities from all over the United States: the Rabbis he met, the halachot he discovered, the *zemirot* he learned, the different types of "Jewish" foods he tasted. Soon gefilte fish appeared on his table, as did chopped liver and chicken soup, alongside the usual *kibbe* and *sambousak*.

This transition coincided with the general American Yiddishisms creeping into the Syrian Jewish vernacular.[15] While the community still felt somewhat estranged from their Ashkenazic brethren, the community began to refer to *k'nees* as shul; their Hachamim were also Rabbis. These words, sprinkled here and there, were more like "Jewish English" to the Syrian community rather than absorption of the Ashkenazic culture.

---

15. In the early years on the Lower East Side, the reality that Sephardic Jewry did not speak Yiddish was an issue. The Ashkenazim could not believe that "real Jews" did not know Yiddish, and were very wary of their Sephardic neighbors. This turned into a blessing, as the Sephardic community remained insular and never became swallowed up into the Ashkenazic majority.

Hacham Murad's *Sefer Torah*

Inner inscription: This *Sefer* has been dedicated in the memory of the soul of Hacham Yosef HaCohen Tarrab Maslaton and his wife Ribka in the year *taf-shin-bet-yud* (1952) – the year Hacham Murad presented it to Ahi Ezer.

For Joe Maslaton, it was different. Joe appreciated Ashkenazic Jewry and purposely adopted much of what he saw. Whenever Joe was home, he had Ashkenazic Rabbis eating at his table. His guests were typically people he had met on his travels. They had different accents, interesting stories, and a whole new dimension of Jewish life. He was interested in all they had to say, where their ideas were coming from, and how they expressed themselves. Sometimes the language of the table turned into Yiddish with Joe as an active participant! Then Joe would invite his guests to share a song. Inevitably, they would begin a tune that he was already familiar with from sharing meals with Ashkenazic families. Even Hacham Murad began singing the new Ashkenazic tunes that Joe belted out at *mazza* on Shabbat.

Hacham Murad paid close attention as Joe described the intense learning he had seen in Telshe Yeshiva of Cleveland and urged him to repeat some *dibrei Torah*. No wonder that Joe Maslaton was one of the first people to send his son outside the Syrian community to learn "by the Ashkenaz." He and his brother Sion sent their boys to Toras Emes, the Kaminetzer Yeshiva in Boro Park.[16]

---

16. "My father ate with Rabbi Eliyahu Meir Bloch and Rabbi Chaim Mordechai Katz when he was in Cleveland. These Roshei Yeshiva were just opening their yeshiva and they asked my father if he had any sons to send to Telshe to learn. My father replied that his first few children are girls and his oldest son is only four years old. So they asked him where I learn. To which my father described to them the public school/kitab combination that existed in our community. Then the Roshei Yeshiva told my father that he must send me to a yeshiva. To my father's credit, even though his father was a Rabbi and a holy man, he listened to the Roshei Yeshiva

Actually, their sister, Ray Tawil, was an even bigger trailblazer. When her husband, Ezra, was alive, he entrusted his father-in-law with their children's education, to everyone's satisfaction. But David was a child when his father Ezra passed away, and by the time he turned 12 the doctors instructed Hacham Murad to stop teaching altogether. Ray panicked. Without a father, who would teach her son?

Ray had her mother's ironclad faith, feisty determination, and wisdom. She ran to Rabbi Kassin (her husband had been *Halabi*). He wrote a letter of recommendation and suggested that she discuss the issue with Rabbi Hecht. She ran to Rabbi Hecht. He wrote a letter and recommended Yeshiva Rabbi Jacob Josef, the most established Ashkenazic yeshiva of the time. With over 1,000 students, it was also the largest yeshiva in New York. Then she went back to her father Hacham Murad, and discussed everyone's advice. Hacham Murad also wrote a letter and supported her decision.

Selim Bibi, Nouri's great-uncle, was one of the old-timers who had come to America as an older immigrant. Here he is marrying off his son Eddie, one of the community kids who had served in the army, and was about to establish a home that was far more American than the home he grew up in. L-R: Frieda Bibi, the bride and groom — Grace and Eddie Bibi — Reuben Bibi, Selim Bibi, Jack Bibi (son of Selim).

Dave Tawil became the only Sephardic boy in RJJ. He had to take three trains in each direction — an hour and a half there and back — and on Sundays as well! It wasn't easy, but he received an education far beyond that of the average boy in the community, and he would always be grateful for his mother's steely determination.

Indeed, the Maslatons were different.

They were courageous fighters, willing to do whatever had to be done to keep Judaism vibrant for themselves and their families. Sending Sephardic children to learn "by the Ashkenaz" was radical in many ways.

---

and sent me to Toras Emes. That was my first step toward becoming a real *ben Torah*," recalled Rabbi Murray Maslaton.

L-R: Rabbi Lezer Levin (Rabbi of Cong. Beth Tefilla of Detroit), Rabbi Eliyahu Meir Bloch and Rabbi Mordechai Katz, Roshei Yeshiva of Telshe Yeshiva in Cleveland. Standing is Rabbi Gavriel Ginsburg, later Rosh Yeshiva of Ner Yisrael of Toronto.

Joe's young son, Murray, who would grow up to have a remarkable effect on the Sephardic community

Joe Maslaton used his trips on the road to connect to other Jews. Besides his acquaintanceship with Rabbanim and Roshei Yeshivos, he also befriended needy people. Here, he is hugging a child orphaned in the Holocaust. Whenever he visited her home, he cheered her up and brought her treats.

The children traveled by public transportation, alone, at a very young age (a nightmare for Syrian mother hens). And the yeshivot taught in Yiddish, a foreign language for most Syrians.

Initially, Nouri was also skeptical about his siblings-in-laws' choices and opted to send his children to public school and then *kitab*, just as he had done.[17] Yet he saw that for some reason, the new generation wasn't

---

17. Though Magen David had opened its full-day yeshiva in 1943, its initial years were very rocky. As long as Hacham Murad was still running his *kitab*, the Dayan children went there.

204 / NOURI

The Maslaton and Tawil families, in the park. The man sitting in the back is Ezra Tawil. The woman sitting more forward is Rebecca (Maslaton) Bibi. [The rest of the girls in this picture are unmarried and therefore their married names are listed in parentheses.] The boy in front of her is Mac Tawil. Esther Maslaton (Safdie) is in front of Mac. Next to her is Sara Maslaton (Massry), then Esther Maslaton (Dayan). The boy slightly above Esther is Saul Tawil. Below him on the far right is Norma Maslaton (Azrak). The front row, L-R: Janet Tawil (Ashear), Irene Tawil (Gindi), Betty Maslaton (Finesmith), Rita Maslaton (Tobias), and Dave Tawil.

growing up as religiously inclined as his generation had been. It was too early to determine exactly why this was so, but if sending to an Ashkenazic yeshiva could help stave the problem, he was going to search for a suitable yeshiva. He discovered Ohel Moshe, an Ashkenazic elementary school that taught in Hebrew, a much more palatable option than Yiddish, and had classes for boys and for girls.

When little Carol came home reciting the entire text of *Yom HaShishi* verbatim, Nouri knew that he had made the correct choice. He proudly had her display her knowledge to her grandparents when they came for the Friday night *seuda*, something that they did on occasion. Hacham Murad was duly impressed.[18]

The Maslatons were one of the crowd — regular people who worked for a living — and yet their willingness to quietly do their own thing in order to keep growing religiously kept them in a class of their own.

---

18. "I don't remember if I said it in a Sephardic accent or Ashkenazic. It didn't matter. We learned to use whichever accent was appropriate in a given situation. My brothers could pray and read from the Torah just as well in an Ashkenazic accent as in a Sephardic accent" (Mrs. Carol [Dayan] Raful).

Rabbi Abraham B. Hecht (1922-2013) came from distinguished Chassidic lineage. He was a Lubavitch chassid who loyally served the Syrian community for over half a century.

Sion Maslaton worked for Morris Bibi as bookkeeper for his fireplace business, English Bellows. As fireplaces went out of style, Morris turned to manufacturing tea carts. He kept the old name, just as he kept the old family policy of using his business as a means to help people in his community.

Morris Bibi combined the attributes of a pious scholar and a businessman. *Yafeh talmud Torah im derech eretz*[19] — "Torah study is good, together with an occupation" was the community creed. Morris personified that ideal and was a neighborhood role model. His business was staffed almost exclusively by religious Jews — Sion and Jack Maslaton among them.

Sion Maslaton began taking over some of his father's classes when he came home after work, and became his invaluable assistant. Nouri also began to take on a more active role in the shul, but very unofficially.

Nouri loved Torah and mitzvos and he couldn't understand why other people were not similarly moved. He reasoned that they were just too distracted, too busy with other things to focus on the beauty of religion.

Maybe if I make it easier for them... That fleeting thought became Nouri's motto. Friday evening, before prayers began, Nouri was busy opening *sid-*

---

19. (*Avot* 2:2). This ideal was lived by some of the leading scholars of the community. Hacham Matloub Abadi was one of the leading Sephardic halachic authorities of the time. Yet he made a living as a salesman. Rabbi Avraham Halioua, Rabbi of the Moroccan community, taught Torah practically all the time, but he earned a living by working for several businesses, among them Bibi and Co. To Sephardic Jewry, this was the fulfillment of the Rambam's teaching: *The way of the world is for one to be involved in earning a living.*

durim to the correct place and stacking them on top of each other so that as soon as a congregant walked into shul, he was greeted with a smile, and a *siddur* ready for him. Shabbat morning, he opened the *humashim* to the correct place and stacked them similarly, as a quiet incentive for congregants to look inside during the Torah reading.

Nouri searched for opportunities to make serving G-d easier and more appealing in a pleasant, non-coercive manner. During Sukkot, Nouri came up with one of his most original and most long-lasting practices.

For years, only the Rabbi had his own *lulav* and *etrog*. The rest of the community used the shul set. After finishing Shaharit, someone would stand on the *teba* holding the shul set, which was called the *mezakeh*. This shul representative said the *beracha* aloud, but with the intention only to be *motzi* himself. Then the rest of the congregation would line up and everyone was given a chance to hold the *lulav* and *etrog* and say the *beracha*. As the shul grew, so did the line. Eventually, some of the men — like Moussa Cohen and Sion Maslaton — began buying their own *lulav* and *etrog*, but that did little to shorten the line.

I want my own as well, Nouri decided one year. Only he had a dual purpose in purchasing his own set. That year, he positioned himself in the hallway at the very beginning of the services. As people walked into the shul, he offered them his *lulav* and *etrog*, reasoning that the more people who made the *beracha* then, the less people would be on line later. People responded with joy and appreciation. It was wonderful to be greeted at the door, as if someone had been waiting for you, and to be handed the *lulav* and *etrog* without having to wait on line. Until Nouri heard the *hazzan* begin *Nishmat*, he stayed outside with his *lulav* and *etrog*.

That year, the line to use the shul set was much smaller than usual.

Nouri was thrilled that his idea had worked.

"We are being *mezakeh et harabbim*, strengthening the community's mitzva observance by making it easier for them," he explained to his children as they walked home from the *k'nees*. "This is a tremendous *zechut*."

Slowly, Nouri was becoming an informal leader, simply by being an encouraging presence. He joined the Ahi Ezer Committee, both the regular committee and the junior committee, and was very active in collecting money for the new synagogue building. He was a quiet complement to his more forceful Uncle Dave, but that would eventually change.

First, there would be more drastic changes, for the Dayan family and for the whole Jewish world.

Chapter 25:
FINDING FAMILY, 1948

"I want to go," Nouri declared to no one in particular.

Dave and Reuben looked up. "To where?" they asked in unison.

"To Eretz Yisrael. To meet my family."

"Our family," Dave corrected him.

Nouri didn't argue, though he knew that for him it was different.

"Let me think about it," Dave said mildly, officially closing the topic for the moment. Nouri went back to his duties, but his dream pursued him.

I want to go… I need to go. It's enough that I never knew my mother or my father, I should never know my brothers and sisters? They are Dave's nephews and nieces, but they are my brothers and sisters… I never had brothers and sisters…

"I want to go," Nouri repeated to Esther later that night.

And, echoing that morning's conversation, Esther asked, "To where?"

"To Eretz Yisrael. To meet my family."

Usually, feisty Esther Dayan had no problem speaking her mind. But for the moment she was at a loss. What could she say? Everyone was excited about the new Jewish State and there were plenty of people who were talking about moving, but for their family, this wasn't an option. Nouri was talking about a visit, not a move. No one was doing that.

Such a trip would be expensive; just the airfare was sky high, literally! Additionally, there would be the time spent away from work, and the time spent away from home. No one made such a trip and then turned right back. She would be left alone with the kids for who knows how long… and yet, how could she stand in his way? Nouri was a quiet man, and, like most men, didn't discuss his feelings. It was almost as if he had none. Yet Esther knew that deep down there was a void, an empty space reserved for the parents he would never know and the siblings he had never met. He had to go, if only to fill that gaping hole in his life.

"Alone?" asked Esther, ignoring the long pause in the conversation.

"If I have to," Nouri answered. "Airfare is expensive, we can't both go. Besides, there would be no one to take care of the kids."

"For how long?"

Nouri shook his head. "I don't know. What do you think? Two weeks?"

"Once you are making the trip, it seems foolish not to go for longer. You need time to really get to know everyone. The trip alone is almost a two-day affair, and then, before you turn around, you will be on your way back."

"But I feel bad leaving you for so long… alone with three little kids…"

Esther permitted herself a small smile. Nouri was a devoted father but she hardly counted on his help in the house; he was simply too busy. Between work, and the shul, and his many projects, he was rarely home. She would certainly miss his company, but taking care of the kids without his help would not be a problem.

"We'll see," was all that she said.

A knock on the door interrupted their conversation. Nouri got up to open the door and returned with Morris and Dave behind him. Esther hid her surprise and quickly offered the men chairs and drinks. After the usual pleasantries, Dave dove right in.

"About this morning's idea…?"

Nouri nodded imperceptibly.

Dave looked sidewise at Morris. "We talked it over and came to a decision…"

Back row, L-R: Morris, Tziyona (Nouri's sister-in-law; his brother Shimon's wife), Dave
Front row: Nouri's uncle, Dod David (his father's brother), and Nouri's brother, Shimon

Finding Family, 1948 / 209

Nouri (right) and his half-brother, Yehoshua

Nouri was mystified. He had not even mentioned the idea to Morris. What decision did he have to make?

"You should definitely go to Eretz Yisrael… but not by yourself. We are coming with you."

"We…?"

"We. You, Dave, and I," Morris stated.

Nouri broke into a wide grin. His two uncles grinned back.

Nouri couldn't stop smiling. His brothers and sisters, nieces and nephews, greeted him with so much love and warmth, it was as if they had been waiting for all those years to meet him. They sat around and talked — in Arabic, their common language. They caught up on so much of life that couldn't be captured in the sporadic letters that had traveled back and forth from America to Israel.

Dave, Morris, and Nouri took the rest of the family on sightseeing tours all over the land. Nouri had brought along two brand-new cameras, bought in honor of his trip.[20] One took regular black and white stills, and the other was a motion picture camera. On every outing, Nouri had one or both of his cameras strapped around his neck as he sought to capture his experience for the folks back home. For most of their time there, the weather was sweltering hot and the Israeli family in their loose fitting, thin cotton, casual clothing were easily distinguishable from their American relatives.

Dave was the consummate gentleman, most at home in a white cotton shirt and pressed pants, even while exploring the dry desert, but certainly when they went to pray at holy sites. He ditched the suit jacket out of deference to the weather, but he kept his tie, though it was wound a bit looser around his neck. He was a great sport, climbing the dry boulders and sitting atop the sandy dunes, teasing his nieces and nephews and cracking jokes, still with his tie neatly fastened. Morris also cut a formal figure. His

---

20. "The motion picture camera was new on the market and very inefficient. When we watched the films, there were so many blank frames, we often waited 10 minutes for something to appear. Then we'd see an Arab lady, walking with this huge jug on her head, through the open, empty desert, and that glimpse of the exotic was so amazing, it was worth the wait. Of course, seeing my father's family was very moving — the first time. We rarely had the patience to sit through it after that" (Mr. Irwin Dayan).

L-R, back: Shimon and Nouri. Front: Morris, Moshe (Nouri's half-brother), and Yaakov Nizri (Nouri's brother-in-law; his sister Sara's husband).

light grey shirt was always buttoned at the neck and, like Dave, white shirt and tie was *de rigueur* for holy places.

Nouri was different. His shirt was open wide at the neck, and it matched his wide-open smile that seemed permanently affixed. It was as if something inside him had loosened now that he finally met his family. No, he didn't have a father or mother, but boy did he have siblings! There were six of them — three whole, and three half. The older ones were married, some with big children. The younger three were young men, barely out of their teens.

He also met some of his uncles — brothers of his father — and their children. Their father — Nouri's grandfather — had lived a long and full life, and passed away only about seven years earlier.

L-R: Mordechai Dayan (Nouri's half-brother), Dave, Nouri, and Morris

Finding Family, 1948 / 211

Walking up to the *kever* of Rabbi Meir Ba'al HaNess

Though he had come to Eretz Yisrael with most of his children, only three were still living in Israel. The others had immigrated to Lebanon and Argentina.

Meeting his father's siblings unlocked a hazy mystery. Until then, that side of the family was virtually non-existent. Finally, he could fill in the blanks of his life as he heard them describe their shared childhood and reminisce over memories of the brother and father who was no longer alive. He used their memories to paint a mental image of the father he never knew. He was warmed by their declarations that his father had never forgotten him.

Nouri slung his arm over the shoulder of his brother, Shimon. He urged his sisters — Sara and Rachel — to pose for pictures with their children. He filmed his brothers — Yehoshua, Moshe, and Mordechai — atop the mountain they had just climbed. And then, every so often, he handed over his camera to one of the group, to capture his own awesome joy for eternity.

Nouri's frank awe and wonder came through in every frame he filmed. He filmed the stone ruins of Akko and the famed buildings at Amuka and Rabbi Meir Ba'al HaNess. Though Morris and Dave had left Syria old enough to remember the Old Country, Nouri had been just a baby. Even the Arabs, dressed in their traditional robes and *kaffiyehs*, piqued his interest as he watched them pray.

In Akko, overlooking the sea: Nouri is crouching on the left.
Morris is standing in the front. Dave is standing on the far right.
The two men with their heads covered with scarves are Nouri's brothers.

The only dark spot on that leg of the journey was coming face to face with the extreme poverty of his Israeli family. In truth, everyone in Israel was poor then. It was a young country with few modern amenities and few ways to make a living. People were stoically optimistic but life was incredibly difficult.

As the visit drew to a close, Nouri was profoundly grateful to G-d that he had finally merited meeting his family. He was equally aware of the great ways of the Almighty that had plucked him out of his immediate family circle and placed him in America, in a life that was so vastly different, so physically and spiritually richer than that of his family in Israel.

On the euphoria of that experience, Nouri and his uncles toured Europe. They posed in front of the Leaning Tower of Pisa and the famed Coliseum as they traversed Italy. Nouri tried to capture the famous image of the Jewish people being led out of Jerusalem by the Romans, carrying the Menorah, immortalized on the Arch of Triumph. The film came out fuzzy, but the engraving was still visible. They visited the Eiffel Tower in France

Finding Family, 1948

L-R: Dave, Nouri, and Morris, in front of the Leaning Tower of Pisa

and watched the Changing of the Guard in England. And Nouri meticulously preserved all these memories in moving pictures.

When they finally arrived home, after a month of being in Eretz Yisrael and two weeks of touring Europe, they joyfully greeted their family who came to pick them up at the airport. Irwin's good behavior was finally rewarded as he was the only child allowed to accompany his mother in the taxi. He dressed for the occasion in his favorite cowboy hat and a face-splitting grin.

After a welcome-home barbecue at Reuben Bibi's house, and much rehashing about the trip, life settled back to normal. "Normal" for Nouri meant: How can I help my family back in Israel?

After much investigation, Nouri purchased several washing machines, and shipped them to Eretz Yisrael. One was for his sister Sara who had a large family and was still washing their clothing by hand. The rest were for his brother Shimon to open a laundromat and, hopefully, earn a decent living. To other family members he began sending packages, mainly with food that he thought they would enjoy.

The trip to Eretz Yisrael remained an unforgettable experience that forged a lifelong connection between Nouri and his family. Nonetheless, the resilience of that connection was to Nouri's credit as he consistently helped out his family, even though he would not see most of them for many more years.

This was vintage Nouri. Actually, it was one of the defining characteristics of the Bibi family. Both in business and community work, they were constantly seeking needs and filling them… and inspiring others to do the same.

Chapter 26:
BENSONHURST, 1949

"I want an open house," Nouri had told Esther, years earlier, "a place where anyone can get a warm meal or a bed. Uncle Reuben and Auntie Esther took me in — an orphan with nowhere to go — and they gave me a home. I want to give back by giving to others."

Esther nodded, hoping to help make that dream a reality one day.

Esther was a younger, softer version of her mother, also fiercely loyal to G-d, also bluntly honest, also tougher on her own family than on her friends from the community. Like her mother, she was strikingly clear about her role in this world: She was her husband's helpmate, the one who enabled him to accomplish all that he did because she was running the home. To Esther, that meant raising her children properly while giving her husband the freedom to devote as much time as he wanted to Torah and mitzvot. It also meant participating in tasks that she might not have chosen but did with equanimity anyway. Like the time Morris showed up with a chicken a few days before Yom Kippur…

There goes baths for tonight, Esther sighed, as she wrestled the squawking chicken into the tub. The real "fun" happened the next morning, when Morris slaughtered the *kapparot* chicken right in the apartment! Then Esther plucked the feathers and *kashered* the chicken before cooking it and sending it off to poor people.

All this, Esther did with aplomb. True, she was used to these things from her own home, but there were many practices that her friends had seen in their homes that they discarded when they got married. Not Esther Dayan. She was proud that her husband was continuing in their traditional ways and was a loyal partner. She was also a good sounding board for her husband's ideas, like when Nouri wanted to initiate new classes in the shul.

Morris Bibi slaughtering a chicken

The late 1940's brought many Holocaust refugees to America. By far, the majority was Ashkenazim who settled among their own people. Yet the arrivals affected the Sephardic community. The group to have the most profound affect was that which came from Shanghai, China. The Mirrer Yeshiva's miraculous survival in Shanghai was fast becoming a legend. Joe Jacobs regaled everyone with stories of their stay there and the unusual impact they had on the Iraqi community.

Nouri took note of these reports. From his learning sessions with Solomon Maimon, he knew that the Ashkenazic yeshivot learned differently than the Sephardim. He wondered if some of these Shanghai Rabbis would be interested in bringing that type of learning into the Sephardic community. He sought out these scholars and convinced some of them to give lectures in the community.[21]

"Are you going to hear the new Rabbi?" Nouri asked his brother-in-law and friend Jack Maslaton.

"Yes," he answered. "I take it that his classes are geared to us."

Nouri nodded. That is what he had been told as well.

They were not disappointed. Rabbi Tzadok Shaingarten was fresh from Shanghai, from years of intensive Torah study. He had to simplify his *shiurim* for the Ahi Ezer congregants, most of whom had never learned advanced Gemara. Rabbi Shaingarten opened a whole world of knowledge to them, a completely different way of thinking. After one particularly riveting lesson, Rabbi Shaingarten stopped. "*Ah,*" he declared with his trademark all-encompassing smile, "if only you would know Yiddish. The whole Gemara sounds different in Yiddish!"

The small group erupted in laughter. Many of them knew a smattering of Yiddish from their years on the Lower East Side, and they could bargain with the best of them, but the idea of learning in Yiddish or, even

---

21. The role that the scholars of Mirrer Yeshiva played in transplanting the Torah of Europe on American soil is immeasurable. They became leaders and teachers in all types of yeshivot: Rabbi Shimon Schwab (Rav of the Yekkishe community), Rabbi Yosef Liss (Mashgiach in Lubavitch), and the Mirrer Yeshiva itself, which welcomed Moroccan, Egyptian, and Syrian boys.

more incongruous, that the Gemara was different in Yiddish, was just too funny. Yet the comment was made in a way that made them feel a kinship with their Ashkenazic rebbi. Yes, there were differences in their *mesora*, but if the differences in Torah learning could be bridged by language, then, one day, those differences could fade away.

Nouri and his contemporaries were working people who could devote only a limited number of hours a week to this type of learning. They would not become *talmidei hachamim* of the caliber of Mirrer alumni. But the classes made them pause in contemplation: *What about our children? If our children are given the right background, can they become like the talmidim of Mirrer Yeshiva, who understand Gemara on a far more advanced level than we understand?*

This lingering thought persisted, though it would take time to bear real fruit.

Before World War II, Rav Tzadok Shaingarten (1912-2005) learned in Kletzk under Rav Aharon Kotler and in the Mir under Rav Yerucham Levovitz. He was with the Mirrer Yeshiva in Japan and Shanghai.

Meanwhile, Bibi and Co. continued to grow and change.

They sold the Bensonhurst building and moved the whole operation to Manhattan, where they had rented a six-story building on 26th Street, just

L-R: Rabbi Shaingarten, Hacham Murad, Rabbi Yaakov Kassin

Bensonhurst, 1949 / 217

Bibi and Company's 5th Avenue showroom

two blocks over from the 5th Avenue showroom on 28th Street. The 26th Street building was huge. Bibi and Co. occupied four out of the six floors, plus the basement. The first floor had the offices, the second floor housed the assembly and packing departments, the fourth and sixth floors were used for general storage, and the basement had all the crystals.

The move out of Bensonhurst coincided with other changes. Gone were the days when the Bibi kids quit school at 14 and grew up in the shop, sweeping the floors, stuffing envelopes, or just doing whatever had to be done. The new generation attended high school — some youngsters even went on to college — and then they entered the family business, or went out on their own.

The roster of outsiders in the business continued to grow, although, more often than not, those "outsiders" were members of the community, just not of the Bibi family. Sol Jacobs, one of the immigrants from Shanghai, joined the business as a bookkeeper. Mary Minyan, a single girl who came to stay with her family (Ahi Ezer congregants), was one of the secretaries.[22] Charles ("Charlie") Serouya was another "outsider" employee, a Magen David congregant. And then there were the union workers, most of whom were not Jewish.

---

22. "My mother came from Mexico, hoping to earn some money. She was forever grateful to Mr. Bibi and Mr. Dayan for giving her a job, and always mentioned how nicely they treated her. They made sure that she took a break during the workday. They brought coffee and cake to her desk. She didn't work there long but she spoke of them fondly for the rest of her life" (Mr. Alan Saka).

218 / NOURI

First row, seated, R-L: Ezra Tobias, David Mizrahi, Leon Sultan, Rabbi Binyamin Seruya, Moshe Zafrani, Pinhas Nissim, Charlie Serouya, Joe Dweck, David Cohen, Danny Massry, Jackie Kassin, Rabbi Harvey Barry, Rabbi Ronnie Barry, Joe Esses, Rabbi Isaac Dwek, Abie Kassin, Abie Serouya, Fred Chazanof [others in this row are unknown]. Second row, standing, R-L: Eli Kairey, Nat Kairey, unknown, Jojo Chehaber, David Eddy, David Abady, Molly Seruya (later Haber), Ikey Abadi, Anna Kassin, Sara Kassin (later Sorscher), Genie Serouya (later Amon), Anna Serouya (later Tawil), Shelly Levy (later Esses), Julie Ashkenazi (later Schwecky), unknown, Carol Menahem (later Palacci), Germaine Menahem, Esther Menahem, Barbara Menahem [others in this row are unknown].

The flavor of the business changed. Children could no longer pop in to read *Tehillim* and no one could shoot over to the *k'nees* for Minha and Arbit. Dave Bibi solved this problem by establishing regular *minyanim* at Bibi and Co., a real innovation at the time. Other Jewish businessmen in the area, Sephardi and Ashkenazi, would stop in as well. No matter how big the business became, it still retained a very warm — and very Jewish — atmosphere.

"Hey, Charlie! Gotta customer for you."

"Yes, sir," Charlie Serouya smiled widely as he greeted the dignified gentleman who had just entered the showroom. Charlie was a super salesman, great at making a sale and great at making the customer feel he came away with a bargain. He could sell almost anything — and he did.

"And now, my friend," he continued, after closing the deal. "This pocket? It's for Bibi and Co., the greatest store around. This pocket?" he fingered the other side of his jacket, "is for the greatest organization around. Let me tell you about it..." And he went on to launch into a speech about his pet project, Young Magen David.[23]

---

23. While the original idea came from Rabbi Kassin and Mr. I. Shalom, YMD was Charlie Serouya's baby. One of the prominent Rabbis in Deal, NJ mentioned that Charlie's Shul

Charlie was a great raconteur, attracting children and adults with his warmth. He loved to regale his audience with army stories, like when he served as a gunner alongside Gene Autry, long before the latter became famous as a singing cowboy.

When Charlie noticed that the community kids were very unenthusiastic about attending synagogue, he came up with a plan: a youth synagogue. He created a synagogue just for kids, from teenagers and down. He had the older boys act as *hazzanim* and read from the Torah. He had the girls cook meals for Shabbat, and then they would all eat together after the services. There were get-togethers, activities, and loads of prizes. Sukkot, he lugged a big, brand-new garbage can to the sukka. He opened the can and the kids whooped in delight when they saw that it was filled to the brim with deli sandwiches, a novel treat. Charlie attracted hundreds of young people and forged a whole community structure for them.

Like every good project, "Charlie's Shul" needed money to keep it running, and Charlie was a terrific fundraiser, not just because he was a great salesman but because he believed in his mission, heart and soul. The community joked that YMD (Young Magen David) actually stood for You Must Donate! And everyone did.

Dave Bibi was all for it. "See a need and fill it" was the motto that he lived by, and he was equally happy when someone else filled that need, as long as the need was filled. Charlie wanted to use Bibi and Co. as a way to raise money for his shul? By all means. It was a good cause that Dave was happy to be a part of.

Nouri took note of the success of Charlie's Shul. It was a warm and welcoming place for all Syrian youth. Nonetheless, it highlighted another lack in the community.

What about the older teenagers? These boys have grown up in Ahi Ezer. They are not about to attend a new "kids' shul," and yet they barely come to Ahi Ezer. How do we reconnect with them…? He had no immediate answers to those questions, but he was certain that in time, Providence would show him how.

---

was his first exposure to Torah and mitzvot. The same applied to many of its other members who only attended public school.

Meanwhile, he and Dave Bibi had a more pressing project to tackle.

In 1949, the "need" that had to be filled was the completion of the new Ahi Ezer building. The community was, thank G-d, constantly growing. Children who had grown up in the community had gotten married and moved near their parents. The community needed a full-service synagogue, with room for everyone to pray, and place for classes and social activities.

The social aspect was crucial.

There was an ongoing debate within the greater Syrian Jewish community of how best to meet the social needs of the young people. The older generation noted with dismay that Meyer's Ice Cream Parlor had become a street hangout, something that grated on their traditional sensitivities. There were also reports of youths mingling among gentiles, something that had always been anathema among the close-knit Syrian community. The prevailing attitude was that a full-service social center would keep Syrian youth indoors, socializing among their own rather than on the street.[24] Throughout the 40's, the community was fundraising and campaigning to establish a community center, and in 1950 it finally opened its doors.[25]

The more religiously inclined community members never viewed the establishment of the center as a total solution to the community's problems. True, keeping the youth in a safe social network would prevent

Outside Young Magen David

---

24. This very heated debate pitted the establishment of a parochial school (a full-day yeshiva) against that of a community center, arguing that the community couldn't afford both: ... *Some children are supposed to become "bad" (personally, we don't believe that there is such a thing as a bad child) when they begin to frequent billiard parlors. Build a decent community center with a hall that can be used as a gymnasium, lecture hall, dance floor, with a small English/Hebrew library, with ping-pong and billiard tables, and meeting rooms, and then the leadership of the Talmud Torah will get plenty of "good" children (i.e., there will be no need for a full day yeshiva)* [Victory Bulletin — Feb. 1943].

25. The first Sephardic Community Center (Avenue P and 75th Street) was established with broad community support but it wasn't successful. Magen David Yeshiva eventually took over the building (Sutton, p. 41).

Young Magen David, a happy place on the outside...

...and on the inside. The man facing the camera is Rabbi Harry Rubin.

them from falling into bad company or picking up gentile behaviors, but it would do little to channel them toward a deeper, more meaningful Jewish life. Even as they supported the center, they wanted more: they wanted to pull the youth into the synagogue, to establish Torah classes, to encourage them to be more committed Jews.

The refurbished house that had served the Ahi Ezer community for almost twenty-five years was no longer adequate. Besides its small size, its simplicity would not draw in and inspire the new generation. Though Nouri had no recollection of the glorious synagogues of Damascus, he heard the old-timers reminisce about their former places of worship, their nostalgia indicating a bond that was lasting. A new building for Ahi Ezer would provide more than space. The dedication and love needed to build the new building would, hopefully, forge a connection between its people and G-d.

They would take pride in their accomplishment and come to prayers in the place they had worked so hard to create.

Back in 1943, Dave Bibi and his friends launched a campaign to put a down payment on a suitable building and then acquire a mortgage. This was no small goal. The Damascus community of the 40's consisted mainly of low-income peddlers and small businessmen. Every dollar they donated was a real sacrifice.

"I want everyone to have a share in this mitzva," Dave Bibi announced in the *k'nees*. "We need one dollar per brick. Gentlemen, how many bricks do you want to buy?" The idea drew chuckles, but the Ahi Ezer congregants saved their nickels and dimes and "bought bricks."

"How about sponsoring a window, in memory of a loved one?" asked Dave, with Nouri at his side.

The little boy holding a book on the bottom right is Charlie Saka. He and his friends are sitting on the stoop in front of Ahi Ezer on 64th Street in 1948. Mr. Saka eventually became president of the synagogue in Deal, always emulating both Dave Bibi and Nouri Dayan.

Moussa Didia's sister, Laura Saka, had just passed away, leaving behind a young son, Charlie. The whole family was pained by the loss and Moussa decided that a section of the stained glass dome would be a fitting tribute. Little Charlie Saka often came to the *k'nees* with his father, Sam. He observed Dave and Nouri as they graciously appealed to the people of the community with warmth and nobility.

No wonder we love them, he thought.

But the community contributions were never enough. Dave Bibi appealed to the broader Syrian community as well. "Mr. Bibi," as Dave was known, was a community leader who supported many Syrian institutions and he expected his friends to return the favor.[26]

---

26. Almost everyone interviewed, including family members, spoke about "Mr. Bibi." Since Bibi and Co. was mainly family, even family members used his formal title. Even more unusual, in the same breath, they spoke of his incredible humility and approachability.

But even the *Halabim*, a much larger, solidly middle-class community, had only a handful of truly wealthy individuals. The new Ahi Ezer would only be built with real *mesirut nefesh*.

One of the movers behind this ambitious project was Mr. Morris (Moussa) Mann. When Bibi and Co. still had offices in Brooklyn and Manhattan, Mr. Mann routinely walked into the Manhattan showroom, picked up the phone, and called Dave Bibi in the Brooklyn office.

"Today," he would insist, "someone has to go today."

And Mr. Bibi would stop what he was doing, grab his car keys, collect Nouri, and go out to fundraise.

"Not less than twice a week," Mr. Mann maintained. Sometimes he went himself, sometimes he prodded others. Nonetheless, the most frequent fundraisers for the new building were Dave Bibi, Nouri Dayan, and Nouri Sarway.

"The three musketeers," people joked.

The three musketeers persevered for years. At the cornerstone laying for the new building, 350 people signed up as congregants, a testimony to the need for the new building and the enthusiasm being generated by the fundraisers.

They forged ahead, undaunted, until they reached their goal.

Dave Bibi's philanthropy was well known. "He supported Jewish institutions all over the world," commented Rabbi Yosef Dayan. "I saw Uncle Dave's name on a plaque in Chevron Yeshiva. Rabbi Chevroni told me that whenever he came to America, Uncle Dave invited everyone from Sha'arei Zion for a Sunday morning breakfast, which he turned into a drive for the yeshiva. In appreciation, the yeshiva made him their vice president."

PART IV

Chapter 27:
BENSONHURST, 1951

I want to do something special, Nouri mused.

Long before they had collected enough money for the synagogue, Nouri was confident that it would happen. For years he dreamed of how he might personally contribute to the momentous occasion. He finally hit on the right idea.

A Sefer Torah, he decided. *I will dedicate a Sefer Torah in memory of my parents. It will be housed in a unique case, for which the Bibi family is famous.*

Nouri discussed his idea with his Uncle Reuben, who was enthusiastic. Reuben Bibi had made several *Sefer Torah* cases for the community, usually employing the velvet/metal combination in order to keep costs down. Nouri wanted a similar case, only more unique, designed to command significance.

The entire family was in on the project. After school, Irwin and Carol popped into the factory (when it was still in Bensonhurst) to watch Uncle Reuben's progress. He fashioned a wooden box with doors that were shaped like the *luhot*. He covered the wood with velvet and then covered the doors with a thin sheet of tin, upon which he engraved the *aseret hadibrot*. He decorated the *luhot* with thousands of rhinestones, each one set by hand, with painstaking precision. Every day, Carol would sit by him and watch, as this work of art emerged, a labor of love.

The day finally arrived.
The *Sefer Torah* was finished.
The case was finished.
The *k'nees* was finished — well, almost.

"We will move in anyway," David Bibi announced at a committee meeting. "We all want to be there for the holidays, so we'll just move in. The

Nouri and Reuben Bibi holding the *Sefer Torah* outside the Dayan home. Irwin is left of Nouri.

little things will get done later. We will make a joint *Hanukat Ha'Bayit* and *Hachnassat Sefer Torah*. It will be a beautiful celebration."

Dave was very excited about the new building. It had taken almost ten years of fundraising to get to where they had arrived: from amassing a down payment on the property, to making architectural plans, receiving the permits, perfecting the design, and finally construction. The *k'nees* was in debt but Dave was optimistic that the new building would foster fresh enthusiasm and generate more donations.

The center of the ceiling was dominated by a large dome, inlaid with stained glass beautifully depicting the twelve *shebatim*. The stained-glass windows around the room were styled with Jewish scenes — a Sukkot scene, a Shabbat scene, etc. — with the donors' names written scroll-like beneath each scene. The *heichal* was a cream-colored beige marble with two wooden beams on the sides, painted with intricate designs. On top of the *heichal* were two *luchot* with a fan-like extension behind them, giving the illusion of rays spreading out from behind the *luchot*. The *teba* was carved from rich brown wood and given a shiny finish. The plaque affixed to it proudly proclaimed that the *teba* had been donated by Nouri Dayan, in memory of his parents.

Ahi Ezer finally had a *k'nees* to be proud of.

Dave Bibi ordered special *kippot* to be given out in honor of the occasion and turned to his committee members to come up with a fitting program. Many meetings later, the grand plan was finalized. The entire congrega-

The procession heading toward 64th Street. Note the musicians in front, followed by the *Sefer Torah*, followed by the Rabbis: Rabbi Yaakob Kassin, Rabbi Mordechai (Murad) Maslaton, and Rabbi Isaac Alkalai.[1] They are the three men walking together, wearing black hats.

tion would assemble at the newly purchased Dayan house on 77th Street and Bay Parkway to accompany the new *Sefer Torah* to the old synagogue on 64th Street. There they would take out the *Sifrei Torah* from 64th Street and carry them, decked by rented canopies, to accompany the new *Sefer Torah* to the new building on 71st Street.

Everyone in the Syrian community — *Halabi* and *Shammi* — joined together in tremendous joy: A beautiful *k'nees* was being established, another Torah was being led to its new home.

Early in the afternoon, the doors of the Dayan home were opened wide as hundreds of people came in to wish the Dayans *mabrook* and partake of the refreshments. Esther made gallons of *shrab el loz*, the traditional white drink made of crushed almonds, sugar, and water, generally served at engagements. Amid the singing and dancing, people marched in and out of the house to eat and drink and congratulate the Dayans on the momentous occasion.

---

1. Rabbi Isaac Alkalai (1882-1978) had been Chief Rabbi of Serbia and Yugoslavia and vice president of the World Sephardic Federation. He fled from German occupation in 1942 and settled in New York in 1943. By the 1940's, the Sephardic community in America (immigrants and their descendants who came from Turkey, the Balkans, Greece, and the Middle East) had over 100,000 members, mainly concentrated in the New York area. They formed the Central Sephardic Jewish Community of America of which Rabbi Alkalai became Chief Rabbi. The Syrian community remained generally autonomous but they did consider themselves part of the broader Sephardic community and often participated in community initiatives.

Exiting the 64th Street shul with the *Sifrei Torah*

Nouri emerged from the house carrying the new *Sefer Torah*. The crowd erupted in applause.

The procession left Nouri's home, led by a walking band of drums, flutes, clarinets, and other portable instruments. They made their way to 64th St., where a crowd awaited them in front of the old *k'nees*. All the *Sifrei Torah* were brought out and each one was given its own canopy.

The procession continued on to the new *k'nees*. Nouri's *Sefer Torah* was passed from one dignitary to the next as each one was given the honor of helping bring it to its new home. Basil Cohen led the parade, twirling a baton as he walked backward, facing the *Sifrei Torah*. Bay Parkway was closed off as hundreds of people marched down the street to the festive music playing in the background.

A partial view of the crowd

As President of Ahi Ezer, Dave Bibi opened the door to the new building, to the singing and cheers of the crowd. All those carrying *Sifrei Torah* entered first. The entire crowd followed them into the

L-R: Nat Escava, Isaac Escava (holding the cigar), Nouri, Joe Srour, Rabbi Kassin, Rabbi Alkalai, Rabbi Maslaton, Joe Maslaton

building, up the stairs, to the unfinished room that was lined with folding chairs because the permanent ones were still on order. Eight stunning Maria Teresa chandeliers hung from the ceiling: three on either side of the men's section, one suspended from the dome, and one over the ladies' section. People exchanged knowing glances and appreciative smiles: The chairs were on order, but Bibi and Co. made sure that the chandeliers were hanging.

Hacham Murad prepared a moving program of *pesukim* for the people to recite together and songs to be sung, based on the teachings of the Hida. Everyone found seats as ushers distributed the printed program and the Rabbanim and lay leaders made their way to the dais. There were many speeches and uplifting words, but the most moving part of the ceremony was when Hacham Murad donned the new Rabbinical robes that the congregation had purchased for him and recited the *Sheheheyanu*.

The Rabbanim present called out: *U'Mordechai yasah milifnei ha'melech bilbush malchut, techeilet, vahur, ve'argaman... veha'eer Shushan sahalah vesameiha!*

The congregation erupted in response: *La'Yehudim hayeta o'rah vesimha vesasson veekar!*[2]

---

2. These passages from *Esther* (8:15-16) were particularly fitting, as Hacham Murad's full name was Mordechai: *Mordechai left the king's presence clad in royal garments of blue and white with a large gold crown and a robe of fine linen and purple and the city of Shushan was cheerful and glad!* [Response of the crowd] *The Jews had light and happiness, and joy and honor!*

Bensonhurst, 1951

Approaching the new Ahi Ezer building

The atmosphere was electric. They were establishing a beautiful House of Prayer where they would serve G-d, led by their Hacham — His messenger, their king. The celebration was as much a coronation as a dedication.

"Izzy's *Sefer Torah*" was the talk of the community, and not just because it pinched the fingers if one didn't open and close it carefully. When Nouri walked out of his house holding it, there was a tremendous sense of awe and happiness: No one had ever seen such a unique and magnificent case. The *safrut* of the *Sefer Torah* was also beautiful. Every aspect of the *Sefer Torah* and its case indicated that it had been created with love and devotion.

The pageantry that accompanied the *Sefer Torah* to its new home was unprecedented. Perhaps the *Hanukat Ha'Bayit* of Magen David in 1922 had been equally historic, but that had occurred almost three decades earlier. Much of the community had still been on the Lower East Side; the youth had no recollection of it, and many of the old-timers were no longer around.

The professional photographs, taken by Trainer Studios, vividly captured the festivities. But the impression the event made on the entire community went beyond those photographs. "Izzy's *Sefer Torah*" was an

Isaac Escava (right) is presenting the key to Ahi Ezer to Dave Bibi.

inspiration. It told the story of an orphan who felt indebted to his parents, simply because they were his parents, and who was determined to honor them, even though he never knew them.

Nouri was a deeply spiritual person in a natural and quiet way. To his friends and acquaintances — in the *k'nees* and in the business — he

Hacham Murad is cutting the ribbon before entering the new *k'nees*.

Bensonhurst, 1951 / 233

was one of the boys, someone who could be counted on for a warm smile, a firm handshake, and normal conversation. But anyone who spent Shabbat at the Dayan home saw that there was so much more to this unassuming "regular guy."

His Shabbat schedule never veered: Friday night, after prayers, he and the boys went to Hacham Murad's house, to wish him Shabbat Shalom and receive his blessing. One at a time, they filed in; each one kissed Hacham Murad's hand, after which the elderly man placed his hands over their heads and recited a *beracha*. In turn, they each walked over to Sara Maslaton and kissed her hand as well. Then they headed home.

Nouri's Shabbat table was full of guests, just as he had seen at the tables of his uncles and his in-laws. Before eating, he led everyone in spirited

Dave Bibi opening the door to the new Ahi Ezer for the first time

Hacham Murad, surrounded by dignitaries, as they present him with a plaque dedicated to everyone who enabled the new building to be built. L-R: William Rosen, Joe Cohen, Rabbi Izak E. Levi, Hacham Murad, Rabbi Hecht, Rabbi Klappholtz, Steve Shalom, Isaac Shalom, Rabbi Kassin, Basil Cohen, Dave Bibi, Sam Liniado.

singing. He stood straight, one hand clasped over the other as he sang *Shalom Aleihem,* and continued with other *zemirot* and *pesukim.*

Nouri exuded royalty.

As each dish was brought out, the guests were amazed at the abundance of food, presented with so much warmth and honor. They felt like they were sitting at a royal table where anything they wished to eat suddenly appeared. Yet the atmosphere was sublime as only *dibrei Torah* were spoken and only praises to Hashem were sung.

Shabbat was a day devoted to Hashem.

Hacham Murad speaking

The meals were neither the beginning nor the end of a day that was holy from before it began and remained holy even after it ended. After the evening meal, after accompanying his guests to the door, Nouri gathered his boys around the table and read Mishnayot, each one taking a turn to read a *perek* out loud. Then they learned the *Ben Ish Hai* on that week's *perasha.*[3]

Shabbat morning, Nouri was up very early, before everyone else, so no one ever discovered exactly how early he rose. He sat at the dining-room table and reviewed that week's *perasha* and then he learned from the *sefer* of Rabbi Chaim Vital. On the way to *k'nees* he would sing the *bakashot* softly. After prayers, it was back to Hacham Murad's house for *mazza* with the family before going home.

Then Nouri and the boys read the next eight *perakim* of *Mishnayot Shabbat* and a bit of *Zohar* before beginning the meal. Kiddush was followed by an elaborate *mazza*, once again accompanied by singing. Nouri was scrupulous to begin singing immediately, and to continue throughout the meal, so that there would be no *debarim b'teilim* — idle chatter — to mar the

---

3. "The Syrian custom is to divide the 24 *perakim* of *Mishnayot Shabbat* over the three meals. The first sixteen, we did regularly, every week without fail. The last eight got dropped because we had *seuda shelishit* in the shul," recalled Mr. Irwin Dayan. "In retrospect, I realize how much I gained from this routine. My father trained me to read fluently, without dots, and to recognize abbreviations instantly. Later on, when I learned *Mesechet Shabbat* in depth, it was very familiar to me."

Bensonhurst, 1951 / 235

Nouri is filling in the first letters of the *Sefer Torah*. Note the unique construction of the case. Later on, Nouri had the inside construction of the case changed so that the *klaff* opened toward the reader; this made it easier for him to see the letters without bending forward.

holiness of the day. As he passed around the *hamin* (a variety of dishes that remained on the stove overnight) and people filled their plates, he began another tune. There was a break in the singing as they ate, but unless one of the guests initiated a conversation (the children knew not to speak unless spoken to) everyone ate quietly.

It was early afternoon by the time the meal ended.

By then, Nouri had been up for hours, learning and praying, only "taking a break" as he ate the meal. But he wasn't ready to rest. He sat with his boys and listened as they read the *perasha* of the coming week, with the proper *ta'amim*. Sometimes he seemed to be nodding off… but one incorrectly pronounced word jerked him awake.

He finally did take a short rest in the afternoon, but at least an hour before sunset, he was back in the Ahi Ezer with his boys, following the same schedule he had grown up with: *mishmara,* Minha, *seuda shelishit,* Hacham Murad's *derasha,* and Arbit. In the winter, the *derasha* was after Arbit.

Mosa'ei Shabbat, as Nouri drove the car he had parked in front of the shul before Shabbat, he began singing the *piyutim*, extending the Shabbat atmosphere all the way home. After Habdala, he continued singing as he sliced some leftover *halla*, opened a can of tuna and mixed it with tomatoes and some other vegetables that he had chopped. He happily prepared *seuda rebi'it* and invited everyone to join him, finally finishing all the *piyutim*, down to the very last one.

Nouri's Shabbat was truly devoted to Him.

Nouri never had the chance to learn Gemara in depth, on a long-term basis. Nor did he have practical Rabbinical training or knowledge. Yet he still developed a lifestyle that, at its core, was total devotion to Hashem, and not just on Shabbat.

He never missed a *minyan* — not for Shaharit, Minha, or Arbit — no matter how short the day, or how overwhelmingly busy. After Shaharit, he was one of the regulars at the Rabbi's daily *shiur* of Hok l'Yisrael. Everyone present would take turns reading the daily portion and Hacham Murad would explain the parts of the Gemara. Whenever Nouri had a spare minute (or a not-so-spare-minute) out came his *Tehillim*, which he said so often, he knew it by heart. Even as he went on with the mundane duties of life, Hashem was constantly present.

Yet nothing about Nouri even hinted of religious fanaticism. He was so down-to-earth and real, so incredibly normal. He even had a touch of the revolutionary within him, but he used that attribute to serve Hashem and His people.

"Why don't you send the children to camp in the summer?" Rabbi Mordechai Wertzberger suggested to Nouri one day.

"Rabbi Mordechai," as he was called, had been teaching in Ahi Ezer Talmud Torah for a number of years. Back in the 40's, when Hacham Murad was finding his schedule overwhelming, the shul had hired Rabbi Mordechai to help out. He taught the boys in the back of the *k'nees*, where the ladies sat on Shabbat, while the girls learned across the street in the Gaon's *shteibel* with "the Morah," Miss Bertha. The community was delighted when "Rabbi Mordechai" and "the Morah" became engaged. By then, they were both beloved "adopted" members of the community, and many Ahi Ezer congregants participated in the novel *simha*.[4]

Nouri listened with interest as Rabbi Wertzberger explained, "It's very unhealthy for the children to spend the long summer months completely unstructured. There are wonderful camps being set up specifically for this

---

4. "My parents returned from the wedding amazed and overwhelmed. The enthusiasm and excitement of an Ashkenazic wedding had not yet reached the Sephardic community, where weddings were more sedate. My mother kept talking about how they picked up Rabbi Mordechai on a chair and danced with him and then did the same with the Morah" (Mr. Irwin Dayan).

purpose. Instead of being in the country for a mere two weeks of family time, camp gives them four weeks of structure. It's a wonderful opportunity for them."

Syrian mothers sending their children away from home? Seriously?

But Nouri liked the idea. In the summer of 1950 he sent Irwin to Camp Agudah and Carol to Camp Bais Yaakov. He even convinced Dave Bibi to send his daughter Helen, and Sion Maslaton to send his daughter Miriam. That summer, they all went to camp together for the first — and last — time.

The Syrian Mama hens wanted all their chickens back in the nest, so sleepaway camp, as a community innovation, was an idea that didn't stick. Nouri wasn't discouraged. He was convinced that it was a good idea for the right person at the right time. When his sister-in-law, Betty (Maslaton) Kubie, was ill with a brain tumor, Nouri watched the children suffer — and acted. He showed up at the Kubie house with empty suitcases and a request, "Would you agree to send Joel to sleepaway camp?"

Betty's eyes filled with tears. "We don't have the money," she whispered.

"I'm not asking for money, only for your permission."

Betty nodded. And Joel had an unforgettable summer.

So innovation was good, in the right time, for the right people.

Certainly, when it came to the community, Nouri was creative and innovative — constantly. He was always looking for ways to raise the religious level of the congregation. When he found a way, he went straight to Uncle Dave and hired people whom he felt would help the congregation.

He discovered Rabbi Rosenfeld, who was teaching in the Yeshiva of Brighton. Rabbi Rosenfeld was a scion of a Breslover family. His years in Ashkenazic yeshivot sharpened his Talmudic skills and he was known to be well-versed in all of *Shas*. What could a Syrian Jew have in common with a Breslover chassid? On the surface, nothing. But deep down, where it counted, everything.

Rabbi Tzvi Aryeh Benzion Rosenfeld energized Ahi Ezer with Torah classes.

Nouri heard Rabbi Rosenfeld speak and he felt that his sincerity would speak to his community. He hired Rabbi Rosenfeld to give evening classes in the shul. His classes were well attended by the community and helped effect a higher degree of religious interest.

Nouri brought in other Rabbis. Slowly, Ahi Ezer developed a regular schedule of classes on a variety of subjects. What was distinctly unique about Nouri was that his clinging to tradition never held him back from innovation. He was open to bring anyone into the community; it made no difference if the person was a Breslover chassid, a Satmar chassid, or a yeshivishe Litvak. If the person had an ability to influence for the good, Nouri hired him.

Not every appointment bore immediate fruit but, beneath the surface, a slow revolution was taking place. It would take many more years to connect all the dots and recognize from where the religious renaissance among Syrian Jewry originated.

Many of those roads led back to Nouri Dayan.

Chapter 28:
AHI EZER, 1952

Aaron Levy slid low in his seat, day-dreaming during prayers. The synagogue was new but the singing was familiar. *Like a lullabye. No wonder Albert is snoring, Maybe it's time to wake the little guy up…*

With some fast finger work, the job was done. Albert let out a startled yelp, Aaron's smirk turned into a fit of coughing, and all their friends sitting with them in the back of the *k'nees* shook with suppressed laughter. Mr. Bibi turned around and gave an impressive glare. Some of the boys grew quiet; others shrugged and continued their muted kibitzing.

"Sh!" came a voice from nowhere. Nouri had stealthily made his way down the side of the room and sidled up near the boys. His presence helped — a little. But when the merry undercurrent continued, Nouri glided past the group and gave Aaron a grave look, his new disciplinary tactic now that the boy was too old for a playful ear-tweak. Aaron sheepishly looked back at Nouri, who could somehow look stern and warm at the same time. *I love the man*, was his fleeting thought.

Somehow, Nouri's love always came through.

It's a different generation, Nouri mused philosophically.

Ahi Ezer had moved to a new location, but it retained the same place in Nouri's mind and heart, even as it changed. No longer was Arabic the predominant language. It was still there, especially since occasional new immigrants inevitably flocked to Ahi Ezer. But the congregation was largely American-born, some already second-generation. They were far removed from the Old Country and from the Depression-era mentality as well. The same kids who used to hang around the business to rake in money saying *Tehillim* had grown up and their heads were occupied with sports, movies, and "having fun." A quarter to say *Tehillim* was passé for

16- and 17-year-olds. They needed something more substantial to ignite the spiritual spark that Nouri was certain existed within them.

Nouri tossed ideas over in his mind, backward and forward. *We have to get them more involved. We have to make religion more meaningful for them, like the downstairs minyan for Rosh Hashana and Yom Kippur.*

Ahi Ezer didn't have a regular youth *minyan*; they left that to Charlie's Shul. On a regular Shabbat, the boys who came to *k'nees* were solid kids who did their own thing but were not particularly inspired. Ultimately, some of them stopped coming even on Shabbat and none of them ventured into the *k'nees* during the week. With public school starting at 8 a.m., they felt extremely virtuous if they managed to get to school on time. No one was going to wake up even earlier to go to the *k'nees*.

Sunday, Nouri decided one day. *I'll get the boys to come Sunday.*

This was such a radical idea that Nouri didn't share his plan with anyone. He knew what the naysayers would say: It's a different generation. Be happy when young people come to synagogue on Shabbat, don't bother them during the week. They are good kids, just leave them alone.

All of this was true, but Nouri wasn't going to let reality get in his way. To him, a different generation meant you needed different methods to reach them. No one under the age of 30 came to the *k'nees* during the week? We can change that! Sure, they are good kids, but they could be even better.

"C'mon Irwin, let's go." Nouri had just come home from the regular 7 a.m. *minyan* and needed help loading the car with provisions for his latest project.

Irwin grabbed his jacket and the bag that his father had indicated. He was a wiry 10-year-old with an infectious smile, a toothy grin, and an appetite for the original. Daddy had been talking and planning about "Sunday morning" a whole week. Now that the great day dawned and Daddy was inviting him to tag along, why not? Irwin jumped into the front passenger seat and Nouri drove the green Chevy down the street. He stopped at a modest two-family house, gave a honk, then pursed his lips together and let out his trademark whistle, loud and long.

No one whistles like Daddy, Irwin noted with pride.

A sleepy-eyed youth poked his head outside. "I'm coming! Just a sec…"

Minutes later the boy was flying out of the house and into the Dayan car. From one street to the next, Nouri canvassed Bensonhurst, picking up his boys. He dropped the first group off at the *k'nees* and went for another trip. It took about 20 minutes to round up the fourteen guys, good kids, who warily agreed to come to *k'nees*, just one Sunday morning.

Oblivious to their hesitation, Nouri appointed one of the boys as *hazzan*, and cheerfully handed out *siddurim*, already opened to the correct page. He wanted to make everything as easy for them as possible. The boys began, somewhat shy and suspicious, but as they continued their prayers they felt more natural.

Good, they finally got into it, Nouri noticed with satisfaction. He puttered around in the back of the room, spreading out a clean tablecloth with napkins and cups, while responding *Amen* to the *berachot* and singing along when appropriate. The boys ended on a happy note. Hey, it had not been so bad... and then when they saw the spread that Nouri had prepared for them, they were positively agog.

"Let me just say a few words of *dibrei Torah*..." Nouri began. Then he invited the boys to enjoy fresh danishes, jelly donuts, and milk.

He really cares about us... was the universal feeling that didn't have to be expressed because it was so obvious. The boys joked and ate, and hung around a few extra minutes, warmed by the attention. Then they headed for Seth Low Park, right across from Magen David Yeshiva, where they transformed themselves into the Silver Knights, a cracker-jack baseball team that competed in the neighborhood leagues.

Baseball was a very important part of the life of an American kid in the 50's. Having their own team, on par with the other predominately gentile teams in the area, was a point of pride for the SY boys. Morris Dweck (captain), Aaron Levy (catcher), Mosey Cabasso (pitcher), Jackie Cabasso (right field), and Charlie Shrem (second baseman) were all part of the Silver Knights, as was the rest of the *minyan*. Suddenly, something else united them besides being SYs who loved baseball.

Here was where Nouri's vision was so apparent. Though he had never been part of a baseball team (who had time for such things when he was growing up?) he didn't view their involvement as an impossible stain, just as he didn't view their marginal religiosity as a lost cause. Times had changed and he wasn't about to fight this new value system by rallying against it. Instead, he chose to draw the boys toward religion by making it attractive to them.

The boys responded to Nouri's whole hearted acceptance. Some of them came to the *minyan* already dressed in their baseball uniforms, the silver stripe shining against a blue background. They felt comfortable with themselves and comfortable in the *k'nees*. It was an exhilarating feeling. They were no longer wild kids chafing from the discipline of sitting through Shabbat services in the back of the *k'nees*. They were the *minyan* and the *minyan* was them. Each one felt a part of something special. The 9 a.m. Sunday youth *minyan* was an innovation that became an Ahi Ezer institution. It was Nouri's baby: He personally picked up the boys, prepared (and paid for) the food, and set up the *siddurim*.

He looked for ways to improve on his original idea, eventually expanding his refreshments to include a full breakfast. Erev Shabbat, he dropped off a bag of caraway seeds at Ginsburg's bakery on 68th Street and 20th Avenue. Clad in his white apron and matching beard, Mr. Moshe Ginsburg beamed as Nouri explained his order. Nouri knew that the boys would not have the patience to wash and say *birkat ha'mazon* and yet they would love having fresh rolls. Inserting the caraway seeds into the bagels would allow them to be considered *mezonot*, and avoid the wash/*birkat ha'mazon* issue.[5] The quantity of caraway gave the bagels a distinct flavor that the boys loved.

Mr. Ginsburg was happy to be part of Nouri's new project. He was a community legend: a storybook figure, straight from the shtetl, a *malach* of a man whose piety was well known. For many years, he faithfully baked these unique bagels, fresh every Sunday morning, special for the Ahi Ezer breakfast.

Mosa'ei Shabbat, with love and joy and patience, Nouri sliced and stacked the hard cheese, and washed and sliced the vegetables. If he was overwhelmed with other duties that week, he would ask one of his children to help him, but he made sure that, no matter what, the job got done. Sunday morning, he entered Ginsburg's bakery with a big smile on his face, and a *d'bar Torah* on his lips as he picked up the fresh bagels and danishes and brought them to shul. Then he picked up the boys.

One day, he decided to add the recitation of some *Tehillim* to the routine.

"Here you go," he said as he handed out open *Tehillims* to the surprised boys. "Just five psalms, it will take only a few minutes. C'mon fellas, you can do it."

It was hard to refuse Nouri, especially when he had that infectious glint in his eye. While he was beloved as a warm and positive role model, Nouri was equally stubborn and persistent. He led them in saying *Tehillim* and it instantly became part of the routine. Each week, the *minyan* moved ahead five psalms so that twice a year they finished the entire *Tehillim*.

Then it was off to the ball park as usual.

And Nouri stayed behind to clean up the mess.

The Sunday morning *minyan*/breakfast became very popular.[6] The *mezonot* rolls were the first of their kind and the boys loved them. The routine of going to the *k'nees* on a weekday and saying *Tehillim* made a profound impression on them. Though many boys didn't keep up continuous synagogue attendance as they entered adulthood, many eventually returned to the *k'nees* later in life, largely because of the incredibly positive experience of those Sunday mornings.

---

5. The *beracha* of a dough-based product may change from *hamosi* to *mezonot* if it's kneaded with nuts or spices that give the end-product a distinctive taste (*Shulhan Aruch O"C* 168:7).

6. Today, all the Sephardic shuls in Flatbush follow this system, but it was first initiated by Mr. Dayan.

Like his *Tehillim*-reading incentives, Nouri's Sunday project was his own initiative. Though he was a member of the synagogue board, he never brought up the idea for a vote and never asked that the synagogue defray the costs. He just went ahead and did what he felt was right, with outstanding results. He was barely 35 at the time and his role in the shul was more of an active committee member than a leader. Nonetheless, his revolutionary idea, and the courage he exhibited to get it moving, was an indication for the future.

The Dayan family was growing; Sara and Joyce joined Irwin, Carol, and Murray. When Nouri and Esther first moved into their new home, they rented out the upstairs to Teddy Srour and his family. When the Srours moved out, Nouri and Esther decided to rent out only half of that apartment and keep the back rooms for themselves. With five bedrooms — two upstairs and three downstairs — they had more room for sleep-in guests, Nouri's dream-come-true.

A winter Sunday in Prospect Park. Top row, L-R: Sara Maslaton (later Sankary) and Irwin Dayan. Middle row, L-R: Max Maslaton, Murray Dayan, Miriam Maslaton (later Ozeri), Rachel Maslaton (later Salem). The child in the front is Judy Maslaton (later Elbaz).

"Amazing that he is so happy about all our new living space," Esther told her sister Rebecca. "He is almost never home to enjoy it!"

Nouri popped into the house in the morning to a lavish breakfast and then dashed off to work. He came home for supper, but usually rushed out for a meeting either for the shul or other community initiatives. He returned hours later, tired from a full day, glanced at the news, and then headed off to bed. He was grateful to Esther, who made taking care of the children, the house, and the guests seem easy, but he never took her hard work for granted.

"Can I get you more help?" he asked her, concerned. Then

Relaxing in the summer, back in the 1940's. Back row,
L-R: Hacham Murad, *Stetta*, Nouri with Irwin on his back, Ray (Maslaton) Tawil.
Front row: Morris Bibi, Rebecca (Maslaton) Bibi – holding Carol on her lap.

he hired a maid, loyal Maria, who lived in the Dayan basement for the next twenty years.

They were a team, Nouri and Esther; each appreciated the other immensely. Only one day a week did Esther claim some time from Nouri's busy schedule. Sunday was set aside for the family… well, not completely.

"Ready?" Morris Bibi asked his sister-in-law/niece, as he entered the kitchen where she was making sandwiches. He and Rebecca often came over for company, conversation, or to see the kids. Sundays, they went on outings together.

"Sure," smiled Esther ruefully, "but not everyone else is here…"

"Who's missing?" Nouri asked with a smile as he poked his head into the kitchen, car keys jangling from his fingers. "Okay, everyone, who's coming in my car?"

For Nouri, Sunday was family day, but only after taking care of the second *minyan* in the shul (including sweeping up the mess and taking out the garbage). He never discussed why he came home late on Sundays, just like he didn't talk about the charity that he gave, or the meetings that he attended. That was all part of his *hatzne'a lechet*, his way of doing things in a hidden fashion. Esther understood that there must be a good reason for

Ahi Ezer, 1952 / 245

Nouri and his father-in-law, learning together

Nouri's constant tardiness, but she was relieved when he finally showed up and the extended Maslaton family could go out together.[7]

Morris and Nouri were the drivers (none of the women drove). Often, two cars were not enough for the extended Maslaton family: Betty had a bunch of kids, so did Sion and Joe, and *Jdedda* and *Stetta* (Hacham Murad and Sara) came as well. So Nouri revved up the Dayan shuttle and made another trip. The ladies set out the blankets and the food, chatting amiably while the kids played. Hacham Murad chanted softly from the *sefer*, often engaging Morris and Nouri in a learned conversation. Everyone had a wonderful time.

The hours passed quickly and soon Nouri was back in the car, taking the first shift back home.

While driving back and forth, Nouri had his *Tehillim* handy and, at each red light, out it came. Inevitably, the light turned green while he was reading.

"Daddy," the kids would shout.

Nouri looked up from the *sefer*, gunned the gas, and finished the chapter while keeping his eyes on the road. This was not very difficult for him, as he knew the *sefer* by heart. The reading at the red light was only to keep him on track.

Those Sunday trips were the glue that kept the Maslaton family together. Family meant the world to Nouri, and he kept up with family on the other side of the world as well. He always sent money to his family in Israel, though few people knew about this generosity.[8] He asked Esther to pick

---

7. "Many years later, when he was already elderly, my father told me why he had always been late on Sundays," commented Mr. Irwin Dayan. "Until then, I had no idea."

8. "When I was studying in Porat Yosef, I went to visit Uncle Nouri's family. They were thrilled to meet me and told me, with great appreciation, of the money and packages that he sent to them. It was so typical of my uncle not to give me anything to bring his family. He

out pretty material so that his sisters could sew nice clothing for their girls.

"Tell me what you need," he begged in his letters. If his siblings responded, he was quick to fill their orders. If not, he still found something to send. When he heard that one of his nieces had moved to Canada, he quickly penned an invitation.

"Please come and visit. Stay as long as you want…"

Helen (Sara's daughter) and her Ashkenazic husband, Harry Schwartz, came to New York. They were supposed to stay for one week, but they felt so comfortable in the Dayan house, they stayed for six months! Helen's fondest memory of her stay was the evening when Nouri sat outside, on the deck, with her and Harry, talking about nothing particularly special. Helen let down her guard, and an honest comment about the difficulties of life escaped her lips.

"Don't say 'I can't,' " Nouri chided softly. "Do your best. Put in effort and hard work and the Almighty will take care of the results."

Helen was moved: *I want to tap into that sincerity!*

Sincerity in one's actions, connection to family, and conviction that the Almighty always helps those who serve Him, were some of Nouri's outstanding attributes. They were part of who he was — all day, every day — even in the workplace.

"This line is so unique, we are going to need a show to launch it properly," Mr. Bibi enthused.

Nouri was amazed at his uncle's optimism, and this was just after the Japanese fiasco almost bankrupted the entire business![9] Mr. Bibi had just returned from Spain where he discovered bronze chandeliers — heavy pieces with ornate chiseling — a novelty in the USA, where crystal was king. He was certain that Americans would go for the new look. Bibi and Co. organized their first show at the Statler Hilton on 8th Avenue. Dave Bibi was correct: The bronze pieces were a big hit. There was nothing like them on the market, and the customers loved them.

Chandeliers had become the mainstay of Bibi and Co. They began importing artistic lighting collections from all over the world. The Venetian chandeliers were made by expert glass blowers who maneuvered colored glass into different shapes, forming flowers and leaves that looked very

---

preferred to wire money and mail packages rather than ask messengers who would then know of his kindness" (Rabbi Murray Maslaton).

9. "Mr. Bibi found Japanese crystal parts for a fraction of what Czechoslovakian crystals cost. He pre-sold containers of them to his biggest competitors — Weiss and Biheller, Igmore, Weinstock, and others. Only after he received the merchandise did he realize that it was defective. When one put the crystal in water and then held it up, it sparkled like a diamond… but a few days later, it became cloudy. Bibi and Co. was stuck with all this bad merchandise. It was a very difficult time" (Mr. Irwin Dayan).

Nouri Dayan (right) presenting Dave Bibi with an award at a community event. Hacham Rephael Elnadav, the *hazzan* in Sha'arei Zion, is on the left.

beautiful when displayed properly in a chandelier. The Czechoslovakian collection was famous for its antique crystals. They also used Aurora Borealis (rainbow crystal), painted on one side but left clear on the other, creating a burst of color that was very attractive. The Austrian collection was known for its amber-colored glass, understated elegance that made crystals obsolete. The Versailles chandeliers had bronze frames and large pendalogues, flat crystals with scalloped edges that were engraved with intricate shapes. Even a collection that stood on its own could be dressed up into something unique to "Bibi," as people fondly referred to the growing business.

Luxury lighting was a dynamic frontier and "Bibi" was at the helm.

For both Dave and Nouri, the business was an important part of their lives.

And yet, so was their community, their religiosity, and their family.

For those who interacted with them on the community level, it was difficult to imagine that they were not neglecting their business in favor of other interests. It seemed that almost any community initiative had Dave on the committee. Nouri came in at a close second.

Those who saw Dave Bibi pray wondered how he had managed to create such a profound relationship with G-d. It seemed that only Rabbis prayed with such sincerity. For those who remembered Nouri as a community kid, they wondered when and how he became so religious. He was a regular guy, and yet he was so far above them.

Yet their families saw them as devoted fathers and loving uncles who were not often home, but whose time that they did spend with family was well spent.

1. Reuben Bibi, 2. Esther Bibi, 3. Carol Bibi [later Franco], 4. Dave Bibi, 5. Milli Bibi, 6. Nouri Dayan, 7. Irwin Dayan, 8. Esther Dayan, 9. Rebecca Bibi, 10. Morris Bibi, 11. Joyce Dayan [later Nahem], 12. Sara Dayan [later Salem], 13. Murray Dayan, 14. Sharon Bibi [later Swed], 15. Jack Bibi, 16. Max Maslaton, 17. Elliot Bibi, 18. Carol Dayan [later Harari Raful]

Every Purim, "the uncles" — Nouri included — made their rounds. The children waited at the window for the foursome to walk up to the house. They assembled themselves around the table, already set with goodies, and began their program.

"Okay, Sharon, what was the name of the wicked king of Persia?" asked Uncle Morris.

"Ely, who was the righteous queen?" asked "Uncle" Izzy.

The men would ask questions, the children would shyly offer answers, and the reward was a bright and shiny silver dollar![10] For months after, the children fingered their precious coins… and waited in anticipation for the coming Purim.

The unique relationship between Reuben, Morris, Dave, and Nouri spilled over to the extended families who absorbed the unspoken message: Family is precious. Appreciate one another, nurture one another, care about one another.

---

10. "It was a royal honor to be 'tested' by our uncles. They made Torah so exciting for us kids. In my day, they switched to $10 bills for each question, which really added up to a lot! I was the envy of my other (Maslaton) cousins who marveled at our special Purim," reminisced Mrs. Barbara (Dayan) Ozeirey.

Chapter 29:
MEXICO, ISRAEL, AND BEYOND, 1953

"I'm going to take you somewhere great," Yehoshua Hilu[11] promised. "America isn't that bad."

That's what he said back in Mexico, Jacobo thought grimly.

When Jacobo Halabe, Jacobo Idi, and Moises Nacach agreed to travel from Mexico to far-off New York to learn in Yeshiva Torah Vodaath, it had sounded like an exotic adventure.

The reality was much less exciting.

They were all very young; the oldest among them was 13. They couldn't call home. Not only was the cost prohibitively expensive, but they didn't have phones in their houses. They had already mailed off letters, knowing that a response could take up to four weeks to receive. They were completely cut off from their families, stranded in a different culture where their Spanish and Arabic were both useless and, to top it all off, the food was strange.

"Come on," Yehoshua enthused the next Friday as he guided the whole group of Mexican boys out of Williamsburg for Shabbat. "It's going to be great!"

They rode the Sea Beach line all the way to the other end of Brooklyn, to a large corner house in a neighborhood whose name they couldn't pronounce. Then the door opened and the scent hit them immediately: It was the scent of home.

"Welcome, welcome," a smiling man greeted them in Arabic.

The boys looked at each other, and then back at the smiling man, and then they smiled… all the way to the *k'nees* where they were greeted with more smiles and more Arabic, all the way through the meal where every-

---
11. Later to become the Rabbi of the *Shammi* community in Mexico.

thing was sung exactly as they sang back home, and all the way up to their rooms later that night.

"Like a Yom Tov," Jacobo declared dreamily as he lay in bed, "so much food, and just what we are used to…"

"The *kibbe hamda* was just like my mother's…"

"…and the *keftes* (Syrian meatballs)… they were spiced just right…"

"…the *salata* — just like home…"

"…I never realized how good *tehina* is…"

That special Shabbat gave many of those boys the warmth and courage that enabled them to stay in New York. Some of the boys learned in Torah Vodaath for seven years! Throughout those years, they kept coming to the Dayan house for Shabbat and Yom Tov.

Sukkot was an especially busy time. None of the boys went back to Mexico; it was simply too expensive. Yet no one wanted to stay in Williamsburg. Luckily, the Dayans had an enormous sukka, built on top of their double garage. Nouri built a permanent frame around half the area and every year he covered the frame with curtains and the top with bamboo. Right before Yom Tov, he bought loads of fresh flowers and personally hung them all over the sukka. The red, yellow, pink and purple flowers, accented by loads of greens, turned the sukka into a miniature garden with natural beauty and refreshing scents.

Everyone in the community would come to make Kiddush in the sukka. It was a neighborhood custom for anyone with a private sukka to invite everyone else to come and make a *beracha*. While there were still not many private sukkot (the Bibis, the Cohens, and the Maslatons were among the few), there were enough to keep the people busy and the atmosphere exciting. The Torah Vodaath boys enjoyed being part of the excitement. It made being so far away from home much more bearable.

One Shabbat, twelve of them decided to walk from Williamsburg all the way to Bensonhurst! Nouri happily welcomed them into his home. Similarly, when one of the boys came up with the idea to have a "major" Shabbat and asked if fourteen boys could come at once, for the whole Shabbat, Nouri readily agreed. He would do almost anything to make them happy.

Nouri took an interest in the boys beyond feeding them food. He asked about their families and tried to find them other connections in New York. When the boys graduated elementary school, who were they going to invite to their graduation? Their parents were certainly not coming in from Mexico. And most of the boys didn't have family in New York.

Actually, they did have family.

Nouri and Esther Dayan went down to Williamsburg to attend the graduation.

The Torah Vodaath boys never asked Yehoshua Hilu how he found the Dayan home. After one Shabbat, it was a moot point. There were so many varied people around the Dayan table, clearly the house was a magnet that drew people.

"Like Abraham Abinu's tent," Carol declared happily. "We also have four doors: the front door, two side doors, and the entrance to the sukka from the back!"

Indeed, "Hotel Dayan" was always open. There were always Rabbis coming and going, often *meshulachim* from Eretz Yisrael. Their schedules were erratic, yet Esther always had meals ready for them.

Their guests became part of the family. The Torah Vodaath boys played with the Dayan kids while the older guests turned to Nouri and Esther for advice and companionship. Both Nouri and Esther were good listeners, which was often exactly what a tired guest was looking for. Unbelievably, no matter how long they stayed, the guests never felt like a burden.

Nouri loved people; he loved bringing them enjoyment. Perhaps that was why he seemed to always hit on just the perfect idea to brighten another person's life.

"Remember you once promised me a whistle for saying *Tehillim*?" a young man once chided Nouri. "Well, you never gave it to me."

The next day the man received a package delivered to his door. It contained a whistling tea kettle! While a whistle would have brought joy to a child, it was worthless to an adult. So Nouri found a different way to keep his word and bring the man happiness.

When Purim came around, Nouri was stumped. What could he send to all the people who were so special to him? He didn't want to send the standard wine and fruit that everyone passed around. He wanted to send something that people would really enjoy.

He also realized that some people didn't have the time and patience to have a proper Purim *seuda*. Some people had to go to work. Others stayed home but were satisfied with noshing on the simple foods that came into the house, leaving their main meal for dinnertime when it was well after sundown. How could he combine his desire to bring people joy with the ultimate joy of performing the mitzva of eating a proper Purim *seuda*? Then it came to him. He would order the Mauzonne special for everyone on his list: a fresh, hot, barbecued chicken, with a container of coleslaw and a container of potato salad. And, of course, a bottle of wine — but not the standard bottle that everyone else gave; Nouri gave everyone a half-gallon jug.

Right after the reading of the Megillah (which Nouri read flawlessly, in record time, so that people would not lose their patience)[12] he would drive

---

12. "I never heard the Megillah read so quickly. I think he clocked in at 21 minutes. I felt that he read quickly so that people could go home to eat after the fast, and in the mornings,

over to Mauzonne, load the car with his massive order, and deliver his chickens, piping hot, to all the people on his list.[13]

"Izzy's *mishlo'ah manot*" was the treat of the day, devoured by its recipients almost as soon as it entered their homes. Who could resist barbecued chicken, fresh off the skewer?

Who could resist Nouri?

Certainly not Uncle Dave.

Dave loved Nouri's energy and optimism. He trusted him completely and relied on him, not only in relation to the shul, but in anything that came up in life. They spent most of their days together — at work, in the *k'nees*, at committee meetings.

"They see each other more than we see them," Milo Bibi once commented to Esther. Yet the two wives respected the special relationship that went far beyond blood. The two men would do anything for each other, no questions asked.

Rabbi Avraham Kalmanowitz (1891-1964), Rosh Yeshiva of the Mirrer Yeshiva; he was tirelessly devoted to Sephardic Jewry.

"Izzy, can you do me a favor?" Dave asked. "Someone asked me to pick up a man at the airport. His name is Masheeya (Messiah)... "

"You have to be joking," Nouri cut in.

"Nope. That's his name. He is coming from Israel. I can't get there on time, can you go?"

"No problem," Nouri answered.

Nouri drove down to the airport and instantly identified the lost-looking Israeli. After settling his passenger into the car, Nouri opened the conversation.

"Where to?" he asked good-naturedly.

"Your house," was the response.

Nouri was surprised but, unfazed, drove him to his house.

"How long will he be staying?" Esther asked casually.

---

they should not be unduly delayed" (Rabbi Harry Rubin). Mr. Irwin Dayan recalled that Hacham Murad also read very fast and perhaps his father was merely continuing in that tradition.

13. "I felt so privileged to go on these deliveries with my father. He bought amber-colored cellophane and I wrapped the chicken and salads together. Then I did the delivering, while he followed me inside to wish everyone a Happy Purim. I felt like a million dollars," recalled Mrs. Barbara Ozeirey.

Rabbi Kalmanowitz in Casablanca in 1947,
surrounded by laymen and Rabbis of the community

Nouri shrugged. He had not known when he was coming, how should he know when he would be leaving? Masheeya stayed in the Dayan home for six months! If Nouri and Esther considered his presence an imposition, they never mentioned it. "Hotel Dayan" was open for anyone in need — no questions, no complaints.

Besides, how could they ask "Messiah" to leave?

Unbelievably, nothing seemed to faze Nouri, and this was not because everything in his life went smoothly. Particularly when it came to his involvement in the *k'nees*, there was always a story… about everything! Nouri was constantly smoothing ruffled feathers, building up egos, and cajoling people for cooperation.

Esther was his sounding board. She marveled at how he never got frustrated and always believed in the intrinsic goodness of every Jew. *There has been progress*, she admitted silently. The Sunday breakfasts were a resounding success. The evening classes were becoming popular. And Nouri was always in the background, quietly coaxing and coaching.

Esther wondered at her husband's resilience, how he never became disillusioned, even when his dreams spiraled slowly out of control.

Like when Obadya[14] showed up in the community.

---

14. Not his real name.

He walked into the shul, a medium-height, very slim young boy of about 18. He radiated confidence, though one wondered what he was so confident about. After all, he was young and unknown. But there was a fire in his dark eyes that gave his face an arresting look. He walked over to Hacham Murad and whispered a few words in his ear. The Rabbi nodded, and indicated that the youth go up to the front of the shul. As he addressed the synagogue, everyone took notice.

"I have come as an emissary of Rabbi Kalmanowitz…"

Everyone straightened a bit in their seats. Rabbi Avraham Kalmanowitz, the Mirrer Rosh Yeshiva, was a beloved and revered figure. No one recalled when the community first met the Ashkenazic Rabbi. No one really cared. They just knew him as a great person who loved all Jews. Without knowing the language, without familiarity with their customs and way of life, he had traveled back to the Old Country to help their brothers. No, he had not yet gone to Syria, but Morocco and Tunisia were close enough. Rabbi Kalmanowitz had joined Mr. Isaac Shalom as one of the leaders of Ozar HaTorah. Almost from its inception, he was a main partner in its development as he tirelessly advocated for the spiritual life of the Sephardic communities in North Africa and the Middle East.

Isaac Shalom visiting an Ozar HaTorah school

The Sephardic community of Bensonhurst was impressed by his devotion.

Every Pesah, Rabbi Kalmanowitz walked from Flatbush to Bensonhurst to appeal for funds for his yeshivos. When he first came, they thought a man out of an ancient storybook stepped into the synagogue. From his round Rabbinic hat, to his long flowing white beard, long Rabbinic coat, and down to his thick black boots, Rabbi Kalmanowitz was like no one they had ever seen. Their own Rabbis had trimmed beards and short jackets, and while their special *kippot* were an indication of their Rabbinical status, they still looked similar to their Syrian brethren. Rabbi Kalmanowitz was in a category of his own.

Mexico, Israel, and Beyond, 1953 / 255

Rabbi Kalmanowitz and Isaac Shalom, partners in saving Sephardic Jewry

Yet they eagerly awaited Rabbi Kalmanowitz's yearly visit. In his queerly accented Hebrew mixed with equally strange English, he endeared the Ahi Ezer people to him. It didn't really make a difference what he said; his warm gaze and loving smile won them over. Year after year, they pledged to help him. They were confident that their money was going to a worthy cause.

But why was this year different? Why had he sent a messenger in his place? And who was this youngster whose Arabic was as strange as Rabbi Kalmanowitz's Hebrew/Yiddish/English?

"… the Rosh HaYeshiva wasn't feeling well. He sent me with his apologies…" The teenager then launched into an appeal that piqued everyone's curiosity.

The young man was clearly bright, maybe even brilliant. He quoted from all sorts of *sefarim* and wove a cogent message. He had everyone riveted, and the crazy thing was that his Arabic was atrocious. Rabbi Kalmanowitz, who certainly didn't speak Arabic, must have thought that he was doing the people of Ahi Ezer a favor by sending, in his stead, a boy who "spoke their language." Only he didn't. But his audience was captivated anyway.

The boy returned to the Mirrer Yeshiva and most people forgot he had ever come. Not Nouri. Nouri kept thinking about the youth — so knowledgeable, so learned — and he spoke Arabic! What an inspiration for the community.

Nouri investigated and learned that the boy's name was "Obadya Kohelet," from a Syrian family living in Argentina. Obadya was precocious and ambitious. He had begun teaching in Mexico when he was only 16 years old and became principal of the school the following year. But Mexico was too small for Obadya so he was off to America to study in the Mirrer Yeshiva. His Arabic was heavily influenced by Spanish and therefore came across strange to the Syrians of America.

But Obadya was leaving Flatbush, his sights set on Lakewood Yeshiva. Eventually, he became a regular Shabbat guest at Nouri's house, one of the crowd who stayed at "Hotel Dayan." Perhaps it was the traditional Syrian food that pulled him from Lakewood (then a four-hour drive) to Bensonhurst. Or maybe it was simply the exceptional warmth and homey atmosphere that drew him. Whatever the case, Obadya Kohelet became a familiar figure in the Dayan home. While no one extended Obadya undue attention, he made himself known. He always had an interesting insight to share and his breadth of knowledge was remarkable. Nouri took quiet note of the youth, impressed with his drive to learn.

A Sephardic youth in Lakewood Yeshiva, what a novelty!

Chapter 30:

MOROCCO, 1955

As the Syrian Jewish community of Bensonhurst struggled to regain the religious character that had slipped away in the New World, back in the Old Country, Sephardic Jewry faced different challenges. Middle East and North African society still lived the same poor but traditional lives their ancestors had lived for hundreds of years. While there were always the wealthy elite, in most countries, the majority of the population — Muslim as well as Jewish — were low-income, working-class people, who were staunchly but simply religious. The 1800's brought modernity to the region from multiple directions, inevitably impacting the religiosity of the Jews negatively.[15]

Rabbi Kalmanowitz, under the auspices of Ozar HaTorah, saw the danger to Sephardic youth. He was determined to save whomever he could by sending teachers to these Sephardic countries and by bringing Sephardic youth to learn in America. The latter approach was revolutionary and, once again, Nouri sensed an opportunity to help, and he did, in his own quiet, unassuming way.

Rabbi Kalmanowitz traveled to Morocco and Egypt, where he hand-picked boys with potential. Back in America, his excitement grew: The Moroccan boys were coming! And the Egyptian boys would soon follow.

---

15. The Ottoman Empire implemented the *Tanzmiat*, a series of laws through which they modernized their systems of education, finance, and justice. Other catalysts for change were: the Damascus Affair that brought European involvement into the area, the construction of the Suez Canal, and European colonization. For the Jews, one of the main vehicles of change was the Alliance school system that introduced them to French culture and secular values, and clearly undermined religious life. Sephardic Jewry was swayed by the promises of financial security through Western education. Only the Yemenite community was unaffected by modernity and/or the Alliance schools. They staunchly retained their religiosity and traditions up until 1948.

Rabbi Kalmanowitz greeting the boys from Morocco as they got off the boat.
Back row, L-R: Haim Lalouch, unidentified, Shalom Revah, Avrohom Abergal,
(slightly forward) Rabbi Avraham Portal shaking hands with Rabbi Avraham Kalmanowitz,
(slightly behind) Gabriel Ohayon, Eliyahu Elbaz, Eli Ohana, unidentified, Yitzchak Bensoussan,
Shimon Cohen. Front row, L-R: Shlomo Wanouno, Meir Bensoussan, Gavriel Elgrabi,
(on the other side of Rabbi Kalmanowitz) Isaac Dahan, Rephael Wizman, Eli Cohen.

Some of the Moroccans knew each other but, overall, they came from three different cities, a group of strangers who bonded together as they traveled by train from Rabat to Tangiers, by ferry from Tangiers to Gibraltar, and by ship from Gibraltar to America. Their ship docked in America on Friday morning, June 15, 1956.

They carried their meager belongings in their hands and stood on the New York Harbor. It was a scorching hot day, but the sea air was clean and fresh and the boys looked around curiously. Suddenly, there he was, a man straight out of the Scriptures: long flowing white beard, long black coat in the sweltering heat, black felt hat, and an all-encompassing smile.

"Rabbi Kalmanowitz," murmured one of the boys. They simply couldn't stop staring.[16]

The boys barely understood his Hebrew, his Yiddish was completely incomprehensible, and his English was worse than theirs! But Rabbi

---
16. Some of the information from this chapter was taken from the book, *Where Two Worlds Met*, by Avrohom Birnbaum.

Morocco, 1955 / 259

The Mirrer Yeshiva in the 1950's. Rabbi Ephraim Mordechai Ginsburg (Rosh Yeshiva) is sitting front left. Rabbi Kalmanowitz is standing in the middle (back). The young man with the beard, seated next to Rabbi Kalmanowitz, is his son, Rabbi Shraga Moshe.

Kalmanowitz spoke the language of the soul and all the boys responded to him. After several pictures with accompanying dignitaries, they were on their way to Flatbush.

The boys went to the dormitory to get settled and ready for Shabbat. Then they were taken to the yeshiva, where it was almost time for Minha. They were overwhelmed by the sight of the Bet Medrash, which wasn't very large but was packed with men of all ages, swaying over Gemaras, oblivious to the group of "little kids" staring at them. So began their first Shabbat in America.

The boys were thrust into a jumble of contrasts. On the one hand, they were excited about all the new experiences, the thrill of being pioneers and, of course, the adventure of just being in America. On the other hand, back in Morocco, they had been the religious ones, the ones who had excellent backgrounds in learning and were hand-picked to come to America. Suddenly they felt ignorant and incompetent in this Ashkenazic yeshiva where everything was so different. They read *lashon kodesh* differently. Their prayers followed a different *nusah*. Their tunes (actually, there were not many of those in the yeshiva) were a totally different style. Even the *Sifrei Torah* didn't look like the ones back in Morocco.

The boys went to sleep that night tired and bewildered.

The next day was more of the same: unfamiliar *tefillot*, unfamiliar *minhagim*, unfamiliar foods, and unfamiliar everything. The boys longed for the familiar. They pined for home. Suddenly, a clean-shaven man, in his late 30's, walked into the room. The boys immediately recognized that he was one of their own. What was a young Sephardic gentleman doing in Ashkenaz town?

Rabbi Kalmanowitz accompanied the man over to the new arrivals.

"The Rabbi said that I can take you to a Sephardic *k'nees*. What do you think?"

The boys stared. This man was speaking Arabic! It was a different dialect than what they were used to, but it was way more familiar than the Yiddish or Hebrew of Rabbi Kalmanowitz.

The lunchroom of the Mirrer Yeshiva. At the table on the right are the Roshei Yeshiva. Note the table on the left where the "*bachurim*" are much younger than the others in the room.

"What's your name?" Shimon Cohen piped up.

"Isidore Dayan. And I would be very happy if you would join me."

Nouri led the group of fourteen back to Bensonhurst, to Ahi Ezer. They were greeted by warm smiles and friendly handshakes. Everyone was happy to see boys from the Old Country, nice Sephardic youth who still had that sweet purity they remembered in themselves. A little Arabic was thrown around and that relaxed the boys even further.

"What's your name?" Nouri asked.

"Refael Wizman."

"Okay, Refael. You are going to be the *hazzan* for Minha. Anyone know how to read from the Torah?"

A few boys hesitantly nodded. Proper reading of the Torah was an intrinsic part of Sephardic education. Nouri signaled to Shimon Cohen, "You will be the *ba'al ko'rei*. Anyone here a Cohen?"

"I am," Shimon offered.

Nouri gave the Moroccan boys center stage that Shabbat afternoon — from reading the Torah, to receiving *aliyot*, to leading the prayers. The boys were beyond excited. Suddenly they felt empowered, their previous insecurities washed away by pride in their heritage and the comforting feeling of being among family.

Morocco, 1955

Rabbi Shimon Cohen first came to Ahi Ezer as a young child. He went on to become a beloved rebbi in Magen David Yeshiva and, in that capacity, has had a profound effect on the Syrian community.

After Minha, they joined in *seuda shelishit* and then Arbit and Habdala. Nouri introduced them to Dave Bibi, who gave each of the boys a couple of dollars — a fortune to the penniless children — and a heartfelt invitation to them to return.

Nouri invited the boys back the next week, and then the next. Eventually, Rabbi Kalmanowitz put a stop to it. Reconnecting with other Sephardim had been good for the boys when they first came, but it was time for the boys to become thoroughly immersed in the yeshiva. That meant that all of Shabbat should be spent there as well.

For Nouri, this was fine. If he could help, he was available. If it was better that he step aside, then he was happy to step aside. For the boys, those few times in Ahi Ezer gave them confidence and courage. They were ready to embrace life in the Mirrer Yeshiva totally and completely.

Perhaps it was his exposure to the Moroccan boys from the Mirrer Yeshiva and the Sephardic boys from Torah Vodaath that highlighted for

Sephardic boys, happily learning in the Mirrer Yeshiva with Rabbi Shlomo Brevda

Nouri a distinct lack in his own community. Why was it that there were no Sephardic yeshivot of higher learning? Over the years, Nouri noticed the difference between boys who attended a post elementary-school yeshiva, and those who didn't. Was this higher standard of religiosity only available to Ashkenazim?

Not if Nouri could do anything about it.

Morocco, 1955 /

Chapter 31:
A NEW FACE IN AHI EZER, 1956

"There he is," Nouri noted to Irwin, who was sitting next to him in the front seat of the green Chevy. Obadya Kohelet was leaning on a car, his hand scratching the short beard that he had grown while in Lakewood.

It makes him look older, Irwin mused. At 21 years old, Obadya could use the extra years the beard afforded him. Irwin and his father got out of the car. Nouri stretched out his hand to another man — an older man who had driven Obadya from Lakewood to Brooklyn — and then picked up the suitcase from the sidewalk. Together they walked over to the trunk that Irwin had just popped open.

"You're taking him too young," the man said softly.

Nouri stiffened, momentarily holding the suitcase aloft. Then he continued putting it into the trunk, and slammed it shut. Irwin caught a glimpse of uncertainty in his father's eyes that was quickly replaced by grim determination: Obadya Kohelet was coming to Ahi Ezer.

"You will give an introductory class," Nouri explained. "I want to see how it goes, if the boys will be interested."

Obadya nodded confidently.

The next day Nouri understood why Obadya seemed so confident.

Obadya delivered a philosophical discourse like nothing they had ever heard. He presented one hypothesis after another, tearing apart concepts they had taken for granted, challenging them to think, baiting his audience, sometimes even debating himself. Few were able to follow his train of thought but everyone was dazzled by his novel approach. The introductory class was a resounding success. Many boys signed up for more classes.

Abraham Durrah and one of the Ariyeh brothers

Nouri was pleased with the excitement for learning that the younger man generated and watched the results with cautious optimism.[17]

Obadya began by offering evening *shiurim*, working around Rabbi Rosenfeld's classes. That conflict became moot: the two types of *shiurim* were radically different and attendees to one usually opted out of the other. Rabbi Rosenfeld's *shiurim* used Chassidic works to inspire the listeners toward a closer relationship with G-d which, in turn, translated into a greater adherence to mitzvot. Obadya's *shiurim* were Talmudical analysis. Even his *hashkafa* talks were logic based.

Rabbi Rosenfeld wanted to create pious Jews.

Obadya wanted to create Torah scholars.

Nouri wanted both.

Maybe he is right, Nouri ruminated. *Maybe intensive immersion in learning during one's formative years is what enables Torah knowledge to stick.*

---

17. Magen David Yeshiva had done the community a great service. Many Syrian boys now attended a yeshiva elementary school instead of public school. Nonetheless, this yeshiva education lasted only until the 8th grade. Then, a small percentage of boys went on to Yeshiva of Flatbush, but the majority attended public high school, effectively ending their Jewish education at a very early age.

Front left: Clement Soffer
Back left: Irwin Dayan facing Billy Mizrahi

L-R: Mosie Shamah, David Esses,
Raymond Heiney, Morris Srour

This was one of the main points that Obadya was espousing, thereby convincing boys to quit college — or to graduate high school early — in order to become full-time members of the Bet Midrash.

The boys were attracted to Obadya. Perhaps it was his way of making sensational statements. Or maybe it was the way he turned everything into a philosophical, yet analytical, discussion. If it was energy and charisma that they craved, Obadya had that as well.

Nouri spoke to Hacham Murad, who was always open to new ideas, especially when it came to increasing Torah scholarship and religiosity in his community. While the board did not run every appointment by the Rabbi, Hacham Murad seemed favorably inclined to the whole idea.

Years before, Ahi Ezer had purchased the two-family house adjoining its building. It had been up for sale and Dave Bibi felt it was too good an opportunity to pass up. They gave the upstairs to Hacham Murad as living quarters, a move that made life easier for the elderly Hacham, who was growing weak from various health issues. The downstairs was dubbed the "Annex," as it was treated as an extension to the main synagogue. It was an ideal venue for the classes that Ahi Ezer had been hosting ever since they moved into the new building. Now Nouri went ahead and offered Obadya full use of the Annex. He also put him on the synagogue payroll.

Then Obadya went to work.

I cannot get over this, Nouri surveyed the Bet Midrash in admiration.

The Annex was full. Young men were learning around tables, animated and excited. Many of them had not really learned since they had finished Talmud Torah years earlier, but they had caught the fever and were learning with unprecedented fervor. The night classes were so successful that

Obadya's students began coming to learn in the morning, afternoon, and whenever they could. Obadya built up their confidence and motivation by lauding the *gedolim* of the previous generations who had been of Sephardic descent and reminding them of their illustrious heritage. At the same time, he pointed out that his lectures were a product of his time spent learning from the contemporary Ashkenazic *gedolim* like Rabbi Aharon Kotler.

His excitement was contagious. Some young men disbanded their businesses to learn full time. Others dropped out of college. These were not small sacrifices, they were revolutionary actions. The most learned members of the community had always lauded *yafeh talmud Torah im derech eretz* as the highest ideal. And now the darlings of the community — good boys who had always done what their parents wanted — were defying the old generation and embracing a path that contradicted their upbringing.

That is when parents began getting annoyed.

"I tell you, Izzy, I don't get it. Learning during summer break is one thing. It certainly beats bumming around. Skipping fall semester, I might be able to tolerate. But leaving college altogether? I think that this is getting a little extreme…"

"A little?" interjected another friend. "I would say major extreme. Eddie and Sammy are quitting their jobs, not that they were making much as entry-level salesmen, but it was a start. How do they expect to build themselves up and support a family?"

Nouri listened but, as usual, was quiet. That was his way. Let everyone get their frustrations off their chests and then they would all get on with life. No one expected these boys to learn full time indefinitely but it was a great thing for right now. It allowed them to make up for all the years they had slackened off and then, hopefully, they would re-enter the workforce with a different mindset. Besides, he had more pressing concerns, like how to pay the rising costs of maintaining the Bet Midrash. Ahi Ezer wasn't a wealthy congregation, and since many of the congregants were only grudgingly tolerating the Bet Midrash, raising money to have it continue was bound to be difficult.

And then, one day, something changed.

The Bet Midrash was hopping. Fifteen to twenty young men were learning together, loudly debating their points back and forth. In walked a stranger, an obviously Ashkenazic Rabbi, complete with a full black beard, long coat, and round Rabbinic hat. Everyone stopped, and rose in respect.

"Excuse me," the man looked uncomfortable at having drawn so much attention, "I'm looking for the Rosh HaYeshiva. Is he here?"

"Sure," answered Maurice Zalta. "He has a room in the back."

The man nodded and walked out in that direction. The young men looked around at each other curiously and then went back to their learning.

Fifteen to twenty young men were learning together, loudly debating their points back and forth...

Everyone stopped, and rose in respect.

Left side, front to back: Clement Soffer, Morris Mizrahi, Mosie Shamah, David Esses, Eddie Zafrani, Morris Srour, Murray Dewek, Denis Dewek, Joe Bijo. Right side, front to back: Raymond Heiney, Abraham Dura, Irwin Dayan, Murray Maslaton, Sonny Setton, Billy Mizrahi, Joe Benon (obscured), Mickey Carey, unknown.

About fifteen minutes later, the stranger emerged from the back room and, of course, everyone rose again. Even though they had no idea who he was, he looked like a Rabbi and their ingrained Sephardic training meant: Stand up for the Rabbi.

This time, the Rabbi just passed through the room and left.

Meanwhile, Obadya came out of his office and walked to the desk at the head of the room. He tucked a slim piece of paper into the blotter on the desk. Then he went on to deliver the day's *shiur*. When he finished, he walked out of the room and back to his office. Maurice noticed that he left the paper in the blotter and he could not resist glancing at it as he passed by. His eyes widened in surprise.

It was a check, for $5,400. A veritable fortune in those days.

Who in the world was giving out so much money for their Bet Midrash?

Rabbi Eisenberg (1916-1976). "He was incredibly unassuming. I once asked him about his line of business. 'Boats,' he answered. I later learned that his casual reference referred to major steamship construction!" recalled Mr. Irwin Dayan.

"His name is Rabbi Rafael Eisenberg," reported one of the boys. "He made major money in the Far East and he uses it to support yeshivot. He heard about us through Eli Safdieh — you know, Joe Maslaton's son-in-law. They do business together. They got to talking and this Rabbi Eisenberg mentioned how he spent the war years in the Phillipines where he prayed with a *minyan* of Syrian Jews and was impressed with their sincerity. So Eli tells him to go check out the Syrian community in Bensonhurst. The rest is history."[18]

Rabbi Eisenberg was an unusual person. He and his brother, Shaul, had been part of a wave of German-Jewish refugees that escaped to Shanghai just before World War II. They built up a business empire in the Far East and became fabulously wealthy. Shaul, the more famous of the two,

---

18. It's also possible that he was referred to the Bet Midrash through Rabbi Aharon Kotler. Rabbi Eisenberg was a big supporter of many yeshivot during those years, including Lakewood (ed.).

Rabbi Aharon Kotler (1891-1962), Rosh Yeshiva of Kletzk and then of Lakewood, speaking in learning

became an international tycoon, particularly venerated by the Chinese for his success and generosity. Rabbi Eisenberg was a quieter personality, whose creativity and drive was seen in his religious zeal.

Rabbi Eisenberg owned two houses, one in Monsey and the other in the newly built "Squaretown." Both homes were large but very plain; nothing indicated that their owner was wealthy. The home in Monsey came first, but when Rabbi Eisenberg heard about the New Square project, he was pulled to there as well, and for good reason. Squaretown was a home for idealists. The village was barely built (the post office and shul were housed at the same location). The chassidim who moved there were pioneers, willing to live without the amenities of large Jewish communities in order to create this self-contained Jewish island where the norms of *der alter heim* (Old Country) would rule. The men wore *shtreimlach*,[19] all the married women covered their hair, and the day was structured to keep the genders separate: When the boys were playing outside, the girls were home; and when the boys were in *cheder* the girls were playing outside.

Rabbi Eisenberg fit right into Squaretown. His life was about how best to serve Hashem and raise his children to do the same. He home-schooled his sons, imparting to them his own unique method in learning Mishnayot. Together with his equally idealistic wife, they raised nine daughters to be so refined that when one walked into their home, it seemed as if no one lived there, rather than a gaggle of girls.

---

19. In the 1950's, there were still very few *shtreimel* wearers in America, even in Boro Park and Williamsburg.

He visited the new yeshiva and was impressed with the sincerity of the Sephardic youth. He sat down with Nouri and they spoke at length about the needs of the community and how to help. He began to come to Bensonhurst regularly, to see how the Bet Midrash was doing and to give occasional classes.

"Reb Aharon is coming!"

The news spread fast. Though most of the Syrian community had not a clue as to who Rabbi Aharon Kotler was, the boys knew that a world recognized *gadol hador* was coming to see their progress.

They were excited.

They were ecstatic.

They were working their heads off.

When the great day finally arrived, they were shaking from fear.

The main sanctuary of Ahi Ezer was set up for the occasion. The slight stage in the front, where the *heichal* stood, was set up with chairs for the Rabbanim. Hacham Murad sat there, alongside Hacham Yaakob Kassin, Rabbi Aharon Kotler, and Rabbi Nesanel Quinn. The young men being tested sat at a bridge table, on the level below. Behind them sat the younger boys, the high-school-age students of the Bet Midrash. They were almost as tense as the boys being tested; they so badly wanted them to do well.

Many people of the community showed up to witness this historic event: The Ashkenazic *gadol hador* had come to a small Syrian shul to test their budding scholars. There was a palpable sense of awe and reverence in the room.

Rabbi Aharon Kotler had arrived.

Mosie Shamah, Dennis Dweck, Billy Mizrahi, Elliot Menahem, and Eddie Zafrani were some of the boys fielding questions on *Mesechet Kiddushin* and *Gittin*. They had been told which parts to prepare, but only after the *farher* (oral test) would they know if they had prepared well. For an hour and a half, Rav Aharon asked questions and the boys answered.[20]

With each question they answered, the boys sat up a bit straighter. They were doing fine, better than fine. Their hard work had paid off. They had proved to themselves that they could excel at real Torah learning. They were quietly euphoric, buoyed by their accomplishments.

Something momentous had occurred.

The Syrian community would never be the same.

---

20. Hacham Yaakob Kassin also asked questions and, at one point, the boys asked questions of Rav Aharon.

Chapter 32:
PAINFUL GROWTH, BENSONHURST, 1957

"Izzy," Billy hollered, "do you have any idea what is going on? He's crazy, they're crazy! The whole thing is nuts!"

"Whoa, Billy, calm down. Come, let's go out to the porch." Nouri steered the man outside. *Maybe he will speak more quietly when he realizes that the whole street can hear him.*

"*Moreh Nebuchim*!" he yelled. "Have you ever heard anything so crazy?"

And I thought he'd be quieter outside, Nouri sighed.

"You learn plenty. Have you ever learned *Moreh Nebuchim*? *Moreh Nebuchim* is for… I don't know, maybe Hacham Murad or Hacham Yaakob. But these kids? Why is he teaching them this stuff?"

But you don't want them to learn any other "stuff" either, right?

"And learning full time, it's crazy! Ely was just accepted to college. He wants to give it all up. And if I don't let him, he has threatened to enlist in the air force, a four-year program!"

Nouri settled into his chair. *This is going to be a long night…*

For hours, Nouri listened as Billy ranted. They knew each other from the neighborhood, but Billy was a Magen David congregant and they didn't have much to do with each other… until his son joined the Bet Medrash. Now Billy was a regular visitor, letting off enough steam to power a train.

And he wasn't the only one. Esther Dayan began to dread any knock on the door; it was sure to be an irate parent taking out his frustrations on her husband. But Nouri never lost his cool. He listened patiently, clucked sympathetically, and interjected with an appropriate comment here and there.

The building on West 4th Street that Rabbi Eisenberg bought for the yeshiva

Overall, he felt bad that so many people were upset at the overwhelming interest in Torah learning that was shaking up the community. But that was just too bad. The community was heading downhill out of ignorance and only Torah learning could reverse that trend.

On the other hand, some of their complaints were valid. This business about teaching *Moreh Nebuchim* bothered him as well. And there were other disturbing things going on. But he and Rabbi Eisenberg agreed that while nothing is perfect, Obadya was doing a good job. At the rate that the yeshiva was growing, they would soon outgrow the Annex. Rabbi Eisenberg had already put a down payment on a new building for the yeshiva.

Nouri hoped that the complaints would die down.

That wishful optimism was soon dashed.

"He brought Hacham Murad a potato chip and asked him what *beracha* to make on it. He knew the *beracha*, but he also knew that Hacham Murad doesn't eat potato chips and would not know what it was. He wanted to trip him up…"

"He asked Hacham Yaakob a question on the Gemara, not because he wanted to hear his answer but because he wanted to rip apart his answer…"

Good boys, respectful young men, were showing a defiant streak, and their unsavory behavior was being traced back to their charismatic Rosh Yeshiva.

Painful Growth, Bensonhurst, 1957

Some of the boys outside Ahi Ezer. L-R: Abraham Dura, David Esses, Mosie Shamah, Isaac Churba, Eddie Zafrani, Billy Mizrahi, Maurice Zalta, Uriel Ariyeh, Denis Dewek, Emmanuel Ariyeh.

As Obadya became comfortable in his position, he became convinced that he was indispensable to his students and to the community. Then, his coarse ways emerged. At first his students were so bewitched by him, they didn't pick up on the nuances of his crude behavior. Rather than recognizing his lack of respect for the *hachamim* as a blatant character flaw, they admired Obadya's "courage" in standing up to the old school. They began to follow his lead, to take up his battle cry, even though it went against the awe and reverence for *hachamim* that was intrinsic to who they were.

"Something has to give," Nouri muttered under his breath. He was emotionally exhausted and confused. Just the night before, he had had to exert damage control yet again.

Then, one Friday night, as the extended Maslaton family came for their weekly blessing from Hacham Murad and *Stetta*, Obadya made an inexcusable comment, that was publicly embarrassing to one of Hacham Murad's children sitting there. Nouri's face turned ashen as he stared at the young man. Obadya smirked back brazenly and then breezed arrogantly out of the room.

Nouri was shaking from emotion. He walked over to his father-in-law.

"*Ami* (my father-in-law), I'm so sorry that such a comment was made in your presence..." Nouri grew choked up and could barely get the words out.

"Sh... it will be fine. Don't worry..."

But Nouri was thoroughly shaken up. He was aghast that the person he had brought into the community had publicly embarrassed someone so dear to him.

When Shabbat ended, Nouri was still torn. Should he fire Obadya for his unacceptable behavior? The community was down his back to get rid of him anyway, though he wasn't convinced that their reasons were valid. And if firing Obadya put an end to the Torah learning that had taken root in the community, was that the correct thing to do? Yet how could he allow good people to be publicly shamed?

He decided to gently encourage Obadya to transfer to the building that Rabbi Eisenberg had bought. At the same time, he would inform him that Ahi Ezer didn't have the funds to continue paying his salary. He wanted to ease him out of the community, not by expelling him but by forcing him to become independent.

He was relieved when Obadya didn't put up a fight.

Gradually, the boys also became disillusioned with Obadya as he alienated them, one after another, even as they continued to learn with him. Rabbi Eisenberg realized that he had placed his faith in someone undeserving and he stopped his funding, though he continued to come to Ahi Ezer to give classes in *Tur* and *Shulhan Aruch*. Eventually, the entire yeshiva fell apart. Obadya left America and later aligned himself with controversial movements. Even his biggest followers among the Syrian community distanced themselves from him.

Nouri never spoke about this disturbing period. He was a doer, not a talker, certainly not after the fact, when he saw nothing to be gained from rehashing the pain of the past. He always took the positive parts of life and focused on them… and there always were positive parts. In this case, he looked to capitalize on the excitement for learning that had taken hold of the community and he was certain that with time and patience, something good would come of it.[21] Likewise, he was grateful for his new friendship with Rabbi Rafael Eisenberg and the wonderful impact he had on the community.

In the community at large, there were many mixed emotions in the aftermath of the Obadya debacle. Some people felt validated: Didn't Obadya's fall indicate that religious extremism was a problem?

Those who were more honest with themselves were understandably confused: My son became more religious, is that inherently bad? Where was the ideal middle of the road?

---

21. While this was a period of tremendous pain, it was also a catalyst for growth. Perhaps this was partially in the merit of Nouri's pure desire to see Torah flourish in his community. Even among those community members who were angry at Nouri for bringing a "brainwasher" into their community, no one doubted that he acted sincerely *l'shem Shamayim* (ed.).

Painful Growth, Bensonhurst, 1957

Then there were Obadya's students, sincere young men who had believed in him. Some of them felt betrayed; they had been dazzled by a witty and brilliant person who proved to be of questionable character. They were ashamed that in following his lead, they had acted out of character. They found it difficult to make amends to those to whom they had been disrespectful.

Others were more resilient. They didn't blame themselves for being taken in by a fake; after all, Rabbi Avraham Kalmanowitz and Rabbi Aharon Kotler had also seen potential in him. They decided to take whatever was good, and run with it. They were not going to throw away the Torah they had learned, nor the perspective that they had gained: *Torah lishma* **was** the way to become a *talmid hacham* and the Ashkenazic yeshivot **did** have exceptional methodology in fostering that knowledge.

Perhaps it was Rabbi Aharon Kotler's visit that infused them with strength, or maybe it was their own *zechut haTorah*, or their own *mesirut nefesh*, but, overall, the young men who had been a part of the Bet Midrash continued to grow in Torah knowledge and religious observance. Those who left college or their jobs didn't return. They headed to other yeshivot such as those in Baltimore, Vineland, and Lakewood.

They returned to Bensonhurst with a whole new value system. The boys were on fire and they looked to recruit younger boys to yeshivot as well. Rabbi Eisenberg invited the older boys to bring younger boys to Monsey, to his home on Saddle River Road, right near Bais Medrash Elyon. There, they would see a yeshiva in action, without having to commit to attending. Soon there was a whole group of Sephardic boys camping out at the Eisenberg home by night while learning on the lawn of Bais Medrash Elyon by day.[22] It was an unbelievable experience, and most of those who participated went on to join regular yeshiva programs.

By far, the most popular Ashkenazic yeshiva in the community was Ner Israel.

Mosie Shamah was the first to discover Ner Israel Yeshiva and realize that this might be just the right answer for his community. The yeshiva had arrangements for boys who wanted to take college courses. Parents who had spent a whole year fighting their children who had quit college or abandoned jobs would finally feel vindicated… if they agreed to let their boys go. One large drawback was the tuition issue. Unlike the Ahi Ezer Bet Midrash program, Ner Israel had a large campus with a dormitory and lunchroom. Parents would have to pay tuition plus room and board, a hefty sum compared to city college (which was free) and living at home.

---

22. Some of those who participated in this summer retreat were Charlie Semah and Mark Mishan.

Sephardic boys who attended Ner Israel with the help of the Scholarship Fund. The fund was established with the help of Joe Shamah, from Ozar HaTorah, in conjunction with Rabbi Neuberger of Ner Israel. They divided the duties between the two Sephardic communities but the meetings were held in Ahi Ezer. Nouri Dayan and Dave Bibi represented Ahi Ezer while Joe Kassin and Joe Tawil represented Magen David. Later, the main fundraisers were Leon Sutton and Morris Srour. "Eli Shamah, Joe's son, told our family that we cannot imagine how much my grandfather, Mr. Nouri Dayan, fought for the establishment of the scholarship fund," noted Rabbi Yosef Ozeirey.

Back row, L-R: Yitzchak Srour, Leon Sutton, Dave Bibi, Rabbi Neuberger, Joe Tawil, Elis Jacob, Joe Kassin. Middle row: Charlie Semah, David Dewek, Morris Srour, David Esses, Alex Abadi, Mike Antebi. Front row: Eli Ariyeh, Eliot Barry, Yaakov Yisrael, Sammy Kassin, Mark Mishan, Max Maslaton.

So Mosie approached interested community members with the idea of creating a scholarship fund for boys who wanted to attend a yeshiva.

And who was one of the main fundraisers for the scholarship fund? Nouri Dayan.

Painful Growth, Bensonhurst, 1957 /

Chapter 33:

EGYPT, 1957

While Torah was finally taking root in the Syrian community of New York, thousands of miles away, Jews were leaving places where Torah had been learned for thousands of years. All over the Middle East, Jews fled. Most headed for the new State of Israel. Many came to America.

In 1957, the first wave of Egyptian Jews arrived on American shores.

Their arrival posed questions that would take years to answer: Were the Syrian and Egyptian Jews similar enough to meld together as one community or would their cultural differences keep them apart? And who would bolster the new refugee community until they stood securely on their own?

These questions began back in Egypt.

The answers unfolded in Bensonhurst, New York.

The full moon glowed, illuminating the tranquil Nile River as it flowed softly to the junction where it emptied into the Mediterranean Sea. Soft laughter serenaded the many boats that floated lazily along the calm waters. Sailing on the Nile at night, swimming the Mediterranean by day — such was the life of upper Egyptian society. And the Jews were an intrinsic part of it.

How did this come to pass?

The construction of the Suez Canal (1859-1869) brought foreign funds, foreign citizens, and foreign influence pouring into Egypt.[23] Unsurprisingly,

---

23. This was part of the modernization of Egypt in the late 1800's, which also bankrupted the country, resulting in it becoming a British protectorate. Nonetheless, the Suez Canal remained a magnet for business, creating an unusual situation where Egypt drew a high percentage of non-Muslim immigrants — British, French, Italian, Spanish — who felt secure and empowered in Egypt, though they never became citizens. Understandably, the Jews felt the same way (*The Lost World of the Egyptian Jews*, pp. 8-9). By 1907, one-quarter

it also attracted the Jews. By 1897, the Egyptian Jewish population — which had remained a steady 5,000 souls for decades — increased to 25,000 people. Later on, they were joined by (mainly Syrian) Jews fleeing from the chaos of World War I. They pushed the numbers up to 60,000 Jews.

These immigrants encountered a fast-growing European society that was cosmopolitan, cultured, and comfortable. Foreign businessmen, diplomats, and their families lived in Egypt and enjoyed a very high standard of living, in elaborate mansions, with plenty of domestic help and time for leisure activities. They spurred the proliferation of country clubs and opera houses, unknown entities in the poorer neighboring Muslim countries. While few very wealthy Jewish families shared this elite life, the new Jewish immigrants fueled the growth of the solid middle class, people who earned a respectable living, respectable enough to enjoy a modified version of "the good life."

By the 1940's, the Egyptian Jewish community was close to 100,000 strong. While they lived mainly in Jewish areas and socialized among one another, they were far more Western than the rest of Sephardic Jewry: All children, girls as well as boys, received a well-rounded education, including fluency in at least one foreign language, usually French. Middle-class Egyptian Jews lived in large houses or apartments, with maids and servants, and plenty of time for cultural events and leisure activities. They went swimming indoors and played tennis outside throughout most of the year. For two months they vacationed along the Mediterranean coast where the beautiful sea met the Nile River. Whenever the moon was out, so were they, sailing down the Nile, gazing up at the luminous orb that cast its light over the calm waters.

Life in Egypt was warm and wonderful — and spiritually bereft.

The Jews of Egypt did not see it that way.

By 1948, only a small minority of Egyptian Jewry was truly religious. This had nothing to do with poverty that necessitated working on Shabbat, nor was religious persecution an issue. Life was simply so good, people saw no need to hold onto the ways of the old generation. They were too busy with their theaters, operas, and country clubs to wonder if, perhaps, life could be more meaningful if they paid a little more attention to their Judaism.

Yet there was almost no intermarriage, and atheism existed only among the avid Communists. They were also proudly Jewish and invoked the name of the Almighty many times throughout the day. They believed in G-d. They were certain that He was happy with their pleasant and moral lives.

---

of the population of Alexandria was non-Egyptian (*The Jews of the Middle East and North Africa in Modern Times*, p. 42).

Socially, the Jews remained apart, but this was mainly by choice. Those who wished to mingle among the gentiles did so. Jews were successful in almost every profession and every business. Their mark on the Egyptian economy was disproportionate to their numbers. They wielded influence in the government and felt completely at home, appreciated and accepted, in Egypt.

All this changed in 1948 with the formation of the State of Israel.[24]

But Egyptian Jewry refused to believe that their idyllic life was ending. Indeed, the situation remained quiet for Egyptian Jewry for a few years. It would take a riot in Cairo, a government coup, and the rise of Nasser to make them face reality.

In 1956, Israel launched the Sinai Campaign.[25]

Though the actual military offensive only lasted a few hours, the Egyptian military defeat created a very anti-Semitic climate in Egypt, even months later. Unruly Arabs kept attacking the Jewish ghetto (a de facto ghetto, home to the old, indigenous Egyptian community), specifically targeting the poorest people. These Jews were confused and defenseless. They needed help, badly. Rabbi Abraham Choueka was appointed by the elderly Chief Rabbi of Egypt, Rabbi Nahum Effendi, to deal with the latest crisis.

Most Egyptian Jews had some connection to a foreign country: Brazil, Peru, Cuba, the Congo, Australia, anywhere. Rabbi Choueka had his workers dig up any connection and then go to the various embassies to arrange visas or affidavits in order for the Egyptian Jews to legally enter those countries. Then he purchased tickets and shipped these shell-shocked Jews out of Egypt. After several months, the Egyptian government realized that all these "tourists" were not coming back and they were outraged. The government had no problem expelling Jews, when *they* wanted and how *they* wanted. This business of slipping out from under the government eye was unacceptable. They warned the Rabbinate to stop their activities, which they did, for a while.

But the living conditions for Egyptian Jewry were worsening.

When Nasser first rose to power, he maintained the old Egyptian policy differentiating between Zionists and Jews: Jews were friends, Zionists

---

24. During the Israeli War of Independence, the Jewish quarter in Cairo was firebombed and looted and over 1,000 suspected Zionists were imprisoned. As a result, 20,000 Jews left Egypt (ibid., p. 428). Nonetheless, Mrs. Sara (Choueka) Malka maintains: "Even after 1948, we had a very good life in Egypt. We kept a low profile. Men and boys would not wear a yarmulke in the street and we didn't display our *sefarim* or religious objects but we did not live in fear. We lived a quiet, comfortable life."
25. Egypt had always denied Israel the use of the Suez Canal. In 1956, they also cut off their access to the Gulf of Aqaba and created a military pact with Saudi Arabia and Jordan. In response, Israel launched the Sinai Campaign.

were enemies.[26] Ironically, their method of identifying Zionists ended up targeting religious Jews, many of whom had no Zionistic affiliation at all. Any Jew who learned Hebrew books, spoke Hebrew, or acted identifiably Jewish was considered a Zionist. That was why the government expelled the Ahaba Ve'Ahva Yeshiva and allowed riots in the Jewish ghetto. Westernized Jews were initially left alone, unless they held British or French citizenship. This changed when the lightning victory that Nasser had anticipated turned into a humiliating defeat.[27]

Frustrated by his military and financial losses, Nasser found an attractive way to fill his coffers and take revenge on the "Zionist enemy." He passed legislation which "encouraged" Jews (now synonymous with Zionists) to leave Egypt while requiring them to abandon their property to the Egyptian government. Suddenly, not only poor ghetto-Jews were fleeing Egypt.

While most upper-class Jews left by choice, they couldn't take out any of their wealth. Their departure was a psychological blow: If these powerful and wealthy Jews were leaving, then surely the poor and downtrodden must leave.

Rabbi Abraham Choueka hastily summoned his staff back to the Rabbinate. "I applied to the Swiss embassy to have all of you affiliated with the Red Cross. The paperwork just came in. As Red Cross representatives, we have every right to help Egyptian Jews visit other countries. So, let's get back to work."

Clement Soffer was part of the group busy saving lives.

Until, one day, his own life was on the line.

---

26. It is noteworthy that years earlier the Egyptian Rabbis tried to distance themselves from the Zionist movement, as they were afraid that their community would suffer from Arab resentment (*The Jews of the Middle East and North Africa*, p. 427).

27. Egyptian air power was 60 percent greater than that of Israel. Nasser had good reason to believe that he would easily defeat Israel, even with British and French aid. Through much diplomatic arm-twisting, Israel agreed to give up the Sinai Peninsula and allowed Nasser to present his defeat as a victory. "Nasser won every public relations battle and lost every military one" (*History of the Jews*, p. 534).

Chapter 34:
ALONE IN ATHENS, 1957

Clement leaned against the window and watched his fellow passengers stream off the airplane and onto solid ground. He fingered his *laissez-passe* (travel document) in his pocket. *A good-bye present from my beloved Egypt,* he thought ruefully. *But at least I'm out of jail...*

His feet still hurt from the many beatings that he endured when he refused to sign the paper admitting he was a Zionist. To sign the paper was a death sentence. They would hang the "Zionist traitor" in the street for everyone to see. The charges were false, but if the government wanted him punished for his activities, they would find a way to punish him. And then, miraculously, he was released, with the document that he held in his hand, stamped: Clement Soffer. Stateless. Dangerous to public security.

That, the clothing he wore, and $5, were all he owned. No wonder he wasn't rushing to disembark. Where would he go? But as the plane emptied, he followed the crowd.

"We'll figure it out," he muttered to his friend who had been expelled along with him. They proceeded further.

"Hey, you! Soffer!"

Who knows my name? Clement whirled around to the direction of the voice.

A young man with a Magen David armband was running toward them. He reached them, panting, "I'm Joe, from the HIAS. The Swiss Embassy notified us about your eviction. I'm here to help you. We arranged for a special affidavit for you from the State of Israel. It declares you the responsibility of Israel and allows you a two-week stay in any country. If that country wants to evict you for any reason, they will send you back to Israel, not Egypt. How does that sound?"

It sounded just fine to Clement. With his "danger to society" *laissez-passe,* he was likely to be shipped back to Egypt for crossing the street the wrong way. And if he returned to Egypt, he knew what awaited him there. This affidavit essentially declared him an Israeli citizen visiting another country. The question remained: Which country did he want to go to? And, with $5 in his pocket, how was he going to get there?

As if reading his mind, Joe interjected, "The HIAS will pay your passage either to America or to Israel. Just tell me where you want to go."

Clement could hardly believe his good fortune. America — Malibu, Los Angeles, Beverley Hills — all the glamorous places he had seen in the movies. And now he would get to go there, free!

Clement Soffer

"I would really love to go to America," Clement answered.

Two weeks later, Clement wasn't so sure.

I cannot believe this.

Clement stared up at the drably painted room he shared with five other boys. He closed his eyes and tried to remember the elegant home he had grown up in, with maids at his beck and call, and a luxurious country club just a few blocks away. He had come to America expecting at least that level of comfort and here he was, in a dormitory, sleeping on an uncomfortable bed, eating strange new foods, and learning Torah all day!

"It's good for you," Rabbi Kalmanowitz reassured him. "First you will study Torah, and then you will be more prepared to go out into the world."

Tongue-tied in the presence of such a holy man, courageous Clement — who had just defied the Egyptian government, spent time in jail, and stoically boarded a plane to Athens with no valid port of residence — remained quiet.

I can't believe I did that, the boy ruminated. In the crowded dormitory room, on Avenue R and East 9th Street, his stomach rumbling and his head spinning, he wished he had been more vocal. Learning Torah had sounded very nice back in Egypt when the Rabbi had visited the community. It remained an attractive option when he came from Athens with nowhere to go. But now that he experienced three weeks of life in the Mirrer Yeshiva, he had just one thought: This is not for me.

The Mirrer Yeshiva dormitory, a happy place... but not for Clement Soffer.

He is a great man, this Rabbi, Clement let his thoughts run wild, *He loves Torah. So do I. Only, I cannot take this type of life. I need to catch up in my schooling, improve my English, refresh my math, perfect my business skills. I need to get a job and make some money. I cannot be a penniless refugee, learning like a scholar while living like a beggar. It's just not for me.*

He leapt out of bed, out of the dormitory building, intent on putting Mirrer Yeshiva out of his life. *He means well, the Rabbi, but I have to bring the rest of my family here. Why should I be all alone? Why should they stay back in Egypt when everyone is leaving? For how much longer will they be safe there?*

He walked out of the dormitory and stopped.

Right or left? What will it be?

He shrugged his shoulders involuntarily and turned right, wandering aimlessly down the street. He crossed Ocean Parkway and kept going. It was an overcast December afternoon. The sky was slowly turning dusky grey and the crisp weather was getting colder by the minute. All Clement had for warmth was a thin raincoat without a lining. All he had left from his initial $5 was 15 cents, not even enough to buy a sandwich. He entered a city park and walked around in circles, thoroughly self-absorbed.

Where can I go? I have no family, no friends, no money, no job. I speak the language, but not very well. I'm all alone... On that very short, winter evening, night came quickly. The darkness did little to alleviate the fog of confusion that had engulfed him. He spotted a park bench and decided that it would be his bed. *There is even an overhanging tree for shelter,* he noted before drifting off into a fitful sleep.

The next morning he woke up cold, confused, and hungry. He spent the day wandering around the neighborhood. By evening, he ended up back in the park — colder, hungrier, and even more confused. *But I'm not going back,* he thought grimly as he settled down for another night on the same park bench.

Cold, cold, cold! A startling wet something fell on his face. Clement opened his eyes and tried to orient himself. *It's not rain... could it be snow?* He had never seen snow in his life but the light flurries were a novelty that he could do without. He lay back on his bench, wearily hoping that the night would be bearable. He tried playing mind tricks, convincing himself that the coldness that pierced his bones was actually the same bite that he felt back in Egypt when the temperature outside was 120 degrees in the shade.

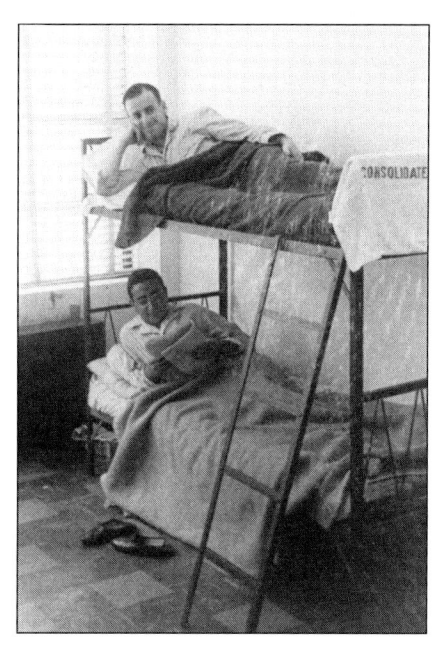

Morris Zafrani is on the top bed. Pinchas Nissim is on the bottom.

I'm not cold. I'm incredibly hot. Extremely hot. Painfully hot. In this way, he lulled himself to sleep. Dawn nudged him awake. Hunger made him weak. He felt glued to the bench.

I can't move... I have to move. I'll wash my face. That will wake me up. Clement walked over to a water fountain and squirted water into his hands.

"Hey kid. Waddaya doin?" A slim, clean-shaven youth began walking over to him. "That water's too cold. You can't wash your face with such cold water, in this freezing weather."

Clement looked back defiantly. "It's all I have."

The man looked him over, curiously. "You've got an accent. Where are you from?"

"I'm from Egypt and I'm looking for a job."

"You're from Egypt? What's your name?"

"Clement Soffer."

"Eddie Zafrani. I'm Syrian."

"Well, my grandfather was a Sultan, also Syrian."

"Listen, three blocks away from here, there's a whole community of Syrian Jews. Let me give you directions to the synagogue. It's called Magen David. I'm sure that someone there can help you."

Alone in Athens, 1957 / **285**

Clement followed Eddie's directions and went to Magen David Synagogue. They were in the middle of prayers, so Clement joined them. Afterward, he went over to the Rabbi, and asked him for help. Rabbi Kassin was a very clear-thinking, sharp person. Within a few minutes he had Clement's whole story out in the open.

"You left the Mirrer Yeshiva? Why?" the Rabbi was too agitated to even wait for an answer. "It's a wonderful place. They give you food and clothing and all you have to do is learn Torah. What can be better? Besides, you are 16 1/2. You cannot legally work in America. With your affidavit, you cannot even *stay* in America. Go back to the yeshiva. Rabbi Kalmanowitz will take care of everything."

Clement stared silently at the dignified Rabbi in front of him, too upset to allow his tangled thoughts to come out coherently. He realized he stood in front of a great man, a special man, who only wanted a better religious future for him. *But I'm all alone here. I can't do it. I can't just sit all day in yeshiva — nothing goes in. I'm too distracted. I need to get a job and bring my family over.*

The 16-year-old boy who, only a few weeks earlier, was cajoling and bribing government officials, stood dumbly, unable to get one word out. He wondered what the Rabbi made of him, this skinny little kid, who had approached him with confidence, and was now suddenly mute.

Rabbi Kassin threw up his hands. "Try Rabbi Aaron Choueka on Ocean Parkway. He is also from Egypt. Maybe he can help you."

Clement walked out of the synagogue, thoroughly frustrated. *Why, why, why? Why could he not just help me find a job?*

Magen David was on 67th Street. Clement walked down the block over to 66th Street. The weakness of his 48-hour fast was getting to him. His eyes began to tear and he couldn't be bothered to rub the drops away.

"Hey kid, why you cryin?" a woman asked as she threw out her garbage.

Clement shrugged, not yet ready to trust his voice.

"C'mon. Tell me how I can help you. Why are you so upset?"

The words tumbled out of his mouth before he could stop them. "I have a problem. I went to the Rabbi, and he wants me to go back to the yeshiva. But I don't want to go back to the yeshiva…"[28]

"Sonny," the woman said with a smile, "you look hungry. You look dirty. You probably have not taken a shower in days. Come upstairs. Take a shower. Eat some breakfast. And then we'll talk."

Clement stared uncomprehendingly. *This woman is going to allow me, a stranger, to come into her house? And take a shower? And eat breakfast?*

---

28. "Now, looking back, I wish I would have stayed [in Mirrer Yeshiva]. Maybe [my life] would have taken a different direction. But when you are young, impatient, and you want to build a future…," lamented Mr. Clement Soffer, explaining that the Rabbis were really correct.

She motioned him inside and, almost in a trance, Clement complied. He took a shower and, over breakfast, explained more about his situation. As he spoke, Sophie Maslaton, Joe's wife, began dialing a phone number.

"Hello, I got a situation here…"

Phones then being what they were, Clement heard the voice on the other end, even though the receiver was far from his ears. "Hold the boy. Tell him that I'm coming to visit him tonight."

Clement was mystified. Should he wait a whole day for this man to come see him? He was exhausted from his two days of living under the stars with no food or shelter. He decided to spend the day resting in the Maslaton house.

That evening, a slim man walked into the house and greeted Mrs. Maslaton in a familiar manner. Clement rose from his chair uneasily and waited to be addressed. The man turned to face the boy and held out his hand. "Isidore Dayan. How can I help you?"

Clement looked deeply into those warm brown eyes and hesitantly extended a hand in return. Nouri clasped his hand in a firm grasp, and motioned the boy to sit beside him. Then he just looked at him — smiling, encouraging, caring.

Clement relaxed into his chair. *Finally, someone who understands. He is really going to help me.*

Nouri was as good as his word. He patiently listened as Clement recounted his saga of wandering, injecting appropriate sympathy. While he probably agreed with Rabbi Kalmanowitz and Rabbi Kassin, and would have liked to see Clement return to the yeshiva, he realized that Clement wasn't changing his mind. And he couldn't allow the boy to spend another night on a park bench.

"For tonight, you will stay here," Nouri decided. "By tomorrow, we will have a more permanent arrangement organized for you."

By the next day, Nouri had leased a room for Clement on 66th Street and enrolled him in classes to improve his English skills. He gave him a stipend, so that he would not feel like a penniless refugee, and then had him legally transferred from Mirrer Yeshiva to Ahi Ezer Yeshiva.[29]

"Make sure to come around," Nouri instructed him.

And indeed, many Shabbat meals in the Dayan home featured Clement as one of their guests. But that wasn't all. Nouri took care of all of Clement's needs for a year and a half, until he was able to legally work. He made sure he had food, board, and clothing and that he was being productive and acclimating to American society. He also introduced him to

---

29. This was the same year that the Ahi Ezer Bet Midrash, a government-recognized institution, had been formed. Initially, some parents were in favor of their sons enrolling in order to get a divinity exemption from the army. Ahi Ezer gave many boys divinity exemptions.

the Ahi Ezer community, where he was warmly welcomed. Reuben and Esther Bibi practically adopted him as a son.

A year and a half later, Clement's parents and siblings joined him in America. By then, he was old enough to legally work. He had everything he had been missing: family, friends, and a respectable income. He entered the business world, married, and became involved in his community, but he never forgot his humble beginnings, or Nouri Dayan's kindness.

Clement Soffer was Nouri's first encounter with a fresh Egyptian refugee. His story indicated that many would soon follow. The Soffers were part of a steady flow of Egyptian Jews emigrating from Egypt to America between 1957 and 1958. While the Suez Crisis had been the force that kicked them out of Egypt, it was, of all things, the Hungarian Revolution that enabled them to enter America.

Once again, the man behind the scenes was Rabbi Avraham Kalmanowitz.

Rabbi Kalmanowitz had been lobbying for the welfare of the Jews in Arab countries since the formation of the State of Israel in 1948, independent of his involvement with Ozar HaTorah. He was afraid that without international intervention, Arab rage against the State could provoke a holocaust of Sephardic Jewry in similar proportions to what had happened to Jews in Nazi-occupied Europe.[30]

Yet bringing these Jews to America wasn't so simple. Immigration quotas didn't allow for the mass arrivals of foreigners, unless they were considered refugees. The 1951 Geneva Convention defined a refugee as a person stranded in a foreign country with a legitimate fear of returning to his country of origin. This didn't apply to people residing in their countries of citizenship who feared for their lives while living in their home countries. In addition, the laws adopted at that convention were specifically designed for refugees from the Holocaust and were not legally applicable to refugees of other lands.

Then came the Hungarian Revolution.

Because of the drama of the event and the many political considerations involved, the United Nations granted refugee status to the Hungarian refugees who had fled to Austria and Yugoslavia and were stranded in those countries because they feared returning to Hungary even after the Revolution ended. This was the first group of non-Holocaust refugees to receive this classification, which ultimately enabled them to immigrate to America and other countries.

---

30. The 1948 pogrom in Aleppo, where mobs of Arab rioters spontaneously ganged up on the Jewish community there, burning down all their *battei k'nessiot* and *Sifrei Torah*, was the catalyst for his involvement. From then on, Rabbi Kalmanowitz continuously lobbied the United States government to recognize the danger facing Jews in Arab lands and to preempt a holocaust.

As usual, Rabbi Kalmanowitz saw an opportunity and jumped at it. He lobbied to confer this refugee status upon Jews from Arab countries as well.[31] Then he let the Egyptian community know that if they left Egypt, and remained stateless for a year, they would eventually be admitted into America as refugees. Thousands of Jews began leaving Egypt. Many of them chose to be stateless in the country whose language and culture was most familiar to them: *Vive la France!*

---

31. This had not been an issue for the young boys whom Rabbi Kalmanowitz brought over as foreign students. There, the only problem they faced was that their student visas were limited to four years, after which Rabbi Kalmanowitz convinced the American government to accept certification from Israel that the boys would be welcome there, essentially ensuring that they would never become a burden on American society.

Chapter 35:

BEYOND PARIS, 1957

Sara Choueka peered outside the window of her Paris boarding school and watched the people walking leisurely by.

Ah, Paris! It was all that she had dreamed and more.

When they had received the letter from her brother Menachem, who had gone to America with Rabbi Kalmanowitz as part of the Moroccan/Egyptian group of boys who came to Mirrer Yeshiva, they had been surprised. Would America actually admit them as "stateless" tourists? Yet Hashem's Hand continued to lead them from one destination to another…

"Enjoy every moment," her father counseled. "When will we have another opportunity to see Greece… Italy… Switzerland… France!"

Her parents' wonderful attitude made being stateless a priceless adventure. Though they had left Egypt with very little money (as per the law), her father had sent money overseas ahead of time. For the first few months, the Chouekas thoroughly enjoyed their impromptu tour of Europe. They stayed a few days in Greece, three months in Italy, and passed through Switzerland on the way to France. All these countries allowed them entry as tourists.

Ultimately, they waited out their "statelessness" in France, the country whose culture was most familiar to them. Sara was in her element. Her French education back in Egypt had been on a very high level and she quickly grabbed a place at the head of the class in her new school, as her siblings did in their respective schools. Wherever she went, she met old friends and acquaintances. Though the Chouekas had been the first to hear about the Hungarian loophole, they quickly passed on the news and thousands of Egyptian Jews followed their lead. While they could have gone to Israel (from France, not from Egypt), the stories they had heard of the

Family and non-family, everyone in Ahi Ezer felt loved by their Hacham. Here is Hacham Murad sharing a light moment with Eddie Safdie and Joe (son of Dave) Bibi.

difficulties facing new immigrants there made them hesitate. Surprisingly, America did not turn out to be the dream haven that they expected.

The Chouekas arrived in New York at the end of November, completely unprepared for a New York winter. The HIAS representative greeted them warmly and took them to Broadway Central Hotel. The hotel was heated and if they stayed indoors all day they would remain warm. But who wanted to stay cooped up in a hotel room when they could sightsee in Manhattan?

So the Chouekas braved the cold weather, with flimsy coats that did little to keep out the cold. They visited the Empire State Building and peered up at all the enormous skyscrapers. It was exciting and exhilarating, but very cold!

They had never really wanted to come to America. The country that was so maligned in the Egyptian press held no allure to the Frenchified Egyptian Jews. With the unrest in Egypt, the poverty in Eretz Yisrael, and their son Menachem being in America, America seemed like the best choice. Now that they were wandering the avenues of Manhattan that seemed endlessly long, treading the shoveled paths where grey cement peered through the snow, listening to people talk and not understanding what they said, confronted with behavior that was boisterous and strange, they felt utterly alone.

How would they ever manage in this terribly foreign land?

"That's it," announced Mr. Moshe (Morris) Choueka. "Tomorrow we're moving to Bensonhurst."

No one reacted. Bensonhurst, Flatbush, who really cared? They were still strangers in a strange land, and none of them felt that there was any

Beyond Paris, 1957 / 291

hope for that changing anytime soon. But, after two weeks in a clean but plain hotel room, their own apartment would be a welcome change.

"Why Bensonhurst?" Mrs. Choueka asked with muted interest. "I thought that Auntie lives in Flatbush?"

"True," Mr. Choueka acknowledged, "but Flatbush is a wealthier area. The houses and apartments are more expensive over there. The old Syrian community is in Bensonhurst and, while many people are moving out to Flatbush, Bensonhurst is still the hub. Besides, that is where I found an apartment."

The Chouekas moved to Bensonhurst just before Shabbat. That Shabbat, Mr. Choueka returned home from synagogue, eyes aglow. "I have found a wonderful *k'nees*. It's called Ahi Ezer. It's a warm and welcoming place.

"I'm telling you," Mr. Choueka turned to his wife, "you cannot imagine what it was like. I walked into *k'nees*, and this man comes straight over to me, as if I'm some sort of long-lost friend. He shakes my hand and introduces himself — Isidore Dayan, but most people call him Izzy. He brings me over to sit up front, right next to him. He introduces me to the Hacham, to the president of the *k'nees*, to everyone and anyone, as if I'm a beloved family member he has not seen for years. It sounds crazy... but I can't wait to go back tomorrow."

The next morning he returned home even happier than the night before.

"I walked into the *k'nees*, and there he was again, Isidore Dayan, in the vestibule, with a *siddur* open to the correct place," he enthused. "He led me inside, brought me to a seat, right next to him, like the night before. He gave me an *aliya* — can you imagine? Instead of treating me like a stranger, he treated me like a dignitary. Some of our friends from Egypt were also there. He gave everyone an honor. Some were given *aliyot*, some held the *Sefer Torah*. He even noticed the young boys. He gave one of them *hemlan* (carrying the Torah), another was given *jilyan* (showing it to the people)..."

"What about everyone else in the *k'nees*? The regular *mitpallelim* didn't get honors?" Mrs. Choueka interjected.

"Some of them did. Most of them didn't. But they all seemed incredibly happy to see us. After prayers, they came over to greet us, and then we had Kiddush with the Hacham downstairs. There was some food, not much, but then there was singing, everyone together, like one family... You know how it was in Egypt..."

They certainly did. In Egypt, they came and went to shul quietly. There was no such thing as a group of Jews singing loudly and uninhibited. Gatherings were limited and in general, there was no real religious fervor on a group level. Even privately, everything was done hidden, low key. To spend Shabbat morning leisurely among friends, singing *zemirot* and *bakashot* together with the Rabbi, was a dream… especially a Rabbi who was so warm and beloved.

"And the Hacham, what a holy person! Just looking at him was uplifting…." Mr. Choueka, normally a reserved person, kept talking, "… and then we walked home and we talked — in Arabic! It was so pleasant to communicate freely and to know that you are understood. Their Arabic is a little different than ours, but my mother spoke a Syrian Arabic so we understood each other just fine. You know what else? One man remembered my cousins from back in Syria. Another is actually related, if you go back several generations. It's all so unbelievable…"

Mr. Choueka's excitement didn't end that Shabbat, but actually increased as time went on. He had found his niche and could hardly believe that he had once been happy in spiritually bereft Egypt. He loved the *tefillot*, even though the services were somewhat different from what he was used to. He loved the people of Ahi Ezer, who not only welcomed him but the entire Egyptian community. He loved the evening classes that Ahi Ezer organized. He had always wanted to study Torah, and would have gone to learn in Yeshivat Porat Yosef in Eretz Yisrael as his brothers did, had he not had to support the family.[32]

And he loved Nouri Dayan who subtly, quietly, enabled all this to happen.

Ahi Ezer — my brother's helper. It truly lived up to its name.

"*Yesiat Mitzrayim* all over again," one Ahi Ezer congregant joked to another.

"Or the Sinai Invasion," kibitzed his friend.

The Egyptians gravitated to Ahi Ezer. Some of them reunited with friends from the Old Country like Ceasar Salama, an Egyptian Ahi Ezer congregant who came to America years earlier. Others were simply grateful for the welcome and were happy to stay.

The new Egyptians were numerous enough to make a difference, especially since there was a slow but steady stream of Syrians moving out of Bensonhurst to Flatbush. The old-timers were warm and welcoming, the good-natured puns all part of the fun. They appreciated the newcomers who injected new life into Ahi Ezer. Some of them, particularly those from the Choueka family, were learned. They were not as learned as their uncle, Rabbi Abraham Choueka, a dynamic *talmid hacham* who had learned in Yeshivat Porat Yosef, but they were more learned than many other people.

---

32. The Choueka family became prominent members of the Sephardic community. Rabbi David Choueka went to Mirrer Yeshiva, learned in Eretz Yisrael, and became a Rosh Kollel in Mexico. Rabbi Shemuel Choueka became a young star in Ahi Ezer, where he grew up. He went on to learn in Mir and then became the Rabbi of Ohel Simha in Deal, where he also runs the girls school.

L-R: Jack Sharabi, Nat Cohen, Nouri, Ceasar Salama

More significantly, these Egyptian Jews were interested in learning. They were excited about the classes offered in Ahi Ezer and their excitement generated enthusiasm in some of the old-timers who had not taken much interest in the classes until then. This cyclical relationship, in which one group benefited the other, forged the Syrians and the Egyptians into a cohesive unit for as long as they were together. When Moshe Choueka joined Nouri Dayan and Jack Maslaton in translating the *Pirkei Abot* for the women during the weeks of *sefirat ha'omer*, it was a symbol of that unity.

This win-win situation was seen in other areas as well. The Egyptians arrived in America essentially penniless. For those who had been poor in Egypt, coming to America was a relief. For those who had been wealthy, it was a difficult transition. They went from being part of a comfortable, elite society, to refugees trying to make a living in a strange new land.

The Syrian community (Bibi and Co. in particular) helped the refugees find jobs. Many of those newcomers later became prosperous pillars of the community, supporters of Ahi Ezer projects, even after they established their own synagogues. They remained forever grateful to Ahi Ezer for giving them a home when they needed one and for helping them move on when it was time to move on.

The Egyptians brought new life into Ahi Ezer.

New life, but no new money.

Ahi Ezer was perpetually in debt. The new building on 71st Street was bought with a mortgage. Construction was paid in loans. The adjoining two-family house that housed the Annex and Hacham Murad's apartment was also bought with a mortgage. The synagogue was paying two mortgages and other expenses as well.

Yet both Dave and Nouri viewed their "debt" positively, as something that pushed them to grow. Buying the second building had been an act of confidence, indicating that they were certain that they would need all the extra space. They just needed some new fundraising ideas and people who would help implement those projects. One of the most popular synagogue fundraisers of the time was Bingo, and Nouri decided to introduce it for Ahi Ezer. Dave Bibi agreed to let him try.

Bingo became an instant hit. The games were open to the public and were mainly attended by the local gentiles. Nouri rented the Rollerama on 86th Street, which had a hall large enough to accommodate 450 people. Other organizations used the same venue but Ahi Ezer offered the highest jackpot, so they attracted a full house every time it was their night. Nouri recruited people from the synagogue to help and soon the shul was making thousands of dollars a week.

Ahi Ezer had two Bingo nights a week, both of which required many communal volunteers and a lot of organization. The atmosphere in the hall was simultaneously excited and tense; the volunteers needed to be firm, cool-headed, and focused. Some workers regularly donated two nights a week to help at Bingo night. Nouri regularly showed up at Bingo, not as a bystander, but as a cashier, working side by side with the others, always one of the gang. That was part of Nouri's charm. His interests were far more spiritual than that of most of his friends and neighbors, but there was never anything "holier than thou" about him.[33]

"Our people mean well," he'd explain to his children, as they walked home on *layl Shabbat*. "We have to help them be what they really want to be."

Nouri saw only good in every Jew, especially those in his community. That was why he began organizing late *minyanim* for Minha on Friday evening, in the vestibule adjacent to the main room. Many men came to shul after the main *minyan* had already prayed Minha, but before sunset. They

---

33. Mr. Joe Jacobs and Mr. Ike Swed both supervised Bingo at different times and they remembered their years of devotion fondly, as they were proud to assist Mr. Dayan. "After a full day's work, Nouri would spend a whole night at Bingo, often twice a week. On other nights there were synagogue meetings and school meetings. You would think that someone devoting three or four nights a week to the community would say 'enough!' Not Mr. Dayan," recalled Rabbi Saul Wolf at an Ahi Ezer graduation. Eventually, the government began to regulate these games and, as the regulations grew cumbersome, many institutions (like Ahi Ezer) stopped using them.

Nouri (front left) with other Ahi Ezer committee members. Joe (son of Reuben) Bibi is next to him, slightly toward the back.

would either pray outside without a *minyan* or shrug their shoulders and not pray Minha at all.

"Wait here a few minutes," he'd cajole a latecomer, "we already have nine."

And when the men looked around and saw others like them, waiting for a quorum, their good intentions won out and they would wait. As soon as one *minyan* began, Nouri was busy organizing a second one, and then a third. And he was busy opening the *siddurim* to the correct places, and handing them out, and going back into the main room for more *siddurim*.

Anything to make it easier for people to serve the Borei Olam properly.

Back in the main sanctuary, Nouri was at it again. He gently encouraged people to focus on their prayers and remain involved in the services. He walked around the room, giving this one and that one a smile (which reminded them to stop talking).

They came here to serve the Borei Olam, Nouri reasoned. *I'm just reminding them how.* And because Nouri was so unassuming, so humble, and so sincere, no one was offended.

B'makom she'ein ish[34] was one of Nouri's mottos. Naturally shy and reserved, he'd force himself forward, but only if he felt that no one else would do what had to be done.

---

34. *Abot* 2:5: When there are no people [to do what has to be done], one must endeavor to be a man.

When Shabbat services ended, many men were eager to go home. It had been a long and tiring week and they were hungry for a good meal. But it's the Sephardic tradition to say *Yigdal* at the end of services on Friday night and *Adon Olam* after services on Shabbat day. They were just ending *tefillah b'tzibbur*, serving G-d in the most ideal way. So why was everyone rushing to leave? Doesn't everyone want to end off properly? Of course they do! They just need some encouragement.

"C'mon everyone, you can't leave," Nouri called out from his seat. "We have to say *Yigdal*, everyone, together, it's only another few minutes." His enthusiasm was infectious. Everyone sat down and sang.

Shabbat morning, he was once again up and down the aisles, offering a *humash* open to the proper place, helping someone else keep up with the reading. Without ever assuming that this is what he was doing, Nouri transformed many people. How? By always being a part of the *tzibbur*, and yet constantly exerting himself beyond his inherent nature, Nouri was transmitting a subtle, yet transforming, message: We need you as part of our group, but look what you can accomplish as an individual.[35]

---

35. There were many wealthy philanthropists whose desire to help the Jewish people was ignited by Mr. Dayan because he helped them out when they were in difficult straits (like Mr. Clement Soffer), or because he encouraged them to become involved in the community when they were young men (like Mr. Seymour Escava), or because he actively molded them for leadership positions (like Mr. Marvin Azrak). They have all noted that their relationship with Mr. Dayan was transforming.

Chapter 36:
BENSONHURST, 1958

The Dayan children were paradoxically aware and unaware of being "different." On the one hand, Nouri was a regular Syrian Jew — a clean-shaven businessman who spoke a Brooklynese English and knew how to appreciate a good joke. On the other hand, in so many other ways he — and they — were different.

The Dayan children were trained by example. Their parents and grandparents were incredibly busy with so many good things, that they assumed that this was what life was all about. They saw it every day, in so many ways.

Esther Dayan rarely had time for frivolous activities; indeed, they didn't interest her. She was much more content being busy. Supper was always ready for the children when they came home from school, for Nouri when he came home from work, and for the guests… whenever.

Then came Shabbat. Esther never knew if they would be having ten or twenty people. And Syrian specialties were very time-consuming to prepare. There was no such thing as grating some potatoes and onions, mixing them with eggs, matza meal, and spices, and producing a huge kugel that could feed an army. Many foods — like *sambousak* and *kibbe* — entailed mixing, rolling, chopping, and stuffing. The multistep recipes ultimately resulted in delicious, individual delicacies that were absolutely essential to the Shabbat *mazza*.

"But they are a real job," Esther commented to Carol one day.

So were the various salads that also required peeling, chopping, roasting, and marinating. But having an elaborate *mazza*, with all the traditional dishes, was intrinsic to a Syrian Shabbat table, almost as important as the *zemirot* and *bakashot* that they sang.

"Why aren't you singing?" *Stetta* asked Murray.

Murray looked ahead. He wasn't in the mood to sing. And so what? Did he have to sing if he didn't want to? According to his grandmother, the answer was yes. On Shabbat, you sang, like it or not. So Murray sang... and *Stetta* beamed.

She is in a class of her own, Murray observed in silent admiration.

"The *safrut*," she explained to Murray when he asked her why she came to *k'nees* Mondays and Thursdays, "it's a *zechut* just to look at it. It's holy."

Jdedda and *Stetta*

Murray had shrugged. What did he know about holiness? He read when he had to read, learned when he had to learn, but he left holiness for the people who understood it, like his grandparents. His grandmother's simple faith was so strong that it encompassed a holiness of its own. She was truly a pious and righteous woman. She also had very clear and exacting standards.

So did Nouri.

"Ashkenazim have it easy," Murray grumbled to Irwin when their father woke them up, bright and early, at 4 a.m. "Don't you think that forty days is a bit much?"

Irwin grunted as he got out of bed... but there was never a question about whether or not to go to *selihot* — the entire month of Elul, and then until Yom Kippur.

Hoshana Rabbah night, the custom was to stay up the whole night learning, saying *Tehillim*, and praying. At 11 at night, they began learning *Sefer Devarim*. At 3 in the morning, they began saying the whole *Sefer Tehillim*. The recital lasted until Shaharit. One year, on Hoshana Rabbah, sometime in the wee hours of the morning, Irwin and Murray decided that they were too tired. They snuck out of shul and ran home. Not a minute after they had gotten under the covers, in walked Nouri.

"What are you doing over here? Come on!"

The two boys scrambled out of bed and ran after their father all the way back to the *k'nees*.

Ohel Moshe had school until 12 on Sundays. When school let out, the boys were free for the afternoon. One Sunday, Murray joined his friends on an excursion to Madison Square Garden to see a much publicized basketball game. He returned late in the evening, when it was already dark outside.

"Where were you?" Nouri demanded.

"I went with the guys to Madison Square Garden."

"Madison Square Garden? Today? Do you know what today is?"

Murray mentally ran through the Jewish calendar and came up blank.

"It was *ta'anit dibbur*[36] today," Nouri answered, clearly exasperated. "You should have been in shul saying *Tehillim* with the rest of us. Instead you were at a basketball game."

His disapproval hurt, even though Murray knew that it was unlikely any boys his age had attended (except maybe his cousin, Maxi Maslaton, Uncle Sion's son, who also had to march to the same drumbeat). That was the way it was. They were part of the Maslaton family, a family with higher spiritual standards than others.

The Pesah Seder at Hacham Murad's house was an experience. He always wanted his sons at his Seder but when it came to the daughters, it was up to their husbands. Inevitably, there was a big crowd. All the daughters and daughters-in-law helped with the cooking, but the real excitement was the aura. Hacham Murad dressed in a *kitel*,[37] unusual among Sephardim, and led a particularly moving Seder. When *netilat yadayim* was brought to Hacham Murad, the majesty of the moment was so elevated, one felt a part of the *geulah* of *yesiat Mitzrayim*.

Shebi'i shel Pesah was another highlight. The *Shammi* custom was to wake up very early in the morning, about 4 a.m., to read all the prayers. They finished at around 8:30, and then they headed for Aunt Ray Tawil's house. Though she was a widow for many years, Shebi'i shel Pesah remained her day. All her brothers, brothers-in-law, and nephews piled into her house where they learned together until the Tawil men came home from prayers. Then everyone sat down and ate her famous *kibbeh-riz*, amid much singing (the Tawils were great singers). This *kibbe* was so rich and filling that, after eating two, they were hardly able to move.

---

36. The Syrian custom is that during the last week of Shovavim, one day is set aside as a *ta'anit dibbur*. The people gather in shul, say the entire *Sefer Tehillim* three times, and they don't talk for the entire day.

37. A *kitel* is a white cotton overcoat worn by Ashkenazic men under the *huppah* when they get married, on Yom Kippur, and at the Pesah Seder. No one in the family knows when Hacham Murad adopted this custom but they all remember his majestic attire at the Seder.

They almost forgot that they had gotten up at 4 a.m.

The girls had their share of duties and privileges. Hacham Murad was *hattan Torah* every year on Simhat Torah, which meant that *Stetta* prepared an elaborate Kiddush for the community. The living room was full of men and the dining room was full of women and everyone loved being a part of all the excitement.

That excitement came with a lot of work. Early in the morning, Carol went to help her grandmother set up for the Kiddush. Later on in the day, while the house was a crush of people, Carol was in the kitchen with her cousins, washing and drying dishes and cutlery, and sending them out to be used over again. There were no disposable dishes and no one had an endless supply of real dishes, so the water ran nonstop, and people kept on coming, and more food had to be sent out, and the girls just kept everything moving.

It was wonderful. It was exhausting. It was part of being a Maslaton.

Nouri's children participated happily, no questions asked, trained by example.

In time, the boys took upon themselves responsibilities that, in the scope of how they lived, just made sense. On Sukkot, during Mussaf, Irwin and his friends — the Didia and Mevorah boys — would run down to the sukka and set up the tables with white tablecloths and plates, rolls and olives and grapes. (For those who wanted to wash, there was a pipe coming out of a hole in the ground that spurted water. Rosh Hashanah, it was used for *tashlich*.) No one actually remembered being told to take care of the Kiddush but, weren't they old enough to help out in the *k'nees*... just because it was the right thing to do?

Mosa'ei Shabbat, after Habdala, most kids ran home to watch the ball game. Not the Dayan boys. While Hacham Murad gave a class to the older men, Nouri gave money to his boys to go to the candy store to buy licorice and potato chips. Then he gathered together the few straggling kids and gave a class. The snacks were their reward and they loved it.

There were men in the community who worked on Shabbat and, paradoxically, considered themselves religious. They sent their boys to shul on Shabbat, even as they went off to work. Who noticed these boys, sitting all alone in the back?

Daddy notices them, Irwin realized one day. *He always greets them and invites them to a class in Humash or halacha, that he creates upon seeing them. Some of these boys have been learning with him for years. He honors them with hemlan or jilyan, and they feel like a million bucks!*

Children gravitated to his warmth.

When someone loves you, you want to be with him... Murray Maslaton (Joe's son) reflected, and joined the Dayan Shabbat table practically every week. He knew that his uncle cared about him, really cared. So he came back, time after time. Other neighborhood kids also stopped by. They just wanted to be a part of that warm and wonderful atmosphere.

Nouri was strict about proper conduct; if he heard that one of the children had acted disrespectfully to their mother, the child would have to ask for forgiveness and kiss her hand, but he was a very warm father.[38] He wasn't home often, but his presence filled the house. When the children walked into the kitchen and saw delicious rolls and danishes, fresh from Ginsburg's bakery, they knew that they were from Daddy. Mini pretzels, exotic fruits, the latest nosh — all appeared on the kitchen counter Friday morning, from Daddy. They were bought in honor of Shabbat, but the children knew that it was in honor of them too (who else would be eating lollypops!).

Though quite comfortable, the Dayans didn't live a rich lifestyle,[39] but Nouri found simple ways to show his love for his children. And the children felt that love.

Daddy's home! Joyce couldn't wait.

Friday afternoon, he came home early and she ran to polish his shoes (a job she happily inherited from Irwin), the ones for Shabbat and for weekday. At the meal on *layl Shabbat*, she pulled her chair over to where he was sitting to be as close to him as possible. In the morning, she woke up early, but he was always up earlier, sitting at the table and learning. She went with him to shul because she loved to go to shul, but also because she loved to walk there with her Daddy.

"What is the name of this week's *perasha*?" Nouri would ask one of the younger children as they walked home from shul. The questions got progressively more difficult, according to age, but the children never felt like they were being tested, especially since they knew that they would be rewarded a nickel for every correct answer after Shabbat! They were warmed by the certainty that he was interested in them, in their lives.

Because he *was* interested in their lives.

Even though Nouri was so busy with so many things, he wanted to know what was going on with his children. He wanted to hear what they felt, how they thought, and if they were learning what he wanted them to know about life.

The 50's was a happening decade. Joey and Barbara joined the Dayan

---

38. This was part of the traditional relationship between children and parents. Many interviewees noted the unusual *chinuch* in the Dayan home and the respect that flowed between husband and wife, parents and children.

39. "We were probably better off than many of our friends and neighbors, but my parents never overindulged us. We never felt wealthy and never poor, only that we had whatever we needed. Someone once gave me a baby sweater. It was white, with soft fur. My father saw it and grimaced; it was too showy for his taste and even though it was for free, he didn't approve of it," explained Mrs. Joyce [Dayan] Nahem. "When I was growing up, my father bought one bicycle, stipulating that Joey and I share it. He could have bought two, but he wanted us to share one," added Mrs. Barbara [Dayan] Ozeirey.

clan, bringing the number of children up to seven. With their ages ranging from 18 years old down to the baby, Esther had her hands full. Yet Nouri's presence, even when he wasn't physically home, gave the house direction.

In the wake of so many things happening at once, that direction was crucial.

While the first Sephardic yeshiva in America had collapsed amid controversy, it still served as an unusual catalyst for growth. The boys' religious fervor extended to the girls and created its own, far more subtle revolution.

The neighborhood girls attended public high school, even those who had attended Jewish elementary schools like Ohel Moshe and Magen David. When their brothers came home all excited about their learning, their sisters wondered if, perhaps, they had learned everything that they should know. Rabbi Eisenberg picked up on this interest and volunteered to bring his rebbetzin into Brooklyn once a week to give classes to teenaged girls.

This was a revolutionary occurrence. Until then, the community assumed that girls didn't need Jewish studies: They knew how to keep a kosher kitchen from their mothers and anything else was old-fashioned and unnecessary in the modern world. But these girls wanted to learn more. Rebbetzin Eisenberg gave classes in the Annex of Ahi Ezer and covered various topics in Jewish thought. The lecture series didn't last long, but the effects of these classes went far beyond their participants, in ways that no one could have foreseen.

Chapter 37:

FLORIDA, 1959

Sara Maslaton puttered around the small hotel room.

Baruch Hashem for Florida, she mused. The frigid New York winters were difficult for her husband. A few weeks of tropical weather rejuvenated his strength.

His strength. She sighed.

She wished Hacham Murad's physical strength matched his spiritual strength.

She had always admired — revered — his spiritual strength, a cage of steel that surrounded his soul, allowing him to be a part of his people and yet never affected by the decaying spirituality around him. Wherever he was — the Pioneer Hotel in the Catskills, Prospect Park, Niagara Falls, Florida — he would glance at the beautiful surroundings, and then right back at whichever *sefer* he held in his hands.

Wherever he went, people gravitated to him, somehow sensing his holiness. They wanted to be in his company. Sometimes they desperately needed his help. Not long ago, Joe and Mitzi Ozeirey had come with their little boy who stuttered terribly, frantic for a cure. Her husband had whispered a few fervent *tefillot* and *berachot* and the child was soon talking beautifully.[40] Over the years, there had been many such stories, too many to remember them all.

Yet Sara was no more impressed by "miraculous recoveries" than she was by her husband's day-to-day life. His everyday actions were so pure, so totally G-d-oriented, that they left her humbled. He was exacting with himself, and forgiving of his people. He greeted everyone with warmth — the spiritually sincere, and those who were not. With the truly devout, he

---

40. The child became Rabbi David Ozeirey, a powerful orator, an influential Rabbi in the community, and Nouri Dayan's son-in-law!

spoke *dibrei Torah*. With the marginally religious, he gave wise advice and counsel. With those who tried to hide their shallowness, he said little, but blessed them when they left, hoping that his blessing would help them mend their ways.

Sara was not like that. She was down-to-earth and shrewd, and saw far more than she wanted to see. She never accepted passing piety, and never minced words. When a relative who was a Shabbat desecrator came to visit, she refused to speak with him. She would not even acknowledge his presence. This was also strength, but it was a different kind of strength than that of her husband.

"She's the strong one," was the constant refrain in the family.

Hacham Murad lighting the menorah. Every action he did had its own unique holiness.

It was both true and false. They were both strong, in different ways.

Hashem, make his physical strength match his spiritual strength!

Hacham Murad and Rabbi Kassin at Meyer Cohen's wedding

Florida, 1959 / 305

Sara gazed out at her husband learning in a wooden chair outside under a tree. At 83 years old, Hacham Murad was relatively healthy, albeit frail. His sugar levels were not great, but he was careful with his medication and kept a busy schedule. He did not teach often but he was an involved Rabbi, who still hosted the community on Yom Tov, was the *hazzan* for the High Holidays, and regularly gave his *derasha* on Shabbat in shul.

But she noticed how slowly he walked when the two of them went out together. And she noticed how labored his breath was when he walked more than one block. And she noticed the expression on the doctor's face when he, once again, adjusted the dosage of medication...

Sara sighed. She was not usually so contemplative. Perhaps it was because they were alone. Usually, they vacationed in Florida together with Dave and Milo. She liked that. When Dave was around, he spent time with her husband. It was like having a friendly companion in an unfamiliar place. And Milo was such a doll.

Hacham Murad in Florida, 1959

And neither of us know the language...
Sara sighed ruefully.

That was why she liked having Dave around. If anything would happen — not that anything ever did — it was good to have someone else around to help communicate. Only this year Dave could not get away from the business.

"You will be fine," he reassured them. "You have already been there many times. Everyone knows you. They'll look out for the Rabbi. Trust me."

And she did.

But she missed his comforting presence.

Back in Bensonhurst, there were feverish preparations going on. The community had sent the Rabbi off for a vacation and they were working on a surprise Testimonial Dinner in his honor.

It was almost 40 years since Hacham Murad had arrived in America to lead the Ahi Ezer Congregation, almost four decades of devotion to his people, concern for their spirituality, and work on their behalf. The committee felt that appropriate appreciation was long overdue and once they made that decision, they were not going to wait another year for the round number to be complete. They were going to honor him now, as soon as he returned from his vacation.

They planned a gala affair, with a full dinner, a journal of warm wishes, and a program of speakers that would do justice to the occasion. They sent out invitations for March 15, 1959.

Vicky (Zalta) Maslaton, Sion's wife, hummed to herself as she cleaned. Her in-laws were away for several weeks, leaving her plenty of time to give the small apartment a complete overhaul. She adored her in-laws. Her own family was from Texas and when she first arrived in New York, she was afraid that she would feel lonely. That fear was easily laid to rest as soon as she met Hacham Murad and Sara.

Hacham Murad with Dave Bibi, vacationing in Florida in a different year

Sara Maslaton was warm in a forthright manner that Vicky appreciated. She immediately felt wanted and loved. Hacham Murad was more reserved but he radiated holiness and Vicky was drawn to him easily. She often stopped by to help her in-laws, to see what they needed, to shop for them or with them.

She felt privileged to be their daughter-in-law.

"Curtains," she said aloud, though there was no one there to hear her. Some nice curtains were just what the apartment needed to give it a fresh, homey look. Neither her father-in-law nor her mother-in-law ever spent money on luxuries. When they were younger, there had never been any extra money to spare. She did not know if they had any extra money now that they were older but, even if they did, they would never spend it on themselves. The trip to Florida only happened because the congregation insisted on paying for it.

They deserve something new and special, Vicky decided. She grabbed her purse and went out shopping, happy that she had thought of the perfect

Florida, 1959 / 307

surprise gift. They were not due back for three weeks but she wanted the curtains up and waiting for their return.

"Izzy, do you have the bill from the printer? They want cash, up front." Reuben Bibi, Ahi Ezer's long-time treasurer, was on the way to the bank to settle the payment for the Testimonial Journal.

Nouri nodded and found the bill. When Reuben left, he perused the journal, scanning the typeset pages. The Rabbis — Rabbi Kassin, Rabbi Hecht, Rabbi Dershowitz — had written truly beautiful letters. The honorary presidents — Nathan, Moussa, and Dave — gave short, appropriate messages. He hoped that his own missive did his father-in-law justice. It was difficult to determine how much to say without overdoing it. The pictures accompanying the letters added a personal touch.

A fitting, dignified journal, Nouri noted with satisfaction.

He sent it off to the printer. It was February 27th.

Hacham Murad was outside learning, same spot as usual. He had left his jacket upstairs, but that was his only sign of informal dress, even on vacation. His ever-present tie, framed by his usual black vest, added just a drop of color to his white shirt. The long sleeves were slightly cuffed, bowing to the warm weather.

The years had colored his beard white but his eyes were sharp and clear. He took off his reading glasses and gazed at the sky. The midday sun was very strong.

Time to go inside.

He pulled himself up and walked slowly to the hotel entrance. He shuffled through the lobby, down a corridor, up the steps. One, two, three... There were not many more to go...

Sara Maslaton was waiting for her husband to come inside for lunch. *He knows better than to stay outside in the hot sun,* she fretted. *Why isn't he home yet? If only Dave were here...*

She checked the window. He was not in his regular spot. *Probably walking slowly.* She put up some hot water for tea and waited.

The water boiled, but her husband had not returned.

Let me go see...

She walked out of her room, down the corridor to the stairwell. She began walking down the steps, and then she let out a scream.

Chapter 38:
AHI EZER, 1959

They entered the *k'nees* Sunday evening, shocked and bewildered.
"She was all by herself when it happened, poor thing."
"Morris Bibi hopped on a plane immediately. He is taking care of all the arrangements down in Florida."
"And here?"
"Dave and Nouri, I suppose."
Sigh.
"So much for the Testimonial Dinner…"
A small crowd had already formed in front of Ahi Ezer. People were subdued, even the children. They shuffled around aimlessly, waiting. Men and women kept going up to the apartment, which was already crowded with people. A long dark station wagon pulled up and parked right in front of the *k'nees*. The passenger door opened and a short, stocky woman emerged, her face a mask of pain.
"*Tahtzmat!* (The king died!)" she cried.
Suddenly, all the women, and even the men, let out a unified wail.
In departure from normal protocol, the men carried the *aron* from the hearse, straight into the sanctuary of the synagogue, and laid the *niftar* on the floor in the front of the room. Yeshiva boys surrounded the *aron*, holding candles, their small flames flickering. The room was packed with people and the crowd spilled over outside. Almost everyone from the Syrian community was there, for Hacham Murad was universally revered. Even some of the local Ashkenazim came.
All the Rabbis of the community spoke.
As the last speaker stepped down, Irwin watched his father lift a *shofar* to his lips. This was an old Syrian custom, rarely done in America in the *Shammi*

community. In organizing the ceremonies, his father and Uncle Sion had decided that for this funeral it was appropriate. There was absolute silence as his father drew in a breath.

Bp...bp...bp

No real sound emerged. Irwin was taken aback.

Daddy blows the shofar like other people blow a whistle...

Nouri lowered the shofar and softly knocked it against his hand. Irwin saw the tears slowly escaping down his cheeks.

He's too overcome. It's not going to go.

Nouri raised the *shofar* to his lips again.

Bp...bp...bp

Nothing doing.

He handed the *shofar* to Irwin, who was also an excellent *ba'al toke'a*. Irwin tried once... twice... Then Nouri took back the *shofar* with new determination, and blew... a plaintive wail, barely heard, a faint cry like the muted weeping of the bereft congregation, overwhelmed with grief, shock, and pain.

Hacham Murad

Our holy Rabbi is no longer with us.

The Maslaton apartment, next door to the synagogue, was packed with women from the community, there to comfort the mourners and to find comfort from one another. They waited at the window for the *aron* to emerge...

They let out a collective wail.

Their cries accompanied the *aron* back into the hearse, and down the block. Their cries accompanied the line of cars inching slowly through the crowds of people still assembled on the street. The women watched as the procession drove slowly toward Bay Parkway from where they would head toward the Staten Island Ferry.

One car, after another, after another...

It seemed that the whole *k'nees* was accompanying the Hacham on his last journey. It would be hours before they returned to sit *shiba'a* with the women waiting back home.

The week passed in a confused mixture of sadness, shock, and togetherness. So many people came — morning, noon, and night. Most people came many times, sitting together with the mourners as one of them. The entire community was in mourning. And when they emerged from mourning, they were different.

"The *kedushah*," Nouri murmured, "it's gone."

"Daddy, what do you mean?" Murray asked.

Nouri shook his head, "It will never be the same… *I* will never be the same."

Hacham Murad had been the soul of the community.

With the soul gone, the community had to change.

PART V

Chapter 39:
MOVING FORWARD, 1960

"Whenever I saw Hacham Murad, I felt overwhelmed by his holiness, humbled and awed by his radiance, by the presence of the Shechina that was with him. Hashem planted him among us, a gift for our generation, a holy soul" [paraphrased from Hacham Baruch Ben Haim's approbation to the sefer, Doresh Tov].

But Hacham Murad was gone.
He was unique in his generation; there was no one like him.

The people of Ahi Ezer mourned their loss. They looked confidently to his son, not as a replacement, but as a successor. They trusted Hacham Sion to continue his father's work, that of maintaining and preserving the *Shammi* traditions.

Perhaps Hacham Murad had a premonition: the year before his passing, he instructed Hacham Sion to deliver the Shabbat *derashot* in his stead. When Hacham Sion stepped up front the first Shabbat after his father's passing, it was far more traumatic for him than for the congregation. When he visited his mother after prayers, he was still overcome with sadness.

"It's forbidden to be sad on Shabbat," *Stetta* insisted to her children and grandchildren sitting around morosely. She turned to Hacham Sion, who sat in front of his father's *kos* but couldn't bring himself to say Kiddush. "Sing!" she ordered. "It's Shabbat!"

As usual, *Stetta's* iron faith was unshakeable.
She gave the family the strength to go on.

Indeed, Hacham Sion rallied to his role, even though he never forgot his father.[1] He did everything as his father had done — not one deviation

---
1. Hacham Sion compiled Hacham Murad's *derashot* in a *sefer, Doresh Tov*. He also compiled his own *derashot* into a *sefer, Torah M'Sion*.

Hacham Sion Maslaton, the new Rabbi of Ahi Ezer. In the foreground, with his back facing the camera, is his brother-in-law, Nouri.

in *minhag* or routine — and the congregation found this consistency very comforting. Hacham Sion had been giving classes for years and had assisted his father in leading the prayers and other Rabbinic functions. Like his father, he was almost always with a *sefer*, even when others were talking or socializing.

Hacham Sion accepted his position with vision and determination. He intended to raise the spiritual level of his congregation in his own way. One of his first projects was something that he had been thinking about for a long time.

"*Et Ratzon* — that is what I want to call the new *siddur*," he told Nouri. "I want to print a *siddur* that will be easy for the people to follow."

This was Hacham Sion's way of nurturing the community: low key, without fanfare, and with projects that he knew would help the people, even though they would not realize it until much later on. The *siddur* took several years to finish, and when it finally came out, it was so clearly an improvement from what they had had, that Hacham Sion immediately set out to make other improvements.

He made the *Et Ratzon* for Tisha b'Ab, designed for the *Shammi* community. Tisha b'Ab had always been an inspiring day in Ahi Ezer, due to the very moving prayers, specific to the *Shammi* tradition.[2] The new *Et Ratzon* was greeted with real appreciation.

Hacham Sion was enormously dedicated, in a calm, diligent manner. He implemented his ideas quietly, without making waves. The congregation was proud of their Rabbi whose *derashot* proved his scholarship and erudition. They enjoyed the seamless transfer of power from father to son… and from uncle to nephew.

Hacham Sion, in front of Ahi Ezer on 71st Street

"It's your turn, Izzy," Dave Bibi decided. "Twenty years of being president of the shul is long enough. It's time for someone younger to step into this role."

Nouri wasn't enthusiastic. He liked remaining in the shadow of his dynamic uncle. Besides, hadn't they just been through enough changes? He preferred to let something remain the same.

"I'm not a speaker," he told his Uncle Dave.

Dave shrugged, "Neither am I. And so what?"

Nouri had nothing to answer. In a small group, Dave was a compelling lobbyist whose gentlemanly manners made every negotiation pleasant. But it was true that he had not been much of a speaker and that never stopped him from accomplishing. Besides, Nouri could never refuse his uncle.

"Well, we'll see if I get elected," Nouri answered.

I guess his recommendation was enough to get me in, Nouri silently noted after he heard the tally. So he took the position… and enrolled in a Dale Carnegie public speaking course to bolster his confidence.

While public speaking wasn't a major part of the job, he found it difficult to even make the short Shabbat announcements about the prayer times and programs. Nouri knew that he couldn't change his nature — he would remain shy for the rest of his life — but if he had to step up

---

2. "When Hacham Murad spoke on Tisha b'Ab, the whole congregation would cry," recounted Mr. Saul Tawil. The Damascus tradition was to recite many moving *kinnot* and Midrashim which, back in Damascus, they translated into Arabic. Even today, many people come to Ahi Ezer on Tisha b'Ab to take part in its heartfelt services.

Like his father before him, Hacham Sion gravitated to holiness. Here he is pictured visiting Hacham Meir Vaknin in Eretz Yisrael.

to a leadership position, he felt obligated to become as qualified as possible. He cared so much about his people that he was willing to fight his own nature in order to help them.

"You should try the course," he told his brother-in-law Hacham Sion. "I might not have become a world-class speaker, but I did pick up a few tricks."

Hacham Sion shook his head. He had no interest. A Rabbi was a spiritual leader. Learning Torah as much as possible was the only preparation that a congregation should want from its Rabbi. Indeed, Hacham Sion spent most of his day learning and his *derashot* reflected his wide-ranging knowledge. Nouri admired his brother-in-law enormously. He had stepped into very large shoes and was working hard to fill them properly. Nouri felt that by taking over Uncle Dave's position, he was doing something similar. They were both dealing with the change thrust upon them.

But the change that Nouri would find most compelling was that which was occurring within his own family.

The year that followed Hacham Murad's passing, Irwin went off to Ner Israel as part of a new trend within the community. What would later be dubbed as "the Yeshiva Movement" slowly grew in the early 60's as intrepid Syrian boys opted to learn in Ashkenazic post-high school yeshivot.

Nouri had been happy to send Irwin to Ner Israel. He was proud of his oldest son, who had already demonstrated leadership qualities. Irwin blew *shofar*, read from the Torah, led the *tefillot*, and wasn't shy to speak in public. If he would round off all his innate talents with advanced Gemara learning, he would certainly be an even more powerful influence on the people.

After a year in Ner Israel, Irwin realized that it wasn't the right place for him. He was restless and unhappy. His friend Eddie Zafrani had been in Vineland and Irwin decided that he also wanted to try it out.

This time, Nouri wasn't happy.

It wasn't just about Vineland Yeshiva being a small, virtually unknown place. Nouri honestly felt that given the values of the day, Irwin would be able to have a greater impact on people if he had a college education.

"The young people have more respect for people who speak polished English and have broad secular knowledge," Nouri explained to Esther. "In Ner Israel, Irwin can advance in Gemara while attending college. In Vineland, that won't be possible."

But, true to form, Nouri didn't argue with Irwin, nor did he forbid him to go. He stated his hesitations and then accepted his son's choice, and waited for the situation to play itself out.

Nouri, the new president of Ahi Ezer

I really didn't count on this, Irwin thought ruefully, as he watched his breath make hazy clouds of smoke in the frigid air. Five blankets didn't dispel the bone-chilling cold of the heatless room on a typically frigid win-

L-R: Irwin, Esther, Nouri, and Carol are standing behind Murray, the bar mitzva boy, who is seated.

Moving Forward, 1960 / 319

ter morning. There was no choice but to dress quickly and run down to the Bet Midrash, where there was heat!

Vineland was an experience, no question. But Irwin liked it. There was something so real about the place, it appealed to him.

Irwin had grown up admiring his grandfather, Hacham Murad, a model of Torah and *yirat Shamayim*. But the Rosh HaYeshiva, Rabbi Moshe Eisemann, added a novel component to that mix. He had mastered a high level of learning and imparted it with energy and clarity. He also had his unique ways of motivating his *bachurim* to grow in Torah and *yirat Shamayim*.

Isolated from the big city with no one but the fourteen *bachurim* in the yeshiva and his own family, Rabbi Eisemann was totally devoted to learning Torah and teaching it to his *talmidim*. He had created an island of holiness where there were no radios, no televisions, and almost no contact with the outside world. In the yeshiva vicinity[3] there was... nothing: no grocery stores, no sidewalks, no baseball diamonds or basketball courts. Except for the occasional bus to nearby Norma, there was no public transportation. Even a trip to the nearest town of Bridgeport was taken by foot, and if one had heavy packages, he balanced them on the top of his head!

There was nothing to do in Vineland except learn, learn, and learn, which, at first, was particularly difficult for Irwin, the lone Sephardic bachur (Eddie Zafrani left before Irwin came and his good friend, Charlie Sultan, left after six weeks).

Every Sephardic *bachur* entering a Litvish yeshiva began with the disadvantage of not knowing Yiddish. This had not been such a problem in Ner Israel where the first-year rebbi, Rabbi Abba Yaakov Liff, taught in English. Had Irwin stayed for the more advanced *shiurim*, lack of Yiddish

Rabbi Moshe Eisemann (1921-1994) was from Germany. Rav Yechiel Michel Schlesinger of Frankfurt encouraged him to go to learn in Ponovezh, Lithuania. He later came to America and became a main student of Rabbi Aharon Kotler. L-R: Rabbi Murray Maslaton, Rabbi Moshe Eisemann, Rabbi Shneur Kotler.

---

3. The yeshiva wasn't actually in Vineland. It was 3 miles from Norma and 7 miles from Vineland.

would have become a problem there as well. Instead, he transferred to Vineland, where he had to deal with the issue immediately.

Fortunately, Rabbi Eisemann spoke very clearly. Every day, Irwin jotted down the words that he didn't understand. Lunchtime, he would go over the list with his new friends — Gavriel Stefansky, Gavriel Mandel, Shlomo Neiman, Yaakov Spector, and others — and then memorized the meanings. By the end of the first *z'man*, Irwin had a list of 120 words, and had no problem understanding *shiur*.

Yeshiva Bais Meir of Vineland was challenging for other reasons as well. For one thing, his father's disapproval was hard for him to handle. It wasn't as if he *said* anything. That wasn't Nouri's way. He gave his children the leeway to make their own decisions but he hoped they would choose how he wanted them to choose. When they didn't, he was disappointed.

Irwin came to Vineland on his own initiative. His meager savings had been used on his bus fare back and forth to Vineland for special occasions. He couldn't ask his father to help him when he knew that his father disapproved of his decision.

But it was hard.

One day, the Rosh HaYeshiva took Irwin aside for a chat. He must have sensed Irwin's struggle. "It will all work out for the best," he comforted him. "A father is the emissary of the son [to bring him to his potential in *kedushah*]. If the son is happy, the father will be happy."

He is right, Irwin noted to himself later on. He knew that his father wanted only what was best for him, only right now they differed in what they thought was best. If he returned after the long winter *z'man* (it was a leap year) happy and mature, he knew that his father would come around.

Indeed, Vineland was a place that made men out of boys. With such a small group, the Rosh HaYeshiva had the time and patience for each *bachur*.

Even familiar practices and teachings took on a new meaning in Vineland. *Rabbeinu Bachye* was regularly studied in the Dayan house, but the Rosh HaYeshiva's way of teaching it was different. Irwin had discovered the *Michtav MeEliyahu* in Ner Israel, but Rabbi Eisemann's Mosa'ei Shabbat classes on that *sefer* added a whole new dimension to what Irwin had already studied. Suddenly he was writing pages of notes, filling one notebook after another.

Vineland Yeshiva had a profound effect on Irwin. He learned new customs, new songs, a new way of learning, and a new way of being. When it was time to go home for Pesah, he was ready to greet his parents.

"Slow down," Eli Shamah[4] told Irwin, who was bubbling over with excitement. The older boy maneuvered the car away from the train station

---
4. Mr. Eli Shamah was the administrator for Ahi Ezer. He was instrumental in helping Eddie Sitt establish B'nei Yosef.

at McDonald Avenue, toward Bensonhurst, the last leg of the 3-hour trip from Vineland. Irwin was coming home after spending six months in Vineland and there were many changes he wanted to initiate.

Eli Shamah understood Irwin's fire, but he also knew that too much too fast would not accomplish anything. "Take it easy," he counseled.

Irwin grew quiet, his steely determination in check. As he exited the car in front of his house, he shyly accepted the usual welcome-home backslaps and hugs, knowing that nothing else about his homecoming was going to be usual.

Esther was pleasantly surprised. Her rambunctious teenager had left like a tiger and returned like a pussycat. *Thank goodness*, she noted, not really caring what had caused the change. Nouri cautiously appraised the mild-mannered adult that had returned. They spoke a bit, went off to Arbit, chatted with the family after prayers, and then turned in for the night.

"It seems that Vineland was good for Irwin," Nouri commented to Esther later that night. Esther nodded. It certainly appeared that way.[5]

The next morning was when the real excitement began.

Nouri went off to work and Irwin began puttering around the kitchen. He had collected a number of cardboard boxes that he began to fill with the contents of the kitchen cabinets.

"What are you doing?" Esther protested.

Irwin looked her in the eye. "Taking them to the *mikva*."

"What!"

"Ma, I don't know why, but this is one of the things that has been forgotten in our community. We are not allowed to use glass and metal utensils for food before *tovelling* them in the *mikva*. It's the halacha."

Stetta happened to be in the house. She began to nod, "Yes, this is our way."

Esther stopped short.

Irwin looked at his grandmother curiously. "What happened?"

Stetta shrugged. It was just one of those things that she couldn't explain.

Irwin heaved the heavy box and walked out the door.

By the end of the day he had dunked the whole house.

One thing taken care of.

The next issue was more complicated.

"Where were you this morning?" Nouri asked Irwin when he showed up just before Kiddush on Shabbat.

"At Magen David," Irwin answered, looking squarely at his father.

---

5. "My mother was forever thankful to Rabbi Eisemann. My father was also very grateful and would help out whenever Rabbi Eisemann came to collect money for the yeshiva," remembered Mr. Irwin Dayan.

Nouri said nothing, but both of them knew that there would have to be a conversation sometime soon. Later that day they had their discussion.

"According to Rabbi Moshe Feinstein, the *mehitza* in Ahi Ezer is problematic. I have no problem praying there during the week, or even on Friday night, when there are no women. But Shabbat by day, I just can't," Irwin explained.

First the dishes, now the shul, what is going on?

This time, Nouri wasn't going to categorically reject Irwin's opinion. Even though Irwin was home barely a week, Nouri realized that Vineland Yeshiva had been good for him and he was broad-minded enough to admit that, perhaps, his disappointment had been unfounded. While he wasn't ready to immediately agree with Irwin's latest craze, he was prepared to explore the issue, especially since he was beginning to realize that while there were certain areas of religion that Sephardic Jewry excelled in, there were some inexplicable gaps that had to be filled. Was this one of them? Perhaps, but he wasn't about to act rashly. He needed to think about the issue and figure out what to do.

For those weeks home, Irwin would not pray in Ahi Ezer when women might be there. And when he returned home for summer break, he continued going to Magen David on Shabbat day.

"How can you do this to your father," Isaac Zaga berated Irwin one Friday night. "His life is the *k'nees*, and suddenly you, his eldest son, won't come? You think you are more religious than him or your grandfather, of blessed memory? They approved of the *mehitza* and you don't?"

Irwin didn't answer. He couldn't answer. It was painful for him to pray elsewhere, but halacha was halacha. He understood that, when the community first built the shul, it would have been prohibitively expensive to gut the entire building and make a women's balcony, as was customary in the shuls back in Syria. But the current setup — with the women in the back of the same room, separated by a very low *mehitza* — was inadequate.

It bothered Nouri that Irwin would not pray in Ahi Ezer. But what bothered him even more was wondering if, perhaps, his son had a point. Irwin had never been impossibly fanatic about his Judaism. If he was taking so strong a stance, maybe the *mehitza* was a problem. And so, rather than rant and rave about the gall of young people to start imposing unnecessary stringencies on themselves while disregarding the feelings of their parents, Nouri decided to do his research.

And then he acted.

Rosh Hashana evening, the men walked into Ahi Ezer and noticed that attractive wooden lattice-work had been added to the *mehitza* in the back of the room. They noticed it, made a few annoyed comments, and went back to their prayers.

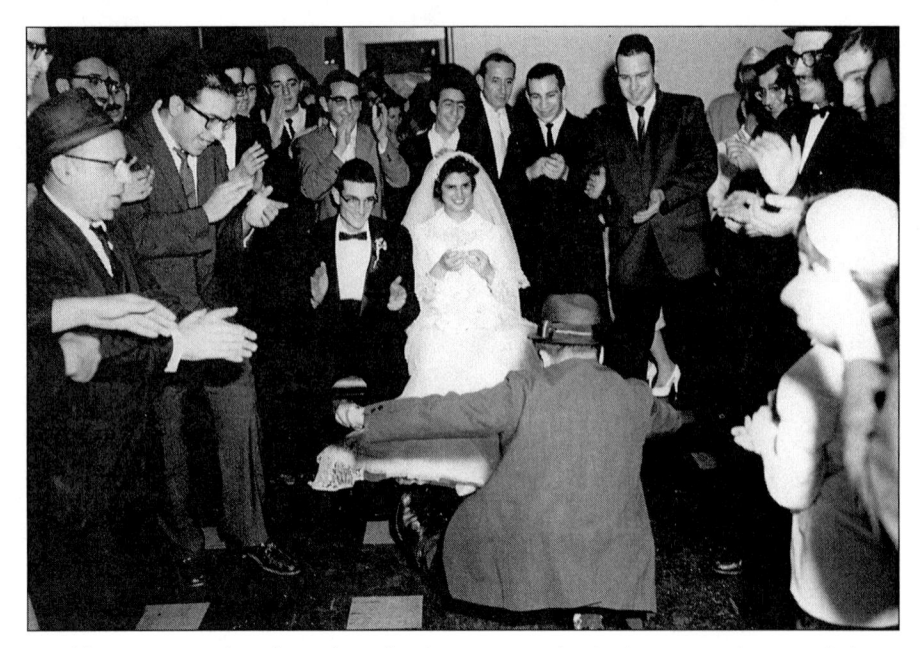

Weddings were another place where the changes occurring in the community were obvious. Pictured here is Rabbi Ezra (Eddie) Zafrani's wedding. With the clear separation of genders and the presence of exuberantly dancing Ashkenazic *yeshiva bachurim*, the affair was the talk of the community long after it ended. Some of the people in this picture include:
L-R: Mike Antebi (second from left), David Srour (standing behind the bride), Charlie Sultan (the third man after David), Morris Srour (the next visible profile after Charlie), and Rabbi Mordechai Goldstein, Rosh Yeshiva of Diaspora Yeshiva.

The next morning, when the women came, the real protests began.
"Who can see through this thing?"
"What, we are being put behind a cage?"
"What was wrong with the way it was before?"
But the *mehitza* stayed.
Yes, there were changes occurring in the community.
The boys went off to some of the growing Ashkenaz yeshivot, and came back spiritually uplifted and ready for halachic growth.
There was an unawareness of practical halachah among the community. The previous generation had been so bogged down with scraping together money for food, they never had time to learn Torah. Syrian Jews had simple but strong faith in the relevance of a fundamental relationship with G-d.[6] This absolute value was imbibed with their mothers' milk and even public school didn't dilute that ironclad belief. But the importance of

---

6. Rabbi Shneur Kotler and Rabbi Rafael Eisenberg both mentioned to leaders in the Sephardic community their wonder as to the innate simple *emunah* of the Sephardim. "We are jealous of you," they said.

adopting halachot with which they were unfamiliar, seemed strange and unnecessary.

The boys were facing a difficult challenge: No matter how carefully they presented their new knowledge, they were inherently questioning the homes where they grew up.

Parents felt threatened and confused by the changes that their children were introducing, whether in halachah, or simply in the way that they were refocusing their lives. One of Irwin's friends had to hide from the private investigator his parents hired when he snuck off to yeshiva. And his parents were not the only ones to act in an extreme manner.

Not Nouri. While he didn't take every new idea that his children brought home at face value, he was ready to listen, learn, and understand. When he saw that Irwin had come back from Vineland more religious but ultimately grounded, he became an ardent admirer of Rabbi Eisemann and gratefully supported the yeshiva. Later on, when Irwin got married and Rabbi Eisemann invited everyone to Vineland for *sheva berachot*, Nouri happily packed the whole family into the car and drove down to New Jersey for an unforgettable experience.

All of this was happening as Nouri was achieving growing recognition as a community leader. Yet he never viewed his success as proof that his way of life was "religious enough." He was a truth-seeker, and his desire for truth allowed him to embrace new ideas and standards in religiosity, not immediately, but slowly, through learning and understanding.

As Nouri embraced change, he looked for ways to help the community grow spiritually as well. Where others were afraid to challenge the status-quo, Nouri was convinced that as long as his goal was *l'shem Shamayim*, for the sake of Heaven, he had to forge ahead, even if other people disagreed with him. It was this attitude that impelled him to embark on one of his most daring projects: the establishment of a religious girls' school for his community.

Chapter 40:
"OSEH HADASHOT, BA'AL MILHAMOT"[7]

Magen David was finally attracting the boys of the community, and that was great, but the girls were just not coming, even though the yeshiva was co-ed. Some girls attended when they were young, but by third grade, most had dropped out. Carol Dayan was amazed to enter a Magen David where there were 25 fourth-grade boys, and two lone girls sitting in the middle of the room!

Nouri contemplated the situation long and hard. He had always tried to help the community youth by luring them to shul and keeping them there. He offered a child $1 to fold the *talletim* left in disarray after prayers. He didn't really need the help, but he wanted to create an opportunity for the child to view the *k'nees* as a positive (and profitable) place.

"You are not doing it for the dollar," he told the child who came to claim his salary. "You are working *l'shem Shamayim*. You want to help keep the shul orderly."

The boy shrugged, but the message seeped in.[8]

Nouri noticed the children not as pesky youngsters who disturbed the services, but as valuable people who would one day be adults. He recognized his own power to influence them through little things. He was still paying kids to say *Tehillim*, often telling them, "You keep track of how much I owe you." He trusted them and they learned to be honest because they appreciated his trust.

---

7. In the blessing of *Yotzer Ohr*, we praise Hashem for bringing renewal to the world and then being the master of war. Mr. Dayan used this to explain that when one wants to do something new, he must be prepared for battle.

8. Jackie Mevorah was one of these boys, as was Mr. Dayan's future son-in-law, Rabbi David Ozeirey.

Hacham Baruch Ben Haim with his class in Magen David Yeshiva. Top row, L-R: Irwin Shamah, Morris Shalom, Mitchel Mansour, Elliot Braha, Eli Ben Haim. Middle row, L-R: Ralph Srour, Joseph Seruya, Joseph Harary, Joseph Elnadav, Ralph Sasson, Yaakov Dewek, Stephen Asher. Front row, L-R: Heywood Chalom, Abraham Safdieh, Ezra Labaton, Hacham Baruch, Julian Koch, Isaac Mizrahi, Morris Rudy.

Nonetheless, he viewed all these projects as band-aids, comforting strips that were multi-functional but not nearly enough to heal a big wound.

And the growing spiritual chasm in his community was a big wound.

"It's not our way," was the dismissive excuse for the disinterest in providing girls with a comprehensive Jewish education.

Not our way? Nouri wondered to himself. *Is it not "our way" for our women to be knowledgeable about Jewish traditions? We are no longer living in Syria where girls stayed home and learned everything from their mothers. We are in America where our girls attend public school and where our traditions are getting lost in this foreign culture.*

"A girls' yeshiva," Nouri kept repeating to anyone who would listen. "We will begin with kindergarten and nursery classes and then continue with a first grade, and in time we will have a full-scale yeshiva. Magen David can keep the boys, while Ahi Ezer will take care of the girls. I think the girls will be happier in a place geared toward them. The Ashkenaz have had schools like these for decades. The girls learn together happily, with their own kind. Can't we learn from our brothers?"

Typical Nouri. He saw, he heard, he learned, and he acted.

With patience.

"I'm telling you, Nouri, what for?"

"It's gonna be a hassle. A girls' yeshiva? You see how difficult Magen David has it, not just getting the girls, but getting the boys. Why do you think that we will succeed where they have not?"

Nouri was unsurprised and unfazed by the skepticism. He knew that he was planting a seed that would take time to germinate. He was convinced that times were changing and that the community was ready for those changes. His proof was in the dramatic outgrowth of the humble Shabbat and Sunday Programs that had been initiated — voluntarily — by the teenaged girls of the community. On the heels of those extraordinarily successful programs, Ahi Ezer had opened a preschool and began offering after-school Talmud Torah classes during the week as well.

No one could explain why the new Talmud Torah was attracting an enrollment when just a few years earlier Ahi Ezer shut down their old Talmud Torah for lack of interest. The facts were there for everyone to see: Within one year, enrollment soared from 40 children to 140 children![9]

"When the girls began organizing groups on Shabbat," he explained to Uncle Dave, "none of us knew that they would become popular. They were acting *l'shem Shamayim*, so Hashem helped them. Then came the Sunday program, which grew so fast we didn't have enough girls to be teachers. That was followed by our preschool and after-school Talmud Torah, both of which are growing as we speak. I keep talking to Rabbi Katz and Rabbi Schachter and I'm convinced that the next step is a full-day girls' yeshiva that will grow from our preschool."

Rabbi Moshe Katz had been a tremendous source of encouragement for Nouri for years. He had arrived in America at the age of three, graduated from the Boyaner Beis Medrash, and went on to Yeshiva University. As a pulpit Rabbi in both Hunter and Liberty, New York, he had inspired many children from irreligious homes to become religious. Now he was using his pedagogical talents as one of the architects of Ahi Ezer Yeshiva. Likewise, Rabbi Schachter was also an incredible help. Practically since he arrived in America from Shanghai, he had been helping Nouri influence his community through educational programs. It was only natural that Nouri turn to him for help in establishing Ahi Ezer Yeshiva.

---

9. "Much credit for this success belonged to Rabbi Saul Wolf, who recruited students through the Public School Released Time program, which allowed students to leave school for a daily hour of religious training. Some of the children who attended these classes were so pleased, they joined the full Talmud Torah program" (excerpted from Ahi Ezer Bulletins, Feb. and Nov. of 1961). Rabbi Wolf spoke movingly at the first Ahi Ezer graduation after Mr. Dayan's passing. Much of the information in this chapter is based on a transcript of that speech and on an interview with Rabbi Wolf.

The "new" Ahi Ezer Talmud Torah and preschool building was housed in a large house, one block over from the synagogue.

While Dave Bibi had stepped down from the presidency, he still played a very active role in the congregation. He was on the board of almost every community initiative, sometimes as chairman and sometimes as a regular member. Nouri continued to run all his ideas by his uncle, both as moral support and because he valued his uncle's input. Dave Bibi liked his attitude. He liked when people forged ahead with their dreams rather than sitting back and complaining about the status quo. And if other committee members objected, well, who said everything had to be done with committee approval?

"*Oseh hadashot, ba'al milhamot* — When a person wants to do something new, he has to be prepared to wage a battle," Nouri often repeated.

And yet no one saw mild-mannered, smiling Nouri as a dictator, ramming his ideas down the community throat. This was because he always introduced his ideas peacefully and quietly. He encouraged people to be on the shul committee, attend meetings, and give their opinions. At committee meetings, he went around the table, asking each person to say his piece. He listened carefully, and only after hearing everyone speak did he offer an opinion. The respect and deference he had for everyone, regardless of their financial situation or spiritual level, engendered respect in return. Therefore, when he went ahead and acted on his own (because he realized that if he waited for everyone to agree to his proposal, nothing would happen), there was little opposition. The community recognized that Mr. Isidore Dayan was their devoted president who cared deeply about every congregant.

Nouri operated with controlled passion. He had a vision that he knew would come to fruition only through patience. When he interviewed Rabbi Wolf for his position as a teacher in the Talmud Torah, he didn't mention his goal of a full-day yeshiva. He just radiated warmth, encouragement, and vision.

"Our Talmud Torah is growing rapidly. We need a person with your background and knowledge to help us grow," Nouri had explained.

Are you certain that you want someone so young...? Saul Wolf couldn't voice the question that might disqualify him from the job.

"I will back you," Nouri continued. "I will be there whenever you need me."

Rabbi Wolf was disarmed by Nouri's charm and he took the job, even though he waved away the flowery words as simply talk. That was a mistake. He soon learned that the clean-shaven businessman, with whom he signed a contract, conducted himself like a Rabbi: Nouri never said anything he didn't mean.

L-R: Eli Shamah, Nouri, Hacham Sion, unknown, and Rabbi Wolf

Whenever Rabbi Wolf called, Nouri was there. And even when he didn't call, Nouri was there. Nouri was determined to see his Talmud Torah grow into a full-day girls' yeshiva, and he understood that something so revolutionary could happen only with constant support and encouragement.

But it had to happen. The community needed a proper school for girls.

The re-establishment of the Ahi Ezer Talmud Torah happened in tandem with other efforts to bring more religiosity into the community. Janet Zalta formed a Ladies Auxiliary, initially established to create a proper Talmud Torah. They campaigned, raised money, and within a year, accomplished their dreams. The Talmud Torah moved out of the Annex and into two newly purchased houses behind it. Nouri recruited some of the community youth, boys who were Sunday morning regulars at the 9 a.m. *minyan*/breakfast, and they cleaned the place up and painted the walls.

The two houses were now a proper school.

Heady with their success, the Ladies Auxiliary revived the Ahi Ezer Bulletin, a community newsletter that had an on-and-off existence for years. They used the paper to publicize their new programs, to update the community on its progress, and as a platform to hear from their leaders. Hacham Sion regularly wrote for the Bulletin, as did Rabbi Wolf. The Ladies Auxiliary wanted to expand their activities.

"We can organize activities, holiday luncheons, and special events, anything that will keep the synagogue in the center of our lives," Janet explained to Nouri.

"Maybe you would like some classes," Nouri suggested casually.

"Classes in what?"

"Well, how about classes in Jewish thought? Or maybe Hebrew language?"

Though many of the women in the community had attended Talmud Torah as children, the general Syrian mentality remained: Boys need to read Torah backwards, forwards, and inside out, with the proper pronunciation, while girls did not. If a girl mastered the *aleph-bet* and learned how to read, that was very nice, but if she did not, that was also fine. She could follow along with the prayers by listening and repeating, as Syrian women had done for centuries. She could read the English transliteration that was in some of the *siddurim*. Anything more was admirable, but not necessary.

Nouri realized the paradox of teaching little girls how to read while their mothers remained illiterate. Yet Rebbetzin Eisenberg's classes had not attracted many participants. Had the atmosphere in the community changed enough to warrant more interest?

Janet considered its merits and agreed that many of her friends would find such classes interesting. Nouri turned to Hacham Sion and Rabbi Wolf, and they designed an adult education program, with separate classes for men, women, teenaged boys, and teenaged girls. Each group received a program geared to its interests and abilities.

The classes for married women were surprisingly popular. Rabbi Wolf taught them how to read and write Hebrew. Then he introduced them to the *perasha* by taking the portion of the week, picking out the important points, and teaching them. As the women advanced, Hacham Sion also began to give classes. Slowly, the women of the community received a Jewish education.

Janet marveled at how Nouri always seemed to sense what the community needed. When she would approach him a few weeks before Hanukah to suggest a party, he immediately offered her funds, and a few more ideas to enhance the occasion. He would do anything to keep the people socializing among their own so that they would not look elsewhere to satisfy their social needs. Janet was inspired by his enthusiasm and organized trips in the summer and indoor entertainment in the winter, besides the seasonal activities, like the Tu B'shebat luncheon and Purim carnival. Most activities were designed for families and Nouri participated in the most humble ways, like flipping frankfurters at the community picnic.

Ahi Ezer Day Camp

Nouri's humility endeared him to his people. He was president of the congregation, inarguably a prestigious position, and yet nothing changed. He still poured coffee for the men who came Sunday mornings, swept the floor if he saw that it was dirty, and sliced watermelon on synagogue field trips. When his first year as president came to an end, he was unanimously re-elected for a second term.

It was time to forge ahead with his dreams.

"Izzy, where are we going to get the money? Bingo is great, but it's not a bottomless pit," complained Nouri Sarway, the third of the musketeers who had relentlessly collected for the 71st Street building. Nouri Dayan could dream a million dreams, but it was Nouri Sarway, the synagogue treasurer, who kept him firmly grounded by reminding him that money had to be a consideration.

"Don't worry," Nouri Dayan answered, "we'll get the money. If we are working *l'shem Shamayim*, it's going to come."

"But Izzy, can't we just breathe a little by paying off the mortgage for the Talmud Torah building? Why pile on more debts?"

But Nouri didn't want to breathe. He wanted to build and build and build. There was a large piece of property up for sale, at a great price, on Ocean Parkway between Avenues X and Y.[10]

---

10. The Syrian community was slowly transferring to Flatbush, mainly from Avenue R down toward Avenue U. This property was farther out, but much closer to Flatbush than to

"Buy it, and then we'll decide what to do with it," Nouri decided. This became his motto. The community would grow, as long as they had a place to grow into.

Ahi Ezer was constantly innovating. In the summer of 1962, they opened their first day camp, also a revolutionary undertaking. It was a resounding success, with a very high percentage of the Talmud Torah students enrolling in the day camp.

It's time for the yeshiva, Nouri decided, *with or without committee approval.*

The years were slipping by. Too many children were already post-elementary school and could barely read Hebrew. Nouri could no longer sit by and watch the trend continue. He had one all-encompassing goal: to see all Syrian children, boys and girls, in a yeshiva, be it Ahi Ezer or Magen David.[11]

"Next year, we are opening our first grade," Nouri announced at an educational board meeting. "Rabbi Katz has agreed to serve as the head of the educational board and Rabbi Schachter will be joining as a board member. Rabbi Wolf will draft an announcement in the Ahi Ezer Bulletin and we will begin organizing our enrollment."

The enrollment drive was an instant success in that most of the parents of the Pre-1A students enrolled their children in the first grade. Rabbi Wolf had invested tremendous energy in the preschool program and parents were impressed that the children were learning so much and came home happy. They were willing to give the yeshiva a try.

Nouri was pleased with the progress, but it always came with aggravation.

"Divine Providence," Esther noted, "there is no way in the world to accomplish so much without Divine Providence." Everything was a hassle: from the spirited board meetings (everyone had an opinion) to dealing with those who cornered Nouri in shul to let him know all the problems (not that they were offering any solutions). There was no euphoria for Nouri and his devoted volunteers. That happiness had to come from within.

And it did.

Nouri's equanimity was legendary. He never lost his temper, always answered people pleasantly, and remained a gentleman. He didn't take

---

Bensonhurst. Ahi Ezer Bulletins report that they bought the lot for a new community center that would unite the whole Syrian community, and give the *Shammis* a Flatbush synagogue.

11. Mr. Dayan always pushed for community cooperation: ..."Thank G-d we have Magen David Yeshiva for boys and the infant Ahi Ezer Yeshiva for girls. Are we proud of these yeshivot? If we are, we would have many more children in them... Don't let the Magen David Yeshiva and Ahi Ezer Yeshiva down. It's your own, it's your backbone, and it's your pride..." (Ahi Ezer Bulletin, April 1964).

"Oseh Hadashot, Ba'al Milhamot" / 333

other people's comments and criticism personally. They had a right to their opinions, and he had a right to his.

Nouri's absolute honesty and integrity was so obvious that even after many decades of community service, he never made an enemy. Everyone knew that he was *l'shem Shamayim*. His friends and congregants saw his unusual dedication and were motivated to volunteer.[12] Many of these people were middle- to low-income businessmen, unable to donate large sums of money. They learned from Nouri that they could donate their time, which was just as precious.

"Why don't you try raising money for the yeshiva?" Nouri suggested to teenaged Seymour Escava. "Anything you bring is good."

Izzy is so easygoing, so likeable, so humble… if he can collect money, maybe I can collect money, Seymour decided.

He went on to become one of Ahi Ezer's most effective fundraisers.

As Nouri forged ahead in battle, he still valued and appreciated every Jew.

---

12. Ahi Ezer had proportionately many more volunteers than any other local congregation. Some of the people motivated by Mr. Dayan's volunteerism include: Ceasar Salama, Freddie Erani, the Escava brothers (Seymour, Bunny, and Nat), Ike Swed, Joe Jacobs, Albert Levy, Dr. Isaac Mohadeb, and Lou Rofe. While by no means complete, this list includes people of varied income levels and backgrounds, all of whom devoted many hours to community service, often crossing cultural lines in their passion to help other Jews.

Chapter 41:
"THE ONE THING THAT YOU SHOULD NEVER MIND IS IF YOUR CHILDREN ARE BETTER THAN YOU."

Nouri worked tirelessly to create Ahi Ezer Yeshiva. Meanwhile, there were changes going on in his own home, some that he effected, some that he accepted, and some that pushed him to grow further.

A few years earlier, his nephew, Joe's son Murray, had been going through a rough time. Being that he dropped by the Dayan home practically every Shabbat, Nouri read the warning signs and decided that Murray needed to go out of town. He also knew that too much talking would derail the whole process, so he simply informed Joe, arranged a passport for Murray, bought him a ticket to Eretz Yisrael, and shipped him off to Yeshiva Porat Yosef. Murray returned to America a year and a half later and went to Ner Israel, much more settled and with a passion for learning.[13]

All because Nouri saw, understood, and acted.

Right after Hacham Murad's passing, fiercely independent Sara Maslaton was determined to live alone. That summer she traveled to Eretz Yisrael on her own, by boat. There, she made the rounds of all her family, and was treated as a queen wherever she went. Her grandson, Murray, watched in amazement as she presided over every discussion, even among *talmidei hachamim* of note. With the rapid Arabic that flashed back and forth, and the heavy hot air flecked with sand, Murray had a taste of what life in Syria must have been like.[14]

---

13. Mr. Dayan took matters in his own hands because he knew that his sister-in-law, Sophie, would never agree to send Murray so far away. At a family *sheva berachot*, Rabbi Murray Maslaton thanked Uncle Izzy for the ticket that changed his life.

14. Some family members said that Sara Maslaton went to Israel in order to visit her grandson, Murray, who had been sent away so young. "I met her at the boat. 'You arrived here

But when Sara Maslaton returned to her empty apartment, the magnitude of her loss came back to her, as jarring and painful as a slap in the face. Not one to hide her feelings, she also couldn't bring herself to acknowledge her situation. So she remained stoic, except when her sadness became overwhelming. Years passed. Her children felt bad that she still seemed so unsettled, but they were at a loss: What was there to do? What was there to say?

As usual, it was Nouri who found the right words.

"*M'rat Ami* (wife of my father-in-law), please move in with us," Nouri said gently.

Sara was startled. How did he know? How did he understand that "Sara the strong" was finding it difficult to live alone? How could she take him up on such an offer... after all, who wanted to be saddled with a live-in mother-in-law?

I'm barely 80. I hope to have many more years on this world, please G-d... if I move in now, they might be stuck with me for a long time. How can I do it to them?

"Please," Nouri softly begged, "I never had a mother. It would be an honor and a privilege to serve you."

Such a plea, Sara couldn't refuse.

Stetta's arrival ushered in a new era in the Dayan home. If Esther thought that life would be less hectic now that her youngest was out of diapers, she was mistaken. Everyone came to visit *Stetta*.

A few years earlier, the Maslaton siblings had begun a Mosa'ei Shabbat routine where they rotated visiting each other's houses. One week they would get together by Hacham Sion, another week by Uncle Jack, the next week at the Dayans, etc. The hostess would set out food, the men would

Murray Maslaton (right) as a young man

---

safely and still haven't called your mother?' was her greeting. Only after I called home was she ready to talk to me. We went all over the place together. Beside those whom she visited, everyone came to visit my grandmother. She was a celebrity. People drew strength from her" (Rabbi Murray Maslaton).

Stetta in Israel, attending a family wedding. The Hacham standing on the far left is Hacham Abraham Fatal, the father-in-law of Hacham Ovadya Yosef. The man sitting next to the groom is Hacham Azur (Ezra) Tarab Maslaton, Av Bet Din of Damascus and then Rabbi of Shechunat HaTikva in Tel Aviv. The groom is his son Yaakov (later a prominent Rabbi). *Stetta* is sitting on the other side of the bride, the daughter of Rabbi Amram Azulai.

sing the Mosa'ei Shabbat songs, and the women would chat. The atmosphere was festive and holy, truly an extension of Shabbat.

Now that *Stetta* was staying by Esther, *seuda rebi'it* was in the Dayan house every week. Esther prepared a full table of salads and rolls and spreads — every week! It was a big job that she tackled good-naturedly.

But hosting *Stetta's* guests wasn't confined to a weekly gathering. Bright and early Sunday morning the phone was ringing. A cousin was in town and wanted to stop by, could he come over right now? Esther quickly put up some more water to boil and set some pastries on the table. An old friend had just come back from Florida and, even though it was already 8 p.m., could she please come to visit?

"Sara," Esther called to her daughter, as she hung up the phone, "I need some more sliced melon."

When Esther called, her girls jumped. That was just the way it was. She and Nouri had built a home founded on hierarchical respect: Nouri was king, Esther was queen, and the children were princes. No matter how noble princes are, they are always subservient to the king and queen.

Nouri and Esther formed one unit. They never contradicted each other, and their respect for each other was so profound, the children simply

Irwin and Shirley Dayan at their wedding. L-R: Nouri, Shirley and Irwin, Selim Shamah, Rabbi Yaakob Kassin, Rabbi Yosef Harari Raful (making the *beracha*), Rabbi Avraham Kalmanowitz.

copied that respect, taking it up a notch as befitting the relationship between parents and children. It was ingrained in the spirit of the house that children listened to parents, whether they liked it or not. The girls often didn't begin doing their homework until after 10 at night, when their grandmother went to sleep. Until then, they were busy preparing refreshments or cleaning up after visitors.

Stetta became a beloved and intrinsic part of the Dayan home.

Carol Dayan became engaged and the Syrian community was delighted with the news. Her *hattan* was a young rabbi who had come from Eretz Yisrael and was teaching in Yeshiva of Flatbush. Rabbi Yosef Harari-Raful barely knew English, but Carol's years in Ohel Moshe had given her a decent background in Hebrew and they managed to communicate just fine.

Not long before their wedding, Irwin became engaged to Shirley Shamah.

"A royal alliance," joked the community. Nouri was president of Ahi Ezer and Selim Shamah was president of Magen David.

Both weddings were to be held in Yeshiva of Bensonhurst. While the couples left the major arrangements to their parents, there was one detail they tackled on their own…

Rabbi Yosef Harari Raful (left) learning with his new uncle, Hacham Sion Maslaton

"I think that's it." Irwin jumped into the back seat next to the last of the boxes. Murray gunned the gas and drove off, his future brother-in-law, Rabbi Yosef Harari Raful, next to him in the front seat.

"Look at this rain," Murray muttered. It was coming down in heavy sheets, too fast and strong for the window wipers to control.

"Too bad we can't just leave everything out in the open and let nature do the job for us," Irwin quipped.

The men chuckled but forged ahead. Murray pulled up in front of the building and parked. Together they carted all the boxes of glasses and silverware (full settings for 800 people!) into the building, running back and forth and getting drenched in the process.

"Eight hundred glasses! Maybe we should have asked Daddy to cut down on the guest list," Murray grumbled.

"Too late," Irwin answered. "And what are you complaining about? Yosef and I are doing most of the work."

After several hours, every single piece was dipped.

"Without breaking one glass," Irwin noted with satisfaction, as they drove back to the hall, mission accomplished.

By then, the family was well aware of the need to *tovel* dishes.[15] After Irwin took care of his house, he went over to his Uncle Jack's house and, when his aunt and uncle were not home, he dunked all of their kitchenware as well. But the young men felt that it was still a new concept and

---

15. The Yeshiva of Bensonhurst was the most religiously stringent hall around. Nonetheless, they relied on a popular *heter*, used by caterers, and didn't *tovel* their dishes.

they didn't want to overburden their parents. Rather than ask their parents to do something that they might feel is overwhelming, they decided to just do it on their own, without telling anyone.

In retrospect, Irwin realized that this, too, he learned from his father. The Sunday morning breakfasts, the many guest lecturers, the raising of the *mehitza*, and even, to a certain extent, Ahi Ezer Yeshiva, had all been established because his father had quietly gone and acted, knowing full well that if he waited for everyone's agreement, nothing would happen. He was a pioneer, and pioneers didn't sit back and wait for everyone to approve of their plans.

Daddy, I'm also a pioneer, Irwin thought as he and his new wife boarded a bus to Lakewood.

Once again, Irwin was following his father's example... against his father's wishes. Irwin replayed the scene that dogged him since it happened a few weeks earlier.

The three of them — Uncle Morris, Nouri, and Irwin — sat awkwardly around the restaurant table. Irwin couldn't remember the last time he had gone out to lunch with his father and uncle. Clearly, they had something on their minds and they thought a nice, over-lunch discussion was the right venue.

Uncle Morris cleared his throat. "Your father mentioned that you have some original plans for after your marriage..."

Irwin sighed inwardly. *I should have known...*

"While we realize that you have gained enormously from the Ashkenazic yeshivot, we have our ways, and some of their ideas are rather different..."

Irwin remained impassive.

Nouri interjected, "We agree that learning is very important, but so is making a living and supporting your family. Living out in Lakewood to learn in Kollel, without any realistic plan of how to support yourself..."

"It's not our way," Uncle Morris continued. "There is a time for everything — a time for learning and a time for working. We all make time to learn, but only within the framework of supporting our families."

"You know that I would be more than happy if you want to be a Rabbi," Nouri quickly added, "but, right now, you don't have a Rabbinic position. How can you think of beginning marriage without any income? Even if the yeshiva will give you a stipend, you know what the Rambam says about being paid for learning Torah."

"We also love to learn Torah," Uncle Morris added, "but providing for one's family is also important."

Irwin inhaled deeply. "Daddy, Uncle Morris, I don't want to argue with you. I can show you all the sources that validate my decision, but I have a feeling that it won't help..."

Nouri began to interrupt but Morris silenced him.

"... I'm very far from where I want to be in terms of proficiency in learning Torah. If I go out to work now, when will I have the time to concentrate on my learning? I don't know how long I will stay, or how it will work out. I only know that right now, I have to try." That conversation continued out the restaurant, in the car on the way home, at home, almost right up until his wedding day.

Irwin showed his father the *Kesef Mishneh* on the Rambam.[16]

Nouri didn't answer.

Unlike the need to *tovel* dishes or the height of a *mehitza*, embracing a Kollel lifestyle wasn't mandated by halacha. Sure, there were many *pesukim* and *dibrei Hazal* supporting the concept but, ultimately, there were many opinions that favored the approach where a man supports his family while finding time to learn. Nouri didn't change his opinion, but he remained quiet when he couldn't change Irwin's mind.

The Dayans were one of the only Sephardic couples in Lakewood. Even among the Ashkenazim, entering Kollel was still a novel idea. Twenty years had passed since the first Kollel in America was established in White Plains, New York. Beis Medrash Govoha of Lakewood, and its affiliated Kollel, was an outgrowth of that first Kollel, and had enjoyed steady growth from its inception. Nonetheless, by 1963, there were fewer than 50 families living in Lakewood. Everyone in Lakewood was a pioneer, but the Sephardic couples had made a more radical change than most of the others.

No matter how deeply religious their parents and grandparents had been, the overall Syrian community had become very American. There was virtually no house without a television, card playing (actually a holdover from Syria) was the standard community pastime, and socializing among genders was considered fine as long as everyone was Jewish. The years that the new generation of young men had spent in Ashkenazic yeshivot had exposed them to a different environment, one that was more isolated, purer, more Jewish. They wanted to live a Kollel life not only for the opportunity to devote themselves to learning, but also to establish their homes on a more solidly spiritual foundation so that when the children came along, they would enter this world in an elevated environment.

Lakewood was their goal for all of these reasons.

Not that it was easy.

There was so much to get used to, and few resources to help them adjust. Lakewood of the 1960's was a vacation area that no longer filled up, neither

---

16. While the Rambam speaks strongly against one who chooses not to earn a living in order to devote himself only to learning Torah, the *Kesef Mishneh* explains that this is only referring to someone who seeks to lead a rich life while living off charity (*Assurot* 17:5).

Rabbi Shneur Kotler (1918–1982),
Rosh Yeshiva of Beis Medrash Govoha
of Lakewood

in the summer nor in the winter. The city was eerily quiet: not a dog in the street barking, not a cat slinking in the alleyways. There were blocks of green lawns, large houses that were old and worn, and not much else. There were no shopping centers and no business districts. The women had nowhere to work, which meant no income, and nothing to distract them from the monotony of living far from family, without jobs. Housework wasn't very time consuming; there wasn't much to cook because they had very little food.

What kept everyone going was their idealism, their sense that they were choosing a different kind of life for all the right reasons. That idealism was constantly tested, particularly during that year right after Reb Aharon passed away. The yeshiva was undergoing tremendous change. Rabbi Shneur Kotler was trying to keep everything running smoothly, materialistically and spiritually, and the burden was enormous.

"He is a great person, really special," Irwin enthused, "warm and encouraging. He is helping me find *habrutot* and often asks me how I'm managing in learning..."

How could he tell the Rosh HaYeshiva that they used up the last of their wedding gifts? The Rosh HaYeshiva already had so much on his shoulders.

And then, one day, a check for $200 came in the mail.

It was postmarked Bensonhurst, and signed by Mr. Isidore Dayan.[17]

Nouri's checks continued to arrive on a monthly basis, not due to a change of heart but from simple compassion. A mutual acquaintance had approached Nouri and told him of how desperately the couple was struggling. Nouri listened to his impassioned description and realized that, no matter how much he disagreed with his son's choice, he couldn't let him struggle in this way.

In a moment of soul searching, he recognized that his son deserved the same compassion that he showered on the rest of Am Yisrael and that anything less would be hypocritical. With rent being $110 a month (before

---

17. Mr. Selim Shamah also helped out.

utilities), there would not be much of his check left over for food, but at least there was the possibility of the couple managing.

Nouri's reaction to Irwin's choices followed a distinct pattern that ultimately led to an overhaul of his entire mentality. At first, he balked at the change in tradition and the assumption that the change was necessary. Slowly, the new ideas grew on him, prompting grudging acceptance, and finally full-hearted change.

Carol had attended public high school after she graduated Ohel Moshe.

"Better to be with *goyim* who you know are different, than with Jews who you don't want to emulate," was her mother's sharp answer when Carol asked why she couldn't attend a local, co-ed yeshiva high school.

Esther Dayan set the tone of her home with her day-to-day comments and life lessons. One subtle message demanded that her children be more religious. She constantly reminded her children that they came from generations of Rabbis and that they were born with the responsibility to follow in their footsteps. She was confident that they could do so even while being a part of the secular world, just as she and Nouri had done. Her children were absorbing the subtle messages, but forging ahead with new interpretations.

When the girls in Sara's eighth-grade class began talking about applying to all-girls Jewish high schools like Central and Esther Schonfeld, Sara realized that there was no way that she was going to go to public school. She wanted to go to an all-girls school, the most religious one around: Bais Yaakov of Boro Park.

Rebbetzin Vichna Kaplan had opened the first Bais Yaakov high school in America in 1944. In less than 20 years, she opened branches in Williamsburg, Crown Heights, the Bronx, and Boro Park. Nonetheless, attending a Bais Yaakov high school was still not a given even among many religious families. Certainly, in the Syrian community, it was a radical idea.[18]

Sara well remembered Irwin's struggle when he went to Vineland and then to Kollel, and she knew that she was also facing a quiet battle. She could already hear the comments: Carol had gone to public school and yet remained a fine Jewish girl who attended *shiurim* and taught Jewish children about Yiddishkeit. She went on to marry a *talmid hacham* and was covering her hair.

Why change a good recipe?

Because there is something better out there, Sara realized.

---

18. In the 40's and 50's, there were still many religious parents who were scared that without a public school education or, at the very least, a Jewish school that had a more accelerated secular studies program than Bais Yaakov, their girls would not be adequately prepared for college. There were a few Syrian girls in Bais Yaakov. Among them was Mrs. Shirley (Shamah) Dayan.

Knowing that her parents would object, Sara went to Boro Park to take the entrance exam without telling them where she was going. She came back later than she expected.

"Where were you?" Esther asked.

"I went to take the Bais Yaakov entrance exam," Sara answered, and casually handed over the application.

Esther was too shocked to comment. Nouri was quiet; he never reacted instinctively. He skimmed the application, which also noted the tuition fee, and grunted, "High tuition." But he didn't say that she couldn't go. Over the summer there were short, quiet comments here and there indicating her parents' displeasure, but they never outright forbade her to go.

Her friends thought she was crazy. "You say you want to be a teacher, but for that you need a college education, not Bais Yaakov."

That was the prevailing mentality: Bais Yaakov education was inferior.

Sara didn't care. She instinctively knew that Bais Yaakov was more religious, more pure.

And that is where I want to be, she decided.

So Sara went to Bais Yaakov, and Nouri paid the tuition. Then Joyce followed Sara, and Nouri paid a second tuition. Then one day, Esther and Nouri realized that their girls had made a choice that wasn't all that bad. They were happy in Bais Yaakov. They were the same good and obedient daughters they had always been. They were learning good things and doing well.

As per the pattern, Nouri and Esther listened, learned, and then embraced something new. As time went on, Nouri would tell his friends and children his new motto: The one thing that you should never mind is if your children are better than you.

Chapter 42:

"I HAVE TO DO MY PART; THE REST IS UP TO HASHEM."

Bensonhurst, 1964

Joe Jacobs noticed a stranger standing in the back of the shul. Almost twenty years had passed since *he* had been a stranger in the back of the shul. That is why he rushed over to welcome the newcomer.

"Joe Jacobs," he beamed, extending a hand. "How can I help you?"

The man followed Joe to his seat, murmuring softly, "My mother is sick. I'd like a blessing from the Rabbi."

"No problem," Joe answered. "First, sit next to me and let's pray. Then I'll take you to the Rabbi."

As the services progressed, Joe realized that his new friend didn't know how to read Hebrew, and was ignorant of most things Jewish. Nonetheless, he took him over to Hacham Sion, who gave him a warm blessing, and then Joe brought him home for a satisfying Shabbat meal.

Two weeks passed.

He's back, Joe thought, as he went to greet his former guest.

"My mother died," the man said softly. Joe didn't know what to do. Then he spotted Nouri and pulled him over to the side.

"His mother died," he whispered. "He does not know anything…"

"He must come to shul every day to say Kaddish. We'll have to teach him."

Nouri walked over to the man and began explaining to him the intricacies of his obligations. "Come tomorrow," he told him. "We will help you."

"But I'm moving out of town in a week."

"Fine," Nouri answered, "you have a week to learn."

The stranger was there, bright and early the next morning. Nouri had already prepared a new *tallit* and a set of *tefillin*. He patiently showed the man how to use both and explained to him the significance of his actions.

He gave him a *siddur* with English transliteration and guided him through the services. Every day, for one week, Nouri taught this man how to pray properly so that he could meet his obligations to his deceased mother. At the end of the week, the man left.

They never heard from him again.

"Izzy," Joe asked, "doesn't it bother you? You bought him a new *tallit*, you gave him *tefillin*, and you took him through the prayers for a whole week, and now he disappeared as if he never came. A little frustrating, no?"

"Joe," Nouri addressed him gently, "the man was a Jew. His mother was a Jew. For one week he prayed. For one week he put on *tefillin*. Maybe he is still praying. Maybe he is still putting on *tefillin*. That is not our business. Our job in this world is to help our fellow Jews in the best way we can, and that is what we did."

Indeed, that was how Nouri viewed his role in this world: *I have to do my part; the rest is up to Hashem.*

When it came to helping his fellow Jews serve Hashem, Nouri never felt that he had done "his part." This was especially true regarding his campaign to give every girl in the community a Jewish education — if not in a full-day yeshiva, at least in a Talmud Torah. He was less worried about the boys, but when it came to the girls, he was obsessed. He wanted to recreate the community mentality. He wanted them to realize that a basic Jewish education was just as important for girls as it was for boys.

Nouri chaired the monthly educational board meetings where many ideas and issues came up. Some of the girls stopped coming to Talmud Torah classes. Perhaps Rabbi Wolf should personally call every girl and encourage her to come back. Parents in the community need additional incentives to send their girls to Ahi Ezer Yeshiva. Maybe cultural classes, like art and music, would draw more interest. We are a new school. How can we be sure that we are up to par? Let us bring in an outside consultant to test our students and give us an honest assessment.

Both Nouri and Rabbi Wolf realized that it was imperative to maintain a top-notch secular studies program. Though their real goal was the Jewish education, they knew that they would not keep any students if their secular studies program seemed inferior to public school. Indeed, Rabbi Wolf took this understanding one step further and worked to keep the preschool reading program above public school level as a powerful attraction. Janet Zalta organized extra-curricular activities, carnivals, and trips, to keep school an exciting and positive place. She brought up every idea to Nouri, whose encouraging attitude motivated her to come up with more ideas. Amazingly, money was never an issue… even though money was always an issue.[19]

---

19. Mrs. Janet Zalta was a most dedicated volunteer. She checked that the secular studies were on the same level as, or ahead of, the public schools and that Ahi Ezer received top-

Nouri viewed every penny spent on bettering the yeshiva a worthwhile investment. On the other hand, he never turned away a child because the parents couldn't, or wouldn't, pay tuition. Some parents paid as little as $5 a month! How was Nouri supposed to run a private school when so many parents were barely paying tuition? Even Bingo didn't bring in enough funds.

As usual, Nouri, Dave Bibi, and their volunteer recruits went fundraising. In establishing Ahi Ezer Yeshiva, Nouri established several ironclad but unspoken policies that he was determined to keep: Every child who wants a Jewish education must receive one, the education must be on the highest possible level, and the staff and teachers **must** be paid on time.

And, as always, Nouri was true to his word.

But raising funds for Ahi Ezer Yeshiva was only one of his many projects.

Ike slid into a chair, just in time for prayers. He came to the *k'nees* only occasionally, but when he did come, he loved the services. That particular day, he didn't know what brought him to the *k'nees*. He was feeling good, could that be it? He was married a few months, had a decent job, and felt refreshingly stable. He prayed with all his heart, and then sat back in his chair, resting for a moment before getting up to leave. Suddenly he noticed two men who sat down squarely alongside him: Dave Bibi on one side and Nouri Dayan on the other.

Uh, oh. I'm in big trouble…

"What can I do for you gentlemen?" he asked brightly.

Dave smiled, "Nothing in particular. We came to say hello."

Right.

Ike smiled back. And waited.

"I want to ask you a question," Nouri casually interjected.

"Okaaaay," Ike prompted.

"We have a free-loan association…" Nouri explained.

Ike nodded. He knew all about it.

"We have a number of contributors.[20] We lend the money to people who are down on their luck and they pay it back when they are able to. The loan is interest free. We want to give people the chance to get their lives back together."

Ike nodded his head. "That's nice. Thank G-d, I don't need it."

"Oh, I know," Nouri answered quickly. "I'm not asking you if you want money, I'm asking you to join the Society."

Ike was floored. He was all of 20 years old — a mere kid next to these older, powerful men — and they were including him in a meaningful project,

---

of-the-line textbooks and government aid. Eventually an assistant principal was hired to take care of these duties.

20. Mr. Leon Levy was also one of the main people involved in this initiative.

essentially indicating that they believed in him, in his ability to make a difference to society. Ike stretched out his hand and grinned, "You got it!"

Dave slapped Ike on the back and the threesome exchanged warm handshakes. Even as the older men left, Ike lingered. He savored the warmth of the moment, the taste of belonging to a group of people who were larger than he was, but who intended to pull him up toward them.

So began Ike's active involvement in the Ahi Ezer community. He had always been a part of the *k'nees* — his good friends were Elliot Bibi (Dave's) and Jackie Bibi (Reuben's) — but now he was involved, and all from a handshake and a slap on the back. He felt relevant and wanted to live up to that image. And his main inspiration was Nouri.

When someone gave Nouri a dollar for the shul, he responded with a warm thank you. When someone gave him a thousand dollars, it was the same warm thank you — no more, no less. He extended himself quietly, in ways that no one else would and therefore, when he encouraged others to extend themselves, they felt obligated to do the same.

Ike had been working on Shabbat but, as time went on, he felt more connected to the *k'nees*, more connected to G-d, more of a man. With that recognition came the desire to make a change in himself that was coming from within himself.

I'll go in through the back door, Ike decided on that first Shabbat. He felt self-conscious, as if showing up for the morning services was making a statement, which, in essence, he was. As he slid in through the back, Nouri spotted him.

"Ike, what are you doing here?"

"Isn't it Shabbat?" Ike said bashfully.

"You are going to come every Shabbat?" Nouri asked.

Ike grinned, "You got it."

Wordlessly, Nouri led Ike into the *k'nees* and sat him up front, right between Hy and Basil Cohen. The older man looked up at Nouri and nodded. Then he took the *siddur* that Nouri held open and showed Ike the place. Ike gratefully followed along as Basil took him through the prayers, one paragraph at a time.

Ike felt warm with belonging.

Basil, he is like my grandfather. And Nouri? He is like my father.

Ike was one of the many Syrian Jews who were slowly returning to their heritage, not because of dissatisfaction in life, but through the pull that was always there and was being nurtured by the warmth and acceptance for which Ahi Ezer, and the broader Syrian community, was known.

Ahi Ezer had its paradoxes: Its members were loyal to G-d and believed in Him with all their heart. The days before the busiest business season, the shul was more crowded than usual as some of the more sporadic attendees suddenly appeared and prayed their hearts out. A week later, those chairs were empty again. The services in Ahi Ezer were deeply traditional (they had the slowest services in the neighborhood). Almost all the yeshiva boys came to Ahi Ezer when they returned home from their Ashkenazic yeshivot, even if their parents prayed elsewhere. In Ahi Ezer, they were happy and accepted and they enjoyed the moving services.

On Simhat Torah, Ahi Ezer was the place to be in Bensonhurst. [21]

Many of the other Bensonhurst congregations were dominated by older people who were happy when each *hakafa* took no longer than a few minutes. Ahi Ezer had Nouri, whose ecstasy on Simhat Torah knew no bounds. He danced vigorously, until he was all sweated up and tired. Then he positioned himself blocking the step up to the *teba*, singing and dancing, and riling up the crowd.

"Keep on going," he'd call, "one more round!"

And because he was blocking the *teba*, no one could put down the *Sifrei Torah* and end the *hakafa*. The spirited dancing lasted for hours and attracted all the neighborhood yeshiva boys who had come home for *bein hazemanim* and were thrilled to find a place where they could express their excitement for Torah uninhibited. The yeshiva boys were grateful to have a place to call home, a place where they felt that their devotion to religion was appreciated and not merely tolerated, and where their enthusiasm and excitement were assets.

Yet, the bulk of the Ahi Ezer congregants were simple Jews who were far from these yeshiva *bachurim* in Torah knowledge and religious aspirations.

Nouri ignored the weaknesses and focused on the strengths.

Rather than launch a campaign barring those who publicly desecrated Shabbat from serving on the synagogue committees, he tapped into their sincerity and purposely recruited them to help the community by giving of their time and opening their wallets. The Ahi Ezer congregants were big-hearted people. By appealing to their goodness, Nouri drafted an army of volunteers who accomplished far more than many other bigger and wealthier communities in the New York area. More poignantly, their good deeds had a transforming effect on themselves and slowly, *shemirat Shabbat* became the normal way of life for an Ahi Ezer congregant.

Nouri never established a formal policy or campaign to turn around his community. He just saw so much good in everyone whom he met and they responded to his belief in them.

---

21. "After our *hakafot*, we ate, and then we went to Mirrer Yeshiva. We wanted to see how the other side lived, especially the Ashkenazim. The *hakafot* in Mirrer Yeshiva were unbelievable. Seeing so many *talmidei hachamim* dancing with love of Torah was an experience. But my father had danced up a storm and he headed for bed, exhausted. He had no need to see what was happening on the other side of the world. He didn't need anything outside his Ahi Ezer" (Mr. Murray Dayan).

He also realized that not everything was within his jurisdiction and not always was his position going to be accepted. That being the reality, he quietly found other ways to accomplish his goals. For example, rather than argue with his brother-in-law, Hacham Sion, about whether having a youth *minyan* was good for the community or not, he went along with the Rabbi's stance… and then found another way to keep the youth in the shul.

"Sure, fellas, right over here, in the social hall." Nouri waved his hand around the room, indicating that they could have the whole thing.

The boys couldn't believe their good fortune. Mr. Dayan was giving them the social hall to set up their own game room just… because. The boys turned the room into a hockey rink. Then they added a ping pong table… and a knock-hockey set… and in general, just wrecked the place.

But Nouri didn't say a word. He wanted to keep them off the streets and in the shul and if this was the way to do it, then he would. Sundays, he got them to come to the 9 a.m. *minyan* and breakfast.

"Where were you?" he'd ask a boy who missed the *minyan*. The boy was abashed by the question, but emboldened by having been noticed and missed.

"Come on guys, it's summer. You have no school. Tell you what, I'll give you the same Sunday breakfast every day of the week if you come to a 9 a.m. *minyan* in the summer," Nouri cajoled the boys. And they came to prayers, every day, the entire summer. Then they went off to play ball in the park, but they were back for Minha and Arbit, even without the refreshments.[22]

The boys learned to regard the shul as their home.

And that was exactly what Nouri wanted.

---

22. Rabbi David Ozeirey was one of these boys.

Chapter 43:
RABBOT MACHASHABOT B'LEV ISH[23]

Bensonhurst, 1965

The spirited *zemirot* filled the room, much as the *mazza* foods filled the table.

There was variety wherever one looked.

Rabbi Eisenberg was back, replete with his flowing coat and distinctive Chassidic hat. He had moved to Eretz Yisrael and returned to America for a visit. Where else would he stay, if not at Hotel Dayan? Rabbi Eliyahu Raful was in town collecting for his Kollel. Rabbi David Ades was in town on business. Both men spoke only Hebrew and Arabic. A few other *meshulachim* from Eretz Yisrael, some yeshiva boys, together with Uncle Jack and his family, filled the room.

There were so many foods on the table, the guests hardly knew from where to start filling their plates. There were two kinds of fresh vegetable salads, pickles, olives, homemade pickled mushrooms, beets, *tehina*, *kibbe*, and *mora* (phyllo dough stuffed with chopped meat, a real treat!), and some chopped liver to help the Ashkenazim feel at home. Rabbi Eisenberg was certain that Syrians put out the whole meal at once, rather than bring in course after course like the Ashkenazim. When the girls brought out the *hamin*, he looked so shocked that they tried hard not to giggle.

The *zemirot* were also varied. Though some Ashkenazic tunes had been part of their meals for years, Irwin had introduced a few new ones that he learned in Vineland. Nouri loved these *zemirot* for they brought an extra *hitlahavut* to the table.

They sang the Sephardic songs in their traditional accent while the Ashkenazic songs were sung Ashkenazic. What was happening at the Shabbat

---
23. "There are many plans in the heart of man, but only the Will of God will endure!" (*Mishlei* 19:21).

table was a reflection of what was happening in the Dayan home: While remaining staunchly Sephardic, the Dayans welcomed Ashkenazic songs and ideas, allowing them to add flavor and depth to their lives.

"*Rabbot machashabot b'lev ish,*" Nouri often said.

The Dayan home was changing and a big factor in this transformation was the Dayan children. They were growing up as a part of the Ashkenazic world, and they were enriching their home with their experiences. Had Nouri ever dreamed that this would happen when he was a young man, learning exclusively from Hacham Murad?

Probably not.

Yet he embraced these changes with love.

Irwin was back in Bensonhurst, living upstairs from his parents. His stint in Lakewood had been rewarding but unsustainable. There had been too many issues to allow for the peace he had yearned for in full-time learning. He was teaching in Magen David in the morning and in Talmud Torah in the afternoon and was grateful that, for now, he was earning a living while still being involved in Torah.

His time in Lakewood had a lasting impact on his perspective of Torah learning and its supremacy in life. He took that back with him to Brooklyn … along with some of the friendships he had cultivated in Lakewood.

Nissim Yagen was one of his Lakewood friends. The Sephardic Israeli *bachur* was an unusual person who immediately captivated everyone who met him. Back in Lakewood, he often came to Irwin's house to eat on Shabbat and they learned together as *habrutot* (perhaps Irwin's Ohel Moshe background, which had stressed Ivrit, made communication with Irwin easier than with the other *bachurim*). They became very close and kept up even after Irwin moved to Bensonhurst.

Whenever the opportunity arose, Nissim Yagen came to Bensonhurst. He was an eloquent and entertaining speaker who gave over meaningful *dibrei Torah*, which Nouri enjoyed immensely. He became a valued family friend. And, of course, Nouri roped him into lecturing in Ahi Ezer whenever he was in town. So when Nissim began campaigning for Murray Dayan to join him in Eretz Yisrael, Nouri took his words seriously, even though the idea was radically new.

Virtually no American-Sephardic boys were traveling to Eretz Yisrael at the time. Even among the Ashkenazim, only a trickle of Americans walked the streets of the Holy Land. Tickets were expensive, parents didn't want to part with their children, and the area was still considered volatile. It was just not done.

But, five years earlier, Nouri had sent Joe's son, Murray, and it had changed his life. Murray returned to America much more grounded and focused and, after a few years in Ner Israel, he married Susie Cohen, one of the new arrivals from Egypt. His fiery spirit had been channeled in the right direction, and he was a rising Rabbinic star in the Syrian community.

Would a stint in Eretz Yisrael accomplish the same for Murray Dayan?

"It will make him into a man," Nissim enthused.

Not a bad idea, Nouri thought, but said nothing.

Murray had been learning by Rabbi Perr in Bais Yosef of Boro Park.[24] It had seemed like a good idea when he went, but now he felt ready for a change. Was Eretz Yisrael the answer?

"I'll take care of him," Nissim insisted. "I'm going to learn in a new yeshiva headed by Rabbi Mordechai Elefant. Have you heard of him?"

Nissim Yagen, in Lakewood. An Israeli-Sephardi learning in Lakewood was a novelty.

He received blank stares.

"He's an unusual person. He's American, learned under some of the greatest *talmidei hachamim* in our generation, and is now living in Eretz Yisrael. He opened a yeshiva in Romema and is attracting some of the greatest minds in Eretz Yisrael. It's a great opportunity for Murray."

Nouri was convinced. Murray was thrilled.

"I'm coming to the airport to meet you," Nissim instructed Murray. "You'll come straight to my parents' house. They live in a new development called Kiryat Sanz. It's right near the border, but no one is afraid."

Fear was the last thing on Murray's mind. He was going halfway across the world, with his parents' approval. What could be better?

I guess, knowing where to go would be nice, Murray mused when he stepped out of customs and into the reception area. Nissim was nowhere in sight. Murray wandered around, wondering if he should wait, or if he should just find his way to Yerushalayim. Then he spotted an old classmate from Ohel Moshe, Aryeh Frimmer.

"What are you doing here?" they asked each other, simultaneously.

"Going to learn in a yeshiva," they answered simultaneously, and then cracked up in laughter.

---

24. Rabbi Yechiel Perr is another Ashkenazic Rabbi who is very involved in the Sephardic community. He has taught Sephardic men and boys for decades.

Rabbi Nissim Yagen's father, Hacham Yaakov – a special, holy man

"You are probably looking for a *sheirut*," Aryeh told his friend. "They are the vans going to Yerushalayim. Why don't you go see if one of them has space?"

Murray found himself a place. By the time he reached Yerushalayim, it was night and the streets were very dark, especially in the new developments where the municipality had not yet put up streetlights (or sidewalks). Kiryat Sanz was so new the buildings did not have addresses. The *sheirut* driver began calling out in the middle of the night, "Mishpachat Yagen! Mishpachat Yagen!"

No one responded to his calls. He drove slowly past the new buildings until he reached the end of the settlement. Then he indicated to Murray that he exit the taxi; he did not know where else to take him. Murray stepped out of the car... and promptly fell into a large pothole. The area was so dark, he could not see where he was going. Just then, someone appeared, seemingly out of nowhere.

"Murray, is that you? Didn't you tell me Thursday?" Nissim greeted him.

Well, I am not about to argue about this in the middle of the night, in the middle of the street, Murray thought wryly, as he returned Nissim's hug.

"Come," Nissim picked up his suitcase and led him toward the house. He introduced him to his father, who Murray right away sized up as a special, holy man, and showed him to his room. The next day, the two of them went to Romema, to Rabbi Elefant's yeshiva, Murray's "home away from home" for the next two years.

Rabbi Elefant was a charismatic and dynamic person who had learned by some of the Torah giants of the generation. He appreciated Torah and wanted to create a yeshiva where any *bachur* could find a mentor to learn from. His plans were grandiose, and he would need many supporters to make them happen.[25]

The Dayan Hotel had a new guest: Rabbi Mordechai Elefant.

Rabbi Elefant spent a lot of time overseas raising money for his many projects. He came to the Dayan home and, like so many others, kept on coming. He was joined by Rav Yankele Galinsky, the irrepressible *maggid* who came around to Bibi and Co. to collect money. Nouri realized that the congregation would love a lecture in Hebrew, so, when Rav Galinsky accepted his invitation for Shabbat, Nouri asked Rav Galinsky to make a guest appearance in the shul. His speech was a hit. From then on, Rav Galinsky was a regular speaker in Ahi Ezer whenever he came to the Dayans.

Rabbi Nissim Yagen (1941-2000) became a living legend. After four years in Lakewood, he served in several Rabbinic positions in Eretz Yisrael and, together with others, went on to found the Arachim *kiruv* organization. He was a noted *talmid chacham* and a dynamic leader.

So many people who ate at the Dayan table became valued friends. Some of them formed relationships so deep and long lasting that they could hardly remember what life had been like before they met each other.

One of those people was a stocky young boy named Marvin Azrak.

"Such a nice boy," *Stetta* announced. Marvin was her great-grandson, the son of Joe's daughter, Norma, who had moved to Panama when she married Raymond Azrak. They came to America to visit but they didn't usually stay long, nor did they always bring the family. Now that Marvin came to study in YU, he would get to know the family.

---

25. Rabbi Elefant's teachers included Rabbi Leib Malin, Rabbi Yecheskel Levenstein, the Brisker Rav, and others. Perhaps it was his exposure to these great people that motivated him to staff his yeshivos with great personalities who became world renowned, such as: Rabbi Shmuel Auerbach, Rabbi Yaakov Galinsky, Rabbi Tzvi Kushelevsky, and Rabbi Shlomo Fischer.

Nouri Dayan (left) and Marvin Azrak, on Purim

There was an almost immediate rapport between Nouri and his great-nephew. Like Nouri, Marvin was a doer. He had dreams and goals and was ever optimistic that he could accomplish them. He was very young, and much more outgoing than Nouri, but had an infectiously encouraging attitude. Nouri saw his spirit and strength and was happy to guide him to use his abilities for the community. Marvin became a constant presence in the Dayan home, listening, asking, and learning from his uncle. Nouri was very taken with the young man who was very different from himself, but similar in what mattered: They shared a deep desire to help their people.

The Dayan home was emptying out and filling up simultaneously. While Murray was overseas, Irwin lived upstairs, and Carol was in nearby Flatbush, though she popped by often. They both had welcomed new additions into the family, making Nouri and Esther grandparents. With *Stetta* still living under their roof, the Dayan home often had four generations eating together.

The Dayans were an anomaly. Most young Syrians were moving to Flatbush and their parents were following them. Bensonhurst was emptying out, and the process was bittersweet.

Back in 1950, when Ahi Ezer built the 71st Street building, 350 families had signed on as members. It was ironic: The 71st Street shul was barely 13 years old (everyone still called it the "new" shul), it had taken almost that long to raise the money to buy the land and build the building, and now many of its founding families (including Dave Bibi) had moved out of the neighborhood. Many of them had joined the Flatbush synagogue, Sha'arei

Zion, which eclipsed Magen David as the *Halabi* center. If Ahi Ezer didn't build a new synagogue in Flatbush, the *Shammi* community would soon be swallowed into the *Halabi* majority.

It would have been understandable for the builders of the 71st Street shul to tenaciously cling to what they had worked so hard to build, and turn a blind eye to the demographic changes and resulting community needs. After all, there was still a community in Bensonhurst. And if everyone would just stay put, there would continue to be a community in Bensonhurst. Let those people who chose to move to Flatbush worry about building a shul in Flatbush.

Not Nouri Dayan.

When he saw the changes happening in his community, he decided to work with them, not fight the trend. It was time to launch a new building campaign: Congregation Ahi Ezer of Flatbush. And once they were doing that, they might as well look for a proper building for Ahi Ezer Yeshiva, which was fast growing out of its refurbished houses in Bensonhurst.

Nouri appointed a committee to look for property in Flatbush, somewhere between Avenues R and U, on Ocean Parkway. The Avenue X building, that the congregation had purchased a few years earlier, was great, but it was far from where most of the community was settling and it was slated as a community center, a different but also important, community need. The committee finally found two buildings that were ideal. One was an apartment building on Ocean Parkway and S, while the other was the Fallas Home (called after the previous owners) right across the street.

The Fallas Home was empty and Ahi Ezer bought it with a nominal mortgage. Nouri hoped to begin construction on the new synagogue within a year.

Nouri was so optimistic about the growth of Ahi Ezer Yeshiva that he designated the large apartment building as its new home. The apartment building lot was huge, spanning almost an entire street block. Ahi Ezer had put down only $25,000 out of the $220,000 that the building had cost. They were counting on the $35,000 in yearly rent to help pay the 10-year renegotiable mortgage. Then they would have to tackle the enormous job of emptying the building of its tenants, gutting the whole place, and reconstructing it into a school.

"After we build the synagogue," Nouri decided.

With each property purchase, Nouri became even more upbeat and optimistic, even though he was constantly undertaking another burden. He was the one negotiating with the owners, dealing with the lawyers, applying for the mortgages, and dealing with the finances. And yet he was so happy. To Nouri, every acquisition spelled growth. Another building meant that another project could be implemented.

Nonetheless, the project most dear to him remained the yeshiva.

Every year, Ahi Ezer Yeshiva added several classes: a new grade, parallel classes in the preschool, and Talmud Torah classes for the children who attended public school and for the older girls for whom there were no yeshiva classes available. As the yeshiva grew and changed, there were constant issues.

"Mr. Dayan, the parents keep on complaining. The women find it difficult to juggle sending their boys and girls to separate yeshivot. They want to wait for one school bus, deal with one tuition committee, and work with one set of schedules. They are begging us to open a boys division."

But Nouri was very reluctant to open a boys division of the yeshiva.[26]

The pre-school had always included boys. From there, Nouri encouraged parents to send their boys to Magen David and their girls to Ahi Ezer. He believed in single-gender schools like he observed by the Ashkenazim. He wanted his Ahi Ezer to be a regular Bais Yaakov and that would not happen if he put boys in the same building, even if they were on different floors.

On the other hand, he didn't want to jeopardize the growth of the school. Ahi Ezer Yeshiva was attracting the community's girls in unprecedented numbers and Nouri didn't want to lose that momentum. He considered opening a boys' division, but encountered surprising opposition.

"The community has a yeshiva," protested Mr. Isaac Shalom, "and if everyone would send, we would not have this problem."

Mr. Isaac Shalom was a community legend. He single-handedly put hundreds of Syrians on their feet by starting them off in business. He traveled around the world on behalf of Ozar HaTorah. He devoted his life to building up the Syrian Jewish community by supporting Magen David Congregation, founding the yeshiva, and backing a host of other community projects.

Nouri wasn't arguing with Magen David's potential. The reality was that in its 20+ year existence, only a handful of girls had attended through the 8th grade. Ahi Ezer had succeeded in attracting the girls. Perhaps now it was time for the community to unite in a way that would enable both yeshivot to thrive.

"Give us your girls and we will give you our boys," Nouri suggested. "I'm not looking to open a boys' yeshiva, but I need to keep the parents

---

26. Mr. Dayan always looked at the total community, not just his school. When Ahi Ezer Talmud Torah girls seemed ready to move on, he and his staff worked to get them accepted into regular Bais Yaakov elementary schools and even funded the considerable transportation costs if necessary. When other Sephardic shuls opened, some offering their own Talmud Torah programs, Mr. Dayan contacted them [Sha'arei Zion, Magen David, Magen David of Ocean Parkway, Sha'arei Torah, and Ahava V'ahva] to discuss how to ensure that all Sephardic children had a Jewish education.

happy. Close your girls' department and let us make a joint drive in the community encouraging everyone to send their boys to Magen David and their girls to Ahi Ezer. Let each school focus on a different gender and we'll see community-wide success."

Over the years, the *Halabi* and *Shammi* communities cooperated with each other on a limited scale that was slowly expanding. In 1961, the Rabbis of the Syrian community formed a Board of Rabbis, a concrete manifestation of that cooperation. Nouri had just donated a *Sefer Torah* to the *Halabi k'nees*, Magen David of Ocean Parkway, jointly with Marco Zalta. He was continuing in the spirit that people like Isaac Shalom, Dave Bibi, and Morris Bibi helped create.

Mr. Shalom was a big supporter of all community endeavors, but when it came to this issue, he couldn't agree. To be fair, Mr. Shalom didn't feel that the overall community would accept the proposal. Magen David parents were happy in Magen David. If the problem was dealing with two schools, then they should encourage all the Ahi Ezer parents to transfer their girls to Magen David.

"But Magen David has never been able to keep the girls," Nouri explained quietly. "I will not risk what we have achieved in order to bolster the existing yeshiva."

So Nouri and Mr. Shalom agreed to disagree.[27]

And Nouri opened a boys' division in Ahi Ezer.

With the addition of the boys' division and the growth of the girls' division, Ahi Ezer Yeshiva outgrew the Bensonhurst buildings. They needed a new building, fast.

They couldn't use the Fallas Home; they needed that for the new synagogue. The apartment building across the street had too large of a mortgage to legally begin construction. They were left with the Avenue X building that they had intended for a community center. With a bit of remodeling, they could turn it into a school building. It was large enough to accommodate many more classrooms, and they could stay there until enough of the mortgage on the Avenue S apartment building was paid off.

"*Rabbot machashabot b'lev ish*," Nouri often quoted.

The *passuk* would apply most appropriately to the saga of Ahi Ezer Yeshiva.

It would also apply to the amazing changes occurring in the Jewish world.

---

27. This was a rare and unusual conflict of interest between the two community leaders. Mr. Shalom was a remarkable person who helped all Jews. He once picked up 50 pairs of *tefillin* on one of his trips to Morocco and donated them to Ahi Ezer. In those days, most men didn't own *tefillin*. The shul had about 12 to 14 pairs, in the back, and people would come in, put on a pair, and pray. If they saw other people waiting to use the *tefillin*, they would then take off the *tefillin* right away and continue praying without *tefillin*. Mr. Shalom's donation enabled everyone to pray with *tefillin*.

Chapter 44:
BENSONHURST AND JERUSALEM, 1967

Murray's roommate crumpled the telegram and threw it across the room. It just missed the wastebasket.

"Hey, waddaya doin?" Murray asked lazily from his bed. He picked up the rolled piece of paper and read it: COME HOME, MAMA

"Oh, another one."

His roommate nodded, "And I am still not going."

"Are you crazy? Your parents are scared sick."

"Survivors… you know how it is. On the other hand, you don't know how it is." He glared at Murray who had yet to receive one urgent telegram from his parents when he was up to telegram number ten.[28] "My whole life, they do nothing but worry."

"It must be hard," Murray sympathized, "but how can you do this to them? What if your mother really gets sick with worry? How are you going to feel then?"

Two thousand miles away, the boys were oblivious to the fear that gripped American Jewry. Egyptian President Nasser had convinced Syria, Jordan, and Iraq to join him in wiping the Jewish State off the map. The news droned on and on about Israel being out-supplied and outnumbered.

"This time," declared Nasser, "we are going to drive them into the sea!"

In every shul, in every Jewish business, on every street corner, American Jews dissected the news and had a difficult time pushing away the nagging fear that the Jewish people would be facing another Holocaust. Of the few American *bachurim* in Israel at the time, a high percentage of them were children of Holocaust survivors. Indeed, a large portion of the country had either lived through the Holocaust or the Israeli War of

---
28. The Dayans did send a telegram telling Murray to come home, but he never received it.

Murray Dayan (on the left) as a *bachur* in Eretz Yisrael, with his friend, Sammy Kassin

Independence, or both. Survivors had settled in Israel under the illusion that, for once and for all, they would be able to live in peace, away from anti-Semitism. Men who fought in the War of Independence thought that they had fought in order that their children would never have to fight a war again. The vitriolic statements coming out of Egypt left an uncomfortable pit in the national stomach. By late spring of 1967, a pall of doom and gloom shrouded the streets of Israel.

And then, the unbelievable happened.

Even before the mobilized nations attacked, Israel bombed almost the entire Egyptian air force, on the ground. While this preemptive action set off the war that the Arabs had been threatening, it crippled the Egyptian army and gave Israeli fighters the morale boost that they so desperately needed. The country was at war, but their fighting spirit was back.

Murray watched the Israeli tanks as they snaked toward the Old City. Five minutes later he heard gunfire. While that should have been a signal to run into the shelter, boys being boys, he ran up to the roof where he trained his binoculars on the sky that was filled with planes… explosions… action. He watched as bomb after bomb rocked the Jordanian positions that were only a few blocks away.

"Are you afraid?" Rabbi Yaakov Hirsch Yellin asked Murray, the lone American remaining in the yeshiva.

"Afraid?" Murray echoed. "No… this is the greatest experience of my life."

From the very first day of the war, morale rose by the hour. Sure, there were painful casualties, and every loss of life was mourned, but there were also unimaginable victories. The atmosphere in the yeshiva and on the street was suddenly optimistic and proudly united... even as the bombs continued to fall.

For six days, the Israelis fought. They conquered the Golan Heights, they annexed the West Bank, and they captured the Old City. That Shavuos was the first time Jews had davened by the Kotel in 19 years.

The Six Day War had wide-ranging ramifications on world opinion of the Jewish State. Israel's stunning victory won it an unprecedented level of awe. The famous Moshe Dayan, war hero turned Defense Minister, was idolized. His name became synonymous with strength which, in a twist of fate, would have ominous ramifications for the Dayan family.

The humiliating defeat of the Arab nations emboldened Palestinian terrorist groups, who were now convinced that they, and only they, could redeem their land and get rid of the Jews in Palestine. They were frustrated that their fellow Arabs seemed more concerned about recouping their losses than on destroying the Jewish State. This, too, would impact the Dayan family in ways that no one would have dreamed.

For Murray, the *z'man* was basically over.

He went back to America three weeks later.

Hacham Ezra Attia

Nouri was euphoric over Hashem's kindness to the Jewish people. Such kindness couldn't go by unmarked. From then on, he took upon himself that on Shabbat, whenever he ate together with two other Jewish men (almost always), he would say the *birkat ha'mazon* over a cup of wine, as is mentioned in the *Shulhan Aruch*, even though no one else in his community did this. This was another one of Nouri's emerging characteristics: He continuously looked to grow and used the circumstances with which he lived as a way to make it happen.

Ever since his first trip there, in 1949, Nouri felt pulled to the Holy Land. He had been back once since then, but the 1967 victory — and the prospect of being able to pray at the Kotel — made him determined to go again.

Next summer, he promised himself.

But Carol and her husband, Hacham Yosef Harari Raful,[29] were not waiting. The euphoria that engulfed the Jewish world was particularly poignant for those who had been born and raised in Eretz Yisrael and remembered the Old City before barbed wire cut it off from the rest of Yerushalayim.

Hacham Yosef Raful was one of those people.

He had been a young *bachur* learning in Yeshivat Porat Yosef during the 1948 war. He and his cousin, Rafael Ades, were going from the New City[30] to the Old City, where the yeshiva was located, when they heard gunfire. They ran for their lives and had not seen the Old City since. Now Hacham Yosef yearned to go back, to see his beloved yeshiva and its venerable Rosh Yeshiva, Hacham Ezra Attia, and to pray at the Kotel once again.

Carol was all for it. She had never been to Eretz Yisrael, but love for the Land had always been a part of her life. She vividly remembered the excitement of her father's trip twenty years earlier and the moving pictures that he had filmed. She was also eager to meet her husband's and her father's extended families.

Hacham Yosef's grandparents moved from Syria to Israel before World War I and settled their family there. Hacham Yosef had grown up in Eretz Yisrael, but his siblings had slowly moved to America. When he came to visit them, he had no intention of staying. But then he began teaching in Yeshiva of Flatbush and then met Carol. His engagement and marriage to Carol brought another sister, Yehudit (Judy), to America, as well as their widowed mother, Rabbanit Rachel. Without ever making a formal decision, the Raful family relocated from Israel to America within a span of a few years.

Rabbanit Rachel had joined her children but she left behind three brothers and many nieces and nephews. Rabbanit Rachel was a daughter of Hacham Abraham Ades (Antebi). The extended Harari Raful family was also a veritable tribe. Carol was planning to spend her summer getting to know Eretz Yisrael and her family.

---

29. Though the full name is Harari Raful, we will be using the shortened version "Raful" for the remainder of the book.
30. The "Old City" of Jerusalem referred to the area surrounded by the Jerusalem Walls. In the late 1800's, the Old City became very crowded and Jews began building settlements outside the walls. Being that the early settlements were virtually alongside the walls and there were no other settlements for miles around, they were naturally considered part of Jerusalem. People referred to these settlements as the "New City." By the time the State of Israel came into being, the New City had eclipsed the Old City in size and population. In 1948, when the Old City was captured by the Jordanians, the only part of Jerusalem left in the Jewish State was the New City, which then lost its title as it was neither old nor new, rather it was Jerusalem.

Hacham Ezra Harari Raful, Hacham Yosef's grandfather

Hacham Aron, son of Hacham Ezra and father of Hacham Yosef

Hacham Yaakob Ades, Rabbanit Rachel Raful's brother

That Tisha b'Ab, she and her husband walked from their apartment on Rechov Yaffo all the way up to the Kotel. Hacham Yosef and Hacham Abraham (who had come without his wife, Marcelle, who had just had a baby) had already been to the Old City. They were heartbroken to see the devastation: Yeshivat Porat Yosef had been destroyed, as were many of the graves on Har HaZeitim, including that of their grandfather, Hacham Abraham Ades.

Now they joined tens of thousands of fellow Jews, walking soberly, quietly, up to Sha'ar Ha'Ashpot, toward the Kotel. It was a march of sadness and joy: They finally had the Kotel but the fact that it was Tisha b'Ab was a painful reminder of its desolation. The Israelis had bulldozed all the houses right in front of the Wall almost immediately after conquering it, leaving an enormous unpaved plaza in front of the Kotel. Everyone sat down on the dirt floor; no one cared about the swirling dust. They just stared in awe at the Kotel, so long inaccessible, standing tall and proud before them. It was so much more than anyone had expected weeks earlier.

It was so little — merely an outside wall — when everyone yearned for the entirety of the Bet HaMikdash.

It was an unforgettable experience.

Hacham Yosef did as he promised and took his young wife to his relatives, among them the venerable Hacham Moshe Ades, who had moved from the Old City in 1948 and now lived in a one-room apartment.

I think that I'm in some kind of time warp, Carol decided, though she kept her shocked thoughts to herself, especially since her husband didn't seem the least bit fazed. She finally understood why her husband had been so proud of their "modern" apartment.

Yeshiva Kol Yaakob was founded by the Ades family in memory of Rav Yaakob Ades. Here they are beginning construction.

A whole different culture, Carol realized with a jolt, as she watched her husband speak with his uncle, two *talmidei hachamim* engrossed in learning, oblivious to the stuffiness of the apartment and to the dimness that hid the dust that was thick on the shelves lined with holy books. They were absorbed in their conversation, on a different plane, in a different world.

It was a long, long way from Brooklyn.

Chapter 45:

"HOW CAN WE HELP OUR BROTHERS?"

Manhattan, 1968

"Where's Charlie?" Irwin called out.

"At your service," Charlie Serouya answered, emerging from somewhere out back. He motioned to the four chandeliers laid out on the floor and turned to the familiar customer. "What'll it be? This one you can have for $100. You know what? Take all four for $400 — a bargain like this you won't get anywhere else."

Irwin grinned to himself. Good ole' Charlie was still doing his thing. Many workers had passed through Bibi and Co. but Charlie was still around and now Irwin was working with him, no longer the boss's kid, getting in the way. Irwin's stint as a rebbi had not lasted long. He wanted to teach in the Sephardic community where he felt he could have an impact. When that didn't work out, he joined his father in the business, which continued to grow and change.

Back in 1960, their salesman, Larry Strack, convinced Bibi and Co. to branch out to national department-store chains. These stores were not buying the luxury chandeliers that were Bibi's specialty. They wanted simple but elegant lighting fixtures that were affordable to the regular guy off the street. And they wanted complete lines, not unique numbers that had to be priced and ordered individually.

"You are too heavily identified with expensive chandeliers," Larry explained. "Open a separate branch, under a different name, with a different showroom, and let the retailers place large orders for their stores from that location. There you can focus on simpler lighting fixtures rather than luxury lighting."

Bibi opened Continental Lighting on the ground floor of the 26th Street building. It was an instant success, and several years down the line it merged with Bibi and Co. The combined business was called Bibi Continental. They moved out of the rented 26th Street building and divided the business between Brooklyn and Manhattan by keeping the 5th Avenue (Manhattan) location as a showroom and moving the factory, warehouse, and offices to a newly purchased building in Bay Ridge, Brooklyn.

Irwin and Charlie worked in the 5th Avenue location, the venue for unique luxury chandeliers. Dave, Reuben, and Nouri spent most of their time in the Bay Ridge building.[31] There they designed, manufactured, and sold whole lines of lighting fixtures, from simple flush domes to large chandeliers. They had become one of the biggest names in the business, and the move to Bay Ridge was a reflection of that growth. The new location was huge, and the business was churning out hundreds of products on a scale that would have been difficult to imagine a decade earlier.

What was the secret to Bibi's success? Perhaps their honest business practices and their focused work ethic had a lot to do with it.

"My word is my bond," Dave Bibi used to say.

When he ordered merchandise from one vendor, and then saw the same merchandise cheaper at another vendor, he would never cancel his original order. By placing his order he had made a commitment on which he would not renege.

Dave was a demanding employer. No matter who you were, you had to work hard and prove your worth. Concurrently, he was an encouraging boss who opened opportunities for friends and family to make a living. Joe and Joe Bibi (his son and nephew) first worked for Dave and then opened Bibi Furniture in rented space on the other side of the Manhattan showroom. Charlie's son, Abie Serouya, opened Bibi Far East and also rented a section off the main showroom. Using the Bibi name and showroom gave these start-up businesses the exposure it would have taken them years to cultivate on their own.

"*All-h ye' Zeedo*! (G-d should give him more!)" Dave would say.

With a warm handshake, Dave wished a departing employee well, even if he was going off to open a competing business. He had full faith in G-d that he would receive whatever he deserved, and whatever belonged to his competitor would end up over there. Dave was happy when the people he trained became independent, even when they resented being forced to move on. He knew that one day they would be grateful for the experience that enabled them to open their own businesses.

---

31. When Mr. Dayan worked in Manhattan, he would take the subway, so he had an hour in the morning to learn and an hour in the afternoon. Before Pesah, he would review ideas connected to the season and, in this way, prepare for the Seder. Whatever he learned on the subway was in addition to his regular learning schedule. When they moved the business to Brooklyn he lamented to his son-in-law, Hacham Yosef, "I lost two hours of learning."

L-R: Reuben, Nouri, and Dave, hosting a Bibi business party.
The man in the black hat is Charlie Serouya.

Taking his uncle's lead, Nouri sought to help people succeed financially, even if he had no benefit from extending himself. He learned of a new invention: plastic zippers. Until then, all zippers were made of metal. Plastic zippers had various advantages, chief among them that they could be produced cheaply. Nouri thought that this idea had tremendous potential. Rather than keep the idea to himself, he told his friends about it and they formed a corporation where, if the invention went public, everyone would triple his investment. The company never got off the ground, but the goodwill that Nouri generated in thinking about others left a lasting impression.[32]

Dave was a positive person who loved encouraging other people to be successful and productive. In an era where business owners stiffened to attention when the union inspector came sauntering around, Bibi Continental maintained a warm and congenial atmosphere.[33] When New Years came around, Dave would make an elaborate party with deli platters from

---

32. Interestingly, this was one of the only times that Mr. Bibi and Mr. Dayan didn't partner together in a business venture. Many of the investors were Mr. Dayan's friends and relatives who had invested from their meager savings. When the corporation didn't work out, Mr. Dayan paid them back from his own pocket, even though he was in no way required to do so.

33. "My father and Mr. Bibi could not think bad of anyone, but sometimes reality forced them to be suspicious. Once, we realized that there was too much of a discrepancy between our inventory and our sales. We hired an investigative agency and discovered that a 'loyal' worker was smuggling out chandelier parts, piece by piece. By the time we caught him, he had set up a whole showroom in his basement!" reminisced Mr. Irwin Dayan.

Crown's and bread from Weiss's, and generous bonuses. The gentile workers were particularly grateful for this attention.

This warm and positive atmosphere extended beyond the employees to the many *meshulachim* who stopped at Bibi in the course of their rounds.

"There is not enough money," Reuben Bibi complained. "We usually give $5 for each *meshulach*, but there are so many of them lately, our charity account is empty too early in the month. I think that we should cut down on each one, rather than run dry before the month ends."

"Take it easy," Nouri said. "If each of us gives just a little more…"

And the two men huddled over the figures to decide how much more they should take off their monthly paychecks in order to be able to give every *meshulach* their usual $5 minimum. But it was more than just the $5 that passed from one person to the other. Reuben greeted each *meshulach* warmly. He sat down and listened to their stories, injecting a kind word, an appreciative comment. The *meshulachim* loved to stop by, not just for the few dollars but for the feeling of being valued and appreciated.

By the mid-60's, Reuben Bibi had retired from designing and building chandeliers. His hours at Bibi were spent taking care of the company's charity account, which included reading all the appeal letters, deciding how much money to donate, and then recording the donation.

Bibi Continental was a new name, but its mission remained unchanged: *How can we help our brothers?*

Nouri still saw his uncle, Reuben Bibi, in the business, though he was coming in less often than before. But for Nouri to see his Aunt Esther, he had to stop by for a visit, which he did at least once a week.

"She has been a mother to me," he explained to his wife. He made sure that Esther and Reuben Bibi knew that they could count on him for anything. Several times during the year, he'd bring the children to visit their great aunt and uncle who were really surrogate grandparents. He never viewed this as a burden but took it for granted that this was the minimal amount of *hakarat hatob* that he owed them.

His devotion to *Stetta* sometimes made his wife, Esther, feel guilty.

Esther took her responsibilities very seriously. She worried that when her mother went out, she might fall. She wondered if she always took her medication and was concerned that she was eating properly.

"It's so difficult to know if I'm always doing what I should be doing…" Esther's voice trailed off wistfully.

As soon as Nouri heard the uncertainty in her voice, he jumped in, "I didn't realize it was so hard for you. Please, don't even consider asking anyone else to take her in. I'll try to be more helpful, but she must stay with us. I never had a mother; this is my only opportunity to fulfill the mitzva of honoring one's mother."

Nouri praying at the Kotel

So *Stetta* stayed in the Dayan house for many more years.

Even as she aged, *Stetta* remained feisty and full of life. When Nouri decided to take the family to Eretz Yisrael to see all the land that had been conquered in the Six Day War, *Stetta* came along. She joined all the "unmarrieds" — Sara, Joyce, Joey, and Barbara — with Nouri and Esther as they went from Gaza to the Golan, with visors to protect themselves from the summer heat. They ate and slept in hotels and visited all of their extended family, with *Stetta* keeping up every step of the way.

Nouri's devotion to his mother-in-law was contagious. His children happily accompanied their grandmother as she trekked with them up to the *kever* of Rebbe Meir Ba'al Ha'ness and other places. They felt privileged to have her along, never burdened.

Nouri's love of mitzvos drew him to mitzvos. In the wake of the 1967 war in Israel, Arab violence drove more Jews to leave Egypt, prompting a second influx of refugees with nowhere to go.

"Let's give them apartments in the Avenue S building," Nouri decided.[34]

The new Egyptians were brought straight to the Avenue S Ahi Ezer apartment complex and were warmly welcomed by Hacham Sion. They paid whatever they could — or nothing at all — until they were financially stable.

---

34. The building had a large mortgage that was covered by the rents. By allowing families to live there rent free, Mr. Dayan was taking on a big burden.

Jackie Cohen was 7 years old, fresh from Egypt.

He stared around the public-school classroom, frankly interested in his new surroundings. *Not bad*, he decided, when he returned home after the first day.

On the second day… The door to the second-grade classroom swung open. A short, stocky man walked up front. He pointed to several of the children sitting in their seats.

"I want this one… and this one… and this one…"

Jackie Cohen and the other chosen classmates meekly followed the man out of the room. They had no idea of the behind-the-scenes arrangements, and didn't question their elders. They piled into the car of the Rabbi whose name they would eventually learn, and rode with him to Ahi Ezer Yeshiva.

"Here they are," announced Rabbi Murray Maslaton with a flourish. He shook hands with Rabbi Wolf, who then welcomed the children and placed them into the appropriate classes. The wheel kept turning: Nouri's protégé, Murray Maslaton, was joining his uncle in spiritually saving Jewish children.[35]

Rabbi Murray Maslaton, with his forceful manner, let nothing stand in his way when it came to giving a Jewish child a Jewish education. In personality, he was very different from his Uncle Nouri, who did everything with gentlemanly diplomacy. But their goals were the same.

Nouri created Ahi Ezer Yeshiva. Rabbi Murray helped bring in the students.

Rabbi Murray Maslaton founded a tuition fund specifically for this purpose. Immigrant families were usually poor, at least upon arrival. They didn't have the money to pay tuition and were not idealistic enough to sacrifice whatever little they did have in order to give their children a yeshiva education. Ahi Ezer took in all these children, and their tuition was covered through Rabbi Maslaton's fund.

"Pay us back when you can," Nouri often told parents.

Ike Swed was on the tuition committee. He sat together with Dave and Nouri as they discussed one man's predicament, and everyone realized that there was no way he could pay four tuitions, or even two. The man was grateful for the understanding attitude. For three years, he paid almost no tuition. The fourth year, he came into the building and handed over $20,000 cash.

"This is for all the tuition I have not paid," he said.

Then he took out a pen and scribbled off a check, "And this is a donation."

---

35. "He saved my life," recalled Dr. Jack Cohen. "Years later, I learned that he also covered our tuition." Rabbi Murray Maslaton put many of the community youth in yeshiva, including the Malkas, the Habers, and Rabbi Mordechai Nahem (who later became Mr. Dayan's son-in-law). He was doing this even before Ahi Ezer Yeshiva was founded. "He dug the ground for all the *bnei yeshiva* in the community," declared Rabbi Shlomo Diamond.

Rabbi Murray Maslaton (far right) with an Ahi Ezer class

Ike read the black scribble: $50,000.

Ahi Ezer does not only educate children, it makes people, mused Ike.

He attributed the $50,000 donation to Dave and Nouri, whose honesty and integrity was so inspiring. When they gave people huge tuition breaks, they did it because they believed their stories, without asking for bank records or any documented proof. They were genuinely concerned about people and hoped that they would emerge from their financial troubles. They believed that when that would happen, parents would want to pay back the yeshiva.

Sometimes, they did. Often, they didn't.

Dave and Nouri never became jaded. They firmly believed that they had an obligation to judge everyone favorably and do all that they could to help them.

They formalized their free loan society. The basic deal was: Borrow $1,000, interest free, for one year, and pay it back through $100 monthly head-checks, beginning two months after taking out the loan. It was meant primarily for businessmen who had to buy extra stock during holiday season and needed some quick cash. In reality, it was available to anyone who needed help and it expanded to include parents from their school, even those who were not members of the Ahi Ezer Congregation.

"Every con artist in the world finds Mr. Bibi," lamented Carol Shapiro.

The sob stories were endless. But Mr. Bibi was so honest, he assumed that everyone else was honest as well. And when an "honest person" disappeared without repaying the loan, his assumption was that the person must have been desperate. How could he not help out a person who was desperate?

Dave Bibi had endless compassion for people in need.

A man in the community owned a store that went up in smoke — literally. He had no insurance and no way to restart his business or pay off his debts. One day, Mr. Bibi walked over to him and handed him an envelope and a message, "Pay your rent. Feed your family. Rebuild! And always remember, from every bad, good will come."[36]

The man eventually became a millionaire, but he never forgot Dave Bibi's kindness. As much as the money — which was considerable — his words of encouragement gave him the comfort that he needed then and remained his motto every time he encountered difficulties in life.

"*B'toch ami anochi yoshabet* — I dwell among my people,"[37] Nouri would say.

And he meant it.

No matter how many people he and Dave helped, no matter how successful their business became, they viewed themselves as just Jews among Jews. He and Dave never held themselves apart, or considered themselves better than anyone else.

Nouri, in particular, had patience for some of the most difficult neighborhood "cases," people no one wanted to deal with, let alone host. That was how Eli Jacobo became one of the family.[38]

Hmmm, I think I have a new brother.

Murray surveyed the table, bemused. He had come back from Eretz Yisrael to find that his seat had been taken by one of the most eccentric characters in the neighborhood.

Eli Jacobo had grown up in the neighborhood, a child of elderly, wealthy parents who had lost their entire fortune. The change of status had been painful for everyone, but Eli was shattered by the loss of prestige and became a bit off. His parents could not control him, and he began to live on his own, floating from house to house for a meal here and there.

Eli was smart and sharp and a ball of fun. He would make jokes and have everyone laughing. He would regale his audiences with stories of his antics, like the time he put a lit match in the garbage can right before the teacher came into the classroom... only no one noticed it until a full-fledged fire had the whole classroom in an uproar.

---

36. *Midrash Rabbah, Shemos* 50:3, explaining *Yirmiyah* 30:17.
37. *Melachim II* 4:13.
38. This is not his real name. "Eli Jacobo" was a fixture in the Dayan home for over twenty years. Not all of these incidents happened in the 1960's. Some of them happened much later.

One day he could carry on a regular, intellectual conversation. The next day he acted like a child, dancing and singing just because he was in the mood, even if the venue was inappropriate. The children loved him. They followed him around and laughed with him, not at him. But Eli was highly unpredictable and unreliable, and even though he was a beloved community character, he could also be a nuisance. Who had patience for a man of so many contrasts and so little self-control?

Nouri Dayan.

Eli Jacobo became a regular at the Dayan table. No matter how many important Rabbis were sitting at his table, Nouri made time for Eli. He spoke to him, coaxed him to take his medication, and brought him into the family circle.

During the week, Nouri tried to guide him toward a normal, stable life. He helped him open a bank account, find a suitable apartment, gave him an allowance, and encouraged him to budget properly. But, no matter what Nouri did, he would find Eli back on the street collecting for himself, often in bizarre ways, like when he walked into a store, wearing a straw hat and holding a cane, and proceeded to dance and sing. The owners quickly slipped "Broadway Eddie" a few dollars so that he would leave. He had various getups (like a white tuxedo complete with a white top hat) and he would dress in whatever he was in the mood to wear and just do his thing.

Esther would shake her head, and Nouri would try again, patiently explaining to him that it would be more pleasant for him to live normally than to engage in inappropriate behavior. Eli nodded and promised to be good, a promise that lasted from Ta'anit Esther until Purim. He could not control himself, no matter how much goodness and patience Nouri showered upon him.

Nouri stopped by the Ahi Ezer office to speak with the secretary — a new addition to the shul — on a regular weekday morning. The phone rang.

"Hello, Ahi Ezer Congregation. How can I help you?"

"Hello, am I speaking to Mrs. Carol Shapiro?"

"Yes."

"I am calling from the Boardwalk Bank in Atlantic City. I have two gentlemen sitting with me, a Mr. Eli Jacobo and a Mr. Isidore Dayan."

"Really…" answered Carol, looking quizzically over at Nouri.

"Mr. Dayan is authorizing you to write out a check for $1,000 and deposit it into Mr. Jacobo's account."

"I hear," Carol paused, "can you hold on, sir? I'd like you to speak to someone…"

Carol handed over the phone to Nouri, who listened quietly. Then he interjected, "Sir, I am sorry for taking your time, but you can tell Mr.

Jacobo that Mr. Isidore Dayan is speaking to you right now, from Flatbush, and he is not authorizing any money transfers and Mr. Jacobo should stop playing such shenanigans!"

Then Nouri got off the phone and began to laugh, his standard reaction to Eli's outrageous behavior. But the next day, he was patiently trying to help him all over again.

"He is a good person," Nouri explained. "He just needs a little more guidance than most people."

Indeed, there was a lot of good in Eli Jacobo. He loved children and used to give them funny little knick-knacks. He made his rounds of the local hospitals to cheer up the Jewish patients. People heard about this jolly Jewish fellow who just walked into the room of a sick person and suddenly the patient was smiling and laughing.

Why didn't we think of that? they wondered sheepishly.

From Eli's humble desire to bring joy and cheer to sick people, the Sephardic Bikur Cholim was born. Dr. Bob Matalon and Freddy Bijou actually got the organization off the ground, but they were acting on Eli Jacobo's initiative. Dr. Matalon guided them as they began more formal programs of sending visitors to sick people and offering services to families with a sick member. Slowly, they became a multi-million-dollar organization that specialized in helping the ill, but also helped the needy. All this came into being through the innate goodness of a person that most people dismissed as being unable to accomplish anything worthwhile.

Most people were not Nouri.

"People don't understand," Eli would say, amused. "I'm not dumb. I'm crazy."

Yet Nouri still believed that Eli could overcome whatever was preventing him from interacting with the world normally. Eli never rose to Nouri's expectations, but Nouri never stopped trying to pull him up. A person is a *tzelem Elokim*, created in G-d's image. How could he give up on him? Besides, was he not a fellow Jew?

B'toch ami anochi yoshabet — Nouri's pride was in being part of a great whole.

He loved all his fellow Jews and rejoiced in simply being a member of the tribe.

Chapter 46:

"WE ARE *L'SHEM SHAMAYIM*; THERE ARE BOUND TO BE SETBACKS."

Bensonhurst, 1968

"Just teach my girls Torah," Nouri implored Rabbi Yehuda Oelbaum.

Rabbi Oelbaum joined Ahi Ezer as assistant principal in 1966. He was constantly impressed with Nouri's passionate plea, one that he repeated at almost every meeting.

By January of 1968, Ahi Ezer had an enrollment of 680 students for the coming year. Yet Nouri never saw this unusual growth (the school was barely six years old!) as a reason to be complacent. He was as passionate as ever, and his loyal assistants — salaried workers and volunteers — mirrored that passion. At the weekly board meetings, which sometimes ran to 1 a.m., all the members pondered ideas, raised motions, and planned programs, anything to attract children to the yeshiva and to provide them with a quality Jewish education. Indeed, Ahi Ezer was growing so fast, it was impossible not to see the Divine Providence.

The rise of the Civil Rights Movement was a clear example.

The Civil Rights Movement of the 1960's claimed as one of its main accomplishments the desegregation of the public schools. Until then, children were assigned public schools based on the neighborhoods where they lived. This meant that a public school in a predominately Jewish neighborhood would have a predominately Jewish student population. The same school in a predominately black neighborhood would have a predominately black student population. Civil rights leaders wanted black children to be bussed into white neighborhoods because, they claimed, there they would receive a better education because they would not be pulled down by the low-income majority.

Hacham Sion, Rabbi Oelbaum, and Rabbi Wolf in Ahi Ezer Avenue X

The atmosphere, decorum, and discipline in the local public schools changed rapidly, practically overnight. Suddenly, Jewish parents who had never considered sending to a yeshiva day school changed their minds. And there was Ahi Ezer, with its passionate Board and warm staff, just waiting to absorb these children.

Ahi Ezer Yeshiva had been founded at precisely the right time, but it was the excitement and devotion of its founders that made a yeshiva education a mainstream concept in the Sephardic community.

Ahi Ezer Congregation had developed into a huge operation. They owned five properties: the 71st Street shul, the Bensonhurst Talmud Torah building, the Avenue X yeshiva building, and the two buildings on Avenue S and Ocean Parkway. Some were mortgaged and some were not, but all were either being used or slated for use.

Almost as soon as they bought the Avenue X building, Nouri and Dave opened a *minyan* for the local Sephardim. Mr. Elie (Lou) Rofe, a 1958 Egyptian immigrant, was the president of Ahi Ezer of Avenue X. Most of the other members were also of Egyptian origin. Though they had been in America for almost a decade, they were still more comfortable speaking French than English. Nouri and Dave began looking for a Rabbi who could speak to them in their language.

"How about one of the Moroccan boys?" suggested Nouri. Both he and Dave still hosted the Mirrer Yeshiva Moroccans on occasion. They continued to be impressed with these Sephardic young men, who had left their families when they were barely teenagers, flourished in an Ashkenazic yeshiva, and even became Rabbis.

"Well," answered Dave, "they speak French."

"We Are L'shem Shamayim; There Are Bound to Be Setbacks."

When Dave bumped into Hananya Elbaz on the street one day and asked him if he would be interested in the job, Hananya protested, "I have no idea what to do."

"Just go. You'll be fine."

And Rabbi Hananya Elbaz became the Rabbi of Ahi Ezer of Avenue X.

The Egyptian *minyan* first prayed in a very small room in the basement of the Avenue X building. The main Ahi Ezer committee members retained an active role. Every few weeks they would meet with Mr. Rofe and discuss how they could help the fledgling congregation. At least once a year, during the holidays, all the big guys — Dave Bibi, Nouri Dayan, Ceasar Salama, and Nouri Sarway — walked to Ahi Ezer of Avenue X. They quietly entered the *k'nees* and someone immediately scrambled to get them seats. They listened respectfully as Lou Rofe made his appeal and then, one of the four would say a few words and the group would leave. Of the group, only Nouri had to walk all the way back to Bensonhurst, easily an hour's walk.

Ahi Ezer Avenue X. Top: Abe Mann. Front: Nat Mann, Lou Rofe, Ceasar Salama.

The visit was to help raise money for the shul, but it also served to connect Ahi Ezer of Avenue X to the main Ahi Ezer. Rather than feeling like they were a small, inconsequential *minyan* in a basement, they felt that they were a part of something bigger than themselves.

Dave and Nouri were proud of the Avenue X *minyan*, but it was far from the Sephardic hub and didn't make up for the lack of a *Shammi k'nees* in Flatbush. Finally, in 1968, the Synagogue Committee announced that there would be a groundbreaking ceremony for Ahi Ezer of Flatbush to be built on the Avenue S property.

The ceremony was scheduled for the spring of 1968.

It was put off due to a setback…

"Izzy, you've gotta come down to the yeshiva."

"Now? It's early in the morning."

"Right now. There's been a fire."

The original Ahi Ezer Avenue X building

"What?"

"You heard me. There was a fire at the yeshiva. The place is a shambles."

Nouri ran over to the Avenue X building. The damage appeared overwhelming, but upon close inspection he realized that the building was salvageable.

"It's not so bad," Nouri noted to Rabbi Wolf. "We have to notify the parents that there will be no school today. Then we have to find temporary locations for classes while we fix the place up. It should not take long. A few weeks, maximum. Look around, there is a lot of water damage, but the basic structure is sound."

Fortunately, Klal Yisrael has each other. School was closed for two days as sympathetic calls from other schools poured into the Ahi Ezer offices.[39] With a little maneuvering, two days later, Ahi Ezer students were placed in four Brighton locations near Avenue X. They learned there until Pesah while cleanup and renovations were done in the Ahi Ezer building. After Pesah, they returned to the Avenue X building, and the postponed synagogue-groundbreaking ceremony was held on May 19, 1968.

It was a gala event, with all the neighborhood Rabbis in attendance, as well as government dignitaries. There were nostalgic speeches, a choir by the second- and fifth-grade boys of Ahi Ezer Yeshiva, and then popular singer, Joe Amar, entertained the crowd. The atmosphere was very upbeat and positive.

Until the next setback occurred a few months later…

---

39. Rabbi Besdin (Marine Park Jewish Center), Rabbi Hecht (Sha'arei Zion), Rabbi Mandel (Yeshiva of Brooklyn), Rabbi Kahan (Hebrew School for Special Children), Rabbis Filler and Lax (Oceanview Jewish Center), Rabbi Langsam (Yeshiva of Brighton), Rabbi Weissman (Young Israel of Brighton), and Rabbi Scheinberg (Hebrew Alliance of Brighton) all generously offered classroom space to help Ahi Ezer.

Rabbi Matloub Abadi speaking at the groundbreaking for the new Ahi Ezer building

Nouri speaking at the same ceremony

It was Hoshana Rabbah, at night.

As usual, Nouri was in the *k'nees*, learning the pieces and saying *Tehillim*. Then he received the phone call that left him reeling in shock.

"Izzy, you gotta come down. There was another fire in the yeshiva."

It cannot be, was Nouri's only thought as he raced through the empty streets in the wee hours of the morning. *Again? Our school has been set on fire again?*

His heart pounded as he saw wispy grey plumes of smoke in the distance. Neighbors had already congregated outside and Nouri quickly spotted one of the members of the Ahi Ezer Egyptian *minyan*.

"The *Sifrei Torah*?" Nouri asked. "Has anyone rescued the *Sifrei Torah*?"

Hacham Sion at the ceremony

Nouri and some of the other men ran up to the entrance of the burning building. The entrance to the shul area seemed clear. They dashed in and saved the *Sifrei Torah*. Then Nouri stood outside, holding one *Sefer Torah*, while one of the other men held another. He stared as the flames continued to spread. He barely heard the sirens echoing through the night, nor did he notice the reporters that had descended on the scene. He simply watched in disbelief.

Ribbono shel Olam, what is going to be now!

The Ahi Ezer choir performing at the ceremony. Front, L-R, begining with the boy slightly obscured by the microphone: David Ozeri, Moshe Cohen, Joey Tourgeman, Joey Dayan. Back row, second from left, is Jerry Sharoff. Soloman Tourgeman is next to him, on the right.

The Hoshana Rabbah fire destroyed the school.

The building needed to be rebuilt from scratch, as there was too much structural damage to fix up the existing shell. Meanwhile, they had over 600 students returning to school in a few days and no place for them.

"We will meet after Yom Tov," Rabbi Wolf decided. "There is nothing for us to do before then anyway."

If Nouri was preoccupied, few were able to tell. As usual, he went with his brothers-in-law, Hacham Sion and Jack, for their bi-annual Yom Tov visit to Hacham Yaakob Kassin. They had been going together for many years, even before the passing of Hacham Murad. It was a treasured part of their Yom Tov. And on Simhat Torah, Nouri was as enthusiastic as always. He returned home from *hakafot*, sweaty and exhausted, but beaming with happiness of having rejoiced with the Torah.

The next day, he had to face the repercussions of the fire.

"We will have to call in all our favors," Rabbi Wolf grimly declared.

In a stroke of Providence, a few years earlier, Nouri had convinced Rabbi Wolf to actively support John Lindsay in his mayoral campaign. Well, Lindsay had won, and now it was payback time. The morning after the fire, Rabbi Wolf called the mayor's office and let them know that the yeshiva had been struck again, and this time it was totally destroyed. In Jewish New York, condemning the burning down of a yeshiva was an excellent publicity opportunity for the mayor.

Within two weeks, Mayor Lindsay had visited the school, ordered an investigation, and publicly donated $1,000 as all the major news agencies filmed the transaction. This immediately created public awareness that a

Mayor Lindsay presenting Rabbi Wolf with a check

yeshiva had been targeted twice by arsonists and created an environment conducive to widespread support.[40] Ahi Ezer began a frantic building campaign and the donations poured in.

"But what about now?" Nouri wanted to know. "Last fire, we kept the school running from several different locations because we knew that the situation was very temporary. This time, we need at least a year, possibly two, to complete the new building. We cannot function from multiple locations for that long."

Once again, Mayor Lindsay came through. He allotted an unused municipal building in Williamsburg for Ahi Ezer to use, rent free. He also provided them with five city busses to bus in all the children. Both Nouri and Rabbi Wolf were relieved with the new arrangements. Unfortunately, not all the parents were as pleased.

"Williamsburg? Are they serious?" one woman complained to her friend. "The kids will be traveling at least an hour in either direction, without traffic."

"Without traffic? In Brooklyn, between 8:00 and 9:00 in the morning?" her friend countered incredulously. "Who is anyone fooling?"

"What do you expect? That is how it is with Ahi Ezer. Well-meaning people but..."

The comments hurt.

Yet Nouri forged ahead, seemingly oblivious.

"We are *l'shem Shamayim*; there are bound to be setbacks. Being *mezakeh et harabbim* is so important and so valuable, Hashem wants to see how hard we are willing to work, how determined are we to accomplish," Nouri explained.

---

40. "Among those who helped us in a big way was the Federation. I believe that this was the only time that the Federation helped build an Orthodox Yeshiva in New York. Their $78,000 contribution jump-started the building campaign and enabled us to build a beautiful, four-story, state-of-the-art building. It was an incredible *kiddush Hashem*," recalled Rabbi Wolf. $78,000 in 1968 is equivalent to about $540,000 in 2015.

He never turned away the people who knocked on his door, looking to air their complaints. He listened patiently and tried to soothe their nerves. The transportation issue was valid. Children had to leave their homes very early and they returned very late. Nouri tried to make their parents realize that a yeshiva education was worth the inconvenience. He persuaded some of them, but others remained frustrated and skeptical. If, in the end, they still wanted to take their children out of Ahi Ezer Yeshiva, he tried to convince them to send their children to a different yeshiva.

"Just give them a Jewish education," he begged them.

Some listened. Some didn't.

It'll be okay, Nouri told himself. *Give it time. They'll be back.*

This was a very difficult period. Nouri and his able staff had to run the yeshiva, pacify the parents, keep the students happy, while working on constructing the new building.

Nothing went smoothly. Though it was gratifying to have the support of the Lindsay administration, unfortunately, the yeshiva was forced to rely on that good will too many times.[41] Rabbi Wolf constantly had to go down to the Board of Standards and Appeals and lobby for leniency regarding various zoning laws. Ultimately, Ahi Ezer received permission to build a four-story building on almost the entire lot. It was to be a far bigger building than what had existed before the fire and it was built without a dime of a mortgage.

As Nouri kept on saying, "HaKadosh Baruch Hu will help."

Along with the setbacks, there were happy occasions.

Sara Dayan married Stanley Salem in the winter of 1969.

A little while earlier, Rabbi Rafael Eisenberg had come to America pitching an interesting idea. He felt that it was time to introduce the concept of Kollel into the Syrian community in a way that would not require them to become part of the Ashkenazic world. He wanted to strengthen the Torah learning in the Syrian community through their own heritage.

For many years, Sha'arei Zion had a *magbid* — a fundraising drive — to raise money for Yeshiva Porat Yosef. Over time, this fostered a connection between the Syrian community and the pre-eminent Sephardic Yeshiva in Eretz Yisrael. Rabbi Eisenberg recognized this connection and arranged for a number of Syrian young couples to go to Eretz Yisrael, where the men would learn in Yeshiva Porat Yosef Kollel and receive a generous stipend, enough that they would not have to depend on parental support and could still live comfortably.

---

41. The authorities never discovered what prompted either fire but they suspected arson by a local resident. Indeed, not all the locals were as sympathetic to the yeshiva as Mayor Lindsay. They lodged complaints about the building and stopped construction many times.

Rabbi Rafael Eisenberg greeting Sephardic Kollel men at the airport in Israel. Front, L-R: Mrs. David Esses, Mrs. Shirley Maslaton, Rebbetzin Eisenberg, unknown, Rabbi Eisenberg, Rabbi David Massry, Menashe Levi, Rabbi Max Maslaton, Rabbi Ezra Zafrani. The child in the front, between Rabbi Maslaton and Rabbi Zafrani, is Shlomo Zafrani. Forty years after Rabbi Eisenberg's passing, his family has continued his devotion to the Sephardic community. Rabbi Elchonon Zelikovitz, a grandson of Rabbi Eisenberg, founded a yeshiva in Haifa for Sephardic youth.

Kollel was still a novel idea. Moving to Eretz Yisrael to learn in Kollel was positively radical. In the Syrian community, children tended to marry and stay close to home, preferably right around the corner from their parents. The fact that several couples signed up immediately created a stir in the community. By the time Sara married Stanley, several young Syrian couples were already living in Eretz Yisrael.

Stanley had put himself on Rabbi Eisenberg's list even though he had not been married at the time and had no idea if learning in Eretz Yisrael after marriage was even realistic. After he was engaged, he suggested to Sara that they go to Eretz Yisrael for a visit. Sara was thrilled. She loved Eretz Yisrael and was happy to visit, even for only a short time.

They planned to leave America three weeks after their wedding.

"Just don't end up in Cuba," was one of the common wisecracks of 1969.[42]

1968 had seen an unprecedented rise in hijackings, mostly to Cuba, and people expected 1969 to bring more of the same. By and large, people were not hurt, but the prospect of an entire aircraft being at the mercy of some petty criminal or a deranged individual was frightening. Yet flying around the world was becoming very popular as the cost of air travel dropped and vacations seemed to mandate boarding a plane. The Salems bought open

---

42. 1969 was "the year of the hijack," when over eighty flights were hijacked, mainly to Cuba. In 1961, America severed diplomatic relations with Cuba and there were no flights between the two countries. Nonetheless, there were a minority of Americans who wanted to go to Cuba, either because of political ideology or simply to evade the American justice system. They created a trend of hijacking aircrafts, diverting them to Cuba where the hijackers disembarked, and then having the planes return to their original destination.

tickets, enabling them to detour to Europe as part of their "honeymoon."

"Why not go to Europe first?" suggested Sara.

Stanley shook his head, "We don't go to Europe and then to Eretz Yisrael as an afterthought. We go to Eretz Yisrael first."

Sara was fine with that. She assumed that they would be touring Europe a few weeks later anyway. But, practically from the first day on Israeli soil, she realized that she didn't want to leave any time soon.

Can I really live here? Sara wondered.

She had no idea. She would soon find out.

L-R: Rabbi Max Maslaton, Rabbi Stanley Salem, Rabbi Ezra Zafrani, learning in Yeshivat Porat Yosef

Living in Eretz Yisrael was nothing like the touring Sara had done the year before. Then, it had been the responsibility of the hotel or their hosts to prepare the food and see to their needs. Now that she was on her own, she noticed so many things that she had not noticed before.

"How do you make *hamoud* without celery? And what about peas? I didn't see any of those either?" Sara asked Rachel Raful, Hacham Yosef's aunt, a warm woman who was quickly becoming Sara's surrogate mother. Rachel had been born in Jamaica and spoke English, a novelty among the older people in Sara's mainly Israeli neighborhood. Sara often came to visit, to share her struggles and learn how to navigate life in Eretz Yisrael. Though her words sounded petty to her own ears, Sara was still frustrated by her disappointing morning when she scoured the *shuk* but couldn't find these ingredients that were crucial to the *layl Shabbat* meal.

The older woman shrugged.

"We adapt," she explained. "Try to figure out how to use what is available instead of dwelling on that which is not."

Wise advice from a wise woman, Sara decided.

She took her words to heart and learned to appreciate the simple life in Eretz Yisrael. During that first year, she was so busy learning about life (and moving three times in half a year) that she hardly had time to be lonely.

Though she was far from the other Sephardic American couples who were based in Givat Shaul, there were other young Americans in the neigh-

Standing, L-R: Murray, Stanley, Sara, Joyce, and Barbara. Sitting, L-R: Esther, Joey, and Nouri.

borhood. Rabbi Chaim Walkin and his wife Henny lived nearby, as did Nechama Tucker, Rabbi Rafael Eisenberg's daughter, who had married Rabbi Yerachmiel Tucker. Rabbi Rosenfeld lived in her building, though he only came to Eretz Yisrael for summers. And though Sara wasn't really related to the Raful and Ades families, they treated her as family because of her connection to Hacham Yosef.

On the other hand, as the "few weeks" stretched into months, Sara had to adjust to the reality of being so far from her family. All the Dayan girls were homebodies; that was part of the Syrian mentality — that girls belonged at home.

Especially a home like our home, was the silent consensus of the Dayan girls.

The Dayan home remained the hive to which all the married children still gravitated. Thousands of miles away, Sara was cut off from everyone. Phone calls were prohibitively expensive and she didn't even have a phone. Every few months, she trooped to the post office to call her parents. If they had anything very important to share, they called her neighbor's phone and one of the children ran to let Sara know that she should come quickly. These rare calls were short and to the point. She and her siblings spent many hours writing letters back and forth, detailing their lives and keeping each other up to date on the news.

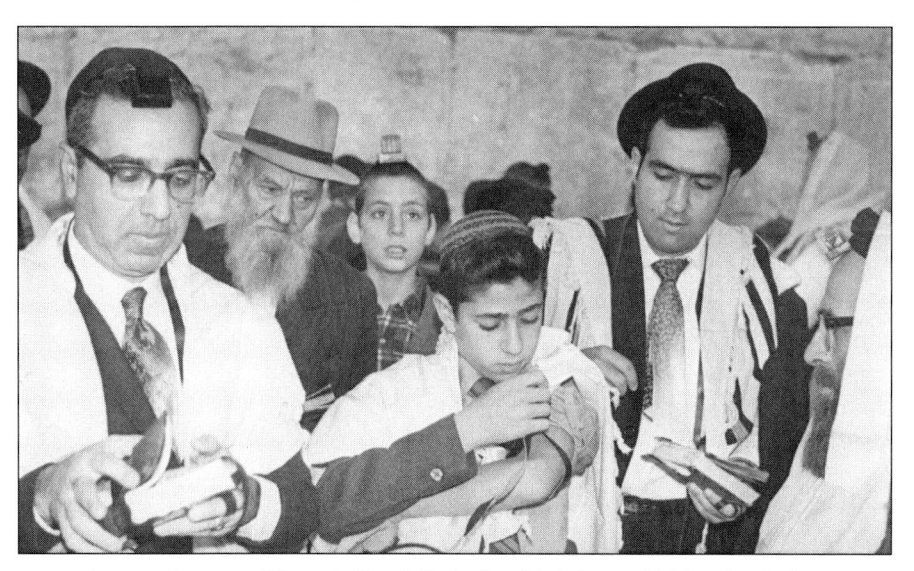

Joey putting on *tefillin* at the Kotel, flanked by his father and his brother-in-law

But when the news was sad, there was that empty, helpless feeling of being far away at a time when you wanted badly to be nearby.

Like when Uncle Morris Bibi suddenly passed away.

Nouri and Joey at the Kotel

...every so often, I feel pain... I wonder what it is...

These few words that Morris Bibi noted in his diary were the only indications that something was wrong. By the time Rebecca Bibi found him in bed, one Shabbat afternoon, it was all over. He had gone to sleep and never woken up.

Nouri and Irwin ran over to the house. Irwin laid the *niftar* on the floor and remained the *shomer* that night, until the funeral the next day. Nouri made all the technical arrangements. Even as he was devastated, he did what he had to do.

The whole community was shocked. Morris had been just over 60 years old and seemed in perfect health. He was one of the de facto

"We Are L'shem Shamayim; There Are Bound to Be Setbacks." / 387 founders of Sha'arei Zion since the Flatbush *minyan* began in his home. Everyone admired Morris Bibi as a role model for the community: a businessman who was very learned and whose spirituality always came first in his life.

For Nouri, Morris's passing was exceptionally painful.

Morris Bibi had been Nouri's uncle, brother-in-law, mentor, and best friend. He and Morris met often, sometimes with their wives and sometimes alone. Inevitably, they would speak *dibrei Torah*, as they exchanged insights about that week's *perasha* or the day's *Hok l'Yisrael*. Their interactions were always spiritually meaningful. Nouri felt like he had lost the one person who understood him on that level.

Sara Salem had to read between the lines to sense what was going on back home. The letters she received were very informative about the day-to-day happenings in the family and in the community, but they were not heart-to-heart conversations. She knew very little about how her father was taking this sudden tragedy. On such occasions, Eretz Yisrael felt very far away from America.

And yet, overall, Sara wasn't overly lonely for family.

In the fall of 1969, Nouri took the family to Eretz Yisrael in honor of Joey's bar mitzva.

Sara was thrilled to host them in her newly purchased apartment. A few weeks later, a new Salem entered the world and Sara's in-laws came in for the *brit*. A month later, Nouri and Esther came in for the *pidyon ha'ben*. Then Sara went back to America for Pesah. There was no time to be lonely for family… especially since so many of them were planning to come that fateful summer of 1970.

PART VI

Chapter 47:
SIMPLE FAITH

June, 1970

"I just bought tickets to Eretz Yisrael," Hacham Yosef Raful announced to his wife. "We are all going this summer."

"We are... what did you say?" Carol asked, really thinking: *I'm in the hospital after having a baby... I'm tired, I can't move; I have nothing to wear; I need clothes; I can't pack... What is he talking about?*

"Don't worry, you just rest up. It's all planned. Abraham and Marcelle will be going, and my mother... everyone!"

"But..."

"*Ken* (Yes)?"

"I'm so tired. How will I travel with the kids? Who will pack?"

He waved his hand dismissively. "Don't worry, it will be fine."

Carol closed her eyes, *I guess so...*

Later on, she looked at the tickets. They were scheduled to leave in six weeks. The TWA flight had two stopovers — one in Frankfurt and one in Athens. *I'm traveling with three children — one an infant — making two stopovers... Besides, those airports...* She shuddered. Just a year earlier there was a highly publicized hijacking of a TWA aircraft that left from Athens airport, and another incident involving the Frankfurt airport.[1]

I'll tell Yosef that we have to change the tickets, she decided.

Marcelle Raful examined the tickets that the travel agent had dropped off. *I don't like them*, she decided as she reached for a phone.

---

1. Given the surprising successes of the Cuban hijackings, terrorist groups began hijacking airplanes and using hostages as leverage over countries that had their members imprisoned. While the vast majority of the hijackings were Cuba-related, there were also some high-profile terrorist hijackings.

"Dave," Marcelle addressed her agent, "I don't want to take this flight."

"What's the problem?"

"I don't want a stopover. We can get hijacked."

"That is ridiculous!"

"Ridiculous or not, I don't want to go. I don't like the whole thing — TWA, stopping in Athens and in Frankfurt — why are we doing this?"

"Marcelle, I'm telling you, these are good tickets. Everything will be fine."

The Raful families were not the only ones going to Israel that summer. Nouri's oldest son, Irwin, and his wife were going on a two-week vacation and scouting trip. Though it was highly unusual at the time, Irwin wanted to leave the business world and join some of his friends who were learning in Yeshivat Porat Yosef. He'd been working for a few years and had enough saved to make a down payment on an apartment. With that, and the generous stipend worked out through Rabbi Eisenberg, he figured that they would be able to manage for a few years. Both sets of grandparents had volunteered to watch the children for the two weeks their parents were abroad.

Murray decided that he needed a change of pace, so he decided that a trip to Israel would be just the right thing. And Joyce was going to spend her summer with her sister Sara. All in all, Nouri and Esther had five out of seven of their children spending all or part of the summer of 1970 in Israel.

It's good that Joyce is coming, thought Carol, relieved. *If I have to have two stopovers, at least it will be with another pair of hands.*

When their flight to Israel arrived uneventfully, she settled down for a wonderful summer, her early premonitions forgotten.

It took time, but soon the Rafuls got the hang of Israeli living. Carol learned to do her errands and visiting either before 11 a.m. or after 4 p.m. She left her house promptly at 8 in the morning in order to capitalize on the cool hours, when it was easier to schlep the laundry back from the laundromat. She hung the wet clothing (the laundromat only **washed** laundry; they did not dry it) on lines on the roof, but made sure to take them down before they were stiff like cardboard and faded beyond recognition.

The midday hours were for straightening up the house, cooking, writing letters to her parents, or just collapsing from the heat. Later in the day, she took the kids out, sometimes braving the 15-minute walk to visit Sara and Joyce on Rechov Hoshea… only to find that they had gone out. Since neither of them had telephones, there was no good way to make sure the other would be home.

It's like growing up in Bensonhurst twenty years ago, mused Marcelle in Bnei Brak. Though she had nostalgic memories of her childhood, running to the candy store for the occasional phone call was one leap backward that she could have done without. Encountering the same situation in Israel wasn't quaint — it was inconvenient, to put it mildly.

Thank goodness for Mom. I think I would go out of my mind from loneliness without her.

Rabbanit Rachel, the matriarch of the Raful family, was beloved and revered. All she wanted to do was to shower her love on her children and grandchildren. She was a quiet woman, not from lack of knowledge, but from lack of desire to make her voice heard. She knew how to speak six languages — French, Spanish, Yiddish, Arabic, Hebrew, and English — but she used them only when she needed, never to show off her knowledge.

To her children, she spoke Arabic or Hebrew. To her neighbors in America, she spoke English. To the butcher on East 4th Street and Kings Highway, she spoke Yiddish, with a perfect Ashkenazic accent! As for French and Spanish, those she spoke when the need arose. And, unlike many Sephardic women, Rabbanit Rachel also read Hebrew. When she wasn't helping out her children, she was praying — constantly.

Rabbanit Rachel (Ades) Harari Raful

"It's a privilege to spend these weeks with her," Marcelle told her husband as they packed to go to Yerushalayim to visit their many Ades and Raful relatives, and where Rabbanit Rachel would move in with Hacham Yosef and Carol.

Carol had settled into a routine that included keeping house and watching the children play outside in the evenings when the air was cooler. Arrangements were informal: Without telephones, most people just knocked on your door to ask if they could come for a meal. Many of their cousins from the Raful and Ades families also came to visit during the course of the summer. Carol was feeling quite comfortable being both a guest of the Land and a hostess to her family.

"Would you want to live here?" Hacham Yosef asked Carol, one particularly pleasant and peaceful evening.

It's so beautiful here… so calm and easygoing… I really love it here…

"Yes," Carol answered slowly. "I think that it would be nice to live here."

"But I have already signed a contract for next year. If you want to stay, I would still have to go back to America and teach this year. Don't worry," he added quickly, "I would come back and forth for the Yamim Tovim…"

Simple Faith / 393

Well, Sara did it. She came for three weeks, and decided to stay... The thought was daunting but doable. Then Carol remembered: *But Stanley stayed with her... she didn't have to navigate Israeli life alone, with three little children... No, I can't do this...*

So the Rafuls stuck to their original plans.

They were scheduled to leave Israel at 6 a.m. on September 6.

Irwin and his wife returned to Bensonhurst, as did Murray. By then, trips to Israel were common, so their homecoming didn't engender much comment, especially in respect to everything else going on.

Nouri was in nightly meetings, feverishly getting ready for the upcoming school year. It seemed incredible, but the four-story, state-of-the-art Ahi Ezer school building was finished. It had everything that he could have dreamed of: large, airy classrooms with central heating and air conditioning, brand-new furniture, fully stocked supply closets, a library with hundreds of Hebrew and English books, a science laboratory, an industrial kitchen, and a synagogue for the yeshiva and the Ahi Ezer Egyptian *minyan*. The Ahi Ezer Day Camp had been using the building even as it was being finished. Now it was time to re-introduce the entire community to Ahi Ezer Yeshiva.

The previous two years in Williamsburg had been rough. Though some parents immediately pulled their children out, a final tally showed enrollment going up, not down. Nouri was convinced that when people saw the new building, enrollment would climb even higher. The building committee sent out fliers and invitations, announcing the Open House Dedication of the new Ahi Ezer Yeshiva.

It was scheduled for September 20, 1970.

Wednesday evening, September 2, Rosh Chodesh Elul

The light grey Jerusalem sky was tinged with yellow and orange. Carol had just gotten the children into bed and was contemplating how to orga-

Hacham Yosef Harari Raful with his sons, Ron and Ezra, in Israel, the summer of 1970

nize her life for the next few days. They had to be in the airport by 4:30 a.m. Mosa'ei Shabbat, which gave her about six hours to clean up from Shabbat and do last-minute packing. The fridge had to be totally emptied out and cleaned so that she could unplug it.

I really should figure out approximately how much food we have left, and how much we still need... A knock at the door interrupted her thoughts. Carol graciously welcomed her husband's cousin and his friend, a prominent Rabbi.

Hacham Yosef invited them to sit down.

"About my dream..." the Rabbi said seriously.

Hacham Abraham Harari Raful

Carol tensed. *Again he is here? But my husband already answered him when he first came, weeks ago. Why does he have to come again and make me nervous?*

Hacham Yosef Raful shook his head. "That is not our way," he said to the man. "*Tamim teheye im Hashem Elokecha.*[2] We don't use dreams to make our decisions in life."

But the Rabbi was persistent. Actually, he was distraught. "But I clearly saw that something bad is going to happen on your flight. I'm frightened for you."

Hacham Yosef politely but firmly reiterated his position.

"And if he comes again," he told Carol after escorting his guests out the door, "I will tell him the same thing. We don't run our lives based on premonitions of the future."

---

2. *Devarim* 18:13. Rashi explains that one must follow Hashem in simple faith and not turn to those who predict the future. One must accept what Hashem does as He does it; then we will be His nation.

Simple Faith / 395

Chapter 48:

"ONE WHO IS ACCOMPANIED WILL NOT SUFFER HARM."

After spending ten weeks in Israel, it was time for the Rafuls to return home. On Saturday night, September 5, so many people came to see them off that it was 12 a.m. by the time the last well-wisher left. Last-minute packing and cleaning took up what was left of the night, and by 2:30 a.m. Carol was waking up the children to dress them. At 3, Rav Yosef Ades, a cousin of the Rafuls and a R"M in Yeshivat Porat Yosef, stopped in on his way to early morning prayers at the Kotel. Carol was touched that he came at that hour.

She continued to pack feverishly, pausing as she held a bag of individually wrapped Splendid chocolates, a present from Uncle Eliyahu Raful.

"For the trip," he had beamed when he handed it to her.

Chocolate? In this weather? Won't they melt? Carol graciously thanked him while mentally erasing the image of melted chocolates on toddlers' hands and faces during a long trip.

"It's good," her husband commented when he saw her hold the chocolate uncertainly. "We need food for the trip. Remember what happened on our way here?"

Yes, she remembered. TWA had run out of kosher meals for the last leg of their journey to Eretz Yisrael. With this in mind, Hacham Yosef added a loaf of bread to the carry-on where Carol had already stashed a buttered loaf of bread, coffee cake, hard-boiled eggs, cheese, and cookies.

"What else is left in the fridge?" he asked.

Carol peered inside. "I guess I overestimated on the apples," she admitted sheepishly.

"Also good," he said. "We'll take them along."

"But we can't bring fresh fruit into America. We'll get fined."

"We're taking them," he decided, placing the apples into the carry-on. "If they don't let us bring them into the country, we'll throw them out over there."

Just as the Rafuls (with Joyce) were boarding the taxi, David Raful (a cousin) showed up. "I'm coming with you to the airport," he announced.

Carol was mystified. As they pulled away from their building, she asked him, "This is all very nice, but why are you bothering to come all the way to Lod?"

"*Kol hamitlaveh eino nizok* — One who is accompanied, will not suffer harm," he told her.[3]

Carol was touched. *Perhaps his efforts will keep us safe...*

Marcelle Raful was waiting in Ben Gurion Airport near the gate with her husband, mother-in-law, and two children.

Where is Carol? she wondered, leaning back in her seat, feeling queasy. She had tried to get a few hours of sleep before the flight, but was struck with a virulent stomach virus that made her wish that she wasn't traveling at all. She refused to think about the trip ahead: two stopovers with two restless children operating on almost no sleep. But at least she was packed and ready to board.

I hope Carol makes the flight...

Carol watched Eretz Yisrael whiz by. She glanced at her watch... No wonder the driver was speeding. Her thoughts wandered back to the Rabbi who had come a few nights earlier, his ominous warnings ringing in her ears. *Why did he have to come back? We heard what he said the first time...*

As they pulled up to the airport, late, the Rabbi's warning haunted her. She ran with her family through the airport, her heart pounding, her thoughts jumbled. The ticketing agent seemed harried and annoyed; she was having a difficult time finding seats for the whole family to sit together.

"It's a very full flight," she muttered. "Large families are supposed to check in earlier. Why did you come so late?"

Carol didn't answer. Finally, the woman found a solution.

"Ma'am, we are going to have to put you into First Class..."

Carol let out a sigh of relief. At least they had made the flight.

Joyce buckled her seat belt and settled in for the ride.

I'm happy for Carol, she mused. Though she had wanted to help her sister with the children during the flight, she was sure that the roomier accommodations in First Class would make up for any help she could have given.

---

3. This is paraphrasing *Hazal*: "*Kol hamelaveh et haveiro eino nizak* — One who accompanies his friend [four cubits in the city] will not suffer harm" (*Sotah* 46b).

Her thoughts kept drifting back to the country she was leaving. She already missed the quiet streets where most of the vehicles were busses or taxis and private cars were very rare. She missed turning off the newly paved roads, onto newly trod dirt paths and sandy open spaces, into a vast emptiness — the Land waiting for her children to return. She missed the warm sunshine that smiled even as it scorched and kept the world brightly lit and cheerful.

But I'll be back, she comforted herself. *We'll all be back — very soon.*

The flight from Lod, as Ben Gurion Airport was known then, to Athens was uneventful. First Class wasn't all that different from coach, only there was a bit more room to spread out. Carol was relieved that at least the baby was sleeping and so, when they landed in Frankfurt, she decided not to join all the people getting off to stretch their legs.

Marcelle was still feeling weak. *Maybe some fresh air will help,* she decided as she and her husband, Hacham Abraham, shepherded their children off the plane. They met Carol and Hacham Yosef on their way out.

"You're getting off?" Carol asked.

"I need some fresh air. You're staying?"

"It's Germany," Carol made a face. "No mitzva to get off here."

"I just want to walk around, maybe buy something…"

"We don't buy things here," admonished Hacham Yosef. "If you are going outside anyway, curse the ground, but don't buy their merchandise."

Marcelle nodded, not really thinking much about anything beyond fresh air.

After walking around the terminal for a while, Marcelle felt just as sluggish as before, only now she was tired from walking, tired from amusing the children, and just plain tired…

"Marcelle, look at those two people."

"Where?" she asked, totally uninterested.

"Over there, just look," Hacham Abraham insisted.

Near the Rafuls, on the tram going from the terminal to the airplane, stood a very striking couple. The man was tall and broad shouldered, his dark features relaxed and impassive. He wore a light-colored suit, a crisp white shirt, and a dark tie. His companion was also dark, or maybe the contrast with her off-white dress made her seem exotic. She stood tall and straight, like a model.

They look like a magazine picture…

"Were they on the plane with us?" Hacham Abraham persisted.

"Who?"

"That couple," he whispered impatiently. "Right over there."

Who cares? And how would I know? I'm trying to take care of two children while I feel sick and weak and he thinks I noticed who was on our flight?

"Were they on the plane with us on the way here?" he repeated.

"I don't know... I think so..." Marcelle answered lamely. She was too muddled to wonder why her husband was so agitated. All she wanted was to return to the plane and collapse into her seat.

The plane gained altitude. Joyce was sitting toward the back. She had been chatting with her seatmate, another Jewish teenager, when suddenly a man stood up and began running down the aisle. A woman followed.

Probably a stewardess, Joyce thought.

"He has a gun!" her seatmate whispered.

Seconds later, screams came from the First Class section.

Carol turned around and saw a stewardess being pushed down the aisle by a tall, well-dressed man who pressed a silver pistol to her back. A slim woman, clutching something, completed the parade as they made their way to the cockpit.

"Duck!" yelled a man from behind. Everyone in the First Class section dropped to the floor, not wanting to be a target.

"Open up!" the hijacker shouted as he banged at the cockpit door, still keeping the gun trained on the stewardess. The door opened, and the two hijackers let themselves in. Moments later, the loudspeaker crackled to life: **This is your new captain speaking. Be calm. The Popular Front for the Liberation of Palestine is now in charge of this plane. We are going to a friendly country with friendly people. Keep your hands behind your head.**[4]

Joyce heard the message and automatically obliged. By then, she was no longer surprised. She had just seen two crewmen stumble out of the First Class section with their hands up, white as ghosts. They were obviously being hijacked, but being so far from America, they couldn't be heading for the standard hijacking destination.

Okay, reasoned Joyce, *at least we are not going to Cuba.*

Marcelle was washing her daughter's hands in the restroom in the back of the plane, oblivious to the drama taking place only a few yards away. A few minutes later, as she led her daughter back toward their bulkhead seats up front, she noticed a passenger staring at her.

"You'd better get to your seat fast," he said.

"Why?" asked Marcelle, puzzled. Then she looked up and gasped.

Mr. Magazine Picture was pointing a gun in her face.

---

[4]. In studying several firsthand accounts published (in *Black September* by David Raab and in *Zman Magazine*) and unpublished (Hacham Abraham Raful's journal, Mrs. Carol [Dayan] Raful's journal, Mrs. Joyce [Dayan] Nahem's letter) and several interviews, we have noticed minor discrepancies, such as exactly what words were broadcasted and when. We have tried to compile an accurate account.

"Sit down. Right now," he said softly.

Yes, sir.

I can't believe it, thought Hacham Abraham, *I knew there was something suspicious about that couple. I should have said something to somebody.*

Not that it would have helped. On that very same day, three other planes were hijacked, two by passengers singled out as being suspicious. Hijacking was a problem that plagued the skies from the very beginning of commercialized travel and the international community had yet to find a solution. With rare exceptions, hijacking had been a dangerous inconvenience, but few people had died as a result. Nonetheless, everyone was frightened, especially since the PFLP was known to be the most extreme terrorist organization in existence.

It's going to be fine, Hacham Abraham calmed himself. *The Ribbono shel Olam will ensure that nothing bad will happen to us. Ima is here. She is a tzaddeket.* He was comforted by her presence.

While the PFLP had declared their authority, the passengers were still clueless as to where they were being taken and why. Then the plane began turning in the opposite direction, back toward the Middle East. Hacham Abraham began to tremble. Having been raised on horror stories of the Damascus Blood Libel and the unusual cruelty of the Syrian Arabs, he panicked: *Ribbono shel Olam, just not to Syria!*[5]

The male hijacker paced back and forth, gun in hand.

Joyce felt sick. As soon as they were allowed to put their hands down, she reached for her *Tehillim* and began to pray.

The crew tried to go about their duties — serving drinks, handing out headphones, serving lunch that few people were interested in eating. They had recovered from their initial shock and were calm, as were the passengers. There was a general sense of "let's just get through this and everything will be fine." The airplane was eerily quiet. Even the many children were subdued.

The airplane flew on.

Hacham Abraham stared out the window, trying to make out their location in the dusky evening that was becoming dark very quickly. He turned to his brother, who had been moved out of First Class when the hijackers took over, and murmured, "I don't see any airport."

Indeed, there was no airport: no lighted runway, no air traffic control tower, just some dimly lit spots (cans of kerosene-drenched cotton, lit like large torches) and vehicle headlights. Was it possible to land safely under these conditions?

---

5. Though the overall feeling of Sephardic Jewry was positive toward the homes they had left, they were quick to acknowledge that when their Arab neighbors decided to be cruel, their cruelty was often barbaric.

The airplane circled and circled, seemingly without direction. Some of the passengers became nauseous from the circling. The pilot tried to keep the descent gradual, hoping to land the airplane safely, without sacrificing the plane itself, so that he could take off as soon as the hijackers allowed it. Miraculously, the plane landed smoothly, as if in a regular airport.

There was silence.

It was hard to feel excited about the safe landing when the passengers were so tense about where they had landed and in whose hands. The pilot shut off the motor, and the entire airplane went black. Hacham Abraham peered out the window. Random automobile headlights gave off enough light to discern what was going on outside. Masses of armed Arabs waved their weapons excitedly. He had a sinking feeling in the pit of his stomach.

Carol leaned back in her seat, now in the regular coach section of the plane. The airplane was a 707 — not the largest airplane of its day, but also not the smallest, either. It had two rows of three seats with an aisle in between. The crew had shuffled some people around and Carol was squashed with two of her children and the three Hirsch children in a row meant for three people. The baby was in an infant seat on one of the pull-out meal trays.

As the hijackers opened the door of the aircraft, the passengers heard whooping cheers as they were greeted by triumphant Arabs, pouring out of the trucks that had pulled up near the airplane. They positioned a wooden ladder onto a truck at the side of the airplane and the hijackers exited the airplane and descended toward the celebrating *kaffiyeh*-wearing crowd.

Moments later, two guerillas boarded the airplane, one female and one male. The woman ordered everyone to hand over his passport and fill out the papers being handed out. The electricity had been shut off and the airplane was black and airless.

"Excuse me, I can't write because I can't see," interjected Hacham Abraham.

"Just write," she snapped.

Marcelle took the forms from her husband and tried to fill them out. There was virtual silence, save the scratching of pens against paper. Children whimpered.

"Ma'am, there are babies on this flight. How are they supposed to manage here?" a passenger called out.

The female commando answered angrily, "For twenty-three years, our Palestinian brothers have lived under these exact conditions. You will also manage. It's not a tragedy."

Her anger instilled fear. Over eighty of the passengers were Jewish.

I'm sure that Yosef is taking care of the passports, Carol mused distractedly. She recalled a conversation that they had after a 1968 terrorist hijacking to Syria. She had asked her husband what he would he do if he were ever caught on a hijacked plane.

"I would dispose of my Israeli passport," he had answered decisively.

Now she wondered how he would accomplish just that.

Joyce was all alone, toward the back of the airplane.

"They want our passports," her seatmate whispered, fumbling for hers.

Joyce nervously began doing the same. Ever since the Six Day War, one of the most hated names in the Muslim world had been Moshe Dayan. What would they say when they saw the name Dayan stamped on her passport?

Bensonhurst, Sunday morning, September 6, 1970

Esther Dayan reached for the ringing phone.

"Mrs. Dayan? It's Judy Raful. I just heard on the news that an El Al plane from Israel has been hijacked."

"Oh my…"

"Do you remember how Carol and Yosef were traveling?"

"TWA," Esther answered confidently.

"Oh good," Judy breathed.

Irwin's car radio blasted the news: "Pan Am Flight 93 from Brussels to New York has been hijacked. The guerillas, members of the PFLP, have requested permission to land in Egypt. We will be reporting details as they come in."

Irwin shut the radio and asked his wife, "Do you remember what flight everyone is on?"

"I'm pretty sure it was TWA, and not through Brussels."

Irwin nodded. But for some reason, he wasn't relieved.

"Did you hear the news?" Rabbi Wolf asked Murray, in Ahi Ezer.

"What news?"

"They've been hijacked."

Can't be… "Are you sure?"

"Go home. I'm sure that everyone knows already."

Indeed, by the time Murray arrived home, his parents were solemnly listening to the news. They had no official confirmation that their family was on any of the hijacked flights, but when they didn't arrive home that afternoon, they knew. Four hijackings in one day — one was thwarted, and three were successful. What was going on?

Actually, "what was going on" was very complicated.

King Hussein of Jordan had been in a very sticky position for quite a while.

Since 1967, his country had been overrun by Palestinians. While the PLO ostensibly cooperated with him, the PFLP made no secret of their disdain for his leadership and their desire to overthrow him. They sowed dissent in Jordan, even carrying out terrorist activities against Jordanian civilians who were loyal to their monarch. Yet King Hussein didn't want to crush the *fedayeen* (literally, *freedom fighters*; actually, terrorists). Their presence kept the people distracted from the poverty that plagued the kingdom. He also hoped that they would help him regain the land that he lost in 1967. He ordered his soldiers to keep law and order but not to reign in the *fedayeen* completely.

Things came to a head in August of 1970 when Egypt, Jordan, and Israel accepted the Roger's Plan, which called for a cease-fire and peace talks between the three nations. The *fedayeen* were outraged at this betrayal. They became increasingly bolder, terrorizing Jordan until they practically controlled Amman. They attempted to assassinate King Hussein twice. Throughout that summer, there were uprisings and agreements. Then came the hijacking crisis.

The PFLP terrorists attempted four hijackings in one day, taking hundreds of hostages.[6] King Hussein appeared foolish and weak: over 300 hostages were in his kingdom, guarded by PFLP soldiers who were dictating their terms to the Western world. The PLO, jealous of the coup, was quick to jump in and show that they were also a player. By now, King Hussein had enough.

It's time to show them who is in charge here, he grimly decided.

He realized that the terrorists were using Dawson Field (a strip of desert once used by the British as a military airport), newly dubbed "Revolution Airport." He ordered the highly professional Jordanian Army to surround the terrorists who were surrounding the airplanes. This wasn't a permanent solution, for he knew that if his army fired on the terrorists, the hostages would be in danger. His goal was to proclaim, loud and clear, that he wasn't in favor of the hijackings, and didn't intend to allow the terrorists to do as they pleased.

He knew quite well that his actions were about to spark a civil war.

---

6. Within two hours of the TWA hijacking, a Swissair flight was hijacked over France, an El Al flight sustained a hijack attempt over England, and a Pan Am flight was hijacked over Amsterdam. The El Al hijack attempt was foiled by air marshals and crew members. The airplane landed safely in London — one hijacker was killed in-flight and the other, the infamous Leila Khaled, was taken into custody. The Pan Am hijacking was unplanned. The PFLP sent four operatives on the El Al plane and all were flagged as being suspicious. Two passengers were body searched and allowed to board (and then hijacked the plane). Two passengers were thrown off the flight, but El Al personnel found them an alternate flight on Pan Am. Those two became the spontaneous hijackers of the Pan Am flight. Ultimately, the PFLP successfully hijacked three airplanes: a TWA flight, a Swissair flight, and a Pan Am flight.

Chapter 49:
"YOU GO WITH YOUR CHILDREN. I'M STAYING WITH MINE."

The hostages began a very difficult night. Outside, in the vast, empty desert, there was nothing to illuminate the deep darkness but the truck headlights that the terrorists flashed on and off at whim. The evening air was cool, and the temperature in the airplane was slowly dropping. Holding flashlights, the Arabs began coming around to collect the passports and the filled-out papers.

Carol started. The sudden light was unnerving, but not as unnerving as the face it illuminated. The glare of the flashlight accented the Arab's stubbly face, bushy mustache, yellowed teeth, and sinister smile. The red-and-white-checkered *kaffiyeh* completed the look. He held out his hand.

Carol gave him her passport.

More *kaffiyeh*-wearing Arabs boarded the plane. They swaggered around with guns and talked excitedly in Arabic. Outside, many more of them trained machine guns on the plane. It was a nightmare.

Marcelle turned to her mother-in-law and, as usual, addressed her in Arabic.

"No," Rabbanit Rachel answered in English, "we must not speak Arabic. If they know that we understand Arabic, they might single us out for trouble."

"What if I slip? Or what if they catch on that I understand?"

"Deny it," her mother-in-law told her emphatically.

Joyce came down the aisle a little while later. "I just overheard the Arabs speaking excitedly about having captured two more planes."

As she spoke, they heard the sound of a plane overhead. Then a crashing noise shook their aircraft. The hostages peered out the window, but it was too dark to make out what was going on. [7] Meanwhile, Hacham Yosef quietly told Joyce, "Don't let on that you know Arabic." Then he turned to his oldest son, Ron, who was 5 1/2. "Don't speak to me in Hebrew. We are Americans and speak only English."

It was very difficult. The Rafuls naturally spoke Hebrew and Arabic. Particularly difficult was when they had to feign ignorance even as the Arabs spoke freely.

"We have just finished wiring the cockpit and the fuel tanks. At the flick of a switch, this airplane will explode," one Arab boasted to his friend.

How could one hear such words and remain impassive?

Everyone was thirsty. The children were scared. The adults, most of whom had never seen a gun up close, were jittery. There was no supper, and people regretted not having eaten lunch. The air was thick with tension.

Sensing the unease, the commandos militantly clamped down on the hostages. No one was allowed to stand up. If they needed the facilities, they had to raise their hands and ask permission. Everyone tried to sleep in their seats.

> *The first night passed in a haze of fear and horror and trauma and suffering that is indescribable,* Hacham Abraham wrote. *Every few minutes more terrorists came onto the plane, flashed light into our faces, and then looked around, talking excitedly. I couldn't close my eyes... Baruch Hashem, in the end, day dawned. We calmed down from the terrifying night. Right away, I washed my hands, put on tefillin, and prayed, as did some other passengers. And then the groups of visitors started up again... They introduced themselves: These are PFLP and these are PLO. The PFLP show the PLO their booty (us!) and because I understand the language, I understood a lot of what they were saying to each other. Referring to the many Jews on the plane, a female terrorist gloated, "Do you have any idea what a catch this is? We never dreamed of such success."*

By 5 in the morning, sun streamed through the windows and people stretched their cramped limbs. The flight was an around-the-world journey that began in the Far East; some of the passengers had been on the same plane over 24 hours. The commandos were in the lounge that separated First Class and Coach, poring over the list of names they had compiled from the

---

7. The next day the hostages saw the Swissair plane. It had landed an hour after the TWA flight but by then it was nighttime and the pilot was basically landing blind, right next to another large plane! It was impossible to accurately judge where the ground began and therefore he "crash" landed and damaged the aircraft. Some of the engines started smoking so people went out the emergency doors and began jumping from the wing. A few got hurt but, overall, the 150+ Swiss Air passengers were miraculously safe, parked alongside the TWA aircraft.

collected passports. Joyce was on her way back to her seat when she heard a female voice say in Arabic, "There is someone named Dayan aboard."

Joyce froze. *Would she really be singled out because of her name?*

The plane began to heat up. The crew opened the back doors and the emergency exits to let in some air. It helped, but for a limited area. The openings also let in a lot of sand. People began walking around, but the commandos kept ordering them back to their seats. Hacham Yosef stood up against the wall to give the women and children more room to sit. Sanitary conditions deteriorated, and the arid air and lack of water slowly dehydrated the hostages.

The fact that TWA was an American airline and most of the crew and passengers were American gave the passengers hope that the American government would not abandon them. On the other hand, it was Labor Day in America, which meant that all government offices were closed. Even the optimists conceded that they would be spending at least another day on the plane.

On Monday afternoon, Red Cross representatives arrived, bringing hope. But then they left, promising to return in two days. The hostages were so let down. Who could hold out another two days under those conditions, in that relentless heat? Members of the Muslim Red Crescent also came on board and asked the women what they needed for the children. There were five babies on board: two infants, an 18-month-old toddler, and two 2-year-olds. The women quickly prepared a list. They needed diapers (crucial) and ointment, Similac, baby food, baby cereal, and powdered or evaporated milk. Meanwhile, the mothers pooled their resources. One woman had baby cereal, another had formula. With a little water that the crew brought from the First Class section, they fed the babies.

Journalists arrived at Dawson Field to find the Jordanian Army surrounding the armed PFLP fighters who surrounded the hijacked planes. There were so many tanks and machine guns, it looked like a war zone. The PFLP held a press conference. They demanded the release of Palestinian prisoners. The reporters were less interested in the Palestinian cause and more interested in hearing how the hostages were faring. They demanded to speak to a crew member, and their request was granted.

Interviewer: Is there enough food and drink?

Stewardess: We have very little to drink, particularly in [view of] the desert heat.

Interviewer: How old is the youngest passenger?

Stewardess: We have two infants who are three months old.[8]

---

8. *Zman Magazine*, September 2010. This was inaccurate. One infant was about 4 months and the other was 9 months.

The hijackers held a press conference. In the background are some of the hostages. The man in the full black beard is Rabbi Yonason David, son-in-law of Rabbi Yitzchak Hutner, and, today, Rosh Yeshiva of Yeshivas Pachad Yitzchak.

Bensonhurst, Monday morning, September 7, 1970

Esther Dayan was glued to the news.

Two infants who are three months old… Rachel! Esther drew in a breath. Her little granddaughter was one of those infants who didn't have enough to drink.

The news droned on as the house slowly filled up with people, family and friends who came to be with them. There were men in one room and women in the other — all day, in and out — as they listened to the news, hoping for more information. Though most of the Sephardic community had grown up in America, the post-1948 Sephardic immigrants arrived with horror stories of Arab viciousness and persecution. Helplessness and fear pervaded the community. They watched the footage of the hijackers making their demands, of the airplane stranded in the desert, of the armed Arabs milling about, but they didn't see the hostages and they didn't know how they were faring. They heard the voices of the hijackers state their ominous threats:

We have wired the airplanes with explosives. Leila Khaled and other Palestinian freedom fighters held in Europe and Israel must be freed within seventy-two hours. The countdown begins retroactively, as of 6 a.m. this morning. If our demands are not met, the planes will be blown up with the passengers aboard.[9]

Esther stared unseeingly as tears poured down her cheeks.

Back on the airplanes, most of the hostages were blissfully unaware that they were sitting on a time bomb — literally. Sure, there were rumors,

---

9. Switzerland and Germany were both holding Palestinian terrorists. Britain was holding Leila Khaled after her attempted hijack of the El Al flight. Khaled had previously hijacked a TWA flight but then had plastic surgery to alter her features, which was why she successfully boarded the El Al flight but was captured in her hijacking attempt. She became a political symbol for the Palestinians.

but those rumors were hard to believe. After all, the plane didn't feel any different than it felt when they first boarded. And the idea seemed so fantastic — like something out of the movies — that it was easier to dismiss than accept. Unlike their families, the hostages were spared the frightening ordeal of listening to the newscasters drone on and on about the wired airplanes that were set to blow up in an instant.

Paradoxically, they all believed that their release was imminent, that the hijacking was just a nuisance or some kind of horrible mistake. So on Monday afternoon, when the commandos boarded the plane and began taking off passengers, the hostages greeted the news with relief but not surprise.

> *The guerillas came to the front of economy class,* Carol wrote, *and called for all citizens of India to come forward with their hand luggage. Instead of letting them leave, they told them to please be seated until after dinner. This was at about 3:30 p.m. We were all pleasantly surprised when there really was dinner: chicken, string beans, salad, pita, boiled eggs, and grapes. I had been wondering how long we could possibly manage without food.*

Ron reached for some of the food.

"No," Carol said, "it's not kosher."

"Why did you tell him that?" Hacham Yosef protested. "He's a child. What is he going to eat?" He turned to the venerable Rabbi Yitzchak Hutner, Rosh Yeshiva of Yeshivas Rabbi Chaim Berlin, sitting behind them, and began discussing the halachic aspects of their situation, mainly, what the adults could or should eat, as opposed to the children.

Carol was silent but wondered, *Don't we have enough fruit and vegetables, bread and cookies in our bags? Aren't we getting off this plane soon?*

Her feelings seemed validated when the Indian hostages were taken off the plane after supper. Then the commandos called all women and children to come forward. The announcement caused quite a commotion. Should they leave their husbands? To where were they being taken? Hacham Yosef advised Carol to leave and go to Amman, the assumed location. She took her suitcase with children's clothes and a TWA bag with bottles, diapers, and Similac. Hacham Yosef kissed the children and they parted. Carol questioningly looked at her mother-in-law, who remained seated.

"You go with your children," Rabbanit Rachel said softly. "I'm staying with mine," she said, referring to Hacham Abraham and Hacham Yosef.

The women and children walked single file to the exit. As they passed through first class, the terrorists told them to state their names.

"Joyce Dayan."

The writing stopped. The terrorist peered closely at Joyce. "Any relation to Moshe Dayan?"

Joyce shook her head, her heart pounding.

The terrorist stared at her, long and hard. Then she let her go by.

Little Ezra Raful, climbing down from the airplane

Bensonhurst, Monday morning, September 7, 1970

The radio blared: "The Jordanian army negotiated with the PFLP to release the women and children. Details will follow."

Esther Dayan paused. *Could it be? Would they be freed so soon?*

As they exited the plane, Carol held Rachel in her infant seat and Joyce took Ezra, the 2-year-old. Ron followed closely behind holding one bag while a helpful girl held another. An Arab guard at the door took the baby from Carol and passed her down to an Arab on the bottom of the ladder that was on top of a jeep. He passed her to another Arab guerilla standing on the ground. Ezra was also passed hand to hand. Carol and Ron followed on the rickety ladder. It was a very steep descent, with the desert winds blowing as they moved down the steps, onto the jeep, where they were helped off by their "accommodating" captors.

It felt good to reach solid ground. Carol looked around and noticed that Rebbetzin Hutner and her daughter, Rebbetzin David, also had not gotten off the airplane. She was relieved that her mother-in-law would not be the only woman staying behind.

She stood together with the other women and children huddled in a circle, the hot desert air blowing in their faces. They were surrounded by terrorists toting machine-guns. The planes loomed large and seemed incongruous against the desert background replete with camels. Several busses stood nearby, awaiting their passengers.

The Arabs directed the hostages toward the busses.

The atmosphere was electric.

Suddenly, everyone was ordered off the busses. Why?

The sun was slipping slowly down the horizon as the commandos read off the names from the pink slips that the hostages had filled out that first night. Name by name, the women and children reboarded the busses.

Camels roamed the desert where the two airplanes were parked.

Then the terrorists stopped reading and ordered the busses to leave. The remaining hostages looked at each other, clarity dawning.

Only non-Jews had left on the busses.[10]

> *At that moment,* Carol wrote, *I recalled what I had read regarding the selections in Auschwitz. When a girl asked me what I thought would happen next, I answered, as if in a stupor, that maybe they will kill us.*

"Mommy, are they really going to kill us," asked 5 ½- year-old Ron.

"No," Carol caught herself, "of course not." She mentally promised herself not to get carried away again, for the sake of the children.

In stoic disappointment, the Jewish women and children reboarded the airplane. By the time they were all inside, it was dusk outside and the plane was dark. The men greeted the women in sad disbelief. They had been so happy when the women and children were taken off the airless plane. They tried to comfort them, though they also felt betrayed and distressed.

Carol gave the children some bread. A young girl sitting across the aisle took baby Rachel from her hands and rocked her. Hacham Yosef helped Carol put the other children to sleep, arranging them on their row of three seats. He then lay down on the floor in front of them.

Carol went walking around the dark plane looking for a better seat than the non-reclining one of the night before. Since many people had been taken off that day, the remaining hostages appropriated their seats. Some people snatched three seats and laid down on all of them. To her dismay, Carol

---

10. The Jordanian army negotiated the release of all women and children, but the terrorists decided that Jewish women and children of the TWA flight were not part of the deal (they did release the ones on the Swiss Air flight). Red Cross representatives observed the process up until the busses were full and then they drove off, expecting full busses to follow. The terrorists re-boarded the busses and separated the Jewish passengers. The hostages taken off the plane that day were not released but were taken to hotels in Amman, where they were more comfortable but very unsafe due to the fighting between the Jordanians and the *fedayeen* taking place there.

found that there were no available seats. Resigned, she went back to the non-reclining seat her son was sleeping in and where she had sat the previous night. She picked up the child and settled his head on her lap and his body scrunched on the adjoining seat where his brother slept.

She sighed. *Another sleepless night ahead.*

"Sir, are you Mr. Raful?"

"Yes," Hacham Abraham mumbled, frustrated. *I cannot believe this...* He had barely slept in 48 hours. Now that he had finally fallen asleep, they were waking him up.

"They have called you for questioning."

Rabbi Yitzchak Hutner (1906-1980).

Hacham Abraham became instantly alert. He heard his brother's name being called as well.

"Yosef, they are calling you," Carol whispered. "Maybe you want to take your jacket? It's cold in the desert at night..."

It was cold on the airplane as well. The temperature rose to over 100 degrees Fahrenheit by day and then dropped to less than half that amount by night. But Hacham Yosef didn't take his jacket, though he took a blanket, as per the guerilla's instructions. He quickly walked off the plane.

"How long will they be outside?" Carol asked the female commando.

"About two hours," she answered.

Carol, Marcelle, and Rivke Berkowitz, whose husbands had been taken off, huddled together, wondering: Why were their husbands singled out for questioning? But, after a few minutes of yawning, Carol decided that she had better get some sleep. Forty-eight hours of no sleep didn't make for a patient mother.

"Carol, wake up," Marcelle shook her awake. "Mom is trying to tear her clothes [as a sign of mourning]."

"What?" Carol asked. "Why?"

"Because they took the boys off," she said.

Oh. That means they haven't come back.

"Marcelle, I haven't slept in two days. I'm so tired. Can't you talk to her?"

"You Go With Your Children. I'm Staying With Mine." / 411

"I tried. I've been talking and talking, but she doesn't stop crying. I've been up with her for hours."

Carol heaved herself out of her awkward position and went over to sit beside her mother-in-law. Rabbanit Rachel was crying uncontrollably, like a child who has been crying for so long, he cannot stop. She looked at Carol with pleading eyes, seeking help.

Carol felt lost. What could she say to her mother-in-law, an unusually strong woman who had lived through so much? The prospect of losing her sons — her pride and joy — must have stirred up painful memories and fears.[11] Just a few hours earlier, this special woman had told her, "You go with your children, I'm staying with mine." *And now, I'm with my children, yet she is not with hers…*

"Ma, they'll be back, don't worry…" Carol's voice trailed off as she realized that her mother-in-law didn't really hear her.

She called over a female commando. "Please, can you explain to my mother-in-law in Arabic that her sons are all right and will soon be back?" she asked, disregarding their previous decision not to let on that they knew Arabic. Right now, it was more important to help her mother-in-law calm down.

The terrorist turned to speak with her, but the Rabbanit preempted her. "My sons don't know anything. All their lives, they sit and study."

"We don't want to do anything to them," answered the woman smoothly. "We just want to ask them some questions."

Though nothing much had been said, Rabbanit Rachel stopped crying and the terrorist walked off. Carol used the opportunity to inject a comment of her own.

"You know, Ma," she said, "maybe they're in a better place than we are. It's crazy here. It's stifling by day, cold at night. We're cramped on a stuffy airplane, with little kids who are going nuts. Maybe it's better for them over there."

Rabbanit Rachel looked hopefully at her daughter-in-law. A little while later, she began praying Shaharit… and she continued to pray for her sons' return, constantly, in the hours and days afterward.

Carol was relieved that her mother-in-law had regained control. Her own words echoed in her mind. *Who knows? Maybe it **is** better for them wherever they are.*

---

11. During World War I, Rabbanit Rachel's husband, Hacham Aharon Raful, and his brothers-in-law, fled to Buchara to avoid the Turkish draft. In those six years, they opened a Talmud Torah and spent their days teaching the local youth and their fathers. Rabbanit Rachel, a young newlywed, left alone in Eretz Yisrael, helplessly watched as her two children passed away from illness and starvation. When her husband returned, they rebuilt a whole new family and put those years of sorrow behind them. Yet she had never completely forgotten her pain.

Chapter 50:
"I JUST WANT MY CHILDREN BACK."

Bensonhurst, Monday evening, September 7, 1970

"Mrs. Dayan? I'm calling from the news network ABC. We understand that you have children and grandchildren being held hostage in Jordan. Would you give us an interview?"

"What for? I don't know anything more than you know."

"The American public wants to hear how you feel about the situation."

How I feel about the situation? fumed Esther for a few silent seconds. *My infant granddaughter has nothing to eat and they want to know how I feel about the situation? I'm going to give them a piece of my mind. The nerve of these people, holding women and children hostage. Do they have any idea what it's like to travel with babies, much less take care of them on a parked airplane in the desert? And what about the trauma, scaring women and children out of their minds? This is crazy, insane!*

"In that case, yes. I will do an interview."

Esther Dayan was not laid back, nor was she timid. When she disagreed with a newspaper article, she wrote a letter to the editor. When she saw injustice, she spoke out. Given the opportunity, even in her grief, she was going to say her piece.

On the plane, the women finished a restless night.

Meanwhile, the six male hostages — Hacham Yosef and Hacham Abraham Raful (dual citizens of Israel and America), Mr. Jerry Berkowitz (an American Jew), Mr. John Hollingsworth (of the State Department), and Mr. Robert Schwartz and Mr. James Woods (of the Defense Department) — had been taken to Irbid, deep in Jordan.

As soon as we arrived, Hacham Abraham wrote, *we were locked into one room. The commander of the base was there to greet us and he offered us*

> supper: pita and hard-boiled eggs, and a cup of tea. After he left, they gave us a few blankets to lie on, to cover ourselves, and as pillows. We slept. When we woke up in the morning, we washed our hands and faces and then asked our guards to bring the commander to us. We begged him to bring us our tefillin from the plane...

He didn't take his tefillin, was Carol's first thought when morning dawned. *Maybe I'll ask the nice lady commando.*

The terrorists began serving dark tea. It was the first hot drink the hostages had had in two days. Carol filled all the bottles with tea, even baby Rachel's. She worried about the baby constantly because she knew how quickly infants can dehydrate. The terrorists then came around with bread and hard boiled eggs.

"Excuse me, where is my husband?" she asked one of the commandos.

"He is in a safe and secure place," the terrorist told her.

Carol dearly hoped that was true, but she couldn't help but notice the whispers around her as a distinct unease settled over the plane. Why had the terrorists taken these men off the plane?

> *In the morning,* continued Hacham Abraham, *the commander came in with a kettle of tea. He assembled us, sitting, on the floor around him, as is customary by the Arabs. Then he asked us what we wanted to eat. We asked him to bring us hard-boiled eggs. We ate breakfast together with the commander and then we started to speak. In the conversation, he let us know that if, within 72 hours from the start of the hijacking, the United States, England, Switzerland, West Germany, and Israel didn't give a positive answer to the PFLP demands, they would blow up the plane with everyone in it. You can imagine our feelings. All of us had our families on the plane! From then on, we lived in a state of constant anxiety...*

The hostages in Irbid were worried about the hostages on the plane.

The hostages on the plane were worried about the hostages in Irbid.

They were all praying for each other's survival, even as their individual ordeals worsened.

"Off the plane," ordered the terrorists. "You need fresh air."

It was 10 a.m. Tuesday morning and getting progressively hotter. Fresh air and wide-open space sounded wonderful until the hostages realized that the air was hot and dry and the open space wasn't wide at all, as it was surrounded by Arabs pointing machine-guns. Carol had her hands full watching the children releasing all their pent-up energy, with machine-guns leveled at their heads.

"They should all be killed," one commando said to another.

"Jim," Carol turned to the co-pilot, "I understand Arabic. They want to kill us!"

"Don't worry," he reassured her, "it's just talk. Ignore it."

But Carol couldn't get those evil words out of her head.

The sun was roasting the desert, so Carol joined the other hostages directly under the plane, where it was cooler. But Ezra managed to wriggle away from his mother. He found oil that dripped on the ground and gleefully stuck his hand in the gooey liquid and then smeared Carol's white and yellow dress with the black gunk. Now her not-too-clean dress was impossibly dirty, her heart still pounded as she relived the sight of the gun pointed at her toddler, and all hope of rejuvenation in the fresh air was gone. She noticed a UPI [United Press International] reporter taking down reports from her fellow hostages. She wanted to go over and tell them about her husband but, just then, Ezra ran toward the sewer[12] and she grabbed him away and held him tightly in her arms.

"Don't worry," Marcelle told her, "we gave him the names of the six men."

A few hours later, the news of the missing hostages was all over the papers.

Bensonhurst, Tuesday, September 8, 1970

"Look — it's right here, squashed in a paragraph all the way in the back." Shaul Raful burst into the Dayan house, extremely agitated. "Six people have been taken off the planes and are being held in an undisclosed location. Yosef and Abraham are two of those six!"

"Calm down," Nouri said soothingly, pulling him over to the table. "Let us read what it says, together."

Nouri scanned the short paragraph, which didn't say much more than what Shaul had reported, and leaned back thoughtfully. *Okay, now what?*

"They are in danger! We must do something!"

"Do what?" Nouri wondered.

"They're being singled out because they're Jewish! We have to go to Washington. America must protect its citizens. Someone has to listen to us."

"If the newspapers are reporting this, then Washington knows about it. Look, three of the six men work for the American government. Washington will have to get involved, without us making a ruckus."

Shaul Raful was slightly mollified.

"Let us see what today brings," Nouri advised.

---

12. Normally, there is an electric suction that draws the refuse from the commode into the waste tanks beneath the airplane. At the end of a trip, enormous vacuums are attached to the valves beneath the waste tanks and the waste is vacuumed out of the airplane. From the very first day, when the electricity was turned off, the crew — and then the passengers — had been manually pushing the waste through the toilet into the waste tanks with hangers and planks of metal. But then the waste tanks became completely full; there was nowhere to push. The captain and his crew members found the valve beneath the plane, opened it, and released all the waste into a pit that the guerillas had dug beneath the plane for this purpose. That was the "sewer."

This was Nouri's way. He preferred to do his part quietly, like when he appealed for help from his brother, Yehoshua, who worked for the Shin-Bet. Ultimately, he believed that only Hashem could help and he turned to his *Tehillim*, his constant comfort.

Back in the Jordanian desert, under the airplane, Carol was still thinking about her husband's *tefillin*. The terrorists had brought out blankets for the hostages to sit on and they gave them water. Carol noticed Hala, a seemingly kind-hearted female commando, going back and forth.

"Hala," she called out, "perhaps I can send my husband the customary boxes that Jews wear when they pray?"

"We are too busy right now," Hala answered hurriedly, and ran off.

Okay, mulled Carol, *that wasn't a "No." I can try again later. But what are they so busy with?*

Unbeknown to the hostages, as they sat outside in the sweltering heat, the guerillas were meticulously going through the airplane. They opened every piece of hand luggage, sifted through every seat pocket, and checked under and over all the seats. It took them two hours. At noon, the hostages were ordered back onto the plane.

Reboarding was a tiring process. The hostages lined up in the hot sun, climbed (one at a time) atop the jeep, up the rickety ladder, and onto the plane. And when they finally got back to their seats, the mood was entirely different.

> *The guerillas were very angry,* Joyce wrote. *They told us, "Your government rejected us and now we're not responsible for you or your lives anymore." Then they told us to take out anything we had from Israel or any notes and books. Anything made in Israel was confiscated. We were checked about a dozen times. They were very disorganized. From some people they took certain things and yet let others keep the same item.*

Though the guerillas had examined all the hand luggage earlier, they pretended that they hadn't, and kept demanding that the hostages give over Israeli passports and anything made in Israel. They waved these items angrily in front of the hostages as "incriminating evidence" of Zionist loyalty. They let them know that they would be examining the regular luggage as well.

The hostages were scared and intimidated, especially when angry guerillas demanded answers. "Why didn't you tell us that your husband is an Israeli citizen?"

"He is not," Marcelle declared, knowing that any other answer would put her husband in mortal danger. "He renounced his Israeli citizenship when he became American."

"We don't believe you." The commando stared at her shrewdly. "You speak Arabic."

"What?" Marcelle asked, playing dumb.

"You speak Arabic, I heard you."

"I know a few words because my mother is from Syria, but I really don't speak anything."

The terrorists let her go.

Whew, Mom was right. They're suspicious of anyone who speaks Arabic...

Actually, the terrorists were suspicious of all Jewish passengers, particularly those who (they decided) had Zionist affiliations. Though they were generally solicitous of *"Hacham Il'kibbir,"* as they referred to Rav Hutner, when they took the six men off on the previous night, they eyed the sage as well. Ultimately, they didn't take him, but they did interrogate him at length.

That Tuesday afternoon, Marcelle saw the terrorists call Rav Hutner aside once again. They found plans for the yeshiva that he was building in Eretz Yisrael which, in their eyes, was proof of his Zionist leanings and cause for intensive interrogation. It was heartbreaking to see the eminent sage forced to stand at length as they fired one question after another at him, barely giving him time to answer. They seemed more intent on instilling fear than in hearing his responses.

Throughout the day and well into the evening, the terrorists grilled many of the prisoners in a process that seemed purposely designed to keep them in a perpetual state of anxiety.

> *There was another guerilla woman we knew as "Palestine,"* Carol recalled. *She always had a kaffiyeh covering her head and often walked around with a rifle or a machine gun slung over her shoulder. She began threatening us... More Israeli passports were found... Still they weren't satisfied...*[13] *There was quiet panic on board. While all of this was going on, my mother-in-law was quietly busy, I didn't know with what. Marcelle suddenly shouted at her to sit in her place.*

Suddenly, Carol noticed three passports in her hands. Her mother-in-law had extracted the Israeli passports from under the seat where she and her sons had hidden them, and she slipped them to Carol, indicating that she decide what to do with them. Carol felt blood rushing to her face and was paralyzed with fright. Thankfully, the guerillas had already moved

---

13. Ironically, while the PFLP successfully hijacked three planes, they had almost no pure Israeli hostages. Though the TWA flight had left from Israel, almost all the "Israeli" passengers were dual citizens of the United States, which meant that the United States was equally — and in Israeli eyes, solely — responsible for them. Yet the main PFLP demands were from Israel. The three terrorists held in Switzerland (for attacking an El Al plane in Zurich), the three in Germany (awaiting trial for their attack on an airport bus en route to an El Al flight), and Britain-held Leila Khaled, were a paltry few compared to the 3,000–4,000 Palestinian prisoners being held in Israel. While the PFLP did not expect Israel to release all their prisoners, they definitely had high expectations, hence their obsession with passengers possessing Israeli passports.

past her row and didn't see what happened. Carol pushed the passports deep into the seat pocket in front of her.

Then fear overcame her and she began to shake and cry uncontrollably.

"Carol," the flight engineer came running over to her. "What's the matter?"

Between sobs, she burst out, "I just can't take it anymore! I can't manage with three children, alone."

This was true. The children were running her ragged. The baby had no bed and was cranky so Carol was always holding her. The toddler was always running up and down the aisles with Carol following behind him. She was frightened, tired, and spent... but that wasn't why she was crying.

"Let us find you some helpers," the flight engineer soothed, and suddenly, Carol found her hands free as he parceled out the children. She calmed down, though her heart still raced.

Marcelle came to sit down next to her. "He should only know what you were really crying about," she said, laughing softly. Carol laughed with her. It was good to feel even-keeled. Then they began seriously discussing what to do with the passports. Until then, Carol was sure that her husband had destroyed them. Now they needed a plan.

She had an idea. Susie Hirsch, who had been holding baby Rachel, brought over the baby to be changed. Carol changed the baby, and then she put the passports on the bottom of the bags provided for nausea. On top of the passports, she placed the dirty diaper, and then she rolled the whole thing up, fastened it with the metal closure, and nonchalantly dumped it into the garbage.

That afternoon, when piles of garbage were removed from the plane, Carol breathed a sigh of relief.

Bensonhurst, Tuesday afternoon, September 8, 1970

The news crew was setting up shop in the Dayan home. Nouri was nowhere to be seen. Even though he was a doer, it was in a behind-the-scenes way. If someone else stepped up to do what had to be done, he was grateful to step aside. Throughout the hijacking ordeal, he was the calming influence, preferring to pray for salvation rather than raise his voice.

"They are terrorists," he commented to no one in particular. "How can you reason with terrorists? Help can only come from the Borei Olam."

But Esther was being given the opportunity to say her piece, and she was going to say it, because justice meant that some things should be said. She spoke for half an hour, bluntly demanding that the Western world protest the incredible injustice being done.

"Why are they holding women and children? Babies need formula, children need food — why isn't anyone saying anything?" No matter what the interviewer asked her, she steered the conversation back to her outrage, laced with emotion.

"I watched when they released some of the non-Jews yesterday. They loaded them onto busses and, all of a sudden, one lady starts crying, 'My dog! My dog! I forgot my dog!' And they went all the way back to pick up the dog. So kind of them; they had pity on a dog. Is that normal? They had pity on a dog but no pity on the rest of the people that they are still keeping captive on the plane?"

The interviewer, who had tried to interject several times, finally succeeded. "Ma'am, you seem upset. Are you seeking revenge for the hijackers? Retribution?"

Esther stared back uncomprehendingly. Revenge? Retribution?

"I just want my children back," Esther whispered, her voice cracking.

In the Jordanian desert, her children were trying to cope.

The tefillin, Carol remembered. *I must take care of Yosef's tefillin.*

She picked up the bag and craned her neck, looking for Hala, the "nice" female commando. Then she hesitated. What if the terrorist took the *tefillin* and didn't pass it on? Might the terrorists desecrate them?

She turned to Rav Hutner, sitting in the row behind hers. "Rosh Yeshiva, should I ask one of the terrorists to bring my husband his *tefillin*? She seems like a decent person…"

"If the woman assures you that she will get the *tefillin* to him, then you may give them to her. But if she seems uncertain, you may not risk it," answered the Rosh Yeshiva.

Carol resolved to find Hala and ask her about the *tefillin*. As she walked down the aisle, bag in hand, she saw Marcelle and Rivke Berkowitz eyeing her suspiciously.

"Carol, what are you doing with the *tefillin*?" Marcelle asked. She was very tense, as was Rivke. "I hope that you are not trying to send them to Yosef. Anything that draws attention to him being a Rabbi can endanger him and the others."

Carol disagreed. "After they searched the plane, Palestine (the other female commando) returned all the *tefillin* back to their owners, unharmed. Arabs realize that *tefillin* have religious importance. And I really don't think that I would be endangering anyone…" But Carol didn't find Hala right away and then she reviewed Rav Hutner's words in her mind: If the outcome is uncertain, don't risk it. In view of all the disorganization around, she certainly couldn't be sure the *tefillin* would get to her husband. She decided not to risk it.

But she was correct in assuming that her husband was distraught about not having his *tefillin*.

> *We asked the commander again for our tefillin,* Hacham Abraham wrote. *He promised repeatedly but never brought them. Praying without our tefillin was very painful. This, too, was ratzon Hashem.*

Every hostage was going through his own unique challenge. The six men in Irbid were isolated and fearful for their families, while the people on the plane were cramped and claustrophobic, though the plane was less crowded than originally.

On Tuesday afternoon, the Red Cross sent boxed lunches from Beirut. There was palpable relief in the air, though that one daily meal could hardly be considered adequate.[14] The "excessive" food that Carol had brought along turned out to be a lifesaver, but now even that supply was running low.

The hostages came to recognize the Arab sub-groups that paraded up and down the plane: Guerillas in camouflage fatigues, Jordanian officers in khaki uniforms and black pointed hats, Iraqis in black berets. The Bedouins dressed in long khaki robes, red-and-white kaffiyehs, with rifles and machine-guns slung across them, back and front. They were very ferocious-looking characters.

A representative of the International Pilot's Association came to see how they were. A sheikh in white came on board. He was particularly interested in seeing the two Rabbis (Rabbi Hutner and Rabbi David). He just stood by their seats, stared for a few minutes, and then left. Quite a few Arabs seemed to fear the Rabbi and respect him as a holy man. Certainly for the religious Jews on board, Rav Hutner's presence was comforting. Indeed, the constant learning of Rav Hutner and his son-in-law, Rabbi David, infused Carol with encouragement. She was convinced that their holiness would keep everyone protected.

The Arab terrorists had no interest in making life liveable for their captives. They paced the aisle of the plane, back and forth, back and forth. The heat was unbearable, and the constant back and forth made it worse. Tensions ran high.

"Look," Carol couldn't resist as she pointed to her 4-month-old baby, while addressing her sister-in-law. "This is their enemy."

The Arabs were oblivious. They just kept ordering their prisoners back to their seats. It wasn't enough that the hostages were confined to an airplane, they were confined to their seats! The prisoners murmured to each other, trying to calm themselves. Sometimes they spoke to the crew, who walked around more freely.

"When I realized that it was a hijacking," one of the crewmen explained, almost apologetically, "my first thought was to jump the man, but the female hijacker had a grenade in her hand. I was afraid she would release

---

14. Actually, later that evening, they received another meal, a plastic bag containing two half-sandwiches, one with butter and jelly and the other with egg salad. Some sandwiches had liver or meat. The religious hostages ate the bread with butter/jelly or egg salad. Some of them did not even eat that. They ate only whole fruits and vegetables such as apples, tomatoes, cucumbers, bananas, and grapes.

the catch. Then I thought to depressurize the airplane, but that action could have killed 10 percent of those on board."

Could have, would have, should have — were all the normal musings of people who had been sitting together in narrow seats for over 72 hours, alternating between fear and boredom, hunger and helplessness.

Chapter 51:

B'TOCH AMI ANOCHI YOSHABET — I DWELL AMONG MY PEOPLE

Wednesday morning, the hostages were permitted to go outside for a short while, though they were not forced to leave. Many welcomed the idea of escaping the terrible smell that permeated the back of the plane. All the expensive duty-free perfumes had been laid out on a cart and the passengers used them to "wash" their hands (in lieu of water) and to camouflage the horrible smell.

Bensonhurst, Wednesday morning, September 9, 1970

"Ma, they're showing your interview now."

Esther shrugged. She knew what she said. The question was, was anyone listening? As it turned out, the news agency cut out almost the entire interview and showed only two minutes' worth.

"Does it bother you?"

"Bother me? They cut it out because everything I said bothers them." Esther shook her head in frustration. "They were scared to offend all the dog lovers out there. Imagine, women and children are being held captive and they are worried about the sensitivities of people who love dogs."

But even her frustrations with the news didn't stop her from tuning in all day, every day. It was her way of being with her children in Jordan — feeling their pain, feeling her own pain. And every day, several times a day, the PFLP reiterated their position: **The airplanes are wired to explode. If our demands are not met by Thursday morning, we will blow up the planes.**

Esther glanced at the clock.

It was Wednesday afternoon in Jordan.

There wasn't much time left.

Ezra was crying. Rachel was crying. Carol didn't know where to put herself.

The stewardesses had become very nasty, blaming "you Jews" for the whole situation. After all, Israel was the Jewish homeland — had they not recreated their State, there would be no Palestinians hijacking airplanes and endangering the lives of innocent gentiles. Not only were the stewardesses particularly unhelpful, but they also made the Jewish mothers feel guilty and responsible for the very-normal-but-sometimes-difficult behavior of their children when, in reality, it was amazing how calm the airplane was, given the high percentage of children. Mrs. Raab was traveling alone with five children. The Hirsch kids — 14, 13, and 10 — were on their own (their parents had been on the almost-hijacked El Al flight) as were a number of others.

Joyce was sitting near a 10-year-old boy traveling alone.

"Where is your G-d?" a terrorist sneered at him. The boy remained silent, but Joyce felt like crying for the child who was all alone and being bullied.

A teenaged girl was beside herself with concern for her father, a Holocaust survivor who had lost his first family in the war. She was his only child, born when he remarried after the war. How was he taking the situation?

In the long and monotonous hours spent together, the passengers got to know each other as they shared their stories, concerns, hopes, and fears. Conversations ran from philosophical to funny, from mundane to imaginative, from cautious optimism to worried despair.

And then, to add more complications to an already complicated story, there was a deafening noise overhead, the unmistakable sounds of an airplane flying low. The hostages peered out their windows and saw a BOAC (British Overseas Airways Co.) airliner almost directly overhead.

A few minutes later, it was parked diagonally in front of the plane.

Now there were three aircrafts parked in the desert: TWA, Swiss Air, and BOAC. The PFLP boasted four successful hijackings in four days. Would this make negotiations easier? If more innocent civilians were in danger would their governments be quicker to capitulate? Or would the governments stand firm in the face of the brazen PFLP, who dared hijack another airplane even as they were negotiating about the other two?

Bensonhurst, Wednesday evening, September 9, 1970

...And now for our continued reporting of the hostage situation. The PFLP have extended their deadline for another 24 hours...

Esther mechanically reached for the boiled water to make herself a cup of coffee. She was grateful for the reprieve but still felt restless and afraid, in a state of constant anxiety. Nouri entered the kitchen, serious and distracted, as usual. Their conversations were short and stilted. What was there to say?

"They called again."

"Who?"

Nouri shrugged. "What's the difference? People who want to know if we would agree to pay money to ransom the kids. They think that if we get enough money together we can ransom our family together with Rav Hutner and his family."

"We already answered them," Esther remarked dismissively. "How can they trust Arab terrorists? Why wouldn't those terrorists just take the money and run? Better to give the money to *tzedaka* as a *zechut* for the captives than risk hundreds of thousands of dollars for nothing."

"If we were dealing with rational people, it would be one thing," Nouri added. "But these are terrorists, people who have proven to be unreasonable." While Nouri was normally active and optimistic, in this case, he saw no way out except Divine mercy. It also went against his nature to allow elitism. Was his children's blood any redder than that of other Jews on the airplane?

"*B'toch ami anochi yoshabet* — I dwell among my nation," he murmured his favorite motto. "My children will share the fate and the fortune of our captive brothers, our fellow Jews. We have to storm the Heavens with prayers to release everyone, not only focus on our family."

In Irbid, Jordan, the six men were moved from their original room to a supposedly bigger one.

> *The real reason,* Hacham Abraham wrote, *was that the first room was their office and they didn't want us to know what was going on. The new room had only one window, so it was stuffier. But what did we do? We thanked them. We thanked them for everything they did for us. Whether it was comfortable or not, it made no difference. We always said "Shukran" (thank you), to which they answered "Ufwan" (you're welcome). We must have repeated these words hundreds of times. That was the only way to feel somewhat safe.*

Bensonhurst, Thursday morning, September 10, 1970

"I'm telling you, Nouri, we have to do something." Shaul Raful came over every day, insisting — begging — that Nouri join him in his plans to save his brothers.

It was very difficult to sit back, hands folded, waiting for something to happen. The news continuously reported on the negotiation impasse between the Red Cross and the PFLP.[15] Then President Nixon dramatically mobilized army, navy, and air force divisions, ostensibly for a military strike, but more widely understood as a warning to all the Soviet-backed Arabs that America would not allow themselves to be terrorized. Meanwhile, the fighting between the Jordanians and the *fedayeen* had escalated into a full-scale civil war.

"Shaul, we have gone over this dozens of times," Nouri said. "Why do you think that anyone in Washington will do more for our family than for their own diplomats? As long as the six men remain in captivity together, we can assume that the government is doing whatever they can. How will going to Washington accomplish anything?"

"Staying here will certainly not accomplish anything," Shaul insisted. "I'm going to Washington, whether you come with me or not."

Nouri remained silent. He felt bad for Shaul, but he was still not ready to join him. "Only the Borei Olam can help us," he told him.

Indeed, the feeling that only Hashem was their Salvation kept the religious Jews praying and hopeful, in Jordan and in America, even as the clock indicated that the deadline was drawing closer. The hostages went to sleep Thursday evening oblivious that they had survived past the next ultimatum.

They woke up to another surprise.

Thursday evening, a number of men had been taken off the plane, among them, Rabbi Yonason David. The reasons for this were, once again, complicated.

Unbelievably — and unknown to the hostages — that Thursday evening, the Iraqi government turned against the *fedayeen*, whom they had been supporting, when they saw that America might intervene militarily. They demanded that the *fedayeen* free all the hostages, unconditionally, and pushed Yasser Arafat (head of the PLO) to announce the release.

While the PLO didn't have control over the PFLP, they were eager to end the hostage crisis so that they could devote their energy to conquering Jordan and creating a Palestinian State that would eventually include Israel. Providing for the hostages and dealing with their countries was distracting them from that fight. That night, the PLO reached an agreement with the PFLP by which they would release all the hostages, except "Israelis of military capacity." The problem was, they had no such hostages in captivity. Consequently, the *fedayeen* made their own creative definition

---

15. The PFLP wanted each country with *fedayeen* prisoners (Switzerland, Britain, Germany, and Israel) to release their prisoners in exchange for their hostage citizens. American hostages would be released when all of that happened. The European countries were itching to give in, but America and Israel refused to deal with the terrorists and both insisted that no country should cut a deal on its own. The Agudas HaRabbanim, led by Rabbi Moshe Feinstein, argued with this uncompromising stance.

which included three of the six men in Irbid (those who were Jewish) and then they took off an additional ten men that Thursday night.[16]

Some PFLP leaders were dissatisfied with a measly thirteen hostages. They decided to take matters into their own hands...

At 8 a.m. Friday morning, the crew served the usual dark, sweet tea, any hard bread that they could find, and some cheese. The guerillas handed out propaganda leaflets. Carol glanced at them. There were statements by Chairman Mao, and statements against Zionism and the Jewish State. *Good scrap paper for the kids...* she decided as she handed them to Ron with a pen.

At about 10 a.m., a wild sandstorm whipped up the desert, invading the plane. Jim Ferguson and Al Kiburis, members of the flight crew, rushed to shut the emergency exits, but sand still swept inside, coating everything in an itchy brown blanket. The plane that had been terribly hot with the doors open became unbearable. The air was so thick with sand, it was difficult to breathe. The hostages wet napkins and kept them over their mouths and noses, trying to get oxygen into their lungs while keeping the sand out. Sand swirled inside the plane. The outside world was obscured by the sand-coated windows.

"How long can this last?" Carol asked a commando.

"Anywhere from a few hours to a few days," was his clipped answer.

I can't believe this, thought Carol as she went back to her seat, dazed. She prayed in her heart that it would let up soon.

"Carol, did you notice that little huddle over there?" asked Marcelle.

Carol nodded, also wondering why the flight crew was in such an earnest conversation with some of the guerillas. A little while later, they found out. One of the crew members came over to where Carol was sitting. He was a nice man who had been a calming presence throughout their ordeal.

"Carol," he said softly, almost apologetically, "I have to tell you something. We are trying to work out a deal. We are hoping that the guerillas will free us today."

"Okay," Carol answered mechanically, wondering why he was singling her out to inform her.

"But we can't include you in the deal."

"Oh." Carol was shocked.

"I hope you understand. It's... you know... because of your husband."

Carol didn't know what to say.

"I'm really sorry," he told her, as he left.

---

16. Actually, all were American citizens. One man was a gentile who happened to have the misfortune of having stamped his passport in Israel. Their ages ranged from 16–40, hardly "military capacity."

Carol sat there, numb. *This is what he tells a woman in my situation, alone with three children? That they are abandoning me because the Palestinians have decided that my husband is Israeli?*

Fortunately, the storm let up two hours later. By then, the hostages were dripping from perspiration in the impossibly hot plane, and the gritty sand stuck to their skin, creating a very uncomfortable layer of dirt. Carol rummaged through her sand-filled hand luggage to find something sand-less for her children to eat. Meanwhile, one of the mustached/kaffiyed guerillas entered coach class and looked purposefully around. He spotted Carol, tending to her children, and walked over to her, his eyes flashing angrily.

"Did your husband have an Israeli passport?" he asked.

It can't be that it was found, it just can't be…

"I don't know," Carol answered vaguely.

He took out two passports from his pocket and looked at Carol and Marcelle accusingly. Then he opened one, and Carol saw that it was her husband's expired passport. The mighty winds had blown everything all over the place, including the garbage gathered in bags outside. The refuse bag had burst open, releasing the passport.

He glared at her and spat out, "Why you lie?!"

The Arab took the passport, reached over behind Carol to where Rav Hutner was sitting, and held it very close to his face.

"You see," he hissed, "your people, they lie!"

> *At that point, I felt nothing,* Carol wrote. *I must have been in a mild state of shock, because I didn't react at all. Then I burst into tears, as if I were relieving myself of all the tension from the TWA crew's scheming, to the found passports. I felt very vulnerable.*

Carol was crying not only out of fear for her husband, but with the humiliation of being branded a liar to Rav Hutner. She couldn't even bring herself to turn around and defend herself, though she was sure that the Rosh Yeshiva understood what had happened. She just sat there, trembling from shame and fear, crying from the whole ordeal. Between the terror of being captive, the fear for her husband, the impossible task of caring for the children who were driving her crazy (for good reason), the lack of food and sanitary facilities, the Arabs, the guns — she broke down. She just cried and cried and couldn't stop.

Ribbono shel Olam, I just can't anymore!

Bensonhurst, Friday morning, September 11, 1970

It was the first week of Elul, the first week of *selihot* in their community. Nouri had not missed a day of *selihot* from the time he learned to pray. During those days of terror, the *selihot* had extra meaning for him. Those constant prayers were a solid reminder that they were mere days before Rosh Hashana, when all believing Jews acknowledge the only real formula for salvation: *teshuva, tefilla,* and *tzedaka.*

Instinctively, in their pure and iron-strong faith, Nouri and Esther had tapped into that magic formula, hoping that their *teshuva, tefilla,* and *tzedaka* would be a *zechut* for *all* the passengers. If anyone mentioned ransom to Esther, she replied that *tzedaka* is the most effective ransom. If anyone mentioned negotiate to Nouri, he replied that prayer is the best method of negotiation.

As Carol cried her heart out to the Ribbono shel Olam out of pain and despair, 2,000 miles away her father was praying with similar passion. Unlike the crew members who were ready to save some but not all, Nouri's prayers encompassed everyone.

B'toch ami anochi yoshabet: He prayed that his children would be saved — along with the rest of the Jewish people.

Chapter 52:
IN EVERY GENERATION OUR ENEMIES RISE UP TO DESTROY US

Carol couldn't stop crying. *Ribbono shel Olam, what is happening to me? Who is going to take care of my children? Who is going to take care of me?*

Marcelle tried to speak to her. Her mother-in-law tried. But the tears just would not stop. Other women came over to her. They kept on repeating, "Don't worry, we won't abandon you."

Slowly, their kind and comforting words seeped in and Carol found herself relaxing. It was hard to know for whom to feel the most sorry: women who didn't know what had happened to their husbands, traumatized children who were traveling alone, mothers whose sons had been taken away.

On top of everything, they were practically out of food. The Red Cross came around twice with whole fruits and vegetables, formula, and baby cereal. But there was never enough for all the religious Jews. The children were becoming weak and lethargic from hunger.

It was heartbreaking to watch.

Shabbat is coming... maybe it will bring us the peace we all need.

Carol took her sister's *siddur* and began to pray Minha.

> *I read the whole Viddui and felt as if I cleansed myself from all wrongdoing,* Carol wrote. *At this point, I felt relieved and joyful that Shabbat was approaching. I gave Ron his clothes to change into; he had a clean pair of green slacks and a white shirt that I had been saving... I was now ready to welcome the Shabbat Queen.*

Marcelle approached the steward. "I have a request that might seem odd to you but will be very meaningful to most of the people on the airplane. Tonight is our Sabbath which we usher in by lighting candles. Perhaps my mother-in-law can light candles for everybody?"

Al Kiburis agreed but he said that they would have to be put out immediately because there was no safe place for them and it would be a fire hazard.

Rabbanit Rachel lit the Shabbat candles. Moments later, Al blew them out.

For those few minutes, those flickering lights lifted the hostages' spirits.

A few hours earlier, miles away, Hacham Yosef struggled to find a way to usher in the Shabbat. He had nothing with him except the filthy clothing he had been wearing the entire week. What could he do in honor of Shabbat? When the terrorists gave him a glass of water, he dunked the shirt into the cup of water, using that meager amount of liquid to wash it.

At least my clothing are somewhat fresher — *lichbod Shabbat Kodesh…*

When night fell and the plane became very dark, most hostages went right to sleep, especially since the plane became light with sunrise at 5 in the morning. Friday evening, the hijackers turned on the electricity (powered by a generator that the terrorists had brought to the desert) and distributed food from the Red Cross. It was an encouraging moment. People woke up to eat, grateful for the food and hopeful that it would be accompanied by good news. The religious hostages scavenged for plain fruits and vegetables.

Then the lights went off.

Just as people began to doze off again, the guerillas re-boarded, announcing that all the men were being taken off. Unbeknown to everyone, this was an independent initiative by some PFLP officers who were determined to be left with more than the measly thirteen hostages being held elsewhere in Jordan.

"This way, the women will be more comfortable," claimed the guerillas as they led the men off the plane.

Right. None of the hostages were convinced that their comfort was uppermost on the minds of the terrorists. By then, there were only eighteen men left on the plane. This was hardly a burden for the remaining women, especially since many of them were family.

It was hard to know what to think. Perhaps the people being taken off were being held in better locations than the filthy, claustrophobic plane… Yet, as the women watched the men leave the airplane, Rav Hutner among them, there was a feeling of overwhelming vulnerability.

"Don't worry," the terrorists reassured them, "you will be leaving tomorrow."

If so, why were the terrorists isolating them? What were their plans?

The PFLP "plans" had been chaotic almost from the beginning. While the initial hijackings were well thought out, everything after that unfolded erratically.

The first group of six men had been taken off by the PFLP in the hope that separating the "Israeli" hostages would give them leverage over Israel and that doing the same to the American diplomats would pressure America. That group was being held in a PFLP stronghold where, as the civil war progressed, they were isolated from the PFLP organizers of the hijackings.

By Thursday, when the PFLP gave in to PLO demands to release everyone except "Israelis of military capacity," they took off the second group of men, ensuring that they had more "Israelis of military capacity" in custody. Those hostages were being held in Wahdat, another PFLP stronghold.

As for the men taken off Friday night, they were taken off by independent PFLP members who felt that their leaders had given in too much. Without notifying their superiors, they smuggled their captives to the outskirts of Zarqa, northeast of Amman.

Meanwhile, according to the Iraqi-negotiated agreements, the hostages who had been staying in Jordanian hotels since Monday were released on Friday while the hostages on the airplanes were to be freed on Shabbat.

As usual, the PFLP had their own interpretation of that agreement.

Bensonhurst, Friday evening, September 11, 1970

We should leave the radio on in the basement, Esther decided.

By then, she was a bundle of nerves, operating mechanically, even as people came to encourage her. She barely heard what people said, barely noticed what was going on. The radio had become her constant companion, even as it droned on and on about the planes being wired to explode. Once, the news actually reported (incorrectly) that the planes had been blown up. Esther let out such a horrific scream, Murray wondered if they heard it in Jordan.

"Ma, it's a mistake — I'm telling you."

The mistake was clarified a minute later, but Esther couldn't get the newscaster's voice out of her head. Would having the radio on in the basement be a comfort? There were times that she was suddenly seized with fear that the terrorists had carried out their threats. Would she then run down to the basement to listen?

"I'm turning it on in the basement," Nouri told her, as if reading her thoughts. She nodded, happy that he had made the decision.

She lit candles and ushered in Shabbat.

Shabbat morning at 10 a.m., the terrorists began coming around asking questions, compiling lists, and having the women sign their names. The commandos signed for the religious women who would not write on Shabbat. Then they began calling people to leave the airplane, one by one.

Finally, the hostages breathed in relief, *we are being freed!*

Marcelle collected her children and helped her mother-in-law disembark. Carol gathered her children together as well. They were used to the routine: Hand over the children to the guerillas who carried them down the ladder, and then go down yourself, onto a truck, where you were "helped" by the terrorists. Carol looked around. Almost all the women and children were with her, standing by the busses, except…

Joyce was still on the plane.

When they began calling names, Joyce listened, semi-interested. After all, they never really knew for certain if it was better to be taken off early or late. While she hoped that this time they would really be set free, she wasn't allowing herself to be too excited… yet.

Then Carol and the kids left.

I hope I'm next.

But she wasn't. Then the guerilla stopped calling out names. She began arguing with one woman who didn't want to leave. Suddenly, it hit Joyce: *This is it.*

She glanced around. The airplane was empty except for six girls, and one woman, and her.

Now I'm nervous…

Carol sat on the van thinking furiously. *They said that they are letting us go free. But Joyce isn't here. How can I go home without my sister? What will I tell my dear mother?*

She made a split-second decision.

"Marcelle," she said, handing her the baby, "I forgot something on the plane. I'll be right back."

Carol let herself off the van, heaved herself up, onto the truck, and then up the rickety wooden ladder. She stepped into the airplane, and stared in horror. A woman guerilla held a grenade in one hand and a gun in the other, leveling them both at an older woman who was facing her resolutely.

"If you don't get off right now…" said the terrorist, in a low, level voice.

"I'm not budging. If you want, kill me — but I'm not leaving my daughter. I'm not leaving these girls."

The girls were crying and looked terrified. Then the terrorist spotted Carol.

"What are you doing here?" she demanded.

"I… I came to get my sister," Carol stammered. "I have three little children. I need help with them. I can't do it myself."

The terrorist stared at her in disbelief. "If you don't get off right now," she hissed, "you are going to stay here."

Carol glanced longingly at Joyce, who was crying hysterically. She admired the woman who refused to leave her daughter. *But I have to go take care of my children. I can't stay here…*

She left the plane and re-boarded the bus with a heavy heart. The busses began driving off, a trail of women and children snaking through the desert under armed guard.

Will I ever see my sister again?
How will I face my mother?

Bensonhurst, Shabbat Morning, September 12, 1970

Esther woke up. As usual, she didn't feel very rested.

Maybe I should go downstairs and listen to the news..., she mused, and then stopped herself. *No! It's Shabbat.*

She began busying herself with her regular Shabbat day routine.

The women and girls on the plane sat silently, petrified.

It was so nice of that woman, mused Joyce, a bit calmer than before. Her presence was comforting; her refusal to abandon them was heartwarming.

They waited.

Finally, the terrorist herded them off the plane... and onto the Swiss Air plane where its crew and the BOAC crew and some other male hostages were all assembled. They were the only non-crew females around.

Why?

They waited. An hour and a half passed.

The guerillas returned. "We are taking all of you to Amman."

There was a mad rush to the door.

"Wait!" screamed the terrorist. "Sit down!"

The hostages obediently returned to their seats. The guerillas began calling people by name... first the BOAC crew, then the Swiss Air crew, then about ten other male Europeans, and finally, five of the girls from the TWA.

Joyce wasn't called.

What is going to happen to me?

Below, that first group was being organized onto busses from where they were driven about 100-200 yards away from the planes. Finally, the terrorists allowed everyone else to deplane... including Joyce.

Joyce sighed with relief as she made her way down the aisle.

"Hurry up... hurry up..." the terrorists urged the hostages, who were running, but not fast enough. Even after everyone was off, the terrorists were still prodding the hostages to board the busses. "Faster," they shouted, "faster."

The busses drove about 100-200 yards away and then stopped.

Suddenly the hostages heard an enormous explosion — one plane, two planes, three planes... all blew up. Joyce stared in shock, struck by the sudden realization: *That could have been me!*

Joyce Dayan watched as the airplane she had been on minutes earlier exploded.

On the bus, all Carol could think about was the sister she had left behind.

"Marcelle, you should have seen those girls. They were terrified. It was heartbreaking."

"Carol, what were you thinking? Leaving me here with Mom and all the kids? I feel bad for Joyce, but what were you supposed to do?"

Carol knew that Marcelle was right, but her heart was back on that plane. During the first few minutes of their bus ride out of the desert, she had been too busy describing what happened to Marcelle to notice anything around her. Now she stared distractedly out the window as their convoy of vans drove on. For a while, there was nothing but them and the desert. Then they came to an Arab village and suddenly there were Arabs all over the place, pushing and shoving at the vans so roughly, they were afraid that the vans would turn over.

They look so angry, Carol realized with a jolt. *Ribbono shel Olam, when is this going to end?*

Joyce stared at the clouds of smoke that reached up in great, grey plumes. All three aircrafts continued to burn while the vanloads of hostages were forced to watch. The PFLP wanted to impress upon them and the Western world that they could have done exactly as they threatened — that they could *still* blow up whatever and whomever they wanted if their demands were not met.

News agencies were filming the explosions.

PFLP terrorists were running around, giving each other orders.

Then the vans with the hostages drove off… toward the circle of Jordanian soldiers who had surrounded the area, from a distance, all week. They had been unable to do anything for fear of harming the hostages. Joyce had no idea that the *fedayeen* were in a bitter civil war with Jordan and that in the past week, the Jordanian army had pounded the terrorists and made a lot of headway. Now the enemies were approaching each other, and the hostages were right in the crossfire.

The terrorists got out of the van and pointed their guns at the hostages inside.

This is it, Joyce thought, *we're finished.*

Carol and Marcelle reached Amman at mid-afternoon.

They were taken to the Intercontinental Hotel where embassy and airline representatives were taking down everyone's names and nationalities because no one had any passports.

"Our husbands were taken away on Monday and we have no idea where they are," Carol and Marcelle told them urgently. Well, the American Embassy officials had no idea either, but they took down the information and said that they would look into it.

Then Carol told them about Joyce. "All through the week, they kept on asking her about her name. I'm scared for her. Maybe this is why she is being singled out…"

The embassy representatives noted this as well. Then they transferred the former hostages to the Philadelphia Hotel where they gave them private rooms. They also gave them food — vegetables and pita, salad and eggs — which the Rafuls ate hungrily.

It had been a grueling week.

Dare they hope that they were coming to the end of their ordeal?

After about an hour of being held in a standoff between the PFLP and the Jordanian army, the vans in Joyce's convoy began to move. Evidently, part of their job was to serve as human shields and allow the PFLP to get out of the desert after they blew up the airplanes.

We are like a parade, Joyce mused, as she watched the local Arabs shout and yell when they saw the vans. *Marching through town… everyone coming out to watch… interesting…*

As they neared Amman, she noticed that the bus behind hers turned off in a different direction. That bus held the remaining women from the TWA flight, most of the flight crews, and a number of men from Swiss Air and BOAC.

Good sign or bad? Who knew?

A short while later, Joyce's bus pulled up in front of the Intercontinental Hotel. They were greeted by embassy and airline personnel who led them into a lobby swarming with news reporters and photographers.

"Just ignore them," an airline representative murmured softly. "Anything you say might affect the people still being held hostage."

That was enough to keep anyone from talking to the papers. Joyce registered with the American Embassy official who, strangely enough, seemed familiar with her name. Then she asked about Carol and the kids.

"They have been taken to another hotel. Would you like to call them?"

I would love to, but it's Shabbat. While it was clear to Joyce that everything up until then had to be done, even on Shabbat, she didn't think that calling Carol fell in that category.

Carol was still very jittery. The hotel was riddled with bullet holes, a silent testimony to the war that was going on around them. They were told that if they heard shooting, they should run into the corridor. Instead, Carol barricaded the door to her room with dressers.

The phone rang.

Carol didn't know what to do. Shabbat was over, but who in the world would be calling her in a hotel in Jordan? The ringing was driving her crazy, but she was too scared to pick up the phone. In the end, she did.

"Hello?"

"Carol?"

"Joyce?"

"Yes, it's me."

"Where are you?"

"At the Intercontinental Hotel."

"Are you okay?"

"Yes."

Carol let out a sigh that Joyce heard on the other end. "Joyce, I was so worried…"

"Carol, one bus, including five of the women, turned in a different direction. They're not here. I think they're still being held captive. I don't know in what *zechut* I wasn't one of them. With my name, I thought that I was finished."

"When did you get here?"

"A little while ago," Joyce paused. "Carol, they blew up the planes."

"What!"

"They blew up the planes, all three of them, right after we got off."

"So they really were wired," Carol breathed.

And we got off them, safely, just in time. A miracle.

Bensonhurst, Mosa'ei Shabbat, September 12, 1970

It was a miracle — a miracle that Esther was still finding difficult to believe. When her neighbor came over to tell her on Shabbat, she didn't believe it. She and Nouri had gone downstairs several times on Shabbat to listen if there was any news and they had not heard anything. After the Shabbat ended, she watched the footage of the hostages being escorted by Iraqi soldiers, and still wondered if her children were really among them, since she couldn't see them. She listened to the reporting in disbelief: Why would the terrorists release so many hostages when they had not yet received any of their demands?

"The PFLP are keeping forty people as political prisoners," explained the newscasters. "The women and children are being released as a humanitarian gesture."

"Where were their so-called humanitarian hearts for the past week?" Esther commented acerbically. But she certainly wasn't complaining, even though the news was only a partial relief.

There were actually 56 people still being held captive.

One of them was her son-in-law.

Carol let out a long breath. She was finally on what was (hopefully) the last part of her journey home. They'd left Jordan at 7:30 Sunday morning and flown to Nicosia, Cypress, where they'd remained overnight. The next morning, they'd flown out.

Her mother-in-law, though still a bulwark of faith, was confused by all the changes: from the airplane at Dawson Field to the hotel (where the sounds of gunfire could be heard throughout the night), to Cypress (also a war zone), to Rome (and a press conference), and then, finally, to America. They all were counting the minutes until they were actually home.

And when they finally arrived, and exited the airplane, the newsmen filmed them smiling to the cameras, belying their real feelings, for as long as the men were still being held captive, they would be as positive as possible and say only nice things about their captors.

But it was Rabbanit Rachel who solemnly and succinctly said what they all felt, immediately upon reaching American soil: *B'chol dor vador, omdim aleinu l'chaloseinu, V'HaKadosh Baruch Hu matzileinu miyadam!*

Yes, in every generation, our enemies rise up to destroy us.

And then the Almighty Himself saves us from their hands.

Chapter 53:

MAMA RACHEL CRIES FOR HER CHILDREN[17]

"You see," Nouri explained to Shaul Raful on one of his many phone calls from Washington, "they were freed without any rhyme or reason. Just like the Ribbono shel Olam freed Carol and the kids and your mother in this way, He will free all the others as well. Come home. There is nothing for you to do in Washington."

But Shaul couldn't hear him.

Though everyone wanted to return to life as usual, it was impossible to do so when so many people were still hostage, particularly family and friends, and the revered Rosh Yeshiva, Rav Hutner.

Only when Carol returned to America did the gravity of what she had escaped hit her. Her stay in the desert had been terrifying and uncomfortable, but at least she had been oblivious to the war going on around her. Now that she was home with the constant news reports, she understood how desperate the situation was for the remaining hostages — including her husband.

The war between Jordan and the *fedayeen* was escalating. Unlike the previous week, when almost all the hostages were concentrated in one location, constantly reported on by the press, now the hostages were being kept hidden and no one seemed to know where they were and under what conditions they were living.

Indeed, the chaos was worse than anyone could have imagined.

The last group (seventeen men from Swiss Air and BOAC and five women from TWA) were being held in Ashrafiyah. The Friday evening

---

17. *Yirmiyahu* 31:14. Rashi in *Vayechi* (48:7) explains that when the Yidden went into Galut, Rachel Imeinu came out of her grave and wept and begged Hashem to have mercy on her children.

group (eighteen men) were being held in Zarqa. The Thursday evening group (ten men) were being held in Wahdat. And the first group (six men) were being held in Irbid.

But the PFLP was in disarray to the extent that, at the time, even they didn't know exactly how many hostages they held and where they were being held. They also claimed that the status of the hostages had changed to that of political prisoners rather than civilian hostages, a statement that was patently false but gave a different public relations flavor that was confusing. Both the PLO and the PFLP were negotiating but nothing was moving.

To complicate matters, Washington was frustrated that it was taking King Hussein so long to reign in the *fedayeen*. They demanded that he take stronger, more drastic measures... or else they would step in.

The hostages were in a very, very, dangerous position.

Luckily, they were unaware just how dangerous.

> *One problem was how to pass the time,* Hacham Abraham wrote. *We were fortunate that we keep Torah and pray three times a day. I was particularly busy saying Tehillim for it encouraged me tremendously and I was certain that it would help release us from our exile. I said so much Tehillim that one of the guards told my brother, "Your brother likes to pray the whole time." I enjoyed that comment and continued even stronger. By the third day, we had made ourselves a daily schedule. My brother and I woke up early in the morning, washed our hands and face, and finished praying. Throughout the day, we tried to keep the room as clean as possible. The first thing we received in the morning was a cup of sweet tea. Sometimes we got it at 8 in the morning, sometimes we got it at 10 in the morning, and there were some days (at least twice) that we got our first cup of tea at 2 in the afternoon. It depended on the terrorists' moods. Meals were sometimes twice a day, sometimes three times a day, and sometimes once a day. We usually ate bread with hard-boiled eggs. Sometimes we had potatoes. During the first few days, we also received tomatoes and bananas. Afterward, there were no vegetables.*

There were no vegetables because all of Jordan had become a war zone.

The hostages' living conditions might have been less claustrophobic than the plane but became increasingly dangerous as the fighting escalated.

For those still in Jordan, the hostage crisis was far from over.

For those back in America, carrying on with life wasn't so simple.

"Where are you going?" Esther asked Joyce, all dressed up, the night after her return.

"To the wedding."

"You can't go to the wedding."

Joyce was taken aback. "Why not?"

"Listen, Joyce, everybody is so happy that you are back. They can't wait to see you. If you go to the wedding, you will make a real splash. Everyone will be coming over to you, hugging you and kissing you…"

What is wrong with that? wondered Joyce, *after all I have been through…*

"You will distract them from the bride. It is her night, Joyce, not yours. You cannot go to the wedding and take attention away from the bride."

Joyce guiltily conceded that her mother was correct. Her safe return did not mandate forgetting about everyone else's feelings. The ensuing weeks found the freed hostages, and the families of those who were not yet free, dancing a difficult dance, where they were required to go back to normal life, when life was not yet normal.

Weeks before the hijackings, Nouri had scheduled an Open House for the newly completed Ahi Ezer building, to take place on September 20, just after the start of the new school year.

The event was very important.

Nouri couldn't deny that in terms of public relations, the wandering school had suffered. Enrollment had not decreased, but it had not increased at the same pace as before. He hoped that when parents would see the state-of-the-art building, and they would hear about all their new programs, they would become enthusiastic about the yeshiva and that enthusiasm would spread to others in the community.

In terms of a yeshiva education, Nouri had become a man possessed. Here was a problem that he could do something about. He felt that every Jewish child who attended public school was almost guaranteed to be lost to the Jewish people. With every year that passed, more children were lost. He was a tireless campaigner and the new building was the cornerstone of his latest campaign.

Yet, amid the hostage crisis, how could they celebrate this happy occasion?

Nouri rose to the occasion, putting his personal worries behind him and focusing solely on the yeshiva and the milestone that he and the community had reached. A week after the first of the hostages had returned home, he was hosting the Open House, showing parents around the yeshiva building, encouraging them to send their children. Indeed, the Open House Dedication was a resounding success as hundreds of parents, benefactors of the school, community members, and well-wishers explored the new school building — from the basement dining room to the rooftop playground — and every crevice in between. They were thoroughly impressed with the modern building that had every educational amenity that they could have imagined.

But when Nouri came home and saw Carol and the children, he was brought back to the grim reality once again: Where was his son-in-law and when would he be freed?

Irbid, Jordan, Sunday afternoon, September 20, 1970

"What if we're here for Rosh Hashana?" Hacham Abraham wondered.

"Heaven forbid," Hacham Yosef answered, but he began thinking of ideas as to how to make a holiday meal, and what to use for *simanim*. He asked his captors for two potatoes, a can of coconut shortening, a knife, and some matches. He koshered the knife with the fire and felt prepared.

"We will heat up the shortening in the can," he told his brother, "put in slices of potato, and let them cook in the shortening until they are edible. That will be our Yom Tov meal. We will even have a *Yehi Ratzon*," he added with a smile. "*She'yipatpitu* (a play on the word *potato*) *o'yeveinu v'soneinu v'kol mevakshei soneinu* — Our enemies should be reduced to nothing!"

While the hostages tried to keep up their spirits, their reality was bleak. The war in Jordan had accelerated into a major conflict with the hostages, held in the PFLP strongholds, directly in the line of fire. They heard the shelling and the machine-gun fire all around them.

Then another ingredient was added to the pot. Syria, with Soviet backing, disguised as *fedayeen*, invaded Jordan to help the PLO. The fighting became even fiercer. Jordan claimed that as many as 5,000 people had been killed. The stench of dead corpses burning in the streets permeated the rooms where the hostages were being held. Miraculously, not one hostage was hurt, even while bombs fell all around them. But they were in terrible danger.

Jews all over the world continued to pray.

"Hello. My name is Marcelle Raful. My husband is an American citizen who is being held hostage in Jordan…"

"American citizen? I believe he is an Israeli citizen," answered the embassy official. "Call the Israeli embassy."

Marcelle slammed down the phone in frustration. She had just gotten off the phone with the Israeli embassy who insisted that her husband was American and she should turn to the American embassy for help.

Hashem! You must help us! We have no one else!

Finally, after two weeks of fierce fighting, and obvious Divine Providence, the tide turned. The Syrians retreated and the Jordanians triumphed over the *fedayeen*. They released most of the remaining hostages, including Rav Hutner. Hundreds of yeshiva students went to greet the Rosh Yeshiva but, as per Rabbi Moshe Feinstein's instructions, no music was played celebrating their safe arrival.

How could they play music when there were other Jews still in danger? The original six hostages had not yet come home.[18]

---

18. The released hostages were held in areas that the Jordanian army conquered from the *fedayeen* and were freed by Jordan. The remaining six hostages were still held by the terrorists.

Irbid, Jordan, September 28, 1970

Suddenly, Nasser died.

"We will soon be freed," Hacham Abraham confidently quoted the Gemara [*Ta'anit* 29a] to his brother Hacham Yosef, "When one who decrees a bad decree dies, the decree is nullified. Nasser has certainly been a major cause of our being held hostage. I'm sure that his death indicates that our ordeal will soon be over."

Unfortunately, back in Flatbush, all this didn't seem so clear.

The phone rang in the Dayan home.

"Carol," Judy Raful was practically hysterical, "I think that Mom has had it. I'm afraid for her life. She is leaning out the window, raising her hands to the heavens and crying *'Abi! Abi!'*"

Truly, Mama Rachel is crying for her children, Carol reflected.

"I don't know what to do," Judy said. "Maybe you should take her to the Rabbi and ask for his blessing. We need to calm her down."

"I'm coming over right now," Carol answered. She hastened to her mother-in-law's apartment on Ocean Parkway. Judy was already standing outside with her mother, who was still agitated. She ushered her into the car and Carol drove her to the home of Hacham Yosef Tawil. Rabbanit Rachel sat in front of the Hacham and continued to cry.

"It's going to be fine," Hacham Yosef said soothingly. "We are all praying for them…"

He continued along this vein for a few minutes. Then he paused thoughtfully.

"Many years ago, I went to your father, to ask him to pray for my wife, who wasn't well. She recovered. Now I'm praying for your father's grandchildren. I'm sure that they will also emerge from this ordeal, healthy and safe," he declared.

Rabbanit Rachel calmed down. Carol thanked the Hacham and led her mother-in-law outside and into the car. As she began pulling away from the curb, she heard some noise behind her.

"Wait, wait…"

She turned around and saw Hacham Yosef Tawil running down the steps in front of his house, out to their car. "They are free! They are free! I just heard it on the news!"

Indeed, Mama Rachel's prayers were answered.[19]

---

19. Exactly why the last hostages were released then is unclear. Some people felt that the terrorists wanted to attend Nasser's funeral so they decided to get rid of them. Others point out that when Arafat realized that he had lost his war against Jordan, he smuggled himself to Cairo, where he accused King Hussein of genocide against the *fedayeen*. King Hussein flew to Cairo to explain his position and work out an agreement that would keep the *fedayeen* out of his country. Suddenly, the *fedayeen* were leaderless and being driven out of Jordan. They turned over the hostages to the Red Cross as a goodwill gesture.

Esther also heard the news, but didn't know whether to get excited or not. There had been so many disappointments. *Hashem will certainly bring them home before Rosh Hashana,* she decided, glancing at the clock. It was 4:10 p.m. Candle-lighting was at 6:20 the next evening. She tried to calculate the hours. Was it possible?

It was a race against time. The plane was scheduled to land at 5:50 and there were police cars waiting to take them. Rabbi Moshe Feinstein and Rabbi Hutner tried to arrange everything in case they couldn't make it home in time for Yom Tov. They had reservations in the International Hotel right near the airport with a *minyan,* kosher food, *machzorim,* and a *shofar.* They even tried to get a helicopter from the airport but, in the end, the police escort was enough to bring the men home on time for Yom Tov.

Hacham Yosef Tawil

Hacham Yosef arrived home at 6:25; candle-lighting was 6:20.

"They can do all their preparations until 6:55," Rabbi Moshe Feinstein had told the family earlier.

Hacham Yosef quickly put on his *tefillin,* inordinately grateful to do so after 23 days without them. He raced against the clock as he showered and shaved — the first time in weeks. Then he ran off to Sha'arei Zion.

Hacham Abraham reached "the Dome" (the main sanctuary of Sha'arei Zion) a few minutes before his brother. As soon as he entered, the whole congregation, hundreds of people, rose from their seats and clapped thunderously. When Hacham Yosef walked in a few minutes later, the clapping continued. It was an amazing standing ovation, a tribute to all the prayers that the community had said that entire month of Elul, when the Raful brothers had been in constant danger. The spontaneous clapping lasted for almost 15 minutes; its memory lingers on in the minds and hearts of everyone who was there.

As for Nouri, where was he when his son-in-law was being so nobly welcomed?

He was praying in Ahi Ezer.

Where else?

Mama Rachel Cries for Her Children / 443

Chapter 54:

BLESSING IS FOUND ONLY ON THAT WHICH IS HIDDEN FROM THE EYE

It's good to be out of the limelight, mused Nouri, when all the excitement over the hijackings died down. But there definitely were lingering effects.

Sara, living in Israel, found the ordeal very difficult. She couldn't sleep during the time that her family had been hostages and, even after they were safe, she felt jumpy. Then, barely two weeks later, she surprised a robber in her house in the middle of the night. Though he ran away without taking much, she remained agitated for days. There were also other unusual circumstances that were emotionally draining.

"Daddy, I've had enough. I want to come home," Sara cried to her father. She knew that, surrounded by parents and siblings, life would be different.

Nouri didn't see it that way.

"Now is not a good time," he answered softly.

Sara was shocked. Her mother was always nudging her to come back to America. Now that she made up her mind to return, why was her father not jumping to agree?

"You are feeling weak. Wait until you are stronger," he urged gently. "You can come home Pesah time."

Sara was bewildered as she hung up. But without her parents' sponsorship, she had no money for tickets. So Sara stayed in Israel. And by the time Pesah rolled around, she was completely rejuvenated from that rollercoaster period where one drama after another had made life seem so bleak. A few months later, she happily joined in the Seudat Hoda'ah held in the newly finished Yeshiva Kol Yaakob, celebrating the survival of the hostages.

Maybe that was what Daddy meant, she reflected many years later. *Maybe he didn't want me to make such an important decision out of weakness.*

Sara (Dayan) Salem is sitting in the middle with Yocheved Raful to her left. Behind them, standing, L-R: Hacham Yosef Raful's Aunt Eenie, Hacham Abraham Raful's (an uncle of Hacham Yosef) second wife, Yolanda Raful.

Rabbi David Attia is speaking. Sitting below the window in the corner is Rabbi Yehuda Ades. Next to him is Shalom Raful. Seated in the middle, at the front table, is Stanley Salem. To his left is Rabbi Rafael Ades.

A different view of the affair. Hacham Abraham Raful (a noted *mekubal*) is seated in the middle. Gideon Raful is speaking.

Seudat Hoda'a at Yeshiva Kol Yaakob

Blessing Is Found Only on That Which Is Hidden From the Eye / 445

Nouri and Esther were a strong and guiding presence in the lives of their adult children without ever being intrusive. For Nouri, that was all part of his approach to life: Stay in the background as much as possible but step up to the plate when necessary. He and Esther stated their opinions, even if they knew their children would not be happy, but they also made it clear that they expected their children to make their own decisions. There was no way that Nouri would act on Sara's emotional plea and bring her to America because he wanted her to return. He wanted her to regain her strength and then make a rational decision, even if that rational decision would be different from what he believed to be correct.

Nouri came to Israel that summer, delighted to find Sara happy and settled.

He arrived with Uncle Dave and the two of them had many plans on their agenda. Nouri was pulled to Israel. He loved being there, spending time with his family, and scouring the Land for more ways to help build it up — physically and spiritually. Back in 1966, he met Rabbi Reuven Elbaz and encouraged him to open a yeshiva.

"We'll help you," he insisted.

The "royal we" always consisted of himself and Dave Bibi. Indeed, Rabbi Elbaz went on to open Yeshivat Ohr HaChaim and had enormous success. Dave and Nouri quietly helped support the yeshiva for many years.

Rabbi Mordechai Elefant was another kindred soul, with incomparable energy and vision and a desire to build. Dave and Nouri became his loyal

L-R: Dave and Nouri at the Kotel

supporters and partners in many of his ventures. On their 1971 trip, they planned to spend Shabbat with him in his newly built yeshiva called Itri [**I**srael **T**orah **R**esearch **I**nstitute]. In the aftermath of the Six Day War, Rabbi Elefant had acquired a large tract of land in Bet Tzafafa and was building a sprawling campus.

"Join us there," Nouri invited Sara. "There is plenty of room."

"Sounds good," Sara answered. But, to her disappointment, she realized the next day that spending Shabbat in Itri wasn't going to work out.

"Don't worry about it," Nouri told her. "We'll walk to you for Shabbat lunch."

"Daddy," Sara protested, "it's an hour's walk and the weather is boiling."

"We're coming," he insisted.

When he and Uncle Dave walked through the door, smiling, with beads of sweat on their faces, Sara was moved. *I can't believe that they came all this way, just for me.*

Indeed, both Nouri and Dave went out of their way for family and friends, often behind the scenes, where only the direct recipient knew of their unusual thoughtfulness. When Eli Levy passed away suddenly, his oldest son, Aaron, was thrust into the position of head of the family, the one making decisions for his widowed mother and orphaned brothers. Aaron was newly married, no longer a child. Yet, standing in the chapel, he felt lost and vulnerable.

Suddenly, there was a tap on Aaron's shoulder.

Dave Bibi and Nouri Dayan had appeared out of nowhere.

"Listen," Dave said, "anything you need, we will take care of. Just call."

A warm feeling of relief engulfed Aaron. He had lost his father, but he still had people who cared about him and would not let him and his family buckle under. He was part of a much larger and broader family — the Ahi Ezer family.

The Ahi Ezer family was expanding, in all directions.

The new yeshiva building was a resounding success, attracting increased enrollment and prompting the committee to offer new programs. Rabbi Wolf used the school to reach out to the parents. He had the PTA organize assemblies, plays, carnivals, and fairs which were used as forums to encourage the parents to be more involved in their children's lives.

"We teach your children about Shabbat and *kashrut*, and their eyes light up in excitement. They want to share that excitement with you, their parents. But their mothers are busy running the house and their fathers come home late at night, after a long and tiring day. No one has the time or patience to listen to the children share their excitement. Slowly, what we teach becomes lost…" Rabbi Wolf let his message seep in before expounding, "You must find time for your children! Have a long and leisurely meal

Ahi Ezer of Ocean Parkway

on Shabbat, where everyone has a chance to discuss what they learned. Develop a relationship with your children through what is going on in their lives. If not, one day you might wake up and find that they are all grown up, with lives of their own. By that time, what you say will have very little impact."

Rabbi Wolf rarely mentioned religion; he was afraid that parents would be turned off if they felt coerced into taking on higher standards of religiosity. He simply encouraged and coached parents to have meaningful relationships with their children. As parents worked on interacting with their children, they realized how many gaps existed in their own religious knowledge. They began enrolling in Rabbi Wolf's adult education classes. Some parents retained a connection to the yeshiva long after their children graduated, even if they were not Ahi Ezer congregants.

Nouri constantly credited Rabbi Wolf for the success of Ahi Ezer Yeshiva and downplayed his own role. "There are so many people devoted to the yeshiva," he would tell Esther. "They deserve all the credit, not me."

He felt the same about the new shul that was nearing completion.

Ahi Ezer of Ocean Parkway was magnificent. Nouri had been involved in every step of the process, even watching the workers as they installed the windows. The building façade was a modern motif, imposing but not ostentatious. The inner sanctuary was special. Nouri had traveled to Texas, where he ordered the unusual synagogue windows from an artist

These are two of the unique windows that still attract viewers, over forty years after they were built.

who specialized in designing stained-glass mosaics that depicted Judaica themes. The result was breathtakingly beautiful.

Thank G-d, the community had grown, not just in size but in financial standing. Ahi Ezer had become solidly middle class. With that in mind, they undertook a larger, far more expensive building than what they had built twenty years earlier in Bensonhurst. Understandably, money remained an issue.

One of the main shul fundraisers of the time was the selling of permanent seats. Nouri was in favor of this not only from the monetary perspective but in the hope that when a family purchased a few seats, they were solidifying their connection to the shul. After all, they had spent good money on those seats.[20] Nouri was willing to try almost any gimmick to raise money but, equally important, he also wanted to bolster synagogue attendance. With the new building nearing completion, he searched for a compelling draw, something to keep people coming every Shabbat, not just for the holidays.

He set his sights on Cantor Meir Levy.

---

20. The flip side of this system was that sometimes people became possessive of their seats, unwittingly making it uncomfortable for a guest who accidentally sat in a pre-purchased seat. Mr. Dayan was famous for looking away if someone sat in his seat, for volunteering his seat to guests who came for a happy occasion, and for leading someone to his seat simply because the shul was full.

Cantor Meir Levy as a young man (in 1960), performing before a crowd of 100,000 people.

Meir Levy had been singing professionally since he was six years old. He sang and led choirs in many high-profile venues, such as the huge Simhat Torah celebration in 1960, and at the Kotel in honor of the reunification of Yerushalayim in 1968. He was a celebrated *hazzan* who had sung in concerts all over the world. Nouri met him on one of his trips to Israel and decided that he would be the latest Ahi Ezer attraction.

When Nouri offered him the job, he was very candid.

"Look," Nouri told him, "I want you in Ahi Ezer and I'm prepared to pay you as much as you ask. But if you decide to leave Eretz Yisrael to come to America, that will be your decision. I take no responsibility for that."[21]

Despite Nouri's frank disclaimer, Meir Levy accepted the position.

Suddenly, Ahi Ezer became the place to be.

For Meir Levy's first Rosh Hashana, construction of the new shul wasn't yet complete. Nouri rented a huge tent, set up right outside the incomplete building, so that Ahi Ezer could already have services. He reasoned that once people heard Meir Levy's services, they would clamor to buy their permanent seats.

Meir Levy was a smashing success. He had an extremely powerful voice that filled the room. As soon as the building was finished, people from other local shuls would come to Ahi Ezer on Friday nights, just to pray

---

21. The Rambam discusses the prohibition of a person who lives in Eretz Yisrael leaving the Land to settle outside of it. He also explains when it is permitted (*Hilchos Melachim* 5:9).

Cantor Meir Levy flanked by Chief Rabbi Yitzhak Nissim at the Kotel in 1967

with Meir Levy. The shul was jammed, and the people walked outside singing his tunes, euphoric from the experience. He led a choir in Ahi Ezer Yeshiva and, when they produced a record, it was an instant community

...and with another huge crowd at the Kotel in 1968

Blessing Is Found Only on That Which Is Hidden From the Eye / 451

The sign announcing the "tent services" of Meir Levy, well before the synagogue was finished

hit. For many years, faithful followers of Meir Levy kept coming to Ahi Ezer, even if they were not Syrian!

And happiest of all was Nouri.

"Brighton Yeshiva wants to merge. What do you think?"

The new Ahi Ezer building attracted many of the local residents and Brighton Yeshiva was losing enrollment. They had a great building with a nice outdoor play area for the young children. Buying them out would give Ahi Ezer additional facilities, which they already needed because of their rapid growth.

"What about the center?" asked another committee member.

Somehow, the community center, for which they had originally bought the Avenue X building, was always being pushed off. There were just too many other projects that took priority. Here too, the gentle reminder was waved aside as Ahi Ezer bought out Brighton Yeshiva and put plans for the center on hold.

Actually, Rabbi Wolf had another idea that would also eclipse the building of the center. As young Syrian families moved out of Bensonhurst, the Bensonhurst branch of Ahi Ezer was made up mainly of senior citizens. In response to their needs, Ahi Ezer set up a senior citizen center in the 71st Street building. Again, Ahi Ezer was the pioneer, finding a need and filling it. They began with lectures on diverse subjects and eventually expanded to include a full schedule of activities including arts and crafts, sewing and knitting, drama and singing, games and classes. They also organized regular holiday events and outings, all of which were heavily — and happily — attended.[22]

---

22. By 1976, the Sephardic Multi-Service Senior Center had almost 400 members.

At the same time, Rabbi Wolf had his eye on the future. Soon these senior citizens would want to be closer to their children and the Flatbush housing market was being priced way out of their range. He learned about a Housing and Urban Development (HUD) program that subsidized rent for the indigent elderly. Taking the two ideas together, he proposed to Nouri that they apply to the government for permission to build HUD housing for the elderly (for which they could use the massive Ocean Parkway and Avenue S building), and that would become a fundraiser for the yeshiva and a service to the community.[23] Nouri loved the proposal, though he knew that it could take years to win government approval.

Meanwhile, the Ocean Parkway/Avenue S building was nicely paying

Cantor Meir Levy

off its own mortgage from the rentals. Though each property came with its own list of hassles, Nouri had his eye out for more real estate. Time and experience had proven that each purchase led to more growth.

But growth often came with pain.

"Izzy, it's bad, really bad."

The voice on the line was barely coherent and Nouri had a sinking feeling in his stomach. *What can be so bad?*

The words that finally tumbled out were beyond shocking. An Ahi Ezer boy, a son of one of their most loyal supporters, had gotten off the bus and, as he bent down to pick up the *kippah* that had fallen off his head, the bus ran him over. The child passed away almost instantly.

Nouri was shaken. Like everyone else, he ran to be part of the *levaya* and to comfort the mourners. He was unprepared for the strange looks that people were giving him. Slowly, realization dawned: People were blaming Ahi Ezer.

Ironically, the parents of the child, while overcome with grief, were not upset with the yeshiva. It had been an accident, plain and simple, and they were gracious and forgiving. But other community members struggled

---

23. The only facility for elderly people in the community was the Sephardic Nursing Home on Cropsy Avenue, founded and run by the Spanish Portuguese community. Only people who were truly incapacitated lived there.

with the issue. They wanted answers to their questions: Being that the accident occurred with an Ahi Ezer bus, did that mean that Ahi Ezer hired an incompetent driver? In other words, were their children safe? And if they were not being safely bussed, what else wasn't up to par?

Night after night, people barged into the Dayan house demanding answers. As usual, Nouri responded calmly, even to the most irrational accusations. How people went from one morbid conclusion to the next was beyond someone as levelheaded as Nouri, but he judged everyone righteously, reasoning that this was an emotionally charged event that challenged the community.

"Yeshuat Hashem keheref ayin — Salvation comes as fast as the blink of an eye," he murmured, as the latest irate parent stormed out of his house. He understood their pain, and hoped that the passage of time would enable them to move on.

Some did, and some didn't.

There were definitely those parents who pulled their children out of Ahi Ezer, which pained Nouri. He just prayed that they send their children to another yeshiva and not to public school. Despite this tragedy, the school continued to grow.

Ahi Ezer Congregation consistently lived up to its name. As "my brother's helper," it continued to welcome every immigrant group into their community. The Egyptians of 1958, and then 1968, came to Ahi Ezer, and stayed there until they became numerous enough to start their own congregation. Then Nouri helped them become independent, but their children remained in Ahi Ezer yeshiva.

The Lebanese, who had been coming in dribs and drabs for years,[24] were also welcomed warmly by Ahi Ezer, but they remained only until they were numerous enough to form their own congregation (with Nouri's help, of course). They, too, continued to send their children to Ahi Ezer Yeshiva.

But it was the influx of Russians that ultimately changed Ahi Ezer Yeshiva.

The 1967 war had an impact far beyond the Middle East. The Russian government reacted to it by vehemently denouncing Zionism and virtually banning immigration to Israel. Conversely, Russian Jewry, who had been oppressed for decades, were energized by the Israeli victory and emboldened to flee the Soviet Union. A daring hijack attempt in 1970 drew

---

24. Post 1948, Lebanon became the most modern and politically safe country in the Middle East. Their Jews didn't flee in large numbers; they didn't "flee" at all. They trickled out as the tension between the Christians and the Muslims in Lebanon escalated. But those who remained were much freer than Jews anywhere else in the Arab world. Only after the 1967 war did Jews begin leaving Lebanon in greater numbers because of rising anti-Semitism.

attention to the plight of the Jews in the Soviet Union who were locked behind the Iron Curtain.[25]

In an effort to counteract the bad publicity they were receiving and to improve relations with the West, Russia began allowing limited Jewish emigration. While only 4,000 Jews had left the Soviet Union in the decade from 1960-1970, in the following decade, 250,000 Jews left. The vast majority of these Russian emigrants came to America. Technically, the Russians who arrived in the 1970's should have been an "Ashkenaz" problem. The majority, by far, were not Sephardic. Nonetheless, while many of them settled in New York, they didn't settle near the mainstream Ashkenazic community. They settled in Brighton Beach, eventually dubbed "Odessa by the Sea."

Nearby was a nice Jewish school called Ahi Ezer.

The Russians found Ahi Ezer, not necessarily because they were interested in their children receiving a Jewish education, but because they heard that this was a "free" private school that gave the children an excellent education. Rabbi Wolf and Nouri realized that all these Russian children would be lost to the Jewish people if they attended public school, and they decided to actively entice them to attend the yeshiva, despite the reality that these were not even Sephardic children. Pre-school cost money, even in the secular world. Rabbi Wolf gave the Pre-1A children the secular curriculum of a first grader. The Russians loved it. The following year, when they were ready to pull out the children (mainly because they didn't want to pay tuition), he would question them, "Now you want to take them out? Why? They already know everything that they are going to be learning in public school."

This argument usually won them over. Rabbi Wolf created a branch of Ahi Ezer — exclusively Russian — in the Brighton Yeshiva building. He even hired some Russian-speaking staff to deal with the language issues that were certain to emerge.

But the tuition issue remained. No Russian immigrant was going to pay tuition when public school was free. To be fair, many of the Russians were struggling financially. But the Russians were not an Ahi Ezer problem; they were a Jewish problem, and Nouri was going to get the message out there: We all have to help our Russian brothers. He created a new scholarship fund and sent out teams of fundraisers to solicit from the broader Jewish community. As usual, he and Dave Bibi were the most active and most passionate.

"You've got to give until it hurts," Dave would say. "If giving to your people — of your money, time, or abilities — is easy, it's a sign that you are not giving enough."

---

25. In 1970, 11 people (10 Jewish, among them R' Yosef Mendelevich) tried to hijack a plane and escape the Soviet Union. They were arrested in the airport and all were sentenced to large jail terms.

Joe Maslaton is holding the new *Sefer Torah*. Rabbi Murray Maslaton — "Big Murray" — is on the left, holding the pole. He is the son of Joe. His younger cousin, the son of Rabbi Jack Maslaton, was called "Little Murray" to differentiate between the two of them. They both became influential Rabbis in the community. Front right is Joe Srour, a prominent member of the Ahi Ezer community, and a close friend of Nouri.

Indeed, few people "gave until it hurt" the way that Dave and Nouri did.

With all the big projects that Nouri undertook, he never forgot his smaller, "hidden" efforts. He still paid the children in the neighborhood to read *Tehillim*, only he upped the stipend to a dollar an hour. This was big money for kids in the 70's. They happily raked in up to $10 a week, and felt rich! Only years later did they realize that the spiritual riches they had earned were far more valuable, as saying *Tehillim* became a natural part of their lives.

"Ein haberacha metzuya ela badavar hasamui min ha'ayin — Blessing is found only on that which is hidden from the eye," was one of Nouri's favorite *dibrei Hazal*. He applied it to business, when he refused to take inventory, and he applied it to himself when he tried to fade into the background.

"Don't put yourself forward," he'd counsel his children.

Nouri found that so much could be accomplished from the background. His home was often the venue of secret meetings where he helped people iron out their differences, never saying, "Let them fight it out."

When the Egyptians and the Lebanese sought to create independent congregations, it was no easy endeavor. Though "most roads led back to Syria," there were real differences in the traditions of the various communities, based on their years apart. Nouri felt that people are most comfortable

The other Sifrei Torah coming out to greet the new one

sticking to their own traditions. If people felt alienated in any way, they might break away from the community and then they would be lost. So, no matter how much time and energy it took to put new congregations on their feet, Nouri was willing to help. He knew that, ultimately, he was investing in generations of Jewish people.

"*Ohev shalom v'rodef shalom* — a lover of peace who runs after peace," was how Rabbi Harry Rubin described Nouri.

Nouri believed that the Jewish people are truly good; no one *wants* to fight. Strong-minded people get things done; only sometimes they need help smoothing out their own rough edges. And because Nouri was so clearly *l'shem Shamayim* (he had no personal benefit from being an unpaid mediator) he was often successful.

Even in the private arena, Nouri had an effect. When he sensed that someone was going through a difficult time, or another person was experiencing marital strife, he would intervene quietly. He was so well-liked, no one said "leave us alone" or "mind your own business." They respected him and allowed him to help them.

People who came to Ahi Ezer, even sporadically, were drawn to his sincerity, and some became more *shomer mitzvot* simply from that exposure. One of the biggest Ahi Ezer supporters and fundraisers wasn't *shomer Shabbat*. After years of being around Nouri, one day, this man decided to

Hacham Ovadya Yosef, flanked by Dave Bibi and Nouri Dayan. Behind Dave Bibi is (far left) Nat Escava and Ceasar Salama. Visible from between Nouri and Hacham Ovadya is Basil Cohen.

stop working on Shabbat, and even dissolved a long-standing business partnership as a result.

Ahi Ezer of Ocean Parkway became the new *Shammi* center. Hacham Sion moved over to Flatbush with the rest of the congregation. The new shul became the venue for community events and affairs. When Rebecca (Maslaton) Bibi commissioned a *Sefer Torah* in memory of her husband, Morris, she knew that its home would be the new synagogue in Flatbush, not the old building in Bensonhurst.

Hacham Sion with Hacham Ovadya

Hacham Ovadya, at the luncheon in Ahi Ezer Yeshiva.
L-R (graduated): Steve Shalom, Abe Sarway, Joe Maslaton, Joe R. Bibi, Rabbi Jacob Kassin, Rabbi Martovka, Nat Escava, Hacham Ovadya Yosef, Nouri Dayan, Hacham Sion Maslaton, Basil Cohen, Mr. Bert Chabbot, Meir Levy, Mr. Dweck, Joe Ades, Ceasar Salama.

Without Hacham Sion at the helm, the Bensonhurst shul needed a new Rabbi. Nouri hired Rabbi Harry Rubin, an Ashkenazic Rabbi whose wife was Sephardi. He had served as Rabbi in Magen David and then in Ahaba Ve'Ahva of Bensonhurst. He was very familiar with Sephardic tradition and mentality and was just the right person to give the synagogue direction.

Nouri still prayed regularly in the 71st Street shul, but he was well aware that the shul was growing quiet as the neighborhood thinned out. Nonetheless, he continued his involvement, usually quietly, but sometimes loudly and forcefully, if that was what was needed.

One year, the synagogue caterer decided to book a New Year's Eve party as a way to drum up business. Shortly before the scheduled party, Nouri got wind of what was going on.

"You cannot have a New Year's Eve party here. There is no such thing in our synagogue," Nouri told him.

The caterer was miffed. "I already took money from people. They made reservations and I cannot cancel on them."

Nouri grew agitated and, uncharacteristically, yelled, "There will not be any party here. I'm locking up the social hall. As far as I'm concerned, you can leave!"

The shocked caterer canceled the party.

Nouri's outburst reflected an inner strength that he preferred to keep hidden. He liked taking quiet initiatives and only reacted publicly when necessary... like when war broke out on Yom Kippur and shocked the Jewish world.

On Yom Kippur of 1973, three Arab countries — Jordan, Syria, and Egypt — attacked Israel in an attempt to recapture the land that they had lost in 1967. Unlike the 1967 war, there was no miraculous victory in one week. The Arab nations were armed by the Soviets and far outnumbered the Israelis in both weapons and personnel. During the first few weeks, the situation was very precarious.

Uncharacteristically, Nouri stood up in shul and announced, "Please open the *sefer Tehillim* to Chapter 83, which we will say as a merit for our brothers in Israel."

Rabbi Harry Rubin and Nouri Dayan. "Mr. Dayan was like Aharon HaKohen," noted Rabbi Harry Rubin. "Through his peaceful influence, many people became more religious. In my day, many people came to shul on Shabbat morning, and put on a *kippah*, right outside the shul. Today, look how many people have their *tzitzit* hanging out!"

As the tension filled weeks passed — particularly for the Dayans who had family in Eretz Yisrael — the extra *Tehillim* was recited with fervor. Ultimately, Israel did succeed in defending herself without giving up any land. But she paid for that victory in lives. Over 2,500 Jews were killed, the largest amount since the founding of the State. Almost every Israeli had a relative, friend, neighbor, or acquaintance who had been killed or wounded in battle.

There was no euphoria when the fighting ended, no moment of exultation and relief, only continued prayers for a final end to all fighting, a final cure to all who had been wounded, a final return of all the soldiers missing in action.

So the extra prayers continued — and never stopped.

To this day, Ahi Ezer adds Chapter 83 at the end of Shaharit on Sundays.[26]

Once again, Nouri initiated a *zechut* that endures.

---

26. They continue to read the five chapters of *Tehillim* that Mr. Dayan initiated with the Sunday morning breakfasts, as well.

Chapter 55:

"DO YOU SEE THAT MAN? HE'S A *TZADDIK*."

Bensonhurst, 1975

Sara Maslaton passed away.

Stetta had lived in the Dayan house for eight years.

Nouri never stopped being grateful for that privilege.

Now her feisty spirit, her pithy sayings, her wise comments were gone. She was a link to the Old Country, one of the last members of their community who had come over to America in the 1920's, already a family matriarch with children of marriageable age. Her memories of Syria were vivid and rich and the traditions that she recounted were transmitted with the authority of one who had lived there.

Her absence created a natural change in the Dayan home.

All the relatives who had come to visit her came less often, if at all. All the hours that Esther had spent preparing for those guests were suddenly available. All the thought and time that Esther had invested in her mother's care were now free for others.

By now, most of the Dayan children had married: Murray had married Linda Seruya and moved to Flatbush in September of 1971. Joyce had married Mordechai (Marty) Nahem a month later and moved to Lakewood. A few years later, Barbara married David Ozeirey and moved to Flatbush. Only Joey, learning in Israel, was still single.

Esther had over a quorum of grandchildren. She well remembered the challenges of raising a young family and she looked to make life easier for her married children. Twice a year, she made appointments with each individual family and loaded the children into the car to take them all shoe shopping for the new season. In the early years, that meant buying three

David Ozeirey and Barbara Dayan, at their engagement. In the front center is *Stetta*, in one of her last public appearances.

or four pairs of shoes in total. But, as the years went on, and the children needed shoes for Shabbat and weekday, she was buying many more. Her married children were grateful: They were relieved of the cost of buying shoes and the hassle of shoe shopping with a slew of children.

"Shoe-shopping with Grandma" became a bi-annual treat as the grandkids piled into Grandma's car, where there was always a comfortable blanket spread out back and yummy nosh to munch on. No matter whether it was the height of the shopping season or a slower time, Grandma always found parking, in the busiest of neighborhoods, "Because we are doing a mitzva," she would tell her grandchildren.

To Esther, being a grandmother meant having more people to whom to give. She remembered every grandchild's birthday with an envelope of bills that grew with the child's age. She remembered every child's anniversary in the same manner. When the grandchildren were young, the birthday gifts were a few dollars but, as they grew older, she gave $30, $40, and then $50. The grandchildren waited all year for these gifts. Married grandchildren got larger sums on their anniversary. By then, it wasn't only the thoughtfulness that counted; the gift was a real help.

Though Esther didn't work outside the home and Nouri managed the finances completely, he never acknowledged or even hinted that he had anything to do with all this generosity. He never pointed out, "Oh, what nice shoes...," as if to imply that the child owed him a thank you.

Nouri and his new son-in-law at the Ozeirey wedding

Everything Esther chose to give to the children and grandchildren had his approval, no questions asked.

Nouri and Esther firmly settled into the Grandpa and Grandma roles.

During the week, rarely a day passed without one of the married children popping by, either with or without some grandchildren in tow. Grandma Dayan was almost always home, cooking up delicious dishes and doling them out. Grandpa Dayan was a different story. He was so busy that, unless the grandchildren came on Shabbat, they were unlikely to see him. But when they did see him, he swooped up the little children and swung them around until they laughed. If they dropped by on a weekday and he happened to be running out somewhere, Grandpa would offer the grandchildren a lift, and that was the biggest treat because Grandpa Dayan had adopted Uncle Morris's "candy car" tradition; everyone knew that there was always something good in the glove compartment.

The Dayan grandchildren were inordinately proud of Grandpa. They knew that he wasn't the type of grandfather who would take them out for ice cream or to the park. He was too busy with many big and important things. Sunday morning, he was in shul until early afternoon. After twenty years, he was still supervising (and cleaning up from) the 9 o'clock *minyan*, though now a series of classes had been added following breakfast. Evenings, he was away practically every night, either in meetings or fundraising. His devotion to others took up all of his time, all of his life.

The grandchildren learned as much from his absences as from his presence. They learned that life was about doing, particularly for the community, to enable others to serve the Borei Olam better. And when they did spend time with him, they reveled in his presence — at *seudat Shabbat* when he sang every *pizmon* and said many Mishnayot, on the way to shul when he asked them questions on the *perasha*, or when they woke up Shabbat morning and joined him at the dining-room table

Grandpa is so… so …holy, mused one of the grandchildren on Shabbat morning, way before the sun even glimmered through the clouds. This was his special time with Grandpa. He tried his hardest to wake up first, and run downstairs before Grandpa awakened… but he never succeeded. Yet "losing" this contest didn't spoil the wonderful atmosphere, that taste of Olam Haba that he felt just sitting together with Grandpa, sipping the tea that Grandpa made special for him, and listening as he read from the *perasha… Targum… Zohar… Eitz Chaim…* on and on, for hours.

Not everyone was privileged to get a glimpse of that holiness because, much of the day, Nouri was busy with mundane manners. But there were times that his special soul glowed clearly, and those who saw this were taken aback.

Like when young Asher Hatchuel from Venezuela, a student at the Mir, came for the Seder.

Malchut, he marveled, *royalty!*

The Dayan house was far from royal, by anyone's standard. Though Nouri was a man of means, neither he nor Esther had the time or patience for frivolity. They had good quality furniture but it was simple and plain, as were the walls and floors of their home. The *malchut* that Asher saw was the aura that emanated from Nouri.

"Like an angel," murmured Rabbi Solomon Maimon.

Nouri's first son-in-law, Hacham Yosef Raful (center), was becoming a major force in the Sephardic community. Here he is pictured in Zucker's Bungalow Colony with Rabbi Murray Maslaton, Nouri's nephew and protégé, who was also becoming a community leader. Carol is on the right.

The Dayan s'machot were always graced with the presence of Ashkenazic Rabbanim. Here is Irwin Dayan, dancing at his son's bar mitzva, holding the hand of Rabbi Shlomo Mandel, Rosh Yeshiva of Yeshiva of Brooklyn, who is holding the hand of Rabbi Eisemann, Rosh Yeshiva of the Vineland Yeshiva. Behind Rabbi Shlomo Mandel is Mike Antebi. The two children in the front, on the left, are Ezra and Maoz Raful.

Many years had passed since the two men learned together on Sunday mornings, and Rabbi Maimon had become a powerful figure in the Seattle community. But when he returned to New York for a visit, he often stopped by the Dayan home for a meal on Shabbat and that was when he saw Nouri, in his element.

Rav Ben Sion Abba Shaul was in New York for a short period of time. He was staying at Marvin Azrak's house and therefore prayed in Ahi Ezer. He pointed to Nouri and commented to Marvin, "Do you see that man? He's a *tzaddik*."

Nouri was oblivious.

He just plugged ahead, doing whatever he felt had to be done.

His house was still open to everyone, particularly beloved family for whom he felt it a privilege to host. Ever since Uncle Morris's sudden passing, Aunt Rebecca came often, and moved in for a whole Shabbat. She brought along her cheerful, no-nonsense good humor, and an inevitable basket of delicacies such as sweet Syrian pastries, or her famous *aras*, a salty snack made of thinly rolled dough that — fried correctly — bubbled up like a potato chip. All her great-nieces and nephews whooped in delight when she brought out this treat.

Nouri was genuinely delighted to host all his guests and many became like family. Every *layl Shabbat*, after the meal, he learned with a *habruta*, a practice he began years earlier, after the kids had grown up. His most steady *habruta* was Jose Freue, an Argentinean immigrant who regularly ate at the *layl Shabbat* meal at the Dayan home. Jose came from the very religious Syrian community in Argentina. Jose gravitated to the Dayan house where he saw in practice the type of home he was looking to create but had not yet found the mate with whom to create it. Eli Moseri was another guest/*habruta* for many years.

There were other steady customers who would later point to Nouri as the formative influence in their lives. Perhaps the most prominent among them was Marvin Azrak, Nouri's great-nephew.

Marvin remained a steady presence in the Dayan home, even after he married. He came by for meetings (Nouri had encouraged him to join Ahi Ezer committees) or just to consult with Nouri. As he took on more of a leadership role in the community, he ran every project and every idea by his Uncle Nouri. Though the two men had very different personalities, they shared an enormous drive to accomplish. Similar to the relationship that Nouri shared with Dave, when Marvin came up with an idea, Nouri was quick to back him up with encouragement.

As always, Nouri had his eye on Flatbush real estate for Ahi Ezer. He bought two more apartment buildings near Ocean Parkway and Avenue S, not certain what they would be used for but reasoning that, for now, they would pay off the mortgages through the rents. Marvin admired Nouri's take-charge attitude and vision and the way he would build, build, and build, even without knowing exactly what he was building. That was why, when a joint delegation from all the Sephardic shuls in the community came to Nouri with a proposal, Nouri was able to respond in a way that bowled over his petitioners.

Nouri and his daughter, Joyce Nahem, surrounded by Dayan grandchildren

Nouri with Hacham Ben Sion Abba Shaul, at the Kotel. Back row, L-R: unknown, Nissim Salem, Rabbi Stanley Salem, Rabbi Harry Rubin, Ezra (son of Murray) Dayan, (slightly forward) Mordechai Dayan (Nouri's half-brother), Murray Dayan, Rabbi Saul Maslaton, Rabbi Shlomo Sutton.

"Izzy, we know that Ahi Ezer owns that big apartment building on Avenue S and Ocean Parkway. We have searched all over and we cannot find any other lot large enough and central enough for a community center. We were wondering if we could buy the lot from Ahi Ezer."

Ahi Ezer had been planning to build a community center for years. Nouri could have proposed that the delegation assist Ahi Ezer in raising money for a community center. But Nouri had no need to lead a project if there were other capable people motivated and willing to take it upon themselves. In fact, he was happy that there were others eager to step up to the challenge and, in consultation with Dave Bibi, readily agreed to sell the property.

When the time came to negotiate a price, here is where their generosity of spirit proved boundless: Rather than ask the building committee to buy the building at market value, which was considerably more than Ahi Ezer had paid for it ten years earlier, they asked only that the building committee take over whatever was left of the mortgage. Basically, Ahi Ezer was donating a large chunk of their property to the community without asking for anything in return.

"Why not?" Nouri asked when people questioned his judgment. "We are here to serve the community. What is the difference if we serve our

Nouri, with the Egyptian community, at a reception

Nouri (far right), at the groundbreaking ceremony for the Sephardic community *mikva*, a venture that he took a key role in bringing to fruition. L-R: Sonny Laniado, Rabbi Abraham Hecht, Mayor Abraham Beame, Rabbi Yaakob Kassin, Ike Hidary, Manny Haber, Nouri Dayan.

Nouri was never limited his community involvement to Ahi Ezer. Here he is seen at broader community initiatives.

own Ahi Ezer congregation, or the entire Sephardic community? Besides, we own other buildings that can be used for future projects, while this lot is ideal for the Community Center."

"But Izzy, we drive ourselves crazy raising money for the yeshiva. Why can't we sell the building at a larger profit and cover some of our debts?"

Nouri shook his head, "We are all one community. The yeshiva will get its money in a different way."

The sale took place in 1976.

One year later, Ahi Ezer finally received HUD approval for their Senior Citizens Housing Project. Nouri was delighted. Though it would take many years and much heartache until this project would become productive and profitable, he was already rejoicing in the potential. Indeed, the establishment of these senior citizen facilities would end up being one of the greatest contributions that any one congregation made to the broader Sephardic community in Flatbush.

Perhaps the Ribbono shel Olam was rewarding one *zechut* with another.

Nouri chased after *zechuyot;* the *zechuyot* seemed to chase right after him.

Jackie Cohen was rolling up his *tefillin* after prayers.

The Ahi Ezer *minyan* was full and there were plenty of high school boys — maybe 20 or 30 — in attendance. The community had blossomed over the years. These boys didn't have to be pulled out of bed or convinced to attend *minyan*. Many of them had graduated Ahi Ezer Yeshiva and were in regular yeshiva high schools. Attending *minyan* was a given; praying three times a day was normal. Unfortunately, the same didn't apply to much of the Sephardic youth living outside the New York area. Those in faraway communities without proper yeshivot were years behind the New York youngsters in practical religious knowledge. The fliers that were floating around the local New York shuls were about to bring these two groups together.

Intended more as a cultural gathering than a religious convention, Nessim Gaon of Switzerland was organizing all the Sephardic young people in one Shabbaton, under the auspices of the American Sephardic Federation. He was hopeful that, ultimately, there would be a world convention of Sephardic youth.[27]

Jackie Cohen filled out an application to attend the event. The whole idea sounded cool: free air fare to Los Angeles, a long weekend in a posh hotel, and meeting Sephardic kids from all over America. He and his friends were intrigued, and the nominal fee meant that their parents could hardly object.

One morning, after prayers, Mr. Dayan stopped Jackie before he left shul. Jackie smiled warmly. Nouri was one of Jackie's favorite role models.

"Tell me about this trip," Mr. Dayan said.

So the two of them sat down on two empty chairs and spoke.

---

27. The World Sephardic Federation (WSF) was founded in 1925 at the international convention of Sephardic Jews held in Vienna. In 1952 the American Sephardic Federation formed its own branch, though it remained relatively inactive until 1974, when Nessim D. Gaon became president of WSF.

"We all want to go," Jackie ended off.

"Will it be held in the proper religious spirit?"

"I think so," Jackie answered.

"I need to know… because I have decided to fund most of it."

And that is exactly what happened. Nouri sponsored the Ahi Ezer youth who wanted to participate in the four-day Shabbaton, and everyone who went found it to be an uplifting and fascinating experience. The New York youth became role models for the out-of-towners who watched in frank interest as their contemporaries expertly wound their *tefillin* in seconds, belted out the *tefillot*, and read flawlessly from the *Sefer Torah*. For the less religious youth, seeing kids their own age so religiously savvy made a powerful impression. And the New Yorkers, who took their expertise for granted, were flattered by their interest, and moved when they recognized their ability to influence others.[28]

Once again, Nouri had the *zechut* of making it happen.

Reuben Bibi decided to retire. He was approaching 80 and had various health issues. Once, he had some kind of attack in the office and stopped breathing. One of the women administered first aid while Nouri sat beside him the entire time, like a devoted child taking care of his parent.

Indeed, that was how Nouri saw himself. He never ceased mentioning to his family his gratefulness to the Bibis who took him in as an orphan when he had nowhere to go and treated him like their own child, not a nephew. After Reuben retired, even though Nouri saw his uncle often in Ahi Ezer, he still went over to his house every Thursday evening to visit, help his uncle balance his checkbook, pay the bills, and take care of anything else he or Aunt Esther might need. Nouri knew that they had devoted children of their own, but he wanted the privilege of serving them.[29] He came to the house regularly (in addition to the Thursday evening visits) to shave his uncle, who found it difficult to do on his own.

On the day that one of the Dayan children was getting married, Nouri was very busy. Then he remembered about Uncle Ruby. "Should I go over to shave him?" he asked Esther distractedly.

---

28. "Years later, I became very involved in the Miami community. I ran two youth programs, taught in three shuls during the week, and taught on Shabbat as well. People asked me: 'Where did you get these skills? From where did you have the desire, the energy, the gumption to accomplish?' And I answered that I acquired all of this from Nouri Dayan and Dave Bibi. They inspired me to serve Klal Yisrael," reminisced Dr. Jack Cohen.

29. Mr. Dayan lamented not having parents, specifically because he felt that he lost out on that precious mitzva of honoring one's parents. When Rabbi Harry Rubin moved to Israel, he commented to Nouri that his parents lived in Denmark and he had not seen them in a long time. "Let me pay your ticket to Denmark," offered Mr. Dayan. "That way I will have a part in your mitzva of *kibbud ab*, a mitzva that I was never able to fully acquire because I never knew my parents."

Esther shrugged. Then something else came up and the question was left hanging. Later on, at the wedding, Nouri noticed that his uncle wasn't freshly shaved and he felt very bad. "I should have gone over," he kept repeating to Esther. "I took it upon myself to shave Uncle Ruby and I should have known that if I don't do it, no one else will think of it."

But that was life. There were highs and lows, victories and disappointments. And at times, there was disappointment and victory rolled in one. Rarely was Nouri ecstatic about his successes; rarely was he derailed by the setbacks.

A tzaddik, was how Rav Ben Sion Abba Shaul described him.

But even *tzaddikim* are sometimes tested by Hashem.

Like on that fateful Shabbat of *Perashat Vayeishev*, 1976.

Rabbi Harry Rubin walked through the peaceful streets of Bensonhurst, early Shabbat morning, as he did every week. There was nothing unusual about that morning, nothing out of the ordinary.

Until he entered Ahi Ezer.

The floor was strewn with *talletim* and *humashim* and *siddurim*. The bookshelves had been overturned and their holy contents trampled on. The *heichal* was open and Rabbi Rubin approached it with trepidation.

Two *Sifrei Torah* were missing and two large *yahrtzeit* candles had been placed in the *heichal*, presumably waiting to be lit. A large *Sefer Torah* case had been flung open, and the Torah Scroll yanked out and slashed. Traces of spittle still clung to the torn parchment. It was a shocking scene straight out of the Middle Ages. These things simply didn't happen in America.

The vandalism caused an uproar in the community and in the broader Jewish world. A synagogue had been desecrated and holy Torah Scrolls defiled. The congregation wept as they cleaned up the shul. They cried *Shema Yisrael* as never before and the walls of Ahi Ezer seemed to weep along with them.

But the person who was most devastated was Nouri.

The *Sefer Torah* that had been slashed and spat upon had been his *Sefer Torah* — the *Sefer Torah* he had written in loving memory of his parents, the *Sefer Torah* whose donation had inaugurated the newly built Ahi Ezer building a quarter of a century earlier.

The rip down the middle of the scroll reflected the rip in his own heart.

Rabbi Rubin noticed how shaken up Nouri was, walking around almost dazed, as if he were pondering why his *Sefer Torah* had been desecrated. It was a very personal loss and, even though Nouri quickly had the scroll repaired, the event took a toll on him. He wondered what the Ribbono shel

Olam was trying to tell him. There were over thirty *Sifrei Torah* in the shul. Why had his been singled out in this way?

He knew that he would never have a clear answer.

He prayed to never again be tested in this way.

Chapter 56:

"IT SEEMS THAT THE WHOLE [DAYAN] HOUSE REVOLVES AROUND... ME!"

Syria, 1974

Sheila stared up the steep mountain, incredulous.

"You are going to climb up the whole thing," the Arab guide said, calmly, "and your mother is going to die along the way."

Sheila turned to her mother, who was hyperventilating even before they began the climb. She stared down at her own high-heeled shoes, which she wore because her original contact had said that there would not be any walking. Then she made a quick decision.

"We are going back," Sheila declared.

Luckily, the guide agreed. The Kabarity family was disappointed; they had already given away or sold anything of value, but they were optimistic that they would try again in another week... Then came the gruesome murder of another group of would-be escapees. The sad story of the Sebbagh girls, three sisters and their cousin, shocked the community. Their mutilated bodies were found in a cave, near the border, by police who then deposited them in sacks and delivered the sacks to their parents as a warning to aspiring escapees.

The Kabarity family was resigned to remain in Syria.

Since the Israeli War of Independence in 1948, Syrian Jewry had lived a precarious existence. In August of 1948, the Jewish Quarter of Damascus was bombed; dozens of Jews were killed and many more fled to Lebanon, Israel, and beyond. The Jews who remained suddenly found that their neighborhood had changed drastically: The Syrian government dumped all the Palestinian refugees right in their backyard.

Not only were the Syrian Jews now living next door to hostile Palestinian Arabs, they were subjected to numerous restrictions that remained in place for decades.[30] While they were allowed to have their synagogues and go to prayers, their economic prospects were dim and their prison-like existence chafed. Slowly, Jews began to disappear — one from a family, two from a block — as young Syrian Jews smuggled themselves out of the country. Almost everyone dreamed of leaving.

Over the years, many more males left Syria than females. For women and girls, escaping with Arab men was exceptionally dangerous and only the very brave (or very desperate) attempted to escape. This led to a very uneven situation where the male population was dwindling substantially while the female population grew. By the 1970's there were simply no young men for the girls to marry.

Western activists, who secretly helped Syrian Jews escape, came up with an ingenious plan. President Assad was well aware of the lopsided male/female ratio within the Jewish community. Why not publicize the situation, presenting a solution that would paint President Assad as cruel if he refused to agree? Muslim law recognizes the validity of proxy marriages, where the groom marries his bride through a third party. Why not allow these girls to marry American boys by proxy, and spare them a life of singlehood? The boys and girls would receive pictures of each other and would choose a match accordingly. Then someone in Syria would "marry" the American boy to his Syrian bride. It would look very bad if President Assad refused to grant a young woman the right to join her husband. Who would ever know if the couple actually married each other later on in America?[31]

It looked like Sheila Kabarity found a different way out of Syria.

Pinch me, thought Sheila, as she leaned back in her Air France seat. She could hardly believe that she was leaving Syria as a normal person, not

---

30. The official government policy was that they were not anti-Jewish, only anti-Zionist. They allowed the Jews to teach prayer but not Hebrew language, which meant that it was difficult to teach Jewish subjects. The Jews were not expelled, but they were not allowed to leave either. After the 1967 war, restrictions were tightened even further. Jews were not allowed to travel more than 4km. out of Damascus without a permit. Those caught in restricted areas were sent off to prison. Jews could not work for the government or banks, acquire drivers licenses, or purchase property. Any Jew who left the country legally (for commercial or medical reasons) had to leave behind family members as collateral. The Jewish Quarter of Damascus was closely monitored as the secret police kept a file on every member of the Jewish community, tapped their phones, and read their mail.
31. The community arranged a gala celebration where the community representative, Selim Toto, "married" the brides to their grooms, in a way that wasn't binding according to Jewish law but was valid according to Muslim law. President Assad granted these girls exit visas to join their "husbands" because political activists guaranteed him positive publicity in the Western world.

climbing stealthily over mountains, at the mercy of Arab guides. *I even have two pieces of luggage, stuffed with my own clothing!*

She and the other twelve girls were in awe of their good fortune. They were heading to America as young women with potentially bright futures ahead of them. They were no longer irrevocably doomed to singlehood; they were no longer political pawns in a complicated chess game.

When the airplane touched down in Kennedy Airport, all the news agencies had reporters on hand, snapping pictures of the "brides" as they went out to meet their "grooms." Just to be sure that the Syrian government didn't suspect that the marriages were fake, all the boys who had signed for the girls were present, while the families that would actually take in the girls were nowhere to be seen.

After a few snapshots with the right people and a mini-press conference, the girls were led outside the airport where several cars were waiting. Four girls went in a car heading for Hacham Sion's house, four went to Janet Zalta, two went to Jack Maslaton, two went to Dr. Bob Matalon, and one went to an uncle.

Sheila went to the home of Nouri Dayan.

"Would you like something to eat?" Esther asked the shy young woman. The Arabic slipped easily off her lips and Sheila felt immediately comfortable.

Yet she was tongue-tied for a different reason. In Syria, when one's host offered food, it was first placed in front of the guest and then the host urged the guest to eat. A guest never asked for food, or even reached out for food that was on the table. Sheila stared at the empty table, confused and quiet.

Esther tried a different tack, "Maybe you want to go to sleep?"

"Oh, yes," Sheila answered, relieved.

"Are you sure that you don't want anything to eat?"

"No, nothing. I will go to sleep."

"Surely you must have eaten on the airplane…"

"Yes, yes…"

Actually, she had not eaten much on the plane, but she was still not hungry. More importantly, she was afraid of breaching social etiquette on her first day in her new home. In Syria, if her host had really wanted her to eat, she would not let her get away with refusing. Sheila decided that since Mrs. Dayan wasn't pushing too hard, she obviously preferred seeing her off to bed, rather than serving her a meal. So Sheila kept smiling and nodding, all the way to the room that was prepared for her.

She was so tired, she fell asleep almost instantly.

"Sheila, come quickly! Your parents are on the phone!" Nouri called out excitedly.

Wow! They have a phone in the house! Sheila grabbed the unfamiliar device. Back home, the grocery had a phone and so did the school, but very few families had phones. A private family would apply for a phone and wait for years until it came (if ever). In their close-knit community there had been very little need for a phone anyway. No one was allowed to travel and it was easy to knock on someone's door if one wanted to say something. So now Sheila was holding the receiver but was barely able to get a word out.

"Sheila? How are you? How are you feeling?"

"Okay," Sheila answered, quietly. "I'm fine."

"Talk to them," Nouri urged. "Tell them that you are happy."

But Sheila was overwhelmed and her words came out hesitant. Nouri took the phone from her hand and began talking in Arabic, "She is fine. You don't have to worry about her. She is really doing well."

I really am doing well, Sheila noted in surprise. Though there was an awful lot that was new and different, she felt secure and cared for in the Dayan house. After that first refused meal, Nouri and Esther realized that they had better prod her to eat, or else she would starve! So they prodded, with love and warmth, piling food onto her plate and sitting with her until she finished every last bite.

Nouri took her to Hacham Sion's house where she met up with her friends who were staying in his walk-in apartment. A group of Syrian boys — also in America without parents — had been staying in the apartment before the girls came. In keeping with the Maslaton tradition of generous hospitality, Hacham Sion always had guests and freely gave needy people use of his walk-in apartment. He sent away the boys to make way for the girls, but he still invited them for meals on Shabbat when the Maslaton table expanded to make room for everyone.

At the end of Sheila's first day in America, all the married Dayan children piled into the house to meet her. Sheila was moved by their warm welcome and already felt part of a big extended family. Later that evening, Esther casually mentioned that she would be taking her shopping the next day.

"For what?" Sheila asked curiously.

"For clothing," Esther replied.

"But I have two suitcases of clothing," Sheila protested. She was very proud of all the nice things she was able to take out of Syria, unlike other refugees who left with little more than the clothing they wore.

"Sheila, here, pants are for boys. Women wear skirts."

"Oh." Sheila was quiet. She had noticed that none of the female Dayans were wearing pants but she just assumed that that was a matter of taste. She had no idea that it was some kind of policy. *I have one skirt... and 20 pairs of pants!*

"But what about all my pants?"

"Don't worry about anything," Esther reassured her.

The next day Esther took Sheila to 86th Street — the popular Bensonhurst shopping district — and bought her several skirts. She also discreetly disposed of the pants. And rather than feel censured, Sheila felt cared for.

Every day, Nouri asked Sheila, "What can I do for you?"

He wanted her to be happy and not grow homesick for Syria.[32] He often brought home Arabic newspapers or magazines or an Arabic music cassette, little things to cheer her up. Though Sheila attended ESL classes offered by the NYANA and was picking up English quickly, Nouri knew that her rest and relaxation took place in Arabic. Reading, speaking, and thinking in English was still a strain.

Every Tuesday afternoon, Nouri arrived home early. "Come," he told Esther, "we have to take Sheila out." And he would drive down to Atlantic Avenue where there was a large Arabic community and take her to see an Arabic movie. Eventually, they learned that the movie house on Kings Highway brought in Arabic films one day a week, and then he took them there. Nouri waited in the car while Esther accompanied Sheila inside. Indeed, just seeing scenes from Syria and hearing her mother tongue was comforting.

All they want is that I should be happy, reflected Sheila.

Nouri had her call her parents once a week, though it was prohibitively expensive. He even dialed the number. "Talk to them," he insisted, holding out the receiver.

And Sheila would talk.

And Nouri never told her to stop — 2 minutes, 3 minutes, 5 minutes, 10 minutes — these phone calls could cost over $50.[33] And Nouri still urged her to speak, at least once every week.

Even the Dayan married children were part of Sheila's acclimation. They would chauffeur her around Flatbush, so that she could spend time with her friends. Eventually, Esther taught her how to take the busses and subways, but in the beginning, those offers kept her mobile.

"Bring your friends!" both Nouri and Esther urged, constantly.

Sheila truly felt like she was inviting her friends to her own home.

Sheila loved living in the Dayan house. The children and grandchildren were always coming around, engaging her in conversation, making her feel like family. Nouri and Esther never left her alone. They always inquired as to her plans: How long would she be at the NYANA? What

---

32. Two of the girls became so homesick, they went back to Syria. Neither of them married while all the ones who remained in America married and integrated into the broader Syrian community.
33. The 2015 equivalent would be about $158.

Some of the Syrian brides, in the Maslaton home. Top row, L-R: Stella (Jarradah) Farah, Esther (Swed) Gadah, Frial (Reuben) Mann, Charlotte (Hamra) Rahmani. Sitting: Hacham Sion and his wife, Vicky.

would she be doing later in the day? Perhaps she wanted to go shopping, or be with friends?

It seems that the whole house revolves around... me!

There was always so much delicious food — the same *kibbe* and *laham b'Ajeen* (traditional mini meat pies) that she was used to from Syria — piled high onto her plate. Either Esther or Nouri sat with her as she ate, entertaining her with conversation.

"Is there anything that you need?" Nouri asked, constantly.

Anything she needed, she got, often before she said anything. All of this was inordinately comforting. For so many years, Sheila had been shouldering the burden of her family. The failed escape attempt had been her initiative, and much of the family income had come from her work as a hair stylist. Even in America, she worried about her family (her mother had a heart condition, her father was elderly, and her brother might attempt a dangerous escape) and their future in Syria. But she was being pampered in ways she couldn't believe and that was an incredibly rejuvenating experience.

Like a little girl, she thought bemusedly. She was over 30 years old, an old maid by Syrian standards, and yet this comforting cocoon of love made the future seem beyond bright.

Hacham Sion and his wife, Vicky, flank Abe Farah when he married one of the Syrian brides. Each wedding was a community affair.

Sheila and her friends were enthralled with their new lives. Great credit for that went to their hosts. Hacham Sion looked for ways to integrate the girls into the community and keep them happy. When he realized that the girls couldn't read, he organized nightly classes where he personally taught them. He surprised them with candy and encouraged all of them to come to his house for Shabbat. When Sheila wanted to spend time with her friends, she called the Maslaton house as late as Friday morning. "Mrs. Vicky, I want to come for Shabbat day."

"Okay, Sheila, I'm making one more *kibbe* — just for you!"

And Sheila felt wanted and welcome, not just by the Dayans but by the whole Ahi Ezer community. She joined her friends in the Matalon house, and that of "Rabbi Jack," as many of them called Jack Maslaton. She often went to Janet Zalta, that wonderful woman who had been recently widowed and yet welcomed the girls with love and warmth. Janet talked to them about Syria, urging them to teach her how to read Arabic (though in the end, she gave that up), asking them about the customs in their communities and what had changed in America.[34] Many fun-filled evenings were spent in Janet's apartment, where the girls danced to Arabic music and

---

34. This very kind and generous woman married off these girls from her home and continued to serve as their adopted mother and their children's adopted grandmother.

Hacham Sion dancing with Abe Farah

taught their gracious hostess some exotic steps. All in all, welcoming the "Syrian brides," as they were known, was a community affair.

That didn't mean that the girls faced no adjustments. One day, after they finished their classes in the NYANA, Sheila and her friends walked out of the Manhattan building to the most amazing sight: Snow!

They had never seen snow. None of them owned a pair of boots; none of them even knew that boots existed. But they were thrilled with the new experience and laughed in delight as their feet sunk into the wet, white fluff. They boarded their Brooklyn-bound train chattering animatedly, and then stared at the falling flakes from their window seats. By the time the girls got off the train, a foot of snow had fallen. Even as the snow turned into rain, they trudged happily along, entranced by the fallen foam that was becoming slick and slushy.

But then, as they scanned the street for Janet's house, they couldn't find it. They recognized the house not from the number, but from the white chair out on the porch. That day, Janet had moved the chair. The girls just kept walking, in the freezing, wet, slushy snow, laughing as their teeth clattered together, asking one another, "Where is the chair? Where is the house?"

Finally, one of the girls figured out which house was theirs and they walked inside, dripping, freezing, but smiling. Janet was aghast. "Girls, is this how you go out in such weather? No coats, no boots?"

The girls just laughed from sheer happiness.

"Sheila, I know that it's snowing, but it's not good for you to stay indoors. Come, let's go to 85th Street. Maybe we'll buy a newspaper, or a pair of gloves…" Esther suggested, leading Sheila outside. Esther talked easily with her companion, pointing out different things about America that Sheila would contrast with Syria.

Sheila felt so completely a part of the Dayan home, never a burden. Esther, Nouri, their children, and even the grandchildren treated her as if she had always been a part of their home. One day, Nouri took her to the factory on 86th Street and gave her a tour. Another time he took her to the showroom in Manhattan and showed her their displays. He patiently explained to her the different parts of the business. He didn't want her to feel as if there was a part of the Dayan life from which she was excluded.

Sheila lived in the Dayan house for one year. During that time, they not only eased her into American life, they also tried to find her a husband so that she would be truly settled. She was working as a hair stylist in Boro Park — the same profession she had back in Syria — but didn't feel ready to settle down with any of the young men she had met. Perhaps she was too preoccupied thinking about her family back in Syria. She shared her concerns with Nouri, who encouraged her to persuade her parents to apply for exit permits so that her mother could receive medical treatment. Ever since the Syrian brides left, President Assad was more lenient in allowing other Jews to leave as well, apparently pleased with the positive publicity he had received.

A year after Sheila's arrival, her parents left Syria… and came right to the Dayan house. Nouri made a big dinner and invited the whole community to welcome the Kabaritys and celebrate their arrival. Mr. Kabarity was very reserved and overwhelmed by the attention but Nouri coaxed him to become comfortable. For the next month, the Kabaritys stayed in the Dayan home as Nouri helped them acclimate. He took Mr. Kabarity to and from shul, answered his questions patiently and in Arabic, and helped him look for a permanent home. They finally found an apartment on Avenue T, near the growing Syrian community in Flatbush. Until the rent subsidies from the NYANA came through, Nouri paid their rent.

Sheila moved in with her parents, but Nouri and Esther continued to be involved in her life. Sheila turned to Esther as a confidante when she felt down as all the other "Syrian brides" were finding their mates while she, the oldest, remained single. Nouri suggested Jose Freue, his Friday guest and *habruta* for ten years, as a husband for Sheila. When Sheila finally agreed, Nouri was there every step of the way, making sure that she had everything she needed to build a proper Jewish home.

Indeed, the wedding was a community celebration. Bert Chabot and Steve Shalom, two prominent community activists who lobbied for the

Nouri and Esther Dayan, with Sheila and Jose at their engagement

Syrian brides, attended, as did all the "Syrian brides." In an interesting postscript, years later, Sheila's son married Bert Chabot's granddaughter.

The whole Dayan family came. Nouri and Esther walked Jose down the aisle. Meir Levy sang under the *huppah* and Hacham Sion performed the ceremony. Hacham Sion married off many of the girls, tirelessly raising funds on their behalf.

By the end of the wedding, the Freues and the Kabaritys were officially on their own, two families, beginning anew in America. Nouri and Esther stepped respectfully aside, giving everyone room to grow, while clearly letting them know that they were still available for help, advice, and anything else they might need.

Forty years later, Sheila said, "I still feel like Mrs. Dayan is my second mother and her daughters are my adopted sisters. Anything that happens, I call Mrs. Dayan. And if nothing is happening, I call anyway, at least once a week. We all feel like family."

Chapter 57:
"OUR HOME IS YOUR HOME."

Damascus, Syria, September 1977

"Come Sophie, please, take just a little bite," Maxi Salama coaxed his little sister, lying limply in her hospital bed.

Sophie opened her eyes for a moment and, with great effort, also opened her mouth. Maxi put a piece of banana inside. "Just chew a little, doesn't it taste good? And now swallow... that's a good girl."

For two months Sophie had been sick at home until her uncle, a doctor, realized that she belonged in the hospital. But it didn't seem that the hospital stay was helping her get better. Sophie spent most of her day sleeping, almost as if she didn't have the strength to stay awake. The doctors knew that her kidneys were not functioning properly, but they had no idea how to treat her condition. And then, when her vision began to deteriorate, they all but gave up.

But her family didn't. Sophie was one of nine children. Their father had passed away from a heart attack four years earlier but all the siblings rallied around their mother, supporting her and each other with encouragement and support. Daily, the Salama siblings and Marcelle, their mother, came to visit Sophie in the hospital. They refused to abandon her and prayed constantly for her recovery.

Maxi had brought the banana to entice Sophie to eat, knowing that it was her favorite food. Slowly, mouthful by mouthful, Sophie ate the banana and seemed to regain some strength.

The next day Sophie greeted her mother in joyful surprise, "Mama, I can see!"

"My daughter said that today she can see me," Marcelle told the doctor.

The doctor raised his hand. "If my hand can see, then your daughter can see."

Then he proceeded to examine her, and he was shocked to find that she really could see. At that point, he realized that her condition wasn't irreversible and therefore, not hopeless.

"We can't keep her here," he told Marcelle. "With the right treatment, she can live. We must send her to America where they will be able to treat her."

The hospital registered an emergency request with the government to allow Sophie and her mother to travel to America for treatment. When the permit came through, the Jewish community in Syria contacted the Sephardic Bikur Cholim for financial assistance. Very soon, Sophie and her mother were on their way.

Representatives of the Sephardic Bikur Cholim came to the airport to greet Marcelle and Sophie. Sophie was extremely weak and Marcelle was overwhelmed. They were grateful to be driven straight to the home of Mrs. Gita Sultan, a wonderful woman who spoke the same Syrian dialect that they were used to. Dr. Bob Matalon was Mrs. Sultan's son-in-law. He immediately came to the house to check Sophie and assess the situation.

"Critical," Dr. Matalon murmured, "we must get her to a hospital as soon as possible." But there were still arrangements that had to be made. Meanwhile Marcelle and Sophie were made most comfortable by Gita Sultan, who had warm memories of life in Syria and was happy to share them with her guests.

"But it's really not the best place for them," Dr. Matalon explained to Nouri two days later. "It would be much better if they could stay at your house, where both you and your wife will be better at navigating the hospital instructions, speaking to the doctors, and just getting around."

Nouri arrived at the Sultan house later that day and, very gently, asked Marcelle to come to his house. "I want you to stay with us. We speak Arabic. You will be comfortable by us."

Marcelle became very nervous. *What is happening? Mrs. Sultan also knows Arabic, why is she sending us away after only two days? And what will happen after that? Will we be kicked out after another two days?* With no alternative in sight, Marcelle packed their belongings and went with Sophie to Mrs. Dayan's car, apprehensive and confused.

Then she walked into the Dayan house.

Esther Dayan stood up as Marcelle entered and walked forward as she spoke, "Welcome! You are now a part of our family. Don't be nervous. Come, let me show you to your room. Here, you may do whatever you feel like. Our home is your home." Then she hugged and kissed Sophie, with warmth and love.

All Marcelle's fears dissipated into nothingness.

She felt like she had come home.

Shortly thereafter, Sophie was admitted into the hospital. They performed an operation and, for the first night, Marcelle slept in her room. Later, volunteers from the Sephardic Bikur Cholim showed Marcelle where there was a special room where she could rest at night. Meanwhile, there was already a steady stream of visitors, but few were as constant as Nouri Dayan.

"Sophie," he called out joyfully, "how are you feeling? Tell me, what should I tell the doctor? Does anything hurt you? Look what I brought you." He rummaged into his pockets and brought out a trinket. "Do you like it?"

Then he turned to Marcelle and discussed with her how Sophie passed the night, what he should tell the doctors, and how else could he help her. He never came empty-handed, but it was his sunny optimism and encouraging words that were the greatest gifts. As usual, the Dayan children were also part of the picture. They also took turns coming down to Manhattan and offered to stay with Sophie so that Marcelle could get some rest. They also offered to pick up anything they needed or to speak to the doctors. Marcelle was always grateful when people who spoke Arabic would come. When she had no one around to interpret for her, she felt very lost. She was grateful that her original hostess, Gita Sultan, came almost every day.

Marcelle and Sophie came to America during Hanuka. Around that time of year, Nouri and Esther often went to Florida for a week of vacation. This had been scheduled weeks before they knew that they would be having live-in guests. One day, Nouri appeared at the hospital dangling a set of keys.

"We are going to Florida for a few days, but don't worry, here are the keys to the house. Our home is your home. As soon as you are discharged, you will stay there. Take whatever you want from the fridge and cabinets. Do whatever makes you comfortable. And before you turn around, we will be back home."

Indeed, Sophie was discharged while the Dayans were in Florida. The doctors had started her on a potassium-based treatment and they wanted her to stay in America to monitor her progress. Marcelle and her daughter went straight to the Dayan home and made themselves comfortable, as per their instructions. The Dayans had asked their children and community members to pop in on their guests and make sure that they had whatever they needed. Some of the Syrian brides came regularly, bringing them food and company.

The weeks that Marcelle spent in the Dayan house with Nouri and Esther made a most lasting impression. Marcelle had grown up in Syria of the 1940's. She had only hazy memories of what it was like prior to 1948 when much of the community had fled and when those who remained became virtual prisoners. She only had vague recollections of revered *hachamim*; the new generation was different — more Western, less religiously educated.

She had never met anyone like Nouri.

The first time she woke up at 3 in the morning and heard Nouri learning at the dining-room table, she thought she was dreaming. She peered into the room curiously: It was pitch black and silent outside, there was one light illuminating the dining room, and Nouri was fully dressed, swaying back and forth over a *sefer*, chanting. The room seemed suffused with holiness.

She went back to sleep… and woke up confused, unsure that the scene that she remembered so vividly really happened. The next night was the same, as was the next. Marcelle realized that this was how Nouri started his day, every day. For several hours before his 6 a.m. *minyan*, he learned. Then he dashed out to prayers before returning to begin his day.

"Sophie," he called out, as he walked into the house, "where are you?"

Sophie ran into the room, beaming. The young child never really knew her father, who had passed away when she was 5 years old. Nouri treated her like one of his own and she basked in his warmth.

"Come eat," he instructed her, pulling out some of the fresh rolls and danishes that he bought for breakfast. Everyone ate together — Nouri and Esther, Marcelle and Sophie — like one happy family.

Friday morning, Nouri brought the spirit of Shabbat home with him, right in the beginning of the day. As soon as he came through the door, he began his Shabbat preparations, always including Sophie.

"Come Sophie, do you know what day it's today? It's Erev Shabbat. Let us prepare for Shabbat together." He cleared off the table, spread out a white tablecloth, and put out the *halla* that he had just brought home from the bakery. Together, they took out the plates and the cutlery, with Nouri talking to her about Shabbat as they set the table. "Before I leave for work, I want the house ready *lichbod Shabbat*, and you are my helper!" Sophie felt honored and privileged.

Shabbat morning, after waking up way before the sun, Nouri walked to Flatbush, to the new shul, rain or shine, snow or sleet. By the time he returned, it was 12 in the afternoon, but that was fine; his uplifting *seuda* was worth the wait.

The weeks that Marcelle and Sophie spent in the Dayan home were incongruous in their contrasts. On the one hand, Sophie was ill and had to return to the hospital twice a week for monitoring. On the other hand, she had more energy and life than she had had in months. The treatments were helping her and everyone was hopeful that she would experience a full recovery. This good news was tempered by uncertainty. Marcelle worried about the eight children she had left behind in Syria. The oldest was a 19-year-old boy, but some of the children beneath him were quite young. They had no father and, with their mother in America, they had no mother.

Living with the Dayans was an uplifting experience, one that Marcelle would never forget, yet uncertainty about the future was her constant companion, especially when the doctors informed her that no matter how well Sophie was responding to the treatment, ultimately she needed a kidney transplant as soon as possible.

The community began a drive to search for a suitable kidney. The most logical match would have been one of Sophie's eight siblings, but they were trapped in Syria. People who came for medical treatment had to leave their children as collateral. Despite numerous appeals that they receive permission to leave based on a medical need, their applications were consistently turned down. The Sephardic Bikur Cholim used all their connections both in America and overseas but, as the weeks progressed, there was no progress.

I have to return home, Marcelle realized one day, with complete clarity. It was wonderful to be in the Dayan home where she was able to devote herself totally to her ill daughter, but she had a houseful of children at home and they also needed her.

"If she does not have a kidney transplant within six months, she will die," warned the doctors. Marcelle was torn. There was no kidney donor in America. And there was no doctor or facility in Syria that knew how to perform such a procedure, even if one of the siblings would be a match. Was she supposed to stay in America and wait for a donor? What about her children back in Syria?

Armed with several months' worth of medication, Marcelle felt she had little choice but to return with Sophie to Syria.

The other Salama children greeted them with warmth and happiness. They were so grateful that their mother and sister were back. They were so excited that Sophie looked so strong and healthy. They hoped that if they continued pressuring the government they would receive the proper permit to fly Sophie and her siblings to America for the transplant operation.

The weeks dragged. The government red tape was impossible to get through.

The American medicine ran out. Sophie grew weaker.

"Our sister is dying," Rachel Salama angrily told the doctor when they admitted Sophie into the hospital. "Can't you do something?"

The doctor shrugged.

Marcelle and her children stayed at Sophie's hospital bed, day in and day out, watching her grow weaker by the hour. At some point they realized that even if the permits would come through, she was far too weak to travel. There was nothing they could do but whisper words of love and comfort as they watched her slip away.

After the funeral, the Salamas returned home, brokenhearted. Sweet Sophie was gone, and they wondered if they could have saved her had they pushed harder. They were angry at the government that was holding them hostage, that would rather they die in Syria than live anywhere else in the world. They were frustrated with their lives and wondered when they would be free from the invisible shackles imprisoning them in Syria. They prayed for freedom and a better Jewish life on brighter shores.

Back in America, the Syrian community was devastated to hear about Sophie's death. So many people had rallied around the little girl. So many people were touched by her fragile sweetness.

They were also frustrated.

Sophie had been doing so well in America. The doctors had been hopeful that she could live a normal and productive life if she would just receive a healthy kidney. By not allowing the Salama siblings to come to America to be tested, the Syrian government had essentially signed her death certificate. How dare they treat Jewish lives so callously?

Though the Syrian brides had been very vocal and descriptive in recounting their prison-like existence in Syria, Sophie's story brought the reality to the Syrian community in a much more vivid fashion. The advocacy that they had begun when they championed the proxy bride arrangement had to be continued. Syrian Jews had no future in Syria, and if their fellow Jews in America would not advocate for them, who else would? Syrian Jewry in America had a responsibility to help their brothers get out of Syria. It would take many years of prayers and tears and political activism for that to happen.

Nouri's "my home is your home" motto extended beyond his house. Everything he had — his time, his money, his possessions — he was ready to give to his fellow Jew in an instant.

"Rabbi Cohen" was visiting from Israel and praying in Ahi Ezer. When he finished, he went to look for his coat in the coatroom. To his dismay, it was gone.

Someone must have mistaken it for his own and taken it, sighed Rabbi Cohen.

Nouri walked in and understood what had happened.

"Here," he said, taking out $100, "go buy yourself a new coat."

No amount of protesting would convince Nouri to take the money back. The man needed a coat, did he not?

"Yes?" answered Carol Shapiro, the secretary in Ahi Ezer Yeshiva.

"This is Tom from the Bank of New York. I'm reviewing your application for a mortgage on the summer home that you want to purchase in Upstate New York."

"Oh, thank you for getting back to me. This has really been schlepping for a while. What interest rate can you give us?"

Nouri popped into the office just as Carol was ending her conversation.

"What kind of bank is calling you?" he asked, curiously.

"We need a mortgage for the summer cabin that we'd like to buy. It's not a big house, but we still need a mortgage to pay for it."

"What rate are they giving you?"

Carol rattled off a figure. Nouri nodded and started to leave. As he reached the door, he stopped. "Listen," he said, "I'll give you the money. We'll work out a schedule. You'll pay back a little at a time, but you won't have to pay that big interest." And as he walked out the door, he stuck his head back inside, "But don't ask for a raise!"

Carol laughed out loud. *How like Mr. Dayan. He wants to help me, he wants to help everyone! But don't ask for a raise because the yeshiva comes first.*

Carol Shapiro loved working in Ahi Ezer Yeshiva. In the late 70's the yeshiva was growing so fast that they didn't know where to put the kids. There was a boys' principal, a girls' principal, assistant principals and loads of teachers — and no one wanted to leave Ahi Ezer. There were faculty members who had been with the school since its founding and had no intention of moving, and others who stayed in Ahi Ezer for many years, including Mrs. Shulamit Fedder, Mrs. Toby Teitelbaum, and Mrs. Batsheva Grama. Other prominent figures in the world of Jewish education, such as Rabbi Yehuda Oelbaum (later principal of Machon High School for Girls) and Rabbi Yeruchem Shapiro (later administrator of Bais Yaakov of Boro Park elementary school) got their start in Ahi Ezer.

It was simply a positive place to work in.

And one of the most positive people around was Mr. Dayan.

Mr. Dayan wasn't involved in the day-to-day running of the school, but if anything came up and his opinion was needed, he came running. He also stopped by every once in a while, just to see how things were going. Rather than be nervous or intimidated that "the boss" was coming, the staff of the yeshiva loved him.

A gentleman from A-Z, marveled Carol. In all her many years of working for Ahi Ezer institutions, she never heard him be disrespectful to a worker, or a parent, or a child, no matter how obnoxious or disrespectful the other person might have acted. And if he had to censure someone, he was so diplomatic, often the person didn't realize that he was rebuked until a few hours later!

His clear concern for every Jew — the students of the yeshiva, their parents, the faculty — endeared him to everyone and made him the natural address to go to for any problem. Nonetheless, one of his greatest gifts was being able to anticipate a problem even before people came to him.

Such was the case with the Ahi Ezer Senior Housing Project.

Chapter 58:

"IF THESE BUILDINGS EVER GET BUILT, IT WILL BE ONLY THROUGH DIVINE PROVIDENCE."

With all the projects that Nouri was involved in, the establishment of the senior citizen homes was probably the most ambitious and innovative project he ever took on.

The idea was the brainchild of Rabbi Wolf and was brilliant on many fronts. The community had many elderly residents who were lonely; the social activities in the 71st Street building took up only a small fraction of their day. Some couldn't afford to move near their children in Flatbush. Some were becoming lonely and depressed living on their own. By reconstructing the Ahi Ezer apartment buildings to fit many small units, they would create a mini-village, with tens of seniors living under one roof. The seniors would have a social structure simply by being together, by seeing each other at mealtimes, during activities, or as they hung around in the large lobby. The apartments would be affordable since they were sponsored by HUD. Ahi Ezer would earn a profit through management of the buildings and those profits would be funneled back into the yeshiva. It was a winning proposition from all directions.

Not surprisingly, something so good came with many obstacles.

In order to move forward with their plans, Ahi Ezer had to revamp the buildings, build a floor where there would be an inviting lobby, a lunchroom, offices, and a kitchen. They wanted to redesign each floor so that the hallways, which would be tastefully painted, would lead into modernized units, reconstructed to fit in as many units as possible while still giving the seniors enough living space. They needed to install elevators and emergency exits. Each building needed major construction.

The main obstacle: All three Ahi Ezer apartment buildings were rent-controlled. People had lived in these apartments for many years, paid very low rent, and couldn't be evicted without a court order, something that Ahi Ezer wanted to avoid if possible. But why would anyone want to leave a rent-controlled building?

So began the battle that took several years and much aggravation.

First, the tenants were approached with incentives to leave and there were those people who took a stipend and moved. The majority wanted to fight it out. They felt that, in the long run, they were unlikely to find similar apartments in the price bracket they were paying. Even if the stipend paid for a year's rent, at some point that would not make up for the low rents they were now paying. They stood smugly firm: If the new owners wanted to evict them, let them get a court order.

Every day, there was another story.

A woman who was very vocal riled up all the tenants.

"If we all refuse to leave, they won't be able to get us out," she urged them.

Just before Yom Kippur, the tenants hung up a huge white sheet on the fire escape of the building, stating in bold black letters: **The Jews are kicking us out!** They chose Yom Kippur purposely for they knew that that was a day that the shuls were packed and, being that the buildings were right near several shuls (Ahi Ezer among them), they knew that their sign would be seen instantly and would shake people up.

Everyone walking out of shul saw the sheet.

Jewish guilt kicked in and people began bombarding Nouri.

"Izzy, come on, how can we do this? Kicking old people out of their apartments?"

"Mr. Dayan, is it true that we are evicting these people?"

Nouri kept his cool, as usual, but he was very upset. The signs were designed to embarrass Ahi Ezer and goad them into backing off. He knew that he wasn't doing anything wrong, but at the time, anything he would say would come out bad. So he just kept quiet.

One tenant came to Nouri's house brandishing a shovel. "You are digging my grave! That is what you are doing to me!"

Nouri just kept quiet.

Every encounter was difficult. Nouri was a gentle soul and he knew that he was doing this to help the community, but when he was being painted as a brutal person who was kicking old people out of their homes, it hurt.

"We are *l'shem Shamayim*," Nouri told Marvin Azrak. "When one is working for the sake of Heaven, he does not have to worry about what everyone else says or thinks." This had been his motto when he began Ahi Ezer Yeshiva and through all the years of its growth. Many times, Nouri faced opposition to his projects or ideas. There were always different opinions of how to do things and people didn't always state their opinions in the nicest of ways. But when it came to evacuating these buildings, he was going to war against tens of people, each with their own arguments, agendas, and methods. Even though Nouri wasn't involved with the actual day-to-day negotiations with the tenants, they knew that he was the man at the top and they let him know that they were going to fight him to the end.

"Divine Providence," Esther would sigh. "If these buildings ever get built, it will be only through Divine Providence. There is just no other way."

Finally, Nouri went to court.

Judge Miller listened to all the arguments. She understood that Ahi Ezer was trying to provide a community service — and had government approval to do so — but were being fought by the tenants who had only their own needs in mind. She issued a court order giving the tenants six months to move out.

Did that end the heckling and harassment? Not at all. But it did make the ultimate evacuation of the building possible.

Once the buildings were empty, then came the next phases: design and construction, fundraising to finance these changes, management and planning. Nouri found able assistance from Bunny Escava, who was quick to cosign a loan or provide one if necessary, and Ceasar Salama, who put his heart and soul into seeing the Senior Homes become a reality. When the homes were finally ready, Ceasar was the one who processed the applications, a job no one had dreamed would be so difficult or politically charged.

While the homes were in their planning stage, there was veiled interest, but no one was demanding admittance or even concerned that it might not happen. The prevailing attitude was: Let them finish building the homes and then I will decide if I want to join or not. By the time the buildings were finished, there was enormous interest, and far more applicants than available apartments.

This became another area of aggravation: Who should they admit? An elderly widow really needs the apartment but she applied late and is not affiliated with Ahi Ezer. Should she take priority over an Ahi Ezer congregant who is not as needy? A man just had a stroke and can no longer live in his house because he needs an elevator. His wife is well and mobile, and with a full-time aide the couple can be independent in a ground-floor apartment. Should they have priority over someone who applied earlier but does not have these issues?[35]

---

35. With all the people trying to get into the Senior Center, there were always those who belonged there but were reluctant to make the move. Mr. Dayan knew of someone who needed this type of housing and program but was hesitant. He persuaded her to move in. Years later, this woman praised Mr. Dayan at every opportunity. Had she not moved then, she would have been very alone in her old age.

And when the final decisions were in, then came more aggravation... from the people who didn't get apartments, from the people who didn't get the apartments they wanted, from the people who were angry that they were not near their friends. While they first aired their complaints with those directly in charge, they also cornered Nouri — in shul after prayers, in the office of the Senior Homes where he would pop in every so often, or in the street when they happened to pass him by.

One woman consistently pestered him when he came to the Senior Homes. Over and over, she repeated her complaint, which was somewhat valid, but couldn't be helped. One day, Nouri finally answered her, "You are correct, we made a mistake." Then he paused. "Sometimes, when we read from the Torah, we find a mistake..."

He paused again, and the woman struggled to understand what he was trying to say. "Even a *Sefer Torah* can have a mistake..."

The woman looked startled, but she accepted his answer and even repeated it to others. If a *Sefer Torah* can have a mistake, so can we.

But the complaints continued. Nouri would try to help people out but, most often, he remained quiet. Many complaints had no solutions. There simply were not enough apartments and, no, not everyone could have the exact apartment that he wanted. Irwin marveled at his father's patience, especially since the complaints never came with praise. No one was running to say, "Wow, Mr. Dayan, these Senior Homes are great!" No one was keeping track of how many unpaid, selfless hours Nouri had given to see the homes become a reality.

Yet Nouri took it all in stride, and still looked at how to make the Senior Homes even better. At the board meetings, he asked partners for new ideas. He was ever aware that everything he accomplished wasn't his own, but was dependent on all the people who assisted him with their inspiration, time, and energy. He credited Rabbi Wolf with coming up with the idea of the Senior Center and then all his fellow volunteers for helping to get it off the ground.

For years the 71st Street Senior Center (which had not provided housing) ran a government lunch program which they now transferred to the homes so that all the seniors would have at least one hot and nourishing meal a day. Though they all had their own kitchens, some of the seniors had very meager incomes. Among those who could easily afford to cook themselves a proper meal, some didn't have the gumption or the energy. This was a known problem in the senior population, where many elderly people ate improperly or skipped meals. Yet when they sat around the tables with their friends and were served a fresh, hot meal, they ate with hearty appetites.

This became the hallmark of the Senior Homes: They provided seniors with an environment conducive to living happy, healthy, and productive lives. The Senior Homes offered outings and activities as outlets for their residents. They put in a fish tank in one of the lobbies because they felt it would be a relaxing diversion.

As the community took notice of the wonderful service that Ahi Ezer was providing, others wanted a share in this mitzva. Nathan Mezrahi of Seuda Catering began donating a full meal, every Shabbat, so that all the seniors had a proper Shabbat evening meal in a festive atmosphere. Local boys would pop in to make Kiddush for the residents. This spirit of devotion and volunteerism was the spirit that Nouri and Dave had modeled and cultivated for years. Devotion to the Klal often turned into devotion to Hashem. It became the flip side of the same coin, a brighter, more polished coin than the original.

Ezra Dayan was learning in Yeshivas Rabbeinu Chaim Berlin when he was called to the pay phone one day. It was Marvin Azrak and he wanted the young *bachur* to be the *hazzan* at one of the *minyanim* in Ahi Ezer of Ocean Parkway for Rosh Hashanah and Yom Kippur. Ezra wasn't overly excited.

"I'll think about it," was his noncommittal answer.

I would not normally daven there for the Yamim No'raim... if I do it this year, I would like to be paid, like any other hazzan...

When Ezra told Marvin his reservations, Marvin decided that Ezra had a valid point and he agreed to pay him. Ezra was thrilled. A little while later, he was called to the yeshiva pay phone again.

"Grandpa?"

"Yes."

"Hi. What is going on?" Ezra asked, bewildered.

"I want to ask you something. Did I ever take a dime from the shul?"

Ezra was speechless.

"Did you ever see me take money from the shul?" Nouri demanded. "You have to give to the shul, not take from the shul. Money that is meant for you, will get to you. Why squeeze the shul? Hashem will send you what you need from a different funnel."

Ezra was humbled.

Few people could match Nouri's devotion to the Klal.

Nouri could be seen in the offices of the shul, the Senior Homes, and the yeshiva all in the same day. When did he have time for his business?

"He just manages to do in two hours, what others would do in a whole day," was Esther's explanation. Nouri's job was the financial and mathematical end of the business, areas in which he was exceptionally talented. Even if he came into the office an hour or two late, he always managed to take care of all his duties in record time.

He rarely went on business trips — that was more Dave Bibi's line — but when he did go, he and Dave would typically seek out the local Jewish community and see if there was anything that they could help them with.

Hacham Sion giving a class

That was how they got the Persian *Sefer Torah*.

Dave Bibi heard that Iran was a good place to pick up bargains for the gift department. He decided that it was worth a trip and he asked Nouri to come along with him. Upon arriving there, they sought out the local shul in order to pray with a *minyan*.

The Jews of Iran were known as *Farsi* — Persian — after the old name of the country. The Persian community was living in prosperity and freedom but, with the burgeoning revolutionary movement, that life seemed tenuous.[36] One of the community members approached Nouri and Dave and quietly asked them if there was any way they could take a *Sefer Torah* with them out of the country. As Nouri and Dave toured various factories and made a few orders, they thought about the *Sefer Torah*. From a business angle, the trip was a bit of a disappointment. The biggest bargain of all was the *Sefer Torah*, which they successfully hid among their merchandise and smuggled to America.

When it arrived, Nouri had it assessed and fixed up, and then he looked for someone who would use it. He found Rabbi Sammy Kassin, who

---

36. Mohammad Reza Shah, ruler of Iran in 1948, was officially against the Jewish State, but actually had a good relationship with Israel and with the Jews living in Iran. Iranian Jewry experienced unprecedented prosperity and freedom under the leadership of the Shah (1941-1978). When the Shah was overthrown in 1979, he was replaced by virulently anti-Semitic Ayatollah Khomeini, and Jewish life in Iran became drastically worse.

was running a Rabbinic training program geared to the Sephardic community. The program was organized as a Kollel in the Old City and required the participants to become proficient in many areas of Rabbinical expertise: *mila, shehita, safrut*, etc. His goal was to train qualified men and then send them off to far-flung cities that had Jews of Sephardic descent but no Sephardic Rabbis. The Kollel was still in its early years and Rabbi Kassin was grateful for the donated *Sefer Torah*.

By the end of the 1970's, the change in the Sephardic community was undeniable. Slowly, subtly, over time, the community had simply turned more religious. For Mr. Alan Saka, it began when Jackie Falik convinced him to attend Hacham Sion's class in *Hok l'Yisrael* that took place right after prayers.

Hacham Yosef Harari Raful, as a young man

It is so thoughtful of Hacham Sion to accommodate my presence by translating everything into English, marveled Alan to himself. *He didn't ask me if I understood what was going on, he just changed his method on the spot*. For Alan, that split-second shift was what kept him coming to class. The class took only 10 minutes. But 10 minutes a day for ten years adds up.

There were hundreds of Sephardic children attending yeshivot. Ahi Ezer Yeshiva was bursting. With over 1,200 students (800 in the Avenue X building and 400 in the Brighton Beach building), Ahi Ezer was one of the largest Jewish educational institutions in the country. Magen David had also picked up, and there were more children attending Ashkenaz yeshivot as well. Boys who wanted to go to post-high school yeshivot, rather than attend college, still faced a battle, but more boys were "going to battle" than ever before. The same applied to those opting to learn in Kollel.

A quiet revolution was occurring.

Nouri's son-in-law, Hacham Yosef Harari Raful, was a tremendous force in this quiet revolution.

Back in the late 60's, while he was teaching in Flatbush Yeshiva, Hacham Yosef was giving *shiurim* in Young Sha'arei Zion. Even as he was accomplishing so much in America, he yearned for Eretz Yisrael. Just when he was up for Sabbatical from Flatbush Yeshiva, he was offered a position

Rabbi Avigdor Miller (sitting, wearing a dark suit), with *talmidim*. To his left is Sammy Chamoula, an Egyptian immigrant who credited Rabbi Miller for his spiritual growth, and Nouri Dayan for starting him off in business with a large, interest-free loan, just when he needed it.

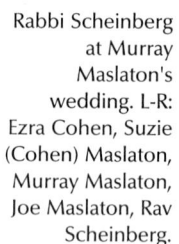

Rabbi Scheinberg at Murray Maslaton's wedding. L-R: Ezra Cohen, Suzie (Cohen) Maslaton, Murray Maslaton, Joe Maslaton, Rav Scheinberg.

Some "outsiders" who had a unique effect on the community include Rabbi Chaim Pinchas Scheinberg, whose yeshiva in Bensonhurst was a magnet for some of the Sephardic youth in the 1960's, and Rabbi Avigdor Miller, whose Thursday night *shiur* attracted a huge following for over thirty years.

that was hard to refuse. He had learned as a young man in Yeshivat Porat Yosef and now his Rabbanim were inviting him to join as one of the Roshei Yeshiva, where he would serve alongside his old friend and *habruta* Hacham Shalom Cohen, another rising star in the Sephardic world. The offer came just when he had a full year off, with a paid salary. He and Carol bought tickets and packed up for the trip. The kids were excited.

One of the boys couldn't stop telling all his friends about the upcoming move, until they began teasing him that he was making it up.

Meanwhile, Hacham Yosef's loyal followers in Young Sha'arei Zion were dismayed. The *mitpallelim* recognized that under his leadership they were changing, and they were scared that if he left they would lose the learning momentum that had been steadily growing. They had offered him a large salary to stay, but he still refused. The night before the Rafuls were scheduled to leave, at the *seudat preida* that the *talmidim* organized for their Rabbi, they begged him once more.

This time, Hacham Yosef answered differently than before. "If you are willing to accept me as your leader, to conform to everything I will demand from you, which will be quite different from what you expect, then I will remain. I will dedicate myself to you completely, but you must follow me completely as well."

The next morning, his *talmidim* returned to his home. They were willing to accept everything he said, unconditionally, if only he would stay.

Hacham Yosef canceled his tickets and became their leader.

Hacham Yosef's main vision was to create Sephardic *talmidei hachamim* and *bnei Torah* from within the community. He wanted to overturn the pervasive mentality that learning Gemara was too difficult and *Hok l'Yisrael* was enough. He wanted to recreate the community through Torah learning.

The Sephardic community was changing, for many reasons.

Not everyone credited a specific person or incident that became their turning point; it was just the atmosphere in the community. There was more learning, more attention to *shemirat Shabbat*, more *hesed*, and simply more of a desire to keep Judaism at the center of one's life. The subtle changes in atmosphere and attitude would continue to influence the community… which was poised for even greater change entering the 80's and 90's.

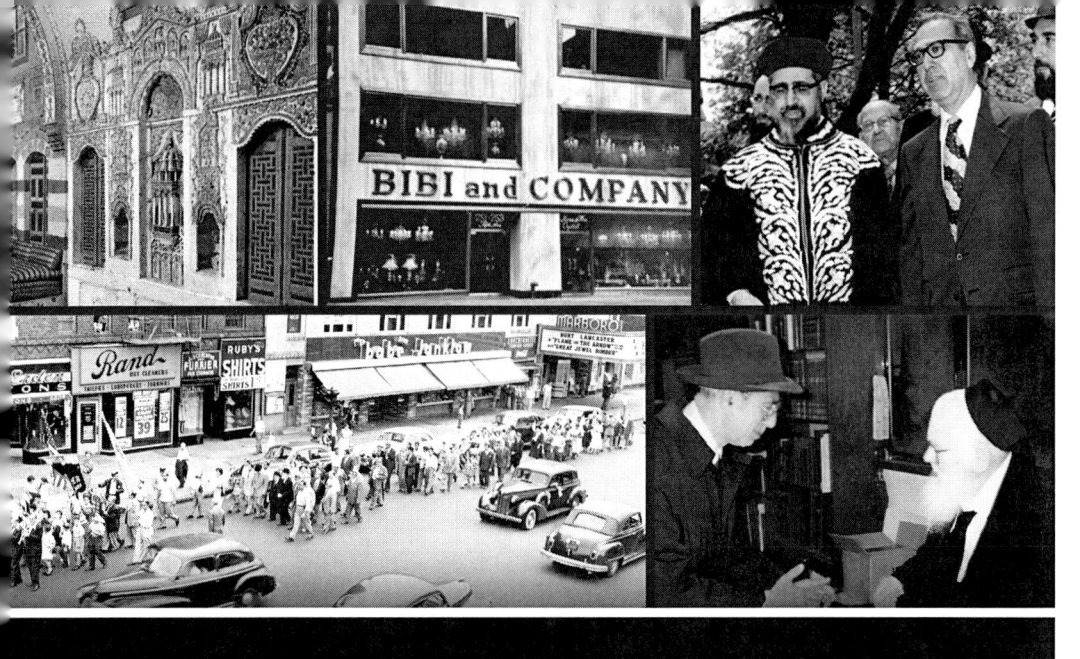

PART VII

Chapter 59:

"HOW CAN I EMULATE AN ANGEL?"

Bensonhurst, 1980

Nouri looked around the 71st Street shul and sighed. They still had regular *minyanim*, but they consisted mainly of elderly men. Irwin was the only Dayan child who still lived in Bensonhurst. Joey, newly married, had moved to Flatbush, where most of his siblings and friends had already settled. For six years Nouri had been walking from Bensonhurst to Flatbush every Shabbat morning. For six years, he had been preparing Sunday morning breakfasts for both shuls. For six years, he had been dividing himself between the two neighborhoods, and he would continue doing so, only differently.

It's time to move on, Nouri decided.

He reluctantly gave Esther the job of looking for an apartment in Flatbush.

Esther had no need for a large house. The children were married and they were not hosting nearly the amounts of guests that they had once hosted. She wasn't looking for something fancy; luxuries had never been an attraction for her or for Nouri. The apartment had to be near the shul on Avenue S and Ocean Parkway, and convenient for visitors. She nixed a corner house on Avenue R because there was an island in the middle of the street that made parking nearby difficult.

"How can I live on a street where my visitors will find it difficult to park?" she told Carol. So they settled on an apartment around the corner, on E. 13th Street between Avenues S and T.

And Nouri continued to travel, only now he drove from Flatbush to Bensonhurst during the week to bolster the 71st Street shul rather than

Nouri and Esther in their new home

walking from Bensonhurst to Flatbush on Shabbat day to pray in Ahi Ezer of Ocean Parkway.

The next change was far more traumatic.

Reuben Bibi passed away.

He was lauded for his years of service as Ahi Ezer's treasurer, and his loyal presence in the shul, not only through the week, but every Erev Shabbat when he assisted Hacham Sion as he checked the *Sefer Torah* that was to be used for that week's reading. He had been a comforting personality, an attentive listener who gave wise advice and artfully kept the peace. Without drum rolls, without honor, without glory, he strove to be a humble servant of Hashem.

Once again, Nouri was in that indefinable position of having lost a parental figure who was, nonetheless, not his parent. Uncle Ruby and Aunt Esther gave Nouri a home and a family. They walked him down the aisle at his wedding. Their older children were like his siblings and their younger children were like his nephews and nieces. They were like grandparents to Nouri's children.

Nouri was devoted to his aunt and uncle, not any less than a biological child. He visited regularly and kept them up-to-date about his life and the lives of his children. Through their shared confidences, they remained close. And, of course, he came to shave his uncle regularly, practically up to his last day on this world. None of this devotion was enough for Nouri.

He was heartbroken when his uncle passed away. He would miss his solid presence but, even more important to Nouri, he could no longer repay Uncle Ruby for taking him in as a child.

"I owe everything that I have — everything that I am — to the Bibi family," he repeated. "There is no way I can ever repay them for their kindness to me."

That was how he felt fifty years earlier, when they took him in.

That was how he felt for the rest of his life.

After Uncle Reuben's passing, Nouri continued his Thursday evening visits to his aunt and took care of her finances. He recommended that every year she should gift at least $3,000 to each child in order not to pay taxes on the money. She began an annual tradition of giving out these funds at a gala Hanuka party that she threw for the family, and Nouri would distribute the checks to his cousins. While Nouri clearly considered himself a son, he never assumed that any of the money was coming to him, not even a token sum for being the family accountant.

"I'm honored to do it," Nouri explained to his children. "She is the mother that I never had."

One year, when the sums were particularly high — $10,000 a child — Aunt Esther insisted that Nouri take a share for himself, which he did, because he saw that she really wanted him to have it. But where he was concerned, she owed him nothing.

The impossible-to-repay debt belonged only to him.[1]

Nouri's relationship with Dave Bibi was more like that of a younger brother to an older brother rather than that of a son to a father. However, Nouri added an unusual measure of respect to that equation. In all their years as equal business partners, Dave remained "the boss"; Nouri deferred to him completely, even as Dave handed more duties over to Nouri.

Dave was used to running the business. It was his vision, his creativity, and his savvy sense of what would or would not sell that turned Bibi Continental into one of the biggest players in the lighting industry. Even as he grew tired of the nitty-gritty work, he wasn't ready to step aside. He began his workday by giving Nouri a list of instructions, which Nouri dutifully took down with utmost respect. It never dawned on him that at 63 years old, and having been in the business for over forty years, he had enough expertise to decide for himself how he wanted to organize his day.

Nouri waited for direction from his uncle, not because he didn't have the confidence to make his own decisions, but because he revered his uncle

---

1. "Though his relationship with her was different, my father was just as solicitous to his other aunt/sister-in-law, Rebecca Bibi. He balanced her checkbook as well and sold her house for her when she decided to move into the Senior Citizen Center," commented Mr. Irwin Dayan.

for taking him under his wing and for guiding him. The fact that they were only eight years apart was irrelevant: Dave was his role model, his mentor, his older brother, and his boss — forever. After Dave finished giving over his instructions, he disappeared into the gift department while Nouri implemented that day's agenda.

The lighting industry had developed and changed over the years.

Whereas forty years earlier, chandeliers and lamps dominated the market, now each of those items commanded a market of its own. There were seemingly endless lighting products: indoor fixtures that were meant only to maximize light and minimize electricity without adding anything to the décor of the room, decorative indoor lighting, ceiling fans that were lighting with a twist, outdoor lanterns that ranged in styles, and much more.

To accommodate that growth, the industry leaders changed their center to Dallas, where Bibi Continental rented an enormous showroom — far bigger than the Statler Hilton in Manhattan — to display its merchandise. For the Grand Opening, Dave and Nouri went to Dallas and even imported an entire luncheon from Bernstein's on Essex Street. After that, Irwin and two sales managers went down twice a year for industry shows, when the owners of large lighting stores came to survey the merchandise and place big orders. In addition, Bibi Continental had salesmen all over the country who sold through catalogues to the "Mom and Pop" stores. They also expanded their retail department by opening a chain of stores in the New York area called Sunday Lighting (so-called because they were open on Sunday, but never on Saturday).

For both Dave and Nouri, the business continued to be a venue to help others. Everyone knew that if a new synagogue was being built, just call "Bibi" and they will come down, explain to you exactly what type of lighting would best suit the décor of the building, give you a choice of styles, and either donate it or sell it at cost price, including installation.[2] If someone in the family was getting married, the young couple just came down to "Bibi" and picked out a pretty chandelier, a whimsical lamp, or anything else that they needed.

When Barbara Ozeirey realized that she would be hosting Hacham Ovadya Yosef in her home, she was embarrassed that her furnishings were so plain.

"Daddy, what can I do to spruce up this place? Hacham Ovadya is coming!"

That same day, a new coffee table and some lamps were delivered to her door, courtesy of Bibi Continental.

---

[2]. Among the many synagogues that are lit by "Bibi" chandeliers are: Magen David of West Deal, Sha'arei Shalom, Mikdash Melech, and Ateret Torah. Mr. Dayan even shipped chandeliers to a synagogue in Mexico!

Nouri and Dave saw nothing wrong with making community-related phone calls from the business, or discussing similar topics during business hours. If Nouri received a phone call from one of his "partners" from the community, all the secretaries knew to put the call right through. There was no such thing as answering "he's busy" when it came to community work.

And of course, the *meshulachim* just kept on coming.

Nouri took over the job of distributing the business's charity funds. In fact, Dave and Nouri were community role models of how to give *tzedaka*, when, and to whom. After they handed over the Ner Israel Scholarship Fund to younger people, they began another fund, which they named the Sephardic Scholars Fund. It was meant for local *talmidei hachamim*, similar to the Ezras Torah fund of the Ashkenazim.

Their ability to sense a need and rise to meet it was noted, and many people turned to them for advice: I have a few thousand dollars that I want to give to charity, to whom should I give it? Organization A has been pestering me for a while, is it a good cause? Dave and Nouri dispensed their advice with the same generosity of spirit that characterized all their encounters.

And, as always, they knew that the biggest service to their people would be to help them come closer to G-d.

Joe Torgumen was looking for a loan to start his business. He approached several men in the community who offered him a large loan at 15-20 percent interest. Then he approached Nouri and Dave.

"Are you going to be open on Shabbat?" they asked him.

"Of course," he answered, surprised by the question. "Shabbat is the busiest day of the week."

The two other men looked at each other and then back at him. "We will give you a $50,000 loan, interest free, as long as you close your business on Shabbat."

Joe accepted their terms, and went on to build a successful business. He was also inspired to be more devoted to his religion and eventually became one of the founders of the congregation Sha'arei Shalom.

Nouri and Dave continued to inspire the people around them.

It was never beneath Nouri to do any of the work that he assigned others. If he had finished what he needed to do for the day, but there was other work to be done, he would help out. He would leave early only if he had a specific reason. He was always asking his employees about their families, their health, and their general well-being.

When Nouri saw the secretary stuffing envelopes he told her, "Let me show you a trick…"

What is there to know about stuffing envelopes? wondered the secretary.

"Watch…" Nouri took a stack of ten envelopes, opened them so that the flap stuck out, and set them up in a graduated way so that each pocket was visible. Then he stuffed them, assembly style; moistened the glue, assembly style; sealed them, assembly style. It only saved a few minutes but it was a cute trick that was useful.

More powerful was the humble and self-effacing way that Nouri related to his employees.

And this was how he came across at the yeshiva, at the Senior Homes, and in the shul.

A grandfather many times over, he would give his seat in shul (for which he paid good money) to a much younger person who was new to the neighborhood and seemed lost. Though he had been president of the shul for more than two decades, he was still out in the lobby, late Friday afternoon, carrying piles of *siddurim*, opened to Minha, and organizing late *minyanim* for the men who came running in from their Manhattan businesses. By the 80's, many people had their own sets of *arba minim*, but Nouri was still waiting for the people who didn't, offering his own set to them to make a *beracha*.

"We have to be *mezakeh et harabbim*," Nouri constantly told his family.

Was he not doing just that by founding Ahi Ezer Yeshiva, by organizing *shiurim* in the shul, and by so many of his other projects? Yet he never felt that he had done enough.

"And to conclude," Nouri paused.

It was Yom Kippur at night, the one time each year that he spoke publicly from the pulpit other than to announce the times for *tefilla* or *shiurim*.

"I would like to ask forgiveness from everyone sitting here…" There was shocked silence. Was that Nouri, the president of the shul, choked up as he lowered himself before the congregation that he served with such devotion? "…It's possible that I might have hurt or offended someone… if so, I'm truly sorry…"

The silence lingered, even as Nouri stepped down.

In an era where boldness, confidence, and self-promotion was valued (and humility was out of style),[3] Nouri's sincere appeal awed the congregation. In those years, for one to publicly ask for forgiveness was unheard of and unlikely to command admiration… except when it came from Nouri.

Nouri was no retiring, meek personality, scared of public opinion. He was a leader, not in a bold, dynamic way, but with solid and silent

---

[3]. Practically every one of the many people interviewed mentioned Mr. Dayan's humility. Dr. Isaac Medab, a Lebanese immigrant who served as vice president of Ahi Ezer under Mr. Dayan, was much younger than Mr. Dayan and considered him his mentor, particularly in synagogue leadership. He recalled: "Mr. Dayan used to tell me, 'Call me Nouri.' I would tell him, 'Call me Isaac.' He laughed, 'No, I will call you Dr. Medab and you will call me Nouri.' That was how humble he was."

strength. He was a courageous pioneer, fighting for religion and fighting for his community. When he stood up and pleaded, the congregation was moved and humbled. Though, at the time, it was unlikely that anyone articulated their feelings (that, too, wasn't in style), many years later they would remember Nouri in awe: *A malach, an angel... how can I emulate an angel? But that is what I would like to do... to be like Nouri Dayan, to emulate his nobility, his humility, his love for the Klal, and his love for the Creator.*

An angel.

An apt description.

Wasn't Nouri on a different spiritual plane than those around him?

His accomplishments — both personal and public — seemed unlimited.

And then, one day, his limitations set in. Nouri ended up in the hospital with a debilitating kidney attack that left him writhing in pain and sapped of his strength. His grandson, Ezra, was with him as he lay in bed, the pain obvious on his face. He lowered his ear to his grandfather's lips and heard him whisper, "*Yissurim shel ahaba* (pain that comes from the Almighty's love)." This became Nouri's mantra through the many cycles of pain he was destined to go through.

Once the medicine kicked in, the pain subsided, but Nouri was still very weak. At that point, he summoned Seymour Escava and Marvin Azrak to his bedside.

"You," he pointed to Seymour, "will take over the yeshiva."

"And you," he pointed to Marvin, "will take over the shul."

When Nouri gave over his dual role he was also acknowledging his mortality. A few years earlier, Nouri began to wake up in the middle of the night, very hot, bathed in sweat. He ended up at a cardiologist who never determined the cause of the sweating, but did discover that he had a leaky valve. This doctor believed in treating a leaky valve with medication rather than surgery. Therefore, even before the kidney attack, Nouri already was being treated for a serious medical condition.

The kidney attack was so debilitating, Nouri suddenly realized that he would not always have the physical strength to do everything that he had been doing, and the responsible thing to do was to give over the reins of leadership while he was still around to guide and mold the future leaders. Indeed, he was once again emulating his Uncle Dave, who turned over the presidency of the shul to him so many years before.

At 64, Nouri didn't consider himself elderly, and time would prove that he still had plenty of energy and drive to accomplish. In fact, even in the hospital, he exhibited a determination that belied his weak state.

Marvin Azrak walked from Flatbush to Maimonides Hospital to blow *shofar* for his Uncle Nouri. As he neared the outside of the hospital room, he heard the long, clear blast of the *shofar*.

Oh no, he thought, *who beat me to it?*

Then he walked into the room and saw Nouri sitting up in bed, blowing the *shofar*.

That was Nouri, focused and determined, even as he was ill.

Yet the kidney attack signaled a dramatic change in Nouri. He left the hospital with more than just physical weakness. During his stay there, a blood vessel burst behind his retina, permanently damaging his eye. Blind in one eye, weak from surgery, he returned to his home in Flatbush to convalesce. Within a short time, he was back to a full schedule, albeit with some changes.

One thing would never change: Nouri remained devoted to Ahi Ezer.

Chapter 60:
AND THEY WERE HONORED BY HIS ATTENTION…

Ahi Ezer of Bensonhurst was struggling.

It had been built at a time when the congregation was poor (not that it ever became rich). Simple working men had gathered their own nickels and dimes, and then went around knocking on doors to collect more nickels and dimes, to build their *k'nees*. People volunteered their time, their energy, and their determination… because that was all that they had.

How could a shul built with so much *mesirut nefesh* close?

So, even after Nouri's kidney attack weakened him, he drove to Bensonhurst every day to pray in the 71st Street shul, to see that it still had a *minyan* and to encourage those who still came to pray there. He often read from the Torah on Mondays and Thursdays and was *hazzan* as well. Irwin still lived in Bensonhurst and, under the leadership of Rabbi Rubin, he and his children kept the *minyan* going.

But Nouri's presence, all the way from Flatbush, was heartening.

The old people waited for him to come; they were honored by his attention.

Eddie was one of the few youngsters who still attended the 71st Street shul even during the week. As he wound his *tefillin* off his arm, he brooded: *Nothing is going the way I expected…*

As usual, the men began filing out of the shul with barely a glance behind them. As usual, Mr. Dayan stayed together with four other men. They sat in the back of the room and began to learn. Eddie had watched this go on since forever. This time, he was feeling so aimless, he decided to sidle up to the group and hear what was going on.

Why not? Nothing better to do…

Mr. Dayan was leading the class, reading the Hebrew, translating the words, and explaining the lessons. Eddie was fascinated. The material was easy to understand and uplifting. He stayed for the entire class and left the shul more optimistic than he had been before.

The next day, he joined the class again. He marveled at how clearly Mr. Dayan explained the material, supplementing it with examples and ideas from other sources. The Torah slipped easily off his tongue as he went from one idea to another. Eddie ended his next class happy and uplifted and resolved to return.

Indeed, these classes gave Eddie purpose and direction and enabled him to keep himself motivated and focused on accomplishing something in life. He became a regular attendee, warmed by the Torah being given over by one so clearly dedicated to Hashem. And this was occurring just when Nouri was slowing down.

For Nouri, the kidney attack subtly changed his life on several fronts. Blind in one eye, he found any visual activity a strain. Even driving was no longer the easy activity that it had once been. He still drove, only he stopped saying *Tehillim* at each red light. With one eye, he had to concentrate more on anything that required vision.

Seymour Escava (middle) with Rabbi David Ozeirey in the Dayan home on Purim. Seymour attributed his upwards pull to religiosity to Mr. Dayan.

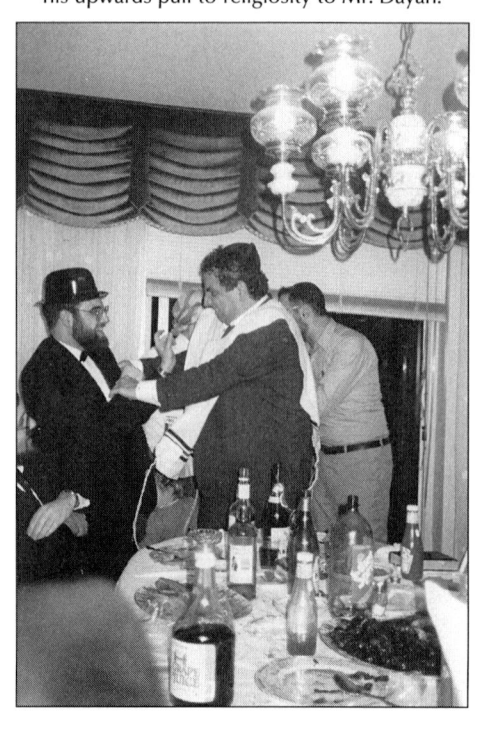

He pushed himself to learn, even more than before. But reading tired him out and he would beg his son Joey to come by to learn with him. And, because he never wanted to ask for favors, even from his children, he added, "I'll pay you money. Just come and learn with me."

Joey came when he could, but Nouri wanted more. He was used to his independence and it was frustrating to be so limited. Then he discovered Dial-A-Daf, and Nouri was excited. After Rabbi Shaingarten's classes way back in the 40's he had never had the time or opportunity to apply himself to real Gemara learning and therefore he stuck to the traditional texts — *Humash* with *Rabbeinu Bachye*, *Nabi* and *Ketubim*, *Mishnayot*,

Nouri, joyous on Purim. L-R, around the table: Murray, Joey (with his son, Shlomo, on his lap), Solomon (Irwin's son), Nouri, Marvin Azrak, Barbara Ozeirey (with her son Avraham on her lap), Seymour Escava, and Irwin.

Zohar, Hok l'Yisrael — but real Gemara learning eluded him. Now that the opportunity arose, he grabbed it, and became a regular listener. He was convinced that this new learning would protect his other eye from failing.

Even as his disability affected him, Nouri's partial blindness wasn't public knowledge. People who were close with him and spoke to him often noticed that there was something different about his eyes but, overall, outside the family the change was kept quiet. Nouri compensated by making quiet changes in his life, things that could be easily attributed to slowing down due to age.

A prime example was the way he changed his community involvement.

Nouri learned from Dave Bibi that a real leader knows when to step back. When he gave over the presidency of the shul to Marvin, it was with complete confidence in his protégé and the determination to let him lead. Nouri still attended board meetings, but as a regular member, not as its president. Marvin came over constantly — practically every evening — to discuss ideas and ask advice. Nouri dispensed both with clarity and wisdom, but still left the implementation up to Marvin. The same applied to the running of Ahi Ezer Yeshiva. Nouri had full faith in Seymour and completely stepped aside. Like Marvin, Seymour was a regular visitor in the Dayan home.

At the Testimonial Dinner: Dave Bibi (left) is shaking Nouri's hand. Joe Bibi (son of Reuben) is in the middle, clapping. Rabbi Harry Rubin is peeking behind Nouri and Basil Cohen is on the far right.

Within two years of taking over from Nouri, Marvin began to finally comprehend all the enormous accomplishments that Nouri had achieved for the community and he was simply overawed. He was also taken aback when he realized that for all these years, Nouri's endless devotion had not really been acknowledged. Over ten years earlier, at the first Ahi Ezer Yeshiva graduation, they had made a tribute to him, but nothing had been done on the community level

"A Testimonial Dinner," he cajoled Nouri, "we will put together an event that will be a testimony to all the work you have done for the community."

"What for?" Nouri answered dismissively. "Nothing I did was my own. Our community is made up of great people who all pitched in. Everyone deserves credit."

"Come on, Uncle Izzy, everyone knows that it was your vision, your optimism, and your energy. I already brought up the idea before the board. They are all very enthusiastic. It's our opportunity to show *hakarat hatob*."

"I don't have to allow myself to be a public guest of honor just because you want to show me *hakarat hatob*. There are many other people who

On the dais, L-R: Rabbi Baruch Ben Haim, Marvin Azrak, Rabbi Wolf, Nouri Dayan, Rabbi Kassin, and Rabbi Maslaton. Typically, Mr. Dayan took the opportunity to ask forgiveness to whomever he might have offended and to express appreciation to all his "partners."

deserve to be publicly thanked and would enjoy it. You know me; I like to stay in the background."

"But we want to honor you," Marvin insisted. Then he added the sentence that he thought would clinch the deal, "and we know that if you are honored, the yeshiva will make money."

Nouri smiled, but shook his head.

It took Marvin many more visits until he finally convinced Nouri to accept the honor, which he did, on one condition. "Make it for Rabbi Wolf as well. Rabbi Wolf is the real hero. He is not even Sephardic and yet he devoted himself to our community for over twenty years. If he agrees to accept the honor, then I will accept it along with him."

Rabbi Wolf had left Ahi Ezer several years before, but there was no question that the yeshiva, the Senior Homes, and much of the growth in the community could be traced back to him. Indeed, Nouri's suggestion was embraced enthusiastically. Everyone in the community loved and appreciated Rabbi Wolf and welcomed the opportunity to honor him.

The joint Testimonial Dinner was held in the downstairs social hall of Ahi Ezer Ocean Parkway. Its smashing success in no way signaled the pinnacle of Nouri's involvement. He was still suggesting, coaching, guiding, and leading from the background.

A community member pointed out that there was another rent-controlled apartment building up for sale on East 7th Street. Nouri well remembered all the difficulties he faced in emptying the other buildings that ultimately became the Senior Homes. Yet look what they built from all of the aggravation? The Senior Homes were a resounding success, the proof being that there was a constant waiting list for people who wanted to get into those buildings.

Nouri's philosophy had always been, "Buy it. Then we will see what to do with it."

With Nouri's prodding, Ahi Ezer bought another building.

As usual, along with the progress, came problems.

The 1980's ushered in some rough times for Ahi Ezer Yeshiva. Initially, when they began admitting Russian students, the Sephardic students remained. Ahi Ezer was known for its excellent education and, unlike other yeshivot, gave generous tuition breaks. These advantages remained dual attractions for low-income Sephardic families. Nonetheless, as the school became overwhelmingly Russian, Sephardic parents began pulling their children out.

"It's a boat school," people muttered.

It wasn't the "Russian" aspect that was unduly disturbing. Rather, the Sephardic community consisted, mainly, of second- and third-generation Americans. They were uncomfortable with sending their children to a school with children who "just came off the boat." They were afraid that the school would have to expend too much time and energy on bringing these children up to par in terms of language and culture and, meanwhile, the quality of the education would go down. They also didn't want their children lumped together with Ashkenazim. Whether these concerns were valid or not were irrelevant: Sephardic parents began pulling their kids out.

In addition, Ahi Ezer always had difficulties with their boys' division (which Nouri had never really wanted to begin with). No matter whom they hired to deal with the boys, they never achieved the level of education and discipline that they wanted. Every other night, someone was over at the Dayan house, discussing how to deal with the situation.[4]

---

4. "My father was more concerned for the Jewish education of these (Russian) children than for his own school, which he built with so much *mesirut nefesh*. He watched enrollment steadily fall from its height of 1,200, down to 1,000... 900... 800... and lower. He still maintained that Ahi Ezer's job was to provide a yeshiva education for every Jewish child seeking to learn" (Mr. Irwin Dayan). Ultimately, the religious world realized that saddling Ahi Ezer with so many immigrant children was unfair to Ahi Ezer, and other New York schools agreed to accept their share of these students. Eventually, Ahi Ezer made a deal with Kingsbay Yeshiva, run by Rabbi Berel Klohr. Kingsbay had been having difficulties

Clockwise, L-R: Marvin Azrak, Rabbi Aharon Schechter (Rosh Yeshiva of Yeshivas Rabbeinu Chaim Berlin), Rabbi Elya Svei (Rosh Yeshiva of the Talmudical Yeshiva of Philadelphia), and Rav Pam (Rosh Yeshiva of Torah Vodaath)

In these pictures, the deal between Ahi Ezer and Kingsbay is being formalized.

Nouri was still very involved, but only from the back seat, not the driver's seat.

Nouri's "back seat" position didn't mean he felt free from responsibilities. He didn't want to be free from responsibilities. He wanted to continue to be *mezakeh et harabbim*, only he chose to do so quietly, leaving the main responsibilities to the younger generation.

There was a sick and lonely man, estranged from his family, living in the Senior Home. But he began to lose his memory and needed more care. He wasn't a poor man, but there was no one to act on his behalf. Nouri used his assets to pay for residency in Scharome Manor. When this man

---

with their girls' department while Ahi Ezer was having difficulty with their boys' department. So Ahi Ezer gave Kingsbay their boys and Kingsbay gave Ahi Ezer their girls.

passed away, Nouri used the remainder of his funds to pay for burial in Eretz Yisrael. He said Kaddish for him an entire year and even bought *sefarim* in his name to perpetuate his memory.

Nouri continued all his old practices and even "upgraded" some of them. His *mishlo'ah manot* were still fresh and piping hot, only he varied his menu. Some years he ordered platters of *kibbe* with *tehina* (from Mrs. Lankry, rather than the Mauzonne chicken special), or a different hot, meat meal (with a bottle of wine, of course). He took a grandchild along, as his messenger, but he always walked in behind him and sat down for a visit, encouraging his host to partake of the fresh food and acquire the mitzva of eating a *seuda* on Purim. His recipients were honored by his attention.

Esther created the backdrop that enabled Nouri to be a family man as well.

"You want to see the kids? You have to cook!" she would say. She never complained that the younger generation was too busy to visit. Rather, she understood that they were leading busy lives. They surely wanted to visit their parents and grandparents, only they needed a little pull… like food.

Friday afternoon, on the way home from the *mikva*, her *yeshiva bachurim* grandsons would pass by and she served them an Erev Shabbat meal: chicken with peas and rice, or whatever else was hot and waiting on the stove. They were often joined by younger cousins holding their mothers' hands as they ran from one errand to another, and stopped off at Grandma's to grab a bite to eat.

Grandma Dayan welcomed everyone with calm warmth and empty plates that she promptly filled. Even as Shabbat drew near, she was unflustered — everything had been ready by *hatzot* anyway — happy to see everyone and pleased to be a help.

But the real excitement was on Sundays.

"Sundays at Grandma's" became a Dayan tradition.

Esther spent the entire week cooking for these Sunday gatherings, when the Dayan family converged on her house. The counters and stove of her small kitchen were lined with pots, pans, and bowls of food. There would be cheese-filled *sambousak*, potato-filled *bourekas*, cheese-filled *calssonets* (ravioli) with noodles, red spaghetti, white spaghetti (for those who don't like tomato sauce), fish cakes, *ejjeh* (quiche), salads, cut-up vegetables, roasted potatoes and sweet potatoes, pickled artichokes, and mini pizzas. Everyone would help themselves to mounds of good food, treats for the little ones (there was always ice cream or ices for dessert), and abundant warmth and love. The adults and children loved the opportunity to see one another, talk, and simply enjoy each other's company.

Grandpa and Grandma Dayan, surrounded by their Israeli grandchildren, the Salems. Mazal and Ezra are on the left. Mordechai and Abraham are on the right.

There were no set times; everyone chose the time most convenient for them. From 10:30 in the morning until 4 in the afternoon, the children and grandchildren popped in and out. To keep some semblance of order in the small apartment, Grandma Dayan bought a video machine, and played videos of family weddings and other momentous occasions. Occasionally, she bought an Uncle Moishy video, or something similar, but she always watched it first to decide if it was appropriate. If she found anything objectionable, it went right back to Mekor Haseforim. The Dayans were such loyal customers, the store owners always accepted her returns.

As part of the "program," Esther would raffle off toys or money, or a scarf or blanket that she had crocheted. Every hour or two she asked someone to pick a raffle. She wanted to generate more excitement, more happiness. Not everyone came every week, but everyone made an effort to participate whenever possible, not because they had to, but because they wanted to.

"You are in yeshiva, right? You are learning? You are learning well?" Esther would ask her grandsons. She made it clear that while she wanted them to enjoy the food and the fun, that wasn't what is important in life. She wanted to hear that they were learning Torah and doing what they were supposed to be doing in life.

How did Nouri contribute to these Sunday gatherings?

"Tell me a *d'bar Torah*," was how he greeted a grandson.

"What did you learn in school?" he asked a granddaughter.

Grandpa with some of Murray's and Joey's children: Shaul, Yosef, Esther (later Hakim), and Jennie (later Nakash)

And the children knew that they had better be prepared with answers. They all wanted to win their grandfather's approval and they knew that that would happen only with *dibrei Torah*. Grandpa Dayan listened with obvious interest to the youngest grandchild. There was nothing patronizing about his manner. He was ready to learn something new even from a small child.

Then Nouri would take out the *Tehillim Mechulak*, pamphlets of *Tehillim* divided into easy-to-read installments, a novelty in the community.

"You know how to read, right?" he'd ask a young grandchild and then hand him a pamphlet. The older ones picked up booklets on their own. By the end of the day, the whole *sefer Tehillim* was said, at least one time.

When he wasn't engaging his grandchildren in saying *Tehillim*, or urging them to tell him a *d'bar Torah*, Nouri was looking for ways to make things easier for Esther.

And how did the Dayan grandchildren relate to Grandpa?

Their respect and love for him was so great that if Grandpa told them to read *Tehillim*, they read *Tehillim*, no questions asked. If Grandpa gave them a rare rebuke, they took it to heart. Like the time one of the grandchildren walked in on Rosh Hashanah and flippantly announced that one of their neighbors had passed away.

When Grandpa came home, he called over the child and admonished him, "You told everyone that he passed away? We don't do that — *motzi diba, hu k'sil* — a fool repeats bad things (*Mishlei* 10:18). Just because you know something does not mean you have to say it."

The Dayan grandchildren were certain that Grandpa was the address for any question. One granddaughter had a friend who often asked her questions, most of which she was able to answer on her own, but some that she couldn't. She went straight to Grandpa Dayan. Sure enough, he took out some *sefarim*, sat down with her, wrote out a seven-part answer and explained it to her.

By the 1980's, Nouri had many grandchildren, some who were already young adults. Many of them had learned with him regularly for years.

"Let us be *mezakeh* this *sefer*," was a phrase they were all familiar with. Grandpa had many old *sefarim* — a tall *Kaf HaHaim* that looked like it came from Syria, a *Zohar* that was probably the same vintage, and many others. He rebound them, preferring to learn with these old volumes than purchasing new ones. In each *sefer* Nouri had stamped: *Kaniti sefer zeh l'avodat Hashem* (I bought this *sefer* in order to serve Hashem). Therefore, he liked to make sure that each *sefer* was used.

The grandchildren loved to go to Grandpa's for Shabbat.

In addition, many grandchildren claimed "special" relationships with Grandpa. While in high school, Maoz Raful came once a week, at 7 in the evening, to learn *Humash* with *Kli Yakar* with Grandpa. They went through the entire *perasha*, every word, every week.

The highlight of my week… Maoz reflected.

When he finished high school, he could no longer come over regularly, so their learning sessions stopped. Nouri purchased him a set of *Kli Yakar*, indicating that he should continue on his own. That set became a cherished possession.

When Ezra Dayan was learning in the Mirrer Yeshiva, he often popped over to Ahi Ezer to learn with Grandpa, and then they'd walk to East 13th for supper. When they walked into the house, Grandpa called out joyfully, "Grandma, Grandma, I have a *habruta*, I have a *habruta!*"

He was radiant with joy.

Another grandson began coming to learn *Kli Yakar* with Nouri every Friday afternoon. Another grandson spent almost every Shabbat at Grandpa's. And with each grandchild, Grandpa was still encouraging and cajoling, "Come, read some more *Tehillim*. Say *birkat ha'mazon* aloud, I'll give you a dollar!"

And They Were Honored by His Attention… / 521

Grandpa Dayan, enjoying a grandson's bar mitzva which, as usual, was enhanced by the presence of *talmidei hachamim*. Top picture, L-R: Murray Dayan, his son Ezra (the bar mitzva *bachur*), Rabbi Elefant, and Nouri. Bottom picture, L-R: Rabbi Hillel Haber, Ezra Dayan, Rabbi Reuven Elbaz, Rabbi Stanley Salem, Nouri.

A dollar for saying birkat ha'mazon out loud? Wow, it must be important! decided little Yosef Ozeirey. So he said it out loud and claimed his dollar after Shabbat from beaming Grandpa.

Everything Nouri did was with princely dignity. Nobody felt coerced. They simply felt encouraged to do what was correct. They felt accomplished when they won their grandfather's approval.

They were honored by his attention.

Chapter 61:

"A SHUL WITH MONEY IN THE BANK IS A BANKRUPT SHUL."

Boro Park, 1988

"Do you know Mr. Isidore Dayan?"

"He's my father-in-law," answered Rabbi David Ozeirey, wondering, *How does this chassid from Boro Park know my father-in-law?*

"Many years ago, I worked in the Ahi Ezer office," continued the chassid. "I will never forget how, every single Sunday morning, he was there, from early morning until mid-afternoon. Besides his own learning and davening, he cleaned up, before the first *minyan* and after. Then he'd help set up for the next *minyan*, breakfast, clean-up — literally, custodial work. And yet, every time he came into the office to make a phone call, he'd leave a dime on the desk, always in an inconspicuous place so that I would not notice it. I have never forgotten him."

To many people, and in many ways, Nouri was unforgettable. Yet he was completely oblivious to the effect he had on other people. He simply did what he had to do in life, without any fanfare. Those fortunate enough to witness his sincerity and dedication became changed people.

Nouri was driving with his son, Joey. He pointed to a building on East 7th Street.

"Ahi Ezer owns it," he told Joey. "What should we do with it?"

Joey looked at the tall building and said, "No problem, Dad, it's very simple. The yeshiva is always in debt. Sell the building and pay off the debts."

Nouri seemed to not even hear him. As if in a trance, he kept repeating, "But I want it for *kodesh*. I just need an idea, how can we use it for something *kodesh*?"

Joey just listened, amazed. *What is wrong with selling the building and having a more financially secure congregation? From where does Daddy have this drive to build, build, and build?*

Neither he nor anyone else could answer that question.

Even as Nouri stepped back, he remained ambitious for his community. And he still pushed others to realize that ambition. From his chair as a regular member of the board, Nouri's opinion counted. As the years passed and the East 7th building still seemed extraneous, there were low grumblings echoing Joey's idea: What was the point of just holding onto real estate when the congregation was constantly in debt? The Senior Homes were financially independent (in itself a huge accomplishment) but the yeshiva lost money, year after year, and was a burden on the shul. Someone had offered Ahi Ezer a huge sum for the East 7th Street building. Why not sell it, pay off the debts, and breathe easy with money in the bank?

Some board members requested bringing up the motion for a vote.

"I must remind everyone that the East 7th Street building is right near the Senior Homes," explained Marvin, who was chairing the meeting, "in the heart of the community. It has enormous potential."

The rest of the board looked unimpressed.

Marvin indicated to each person around the table to state their vote.

"Sell."

"Sell."

"Sell."

"Sell."

"Sell."

It seemed unanimous… until they came to Nouri.

Impassive, Nouri quietly said, "I think that everyone who voted to sell the building and to use that money to pay our debts should resign from the committee. A shul should be using its money to help its congregation. A shul with money in the bank is a bankrupt shul."

There was absolute silence.

Marvin cleared his throat, "Maybe we should vote again."

He went around the room once more.

"Don't sell."

"Don't sell."

"Don't sell."

"Don't sell."

"Don't sell."

It was unanimous: Ahi Ezer would hold onto the East 7th Street building and search for a way to introduce another innovative project to the community. Simultaneously, everyone at the meeting learned a lifelong lesson: If you are working for the community, you should never look to breathe easy. Always look to build.

Perhaps it was because Nouri was always looking to build that the idea of conceding defeat was so difficult. It was already seven years since Nouri moved to Flatbush, and he was still traveling back to Bensonhurst every day to bolster the old *minyan*, even cajoling others to join him to ensure that there would be a *minyan*. But, despite his valiant efforts, the congregation continued to shrink.

Somewhere along the way, Nouri realized that his efforts were futile. Irwin had moved to Flatbush and Rabbi Rubin was ready to retire to Israel. There were simply not enough Ahi Ezer congregants left in Bensonhurst to keep the shul going.

It was time to sell.

But Nouri was determined that if they had to sell the 71st Street building, the proceeds should go to another project that would benefit the community… only he couldn't decide what that would be.

"*Kodesh*," he kept telling people, "we need to use the funds for *kodesh*."

As they negotiated the terms of the sale, as they organized the burial of the *genizah* (the old *siddurim* and *sefarim* that no one wanted) in the newly dug foundation of Har HaLebanon, as they notified people who owned *Sifrei Torah* and asked them where they wanted them transferred, Nouri was still preoccupied with finding a fitting use for the money from the sale.

He surveyed the beautiful interior of the shul and remembered how, almost half a century earlier, he and his Uncle Dave had gone from member to member and appealed to each family to donate a window. Their donations were gifts of love, and he decided to hire a glazier to carefully remove each artistic, stained-glass window, designed in memory of beloved family members, and he personally delivered each window back to the family who had donated it.

"Thank you for your support then, and all the years since," he graciously declared, presenting them with the window. "As you know, the community has moved, and the building has been sold. Please keep this as a memory."

The people were touched by his thoughtfulness and appreciated the gesture.

He removed the beautiful doors of the *heichal* and put them into storage, hoping he would find a fitting home for them… and when he did, he couldn't contain his excitement.

"A Torah Center," he announced excitedly to Uncle Dave.

Dave Bibi was no longer well and no longer active. He had stopped going into the business in 1986 and Nouri had bought him out, leaving the entire business in Dayan hands. Then Dave had a stroke and became wheelchair bound. But Nouri visited regularly, keeping him abreast of everything going on in the community and asking his advice.

"Our shuls are primarily for praying," explained Nouri. "Of course, we have *shiurim* and activities, but the venue is not conducive to real Torah learning. Also, we are losing the youth.[5] In the main shul, only the older people get honors. The whole set-up is geared toward older people. Let's set up a Torah Center where the goal will be a place of learning. We will have prayers there also, but there will be learning before and after prayers and throughout the day. I want it to be a place that will attract the youth to Torah and mitzvot."

From that initial idea, the first Sephardic Torah Center was born.[6]

Nouri finally had a concrete plan for the East 7th Street building. Marvin was all for it and within a few days it was all set up, though over the years it would develop and change.

The Tablets of the Ten Commandments from the 71st Street shul were affixed at the entrance of the Torah Center, and the doors to the old *heichal* were cut down to fit the new *heichal*. The old shul would not be forgotten.

The Torah Center became Marvin's pet project.

Marvin was young and energetic and, by nature, a powerful personality. As soon as an idea captivated him, he was pushing it through, with excitement and enthusiasm. His ambition was contagious and, suddenly, there was an energy in the air, a desire to accomplish. People who in the past had demurred when being asked to pitch in couldn't refuse Marvin.

Like Nouri, Marvin was a visionary.

He expounded on Nouri's idea in various ways. On the first floor, he built the Bet Midrash, meant for learning, with the prayer times scheduled so that they would not conflict with the main Ahi Ezer shul. On the same floor, there was a library for English Judaica — well stocked with practically everything on the market — organized and accessible. It was also the first of its kind in the neighborhood. It became very popular among both Sephardim and Ashkenazim.

On the second floor, he opened a Hebrew library and asked Irwin's son, Ezra, to stock it with every *sefer* a scholar could want. Marvin gave him

---

5. Ahi Ezer did try to attract the youth. During the late 1970's and early 1980's, there was a youth *minyan* in the front hall of Ahi Ezer run by Jack Mevorah and, later on, by Rabbi Shlomo Shalam and Sammy Grazi. For many years, there was robust attendance. The boys learned to lead the prayers, enjoyed a lively *seuda shelishit* with much singing, and after Shabbat they received prizes. Nonetheless, this program also petered out.

6. The Ahi Ezer Torah Center was the catalyst for the many Torah Centers that are now part of the Sephardic community of Flatbush. They all have similar goals: to provide the atmosphere and infrastructure conducive to encouraging the young men and women of the community to embrace a higher standard of Torah and mitzvot.

The *keilim mikva*

Mr. Azrak dedicated the Bet Midrash in memory of his grandfather, Mr. Joseph Maslaton, Hacham Murad's oldest son. He dedicated the *keilim mikva* to his grandmother, Joe's wife, Sophie Maslaton. He wanted to designate the upper floors for *shelichim* from Eretz Yisrael who needed a place to sleep. That never happened. Ultimately, the top floors were used for a girls' high school, called Bnot Rachel, a project that Mr. Dayan always wanted but Rabbi Wolf discouraged. Mr. Azrak opened this high school after Mr. Dayan's passing.

carte blanche to spend whatever was necessary to put together an unbelievable library, the first of its kind in the neighborhood. All of the *sefarim* were categorized by a card system and were easily accessible. It was a large, quiet room with plenty of space to peruse the *sefarim*. The ambience made a person want to sit down and learn. This room was also used for various classes: *Hok l'Yisrael* (after Minha), Daf Yomi with Rabbi Feintuch, evening classes with Rabbi Yechiel Perr, Rabbi Eli Mansour's classes, and others.

Marvin built a *keilim mikva*, reasoning that if he made it easy for people to *tovel* their dishes, they would do so willingly. The *keilim mikva* was built street level, open and accessible throughout the day, so that anyone could come to dip their dishes practically whenever they wanted. There was plenty of room to unload many new purchases and dunk them easily into the water. There was pleasant music playing in the background, a list of basic halachot posted on the wall, and a *tzedaka* box for anyone who wanted to give a donation to help keep the *mikva* running efficiently. The set up was so pleasant and convenient that it instantly attracted a following. People who had viewed dipping their dishes as an unnecessary

A glorious *siyum* in Shaarei Zion, back in the 1970s, was proof of the Torah revolution taking place in the Syrian community. Many of the attendees formed the parent body of the nascent Yeshivat Ateret Torah. In the middle of the head table, slightly raised above everyone seated, with his head turned to the left, is Hacham Yosef Harari-Raful. From him, L-R: unidentified, unidentifed, Rabbi Hecht, Rabbi Yaakob Kassin, Rabbi Saul Kassin, Hacham Sion Maslaton.

stringency became regular customers. As Nouri had always counseled, "Our people want to keep mitzvot. Let's help them!"

The Torah Center took off in a way that no one had imagined.

During the week, the Bet Midrash had learning going on there the whole day with *minyanim* as an added convenience. On Shabbat, there were several *minyanim*, with popular *hazzanim*, to accommodate any type of schedule: early or late Shaharit; early or late Minha (before then, there was no Minha Gedola in Sephardic shuls). Throughout the morning, there was Kiddush available, complete with *sambousak* and *ka'ak*, and then a *shiur*. Some people chose to skip the *shiur* and go to the library to learn. There was also an elaborate *seuda shelishit* in the afternoons.

All Shabbat, people popped in to pray, to learn, to come to a class, to eat together and sing together. The easily accessible libraries were a big draw. You came to Minha a few minutes early? No problem, you just picked up a book from the English library and read for a while. Or you went up to the Hebrew library and learned for a bit. There were classes on Mosa'ei Shabbat with people who went on to become very popular speakers. They also brought in *talmidei hachamim* to give classes and to keep the Bet Midrash alive with learning.

Hacham Sion was worried that the Torah Center was taking people away from the big shul. While this was somewhat true, the sad fact was that the big shul had been losing the youth for many years. Many of the grownup children of stalwart Ahi Ezer families had not been praying in the main Ahi Ezer even before the creation of the Torah Center. Some of them prayed in Sha'arei Zion or in Ateret Torah, the new yeshiva founded by Hacham Yosef Harari Raful.

The first Sephardic sleepaway camp, Camp Shivtei Yisrael, was another indication of community growth. Here Hacham Sion is with Rabbi Yeruchem Kaplan on the camp grounds.

While Nouri was also disappointed in the shrinking attendance in the big shul, he rejoiced in every new shul that opened. To him, each new building was a sign of religious growth in the community, and that could only be good. He still prayed in the big shul, and he was confident that, with the right efforts, attendance would rebound. For example, when Marvin brought in Rabbi Yisrael Reisman to give classes in the main shul on Mosa'ei Shabbat, Ahi Ezer was quickly jammed. Marvin set up screens in the social hall for the overflow crowd. Nouri was amazed at the crowds who came to these new classes and he joined as well.

But the Torah Center became the hub.[7] While it could have rightfully been dubbed "Mitzva Center," it was designed for those who wanted to learn Torah. The Bet Midrash was set up like a yeshiva: a large and simple room without the high-ceilinged ambiance of the typical Sephardic sanctuary. The *heichal* doors of the 71st Street shul were the most impressive parts of the room. Nouri also donated the *teba* — once again, in memory of his parents — and had the plaque that he had made for the 71st Street shul put on the *teba* of the Torah Center.

Nonetheless, the bulk of the money from the 71st Street building didn't go to the Torah Center. It went toward a down payment on the Carvel

---

7. The Torah Center became so busy and crowded that Mr. Irwin Dayan suggested to one of his daughters to organize girls' youth groups (Bnos) so that the children don't run around when their fathers come to pray. The Dayans were so accustomed to volunteerism, the girls readily gave up their relaxing Shabbat afternoons to help the community. Those Bnos groups grew to include seasonal programs, like a gala Purim party and occasional Sunday outings and activities.

Nouri at a *Hachnasat Sefer Torah* at Camp Shivtei Yisrael

building on Kings Highway and East 3rd Street. Typically, when the large lot was up for sale, Nouri recommended that Ahi Ezer buy it. It was an even better acquisition than the other apartment buildings in that it was basically a large parking lot with a small Carvel station. Ahi Ezer would not have the hassle of evicting tenants. As soon as the city approved the building plans, they could go ahead and build.

This was very providential. The waiting list for the Senior Homes was far too long to fill with the two buildings that they had built back in the 70's. They needed to begin building as soon as possible, and they did. Ultimately, Ahi Ezer built 120 units for senior housing.

All this was due to Nouri, who had charted a philosophy that Marvin admired and emulated: If you have the ambition and desire to build for Klal Yisrael, forge ahead and the Borei Olam will help.

Nouri loved Marvin's excitement and energy.

And Marvin continued coming to Nouri for advice and encouragement.

Nouri's impact wasn't only through his words, but through the person he had become. He was constantly learning, constantly growing, constantly becoming, even in his old age.

One evening, as Joey dropped his father off at home, he decided to broach a topic that had been on his mind.

L-R: Rabbi Yaakob Kassin, Rabbi Mordechai Eliyahu, Rabbi Abraham Hecht, unknown, Hacham Sion "digging"

The groundbreaking ceremony for the East 3rd Street Senior Center. On the right is Hacham Sion and next to him is Rabbi Mordechai Eliyahu.

"Daddy, I have been thinking," he began. "Baruch Hashem, I teach in the morning, and that brings in an income. But the family is growing… money is tight… Maybe you want to give me an afternoon job in the business?"

Joey waited for the response that he was sure would follow. After all, since he was a child he had been raised with the understanding that while one must learn Torah, one must also embrace his obligation to support his family.

Instead, Nouri looked at Joey sadly. "All my life I dreamed of having a son who is a *talmid hacham*…" his voice trailed off. "Maybe it's my fault. I have always prayed that my children be accepted by the people and be *talmidei hachamim*. Perhaps I should have reversed that order and prayed

Front row of Rabbis, L-R: Rabbi Shimon Hai Alouf, Rabbi Sydney (Zevulun) Leiberman, Rabbi Chaim Benoliel, Rabbi David Ovadya. Rabbi Hanaya Elbaz is diagonally behind Rabbi Hai Alouf and Rabbi Shlomo Diamond is diagonally behind Rabbi Elbaz. Hacham Sion and Rabbi Kassin are seated on the regal chairs in the center. Mr. Lou Rofe is speaking.

first that my children be *talmidei hachamim* and afterward that they be accepted by the people."[8]

To Joey, his father's words were a revelation.

Had not he, Joey, grown up with the unsaid message that one could be in business and still be a *talmid hacham*? Had his father changed?

That wistful comment indicated that Nouri *had* changed. He now believed that only one who is completely devoted to learning, to the exclusion of all else, could become a real *talmid hacham*. If Joey entered the business world, he would be giving up that goal.

How many people as successful as my father — in both the spiritual and material realm — wake up at 70 years old and re-examine their beliefs and opinions? reflected Joey. *He is not in the same place that he was when I was growing up, and I didn't even realize this.*

Joey scratched his plans to enter the business.

---

8. "Unlike today," Rabbi Joey Dayan explains, "when I was growing up, people in our community didn't appreciate a man who sat and learned, unless he was a famous Rabbi. My father logically concluded that if his children are first accepted by the people, then they will be able to give over Torah, as he had done. But he changed his approach and regretted his 'logic.'"

"A Shul With Money in the Bank Is a Bankrupt Shul." / 533

Chapter 62:

"IN WHAT *ZECHUT* DID HE MERIT TO SEE GENERATIONS OF CHILDREN AND GRANDCHILDREN WHO ARE *BNEI TORAH?*"

Flatbush, 1989

"Something is wrong," Carol told Hacham Yosef, one evening. "My father is not himself. Every time I go over, he seems tired, almost lethargic."

"Maybe it's time for us to visit his cardiologist," ruminated Hacham Yosef. He, together with his brothers-in-law, Irwin and Rabbi David Ozeirey, scheduled an appointment. As expected, the cardiologist still recommended medication. But the Dayan family was convinced that it was time for a second opinion. They took Nouri to a different doctor whose prognosis was grim.

"He needs a triple bypass and valve replacement, both of which require open heart surgery. This is a complicated procedure for someone his age, but without it his condition is almost certain to deteriorate."

After much discussion back and forth, Nouri agreed to the operation. For the first time in his life, Nouri was very nervous. He was warned that until he had surgery he could go into cardiac arrest at any moment. On the other hand, the surgery had its own risks.

Ezra Dayan was right outside Mirrer Yeshiva in Flatbush, his other "home."

Grandpa is about to have a risky procedure done. What can I do? Then he dashed into the yeshiva, straight up to the Rosh HaYeshiva, Rabbi Shraga Moshe Kalmanowitz.

"Rebbe, my grandfather is in the hospital," he panted.

Reb Shraga Moshe was well acquainted with Nouri, who had always been a staunch supporter, not only of the yeshiva, but of the many projects that his father, Reb Avraham Kalmanowitz, had pioneered.

534 / NOURI

"Tell the *chazzan* to say *Tehillim*, immediately," he instructed Ezra.

Ezra did as he was told and the whole yeshiva prayed for Nouri.

Afterward, Reb Shraga Moshe told Ezra, "Your grandfather has merited that which few others merit: He has many children and grandchildren devoted to Torah." Then he paused and asked in wonder, "From where did that come from? In what *zechut* did he merit to see generations of children and grandchildren who are *bnei Torah*?"[9]

The question was rhetorical. The message was powerful.

Thankfully, the procedure was successful, although there were complications.

One of the medications that the doctors gave Nouri immediately following surgery caused him to hallucinate. When Irwin came to visit him in the hospital he was amazed when suddenly Nouri sat up, eyes wide open, and pointed, "There is Rashi! There is Rabbeinu Bachye!"

Irwin was floored: *Daddy is barely conscious, yet the only thing he "sees" are his beloved Rabbis!*

But recovery was long and hard.

After Nouri was released from the hospital, family and friends lined up to help him. While Nouri was too weak to go to shul, the family organized *minyanim* in the house. They also got tapes of the *shiurim* of Hacham Ovadya Yosef, which Nouri listened to over and over again. But Ezra Dayan knew that his grandfather would prefer interactive learning, with a *habruta*, and so he offered to learn with him.

"Listen," Nouri answered, "I want you to find out how much an hour of tutoring costs."

"Grandpa," Ezra protested, "I'm not taking money from you."

"So, I'll find somebody else," Nouri stubbornly insisted.

Left with no choice, Ezra did his investigations and found out the going rate. He learned with his grandfather every day and, without fail, Nouri would check the clock and pay accordingly. He didn't want to take advantage of anyone, even his own grandson. As long as the service being given had a definable price tag, he wanted to pay for it.

As Nouri recovered, he regained his usual optimism, even when there were setbacks. Finally, he was back at the office, only with reduced hours. A few months later, he once again struggled with a traumatic change when his Uncle Dave passed on.

---

9. Mr. Dayan's grandson, Rabbi Ezra Dayan, commented that he felt that his grandfather merited these blessings because of his devotion to *tefillah* and to Torah, and his absolute conviction that nothing he had was in his own merit but that he owed everything to the Almighty. Mr. Irwin Dayan noted that he once overheard his father amending the usual *Brich Sh'mei* at the end of prayers (when we ask Hashem to give us children who are *talmidei hachamim*) to include grandchildren. Perhaps his learned grandchildren were in that merit.

Nouri with his *habruta*-grandson, Ezra Dayan

Though Dave had been struggling with health issues for years, Nouri still sought his wisdom, advice, and companionship. His death left Nouri with an emptiness in his heart. For the first time in his life, he was left without a mentor.

Indeed, Dave Bibi was irreplaceable.

Dave had been a unique person. He had his own difficult childhood where he grew up practically without a father and then, when they finally reunited in America, their time together was teasingly short. One of his children once found a picture of their grandfather, Grandpa Yosef Bibi, stashed away in a drawer.

"Dad," she asked, "why don't you enlarge this? It's a great picture. Make a copy and hang it on the wall."

Dave shook his head. "I can't," he said, and then in a low voice, almost a whisper, he added, "it's too painful."

Yet he went on to become a prince of the community.

Everyone of that generation — *Halabi* and *Shammi* — admired Dave Bibi. When he walked into a room, no matter how inconspicuous he wanted to be, his regal bearing commanded attention. People rose to greet him, to find him a chair, to sit near him. When a stranger walked into a room, he felt flattered when this princely man ran over to welcome him with a smile and a handshake and instructions to "just call me Dave."

Every community initiative had Dave on its board.
Every *tzedaka* fund had Dave on its list of patrons.
And Dave just gave, and gave, and gave… until the last day of his life.
But Dave was gone and only *tehiyat ha'meitim* would bring him back.

"I have no words to express my loss," declared Nouri as he broke down at the *sheloshim*. "Once again, I'm an orphan. Uncle Reuben provided me with a home. Uncle Morris nourished me spiritually. Uncle Dave gave me my livelihood. I worked side by side with Uncle Dave for approximately fifty years. He was a great influence on my life and will always be an inspiration to me. I'm involved in community work because my uncle got me involved. Whatever I am and whatever I do, I owe to my dear Uncle Dave. I'm indebted to the entire Bibi family and, with G-d's help, hope to repay them in happy occasions for all their generosity."

Still weak from his own health scare and, perhaps, more aware of the transiency of life, Nouri cried as he eulogized his uncle. His life flashed before him and he was overcome with the enormity of the kindness his uncles had done for him. Granted, he had repaid them many times over by being a loyal and loving nephew, ready in an instant to serve them. But to Nouri, that would never be enough.

His uncles, each in their own way, had given him life.

Was it possible to repay someone for the gift of life?

Providentially, there were happy occasions coming up in the Dayan family. Sara was making a bar mitzva in Eretz Yisrael and both Nouri and Esther looked forward to making the trip.

Then, on August 22, 1990, Saddam Hussein attacked Kuwait.

"Ma, let me show you how to use the mask…"

Esther fumbled with the mask, and then shrugged, as if to say: *We'll see.*

By the next evening Esther made up her mind. "Sara, if the siren goes off in the middle of the night, don't wake me up. I can't do this…"

Sara understood what she meant. The mad dash to the sealed room crowded with the whole family (including crying babies) in the middle of the night, when everyone was groggy and confused from being woken up, was the most traumatic part of the whole deal. So far, the only civilian to die in the war was an elderly woman who had a heart attack while going into the sealed room!

"… I'm not going into the sealed room. Hashem will protect me."

"Dad?"

Nouri nodded in agreement.

Sara marveled at their faith. They had come to be with her even though few Americans were coming to Israel (the airport had been practically empty) and many opted to flee to America. Their arrival enhanced the

Rav Shach greeting Nouri

simha before it even began. Though there was no way to orchestrate a siren-free night, the Dayans went to sleep surprisingly calm. The next morning, Sara asked them if they had heard the siren.

"No," Esther answered, not nervous at all.

"I heard it," said Nouri. Sara didn't comment on his choice of inaction.

The day of the bar mitzva, they prayed at the Kotel. Then they returned home for an elaborate but impromptu meal. With the shaky security situation, they had canceled the hall, and used word of mouth to invite people to their home for the meal. Over 100 people showed up to the afternoon affair! But the highlight of Nouri's trip turned out to be something else altogether.

"Grandpa, how are you doing?"

"Maoz? Is that you?"

Maoz Raful was in Bnei Brak, learning in Ponovezh, the same yeshiva where his father, Hacham Yosef, had learned as a *bachur*.

"Yes, Grandpa. I had an idea for you. How would you like to meet Rav Shach?"

"Oh, yes," Nouri responded with an excitement that Maoz could feel over the telephone wires, "that would be a treat!"

Maoz knew that his grandfather had had a difficult year and he hoped that a visit to the *gadol hador* would cheer him up. Rabbi Stanley Salem decided that he would accompany his in-laws and that he would take along the bar mitzva *bachur* as well. The enthusiastic group left for Bnei Brak.

Rav Shach greeting Rabbi Salem

Maoz met the family near Ponevezh and they went together to Rav Shach's house. Rav Shach was already old and frail but he welcomed his visitors with tremendous warmth. He asked Nouri about his roots and his life and sat him directly opposite him, attentive to every word. Nouri was surprised that it was so easy to talk to the *gadol hador*. He told him all about himself, from being an orphan in Damascus, to building up the community of Ahi Ezer in America. Rav Shach complimented him on his work.

Then he told Nouri, "You are very fortunate. Look! You have children and grandchildren who are real *bnei Torah*!"

Nouri beamed.

"And I must tell you, your son-in-law [Hacham Yosef Raful], half the world is resting on his shoulders."

As usual, Nouri deflected the compliment with a compliment of his own. "Why is that so special? The Rosh HaYeshiva is carrying the entire world on his shoulders!"

Rav Shach smiled, "One day, you will understand."

"Maoz," Esther whispered to her grandson, "he looks like Moshe Rabbeinu."

"Grandma," Maoz whispered back, "how do you know what Moshe Rabbeinu looked like?"

The two of them laughed and Rav Shach and Nouri looked up from their conversation.

Rav Shach speaking with his guests; Esther Dayan is sitting with her back to the camera.

"I will explain later," Maoz told his grandfather.

Nouri spoke with Rav Shach for about 25 minutes. When they finished, Rav Shach gave each person an individual blessing. He warmly wished Nouri good health until 120 years old.

Nouri left Rav Shach's room ecstatic. He was so happy and excited, he hugged his grandchildren, he hugged the *bachurim* waiting outside, he hugged the *gabbaim*, he hugged almost everyone in sight. Then he pulled out his wallet and began giving out money to everyone, hundreds of dollars.

"I cannot believe the *zechut*," he said over and over, as he continued to give out money, "such a *zechut* has to be paid for."

Soon, more *bachurim* were running over to the American who was handing out money, and Nouri continued to beam with happiness as he gave again and again. His smile was so wide, it seemed to take over his face, and it remained in place even as they drove all the way back to Yerushalayim.

That night, he called each of his children to tell them about his wonderful visit. They were all amazed at the lilt in his voice, a happiness that they had not heard in a very long time. The visit rejuvenated and revitalized him. It became not only the highlight of his trip, it became the highlight of his life: *I, Nouri Dayan, met with the gadol hador and received his blessing.*

Chapter 63:

"YOUR GRANDFATHER, HE KNEW IN WHAT TO INVEST."

Damascus, Syria, 1991

"And please, Hashem, watch over Nouri Dayan and his dear wife, Esther," whispered the middle-aged woman, as she completed her prayers.

While Nouri reveled in Rav Shach's blessing, only a few hundred miles away, but in a place that was like a different planet, Marcelle Salama, Sophie's mother, reverently remembered Nouri Dayan in her daily prayers. She was still grateful for the kindness he did for her so many years before. Even though her daughter tragically passed away, just recalling the weeks of kindness she experienced in America warmed her soul. Marcelle was still in Syria with four of her children. Her other children had succeeded in leaving — each with their own story — but Marcelle and the others remained. Throughout the 70's and 80's, there had been several prominent American and Canadian activists involved in raising a public awareness about the plight of Syrian Jewry.[10] Yet the doors seemed irrevocably locked.

Resigned to their fate, Syrian Jews began fixing up their houses, investing in their businesses. If they couldn't leave Syria, they might as well live in gilded cages.

And then, in 1992, the impossible happened.

---

10. Mrs. Judy Feld-Carr of Canada helped many young Syrian girls leave Syria. In 1988, Dr. Mayer Ballas began an American initiative called SOSJ – Save Our Syrian Jews. This turned into the Council for the Rescue of Syrian Jewry (CRSJ) and became a tremendous contributor to the changed political climate. Some community members who were active in the CRSJ included: Mr. Albert Ayal, Mr. Maurice Hedaya, Mrs. Janet Zalta, Mr. Marcos Zalta, Mr. Clement Soffer, Dr. Gilbert Kahn, and Mrs. Alice Sardell Harary.

Albert Ayal made the announcement in Ahi Ezer on the night before the last days of Pesah.

> *The people at Ahi Ezer synagogue burst out in laughter and tears. They hugged each other and shouted "Mabrook!" upon hearing the news: The Syrian government had suddenly given its 4,000 Jews freedom to travel.[11]*
>
> *The timing of the announcement wasn't lost on the deeply observant, tightly knit Syrian Jewish enclave tucked away in the Midwood section of Brooklyn. It came on Passover, which marks the Jewish liberation from Egypt 3,200 years ago...*
>
> *Since that first flash of euphoria, the enthusiasm has been tempered by a sense of the delicate road ahead. Quietly, the largest community of Syrian Jews in the world prepares for the daunting task of welcoming and helping integrate the families who will surely come... [paraphrased from New York Times 5/6/91].*

I can't believe it... I don't believe it... Rachel (Salama) Alfie walked around in a daze. Had she just heard that Syrian television had broadcasted President Assad granting permission to any Jew who wanted to leave? Was it possible?

"What do you think, Rachel? Do you think it's true?" Marcelle's voice lilted over the telephone lines.

"I don't know, Ma... I don't know. What is Rabbi Hamra saying?"

"He is telling us to go! Buy tickets. Apply for visas. They are letting us out..."

At first, everyone was like Rachel, too shocked to react. But then they began filling out applications and, wonder of wonders, permission was granted! The government demanded a high exit fee and the tickets were also costly. Some people paid the tax and purchased their tickets immediately. But if anyone came to Rabbi Hamra and said that he couldn't afford to leave, Mr. Edmond Safra paid for their tickets, ultimately $1.5 million in total. Rachel could hardly believe that after all those years of fighting the Syrian government, her family would finally be together again.[12]

---

11. The actual number of Syrian Jews was over 4500. Historians and political analysts have many ways to explain why President Hafez Assad completely changed his decades old policy regarding Jewish emigration. While the tireless dedication of political activists certainly helped, no one expected a complete policy reversal. Being that the declaration happened on Pesah, it reinforced the conviction within the Syrian community that this was their personal exodus — not from Egypt, but from Syria. Indeed, this proved to be the end of the centuries-old Jewish community in Syria. By 1994, almost the entire Jewish community of Syria had left its birthplace.

12. "I still don't believe it," Mrs. Rachel Alfie emotionally declared almost twenty years later. Her story was particularly unique in that she had been separated from two of her own children for six years! In the 1980's, Rachel and her husband came to America with their two youngest children and then waged an international battle to have their two older children, who were still in Syria, returned to them in America.

Indeed, a mass exodus ensued.

Most of the emigrants came directly to America.[13]

Originally, President Assad agreed to let out seventy-five families per month. Perhaps the flood of applications changed his mind but, almost immediately, he began issuing hundreds of permits and sending off one planeload of emigrants a week, 200 people at a time. Within a few months, over 2,400 Syrians had arrived.

The Syrian community of Flatbush united to welcome the newcomers. Every Sunday, tens of cars flooded the airport as volunteers came to welcome the new arrivals. Brothers and sisters — some, like Sophie Maslaton and her brother, had been separated for over sixty years — now embraced as they cried. They couldn't believe that they were finally together again. Parents, children, and grandchildren who had been separated from each other, and those who had never before met, were overcome with emotion. Aunts, uncles, and cousins met their relatives for the first time. Almost everyone had a relative in the community.

But the emotional reunions were only the beginning.

Then the community began the mammoth job of settling the newcomers.

The American-Syrian community embraced the new Syrians with warmth and love. Mr. Albert Ayal, an Ahi Ezer congregant, went every single Sunday to meet, welcome, and help the new immigrants. Mr. Solomon Sasson became Chairman of the Resettlement Committee at the Sephardic Bikur Cholim and, in that capacity, worked to find apartments and employment for the new immigrants and helped them navigate government bureaucracy. They were assisted by many community members.

The Sephardic Bikur Cholim rallied their staff of volunteers and rented out the Golden Gate Hotel as temporary housing. Then they canvassed the neighborhood for empty apartments and, as soon as they found one, they paid the rent and stocked the apartment with donated mattresses that they spread out on the floor. They also gave the newcomers pots and pans, tables and chairs, and major appliances.

But the immigrants were arriving in rapid succession and it was very difficult to find so many suitable apartments. The majority of the new immigrants stayed in the hotel for months. The hotel was in Sheepshead Bay, far away from the community in Flatbush. Whole families were crowded into small rooms, which was fine for the evenings, when everyone went to sleep, but difficult for the rest of the day. Once again, Ahi Ezer rose to the occasion.

---

13. Part of the deal was that the immigrants were not allowed to go to Israel. When Jewish activists realized what was happening, they lobbied the Israeli government to waive any debt or mortgage on an apartment bought by immigrants who went to Israel within a year of leaving Syria. 1,200 Syrians immigrated to Israel.

Albert Ayal and other members of the Ahi Ezer community welcoming the new Syrian immigrants at the airport

Bright and early one morning, busses arrived at the newly built Kings Highway Senior Citizen Home. Tens of women, most with several children, came into the lobby. They settled themselves on the chairs and couches and seemed happy to be there. The seniors cautiously joined them, delighting the new immigrants with Arabic greetings.

The Sephardic Bikur Cholim organized a toy drive and soon, there were toys for the children. The seniors loved playing with the children, engaging them in conversation, teaching them how to play some of the games and use the toys. The new immigrants spent from 9 in the morning until 4 in the afternoon in the Senior Home where they even received a hot Syrian-style lunch (except on the one day a week that they were served pizza), donated by Nathan Mezrahi of Seuda Catering. The seniors and the resident staff served the lunch and helped amuse the children.

Where were Nouri and Esther Dayan in this picture?

Nouri came around occasionally to see how Carol Shapiro, the manager of the Senior Home, was managing. As usual, he always wanted to know, "Do you need anything? Is there anything I can do to help?"

Esther came up with her own contribution. She turned every Wednesday into "snack day." She came with a big shopping bag — mainly for the kids — stocked with orange juice, cookies, candy, tea, and anything else she thought the kids would enjoy. The children couldn't wait for her to come.

As the weeks went by, new people came, old-timers found apartments and settled their children in schools, and the faces in the Senior Home changed. It took two years for the community to completely settle in America.[14]

Most of the new Syrians settled in Flatbush, near the old Syrian community.

Many of them began praying in Ahi Ezer.

Ahi Ezer welcomed the new Syrians with the same warmth and excitement with which they had welcomed the Egyptians, the Lebanese, and all the other newcomers over the years. This time, everyone was family — literally. Emotional reunions, often surprise encounters, were taking place daily, to the joy and amazement of everyone around.

Nouri beamed.

Just a few months earlier, Ahi Ezer had many empty seats, as the congregation had been gradually losing its youth for years. Suddenly, the sanctuary was packed and Nouri couldn't stop smiling. Every Shabbat, there was a line-up to the Torah as the new immigrants, one by one, said the *Hagomel* blessing.[15] The tearful emotion with which those blessings were recited prompted a resounding "Amen!" that reverberated through the shul.

Beautiful, breathed Esther Dayan, watching from the women's gallery.

A few months after the first of the new Syrians arrived was Rosh Hashana. Just walking past Ahi Ezer was uplifting as crowds of happy people jammed the entranceway. Though there had been very little real Torah scholarship in Syria in the previous fifty years, Syrian Jewry connected to Hashem through prayer. They loved to sing, and the services that year were rousing and fervent.

For Simhat Bet Ha'Sho'eiba, the broader Syrian community joined together in Ahi Ezer and made a massive celebration. The old Syrians and the new Syrians celebrated as one large family. The euphoria of everyone being together, something that no one had dreamed possible the year

---

14. One major job was placing all the children in yeshivot. Dr. Mayer Ballas, Albert Ayal, and Sol Sasson interviewed all 900 immigrant children and, by September, only 52 boys had not been placed. Dr. Ballas asked Mr. Dayan to accompany him to Hacham Yosef Raful for a meeting. Hacham Yosef agreed to open a temporary yeshiva in Mikdash Melech provided that Dr. Ballas fund it. They had classes there for two years, after which the children were mainstreamed into local schools. To the community's credit, none of the immigrant children went to public school.

15. One says the *Hagomel* blessing when emerging safely from a dangerous situation such as prison (*Orach Chaim* 219).

Nouri, sitting in the front row, clapping joyously

before, was overwhelming. There was music and dancing and singing as everyone turned to one another in happy disbelief.

And few people were happier than Nouri Dayan.

"It's unbelievable. Daddy is on a high," Irwin commented to Murray.

Since his open-heart surgery, and then Uncle Dave's passing, Nouri seemed older, frailer, than ever before. The trip to Rav Shach had definitely rejuvenated him, but the arrival of the new Syrians made him positively euphoric. The jubilance came from a combination of finally seeing his brethren safe in America after all those years, and the rebirth of Ahi Ezer as a strong and vibrant synagogue.

"Mr. Ahi Ezer" was how many people referred to Nouri.

Indeed, Nouri had devoted most of his life to the community's growth and development. Though he never spoke pessimistically, it clearly pained him when the beautiful Ocean Parkway shul, which he pushed so hard to build, had become dry and empty within twenty years of its existence. No matter what he tried to do to boost attendance, it seemed to be in a downward spiral that no one knew how to reverse. The last thing that anyone expected was that President Assad would one day release all his Jews and a large portion of them would fill the seats of Ahi Ezer practically overnight!

"Definitely a miracle," Murray agreed.

"Murray, I need your help," Nouri greeted his son as he walked into the house. "Check these lists. Each child gets an envelope with his name on it.

Marvin Azrak, dancing with Rabbi Hamra

Then put in a dollar for every hour that he said *Tehillim*. And check that his mother signed for him."

Nouri was in his element. For years, he had barely a handful of "customers" for his *Tehillim* incentives. With the arrival of the new Syrians who had young children eager for a few dollars, Nouri's "customer list" grew from ten to twenty to thirty participants, and the number rose by the day. Every week, he made another trip to Mekor HaSeforim to order more personalized, leather-bound *Tehillims*, and to pick up the previous week's order. This was his newest incentive, in addition to the monetary allowances. The owners of Mekor HaSeforim were constantly amazed at the quantities of *sifrei Tehillim* that he bought.

As Murray stuffed the envelopes, his mind reeled: *The business is going down... and Daddy is giving away hundreds of dollars a week to kids who say Tehillim!*

And yet neither he nor Irwin, who also assisted their father in distributing the *Tehillim* money, would ever say a word. This was what their father wanted to do, and they graciously helped him... even when it was frustrating.

Irwin shook his head, bewildered. For some odd reason, Syrian women signed with their maiden names and he found it impossible to match the boys with their mothers. Each Mosa'ei Shabbat, as he distributed the envelopes to the children, he asked them again, "What is your name? What is

View of the entrance from the Ahi Ezer women's gallery

your mother's name? Is this your list from last week?" But as he looked at their shining faces when they received their envelopes, he remembered the words that Rav Reuven Elbaz once told his son, Ezra, "Your grandfather, he knew in what to invest."

Yes, Daddy is investing in generations of Jewish children.

Unfortunately, on the business end, Nouri's investments were not doing as well. Both Irwin and Murray had been working full time in the business for years, way before Dave had passed away. When Nouri bought out Dave Bibi back in 1986, it was just after Irwin had brought sales up to an all-time high of over $6 million. He had done this through expanding their line of affordable luxury chandeliers. By 1990, Bibi Continental published an impressive 150-page catalogue of glossy, full-color pictures of their products.

Then, within a year, the whole industry turned around.

The first blow came when Irwin noticed his competitors had copied practically his whole catalogue. *Inferior quality,* he noted, when he examined one of their pieces, *Taiwanese copies.*

Perhaps. But he soon realized that people preferred cheaply priced "Taiwanese junk" than high-priced Spanish or Italian quality. The buyer's whole mentality had changed. America was becoming a disposable society where people wanted to redo their houses every few years rather than decorate once and forever. People were moving away from luxury lighting — timeless pieces that cost thousands of dollars — and were buying cheap

View of the crowd

imitations that were easy to discard a few years down the line when they wanted to redecorate. New technologies made it easier for companies to copy original designs (almost instantly) and reproduce crystals, and other high-end materials, in plastic versions that were so close to the original, only an expert could tell the difference. These imitations were sold at a fraction of the price of an original and basically killed the market for economically priced luxury lighting.

Bibi Continental was suddenly struggling to keep up with the competition. Their main wholesale customers, the "Mom and Pop" stores spread across the country, were dying out because the chain stores, who bought huge quantities of imitation fixtures, were heavily out-pricing them. This happened to Bibi's retail chain, the Sunday Lighting stores, as well.

Irwin kept looking for new angles for the business. The 65th Street building was huge and no longer being fully used. He had a wall built and cordoned off part of the building to rent it out. When that proved profitable, he rented out another area, mainly to businesses who needed factory space. He also expanded their retail showroom in the 65th Street building. The local customers loved the artistic and original chandeliers that he designed and manufactured, still made mainly from the original Czechoslovakian crystals. Decorators came to order custom-made pieces to match a specific décor; only Bibi specialized in colored crystals that could be custom coordinated.

Some of the immigrant children

Everything was selling… but not enough. The business wasn't generating enough funds to compete with the big lighting companies. And on top of it all, they were still paying out the Bibi family.[16]

Nouri, the eternal optimist, was quick to forecast better times ahead.

"Things will turn around," he'd say. "We just have to forge ahead."

Then one day, Nouri proposed another idea. "I think that we should set aside an hour a day to learn — all three of us together — me, you, and Murray."

And that is exactly what they did. In the middle of every day, for one hour, Nouri, Irwin, and Murray instructed the secretaries to hold all the phone calls as the three of them congregated in Nouri's office for a midday *seder*.

Did business improve? Not really. But there was no significant downturn either, and at least they were spending more time learning Torah.

Once again, Nouri hit on the best investment.

---

16. The deal with Dave Bibi was fair and the payment plan was reasonable, based on the reality then. No one could have forecasted all the changes that would occur in the retail world — particularly in the lighting industry — that would precipitate a steady decline in their profits, year after year.

Chapter 64:

"HIS RADIANCE SHINES; HIS WAYS MAKE YOU CLING TO THE *SHECHINAH*."

Flatbush, 1993

"Good morning, Eddie."

"Good morning, Mr. Dayan."

Both men were putting away their *tefillin* and getting ready for their regular learning session.

"How is the family?"

"Fine, thank G-d."

Eddie marveled at the same routine, every day, for... how many years was it? Four in the Ocean Parkway shul, but probably more than ten if he counted all the years that they learned together at 71st Street. Day in and day out, except for the times that Mr. Dayan had been recovering from illnesses, they learned together. And their learning sessions never began without Mr. Dayan first inquiring about everyone's health and general well-being. They would begin in the back of the room, but if there was a *brit* taking place, Mr. Dayan would motion to Eddie that he follow him out and they would continue the class sitting on the steps in the back, leading upstairs.

"Let me get you a chair," Eddie protested.

But Mr. Dayan just shook his head and continued to teach. Eddie sat down beside him and listened as the Torah flowed effortlessly from his lips.

"Let me take you home," Eddie offered, after they finished learning.

Nouri had stopped arguing years ago. This, too, was part of the routine.

It's a privilege, Eddie noted, as he watched people stop Mr. Dayan as they left the building. Some people wanted to ask him a question; others

Nouri and Esther Dayan at their 50th anniversary. L-R: Shirley Dayan, Esther Dayan, Grandma Dayan, Grandpa Dayan, Rabbi Eli Dayan, Rabbi Ron Raful, Carol Raful.

just wanted to say hello. Eddie watched his interactions: *He never says anything negative about anyone… He never tells me to change. I want to change myself just by watching him and learning from his ways! My holidays are different holidays because of him. He teaches me the meaning of life. He teaches me to enjoy life through the Torah. His radiance shines; his ways make you cling to the Shechinah.*

Despite all the suffering that Nouri endured during those years, Nouri consistently found his life "sweet."

"Even I didn't merit a son-in-law like Hacham Yosef," Hacham Ovadya Yosef commented to Nouri fifteen years earlier, when he visited Ahi Ezer Yeshiva. Nouri smiled at the compliment but was fully cognizant of his gifts even without it.

Many times, he commented to his children, "Who am I to deserve anything? My merits? Maybe my forefathers…"

He took credit for nothing. He thanked Hashem for everything.

A few years earlier, when his family organized a 50th anniversary celebration, he was touched by the outpouring of love. He was blown away when they flashed a picture of his parents on the video screen.

My mother?! He stared at the photograph, the first he had ever seen.

He inched closer and put on his glasses to see more clearly.

Then they flashed another picture.

My father?! He stared again. His eyes welled up with tears.

552 / NOURI

More pictures followed, some evoking emotion, others evoking laughter. But no one forgot those precious moments, when the room turned silent as Nouri stared at the parents he had never known but always strove to honor. When the celebration ended, Nouri was pensive. He was overwhelmed with finally seeing a picture of his parents, concrete images to match the faces and feelings he had imagined. He was just as overwhelmed by the efforts that had brought those pictures to him.

"Where did you get them from?" he asked his daughter in wonder.

"Sara called Aunt Rachel in Eretz Yisrael. She was surprised that they never showed you the pictures and happily sent them," Carol answered.

Nouri and Esther Dayan at their 50th anniversary

"So much preparation... so much effort," Nouri marveled. "Everyone worked so hard to make this celebration... it's unbelievable. Thank you."

Daddy, you are the one who is unbelievable, thought Carol fondly.

Nouri's sincere belief that everything he had was a gift, including the warmth and love of his family, was unbelievable. The anniversary celebration only enhanced his feelings of gratefulness and obligation. He was a servant of Hashem; is not the servant of the King grateful for the privilege of serving Him?

Nouri still woke up very early in the morning and began his day by learning the Daf over the phone, in itself a lesson in *mesirut nefesh* for Torah. He leaned over the page of the Gemara with a huge magnifying glass as he tried to read the tiny letters even as his vision was deteriorating. He strained to hear the words (his hearing was also going) and follow along. His face was furrowed in concentration. For Nouri, learning the Daf required intense effort.

Then it was off to Ahi Ezer for more praying and learning, after which he returned home for breakfast with Esther before going to work. His life was regimented, from early in the morning until late at night.

"Because you can't become a great person without routine," Esther explained to her grandson, Ezra, years earlier. "A person must have a schedule — when to get up, when to pray, when to eat, when to learn, when to work — only through discipline can one become great."

Disciplined living was the framework from which Nouri's spirituality flourished. In the evening, when there were no meetings to attend, Nouri sat down with a *sefer* and continued to learn, until he was nodding off from fatigue. Even when he got ready for bed, he wore *tzitzit*. On his night table next to his bed, there was a Mishnayot. He went to sleep reading from the Mishna, and when he woke up in the morning it was the first thing that he saw.[17]

All his actions were calculated; nothing was random.

But it was from Erev Shabbat until after Shabbat that Nouri's spirit soared.

Friday morning, after learning, Nouri waited as the shul emptied out. He tidied up the place, replacing some of the *siddurim* that the *shamash* had forgotten, straightening up the *sefarim*. Nouri's love of his shul only deepened over the course of his life. He wanted everything to be perfect when he came back later to welcome the Shabbat Queen.

Finally, he and Hacham Sion were the only ones left.

Hacham Sion opened the *heichal*, took out a *Sefer Torah*, and read the Torah portion for that week. Nouri followed as Hacham Sion read through that week's reading to make sure that there were no problems with the *Sefer Torah*. He was already focused on the approaching Shabbat.

Yosef Ozeirey walked toward the Dayan home early Friday afternoon.

It was 1 o'clock. He quickened his pace, eager to open the door and have that simple serenity overwhelm him. He could smell the Shabbat foods, fully cooked and resting in the oven. He could see the Shabbat table, decked in white, completely set. He could hear Grandpa learning from a *sefer* while Grandma sat silently nearby, peacefully crocheting something pretty while awaiting the Shabbat Queen.

Sure enough, Grandpa had showered, shaved, cut his nails, shined his shoes, and dressed in his Shabbat best, hours before candle-lighting. Grandma was also fully prepared for Shabbat, but as soon as Yosef came in, Grandma went into the kitchen to bring him an early taste of Shabbat.

"A *beracha* out loud," Grandpa reminded Yosef.

He was soon joined by some more cousins but, no matter who popped in Erev Shabbat, nothing marred that blissful peacefulness. They were partaking not only of the food, but of the spiritual ambience.

Yosef counted the settings around the table. As usual, there was one extra.

---

17. The Arizal recommends wearing *tzitzit* even at night as a *segula* for *yirat Shamayim*. (*Shaar HaKavanot, Drush* 1). The letters of Mishna and *neshama* (soul) are the same, alluding to the value of learning Mishna before going to sleep [giving up one's *neshama*].

"Just in case Grandpa brings home an unexpected guest," Grandma had explained to Yosef. Lately, that wasn't happening, though they had plenty of scheduled guests, usually children and grandchildren. Nonetheless, Esther faithfully set an extra setting, just in case.

Shortly before candle-lighting, Nouri headed to shul.

"Come, Yosef," he invited his grandson.

Inevitably, they were the first ones to arrive.

"Here," Nouri opened a bottle of rose-water, "let us make a *beracha*, another *zechut*!"

And the two of them said a *beracha* over the *besamim* and answered "Amen" to each other's *berachot*. Slowly, the shul filled up. They prayed Minha and Kabbalat Shabbat.

"Let us be *mezakeh et harabbim*," Nouri instructed Yosef as he opened *siddurim* to Minha. Yosef knew the routine, and hastened to help his grandfather who, even after his open-heart surgery, insisted on helping the people.

Once the prayers started, Yosef was glued to his grandfather's side. From the time he was old enough to read, when he went to shul with Grandpa, he never wanted to run around and play, but was proud to remain next to him the entire time. He loved watching Grandpa pray: He stood absolutely straight as he said the *amida*, a servant facing his Master, his concentration evident on his face. Yet he never went overtime; if he took too long, maybe someone would think that he was a Rabbi.

Yosef stayed with Grandpa all the way until after *Aleinu*, when the entire congregation sat down and sang *Yigdal* together. Then, as everyone approached Hacham Sion to wish him a Shabbat Shalom, they stopped by "Mr. President" as well. Though Nouri had abdicated that position years before, the congregation still looked to him as their leader.

Nouri was the first to arrive and the last one to leave, as he lovingly put away stray *siddurim* so that the next morning the people would all return to a perfectly prepared shul.

"Shabbat Shalom," Nouri called out as he opened the door to his home.

"Shabbat Shalom," answered Esther, rising from her seat with a smile.

He brings the kedushah into the house with him, noted a granddaughter, as Nouri walked to his seat — in the middle of the table, never at the head, a practice he adopted years ago when all the children wanted to sit near him — and proceeded to sing *Shalom Aleihem*. Then it was onto the next song, and the next… It took at least a half hour until he actually made Kiddush. Esther felt bad for the grandchildren who might be hungry, but her guests loved the holy atmosphere and kept coming back, week after week.

Over time, Nouri had taken on more customs until he kept every *humra* of the *Kaf HaHaim* and more. He made Kiddush over 12 challos. He used a *kos* for *birkat ha'mazon*. He did everything slowly, lovingly, demonstrating how each action was a pleasure. The meal was a royal feast, not just because of the many elaborate dishes that were always fresh and delicious, but because each course was an event, drawn out through singing and *dibrei Torah*. There was no idle talk, and certainly no negative talk. No one dared ruin the sublime atmosphere.

Yosef slept on the couch in the living room.

He heard his grandfather learning.

He rolled over to check the clock. 4:30 a.m. He closed his eyes for a few more minutes. Then he leaped out of bed, washed his hands, dressed, and joined Grandpa at the table. Grandpa beamed. "Birchot HaShahar — come on, I want to say Amen to your *berachot*."

So Yosef said *Birchot HaShahar* out loud and Nouri answered Amen. Then Nouri went to the kitchen and took out seven-layer cake, or checkerboard cake, and he cut a slice for Yosef and served it to him with a cup of tea. He answered Amen to his *berachot* and then went back to his learning while Yosef sipped his tea and ate his cake and wondered if there could be anything holier than Shabbat with Grandpa.

Slowly, the sun rose and they were off to shul.

Once again, they were the first ones there and the last ones to leave.

And, all the way there and back, they only spoke *dibrei Torah*.

The day meal was also lovingly drawn out as Nouri read all the Mishnayot, sang the *pizmonim*, and said more *dibrei Torah* in between eating all the delicious foods. Though he was elderly and weak, he couldn't imagine sleeping his Shabbat away. After the *seuda*, he lay down on the couch, his *kippah* pulled over his eyes as he dozed off... but only for a short time.

Soon, another grandson, Shaul Dayan, was knocking at the door, waiting to accompany Grandpa to *Mishmara*, a task he loved. Though it was far from common in their community, Grandpa Dayan always wore a hat in the street. He was always well dressed and dignified, even as age had rounded his shoulders. People stopped him in the street to greet him respectfully.

His life has always been about respect for others. No wonder everyone respects him! Shaul decided.

From *Mishmara*, to Minha, to *seuda shelishit*, to Arbit, to another *shiur*, and then finally home for *seuda rebi'it*, which Nouri still prepared on his own, singing the *pizmonim* as he diced the tomatoes, mixed the tuna, sliced the *halla*, and ate.

Holiness: from before Shabbat began until way after it ended.

Rabbi Joey Dayan happened to stop by for a visit one day. Years had passed since he had asked to join the business, and he was still grateful for his father's answer, which kept him firmly in the Bet Midrash. He taught in Ateret Torah, which gave him the *zechut* of teaching Torah to others, and spent the rest of his day also learning and teaching.

Nouri was in a thoughtful mood.

"I want to tell you something... two very important things," Nouri began.

Joey was mystified. Never did his father speak to him in this way.

"You have no idea how important it is to be *mezakeh et harabbim*," Nouri said emphatically. "The second thing I want to tell you: You work with the *tzibbur*, you must always be *l'shem Shamayim*."

Joey was startled.

It's as if he is handing me his final will... he mused. While neither of these concepts were new to Joey, the way his father seemed to be talking to himself, and yet addressing his child, lent the statement greater force.

He is telling me his expectations of me... now and forever.

Chapter 65:
"HOW CAN I EXPRESS MY GRATEFULNESS TO THE BOREI OLAM?"

Imagine a man sitting in mud up to his waist. He takes a washing cup, washes his hands, and says, "Now I'm all clean." Ridiculous! He is sitting in mud. There is no way that he is going to become clean by washing his hands. Imagine a different man, dressed in a beautiful white suit, walking down the street. A car speeds by and splashes some mud on this man's pants. It does not take much to clean up those little stains; a trip to the dry cleaners and the suit is pure white once again.

People who, in this world, are "in the mud" up to their waists, toward the end of their lives find it very hard to "become clean." At that point, there are not enough troubles in the world to cleanse them from their sins, so Hashem leaves them alone. Tzaddikim are compared to the man who is wearing the white suit. Over the course of his life, there are only a few minor stains that have soiled the suit. Hashem gives these tzaddikim a hard time at the end of their stay in this world, and through those hardships those "small stains" are cleansed. After they pass away, they go straight up to claim their portion in Gan Eden. [Paraphrased from the hesped that Hacham Yehuda Ades said on Mr. Nouri Dayan.]

Flatbush, 1994

Rabbi David Ozeirey was walking with his father-in-law.

"I thought that I accomplished things in my lifetime," Nouri commented suddenly. "I built the shuls, the yeshiva, the Senior Homes... But I just heard of a Rabbi in Eretz Yisrael who accomplished much more than that..." He lapsed into silence.

Rabbi Ozeirey was too taken aback to answer. What do you answer someone who feels that he could never do enough for Hashem and His people?

Nouri and Esther spent Purim with Rabbi Mordechai and Joyce Nahem, their children in Deal. Their son, Murray, was also there with his family.

"Dad," Murray addressed his father, "what is the matter? You don't look good."

Nouri sighed, "I didn't learn enough Torah in my life."

Elderly, weak, and beset by health issues, Nouri still expected to grow and improve. When he felt that wasn't happening, he grew thoughtful and somewhat sad. Even as he went from one health issue to another, he kept pushing himself.

The years that had passed only strengthened his love of mitzvot, even as they dulled his physical abilities. A few days before Sukkot, two of his grandsons came to help him decorate the *sukka*. A plain *sukka* was never enough for Nouri. Every mitzva had to be done with the greatest *hiddur* that he knew about. He was determined not only to have a decorated *sukka*, but to be involved in the mitzva. So Nouri worked with them, holding the decorations as the boys climbed up the ladder and commenting on where to hang them. But the expression on his face seemed strained…

"Grandpa, are you okay?" one of the boys asked.

"I'm fine," Nouri answered dismissively, "it's just a headache."

But the headache became overwhelmingly painful.

Nouri went to lie down. When he didn't come out of his room for a while, his son-in-law, Rabbi Ozeirey, went to see how he was feeling. Nouri was very still and sweating profusely. Then he lost consciousness and was rushed to the hospital.

"He seems to have suffered from an aneurism," noted the doctor grimly. "We cannot operate since the aspirin that he takes for his heart condition has thinned his blood. We have to pray that the bleeding stops on its own."

The next few days were very tense.

Then the hospital staff noticed that Nouri seemed somewhat conscious.

"Draw him out," they urged the family. "Give him familiar cues."

Joyce began reciting a *passuk* in *Tehillim*… and Nouri murmured its ending.

Baruch Hashem, Daddy is back.

But the road to full recovery proved to be long and tedious.

When Joey came to the hospital, his father was lying so still, he wondered if he was conscious. His eyes were closed and his lips were moving, so Joey lowered his ear to his father's lips to hear if he was speaking coherently. His eyes widened in surprise: *Daddy is murmuring the derasha that we were speaking about before he had his aneurism!*

When Irwin came to visit, Nouri's eyes were open, but he seemed far away.

"Dad, do you know who I am?" Irwin asked.

"*Yisrael asher b'cha etpa'er,*"[18] Nouri said weakly.

Irwin — whose name was Yisrael — smiled in relief: *Daddy is okay.*

Indeed, Nouri was on a slow journey to recovery. Yet it was specifically in his weakened state that his exalted soul was being revealed. During those first few days, he only spoke *lashon kodesh*. On a subconscious level, that was the language most natural to him, though it was neither his mother tongue nor the language he spoke most often. But it was the language of his soul.

In his weakness, it was his soul that shined through.

Nouri remained in the hospital for a few days so that the doctors could monitor his condition. In his weakness — or perhaps due to the medication — he cried easily, a situation that was painful for the family who was used to seeing their father and grandfather always stoic and in control. They tried to cheer him up by singing, but the tears continued to flow.

Irwin brought his *tefillin* and Nouri began to cry once again.

"Dad, what is wrong? What did I do?"

Nouri just shook his head weakly. It was then that Irwin realized that he had taken an unfamiliar *tefillin* bag. He looked more closely and was amazed.

My father has Rabbeinu Tam tefillin?

In their community, only great Rabbis wore Rabbeinu Tam *tefillin*. Irwin still remembered his grandfather, Hacham Murad, praying with both *tefillin* on his forehead at once, as was customary among the great Syrian Rabbis. But his father?! As the tears continued to fall, Irwin understood: His father had been putting on Rabbeinu Tam *tefillin* for years, in the privacy of his home, so that no one would know about it. Now the secret was out and that pained Nouri.[19]

"What is going on?" Esther asked Irwin, who stood silently by as his father cried. After Irwin explained to her why his father was crying, Esther exclaimed, "You mean that is what he was doing? Every morning, after he came back from shul, he would go to his room for about three minutes, and then he would come out for breakfast. I never asked him about it. I figured that it wasn't my business."

Nouri wanted to remain hidden. Esther, as usual, respected his will.

Though Nouri was out of danger, he was clearly not himself. The doctors explained that it would take him time to recover and they released

---

18. Yisrael, in you, I (Hashem) am glorified (*Yeshayah* 49:3).
19. When Rav Yehuda Ades heard this story, he was amazed. "This is the type of story said over about our great, hidden *tzaddikim*," he declared.

Rabbi Maimon Elbaz visiting Nouri with a delegation of students from Ahi Ezer Torah Center and Ateret Torah; Yosef (son of Murray) Dayan is on the far right.

him to RUSK, NYU's rehabilitation center, where he would "relearn" how to walk properly and improve his cognitive function. Nonetheless, the prognosis was good.

"A miracle," agreed the doctors.

Indeed, Nouri felt that he had truly faced death and had been spared. As he astonished the doctors with his quick command of numbers so soon after a cerebral event, as he caught the ball the therapists threw at him and then threw it back to them, as he took baby step after baby step — first with an aide, then with a walker, then with a cane, and then by himself — he was inordinately grateful to the Borei Olam for keeping him alive.

How can I express my gratefulness to the Borei Olam? he wondered.

This thought preoccupied him constantly.

When he returned home, his children and grandchildren were always around, encouraging and helping him... and learning from him.

No matter how difficult the exercises, how painful it was to conquer his weakness, Nouri never complained about his ordeal. He accepted his challenges with dignity and was determined to overcome his limitations. One day, Nouri greeted Irwin with excitement. "I know how I want to express my gratefulness to Hashem."

Irwin waited patiently.

"I'm almost ready to return to shul. On my first time returning, I want you to hold me on one side, your brother on the other side, and I want to go up to the *heichal* and prostrate myself."

"Daddy," Irwin protested, aghast.

Nouri's request seemed a bit extreme; Irwin couldn't believe that he was serious. It was so like his father to want to do something concrete, but so unlike him to want to do something so unusual in public. Irwin marveled at his father's effusive gratefulness. Nothing short of a public display of that gratefulness would satisfy him.

Jack walked into the Ahi Ezer Synagogue office. He looked very annoyed.

"Where is my money?" he asked the secretary.

"Excuse me, sir?"

"Where is my envelope for the month? From the organization?"

"What envelope? What organization?" The secretary was puzzled.

"The Ahi Ezer Fund," Jack told her, clearly exasperated.

"Fund for what?"

"For what? I don't know. The fund for people down on their luck, like me."

"I'm sorry, sir, there is no such organization," apologized the secretary.

"What do you mean? Every month, for the past — I don't know how many — years, I get an envelope with cash…"

"I'm working here for ten years, there is no such organization." Then the secretary paused. "Maybe you know which gentleman gave you this envelope? What was his name? What did he look like?"

Jack shrugged. "I don't know… a slim man… elderly… clean shaven."

The secretary smiled. "It sounds like Mr. Dayan. That would be just like him."

Nouri had been out of circulation for a while and his family began to learn about some of the projects that he had worked so hard to keep secret. Now Hashem was revealing small glimpses of that hidden goodness.

"Three *Sifrei Torah*," murmured Nouri. "Tomorrow, I have to go to shul. Three *Sifrei Torah*…"

"What's he saying?" Esther asked Shaul, the grandson on duty that night.

He's confused, reasoned Shaul. *I mean, tomorrow, we take out three Sifrei Torah, but there is no way Grandpa is going to shul. He can barely walk.*

"Shaul, wake up," Esther shook her grandson awake the next morning, "Grandpa's not in bed. He's gone to shul."

Shaul stared at her in disbelief.

"Go to shul! Find out what happened to him."

Shaul scrambled out of bed and off to shul. *I can't believe it… How did he get out of the house, down two flights of stairs… and then what?*

"Then he got to the end of the block, but he couldn't go anymore," explained Rabbi Leib Keleman. "I found him there, lying on the floor. I asked a child to bring a wheelchair and wheel him to shul. You should have heard the standing ovation he received when he arrived!"

Nouri beamed at his grandson: He had gotten to shul for the three *Sifrei Torah*.

Nouri was still determined to come up with a concrete way to express his gratefulness to Hashem. He hit upon the idea of printing up a unique *Tehillim* card he entitled: *Tefillah l'kol tzorech* — a prayer for all needs. He included several passages of *Tehillim* plus a prayer for the ill to be healed. It was conveniently wallet sized and laminated, with the Hebrew words on one side and the English translation on the other. Norman (Nochum) Kornfeld of Simcha Graphics designed and produced the card according to Nouri's instructions.[20]

Nouri began distributing these cards to everyone he met. People appreciated the convenience of having these prayers so easily accessible. If they were in the car or waiting for a bus, they could take out this little card and say some *Tehillim* during that time. And, once more, Nouri was being *mezakeh et harabbim*.

It took a while until Nouri began to walk unattended, but he refused to put his life on hold. When Seymour Escava was honored by Ahi Ezer, Nouri insisted on attending the dinner, even confined to a wheelchair.

When Nouri was finally ready to discard the wheelchair, life still didn't revert to what it had been. Nouri was unsteady on his feet and sometimes would fall, but he was determined to go to shul. Many people would have loved to give him a ride, or accompany him on Shabbat, but Nouri was still fiercely independent and he didn't want to have to depend on other people for his day-to-day activities.

One time, Nouri tripped on the steps of the shul and broke his glasses. An acquaintance who was passing by ran to pick him up. Nouri's face was bloody from the fall, but he seemed not to notice.

"Please," he begged his friend, "don't tell my wife; she won't let me come to shul anymore."

Of course Esther wanted Nouri to go to shul, but only accompanied by another person. She arranged for children, grandchildren, neighbors, and friends to accompany him. But if they arrived a few minutes late, Nouri was usually gone.

"Nouri, are you ready to go?"

"Almost, Albert, but don't worry, you don't have to wait."

---

20. Albert Levy regularly visited patients in Maimonides Hospital. He loved Mr. Dayan's cards, and asked for many more cards to give out to people in the hospital. Mr. Dayan was happy to oblige.

But Albert Levy waited because he wanted to walk Nouri home. They were inevitably joined by Rabbi Avraham Travitsky, who lived nearby and loved to discuss that week's *Rabbeinu Bachye* with Nouri.[21] From Ocean Parkway until East 12th Street, they were absorbed in their conversation, only talking *dibrei Torah*. But when they hit East 12th Street, Nouri noticed immediately.

"Here is where you turn off," he reminded Reb Avraham.

"No," Reb Avraham insisted. "I want to continue our discussion."

And I want to make sure that you get home safely, was his unsaid goal.

When they reached the Dayan home, and stood in front of the steep staircase leading to the door, Nouri turned to his escorts. "Shabbat Shalom," he wished them.

"I want to go up and say Shabbat Shalom to Esther," Albert insisted.

And I want to help you get up all those stairs safely...

And that was how, inevitably, Nouri was escorted home by at least two escorts.

In so many ways, he was the same old Nouri. In shul, "Mr. President" still felt responsible to keep things running smoothly. One week, there was a low rumbling during Arbit.

"He's too low."

"Tell him to pray louder."

"I can't hear a thing."

Nouri was becoming frustrated by the lack of decorum. Even if the new *hazzan* didn't have a very powerful voice, that wasn't the real reason that people couldn't hear him...

Nouri walked up to the middle of the room and addressed everyone. "If all of you would stop talking, you will be able to hear the *hazzan*!" And then he went back to his place.

Even as he slowed down, Nouri still came into the business every day.

"Why, Grandpa?" asked Yosef Ozeirey on a visit to the office. After Grandpa's aneurism, Yosef spent a lot of time in the Dayan house. He knew that Grandpa was weak and needed help for many activities. Besides, he was way past retirement age.

Irwin and Murray also listened with interest as their father answered.

"*Yafeh talmud Torah im derech eretz* — it's good for a person to work and learn Torah. The Mishna in *Abot* says that when one works even as he learns, he will not come to sin. Every day that I come into the office, I'm protecting myself from sinning."

---

21. "Escorting him was a treat, never a burden," wrote Reb Avraham Travitsky in a letter to the family. "Once, in a conversation about how people suffer, I mentioned a Rosh HaYeshiva who was in great need as an illustration of the principle under discussion. It was never my intention to ask for a donation. But it was too late! Mr. Dayan insisted on giving this man a contribution. Mr. Dayan's simplicity and sincerity was from generations ago. He served both Hashem and His people with the same zeal."

Nouri's simple sincerity shone through.

This was even more amazing given that, at that point, only an incorrigible optimist like Nouri could find it uplifting to go into the office while the business continued to decline. His only bow to old age was that he spent less hours in the office and had given up most of his management duties. He came to the business and headed straight to his office where he learned until noon. Then he met with "the boys" — Irwin and Murray — to speak about the state of the business and what steps they were taking to build it up. He offered insights and optimism and busied himself anywhere that he thought he could be useful.

When the business had been doing well, he faced the test of recognizing that its success was from Hashem and therefore should be shared with Hashem's people. This had been his attitude for over fifty years. Now that the business was declining, he faced a different test: How does one deal with going from riches to rags?

For Nouri, there was only one way to view the situation: Everything is from Hashem and therefore it must be good. Besides, just because the business is suffering, why should the community suffer? No matter how poorly the business was doing, Nouri was still donating his time, his money, and his chandeliers. His approach to charity distributions was similarly unchanged. Late in the morning, the cars would pull up in front of the building — five *meshulachim* at a time; each one would come in, one at a time, and say his story. Nouri listened patiently, always asked for a *d'bar Torah*, and always responded with a donation.

Just before 3 in the afternoon, Nouri would call a car service to take him to Ahi Ezer. Inevitably, the taxi driver was an unaffiliated Russian or Israeli Jew. Nouri would engage the driver in conversation by telling him a *d'bar Torah* or encouraging him to send his children to yeshivot. In Ahi Ezer, he learned with his brother-in-law, Rabbi Jack, in a small library off the main shul. Their nephew, Rabbi Maxi Maslaton, gave a mini-class to his two uncles.

Nouri was still in Ahi Ezer every day, twice a day (he always prayed Arbit and Minha together). He was still attuned to what was going on there. When he met a *meshulach* from Eretz Yisrael who also happened to be a *sofer*, he offered him a proposal, "Perhaps you would like to stay here for a while to check and repair all our *Sifrei Torah*?"

The shul housed well over 30 *Sifrei Torah*, many of which were old and needed to be checked. The *sofer* readily agreed and, for the next half a year, worked daily in one of the side rooms in Ahi Ezer.

As usual, Nouri sensed a need and went to meet it.

Chapter 66:
"I THINK THAT THIS IS GOING TO BE MY LAST TIME..."

Flatbush, 1997

"Uncle Nouri," cajoled Marvin, "it's been over a decade since the Testimonial Dinner. Besides, that honor came mainly from the yeshiva. Now we want to honor you at the shul dinner. We have never done that before."

"I'm really uncomfortable with this," Nouri sighed.

"I know, so I'm not asking you to accept this alone. We'll honor you together with Hacham Sion. The two of you have lived together, learned together, and built up the community together, for over sixty years. It will not be a standard dinner with standard honorees. We want to donate a *Sefer Torah* as a tribute to you." Marvin spoke fast, excited.

Nouri sighed again. He really didn't want this.

"Hacham Sion seems ready to agree…"

Nouri shrugged. If his brother-in-law agreed, he would not be left with much of a choice. But he really didn't want this public display of honor. His short message at the dinner encapsulated that feeling: "Give honor to the Torah," he began. "Though Hacham Sion and I are being honored tonight, the real honor belongs to the Torah. Those who toil in learning Torah, and those who support them, are the true servants of Hashem."

Nonetheless, the outpouring of love and generosity from the community toward their leaders was overwhelming. Marvin had organized a gala affair that was poignant and uplifting. Nouri was abashed at the attention, but appreciated the warmth and good-will of everyone involved. Hacham Sion seemed particularly overcome by the spirit of the occasion. No one

Hacham Yosef Harari Raful writing a letter in the *Sefer Torah*

could foresee that this would be the last major public appearance for both of them.

I must be getting old, Nouri sighed.

He had stopped driving; it was simply too much of a strain. No one let him walk to and from shul alone anymore. Though there was never a shortage of volunteers for this honor, Nouri was very aware that he needed the companionship, especially when the weather was wet or icy.

His hearing was going.

His children convinced him to get a hearing aid but it sometimes emitted a screeching sound that was annoying, so he often opted not to wear it. Every time there was *keri'at haTorah* in shul, he walked up to the *teba* and stood right nearby, to make sure that he heard every word. It was an amazing sight: Nouri, still a pillar of the community, humbly walking over to the *teba*, standing for the entire reading, concentrating on every word.

When he came to the *teba* for his *aliya*, the whole shul stood up for him.

Nouri hated receiving this honor, but honor pursued him.

The *Yamim No'raim* arrived.

As usual, Nouri bought the honor of holding the *Sefer Torah* by *Kol Nidrei*. It was part of the routine, an intrinsic part of the Ahi Ezer services. After he returned the *Sefer Torah* to the *aron*, he seemed pensive.

"I think that this is going to be my last time," he told Ike Swed.

"Nouri," protested Ike, "you are not going anywhere! You are going to be around for a long time. They will dedicate statues in your honor before you leave this world."

Nouri and Hacham Yosef, next to the *Sefer Torah*

"I don't want statues," Nouri shook his head vigorously, "I don't want anything. All I want is that everyone should live in peace."[22]

The first day of Sukkot arrived.

"Please, do me a favor," Nouri begged an acquaintance who normally prayed in Ateret Torah. "Pray in Ahi Ezer. I can't stand on my feet for so long, but I have this *lulav* and *etrog* that I bought for the people. Make sure everyone who walks in makes a *beracha* on the *lulav* and *etrog*."

He had been *mezakeh et harabbim* with this mitzva for so many years, he couldn't bear the thought that someone might not say the blessing, because he was too weak to help him.

Nouri was in pain.

Dr. Ballas, his cardiologist, recommended that he check into the hospital for some tests. They discovered that he needed a surgical procedure, only they first had to take him off Coumadin, the blood thinner that he was taking for his heart condition, before they could operate. They put him on Heparin, a blood thinner that wears off after 24 hours, and then they operated. The surgery was successful, but the doctors saw that the blood

---

22. "Mr. Dayan was a visionary, but he always worked with his people. If someone disagreed with an idea, he made it his personal mission to find out why and then he would decide if he should change his idea, or convince the other person to accept it. He wanted everyone to be happy" (Mr. Ike Swed).

wasn't coagulating and there was internal bleeding. They had no choice but to take him off the Heparin as well.

Twenty-four hours later, there was a marked improvement.

Thirty-six hours later, Nouri was feeling even better.

One of his grandsons rattled off the beginning of a Mishna in *Abot*.

Nouri smiled and finished off the Mishna easily.

Everyone was relieved: *Grandpa would be fine.*

Hacham Yosef came to visit his father-in-law in the hospital.

"A *d'bar Torah*," Nouri asked him. "Please, share some Torah with me."

Hacham Yosef was amazed that, in his weakened state, the only thing that Nouri wanted to discuss was Torah.

The next morning, Nouri was transferred to Metropolitan Hospital for rehabilitation. The Dayan family hired a *yeshiva bachur* to be with him the entire time, especially on Shabbat when it was hard for a family member to be there constantly.

Shabbat morning, Nouri had a surprise visitor.

"What are you doing here, Maoz?"

"*Mabrook*, Grandpa! Adele had a baby girl a couple of hours ago," announced Maoz Raful, somewhat breathless after climbing up several flights of steps.

"*Mabrook! Tizkeh l'gadla l'Torah l'chuppah u'l'maasim tovim!*" Nouri called out effusively. Then he changed tracks, "Where is your Uncle Irwin?"

"I don't know," Maoz apologized, "but I will try to find him for you. I'm walking back to Flatbush. Maybe I'll meet him along the way."

Indeed, Maoz bumped into Uncle Irwin on Ocean Parkway. "Grandpa is asking for you," he told him.

Irwin nodded and began walking faster. When he arrived at the hospital, he found his father alert and in a good mood. Irwin walked around with him, as per the doctor's recommendation that, after surgery, a patient recovers more quickly if he becomes mobile. Irwin returned home after Shabbat very optimistic.

"Dad," Irwin greeted Nouri jovially on Monday morning, "how are you feeling?"

Nouri didn't respond. Even more disturbing, his eyes were glassy and he wasn't moving. Alarmed, Irwin called the doctor.

"He had a stroke," pronounced the doctor, grimly. "We'll have to transfer him to Maimonides."

From that point on, Nouri was comatose.[23]

---

23. "I did a little digging to find out what happened. He had been doing so well, why the sudden downturn? I saw that when they transferred him to Metropolitan after the surgery, on his list of medications they forgot to write down Coumadin. When our lawyer heard this story, he told us that we had an unbelievable case of negligence, but my mother refused to sue," recalled Mr. Irwin Dayan. Fittingly, Mr. Morris Srour recounted the following

Esther was in the hospital all day, every day. Irwin was there every morning for three hours. Murray would take over in the afternoon. All the Dayan children took turns keeping their mother company at Nouri's bedside as they tried to stimulate their father to wake up.

Irwin said *Tehillim* aloud, singing it with different tunes, anything to illicit some response from his father. All the volunteers from the Sephardic Bikur Cholim and Satmar Bikur Cholim loved to listen to Irwin's singing, but Nouri remained unresponsive. Irwin also read the *Hok l'Yisrael* of the day, just as his father had done every day, practically from the time he was able to read.

One day he came to the passage, *v'ein shilton b'yom ha'mavet*.[24]

"Irwin, look!"

A lone tear rolled down Nouri's cheek.

On some level, he is with us, marveled Irwin. That knowledge drove him to find other ways to draw his father out of his seemingly endless sleep. He encouraged everyone to visit — children, grandchildren, other relatives, and friends. Hacham Sion was admitted into the hospital for a minor condition. While he was a patient, he came to visit Nouri. With his usual jovial good humor, he talked to him and tried to encourage a response, but none was forthcoming.

"I can't stand it," Esther told Joey. "He needs a haircut. And when he is not shaved, he looks unkempt." For almost sixty years, Esther had taken care of her husband. His food was always on the table at precisely the time they arranged. His clothing were always cleaned and pressed. She viewed the role of wife as being a holy obligation, an honor and a privilege. Suddenly, she couldn't take care of him the way she felt he should be cared for and it bothered her.

"Ma, I'll take care of it."

Joey began coming every Friday, together with his son. They would wash Nouri's hair and shave him, and Esther was able to relax when she saw that her husband was being cared for properly.

People from the community and the family came constantly. Grown men — millionaires — sat at his bedside and cried as they said *Tehillim*. One of them kissed his forehead and then turned to the family members who were with him, saying, "He made me. Everything that I am today is because of Nouri."

This sentiment was repeated over and over by the many visitors who came to say *Tehillim* at Nouri's bedside. They were broken when they saw

---

incident: One time in the shul, when Irwin was a little kid, one of the other kids pulled out the chair from under him and he fell on the floor. Another kid cried out, "Sue him!" Mr. Dayan helped him up, brushed him off, and said very firmly, "We don't sue."

24. And one has no control over the day of his death (*Kohelet* 8:8).

their mentor so ill and yet they kept coming, some regularly and some sporadically, but rarely was there a day without visitors from the community.

Family members were there constantly. One grandchild would sleep over one night and the next night a different one took over. They scheduled slots so that Nouri was never alone and Esther always had company when she was there.

They never gave up trying to stimulate him to react.

Irwin held his father's hand as he read the *Tehillim*, or the *Hok l'Yisrael*. Sometimes he felt him move, but the doctors said that any reaction was only a reflex. One time Irwin brought a very sweet-smelling flower and held it under Nouri's nose to coax a reaction. There was none.

Months passed with no change.

On Rosh Hashana, Irwin walked from Flatbush to blow the *shofar* for Nouri.

There was no response.

On Hol Ha'moed, Hacham Sion passed away.

Nouri still hung on.

Every once in a while, something encouraging occurred.

Rabbi Avraham Travitsky was a regular visitor. *I finally understand the meaning of HaShechinah lemalah meiroshotav shel holeh,*[25] he mused after a visit. In his unconscious state, Nouri's face radiated holiness.

Even though it seemed futile, every time he visited, Reb Avraham read aloud the words of the Rabbeinu Bachye, which Nouri loved so much. One day, months after Nouri was in a coma with no sign of change, as Reb Avraham hollered the words of Rabbeinu Bachye, he and Esther noticed, in shock, tears flowing from Nouri's eyes. Such was his yearning for Torah! Reb Avraham was dismayed. He had hoped to provoke a reaction, but he was upset that the reaction seemed to indicate that he had caused Nouri pain.

"It's my father's tremendous love of Torah that provoked those tears," Murray explained. "Please continue to yell Torah into his ear. These words of Torah keep him alive."

As long as there was life, there was hope.

They never stopped hoping.

Esther asked Hacham Baruch Ben Haim for tapes of him saying the whole *Tehillim* and she would play those tapes for Nouri constantly.

"He hears it," she would insist. "I'm sure of it."

The children and grandchildren walked in on Shabbat. The girls would sing *zemirot* for him. One week, as they were singing *Yedid Nefesh*, tears began falling down Nouri's cheeks. When Joyce came to visit, and one of her brothers was "praying with him," they noticed that Nouri seemed to be counting the *Pittom Ketoret* with his hands.

---

25. His Holy Presence rests above the head of an ill person (*Shabbat* 12b).

"*Kedusha*, he only responds to *kedusha*," they commented in wonder.

As difficult as those months were, these glimpses of greatness were uplifting.

Nouri continued to physically deteriorate. He developed terrible bedsores that became infected. It was heartbreaking for the family to discuss with the doctors whether to amputate his foot, which had turned black from gangrene. But then they would see how, even in his unconscious state, Nouri's purity shone through, and that gave them encouragement.

Every day that he was with them was a gift.

Ezra Ozeirey came to the hospital to spend Shabbat with Grandma and Grandpa. Next to Nouri's bed was the small hospital table, usually covered with paraphernalia, now decked in a small white tablecloth. He began singing *Shalom Aleihem*, and then the other *zemirot*, softly. Tears escaped from Nouri's eyes.

Ezra looked up and met his grandmother's gaze, while he still sang.

He hears me. We know it.

Ezra made Kiddush… *Hamosi*… He and Esther ate and sang and felt that Nouri was with them. Ezra read the *perasha* with the proper tunes. The atmosphere in the room was holy, sublime, and yet electric.

Two nights later, it was all over.

Chapter 67:

"HE HAD MERITS, AND BROUGHT MERITS TO MANY..."

Flatbush, the 6th of Adar, 1999

They stood together — children, grandchildren, great-grandchildren, family, and friends — in shock. Though a year had passed since Nouri had lapsed into a coma, they couldn't believe that he was gone.

He passed away the day before the *yahrtzeit* of Moshe Rabbeinu.

The burial was scheduled for the next day, in Israel, on the *yahrtzeit* itself.

How fitting: *Hazal* explain that Moshe Rabbeinu was *zaha v'zeekah et harabbim* — he had merits, and brought merits to many. Did that not describe Nouri and his life?

Even after his passing, he continued to inspire people to take on and strengthen their performance of mitzvot and learn from his ways:

...Like the man who attended many of the *minyanim* in the *shiba'a* house and, upon noticing the *tzitzit* worn by the Dayan family members, decided to begin wearing *tzitzit* as well.

...Like the many people who took upon themselves to say extra *Tehillim* during the year of his *yahrtzeit*.

"He Had Merits, and Brought Merits to Many..." / 573

…Like the president of the shul, who dedicated a yeshiva in Nouri's name and designed an easy-to-use *Tehillim*, which he then donated to all the Sephardic shuls.

…Like his family and friends who felt that the rest of the Jewish people should learn from Nouri Dayan's life and exemplary ways…

And that is why we decided to write this book.

GLOSSARY

Adon Olam — prayer recited at the beginning of the morning service and at the conclusion of other services

Aleinu — prayer recited at the conclusion of each of the daily prayers

aleph-bet — the letters of the Hebrew alphabet

aliya (pl. *aliyot*) — act of being called to recite a blessing at the public reading of the Torah

amida — the 19-blessing prayer recited three times a day; it is the main part of the daily prayer service

Arbit — the evening prayer service

aron kodesh — the ark in which the Torah Scrolls are kept

aseret hadibrot — the Ten Commandments

ba'al ko'rei — one who reads aloud from the Torah Scroll on behalf of the congregation

ba'al toke'a — one who blows the shofar during the prayer service

bachur (pl. *bachurim*) — unmarried young man, often used to denote a student in a yeshiva

bakashot — prayers recited on Shabbat, usually early in the morning

bein hazemanim — vacation break between semesters in yeshiva

Beit Knesset (pl. battei k'nessiot) — shul

beracha (pl. *berachot*) — blessing

brit mila — circumcision

besamim — spices (used during Habdala at the end of Shabbat)

Bet Din — rabbinic court

Bet HaMikdash — the Holy Temple

Bet Midrash — study hall

Birchot HaShahar — the blessings recited during the morning prayer service

birkat ha'mazon — Grace After Meals

bnei Torah — those who learn, and observe, the Torah

Borei Olam — lit., "Creator of the world"; i.e., G-d

bourekas — flaky-dough pastry, usually filled with potatoes or cheese

Brich Sh'mei — prayer recited when the Torah is taken out of the *aron kodesh*

d'bar Torah (pl. *dibrei Torah*) — a Torah thought

debarim b'teilim — idle chatter

der alte heim — "the old home"

derasha (pl. *derashot*) — lecture on a Torah topic

dibrei hazal — Torah thoughts of our Sages

emunah — faith; belief in G-d

Erev Shabbat — the eve of Shabbat; i.e., Friday

etrog — citron; one of the Four Species taken on Sukkot

farher — oral exam on a Talmudic topic, often required for admission into a yeshiva

fedayeen — terrorists

gabbaim — synagogue sextons

gedolim — great Torah scholars

Habdala — lit., "separation"; separation service recited at the end of Shabbat

habibi — my friend

habruta (pl. *habrutot*) — study partner

Hacham — sage; scholar; wise person

Hachnassat Sefer Torah — celebration marking the bringing of a new *Sefer Torah* into a synagogue

HaKadosh Baruch Hu — lit., "the Holy One, blessed is He"; i.e., G-d

hakafot — the encircling of the *bimah* seven times on the holiday of Simhat Torah, while dancing with the Torah Scrolls

hakarat hatob — acknowledging and being grateful for good
Halab, Halabi — referring to the Jews who came from Aleppo, Syria
halacha (pl. *halachot*) — a Torah law
halla — braided loaf of bread traditionally used at Shabbat and festival meals
hametz — leavened food, forbidden on Pesach
hamin — stew cooked on Friday and kept simmering until the Sabbath lunch meal
hamosi — blessing recited before eating bread
hamoud — a lemon mint soup made with various vegetables
Hanuka — festival commemorating the victory of the Jews over their Syrian oppressors, and the miracle of the oil
Hanukat Ha'Bayit — celebration of the dedication of a building
hashkafa — Jewish outlook; worldview; ideology
hattan Torah — lit., "the bridegroom of the Torah"; the one given the honor of coming up to the Torah on Simhat Torah when the last Torah portion is being read
hatzot — halachic midday or midnight
hazal — our Sages, of blessed memory
hazzan (pl. *hazzanim*) — cantor; leader of prayer services
heichal — ark in which the Torah Scrolls are kept
hesed — kindness; acts of beneficence
hesped — eulogy
heter — halachic ruling that deems something permissible
hatzne'a lechet — acting in a hidden, modest fashion
hiddur — enhancement or beautification of a commandment
hitlahavut — enthusiasm
hohsh — communal courtyard
Hok l'Yisrael — a daily study program which includes selections from Scripture with commentary, Mishnah, Talmud, Kabbalah, Jewish Law, and Ethics
Hol Ha'moed — intermediate days of Pesah and Sukkot
humash (pl. *humashim*) — the Five Books of Moses
humra — a stringency in observance
huppah — canopy under which the marriage ceremony takes place; the marriage ceremony itself

Jdedda — grandfather

k'nees — synagogue
ka'ak — sweet pastry
Kabbalat Shabbat — prayer service welcoming the Sabbath
kaffiyeh — Arab man's headdress
kapparot — ceremony performed before Yom Kippur as an atonement for sin
kashered — made kosher
kashrut — Jewish dietary laws
keilim mikva — a pool of water for ritual immersion of utensils
keri'at haTorah — the reading of the Torah in the synagogue
Ketubim — lit., "the Writings"; the third division of the Biblical Books
kibbe — ethnic Syrian food; traditionally, meat-filled dumplings
kibbud ab — reverence (or respect) for one's father
Kiddush — sanctification of the Sabbath and festivals, usually recited over a cup of wine
kinnot — lamentations, recited on Tishah b'Ab
kippot — skullcaps
kitab — school, usually elementary school
Klal Yisrael — the Jewish people in general
kodesh — holy
Kol Nidrei — opening prayer of the Yom Kippur service
Kollel — an institute of higher learning, usually for married men
kos — cup

l'shem Shamayim — for the sake of Heaven
Lag ba'Omer — a minor festival celebrated on the 33rd day of the Omer
lashon kodesh — the holy tongue; i.e., Hebrew
layl Shabbat — Shabbat night; i.e., Friday after candle-lighting
levaya — funeral
lichbod Shabbat Kodesh — in honor of the holy Sabbath
luhot — tablets (of the Ten Commandments)

mabrook — congratulations!
magbid — fundraising drive
malach — angel
mazza — traditional Kiddush buffet
Megillah — the scroll of Esther, read on Purim
mehitza — partition used (in a synagogue) to separate men's and women's sections

melaveh malkah — meal eaten on Saturday night in honor of the departed Sabbath Queen

mesader — the official in shul who gives out the honor of being called to the Torah

mesechet — a volume of Talmud

meshulach (pl. *meshulachim*) — itinerant fund-raiser

mesirut nefesh — physical or spiritual self-sacrifice; unusual effort or devotion

mesora — tradition

mezakeh et harabbim — strengthening mitzvah observance of others

mezonot — blessing recited on foods made from grains

mikva — a pool of water for ritual immersion (of people or utensils)

Minha — the afternoon prayer service

minhag (pl. *minhagim*) — custom

minyan — quorum of ten men necessary for conducting prayer services

mishlo'ah manot — gifts of food sent on Purim

Mishna (pl. Mishnayot) — the teachings of the Oral Law that form the basis of the Talmud

mitpallelim — those who are praying

mitzva (p. mitzvot) — a Torah commandment; loosely, a good deed

Mosa'ei Shabbat — Saturday night after nightfall

muktza — items forbidden to be touched or moved on the Sabbath

Mussaf — additional prayers recited on Shabbat, festivals, and Rosh Hodesh

Nabi — Books of the Prophets

neshama — soul

netilat yadayim — ritual washing of the hands

Nishmat — prayer recited on Sabbath and festivals expressing lofty praise of G-d

nusah — version; style of prayer service

Olam Haba — the World to Come

parochet — curtain that hangs in front of the aron kodesh

passuk (pl. *pesukim*) — verse

perasha — the portion of the Torah read weekly

perek — chapter

pidyon ha'ben — redemption of the firstborn son

Pirkei Abot — Ethics of the Fathers

Pittom Ketoret — liturgy regarding the incense service performed in the Holy Temple

pizmonim — lyrical religious songs

Rabbanim — Rabbis

Ribbono shel Olam — lit., "Master of the world"; i.e., G-d

safrut — the writing of Torah Scrolls, *tefillin*, and *mezuzot*

sambousak — Syrian ethnic food

sandak — one who holds the baby at a circumcision

se'kach — sukka covering, such as branches

Seder — Pesach-night ritual during which the Haggadah is recited on Pesah

seder — study session

sefer — book, esp. on a learned topic

Sefer Torah — Torah scroll

sefirat ha'omer — the counting of the Omer, which takes place between Pesach and Shabu'ot

segula — spiritual remedy

selihot — prayers asking for forgiveness, recited before Rosh Hashana

semahot — happy occasions; celebrations

seuda rebi'it — meal eaten after the conclusion of the Sabbath; i.e., melaveh malkah

seuda shelishit — the third meal eaten on the Sabbath

Seudat Hoda'a — lit., "meal of gratitude"; a festive meal served on the occasion when one wants to give thanks to Hashem

seudat preida — a meal marking the departure of a person from a place or position

Shabbat Shalom — traditional Sabbath greeting

Shabu'ot — festival celebrating the Giving of the Torah

Shaharit — the morning service

Shalom Aleihem — traditional greeting; Friday evening song of welcome to the ministering angels

Sham, Shammi — referring to the Jews who came from Damascus, Syria

shamash — synagogue caretaker

Shas — the Talmud as a whole

shebatim — tribes (of Israel)

Shebi'I shel Pesah — the seventh day of Pesah

Shechina — Divine Presence

sheheheyanu — blessing recited on festivals and certain special occasions

shehita — kosher ritual slaughter

Glossary / 577

sheirut — a taxi service in Israel that takes many passengers at one time

sheloshim — the 30-day period of mourning observed for a deceased close relative

shemirat Shabbat — the observance of Shabbat

sheva berachot — a festive meal honoring the bride and groom during the week after their wedding

shiba'a — the seven-day period of mourning observed after the death of one's immediate relative

shiur (pl. *shiurim*) — lecture on a Torah topic

shofar (pl. *shofarot*) — ram's horn, blown on Rosh Hashana

shomer — one who watches or guards

shomer mitzvot — one who observes the Torah laws

shomer Shabbat — one who observes the Sabbath

Shovavim — the weeks during which the first six portions of *Shemos* are read in the synagogue

shteibel — small synagogue, used mainly in Chassidic circles

shtreimel (pl. *shtreimlach*) — fur-trimmed hat worn by chassidim

shul — synagogue

siddur (pl. *siddurim*) — prayerbook

simha — joy; joyous occasion

Simhat Bet Ha'Sho'eiba — gathering held on the intermediary days of the Succos holiday, which includes music, dance, and refreshments, commemorating the Water Libation Ceremony performed in the Holy Temple in Jerusalem

Simhat Torah — Festival of Rejoicing with the Torah

sofer — scribe who writes Torah Scrolls, *tefillin*, and *mezuzot*

souk — market

Stetta — grandmother

sukka — booth in which Jews dwell during Sukkot

Sukkot — one of the three pilgrimage festivals, marked by living in a *sukka*

ta'amim — cantillation notes for reading from a Torah Scroll

ta'anit dibbur — refraining from speaking (for a spiritual cause)

Ta'anit Esther — the fast of Esther, observed on the day before Purim

tallit — prayer shawl

talmid (pl. *talmidim*) — student

talmid hacham (pl. *talmidei hachamim*) — Torah scholar

Tanach — Scriptures; the Written Torah

tarboush — a type of turban worn in Arab countries

tashlich — ceremony performed on Rosh Hashana in which one "throws away" his sins

tefillin — phylacteries; small black leather boxes containing parchment scrolls inscribed with Biblical passages

tefillot — prayers

Tehillim — Psalms

tehina — a spicy paste-like dip made from sesame seeds

tehiyat ha'meitim — revivification of the dead

teshuva — repentance

Tisha b'Ab — the 9th day of Ab, a day of mourning for the destruction of the Holy Temple

Torah lishma — studying Torah for the sake of pleasing G-d, without ulterior motives

tovel, tovelling — immersing utensils in a *mikva*

Tu B'shebat — the 15th day of Shebat, the "new year" of the trees

tzaddeket — a righteous woman

tzedaka — charity

tzibbur — congregation

tzitzit — four-cornered garment with fringes, worn by men and boys

Viddui — prayer recited on Yom Kippur and by one who is near death

wan-neseh — an oil lamp

yahrtzeit — anniversary of a person's passing

Yamim No'raim — the Days of Awe; i.e., Rosh Hashana and Yom Kippur

Yesiat Mitzrayim — the Exodus from Egypt

Yiddishkeit — Judaism

Yigdal — prayer recited at the beginning of the morning service and at the end of other services

yirat Shamayim — fear of Heaven

yissurim shel ahaba — suffering that is experienced as coming from G-d's love

Yom HaShishi — lit., "the sixth day"; the opening words of the Friday night Kiddush

Yom Tov — Jewish holiday

z'man — semester; time frame
zechut — privilege; merit

zemirot — songs sung at Sabbath and festival meals

BIBI FAMILY

JOSEPH ABDULLAH BIBI & FARHA (BAKAL)

Reuben & Esther (Mizrahi)
- Lillian (Grossman)
- Morris (Moe)
- Joseph
- Isaac
- Charlotte (Zeitoune)
- Eli
- Florence (Deutsch)
- Sara (Cain)
- Evelyn (Tawil)
- Rita (Polisky)
- Jack

Shafikah & Yisrael Dayan
- Shimon
- Sara (Nizri)
- Rachel (Levy)
- Ezra/Nouri & Esther (Maslaton)
  - Irwin
  - Carol (Harari-Raful)
  - Murray
  - Sara (Salem)
  - Joyce (Nahem)
  - Rabbi Joseph (Joey)
  - Barbara (Ozeirey)

Morris & Rebecca (Maslaton)

David & Milo (Salem)
- Florence (Safdieh)
- Joseph
- Helen (Dweck)
- Carol (Franco)
- Sharon (Swed)
- Elliot

580 / NOURI

DAYAN FAMILY

SHIMON DAYAN & SARA

- Yisrael
- Moshe
- Miriam (Hadid)
- Yosef
- Chanum
- Kachila (Naberzilah)
- Leah (Mitzri)
- David
- Haim
- Rachel

Shafikah (Bibi) — Miriam (Peretz)

Children of Miriam (Peretz):
- Moshe
- Yehoshua
- Mordechai

Children of Shafikah (Bibi):
- Shimon
- Sara (Nizri)
- Rachel (Levy)
- Ezra / Nouri & Esther (Maslaton)

- Irwin
- Carol (Harari-Raful)
- Murray
- Sara (Salem)
- Joyce (Nahem)
- Rabbi Joseph (Joey)
- Barbara (Ozeirey)

Family Trees / 581

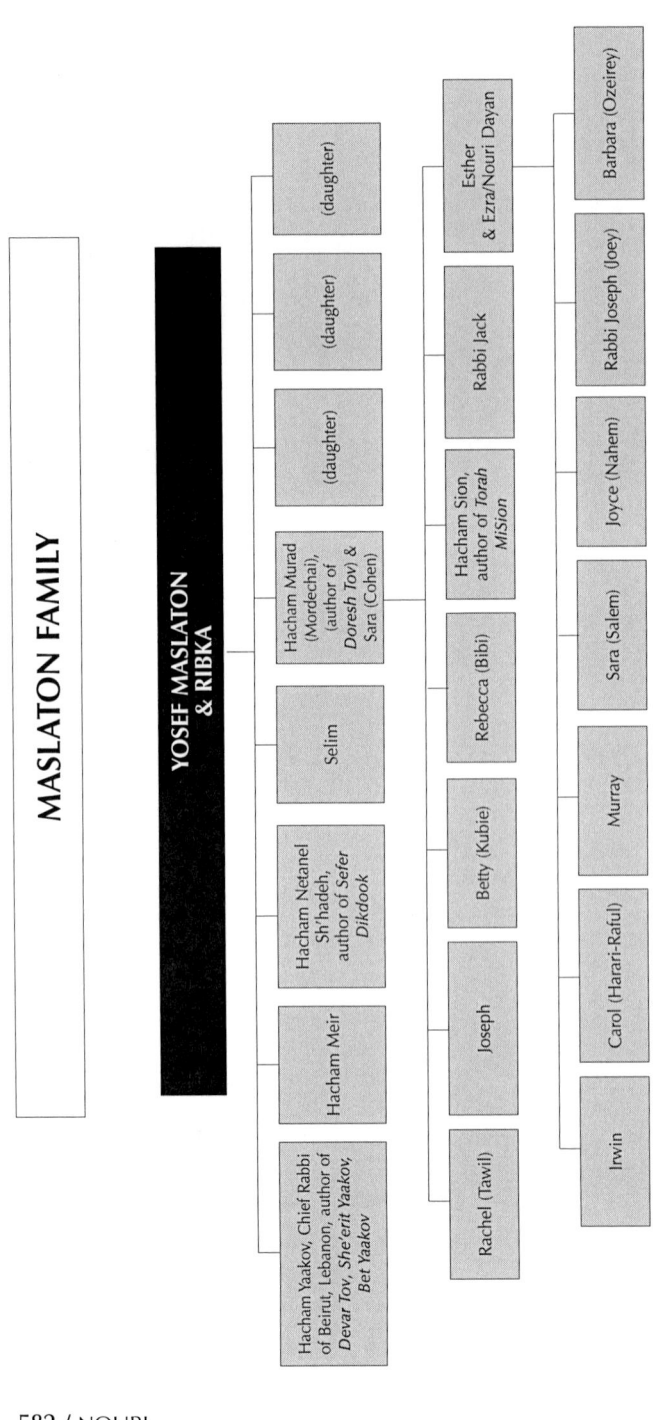

MASLATON FAMILY

YOSEF MASLATON & RIBKA

- Hacham Yaakov, Chief Rabbi of Beirut, Lebanon, author of *Devar Tov, She'erit Yaakov, Bet Yaakov*
- Hacham Meir
- Hacham Netanel Sh'hadeh, author of *Sefer Dikdook*
- Selim
- Hacham Murad (Mordechai), (author of *Doresh Tov*) & Sara (Cohen)
  - (daughter)
  - (daughter)
  - (daughter)

Children of Hacham Murad & Sara:
- Rachel (Tawil)
- Joseph
- Betty (Kubie)
- Rebecca (Bibi)
- Hacham Sion, author of *Torah MiSion*
- Rabbi Jack
- Esther & Ezra/Nouri Dayan

Children of Esther & Ezra/Nouri Dayan:
- Irwin
- Carol (Harari-Raful)
- Murray
- Sara (Salem)
- Joyce (Nahem)
- Rabbi Joseph (Joey)
- Barbara (Ozeirey)

582 / NOURI

COHEN FAMILY

HACHAM DAVID HAIM COHEN

- Salha
- Rachel
- Sanyar & Hacham Meir Maslaton
  - Ezra (Azuri)
- Basil & Louise
  - David
  - Hyman
  - Ely (Sonny)
  - Rachel (Benet)
  - Gloria (Horowitz)
  - Grace (Pearlman)
- Jamileh & Michael Zonanan
  - Sara (Feldman)
  - Rachel (Hesney)
  - Vicky (Ancona)
  - Esther (Zeller)
  - Effie (Shwekey)
  - Frieda (Daniels)
  - Hyman
- Isaac (Zaki) & Regina (Maslaton)
  - Rachel (Weinberg)
  - Nettie (Kastel)
  - David
  - Celia
  - Meyer
  - Joseph
  - Ezra (Sonny)
  - Adele
  - Maurice (Mersh)
- Sarah & Hacham Murad Maslaton, author of *Doresh Tov*
  - Rachel (Tawil)
  - Joseph
  - Betty (Kubie)
  - Rebecca (Bibi)
  - Hacham Sion, author of *Torah Mision*
  - Rabbi Jack
  - Esther & Nouri Dayan
    - Irwin
    - Carol (Harari-Raful)
    - Murray
    - Sara (Salem)
    - Joyce (Nahem)
    - Rabbi Joseph (Joey)
    - Barbara (Ozeirey)

Family Trees / 583

MASLATON FAMILY STARTING FROM HACHAM MURAD

HACHAM MURAD (AUTHOR OF *DORESH TOV*) & SARA (COHEN)

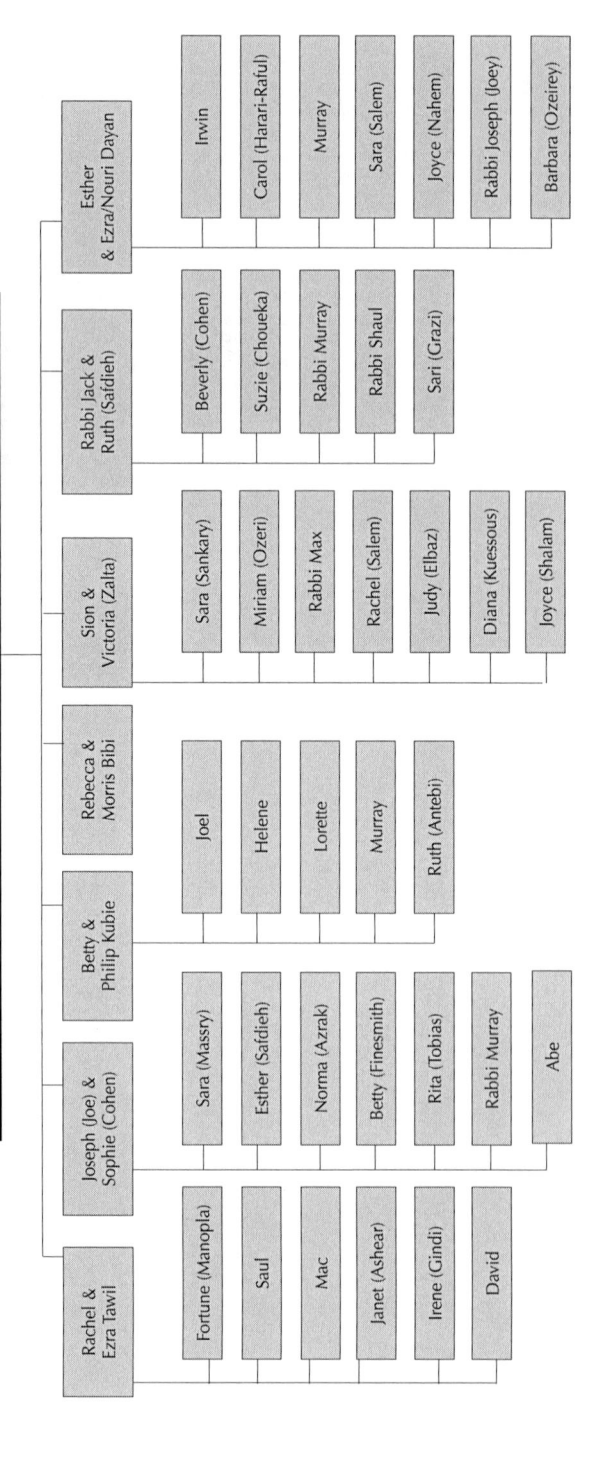

Rachel & Ezra Tawil
- Fortune (Manopla)
- Saul
- Mac
- Janet (Ashear)
- Irene (Gindi)
- David

Joseph (Joe) & Sophie (Cohen)
- Sara (Massry)
- Esther (Saidieh)
- Norma (Azrak)
- Betty (Finesmith)
- Rita (Tobias)
- Rabbi Murray
- Abe

Betty & Philip Kubie

Rebecca & Morris Bibi
- Joel
- Helene
- Lorette
- Murray
- Ruth (Antebi)

Sion & Victoria (Zalta)
- Sara (Sankary)
- Miriam (Ozeri)
- Rabbi Max
- Rachel (Salem)
- Judy (Elbaz)
- Diana (Kuessous)
- Joyce (Shalam)

Rabbi Jack & Ruth (Saidieh)
- Beverly (Cohen)
- Suzie (Choueka)
- Rabbi Murray
- Rabbi Shaul
- Sari (Grazi)

Esther & Ezra/Nouri Dayan
- Irwin
- Carol (Harari-Raful)
- Murray
- Sara (Salem)
- Joyce (Nahem)
- Rabbi Joseph (Joey)
- Barbara (Ozeirey)

584 / NOURI

This volume is part of
THE ARTSCROLL® SERIES
an ongoing project of
translations, commentaries and expositions on
Scripture, Mishnah, Talmud, Midrash, Halachah,
liturgy, history, the classic Rabbinic writings,
biographies and thought.

For a brochure of current publications
visit your local Hebrew bookseller
or contact the publisher:

Mesorah Publications, ltd

4401 Second Avenue
Brooklyn, New York 11232
(718) 921-9000
www.artscroll.com